AF698355

THE LAW AND THEORY OF TRADE SECRECY

RESEARCH HANDBOOKS IN INTELLECTUAL PROPERTY

Series Editor: Jeremy Phillips, *Intellectual Property Consultant, Olswang, Research Director, Intellectual Property Institute and co-founder, IPKat weblog*

Under the general editorship and direction of Jeremy Phillips comes this important new Handbook series of high quality, original reference works that cover the broad pillars of intellectual property law: trademark law, patent law and copyright law – as well as less developed areas, such as geographical indications, and the increasing intersection of intellectual property with other fields. Taking an international and comparative approach, these Handbooks, each edited by leading scholars in the respective field, will comprise specially commissioned contributions from a select cast of authors, bringing together renowned figures with up-and-coming younger authors. Each will offer a wide-ranging examination of current issues in intellectual property that is unrivalled in its blend of critical, innovative thinking and substantive analysis, and in its synthesis of contemporary research.

Each Handbook will stand alone as an invaluable source of reference for all scholars of intellectual property, as well as for practicing lawyers who wish to engage with the discussion of ideas within the field. Whether used as an information resource on key topics, or as a platform for advanced study, these Handbooks will become definitive scholarly reference works in intellectual property law.

Titles in the series include:

Copyright Law
A Handbook of Contemporary Research
Edited by Paul Torremans

Trademark Law and Theory
A Handbook of Contemporary Research
Edited by Graeme Dinwoodie and Mark D. Janis

Patent Law and Theory
A Handbook of Contemporary Research
Edited by Toshiko Takenaka

Research Handbook on the Future of EU Copyright
Edited by Estelle Derclaye

The Law and Theory of Trade Secrecy
A Handbook of Contemporary Research
Edited by Rochelle C. Dreyfuss and Katherine J. Strandburg

The Law and Theory of Trade Secrecy

A Handbook of Contemporary Research

Edited by

Rochelle C. Dreyfuss

Pauline Newman Professor of Law, NYU School of Law, USA

Katherine J. Strandburg

Professor of Law, NYU School of Law, USA

RESEARCH HANDBOOKS IN INTELLECTUAL PROPERTY

Edward Elgar

Cheltenham, UK • Northampton, MA, USA

© The Editors and Contributors Severally 2011

All rights reserved. No part of this publication may be reproduced, stored in a retrieval system or transmitted in any form or by any means, electronic, mechanical or photocopying, recording, or otherwise without the prior permission of the publisher.

Published by
Edward Elgar Publishing Limited
The Lypiatts
15 Lansdown Road
Cheltenham
Glos GL50 2JA
UK

Edward Elgar Publishing, Inc.
William Pratt House
9 Dewey Court
Northampton
Massachusetts 01060
USA

A catalogue record for this book
is available from the British Library

Library of Congress Control Number: 2010939249

MIX
Paper from
responsible sources
FSC® C018575
FSC
www.fsc.org

ISBN 978 1 84720 899 6 (cased)

Typeset by Servis Filmsetting Ltd, Stockport, Cheshire
Printed and bound by MPG Books Group, UK

Contents

Contributors

Robert G. Bone is Professor of Law and holds the G. Rollie White Excellence in Teaching Chair at the University of Texas School of Law. He joined the University of Texas faculty in January 2010 and was previously the Robert Kent Professor in Civil Procedure at Boston University School of Law, where he served from 1986 to 2009. Professor Bone received his B.A. degree from Stanford University in 1973 and his J.D. from Harvard Law School in 1978. He is a leading scholar in the fields of intellectual property, civil procedure and complex litigation. In intellectual property, his writing focuses primarily on trade secret law and trademark law. Professor Bone gave the 2000–2001 Boston University Lecture in honor of his scholarly achievements and received Boston University's highest teaching award, the Metcalf Award for Excellence in Teaching, in 1991. Professor Bone is a member of the American Law Institute.

Carlos M. Correa is Director of the Center for Interdisciplinary Studies on Industrial Property and Economics and of the Post-graduate Course on Intellectual Property at the Law Faculty, University of Buenos Aires and Professor of the Master Program on Science and Technology Policy and Management of the same university. He has been a visiting professor in post-graduate courses of several universities and consultant to UNCTAD, UNIDO, UNDP, WHO, FAO, IDB, INTAL, World Bank, SELA, ECLA, UNDP, and other regional and international organizations. He has advised several governments on intellectual property, innovation policy and public health. He was a member of the UK Commission on Intellectual Property, of the Commission on Intellectual Property, Innovation and Public Health established by the World Health Assembly, and of the FAO Panel of Eminent Experts on Ethics in Food and Agriculture. He is the author of several books and numerous articles.

Robert Denicola is the Margaret Larson Professor of Intellectual Property Law at the University of Nebraska, where he teaches courses in Copyright Law, Trademark and Unfair Competition Law, and Contract Law. Professor Denicola received a B.S.E. degree from Princeton University and J.D. and LL.M. degrees from Harvard University. He is the author of a casebook on Copyright Law published by Foundation Press. He is also the Reporter for the American Law Institute's Restatement of the Law of

Unfair Competition, which covers trademark law, trade secret law, false advertising and the right of publicity.

Rochelle C. Dreyfuss is the Pauline Newman Professor of Law at New York University School of Law and Co-Director of the Engelberg Center on Innovation Law and Policy at NYU. Her research interests include international and domestic intellectual property law and civil procedure. She holds B.A. and M.S. degrees in Chemistry and was a research chemist before entering Columbia University School of Law, where she served as Articles and Book Review Editor of the *Law Review*. She was a law clerk to Chief Judge Wilfred Feinberg of the U.S. Court of Appeals for the Second Circuit and to Chief Justice Warren E. Burger of the U.S. Supreme Court. She is a member of the American Law Institute and was a co-Reporter for its Project on Intellectual Property: Principles Governing Jurisdiction, Choice of Law, and Judgments in Transnational Disputes. She was a consultant to the Federal Courts Study Committee, to the Presidential Commission on Catastrophic Nuclear Accidents, to the Federal Trade Commission and was a member of the Secretary of Health and Human Services' Advisory Committee on Genetics Health and Society. She is a past chair of the Intellectual Property Committee of the American Association of Law Schools. She was also a member of the National Academies committees on Intellectual Property in Genomic and Protein Research and Innovation and on Intellectual Property Rights in the Knowledge-Based Economy. She is presently on the Academies' Committee on Science, Technology, and Law.

Rebecca S. Eisenberg is the Robert and Barbara Luciano Professor of Law at the University of Michigan Law School, where she has been a faculty member since 1984. She is a graduate of Stanford University and Berkeley Law (Boalt Hall), University of California. Her research focuses primarily on regulation of biomedical innovation. She has written and lectured extensively about patent law as applied to biomedical research and the interaction of patent law with drug regulation. She has also played an active role in public policy debates concerning the impact of intellectual property on biopharmaceutical research. She teaches courses in patent law, trademark law and food and drug law.

Valeria Falce is Associate Professor of Intellectual Property and Competition Law at Università Europea di Roma. She received a Ph.D. in Competition Law from the University of Perugia and an LL.M., with merits, in Intellectual Property from the London School of Economics. In 1996 she joined the Osservatorio di Proprietà Intellettuale, Concorrenza e Comunicazioni chaired by Professor Gustavo Ghidini. Author of two monographs, Professor Falce's current fields of interests include intellectual property, competition, regulation and law and economics. She is a member of the International Association for the Protection of Intellectual Property (AIPPI), the International Association for Teaching and Research in Intellectual Property (ATRIP) and the Academic Society for Competition Law (ASCOLA).

Harry First is the Charles L. Denison Professor of Law at New York University School of Law and the Director of the law school's Competition, Innovation, and Information Law Program. From 1999–2001 he served as Chief of the Antitrust Bureau of the Office of the Attorney General of the State of New York. Professor First's interests include antitrust, international and comparative antitrust and innovation policy. He is the co-author of law school casebooks on antitrust and on regulated industries, and the author of numerous articles involving antitrust law. Professor First is a Contributing Editor of *Antitrust Law Journal*, Foreign Antitrust Editor of *Antitrust Bulletin*, and a member of the Advisory Board and a Senior Fellow of the American Antitrust Institute. Professor First has twice been a Fulbright Research Fellow in Japan and has served as an Adjunct Professor of Law at the University of Tokyo. Prior to entering law teaching Professor First was an attorney with the U.S. Department of Justice, Antitrust Division. He has also been Counsel to Loeb & Loeb in New York City.

Jeanne C. Fromer is an Associate Professor at Fordham Law School. Professor Fromer previously served as a law clerk to Justice David Souter of the U.S. Supreme Court and to Judge Robert Sack of the U.S. Court of Appeals for the Second Circuit. She also worked at Hale and Dorr LLP (now WilmerHale) as an intellectual property attorney. Professor Fromer earned her B.A. in Computer Science from Barnard College, Columbia University; S.M. in Electrical Engineering and Computer Science from the Massachusetts Institute of Technology; and J.D. from Harvard Law School. She specializes in intellectual property and information law, with particular emphasis on unified theories of patent and copyright law.

Gustavo Ghidini is Full Professor of Intellectual Property and Competition Law at University of Milano, Faculty of Law. He teaches the same subject at LUISS University in Rome, where he also serves as Director of Observatory of Intellectual Property, Competition, and Communication Law. Past President of the International Association for the Advancement of Teaching and Research in Intellectual Property (ATRIP), he has written several books and articles. His latest book is *Innovation, Competition,* *and Consumer Welfare in Intellectual Property Law* (Edward Elgar, Cheltenham, UK, 2010).

Charles Tait Graves is a partner at Wilson Sonsini Goodrich & Rosati in San Francisco and an adjunct professor at the University of California, Hastings College of the Law. He has published widely on the history, theory and practice of trade secret law and related doctrines.

Mark A. Lemley is the William H. Neukom Professor of Law at Stanford Law School, the Director of the Stanford Program in Law, Science and Technology, and the Director of Stanford's LL.M. Program in Law, Science and Technology. He teaches intellectual property, computer and Internet law, patent law and antitrust. He is the author of seven books (most in multiple editions) and 111 articles on these and related subjects, including the two-volume treatise IP *and Antitrust*. His works have been reprinted throughout the world, and translated into Chinese, Japanese, Korean, Spanish and Italian. He has taught intellectual property law to federal and state judges at numerous Federal Judicial Center and ABA programs, has testified seven times before Congress and numerous times before the California legislature, the Federal Trade Commission and the Antitrust Modernization Commission on patent, trade secret, antitrust and constitutional law matters, and has filed numerous *amicus* briefs before the U.S. Supreme Court, the California Supreme Court and the federal circuit courts of appeals. He has been named California Lawyer's Attorney of the Year (2005), Best Lawyers' San Francisco IP Lawyer of the Year (2010), and a Young Global Leader by the Davos World Economic Forum (2007). In 2009 he received the California State Bar's inaugural IP Vanguard award. In 2002 he was chosen Boalt's Young Alumnus of the Year. He has been recognized as one of the top 50 litigators in the country under 45 by the *American Lawyer* (2007), one of the 100 most influential lawyers in the nation by the *National Law Journal* (2006), one of the 10 most admired attorneys in Intellectual Property, one of the top intellectual property lawyers in California (2003, 2007, 2009, 2010) and one of the 100 most influential lawyers in California (2004, 2005, 2006 and 2008) by the *Daily Journal*, among other honors. Professor Lemley is a founding partner of Durie Tangri LLP. He litigates and counsels clients in all areas of intellectual property, antitrust and Internet law. He has argued six federal appellate cases and numerous district court cases, and represented clients including Comcast, Genentech, Google, Grokster, Hummer Winblad, Impax, Intel, NetFlix, Palm, TiVo and the University of Colorado Foundation in 75 cases in nearly two decades as a lawyer. After graduating from law school, he clerked for Judge Dorothy Nelson on the U.S. Court of Appeals for the Ninth Circuit, and has practiced law in Silicon Valley with Brown & Bain and with Fish & Richardson, and in San Francisco with Keker & Van Nest. Until January 2000, he was the Marrs McLean Professor of Law at the University of Texas School of Law, and until June 2004 he was the Elizabeth Josslyn Boalt Professor of Law at the Boalt Hall School of Law, University of California at Berkeley.

David S. Levine is an Assistant Professor of Law at Elon University School of Law and an Affiliate Scholar at the Center for Internet and Society at Stanford Law School (CIS). His scholarship focuses on the operation of intellectual property law at the intersection of technology and public life and intellectual property law's impact on public and private transparency and accountability. Professor Levine founded and hosts *Hearsay Culture* on KZSU-FM (Stanford University), a technology and intellectual property law radio show and podcast that was chosen as one of the top five podcasts in the American Bar Association's Blawg 100 of 2008. Prior to becoming a law professor, Professor Levine was a resident fellow at CIS. He also practiced intellectual property, entertainment, labor/employment and commercial litigation as an associate in the Manhattan offices of Pryor Cashman LLP and Windels Marx Lane & Mittendorf LLP and as Assistant Corporation Counsel for the City of New York. He holds a B.Sc. in industrial and labor relations from Cornell University and a J.D. from Case Western Reserve University School of Law.

Doris Estelle Long is Professor of Law and Chair of the Intellectual Property, Information Technology and Privacy Group at The John Marshall Law School. She has lectured in 31 countries on five continents and served as a consultant on intellectual property right issues for diverse U.S. and foreign government agencies, including as attorney advisor in the Office of Legislative and International Affairs of the USPTO. She has taught in eight countries, including serving as a Fulbright Professor at Jiao Tung University in Shanghai. Professor Long is the author of numerous books and articles in the area of intellectual property law, and a monthly columnist on international intellectual property law for the *Chicago Daily Law Bulletin*. Before joining the faculty, Professor Long was an attorney with the Washington, D.C. law firms of Arent Fox Kintner Plotkin & Kahn, and Howrey and Simon. She is a graduate of Ithaca College, B.A. *summa cum laude*, Cornell Law School, J.D. *cum laude*, and holds an Executive Education Certificate from the Kennedy School of Government/ Harvard University in Science, Technology and Innovation Policy.

Mary L. Lyndon is a Professor of Law at St. John's University School of Law. Her research and writing have concentrated on the production and availability of health, environmental and safety information, the effects of proprietary claims on the dissemination of this information, and the relationship between intellectual property and environmental law. Professor Lyndon's work has appeared in a variety of journals and reports and she has contributed to several books. She teaches Environmental Law, International Environmental Law and Tort Law. Prior to joining the law faculty, Professor Lyndon first practiced broadcasting and telecommunications law and then was an Assistant Attorney General for the State of New York. In that capacity she headed a group of attorneys working on acid rain and other environmental problems. In 1985–1986 she was the Silver Fellow in Law, Science and Technology at Columbia University. She received a J.S.D. from Columbia University and her J.D. from Northeastern University. Professor Lyndon is a member scholar of the Center for Progressive Reform.

Michael J. Madison is a Professor of Law at the University of Pittsburgh School of Law, specializing in the law, policy and theory of intellectual property. His work on copyright law, property theory and governance has appeared in law reviews at Cornell University, Fordham University and the College of William and Mary, among other leading law schools, and he is the co-author of a casebook on intellectual property law published by Aspen Publishers. He received his law degree from Stanford University and undergraduate degree from Yale University. A complete biography and list of scholarship can be found at http://madisonian.net/home.

Frank Pasquale is Schering-Plough Professor in Health Care Regulation and Enforcement at Seton Hall Law School and a Visiting Fellow at Princeton University's Center for Information Technology Policy. He has been a Visiting Professor at Yale and Cardozo Law Schools. He received his B.A. *summa cum laude* from Harvard, attended Oxford on a Marshall Scholarship, and received his J.D. from Yale. He has written several articles on Internet law and intellectual property. In 2008, he testified before the Task Force on Competition Policy and Antitrust Laws of the House Committee on the Judiciary, appearing with the General Counsels of Google, Microsoft and Yahoo. Professor Pasquale is particularly concerned with opaque decision-making at large intermediaries, including insurers, search engines, Internet Service Providers and financial institutions. He is writing a book on the topic tentatively titled *The Black Box Society*.

Jerome H. Reichman is the Bunyan S. Womble Professor of Law at Duke Law School, Durham, North Carolina. He has written and lectured widely on diverse aspects of intellectual property law, including comparative and international intellectual property and the connection between intellectual property and international trade laws. In collaboration with Keith Maskus, he published *International Public Goods and Transfer of Technology under a Globalized Intellectual Property Regime* (Cambridge Press, 2005). He serves as a consultant to numerous intergovernmental and non-governmental organizations and on the board of editors for various journals, including the *Journal of International Economic Law* and *Il Diritto D'Autore* (Rome). In recent years, he has written extensively on the tensions between intellectual property rights and the needs of both scientific research and public health. His articles in this area include *Pathways Across the Valley of Death: Novel Intellectual Property Strategies for Accelerated Drug Discovery* (with Rai, Uhlir and Crossman, 2008); *Compulsory Licensing of Patented Pharmaceutical Inventions: Evaluating the Options* (2009); *Rethinking the Role of Clinical Trial Data in International Intellectual Property Law: The Case for a Public Goods Approach* (2009); *When Copyright Law and Science Collide: Empowering Digitally Integrated Research Methods on a Global Scale* (with Ruth Okediji, 2011); *The Doha Round's Public Health Legacy: Strategies for the Production and Diffusion of Patented Medicines under the Amended TRIPS Provisions* (with Fred Abbott, 2007); and *A Contractually Reconstructed Research Commons for Scientific Data in a Highly Protectionist Intellectual Property Environment* (with Paul Uhlir, 2003). He and two co-authors (Paul Uhlir and Tom Dedeurwaerdere) are currently finishing a book entitled *Designing the Microbial Research Commons: Global Intellectual Property Strategies for Accessing and Using Essential Public Knowledge Assets* (Draft version presented at the International Symposium on Designing the Microbial Research Commons, National Research Council, Washington D.C., October 8–9, 2009).

Michael Risch is an Associate Professor of Law, Villanova University School of Law. Professor Risch's teaching and scholarship focus on intellectual property and cyberspace law, with an emphasis on patents, trade secrets and information access. His articles have appeared in the *Stanford Law Review*, *Indiana Law Journal*, *BYU Law Review*, *Yale Law Journal Online*, *PENNumbra*, *Tennessee Law Review* and *Harvard Journal of Law and Technology*, among others. Prior to joining the Villanova faculty in 2010, he was an Associate Professor at the West Virginia University College of Law, and an Olin Fellow in Law at Stanford Law School. Professor Risch graduated from Stanford University with honors and distinction in public policy and distinction in quantitative economics. He earned his law degree at the University of Chicago, where he graduated with high honors and was an Olin Fellow in Law and Economics and a Bradley Fellow in Law and Economics.

Pamela Samuelson is the Richard M. Sherman '74 Distinguished Professor of Law and Information at the University of California at Berkeley and a Director of the Berkeley Center for Law and Technology. She is a Fellow of the Association for Computing Machinery (ACM), a Contributing Editor of Communications of the ACM, a past Fellow of the John D. and Catherine T. MacArthur Foundation, and an Honorary Professor of the University of Amsterdam. She is a member of the Board of Directors of the Electronic Frontier Foundation and of the Electronic Privacy Information Center, as well as a Fellow of the Center for Democracy and Technology. She has been a member of the Berkeley faculty since 1996, and prior to that, with the University of Pittsburgh Law School. She has visited at Columbia, Cornell, Emory and Harvard Law Schools.

Sharon K. Sandeen is a Professor of Law at Hamline University School of Law in St. Paul, Minnesota, where she teaches a variety of intellectual property law courses. Prior to beginning her teaching career, Professor Sandeen practiced law in California, specializing in intellectual property litigation and counseling. A native of northern California, she received a B.A. in Political Science from the University of California, Berkeley, a J.D. from the University of Pacific, McGeorge School of Law, and an LL.M. from the University of California, Berkeley School of Law (Boalt Hall). Her research interests and recent scholarship focus on trade secret law, including the history, purpose and scope of the Uniform Trade Secrets Act and Article 39 of the TRIPS Agreement. She currently serves as the Chair of the Intellectual Property Transactions Committee of the Business Law Section of the American Bar Association.

Katherine J. Strandburg is Professor of Law at New York University School of Law. Her research and teaching focus on patent law, cyberlaw and information privacy law. In particular, she has written extensively about the intersection between research science and the patent system. Recent publications focus on the implications of user innovation and collaborative innovation for patent law and on the privacy implications of networked communication. She has also authored a number of *amicus* briefs on patent issues, most recently on behalf of a group of medical associations. Professor Strandburg obtained her law degree from the University of Chicago Law School with high honors in 1995 and served as a law clerk to the Honorable Richard D. Cudahy of the U.S. Court of Appeals for the Seventh Circuit. Prior to her legal career, Professor Strandburg was a Ph.D. research physicist at Argonne National Laboratory.

Geertrui Van Overwalle is Professor of Intellectual Property Law at the University of Leuven, Belgium and Professor of Patent Law and

New Technologies at the University of Tilburg, the Netherlands. In her recent work, she focuses on patents, genetics and their impact on access to healthcare. The results of this research are published in her book *Gene Patents and Public Health* (Bruylant, Brussels, 2007) and in *Gene Patents and Collaborative Licensing Mechanisms: Patent Pools, Clearinghouses, Open Source Models and Liability Regimes* which she recently published with Cambridge University Press (2009). Professor Van Overwalle is a member of the national Belgian High Council for Intellectual Property. She is a member of the European Commission's Expert Group on Biotechnological Inventions. She contributed as an expert to the Report *Policy options for the improvement of the European patent system* commissioned by the European Parliament. At present, she is also an external advisor to the Unitaid Medicines Patent Pool Initiative.

Eric von Hippel is T. Wilson Professor of Innovation Management, and also Professor of Engineering Systems at MIT. Professor von Hippel is known for his research into the sources of and economics of innovation. He and his colleagues find that product development is rapidly shifting away from producers to users and to open user collaborations in the Internet Age – is being 'democratized'. This shift in the locus of innovation requires responsive changes in government policy-making and corporate business models. For example, policy must be altered to support an information 'commons' model of innovation rather than only a model based upon proprietary intellectual property. Professor von Hippel's book, *Democratizing Innovation* (2005) is available free at http://mit.edu/evhippel/www/books.htm.

Georg von Krogh was born in Oslo, Norway. He is a Professor at ETH Zurich and holds the Chair of Strategic Management and Innovation. He is also the Head of ETH Zurich's Department of Management, Technology and Economics. Professor von Krogh specializes in competitive strategy, technological innovation and knowledge management. He has conducted research in various industries including financial services, media, computer software and hardware, life-sciences and consumer goods. Professor von Krogh has published books on strategic management, knowledge creation, innovation, as well as organization and management theory. *Enabling Knowledge Creation* with Professors Nonaka and Ichijo, focused on how firms can build an organization culture and infrastructure that support product and process innovation. His awards and recognitions include the Association of American Publishers' 'Best Professional Business Book Award', the Organization and Management Theory Division's 'Best Symposium Award' at the

Academy of Management, Harvard Business Review's 'Breakthrough Idea' and the ETH Teaching Award 'Goldene Eule'.

Diane Leenheer Zimmerman, a graduate of Columbia Law School, is the Samuel Tilden Professor of Law Emerita at New York University. Her scholarship focuses on the First Amendment, intellectual property and gender issues. Professor Zimmerman has served as the Inaugural Hosier Distinguished Visiting Professor of Intellectual Property at DePaul's Law School, Distinguished Lee Visiting Professor of Constitutional Law at the George Wythe School of Law, College of William and Mary, and as a research fellow at the London School of Economics. She taught in the Aspen Institute Law and Society Program, and has served as the Reporter on Gender for the Second Circuit Task Force on Gender, Racial and Ethnic Fairness in the Courts. She is a co-editor of *Working Within the Boundaries of Intellectual Property* (2010), *Expanding the Boundaries of Intellectual Property* (2001) and of a casebook, *Intellectual Property: Cases and Materials on Trademark, Copyright, and Patent Law* (new edn, forthcoming 2012).

Acknowledgements

The chapters in this volume are based on essays that were first presented at a Conference sponsored by the Engelberg Center on Innovation Law and Policy and New York University School of Law. The Conference provided a unique opportunity for contributors to test their theories, consider opposing viewpoints and modify their positions. The final product therefore owes a great deal to those who contributed to this volume, as well as to the practitioners and academics who were present at the Conference but did not memorialize their input in writing. We also owe a debt of gratitude to Alfred B. Engelberg, whose vision and generosity created the Center, and to Dean Ricky Revesz, who supports its work. We are grateful to our students who provided invaluable research assistance: Jason Liu, NYU Class of 2012, and Simon Kung, Meera Nair, Darryl Tam and Natalie Thomas, NYU Class of 2011. In particular, we would like to thank Nicole Arzt. Without her incomparable organizational skills, neither the Conference nor the volume would have been possible. When we started on this project, trade secrecy was barely on the scholarly agenda. We would like to acknowledge Luke Adams for having the insight to see its importance and persuading us to bring his vision to fruition.

Introduction

Rochelle C. Dreyfuss and Katherine J. Strandburg

Surveys of the creative sector repeatedly demonstrate that innovators regard trade secrecy as one of their most important information management strategies. Surprisingly, however, there has been relatively little academic writing in this area. The reasons why are telling, for they shed light on the issues with which the chapters in this volume deal.

The absence of a deep literature may, in fact, be overdetermined. Thus, one reason for the absence of a robust scholarship is that the legal landscape is difficult to evaluate. The major intellectual property regimes (patent, trademark and copyright law) are based on federal statutes, making both the legislation and case law easy to collect, survey, and categorize. But because trade secrecy is largely a creature of state law (and until recently, mostly state common law), it is less available as a target for doctrinal analysis. Nor is trade secrecy appealing to empiricists. After all, the hallmark of the legal strategy is secrecy. Thus there is little data with which to work: there are no registries of trade secrets and few available indicators of their economic significance. In contrast, the patent system gives economists and lawyers a vast trove of information to study.

Even more importantly, trade secrecy lacks a central theoretical organizing principle. In a sense, trade secrecy functions as an umbrella covering a variety of distinct concerns. Promoting honest business practices is one clear theme. Other concerns involve the relationships between a firm and its employees, commercial partners, and customers. Still others are animated by interests in promoting efficient investment in research and development, human capital, and security. Because it is an umbrella concept, trade secrecy lies at the intersection of many legal doctrines, among others, labor and employment law, torts, contracts, and criminal law.

The plethora of legal regimes, lack of theoretical clarity, and paucity of scholarship and empirical data make it hard for lawmakers to grapple with many of the central questions of trade secrecy law. Open issues include the types of information that fall under trade secrecy protection, the degree to which the information must be kept secret, the respective rights of parties with access to the information, the appropriate measures and types of relief, and the relationship between trade secrecy and other intellectual property laws.

The murkiness of trade secrecy doctrine also makes it difficult to balance the interest in trade secrecy against other societal values. In particular, there are many contexts in which openness is crucial. Sharing is critical to collaborative and cumulative research. Information flow is the basis of a competitive economy. Democratic governance requires a vibrant marketplace of ideas and a degree of transparency regarding critical platform technologies, such as voting machines and search engines. Some social problems are so large that they require the efforts of multiple parties, and therefore broad access to key information. Forging domestic law that takes all of these interests into account is no easy task. International lawmaking is equally affected. Trade secrecy has been the subject of both bilateral and multilateral negotiation efforts, but the premier international intellectual property instrument – the TRIPS Agreement – treats trade secrecy in only one, rather vague, provision and fails to fully account for important categories of secrets, such as traditional knowledge and regulatory data.

The chapters in this book begin to address these issues. Drafts of the chapters were presented at a workshop attended by the authors and a number of commentators. The chapters provoked a lively discussion highlighting the problematic nature of the trade secrecy regime, but also clarifying the sources of those difficulties and illuminating the policy options. We hope the resulting volume, which reflects that conversation, will act as a springboard for further scholarship in this critical area.

PART I

FOUNDATIONS

1 Trade secrecy in Willy Wonka's Chocolate Factory

*Jeanne C. Fromer**

Roald Dahl's *Charlie and the Chocolate Factory* is well-known as a dark fantasy in which five children win a visit to a whimsical candy company.[1] Less conspicuous is the legal issue of trade secrecy driving the novel's plot. Secrecy is not indigenous to fictional representations of the candy industry, but is widespread throughout its real-world confectionary counterparts of today and yesteryear. An investigation of the need for secrecy in this commercial sphere raises fundamental questions about the role of legal protection for misappropriations of secrets when actual secrecy seems to be paramount and about the relationship between trade secrecy and patent law.

Dahl's story depicts Willy Wonka as an extraordinary innovator of candies. Early in the story, the novel's title character, Charlie Bucket, receives a mere taste of some of Wonka's many creations from the descriptions of Grandpa Joe, Charlie's grandfather, of 'a way of making chocolate ice cream so that it stays cold for hours and hours without being in the icebox',[2] 'marshmallows that taste of violets, . . . rich caramels that change colour every ten seconds as you suck them, . . . chewing gum that never loses its taste, and candy balloons that you can blow up to enormous sizes before you pop them with a pin and gobble them up'.[3]

In his depictions, Grandpa Joe is careful to stress that many of Wonka's methods for producing his candies are 'most secret'[4] to protect his ideas from appropriation by others. In fact, Wonka's methods and his perpetual stream of product ideas are so coveted that three of his competitors, Fickelgruber, Prodnose and Slugworth, have tried to steal these ideas. As Grandpa Joe tells it:

---

* Associate Professor, Fordham Law School. I am grateful to Audrey Ajdler, Eric Ajdler, Olivia Ajdler, and Sonia Katyal for their comments, and I thank Benjamin Arrow for excellent research assistance.

[1] Roald Dahl, Charlie and the Chocolate Factory (Puffin ed. 1998, orig. ed. 1964).

[2] *Id.* at 10.

[3] *Id.* at 11.

[4] *Id.*

> All the other chocolate makers, you see, had begun to grow jealous of the wonderful candies that Mr. Wonka was making, and they started sending in spies to steal his secret recipes. The spies took jobs in the Wonka factory, pretending that they were ordinary workers, and while they were there, each one of them found out exactly how a certain special thing was made.[5]

The spying had been successful, as:

> soon after th[e spying], Fickelgruber's factory started making an ice cream that would never melt, even in the hottest sun. Then Mr. Prodnose's factory came out with a chewing gum that never lost its flavour however much you chewed it. And then Mr. Slugworth's factory began making candy balloons that you could blow up to huge sizes before you popped them with a pin and gobbled them up.[6]

Unsurprisingly, Willy Wonka grew frustrated and feared financial ruin were his competitors to persevere in the thievery of his ideas.[7] As things stood, he would be investing his resources and energy to produce new types of candies and novel ways of making them, while his competitors would be reaping a good deal of his creativity's sweet rewards, so to speak. Not content with that result, Wonka opted to cease all operations at his chocolate factory, by firing all of his employees, 'shut[ting] the main gates and fasten[ing] them with a chain', and stopping the factory's machines and chimneys.[8] With no chocolates or candies being made, Wonka disappeared from sight for months.[9]

While Wonka was not applying his creative talents to making chocolate, he was using them to find a solution to his competitors' stealing. He located a tribe of Oompa-Loompas, tiny song-loving people from Loompaland.[10] The Oompa-Loompas loved cacao beans, a prime ingredient for chocolate, but hardly any of the beans were available in Loompaland.[11] Willy Wonka was therefore easily able to convince them to leave the dangerous jungles of Loompaland and come and live in his candy land of a factory,

---

5 *Id.* at 15.

6 *Id.* at 16.

7 *Id.*

8 *Id.*

9 *Id.*

10 *Id.* at 68–9, 80. In the original publication in the 1960s, the Oompa-Loompas were 'depicted as Congolese pygmy slaves'. JEREMY TREGLOWN, ROALD DAHL: A BIOGRAPHY 39, illus. 19 (1994). Following accusations in the 1970s that Dahl's portrayal was racist, Dahl revised the book and the Oompa-Loompas were instead illustrated as 'dwarfish hippies with long "golden-brown" hair and "rosy-white" skin'. *Id.* at 39, 203, illus. 20.

11 DAHL, *supra* note 1, at 69–70.

working for him there in exchange for an unlimited supply of cacao beans and chocolate.[12]

With the immigration of the Oompa-Loompas, Wonka was able to reopen his chocolate factory. He had found a way to get distinctive-looking laborers who would not leave the factory, which protected him in two ways from divulgence of information about his candy-making processes and products. First, as the Oompa-Loompas would be living at the factory and without access to outsiders, there would be little to no chance for them to reveal Wonka's sweet nothings to his competitors. Second, because Wonka would not be letting in any employees other than the Oompa-Loompas and because they had a unique look, it had become exceptionally difficult, if not impossible, for Wonka's competitors to sneak spies into the factory under the guise of employment.

Although Willy Wonka could now restart his factory's machines and chimneys, producing delectable treats once more for mass consumption, it might seem remiss for him to throw open the factory's main gate. But that is just what he did. Ten years after he recommenced factory operations,[13] Wonka announced a contest for five children to visit the factory (along with one or two family members[14]) and get a lifetime's supply of his candies.[15] To win, a child had to find one of five golden tickets hidden underneath the wrapping paper of a Wonka candy bar.[16] The contest piqued the world's curiosity, not in small part because of the passion for Wonka's candies, but also because, according to Grandpa Joe, 'people are actually going to be allowed to go inside the factory'.[17] There was interest in the factory's innards, both to see the secretive candy-making and also to get a better sense of just how, without any employees going in and out, the candies and chocolates were being made. Because the public did not know that Wonka had brought Oompa-Loompas to work for him, people could not understand how the factory's operations had been restarted.[18]

The golden-ticket contest was an inspired marketing tactic, as Wonka candy bars flew off the shelves in response to worldwide interest in the chocolate factory.[19] And so five children – Augustus Gloop, a gluttonous boy; Veruca Salt, a spoiled, rich girl; Violet Beauregarde, a non-stop

---

12 *Id.* at 69–71.
13 *Id.* at 18.
14 *Id.* at 51.
15 *Id.* at 19–20.
16 *Id.* at 20.
17 *Id.* at 19.
18 *Id.* at 14, 16–18.
19 *Id.* at 20.

gum-chewer; Mike Teavee, an incessant television viewer enamored of gunfights; and Charlie Bucket, the poor and hungry title character – successfully spent wildly divergent amounts of time and energy to secure a golden ticket.[20]

The children's tour of the factory revealed to them imaginative candy products and processes and mechanisms. The children start out in a chocolate room, 'the nerve center of the whole factory, the heart of the whole business', with a 'great brown river' of chocolate flowing both into a 'tremendous waterfall' and glass pipes carrying away the chocolate mixed in the waterfall into a 'light and frothy' state to other parts of the factory.[21] In the factory, the children see or learn of, among other things, everlasting gobstoppers, a candy that never gets smaller and changes color weekly; hair toffee, a candy producing on the consumer a full head of hair, a mustache, and a beard; a piece of chewing gum that, in the chewer's mouth, feels like a meal with appetizer, entrée, and dessert; lickable wallpaper for nurseries; and edible marshmallow pillows.[22]

The contest winners also experience some of Wonka's mechanisms for keeping secret these products and the processes that make them. In addition to the Oompa-Loompas, Wonka built most of his factory underground, taking particular care to place the most important rooms there.[23] He justifies building downward to generate more space,[24] but it has the important benefit also of making it that much harder to observe the factory's operations from the outside. Wonka keeps his factory rooms locked, as evidenced by the keys he produces to open up the rooms the children enter with him.[25] Finally, in addition to being locked, the door of the most vital room of the factory – where inventing takes place – is labeled, 'private – keep out'.[26] Wonka acknowledges the room's importance by remarking, 'Old Fickelgruber would give his front teeth to be allowed inside just for three minutes! So would Prodnose and Slugworth and all the other rotten chocolate makers!'[27] In fact, the contest winners are the first people ever to enter the room, other than Wonka himself.[28]

---

20 *Id.* at 21–2, 24–5, 30–2, 32–4, 44.

21 *Id.* at 63–6.

22 *Id.* at 87–95, 104.

23 *Id.* at 62.

24 *Id.*

25 *Id.* at 63 (chocolate room); *id.* at 87 (inventing room); *id.* at 106–7 (room for square candies that look round).

26 *Id.* at 87.

27 *Id.*

28 *Id.*

Although it is apparent that Willy Wonka would go to great extremes to guard his candy secrets from his competitors and his competitors to similar lengths to steal Wonka's ideas, some aspects of the story are baffling from the vantage point of trying to understand how Willy Wonka and his competitors act. First, given the value of the information inside the chocolate factory to Wonka's competitors, it is surprising that they did not try to win golden tickets to enter and spy in the chocolate factory. They could, in theory, have bought up hundreds of thousands of candy bars just as Mr Salt did to indulge his daughter, Veruca,[29] to maximize their chances of winning a ticket worth its credential in gold.

Second, it is surprising to see that Wonka put little to no restriction both on who could win the contest and on what the winners could see inside the factory and do with that information after they left. Even though Wonka assumes that only children would win golden tickets, it was theoretically possible under the terms of the golden ticket for a competitor to enter the factory. Even if no competitor were to secure a golden ticket, Wonka left himself vulnerable to the contest winners cashing in on their valuable tour by divulging their experiences inside the chocolate factory to friends, strangers, Wonka's competitors or the media, something Wonka did not forbid. Perhaps Wonka (otherwise quite paranoid and obsessed with maintaining a veil of secrecy over his factory) was distracted by his true purpose for the contest, revealed toward the end of the story. After the four winners other than Charlie get themselves in varied forms of trouble at the factory based on their particular personality quirks,[30] Wonka names Charlie the true winner of the contest and gifts the chocolate factory to him.[31] The true purpose of the contest, according to Wonka, was to find a winning child to take over the factory when that child would get older.[32] Wonka wanted to turn over the factory to a child so he could share his candy-making secrets with someone who would listen to him, as compared with an adult who might not, and have the factory continue operations long after Wonka is gone.[33] The intimation, of course, is that Wonka

---

29 *Id.* at 24.

30 Augustus Gloop drinks from the chocolate river in the chocolate room and is carried away by one of the glass pipes. *Id.* at 72–80. Violet Beauregarde cannot resist chomping the chewing-gum meal before the invention is sufficiently refined and turns into a giant blueberry. *Id.* at 96–9. Veruca Salt is thrown down a garbage chute by squirrels after she tries to grab one to keep. *Id.* at 112–13. And Mike Teavee sends himself in tiny pieces through the air into a television and is then reassembled into a shrunken version of himself. *Id.* at 129–37.

31 *Id.* at 142, 150–1.

32 *Id.* at 151.

33 *Id.*

would pass on his candy-making secrets to Charlie, who would maintain their confidentiality so as to carry on Wonka's thriving operations. The secrets, then, would endure, outliving Wonka.

Roald Dahl's story of whimsical candy-making and cut-throat competition is not pure fantasy, but is grounded in real-life events. Dahl seemed to have a sweet tooth dating to his childhood. At the age of nine, he and his friends would loiter at a local sweet shop and spend their pocket money on treats like liquorice bootlaces, 'a flat black tape about half an inch wide', and gobstoppers, a sucking candy lasting for about an hour that would change color every five minutes.[34] Dahl clearly drew inspiration from these and other candies in filling in the details of *Charlie and the Chocolate Factory*. For example, he merely extended the gobstoppers of his childhood to become everlasting in his novel.[35] In what may have triggered some of the intricate and whimsical ways for making candies in *Charlie and the Chocolate Factory*, Dahl's friend told everyone that the liquorice bootlaces were made from rats' blood extracted in an elaborate way from tens of thousands of dead rats and that eating the bootlaces would cause ratitis, an incurable condition of getting sharp, pointed teeth and a stumpy tail.[36]

When Dahl was a teenager studying at boarding school in England, he and his fellow students would periodically receive individual packages from Cadbury, the chocolate company, containing twelve different types of chocolate bars.[37] Eleven of them were new types of chocolate bars and one was an existing chocolate bar to serve as a control.[38] Along with the chocolates, the boys would receive a sheet to rank each of the chocolate bars and provide comments.[39] It was at this point that Dahl realized that 'the large chocolate companies actually did possess inventing rooms and they took their inventing very seriously', and he would daydream about inventing a great new type of chocolate bar.[40] Dahl pinpoints this experience as the seed from which he grew *Charlie and the Chocolate Factory*.[41]

Dahl's experience with Cadbury was situated more broadly in a hyper-competitive chocolate industry in England, which may very well have motivated the details of spying in Dahl's novel. Joël Glenn Brenner, who

---

[34] ROALD DAHL, BOY: TALES OF CHILDHOOD 28–31 (1984).
[35] DAHL, *supra* note 1, at 88–90.
[36] DAHL, *supra* note 34, at 29–30.
[37] *Id.* at 133.
[38] *Id.*
[39] *Id.*
[40] *Id.* at 134–5 (describing his vision of such a laboratory).
[41] *Id.* at 135.

has written about the contemporary business of chocolate in the United States, indicates that the two top chocolate companies in England at the time of Dahl's writings, '[t]he Cadburys and Rowntrees[,] sent so many moles to work in each other's factories that their spying became legendary'.[42] Because spying had become so extensive, according to Brenner, these and other candy companies in Europe 'began hiring detective agencies to investigate their employees. Sensitive manufacturing processes were designated off-limits to all but the most loyal workers. And businesses that dealt with candy makers were forced to sign confidentiality agreements'.[43]

Spying and extreme secrecy seem not to be merely a relic of early twentieth-century British candy-making, but endemic to the business historically and currently. In the sixteenth century, the explorer Hernán Cortés returned to Spain from Mexico with some cacao beans and an Aztec recipe for chocolatl, a bitter drink made from the beans, which was said to build its drinker's resistance and protect him from fatigue.[44] Because of its new flavor and desirable qualities, the Spanish leadership had its resident monks guard and refine the chocolatl recipe to make it less bitter.[45] By entrusting the recipe to its cloistered monks, Spain was able to keep others from learning of a drink it thought to be valuable, thereby maintaining a competitive edge. The monks managed to keep the recipe a secret from the rest of Europe for over one hundred years.[46]

In present-day United States, candy companies are no less secretive. Generally, to protect candy innovations, recipes are shielded in alarmed safes and shared in a company only if absolutely necessary, so that workers cannot easily reveal them to competitors.[47] Companies will not even disclose how many cacao beans they buy, regarding that as a proprietary secret.[48]

The two biggest candy companies, Mars and Hershey, illustrate the lengths of secrecy to which these companies will go. Mars, the maker

---

42 Joël Glenn Brenner, The Emperors of Chocolate: Inside the Secret World of Hershey and Mars 61, 65 (1999).

43 *Id.* at 61–2.

44 *Id.* at 92–3.

45 *Id.* at 93.

46 *Id.* This interval exceeds the current patent term of approximately 20 years, see 35 U.S.C. § 154, and possibly also surpasses present copyright protection for the author's lifetime plus 70 years, see 17 U.S.C. § 302(a), indicating that secrecy would likely have been preferable to those forms of intellectual property protection.

47 Brenner, *supra* note 47, at 27.

48 *Id.* at 238.

of M&M's, Snickers, Twix and Starburst, is so guarded that it has no company representative for outsiders to contact.[49] The company will not answer who the president of the privately held company is when a member of the public calls the company to ask.[50] To prevent anyone from learning about its candy-making process, Mars designs, makes and operates all of its factory machines itself.[51] The few outsiders Mars has allowed into its factories must sign prohibitive confidentiality agreements.[52] In fact, it has a policy of blindfolding outside contractors coming in to make repairs at the factory so they can see only the area where the repairs are to be done.[53] Mars is so secretive about the special cacao bean at the base of its Dove bar that the bean has no official name and is not directly mentioned in company records; only a small select number of executives know the bean's origins.[54]

Hershey, maker most popularly of Hershey and Kit Kat bars and Reese's Peanut Butter Cups, is similarly furtive, despite the fact that it is publicly traded.[55] When in 1990, Hershey made a Desert Bar for the U.S. military in the Persian Gulf – a chocolate that 'tasted just like an original Hershey bar but could withstand temperatures up to 140 degrees Fahrenheit' – the heads of the company refused to explain the decades-in-the-making technology that created the bar.[56] Even the method of making an original Hershey bar is kept under wraps. As former CEO Richard Zimmerman explains, 'Anyone can read the ingredients on a Hershey bar . . . But to actually make a Hershey bar, you have to know a lot more than that', like how to process milk, which types of cocoa beans to use, and how long to mix the chocolate, information which is not publicly disclosed.[57] Not a single Hershey employee knows the exact proportions of ingredients to mix to create the different chocolate bars.[58] Instead, that information is locked away in a computer.[59] Company information, even about sales and

---

49 *Id.* at ix.

50 *Id.* at 21.

51 *Id.* at 28.

52 *Id.*

53 *Id.*

54 *Id.* at 121.

55 *Id.* at ix (justifying its secrecy based on its competition with Mars, which is so secretive).

56 *Id.* at 10. In fact, a black market had developed to trade information about a predecessor invention in a Swiss laboratory for a tasty chocolate that would not melt at 100 degrees Fahrenheit, with Mars and Hershey very interested in developing a similar chocolate. *Id.* at 11–13.

57 *Id.* at 27.

58 *Id.* at 121.

59 *Id.*

profits, has been so hard to come by to employees, making it extraordinarily hard to do internal marketing.[60] And as with Mars, very few outsiders can come into the factory's main areas.[61]

Just as in Dahl's concocted world of competition between Wonka, Fickelgruber, Prodnose and Slugworth, the motivation for so much secrecy is the constant attempts at, and occasional successes of, spying and thievery of ideas. For instance, to learn how to make chocolate properly, Forrest Mars, Sr, the driving force behind the Mars empire that his father began, spent time in the 1930s working in Switzerland at the factories of Jean Tobler (originator of the Toblerone bar) and Henri Nestlé (inventor of milk chocolate).[62] To do this, Mars posed as a regular factory worker without revealing his true place in the world of chocolate.[63] In turn, it would seem, years later, Mars's European operations were infiltrated by other European manufacturers.[64]

It appears that each candy company has stolen something from another at some point in time. Mars stole the idea for its Bounty bar, a chocolate bar with a coconut filling, from Peter Paul Candies.[65] After the Heath company refused to sell Hershey its recipe for the Heath bar, Hershey bought one for its Skor bar, butter toffee covered in milk chocolate, from a Norwegian candy-maker that had copied its recipe from the Heath bar.[66] Mars and other candy companies are known for trying to extract information about competing candy products from candy suppliers, brokers and buyers.[67] And the companies would recruit their competitors' employees, including top-level ones, as Hershey did when it hired Mars's heads of marketing and sales in 1968,[68] prime sources of proprietary information.[69]

---

60 *Id.* at 215.

61 *Id.* at 62.

62 *Id.* at 60–1.

63 *Id.* at 61.

64 *Id.* at 62–3.

65 *Id.* at 25 ('Given the finite number of available ingredients, the limited understanding of science and manufacturing and the relatively narrow range of consumers' candy preferences, it made perfect business sense to borrow hot-selling products from the competition, alter them slightly and resell them as one's own.').

66 *Id.* at 25–6 (listing also many more examples of such copying).

67 *Id.* at 62.

68 *Id.* at 220.

69 At some points in their histories, Mars and Hershey engaged in a rare collaboration to produce M&M's. *Id.* at 47 (noting that one 'M' stood for R. Bruce Murrie, the son of Hershey's president at the time, and the other for Mars). The companies agreed that Mars would contribute 80 percent of the capital and Murrie's son the other 20 percent, and Hershey sent machinery to Mars to make the M&M's. *Id.* at 48, 151. Perhaps the explanation for this collaboration in the

In many industries, when there is the possibility of competitors stealing a company's innovations, the company relies on patents or copyrights to protect itself. But this is not the *modus operandi* of the candy industry. Willy Wonka would likely have satisfied today's patentability standards of novelty, non-obviousness, and utility[70] for many of his candy-making processes, like the gigantic and complicated machine that would produce the chewing-gum meal with appetizer, entrée and dessert;[71] and resulting products, such as his non-melting ice cream and chewing gum that does not lose its taste.[72] There is, nonetheless, nary a mention of patent (or copyright) law in Dahl's story. Although that, of course, might be attributable to *Charlie and the Chocolate Factory* being a children's fantasy, not a legal brief, things are not much different in the real-world candy industry. As one pertinent example, Forrest Mars would never seek patents on the machinery his company would initiate, improve and adapt.[73] Getting a patent would mean disclosing to the public the innovation,[74] something Mars, like other candy-makers, was loath to do because of the help it would give his competitors.[75] Moreover, protection would last only for approximately two decades, while a secret might be eternally durable if properly protected.[76]

Nor is copyright a sought-after form of protection in the candy industry. Copyrights are likely proper for some aspects of the business, namely,

face of the usual tough competition was that, at the time, Hershey was supplying Mars with chocolate for the M&M's, *id.* at 58, meaning it was in both companies' interest to see M&M's succeed.

70 35 U.S.C. §§ 101–103.

71 DAHL, *supra* note 1, at 91–6.

72 *Id.* at 10–11. Though possible to get a patent on a food product, it can be difficult for it to satisfy the standards of patentability. See 1 DONALD S. CHISUM, CHISUM ON PATENTS § 1.02[6] (2009) (citing cases). Some recent food patents are for sugarless baked goods, U.S. Pat. No. 5,804,242 (issued September 8, 1998), and meat steak, U.S. Pat. No. 5,690,989 (issued November 25, 1997).

73 BRENNER, *supra* note 42, at 183.

74 See 35 U.S.C. § 112. See generally Jeanne C. Fromer, *Patent Disclosure*, 94 IOWA L. REV. 539 (2009).

75 BRENNER, *supra* note 42, at 183. Mars, though, will secure design patents to protect the look of their candy bars. See, e.g., U.S. Pat. No. D565,827S (issued April 8, 2008). The information in a design patent about a candy bar's look does not give Mars's competitors any information they would not otherwise have from buying the candy bar at a store, so there is little downside to Mars in securing design patents.

76 See 35 U.S.C. § 154(a). Mars will secure patents from time to time on machinery that will be in public view, such as vending machines, U.S. Pat. No. 5,831,862 (issued November 3, 1998), and occasionally even for peripheral chocolate products, such as a cocoa extract and a method of making it to prevent and treat cancer, U.S. Pat. No. 5,554,645 (issued September 10, 1996).

'substantial literary expression – a description, explanation, or illustration, for example – that accompanies a recipe or . . . a combination of recipes, as in a cookbook'.[77] Copyright protection, however, subsists in the particular expression and prohibits only substantially similar expression.[78] The idea underlying a recipe – that is, the food itself – can be freely made despite copyright protection. Therefore, copyrighting the recipes for a candy company's products is unlikely to leave the company sated that it is protected against copiers. Moreover, despite some academic argument to the contrary, copyright protection is not currently recognized for food products themselves.[79] Although copyright protection is likely available for certain aspects of what the candy industry does, its downsides guarantee that it will not be invoked much.

Because copyright and patent laws are unsatisfying or unavailable ways to protect the central innovations in the candy industry, the industry and Dahl's depiction of it have turned to secrecy to protect their processes and products. Unlike copyright and patent, which protect only for a limited time, so long as a secret remains unrevealed, its cloak is everlasting.[80] Of course, the information comprising the secret might always be properly revealed through independent discovery or reverse engineering of an available product.[81] But information is shielded by the law as a trade secret from certain types of misappropriation if the underlying information 'derives independent economic value, actual or potential, from not being generally known to, and not being readily ascertainable by proper means by, other persons' and is 'the subject of efforts that are reasonable under the circumstances to maintain its secrecy'.[82] Information about a company's process for making particular candies and about future candy

---

[77] U.S. Copyright Office – Recipes, www.copyright.gov/fls/fl122.html (last visited January 18, 2011).

[78] See, e.g., Whitehead v. Paramount Pictures Corp., 53 F. Supp. 2d 38, 46 (D.D.C. 1999).

[79] Christopher J. Buccafusco, *On the Legal Consequences of Sauces: Should Thomas Keller's Recipes be Per Se Copyrightable?*, 24 CARDOZO ARTS & ENT. L.J. 1121 (2007); J. Austin Broussard, Note, *An Intellectual Property Food Fight: Why Copyright Law Should Embrace Culinary Innovation*, 10 VAND. J. ENT. & TECH. L. 691 (2008); *cf.* Emanuelle Fauchart and Eric von Hippel, *Norms-Based Intellectual Property Systems: The Case of French Chefs*, 19 ORG. SCI. 187 (2008) (exploring how French chefs use certain norms to protect their valuable recipes).

[80] David S. Levine, *Secrecy and Unaccountability: Trade Secrets in Our Public Infrastructure*, 59 FLA. L. REV. 135, 145 (2007).

[81] Kewanee Oil Co. v. Bicron Corp., 416 U.S. 470, 476 (1974) (independent discovery); Cal. Civ. Code § 3426.1(a) (West 2006) (reverse engineering).

[82] Unif. Trade Secrets Act § 1(4) (amended 1985) (adopted in 46 states and the District of Columbia); *accord* 18 U.S.C. § 1839(3)(A).

products undoubtedly meets the first requirement, by giving the company an advantage over its competitors if the information is kept secret.

Secrecy need not be absolute to meet the second requirement, particularly as companies can share information with employees or outsiders so that they can make the most of the information commercially, so long as they protect against unauthorized uses.[83] The Uniform Trade Secrets Act explains that 'reasonable efforts to maintain secrecy have been held to include advising employees of the existence of a trade secret, limiting access to a trade secret on "need to know basis", and controlling plant access. On the other hand, public disclosure of information through display, trade journal publications, advertising, or other carelessness can preclude protection'.[84] Distilled, it is understood that efforts are reasonable if they '(1) control access to the secret; (2) do not disseminate the secret more widely than necessary; (3) do not give access to individuals who fail to hold the information in confidence; and (4) establish, update and follow security guidelines for keeping it safe'.[85]

There are a number of justifications proffered for the reasonable-efforts requirement. For one thing, it ensures that legal protection is granted only to those who value and treat the information as secret.[86] Relatedly, the efforts broadcast a message to both outsiders and insiders that the protected information ought not to be taken wrongfully, frequently also helping the information holder detect misappropriations.[87] And by imposing this requirement on the company holding the information, the expended efforts will prevent many potential episodes of misappropriation.[88] The requirement also encourages companies not to over-invest in keeping secrets or to behave impracticably, as efforts need only be reasonable.[89] For example, in a case in which the defendant flew an airplane over the plaintiff's chemical plant under construction to obtain otherwise proprietary information, the Fifth Circuit found that the plaintiff had undertaken reasonable efforts toward secrecy, even though it theoretically

83 1 Roger M. Milgrim, Milgrim on Trade Secrets § 1.04 (2009).

84 Unif. Trade Secrets Act § 1 cmt (2005).

85 Victoria A. Cundiff, *Reasonable Measures to Protect Trade Secrets in a Digital Environment*, 49 IDEA 359, 363–4 (2009).

86 Rockwell Graphic Sys., Inc. v. DEV Indus., 925 F.2d 174, 178–9 (7th Cir. 1991).

87 Michael Risch, *Why Do We Have Trade Secrets?*, 11 Marq. Intell. Prop. L. Rev. 1, 45–7 (2007).

88 Cundiff, *supra* note 85, at 363.

89 Whether or not this requirement ought to be an element of trade secrecy is disputed. See Mark A. Lemley, *The Surprising Virtues of Treating Trade Secrets as IP Rights*, 61 Stan. L. Rev. 311, 348–50 (2008).

could have spent much money building a temporary roof over the construction.[90] The law thus encourages a company constructing a plant not to undertake the expense of a temporary roof by providing trade secrecy protection without it.[91]

Quite interesting, then, about the depiction of Willy Wonka's operations and its real-world analogues is that some of the secrecy measures taken are extreme, apparently well beyond that which is reasonable.[92] Although it seemed quite reasonable to lock and mark as private important rooms in his chocolate factory and perhaps to build underground to conceal any public view, Wonka seemed to go well beyond that by firing all of his employees and hiring Oompa-Loompas, keeping the factory gates shuttered all of the time.[93] Also appearing excessive are Mars's practices of having no company representative and designing and producing all of its own machines for purposes of secrecy, especially if Mars is not the most efficient designer of these machines. Hershey's efforts at protecting secrecy, such as by not revealing its production methods, seem reasonable in comparison, although probably not with regard to the difficulty of getting information internally to help build the business.

Given that legal protection is available for misappropriation of trade secrets, which the candy companies' production methods and future product ideas would appear to be, why do companies in this industry seem to be going above and beyond what the law requires for protection by over-investing in secrecy? Some of the personalities behind these fictional and real companies, Willy Wonka and the Mars family in particular, are sufficiently eccentric and paranoid that perhaps they value secrecy at all costs. Relatedly, it might be the case that the candy companies are far from indifferent between the legal remedies for trade secrecy misappropriations[94] and avoiding an actual misappropriation in the first instance,

---

90 E.I. duPont de Nemours & Co. v. Christopher, 431 F.2d 1012, 1016 (5th Cir. 1970).

91 See Lemley, *supra* note 89, at 334–5 (noting also that over-investment in protection of information tends to occur in countries where there is no legal protection for trade secrets).

92 Given the degree of secrecy in the candy industry, it is perhaps unsurprising that the earliest reported American case on misappropriation of trade secrets involved a method for making chocolate. See Vickery v. Welch, 36 Mass. 523 (1837).

93 That said, Wonka possibly saved money by taking this measure, given that he was paying the Oompa-Loompas in cacao beans and chocolate instead of paying cash as to his previous employees.

94 Possible remedies for misappropriation of a trade secret include criminal penalties, injunctive relief and damages. Lemley, *supra* note 89, at 319.

in that they are of the opinion that the former under-compensate for misappropriation. Perhaps the sentiment is that once the Kit Kat is out of the bag, the ballgame is over.[95] There is also always the risk that legal recovery is too unpredictable, given gray areas in the law of trade secrets. Moreover, perhaps the time and energy to be spent on litigation are considered too costly. Alternatively, maybe it is wrong to consider the industry's efforts at secrecy as going beyond that which is reasonable, given the extravagant and persistent attempts of thievery in the industry.

This industry's practices, as per Dahl's colorful depiction of Wonka and his competitors in *Charlie and the Chocolate Factory* and the ways of their factual counterparts, provide some brain candy for trying to understand the role and operation of trade secrecy. They raise central questions about trade secrecy. When, if ever, will companies draw the line of efforts to protect secrecy at that which is reasonable, without over-investing? Is the legal protection of trade secrecy desirable or is there a strong preference instead for deterring any actual misappropriations through perhaps extreme efforts of protecting important information? Perhaps in certain industries, like candy, trade secrecy acts typically as a fail-safe should extravagant attempts at secrecy somehow fall short.

The tale of the candy industry also seems to serve as a counterexample to key assumptions made by the U.S. Supreme Court on when the availability of trade secrecy protection provides an incentive to innovate in the first instance.[96] In holding that patent laws do not pre-empt state laws on trade secrecy, the Supreme Court assumed that trade secrecy is a far weaker form of protection than patent law when both might be invoked.[97] Reasoning that trade secrets are at risk of honest discovery and failed lawsuits even when misappropriated, the Supreme Court stated that '[t]he possibility that an inventor who believes his invention meets the standards of patentability will sit back, rely on trade secret law, and . . . forfeit any right to patent protection is remote indeed'.[98] Based on that assumption, the Supreme Court concluded that there is no sufficient conflict between states' laws of trade secrecy and federal patent law.[99] Counter to the Court's assumption, many of the innovations of the fictional Willy Wonka and the factual Mars and Hershey appear to be patentable, yet their creators opt for secrecy on the basis that its protection will outlast the term of patent protection. If the candy industry's practices are sufficiently

---

95 *Cf.* Gambale v. Deutsche Bank AG, 377 F.3d 133, 144 n.11 (2d Cir. 2004).
96 Kewanee Oil Co. v. Bicron Corp., 416 U.S. 470, 484–93 (1974).
97 *Id.* at 489–90.
98 *Id.* at 490 (citation omitted).
99 *Id.* at 491–3.

widespread, the law ought to recalibrate patent and trade secrecy law by considering both how much trade secrecy laws provide an incentive to invent patentable, but unpatented, inventions and how concerned to be with a flight from the disclosure of innovations that patent law requires to secrecy.

2 The Restatements, the Uniform Act and the status of American trade secret law

*Robert Denicola**

I. INTRODUCTION

Patents in America are governed exclusively by federal law. Federal control over copyrights is only slightly less complete.[1] Trademark law remains a mixture of federal law and state statutory and common law protection, but the federal scheme clearly predominates.[2] Trade secret law, however, is state law.[3] For most of its history trade secret law was also common law, consisting of a gradual accretion of precedents arising through the resolution of disparate disputes between owners and users of alleged trade secrets.[4] As a creature of state law, it was never quite accurate to speak of *the* law of trade secrets; there were instead numerous trade secret laws produced as courts in separate jurisdictions experimented with the theories and scope of protection for confidential business information. In some places, and at some times, decisions put emphasis on the property

* Margaret Larson Professor of Intellectual Property Law, University of Nebraska.

[1] Under the pre-emption provision in the federal copyright act, only 'works of authorship not fixed in any tangible medium of expression' remain open to state copyright protection. 17 U.S.C. § 301(b).

[2] Trademark registration under the federal Lanham Act, for example, allows trademark owners to secure rights in a mark earlier than under state law, 15 U.S.C. § 1051(1), and can substantially increase the geographic scope of protection. *Id.* § 1057(c). It also enables the owner to prevent the importation of infringing goods. *Id.* § 1124. Even for marks that have not been federally registered, the causes of action against infringement and dilution provided in § 1125 of the Lanham Act have largely superseded similar actions under state law.

[3] The only significant source of federal protection for trade secrets are the criminal provisions of the Economic Espionage Act, 18 U.S.C. §§ 1831–9, and the prohibition against disclosure of trade secrets by federal employees in 18 U.S.C. § 1905.

[4] The first trade secret case in America was probably Vickery v. Welch, 36 Mass. 523 (1837), holding that an agreement for the sale of a secret process was not void as a restraint of trade. The most well-known of the early trade secret cases is Peabody v. Norfolk, 98 Mass. 452 (1868), which enforced the promise of a former employee not to disclose the employer's trade secrets.

rights of the trade secret owner,[5] on a breach of a duty of good faith,[6] and on principles of unfair competition,[7] although the different perspectives typically had little impact on ultimate outcomes.[8] The absence of precedent in some jurisdictions meant in effect that they had no trade secret law at all.[9] The lack of uniformity inherent in a common law system of trade secret protection became increasingly problematic with the growth of interstate commerce throughout the twentieth century.

A measure of uniformity was introduced into trade secret law with the publication of the fourth and final volume of the Restatement (First) of Torts in 1939, although only two of the Restatement's 971 sections dealt specifically with trade secrets. Section 757 treated the general principles of liability for the use or disclosure of another's trade secret, while § 758 stated a narrow rule limiting the liability of persons who learned a trade secret without notice of its secret character. The Restatements, promulgated under the auspices of the American Law Institute, are not a source of primary law. Their influence rests on their persuasiveness. As the Institute put it, 'The object of the Institute is accomplished in so far as the legal profession accepts the Restatement as prima facie a correct statement of the general law of the United States'.[10] The 'object of the Institute' was not, at least overtly, substantive reform. 'The object of the Institute in preparing the Restatement is to present an orderly statement of the general common law of the United States' – an object prompted by concern 'that the ever-increasing volume of the decisions of the courts, establishing new rules or precedents, and the numerous instances in which the decisions

[5] E.g., *Peabody*, 98 Mass. at 452 (1868); Elaterite Paint & Mfg. Co. v. S.E. Frost Co., 117 N.W. 388 (Minn. 1908); Mann v. Tatge Chemical Co., 201 Kan. 326, 440 P.2d 640 (1968); Microbiological Research Corp. v. Muna, 625 P.2d 690 (Utah 1981).

[6] E.g., Northern Petrochemical Co. v. Tomlinson, 484 F.2d 1057 (7th Cir. 1973) (Illinois law); Valco Cincinnati, Inc. v. N & D Machining Serv., Inc., 492 N.E.2d 814 (Ohio 1986); Smith v. Snap-On Tools Corp., 833 F.2d 578 (5th Cir. 1987) (Wisconsin law).

[7] E.g., Eastman Co. v. Reichenbach, 20 N.Y.S. 110 (Sup. Ct. 1892), *aff'd*, 29 N.Y.S. 1143 (1894), Chicago Lock Co. v. Fanberg, 676 F.2d 400 (9th Cir. 1982) (California law).

[8] 'The differences between the theoretical bases of trade secret protection are often academic and practically meaningless'. 1 M. Jager, Trade Secrets Law § 4:3 (2010).

[9] See Briefing.com v. Jones, 126 P.3d 928 (Wyo. 2006) (adopting the cause of action for trade secret misappropriation as set out in the Restatement (Third) of Unfair Competition). The Wyoming state legislature later adopted the Uniform Trade Secrets Act. Wyo. Stat. Ann. §§ 40-24-101 *et seq.*

[10] 4 Restatement (First) of Torts x (1939).

are irreconcilable, taken in connection with the growing complication of economic and other conditions of modern life, are increasing the law's uncertainty and lack of clarity'.[11] At least with respect to trade secrets, the Restatement (First) of Torts has been persuasive indeed, and its formulation of trade secret law in § 757 has been cited by courts in hundreds of decisions. Perhaps the most influential aspect of § 757 was the attempt in comment b to articulate an operative definition of a 'trade secret':

> A trade secret may consist of any formula, pattern, device or compilation of information which is used in one's business, and which gives him an opportunity to obtain an advantage over competitors who do not know or use it.[12]

A Westlaw search reveals that this definition has been recited in over 500 trade secret cases. Despite the influence of the Restatement (First) of Torts, the topic of trade secret law was not included in the subsequent Restatement (Second) of Torts completed in 1979. Trade secret law, along with the law of trademarks and false advertising, was deleted by the American Law Institute on the rationale that the subjects 'have become substantial specialties, in their own right, governed extensively by legislation and largely divorced from their initial grounding in the principles of torts . . . If restatement is attempted in these fields, it will be done by separate projects'.[13] The deletion contributed to the next major development in trade secret law.

The law of trade secrets was dramatically transformed in 1979 with the approval of the Uniform Trade Secrets Act by the National Conference of Commissioners on Uniform State Laws. Like the American Law Institute, the National Conference has no law-making authority. Unlike the Restatements, however, the work products of the National Conference are intended for adoption into law by the legislatures of the states. The rationale offered for the Uniform Trade Secrets Act by the National Conference is reminiscent of the Restatement of Torts:

> Notwithstanding the commercial importance of state trade secret law to interstate business, this law has not developed satisfactorily. In the first place, its development is uneven. Although there typically are a substantial number of reported decisions in states that are commercial centers, this is not the case in less populous and more agricultural jurisdictions. Secondly, even in states in which there has been significant litigation, there is undue uncertainty concerning the parameters of trade secret protection, and the appropriate remedies for

---

11 *Id.*

12 *Id.* § 757, cmt. b.

13 4 Restatement (Second) Torts, introduction, vii–viii (1979).

> misappropriation of a trade secret . . . In spite of this need, the most widely accepted rules of trade secret law, § 757 of the Restatement of Torts, were among the sections omitted from the Restatement of Torts, 2d (1978).[14]

Beginning with Minnesota in 1980 and concluding for now with Wyoming in 2006, the Uniform Trade Secrets Act has become a statutory source of trade secret protection in 45 states as well as the District of Columbia and the Virgin Islands. (The holdouts as of 2010, however, are the commercially important states of Massachusetts, New Jersey, New York, North Carolina and Texas.)

When the American Law Institute embarked on a third series of Restatements in the 1980s, the 'separate project' on unfair trade practices anticipated in the Restatement (Second) of Torts was part of the agenda. A request that I received from the Institute for a project proposal in 1985 began a process that ultimately resulted in the publication of the Restatement (Third) of Unfair Competition. Harvey Perlman soon joined me as a Reporter for the project. During the ensuing decade, our drafts were reviewed at a series of seven meetings by a panel of prominent Advisers appointed by the Institute. The drafts were also reviewed six times by a Consultative Group consisting of interested members of the Institute, four times by the Council of the Institute, and four times by the Institute's membership at its annual meeting. Every meeting yielded significant improvements, and the final product, published in 1995, is clearly the Institute's and not our own.[15] In addition to trade secret law, the Restatement (Third) of Unfair Competition includes sections on deceptive marketing, trademark law and the right of publicity, although the full scope of 'unfair competition' and its status as an independent source of liability remains controversial.

In one sense, the inclusion of trade secret law in the Restatement (Third) seems odd. With the promulgation and rapid success of the Uniform Act, trade secret law is now largely statutory law, and the Restatements have traditionally focused on the common law. Even the original Restatements, however, recognized the desirability of analysing 'not only the law

---

[14] Uniform Trade Secrets Act, prefatory note (1979) (hereinafter 'Uniform Act').

[15] The creation of a Restatement is describe, in S. Abrahamson, *Refreshing Institutional Memories: Wisconsin and the American Law Institute, The Fairchild Lecture*, 1995 Wis. L. Rev. 1 (1995). See also R. Denicola and H. Perlman, *A Foreword to the Symposium on the Restatement of Unfair Competition,* 47 S.C. L. Rev. i (1996). For a discussion of some of the criticisms directed at the American Law Institute and the Restatement process, see K. Adams, *Blaming the Mirror: The Restatements and the Common Law*, 40 Ind. L. Rev. 205 (2007).

developed solely by judicial decision, but also the law that has grown from the application by the courts of statutes that have been generally enacted and have been in force for many years'.[16] The analysis of trade secret law offered in the Restatement is applicable both to actions at common law and to the interpretation of the Uniform Act, which itself relies, often without significant elaboration, on concepts developed through common law adjudication. The trade secret sections of the Restatement do not substitute for the statutory language of the Uniform Act, but are useful aids in interpreting and applying the statutory law. As with any statutory text, the generalizations and ambiguities of the Uniform Act present occasions for disagreement. In considering such issues in the Restatement, we took our guidance from Professor Herbert Wechsler, who as Director of the American Law Institute in 1966 advised the Institute in its Restatements 'to weigh all of the considerations relevant to the development of the common law that our polity calls on the courts to weigh in their deliberations'.[17]

II. THE RESTATEMENT (THIRD) AND THE UNIFORM ACT

The Uniform Act emphasizes codification over innovation, but even codification requires difficult choices. The more expansive format of the Restatement (Third) offers an opportunity to examine the implications of some of the drafters' decisions.[18] For example, the Act excludes from the definition of 'trade secret' information that is 'generally known . . . [or] readily ascertainable by proper means'. Since only misappropriation of a 'trade secret' is actionable under the Act, the Restatement (Third) interprets the statute as rejecting a series of common law decisions that imposed liability for the use or disclosure of confidentially acquired information even after the information had become available from public

---

16 4 Restatement (First) of Torts x (1939).

17 H. Wechsler, *Report of the Director*, 43 A.L.I. Proceedings 27 (1966).

18 Some issues are arguably left unattended by the Uniform Act, particularly those that are removed from its commercial orientation. It is unclear, for example, whether the Act imposes liability for disclosures that are unrelated to commercial exploitation of the information. While a disclosure solely for the purpose of causing harm to the trade secret owner would undoubtedly be actionable, some disclosures may raise substantial free speech or public interest issues. The Restatement therefore cautions that a privilege may well be recognized by the courts in connection with the disclosure of a trade secret that is relevant to public health or safety, or to the commission of a crime, or to other matters of substantial public interest. Restatement (Third) Unfair Competition § 40, cmt. c (1993).

sources.[19] While the secrecy requirement is sometimes questioned,[20] trade secret law is designed to protect owners only from unfair methods of competition and to prevent unjust enrichment attributable to an appropriator's misconduct. It also encourages investment in innovation and promotes efficient exploitation by facilitating confidential disclosures to employees and licensees.[21] However, as the Restatement cautions, '[t]he subject matter and scope of trade secret protection is necessarily limited by the public and private interest in access to valuable information'.[22] Thus, the Restatement adopts the view that '[t]he public interest in avoiding unnecessary restraints on the exploitation of valuable information supports the conclusion that protection as a trade secret terminates when the information is no longer secret'.[23] The Restatement also rejects the imposition of any obligation on the user to rely on public domain sources rather than on the original confidential disclosure.[24]

The Restatement (First) of Torts in § 757 limited liability to a person who 'discloses or uses' another's trade secret;[25] many common law cases similarly list 'use or disclosure' as an element of the cause of action.[26] The Uniform Act in § 1(2)(i) now explicitly extends liability to the *acquisition* of a trade secret by improper means. As the Restatement (Third) of Unfair Competition explains, however, the new rule is largely consistent with the prior case law.[27] The Uniform Act also adopts the rule from cases such as

---

19 See, e.g., Goldberg v. Medtronic, Inc., 686 F.2d 1219 (7th Cir. 1982); Franke v. Wiltschek, 209 F.2d 493 (2d Cir. 1953); Smith v. Dravo, 203 F.2d 369 (7th Cir. 1953); Kamin v. Kuhnau, 374 P.2d 912 (Or. 1962); Reading & Bates Constr. Co. v. O'Donnell, 627 S.W.2d 147 (Tex. App. 1982).

20 See further Robert G. Bone, Chapter 3.

21 'The maintenance of standards of commercial ethics and the encouragement of invention are the broadly stated policies of trade secret law.' Kewanee Oil Co. v. Bicron Corp., 416 U.S. 470, 481 (1974). The U.S. Supreme Court also emphasized another rationale for the protection of trade secrets: 'A most fundamental human right, that of privacy, is threatened when industrial espionage is condoned or is made profitable'. *Id.* at 487.

22 RESTATEMENT (THIRD) UNFAIR COMPETITION § 39, cmt. a.

23 *Id.* § 39, cmt. f.

24 'Even those courts that decline to take into account a loss of secrecy following a confidential disclosure to the defendant often assert in dicta that no liability attaches if the defendant actually extracts the information from public sources. When the information is readily ascertainable from such sources, however, actual resort to the public domain is a formality that should not determine liability.' *Id.*

25 RESTATEMENT (FIRST) OF TORTS § 757 (1939).

26 See, e.g., Texas Urethane, Inc. v. Seacrest Marine Corp., 608 F.2d 136 (5th Cir. 1979); E.W. Bliss Co. v. Struthers-Dunn, Inc., 408 F.2d 1108 (8th Cir. 1969); Heyman v. A.R. Winarick, Inc., 325 F.2d 584 (2d Cir. 1963).

27 RESTATEMENT (THIRD) UNFAIR COMPETITION § 40, cmt. b.

E.I. duPont de Nemours & Co. v. Christopher[28] that 'improper means' can include conduct that is not independently wrongful.[29] The Restatement (Third) adds that the propriety of the means of acquisition may depend in part on the extent to which the acquisition was facilitated by the owner's failure to take precautions against discovery of the information by the means in question, taking into account the foreseeability of the conduct and the availability and cost of effective precautions.[30] Although the general obligation of a trade secret owner to take reasonable precautions remains subject to debate, in some instances the absence of precautions may permit access by unobjectionable means.

In its remedial provisions, the Uniform Act struggles to maintain an appropriate balance between protection and access. In § 2, the Act follows those common law decisions that permit injunctive relief against 'threatened' misappropriation.[31] However, in order to avoid undue restraints on former employees, the Restatement (Third) Unfair Competition urges caution in the issuance and formulation of any such injunction.[32] Section 2 of the Act also deals with the appropriate duration of injunctive relief in trade secret cases, specifically rejecting those common law decisions that perpetually enjoin a defendant's use.[33] According to the drafters, 'an injunction should last for as long as is necessary, but no longer than is necessary, to eliminate the commercial advantage' obtained through the misappropriation.[34] The Restatement (Third) analyses the application of this limiting principle in cases where the trade secret subsequently becomes public or where the defendant could have eventually obtained the information through reverse engineering or independent discovery.[35] Monetary relief under § 3 of the Act, which is subject to similar durational

---

28 431 F.2d 1012 (5th Cir. 1970), *cert. denied*, 400 U.S. 1024 (1971) (aerial reconnaissance of a manufacturing plant during construction was an improper means of acquisition).

29 'Improper means could include otherwise lawful conduct which is improper under the circumstances.' Uniform Act § 1, cmt.

30 Restatement (Third) Unfair Competition § 43, cmt. c.

31 Uniform Act § 2 ('Actual or threatened misappropriation may be enjoined'). See, e.g., Baxter Int'l, Inc. v. Morris, 976 F.2d 1189 (8th Cir. 1992); Allis-Chalmers Mfg. Co. v. Continental Aviation & Engineering Corp., 255 F.Supp. 645 (E.D. Mich. 1966); B.F. Goodrich Co. v. Wohlgemuth, 192 N.E.2d 99 (Ohio Ct. App. 1963).

32 Restatement (Third) Unfair Competition § 44, cmt. c.

33 See, e.g., Franke v. Wiltschek, 209 F.2d 493 (2d Cir. 1953); Valco Cincinnati, Inc. v. N & D Machining Serv., Inc., 492 N.E.2d 814 (Ohio 1986); Elcor Chemical Corp. v. Agri-Sul, Inc., 494 S.W.2d 204 (Tex. Civ. App. 1973).

34 Uniform Act § 2, cmt.

35 Restatement (Third) Unfair Competition § 44, cmt. f.

limitations,[36] may consist of damages for actual loss and the recovery of unjust enrichment. The Restatement (Third) in § 45 examines the relationship between compensatory and restitutionary remedies and reviews the measures of recovery typically employed in trade secret litigation, which can present unique remedial issues distinct from other unfair competition torts.

In at least one instance, the Uniform Act is self-consciously innovative. The comment to § 1 of the Act states, 'The definition of "trade secret" contains a reasonable departure from the Restatement (First) of Torts definition which required that a trade secret be "continuously used in one's business"'.[37] The immediate objective of the drafters seems relatively modest. Their comment states that a 'trade secret' under the Act now includes 'negative' information – knowledge that certain processes or methods will *not* work – which by its nature perhaps cannot be 'continuously used' by its owner. The comment also indicates that the Act includes information that an owner has not yet had the opportunity to put into 'use'.[38] The full implications of the change, however, are more far-reaching.

The Restatement (First) of Torts in § 757 had employed the 'continuous use' requirement to exclude from the scope of trade secret law what it described as 'information as to single or ephemeral events'.[39] However, the exclusion of information relating to 'single or ephemeral events' from the scope of trade secret protection did not mean that confidential business

---

[36] Uniform Act § 3, cmt. ('[A] monetary recovery for trade secret appropriation is appropriate only for the period in which information is entitled to protection as a trade secret, plus the additional period, if any in which a misappropriator retains an advantage over good faith competitors because of misappropriation.').

[37] According to the Restatement (First) of Torts, 'A trade secret is a process or device for continuous use in the operation of the business'. Restatement (First) of Torts § 757, cmt. b (1939).

[38] Uniform Act § 1, Comment. The elimination of the 'use' requirement is discussed in Restatement (Third) Unfair Competition § 39, cmt. e. Even before the Uniform Act, a number of cases had rejected 'use' by the owner as an element of the common law action. See, e.g., Syntex Ophthalmics, Inc. v. Tsuetaki, 701 F.2d 677 (7th Cir. 1983) (Illinois law); Ferroline Corp. v. General Aniline & Film Corp., 207 F.2d 912 (7th Cir. 1953), *cert denied*, 347 U.S. 953 (1954) (New Jersey law); Sinclair v. Aquarius Electronics, Inc., 116 Cal. Rptr. 654 (1974).

[39] '[A trade secret] differs from other secret information in a business (see § 759) in that it is not simply information as to single or ephemeral events in the conduct of the business, as, for example, the amount or other terms of a secret bid for a contract or the salary of certain employees, or the security investments made or contemplated, or the date fixed for the announcement of a new policy or for bringing out a new model or the like.' Restatement (First) of Torts § 757, cmt. b (1939).

information such as executive salaries or secret bids were fair game for competitors. Section 757 itself disclaimed any intent to pre-empt the protection of other types of confidential information,[40] and § 759 announced a separate rule of liability for those who used 'improper means' to acquire business information if their possession, disclosure or use caused harm to the other's interests.[41] 'Improper means' here was intended to have the same meaning as in the rule that protected trade secrets.[42] Similarly, the Restatement (Second) of Agency in § 396 protects both trade secrets 'or other similar confidential matters' from unauthorized use or disclosure following the termination of an employment or other agency relationship.[43] Thus, the Restatements envisioned protection for confidential business information that fell outside the scope of trade secret law on terms similar to the protection enjoyed by trade secrets. The Restatement (Third) of Unfair Competition interprets the Act's elimination of the 'continuous use' requirement as rejecting the Restatement of Torts categorical exclusion of information about 'single or ephemeral events' from the scope of trade secret law.[44] Cases under the Uniform Act now demonstrate an

---

[40] 'Although given information is not a trade secret, one who receives the information in a confidential relation or discovers it by improper means may be under some duty not to disclose or use that information.' *Id.*

[41] *Id.* § 759. See, e.g., Seismograph Serv. Corp. v. Offshore Raydist, Inc., 135 F.Supp. 342, 354 (E.D. La. 1955) (both 'business information' and 'trade secrets' are protected against improper acquisition, citing § 759), *aff'd*, 263 F.2d 5 (5th Cir. 1958); USM Corp. v. Marson Fastener Corp., 393 N.E.2d 895, 903 (Mass. 1979) (dicta stating that 'business information' not protectable as a trade secret is still protected against improper acquisition, citing § 759).

[42] Restatement (First) of Torts § 759, cmt. c (1939).

[43] Restatement (Second) Agency § 396 (1958). See Nucor Corp. v. Tennessee Forging Steel Serv., Inc., 476 F.2d 386 (8th Cir. 1973) (employees have a duty not to disclose confidential information regardless of whether it is a trade secret, citing Restatement (Second) Agency §§ 395–6).

[44] 'The definition of "trade secret" adopted by the Uniform Trade Secrets Act does not include any requirement relating to the duration of the information's economic value . . . The definition adopted in this Section similarly contains no requirement that the information afford a continuous or long-term advantage.' Restatement (Third) Unfair Competition § 39, cmt. d. See also E. Kitch, *The Expansion of Trade Secrecy Protection and the Mobility of Management Employees: A New Problem for the Law*, 47 S.C. L. Rev. 659, 661–2 (1996) (emphasizing that neither the Restatement nor the Uniform Act continue the 'single or ephemeral events' limitation from the Restatement of Torts and concluding, 'The Restatement of Unfair Competition, following the lead of the Uniform Trade Secrets Act and the cases following the Act, eliminates the distinction between information that is a trade secret and other confidential information') (footnotes omitted); R. Klitzke, *The Uniform Trade Secrets Act*, 64 Marq. L. Rev. 276, 288 (1980) (noting the

increasing willingness to protect as trade secrets information with a relatively short shelf-life.[45] The Restatement (Third) position may also influence results in common law jurisdictions.[46]

Since the Restatement of Torts and the corresponding common law cases already extended protection to confidential business information that was outside the former scope of trade secret law, the expansion of the definition of 'trade secret' in the Uniform Act may seem academic. Whether or not technically a trade secret, confidential business information would in any case be protected from improper acquisition or use in breach of confidence. Paradoxically, however, the expansion of the definition of a trade secret in the Uniform Act may actually enlarge the public domain. Bringing all confidential business information within the scope of

---

former distinction between trade secrets and 'business information . . . not used continuously in the operation of the owner's business', but concluding that the Uniform Act now 'extends protection to valuable information not continuously used in the trade or business. Thus, the Act would provide trade secret protection for 'single event' information, such as a current status report').

[45] See, e.g., Camp Creek Hospitality Inns, Inc. v. Sheraton Franchise Corp., 139 F.3d 1396 (11th Cir. 1998) (hotel occupancy levels, daily rates and operating expenses as trade secrets under the Georgia Act); PepsiCo, Inc. v. Redmond, 54 F.3d 1262 (7th Cir. 1995) (marketing and distribution plans protected under the Illinois Act); H & R Block Eastern Tax Servs., Inc. v. Enchura, 122 F.Supp.2d 1067 (W.D. Mo. 2000) (information about upcoming advertising and marketing plans and new customer services treated as trade secrets under the Missouri Act); Ovation Plumbing, Inc. v. Furton, 33 P.3d 1221, 1224 (Colo. App. 2001) (details of a bid on a plumbing contract found protectable under the Colorado Act, specifically rejecting an argument that it 'cannot be a trade secret because it was not used continuously in the operation of [plaintiff's] business'. 'Section 7-74-102(4) does not contain a continuous use requirement . . . We will not read a continuous use requirement into this statute when it does not contain such language nor any indication of legislative intent to include this concept'). But see Enterprise Leasing Co. v. Ehmke, P.3d 1064, 1068 (Ariz. App. 1999) (limiting trade secrets under the Arizona Act to information 'that is continuously used or has the potential to be used in one's business' and excluding 'information as to single or ephemeral events'); State *ex rel.* The Plain Dealer v. Ohio Dept. of Ins., 687 N.E.2d 661 (Ohio 1997) (citing the requirement of continuous use from the Restatement of Torts as applicable under the Ohio Act).

[46] See Storage Tech. Corp. v. Custom Hardware Eng'g & Consulting, Ltd., 2006 WL 1766434 (D. Mass. 2006) ('However, it is unclear whether Massachusetts courts would still apply the continuous-use requirement. *See* Restatement (Third) of Unfair Competition § 39, cmt. d.'). But see Portfolioscope, Inc. v. I-Flex Solutions Ltd., 473 F.Supp.2d 252, 255 (D. Mass. 2007) ('Whatever its wisdom, the continuous use requirement is part of Massachusetts law and this court is powerless to remove it'). *Cf. In re* Bass, 113 S.W.3d 735 (Tex. 2003) (seismic data for a ranch protected as a trade secret under Texas common law).

trade secret law means that protection for such information will now be subject to all of the limitations imposed by the Uniform Act. Information that is 'readily ascertainable by proper means', for example, or that is not the subject of efforts 'reasonable under the circumstances to maintain its secrecy', should no longer be protectable.[47]

Case law offers examples of the risks associated with protecting confidential business information under separate tort actions independent of the limitations of trade secrets law. In one case, for example, a plaintiff complained that a former employee had disclosed to a competitor the plaintiff's 'bid range' on an upcoming contract along with details of the plaintiff's production process. The trial court held that the plaintiff had not established the existence of any trade secrets protectable under the Louisiana Trade Secrets Act, specifically finding that the production process involved mere refinements of techniques generally known in the industry. Although the trial court's decision on the trade secret count was not appealed, the appellate court held that both the bid range and the production process were nevertheless protectable under a claim for breach of fiduciary duty, although it ultimately held that there had been no unlawful disclosure.[48] In another case, an appellate court upheld a summary judgment that 'know-how' relating to a training course for the unemployed consisting of techniques such as conducting the course on consecutive days, critiquing thank-you notes, and holding dress rehearsals for job interviews were matters of common knowledge and not protectable as trade secrets. However, the court remanded the case with directions to the trial court to consider claims for breach of confidence and misappropriation with respect to the same information.[49] Cases protecting more traditional trade secret subject matter under alternative tort theories can

---

[47] According to the Restatement, '[I]n the absence of interests justifying broader duties, the plaintiff should be required to demonstrate that the information qualifies for protection as a trade secret under the rule stated in § 39'. RESTATEMENT (THIRD) UNFAIR COMPETITION § 41, cmt. c. Other consequences of the expanded definition of trade secret under the Uniform Act and the Restatement are pursued in Kitch, *supra* note 44.

[48] Defcon, Inc. v. Webb, 687 So. 2d 639 (La. App. 1997).

[49] Self Directed Placement Corp. v. Control Data Corp., 908 F.2d 462 (9th Cir. 1990). See, e.g., Seismograph Serv. Corp. v. Offshore Raydist, Inc., 135 F.Supp. 342 (E.D. La. 1955) (involving the improper acquisition of information such as the financial condition of a business and the status of a pending patent application), *aff'd*, 263 F.2d 5 (5th Cir. 1958). 'The fact that the business information is otherwise available is no defense. The improper acquisition itself creates the liability in damages.' *Id.* at 354.

produce equally problematic results.[50] Although the instinct to condemn a defendant's improper conduct is understandable, channeling business information cases through the Uniform Act insures equal attention to the public interest in preserving access to material that should be considered part of the public domain.

Elimination of the 'continuous use' requirement under the Uniform Act and the Restatement (Third) enlarges the scope of trade secret law in another way. As the drafters of the Uniform Act noted, 'The broader definition in the proposed Act extends protection to a plaintiff who has not yet had an opportunity or acquired the means to put a trade secret to use'.[51] A company that has developed a new manufacturing process that it has not yet put into practice may thus be entitled to protection under the Act. However, the expanded definition of trade secret now also apparently subsumes inventors and other creators who develop valuable information with the intention of selling it to someone who can put the idea to use. Cases involving ideas for new or improved products submitted to manufacturers or programming ideas offered to the entertainment industry have traditionally been analysed under unique rules often described as 'the law of ideas'.[52] As the Restatement notes, 'With the rejection under the Uniform Trade Secrets Act and this Section of any requirement of use

---

50 See, e.g., Roboserve, Ltd. v. Tom's Foods, Inc., 940 F.2d 1441 (11th Cir. 1991). The appellate court held that the trial court had erred in denying the defendant's motion for judgment notwithstanding the verdict on a trade secret claim brought by a vending machine manufacturer. Once the machines had been sold by the plaintiff to a customer, it could not invoke trade secret law to prevent reverse engineering. However, the court proceeded to uphold a jury verdict on a breach of a confidential relationship count based in part on the defendant's transfer of the machine to a competing manufacturer. In USM Corp. v. Marson Fastener Corp., 379 Mass. 90, 393 N.E.2d 895 (1979), the trial court had dismissed the plaintiff's claim for misappropriation of trade secrets embodied in a machine used to manufacture rivets, finding that the plaintiff had not taken adequate precautions to preserve its secrecy. The appellate court reversed, holding that plaintiff's precautions were sufficient. However, the court went on to assert, 'A plaintiff who may not claim trade secret protection either because it failed to take reasonable steps to preserve its secrecy or because the information, while confidential, is only "business information", may still be entitled to some relief against one who improperly procures such information. The law puts its imprimatur on fair dealing, good faith, and fundamental honesty. Courts condemn conduct which fails to reflect these minimum accepted moral values by penalizing such conduct whenever it occurs'. *Id.* at 903.

51 Uniform Act, § 1, cmt.

52 See, e.g., M. AND D. NIMMER, NIMMER ON COPYRIGHT ch. 19D ('The Law of Ideas') (2010); *cf.* P. GOLDSTEIN, COPYRIGHT § 17.7 ('Protection of Ideas') (2011); R. MILGRIM, MILGRIM ON TRADE SECRETS § 9.05 ('Submission of Ideas') (2010).

by the owner of a trade secret . . . there is no longer a formal distinction between trade secrets and the ideas that form the subject matter of the idea submission cases'.[53]

Prior to the Uniform Act, trade secret claims based on the submission of product or marketing ideas were regularly rejected, often with the explanation that the information was not subject to continuous use as a trade secret since implementation would expose the new idea to the public.[54] Other cases denying protection for ideas drew analogies to 'information as to single or ephemeral events' which could not be protected as trade secrets.[55] Plaintiffs seeking compensation for their ideas most often rely instead on contract claims. Indeed, in many industries, idea recipients endeavor to control the terms of their potential liability through the use of standardized idea submission forms.[56] In the absence of an express contract, idea submitters often assert the existence of an implied-in-fact contract to pay for an idea, although there is no consensus as to the circumstances that justify the implication of such a promise.[57] In addition,

---

[53] Restatement (Third) Unfair Competition § 39, cmt. h. See Kitch, *supra* note 44, at 663 ('Now instead of one set of rules for the protection of trade secrets, another for the protection of confidential information from business rivals, and yet a third applicable to idea submitters, all are handled under a single rubric: trade secrecy law'); Milgrim, *supra* note 52, § 9.05[4] (the Uniform Act's definition of a trade secret 'is broad enough to encompass matter traditionally analyzed at the common law under "submission-of-idea", not trade secret principles').

[54] See, e.g., Hudson Hotels Corp. v. Choice Hotels Int'l, 995 F.2d 1173, 1176–7 (2d Cir. 1993) (stating that 'the commonly accepted common law definition of a trade secret "does not include a marketing concept or new product idea"' and noting that plaintiff's idea for a micro-hotel could not be 'secretly and continuously used in commerce' since once marketed, the hotel features would necessarily be disclosed); Richter v. Westab, Inc., 529 F.2d 896, 900 (6th Cir. 1976) ('a marketing concept does not by confidentiality create a continuing competitive advantage because once it is implemented it is exposed for the world to see and for competitors to legally imitate'). But see Smith v. Snap-On Tools Corp., 833 F.2d 578 (5th Cir. 1987) (applying trade secret law to a plaintiff's submission of a new product idea); Sikes v. McGraw-Edison Co., 665 F.2d 731 (5th Cir.) (specifically rejecting both the argument that a 'new product idea' cannot be a trade secret and that the ability to reverse engineer the product after it is marketed deprives the product idea of competitive value), *cert. denied*, 458 U.S. 1108 (1982); Mann v. Tatge Chemical Co., 440 P.2d 640 (Kan. 1968).

[55] See Lehman v. Dow Jones & Co., 783 F.2d 285 (2d Cir. 1986) (information about the availability and attractiveness of a corporate acquisition could not be a trade secret under the Restatement of Torts).

[56] See Milgrim, *supra* note 52, § 9.05[5].

[57] See, e.g., Reeves v. Alyeska Pipeline Serv. Co., 926 P.2d 1130, 1141 (Alaska 1996) ('Under California law, if the recipient at the time of disclosure understands that the idea person expects to be paid for the disclosure of the idea, and does not

there is disagreement over whether the idea must satisfy additional criteria such as 'concreteness' or 'novelty' in order to support recovery under an implied-in-fact contract theory.[58] Since the Uniform Act does not displace contractual remedies,[59] these uncertainties will persist despite the broadened definition of trade secret.

In addition to express and implied-in-fact contract claims, idea submitters have also asserted various tort and restitutionary theories, including breach of confidence,[60] misappropriation of property,[61] and implied-in-law contract (quasi-contract).[62] Plaintiffs pursuing these non-contractual claims have been required to establish that their idea is 'novel' and sometimes also 'concrete'.[63] The 'novelty' requirement excludes from protection ideas that are generally known and thus seems analogous to the secrecy requirement of traditional trade secret law.[64] The novelty of an idea can

---

attempt to stop the disclosure, inaction may be seen as consent to a contract. This view has been criticized as unfairly placing a duty on the recipient to take active measures to stop the submission . . . We believe that a contract should not be implied under this scenario') (citations omitted).

[58] '[D]isagreement persists whether "concreteness" is necessary in idea-submission cases based on implied contract.' NIMMER, *supra* note 52, § 19D.06[A][2]. 'When protection for an idea is sought by *implied* contract, there is a split of authority whether the idea must be novel.' *Id.* § 19D.06[B][2][b] (emphasis in original).

[59] Uniform Act § 7.

[60] See Tele-Count Engineers, Inc. v. Pacific Tel. & Tel. Co., 168 Cal. App.3d 455, 214 Cal. Rptr. 276 (1985); Faris v. Enberg, 158 Cal. Rptr. 704 (1979).

[61] See Murray v. National Broadcasting Co., 844 F.2d 988 (2d Cir.), *cert denied*, 488 U.S. 955 (1988); Kleck v. Bausch & Lomb, Inc., 145 F.Supp.2d 819 (W.D. Tex. 2000); John W. Shaw Advertising, Inc. v. Ford Motor Co., 112 F.Supp. 121 (N.D. Ill. 1953).

[62] See Matarese v. Moore-McCormack Lines, Inc., 158 F.2d 631 (2d Cir. 1946); Kleck v. Bausch & Lomb, Inc., 145 F.Supp.2d 819 (W.D. Tex. 2000); Werlin v. Reader's Digest Ass'n, 528 F.Supp. 451 (S.D.N.Y. 1981).

[63] See Duffy v. Charles Schwab & Co., 123 F.Supp.2d 802 (D.N.J. 2000) (novelty required for misappropriation, unjust enrichment and unfair competition claims); Tele-Count Engineers, Inc. v. Pacific Tel. & Tel. Co., 214 Cal. Rptr. 276 (1985) (breach of confidence claim requires novelty); Werlin v. Reader's Digest Ass'n, 528 F.Supp. 451 (S.D.N.Y. 1981) (quasi-contract claim requires that the idea be novel and concrete); *Kleck*, 145 F.Supp.2d at 819 (quasi-contract claim requires novelty); *Murray*, 844 F.2d at 988 (property claims require novelty), *cert. denied*, 488 U.S. 955 (1988); *John W. Shaw Advertising, Inc.*, 112 F.Supp. at 121 (property claims require that the idea be novel and concrete).

[64] See *Duffy*, 123 F.Supp.2d at 802 (including the idea's commonality, commercial availability and secrecy as factors in determining 'novelty'); *Tele-Count Engineers, Inc.*, 214 Cal. Rptr. at 280 (equating novelty with 'substantially secret').

also be evidence of its competitive value[65] and may aid in proving subsequent use by a recipient.[66] 'Concreteness' insures that the boundaries of the plaintiff's idea can be suitably defined,[67] thus enabling an assessment of its value and the fact and extent of a recipient's use.[68]

Relocating the idea cases to the Uniform Act is a significant improvement. Novelty is a poor substitute for the more nuanced secrecy standard embodied in the Act, particularly since the idea cases have failed to achieve a common understanding of 'novelty'.[69] In one common law case, for example, protection was granted under a quasi-contract theory to an idea for a magazine story after the court found that the idea was novel to the defendant, although a similar story had already been published by the plaintiff.[70] Cases analysing idea submissions under the Uniform Act ask instead if the idea is 'generally known' or 'readily ascertainable', thus excluding from protection ideas that should be considered part of the public domain.[71] Similarly, a direct evaluation of the idea's 'economic value, actual or potential'[72] under the Uniform Act seems preferable to reliance on a standard of 'concreteness'.[73] As to 'misappropriation', the elaborate rules focusing on the circumstances of the recipient's acquisition

---

65 A. Miller, *Common Law Protection for Products of the Mind: An 'Idea' Whose Time Has Come*, 119 HARV. L. REV. 703, 728 (2006).

66 *Id.* at 728–9; NIMMER, *supra* note 52, § 19D.06[B][3].

67 John W. Shaw Advertising, Inc. v. Ford Motor Co., 112 F.Supp. 121, 123 (N.D. Ill. 1953) ('Since courts could not define and enforce a right in an abstraction, it is uniformly held that an idea must be reduced to concrete form in order to qualify as the subject of a protectible property interest.').

68 RESTATEMENT (THIRD) UNFAIR COMPETITION § 39, cmt. h; see Miller, *supra* note 65, at 724–5.

69 See NIMMER, *supra* note 52, § 19D.06[B][1].

70 Werlin v. Reader's Digest Ass'n, 528 F.Supp. 451, 466 (S.D.N.Y. 1981).

71 Uniform Act § 1(4). See, e.g., Auto Channel, Inc. v. Speedvision Network, LLC, 144 F.Supp.2d 784, 797 (W.D. Ky. 2001) (specifically cautioning that 'all of these misunderstandings, deceptions, and disappointments must be carefully examined to determine whether the law provides a remedy for the natural rough and tumble consequences of the business world'); Wal-Mart Stores, Inc. v. P.O. Market, Inc., 66 S.W.3d 620, 633 (Ark. 2002) ('The question then that confronts this court is whether the O'Banion concept is indeed unique information or whether it is, at its core, a variation of other economic models already in the public domain and readily ascertainable'); Pope v. Alberto-Culver Co., 694 N.E.2d 615 (Ill. App. Ct. 1998).

72 Uniform Act § 1(4).

73 See, e.g., Learning Curve Toys, Inc. v. Playwood Toys, Inc., 342 F.3d 714 (7th Cir. 2003); Penalty Kick Management Ltd. v. Coca Cola Co., 318 F.3d 1284 (11th Cir. 2003); and Olson v. Nieman's, Ltd., 579 N.W.2d 299 (Iowa 1998), all relying on market-oriented evidence of the idea's potential value to determine eligibility for protection under the Uniform Act.

and use of the idea in the Uniform Act[74] and the Restatement (Third)[75] offer a sounder basis for decision than generalized notions of 'unjust enrichment'.[76] Most significantly, the shift in analysis furthers the ultimate purpose of the Act by substituting uniform statutory standards for the uncertainty and inconsistency of the common law rules on idea submissions.[77] Although there are still holdouts, the trend toward application of the Uniform Act in idea submission cases continues to strengthen.[78]

III. DISPLACING THE COMMON LAW WITH THE UNIFORM TRADE SECRETS ACT

With its rigorous standards for protection and careful calibration of remedies, the Uniform Act offers an analytic structure that seems far superior to the common law. The elimination of the 'continuous use' requirement

---

[74] Uniform Act § 1(2).

[75] RESTATEMENT (THIRD) UNFAIR COMPETITION §§ 40–3.

[76] See, e.g., Penalty Kick Management Ltd. v. Coca Cola Co., 318 F.3d 1284 (11th Cir. 2003) (finding no use or disclosure by the recipient under the Uniform Act and Restatement); Nilssen v. Motorola, Inc., 963 F.Supp. 664 (N.D. Ill. 1997) (analysing the recipient's duty of confidentiality under the Uniform Act).

[77] See Miller, *supra* note 65, at 719–20 (commenting on the vagueness, uncertainty and inconsistency of the novelty and concreteness requirements and recommending their elimination). See also NIMMER, *supra* note 52, §§ 19D.06[A] and 19D.06[B].

[78] *Compare* Stromback v. New Line Cinema, 384 F.3d 283, 305 (6th Cir. 2004) (dicta concluding that the plaintiff's movie idea could not be a trade secret under the Michigan Act since it could have 'economic value' only if it was publicly exploited) and Mainardi v. Prudential Insurance Co., 2009 WL 229757 (E.D. Pa. 2009) (following *Stromback* and holding that 'a product cannot constitute a trade secret when it provides its creator with economic value only when disseminated – or, as here, sold – to third parties'); *with* Olson v. Nieman's, Ltd., 579 N.W.2d 299, 314 (Iowa 1998) (specifically noting that despite later public disclosure through marketing, an idea can have pre-release 'economic value' under the Uniform Act since it can be sold to potential exploiters). See also Daktronics, Inc. v. McAfee, 599 N.W.2d 358, 361 (S.D. 1999) (refusing relief to an idea submitter under the South Dakota Act since 'a trade secret does not include a marketing concept or new product idea submitted by one party to another', quoting Hudson Hotels Corp. v. Choice Hotels Int'l, 995 F.2d 1173, 1176 (2d Cir. 1993), which had been decided under the common law of New York). But see Niemi v. NHK Spring Co., 543 F.3d 294 (6th Cir. 2008) (reversing a summary judgment under the Ohio Act against a plaintiff who disclosed a new manufacturing technique to an automobile parts maker); Learning Curve Toys, Inc. v. Playwood Toys, Inc., 342 F.3d 714, 727 (7th Cir. 2003) (protecting a new product idea by noting that actual use by the submitter is not required for protection under the Illinois Act).

extends the advantages of that structure beyond the former boundaries of trade secret law. Uniformity itself is also a major contribution of the Act.[79] However, all these benefits are at risk if plaintiffs can too easily escape the reach of the Act and fall back on the diverse contours of the old law. The Uniform Act makes a clear attempt to safeguard its achievements. According to § 7, 'Except as provided in subsection (b), this Act displaces conflicting tort, restitutionary, and other law of this State providing civil remedies for misappropriation of a trade secret'.[80] Unfortunately, this effort to preserve the integrity of the Act has been less effective than its drafters undoubtedly hoped.

Plaintiffs have been surprisingly successful in avoiding the limitations of the Uniform Act. In one line of cases they have persuaded courts that pre-emption does not apply if the information they seek to protect fails to satisfy the statutory definition of a 'trade secret' and hence their alternative claims do not seek 'civil remedies for misappropriation of a trade secret'. *Burbank Grease Services, LLC v. Sokolowski*[81] is a prominent example. An employer's trade secret claim under the Wisconsin Act against a former employee who allegedly misappropriated customer information was dismissed on a summary judgment motion after the trial court concluded that the information did not satisfy the statutory definition of a trade secret. The trial court also dismissed common law claims for breach of a duty of loyalty and interference with business relationships, citing the Act's displacement provision. The Court of Appeals affirmed, but the common law claims were reinstated by the Supreme Court of Wisconsin. Citing the 'plain language' of the displacement provision, the Supreme Court concluded that 'any civil tort claim not grounded in a trade secret, *as defined in the statute*, remains available to Burbank'.[82] The majority opinion elicited a strong dissent arguing that the Act was specifically intended to preclude protection for 'confidential information' that did not satisfy the statutory

---

[79] 'The contribution of the Uniform Act is substitution of unitary definitions of trade secret and trade secret misappropriation, and a single statute of limitations for the various property, quasi-contractual, and violation of fiduciary relationship theories of noncontractual liability utilized at common law.' Uniform Act, prefatory note.

[80] Uniform Act § 7(a). The statutory exception in subsection (b) covers 'contractual remedies', 'civil remedies that are not based upon the misappropriation of a trade secret' and 'criminal remedies'. *Id.* § 7(b). The pre-emption section of the Uniform Act was omitted by the legislatures of Iowa, Nebraska and New Mexico. See Iowa C.A. §§ 550.1–550.8; Neb. R.R.S. §§ 87-501–87-507; N.M.S.A. §§ 57-3A-1–57-3A-7.

[81] 717 N.W.2d 781 (Wis. 2006).

[82] *Id.* at 793–4 (emphasis in original).

definition of a 'trade secret'.[83] The dissenters also lamented the decision's impact on national uniformity.[84] A district court judge who refused to dismiss a conversion claim joined with a trade secret count under the Pennsylvania Act succinctly captured the consequences of *Burbank,* with no acknowledgment of the resulting irony:

> Preempting plaintiff's conversion claim at the motion to dismiss stage risks leaving the claimant is [*sic*] without a remedy for information he proves has been stolen. For example, in this case, if the Court were to dismiss plaintiff's conversion claim and later make the finding that, although plaintiff had proved that defendants took its pricing structure and business proposals, such information was not a protected trade secret under the PTSA, the Court would be in the difficult position of telling the plaintiff that it had no remedy.[85]

As summarized by Tait Graves, 'The paradoxical result of such UTSA preemption rulings is that a plaintiff who cannot prove trade secrecy has more claims, and stronger claims, than a plaintiff who succeeds in establishing trade secrecy'.[86] Nevertheless, there is considerable authority for the proposition that claims relating to information that does not qualify for protection as a trade secret under the Uniform Act are not pre-empted.[87]

---

83 *Id.* at 802–3 (Bradley, J., dissenting).

84 'If litigants in the various states could maintain common law claims for misappropriation of "confidential information" that does not rise to the level of a UTSA-defined "trade secret", then trade secret law across jurisdictions would continue to depend on the varying common law as to misappropriation of economically-valuable secret information.' *Id.* at 803. The *Burbank* decision is criticized in S. Gettings, Note, *Burbank Grease Services, LLC v. Sokolowski: Frustrating Uniformity in Trade Secret Law*, 22 Berk. Tech. L. Rev. 423 (2007).

85 Cenveo Corp. v. Slater, 2007 WL 527720 (E.D. Pa. 2007). 'This Court respectfully declines to join other courts in the assumption that the legislatures adopting the act intended to remove liability for any theft of non-trade secrets.' *Id.*

86 C. Graves, *Trade Secrets as Property: Theory and Consequences,* 15 J. Intell. Prop. L. 39, 57 (2007).

87 See, e.g., Motorola, Inc. v. Lemko Corp., 2009 WL 383444 (N.D. Ill. 2009) (Illinois Act); ClearOne Communications, Inc. v. Chiang, 2008 WL 4153767 (D. Utah 2008) (Utah Act); Combined Ins. Co. v. Wiest, 578 F.Supp.2d 822 (W.D. Va. 2008) (Virginia Act); Binary Semantics Ltd. v. Minitab, Inc., 2008 WL 763575 (M.D. Pa. 2008) (Pennsylvania Act); Stone Castle Financial, Inc. v. Friedman, Billings, Ramsey & Co., 191 F.Supp.2d 652 (E.D. Va. 2002) (Virginia Act); and Combined Metals of Chicago Ltd. Partnership v. Airtek, Inc., 985 F.Supp. 827 (N.D. Ill. 1997) (Illinois Act), all refusing to dismiss common law claims seeking to protect information whose status as a statutory trade secret had yet to be determined. Terarecon, Inc., v. Fovia, Inc. 2006 WL 1867734 (N.D. Cal. 2006) (California Act) apparently goes further, refusing to dismiss a conversion claim that accompanied a trade secret claim under the California Act because the

Fortunately, there is also considerable authority supporting a broader interpretation of the pre-emption provision. A thorough analysis of the Kentucky Act lead the court in *Auto Channel, Inc. v. Speedvision Network, LLC*[88] to reject the argument that common law protection for 'commercially valuable information' that does not meet the statutory definition of 'trade secret' survives pre-emption:

> While a selective reading of KUTSA might seem to support such an argument, the history, purpose, and interpretation of the statute absolutely precludes it . . . Such a result would undermine the uniformity and clarity that motivated the creation and passage of the Uniform Act. For our purposes, therefore, KUTSA replaces other law relating to the misappropriation of trade secrets, regardless of whether the Plaintiffs demonstrate that the information at issue qualifies as a trade secret.[89]

Similar sentiments were expressed about New Hampshire's Act in *Mortgage Specialists, Inc. v. Davey*:[90]

> [S]uch a narrow construction of the preemption provision ignores not only the overall legislative scheme reflected in the NHUTSA, but also the statutory directive that we must construe the NHUTSA 'to effectuate its general purpose to make uniform the law with respect to the subject of [the NHUTSA] among states enacting it'.[91]

Other cases agree.[92] In addition, the commentators appear unanimous

---

plaintiff 'did not incorporate by reference its allegation that its proprietary materials are trade secrets in its proposed claim for conversion'. See also SKF USA, Inc. v. Bjerkness, 2009 WL 1108494 (N.D. Ill. 2009) (other common law claims that do not 'even contain the phrase "trade secret"' are not pre-empted by the Illinois Act). Other cases, like *Burbank*, have allowed common law claims to proceed after finding that the information was not eligible for protection as a statutory trade secret. See, e.g., Vigoro Indus., Inc. v. Cleveland Chemical Co., 866 F.Supp. 1150 (E.D. Ark. 1994), *aff'd*, 82 F.3d 785 (8th Cir. 1996) (Arkansas Act); Defcon, Inc. v. Webb, 687 So.2d 639 (La. Ct. App. 1997).

88 144 F.Supp.2d 784 (W.D. Ky. 2001).

89 *Id.* at 789.

90 904 A.2d 652 (N.H. 2006).

91 *Id.* at 662. 'We conclude that [the pre-emption provision], viewed in the context of the overall legislative scheme and construed in a manner that effectuates the purpose of making uniform the law among states that have adopted the UTSA, provides that the NHUTSA preempts claims that are based upon the unauthorized use of information, regardless of whether that information meets the statutory definition of a trade secret.' *Id.* at 664.

92 E.g., Thermodyn Corp. v. 3M Co., 593 F.Supp.2d 972 (N.D. Ohio 2008) (Ohio Act); Cardinal Health 414, Inc., 582 F.Supp.2d 967 (M.D. Tenn. 2008)

that pre-emption should extend to information that does not qualify for protection as a trade secret.[93]

An analogy can be drawn to federal pre-emption of state protection for works that 'come within the subject matter of copyright' as specified in the federal copyright statute.[94] A few early cases held that the copyright pre-emption provision did not apply to subject matter that was expressly excluded from protection under the federal Copyright Act.[95] Later cases have interpreted the pre-emption section more broadly to cover works and aspects of works that Congress, through the copyright statute, has chosen not to protect.[96] The latter position is in accord with

---

(Tennessee Act); Opteum Financial Serv., LLC v. Spain, 406 F.Supp.2d 1378 (N.D. Ga. 2005) (Georgia Act); Bliss Clearing Niagara, Inc. v. Midwest Brake Bond Co., 270 F.Supp.2d 943 (W.D. Mich. 2003) (Michigan Act); AutoMed Tech., Inc. v. Eller, 160 F.Supp.2d 915 (N.D. Ill. 2001) (Illinois Act); Thomas & Betts Corp. v. Panduit Corp., 108 F.Supp.2d 968 (N.D. Ill. 2000) (Illinois Act), all pre-empting common law claims without determining whether the information qualified for protection as a statutory trade secret. Other cases have applied the pre-emption provision to common law claims when the information has already been found ineligible for protection under the Act. See, E.g., Web Communications Group, Inc. v. Gateway 2000, Inc., 889 F.Supp. 316 (N.D. Ill. 1995) (Illinois Act); Dicks v. Jensen, 768 A.2d 1279 (Vt. 2001).

93 See M. Ahrens, Note, *Wisconsin Confidential: The Mystery of the Wisconsin Supreme Court's Decision in* Burbank Grease Services v. Sokolowski *and its Effect upon the Uniform Trade Secrets Act, Litigation, and Employee Mobility,* 2007 WIS. L. REV. 1271 (criticizing the pre-emption analysis in *Burbank Grease*); Graves, *supra* note 86, at 54–7; Gettings, *supra* note 84; J. Piper, *I Have a Secret?: Applying the Uniform Trade Secrets Act to Confidential Information that Does Not Rise to the Level of Trade Secret Status,* 12 MARQ. INTELL. PROP. L. REV. 359, 380 (2008) ('Upon balancing the interests of employers, employees, and competitive businesses, the most efficient and fair interpretation of the current version of the USTA is that it does, or should, abrogate all other civil remedies for the misappropriation of confidential information deemed not to be a trade secret'); R. Unikel, *Bridging the 'Trade Secret' Gap: Protecting 'Confidential Information' Not Rising to the Level of Trade Secrets,* 29 LOY. U. CHI. L.J. 841, 888 (1998) ('Permitting litigants in USTA states to assert common-law claims for the misappropriation or misuse of confidential data would reduce the USTA to just another basis for recovery and leave prior law effectively untouched'). However, since the Uniform Act deals only with information that has 'independent economic value, actual or potential', Uniform Act § 1(4), it should not pre-empt claims relating to non-commercial information.

94 17 U.S.C. § 301.

95 See, e.g., Bromhall v. Rorvik, 478 F.Supp. 361 (E.D. Pa. 1979); Vermont Castings, Inc. v. Evans Prod. Co., 215 U.S.P.Q. 758 (D. Vt. 1981); H_2O Swimwear, Ltd. v. Lomas, 164 A.D.2d 804 (N.Y. 1990).

96 E.g., National Basketball Ass'n v. Motorola, Inc., 105 F.3d 841 (2d Cir. 1997); United States *ex rel.* Berge v. Board of Trustees of Univ. of Alabama, 104

the U.S. Supreme Court's intellectual property pre-emption jurisprudence under the Supremacy Clause, which distinguishes between subject matter attended and unattended by the federal copyright statute.[97] The Uniform Act clearly attends to confidential commercial information, specifying the circumstances under which it is or is not entitled to protection. Deference to the legislative decisions embodied in the Act – and to the objective of uniformity – should preclude recognition of common law protection for commercial information that fails to satisfy the statutory criteria for protection as a 'trade secret'.

According to § 7, the Uniform Act displaces state laws 'providing civil remedies for misappropriation of a trade secret'.[98] Litigants seeking alternative grounds for relief against appropriations of commercial information have invoked a dizzying array of common law theories, including conversion, common law misappropriation, breach of confidence, fraud, unjust enrichment, unfair competition, intentional interference with contract or economic relations, breach of a duty of loyalty and conspiracy. The issue in each instance is whether the cause of action, however denominated,[99] has been invoked to obtain relief for the misappropriation of commercial information. A few cases purport to determine pre-emption by comparing the 'elements' of the cause of action with those of an action under the Uniform Act.[100] The comparisons, however, can be problematic given the wide variety of conduct actionable as 'misappropriation' under the

F.3d 1453 (4th Cir.), *cert. denied*, 522 U.S. 916 (1997); ProCD, Inc. v. Zeidenberg, 86 F.3d 1447 (7th Cir. 1996).

[97] 'The standards established for granting federal patent protection to machines thus indicated not only which articles in this particular category Congress wished to protect, but which configurations it wished to remain free. The application of state law in these cases to prevent the copying of articles which did not meet the requirements for federal protection disturbed the careful balance which Congress had drawn and thereby necessarily gave way under the Supremacy Clause of the Constitution. No comparable conflict between state law and federal law arises in the case of recordings of musical performances. In regard to this category of "Writings", Congress has drawn no balance; rather, it has left the area unattended, and no reason exits why the States should not be free to act.' Goldstein v. California, 412 U.S. 546, 569–70 (1973) (footnote omitted).

[98] Uniform Act § 7(a).

[99] 'The majority of courts that have examined this issue have not relied upon the label attached to the claim, but have examined the facts underlying the claim to determine whether it is preempted by the UTSA.' Mortgage Specialists, Inc. v. Davey, 904 A.2d 652, 665 (N.H. 2006).

[100] See, e.g., Craig Neon, Inc. v. McKenzie, 25 Fed. Appx. 750 (10th Cir. 2001) (fraud claim not pre-empted); Powell Prods., Inc. v. Marks, 948 F.Supp. 1469 (D. Colo. 1996) (conspiracy claim not pre-empted).

Uniform Act. Fraud, for example, is not a necessary element in an action under the Act. However, fraud can be an 'improper means' of acquiring a trade secret that is actionable under the Act, and thus a common law fraud claim brought to remedy the acquisition of commercial information by fraudulent means should be pre-empted.[101] Other cases focus on whether the alternative claims 'are based on the same nucleus of facts as the misappropriation of trade secrets claim'.[102] A comparison of the 'facts' underlying the claims is also problematic, however, since the same conduct can invade distinct interests. A defendant who steals a laptop computer in order to acquire trade secrets is liable under the Uniform Act for acquiring the information by improper means; a common law conversion claim seeking a remedy for loss of that information would be pre-empted.[103] However, the same conduct also intrudes on the owner's interest in its tangible property, and a conversion claim seeking to recover the cost of the laptop should not be displaced by the Uniform Act.[104]

The language of the Uniform Act itself offers the surest point of departure. The Act targets state laws 'providing civil remedies for

---

[101] See, e.g., On-Line Tech., Inc. v. Bodenseewerk Perkin-Elmer GMBH, 386 F.3d 1133 (Fed. Cir. 2004) (claim alleging that fraud was used to induce disclosure of trade secrets pre-empted); Auto Channel, Inc. v. Speedvision Network, LLC, 144 F.Supp.2d 784 (W.D. Ky. 2001) (claim for fraudulently inducing the disclosure of information pre-empted); Thomas & Betts Corp. v. Panduit Corp., 108 F.Supp.2d 968 (N.D. Ill. 2000) (fraud claim based on misrepresentation and concealment relating to the acquisition and use of information pre-empted); Weins v. Sporleder, 605 N.W.2d 488 (S.D.) (fraud and deceit claim pre-empted), *cert. denied,* 531 U.S. 821 (2000). But see Craig Neon, Inc. v. McKenzie, 25 Fed. Appx. 750 (10th Cir. 2001) (elements of a USTA claim differ from fraud and deceit); Paint Brush Corp. v. Neu, 599 N.W.2d 384 (S.D. 1999) (deceit claim based on 'trickery' in acquiring information is not pre-empted because deceit is not a conflicting tort remedy for the misappropriation of a trade secret).

[102] Digital Envoy, Inc. v. Google, Inc., 370 F.Supp.2d 1025, 1035 (N.D. Cal. 2005); K.C. Multimedia, Inc. v. Bank of America Tech. & Operations, Inc., 171 Cal.App.4th 939, 90 Cal. Rptr.3d 247 (2009). See also Thermodyn Corp. v. 3M Co., 593 F.Supp.2d 972 (N.D. Ohio 2008) ('claims are no more than a restatement of the same operative facts'), Ali v. Fasteners for Retail, Inc., 544 F.Supp.2d 1064 (E.D. Cal. 2008); Chatterbox, LLC v. Pulsar Ecoproducts, LLC, 2007 WL 1388183 (D. Idaho 2007); Hertz v. Luzenac America, Inc., 2006 WL 1028865 (D. Colo. 2006).

[103] See, e.g., Bliss Clearing Niagara, Inc. v. Midwest Brake Bond Co., 270 F.Supp.2d 943 (W.D. Mich 2003); Thomas & Betts Corp. v. Panduit Corp., 108 F.Supp.2d 968 (N.D. Ill. 2000); Mortgage Specialists, Inc. v. Davey, 153 N.H. 764, 904 A.2d 652 (2006).

[104] See, e.g., Powell Prods., Inc. v. Marks, 948 F.Supp. 1469 (D. Colo. 1996); Tronitec, Inc. v. Shealy, 249 Ga. App. 442, 547 S.E.2d 749 (2001).

misappropriation of a trade secret'.[105] The question is thus whether, under the facts of the particular case, the alternative claim protects the plaintiff's interest in safeguarding commercial information from 'misappropriation' as defined in the statute.[106] Like claims for conversion of commercial information, a claim for common law misappropriation of information[107] or for 'unjust enrichment' resulting from an appropriation of information[108] should be pre-empted. Claims for 'unfair competition' should also be pre-empted to the extent that the claim is based on allegations relating to the misappropriation of confidential information.[109] A few plaintiffs have added claims for 'civil conspiracy', but they too should be pre-

---

[105] Uniform Act § 7(a).

[106] See, e.g., *Thomas & Betts Corp.*, 108 F.Supp.2d at 971 (Act applied 'to preempt non-contract claims to the extent that they are based on a misappropriation of trade secrets'); R.K. Enter., LLC v. Pro-Comp Management, Inc., 158 S.W.3d 685, 689 (Ark. 2004) ('As a general rule, courts examine whether the claim is based upon the misappropriation of a trade secret.'). The Restatement takes an analogous view, applying its rules to actions under the Uniform Act and to 'common law actions in tort or restitution for the appropriation of another's trade secret, however denominated, including actions for "misappropriation", "infringement", or "conversion" of a trade secret, actions for "unjust enrichment" based on the unauthorized use of a trade secret, and actions for "breach of confidence" in which the subject matter of the confidence is a trade secret'. RESTATEMENT (THIRD) UNFAIR COMPETITION § 40, cmt. a.

[107] See, e.g., Bliss Clearing Niagara, Inc. v. Midwest Brake Bond Co., 270 F.Supp.2d 943 (W.D. Mich 2003); AutoMed Tech., Inc. v. Eller, 160 F.Supp.2d 915 (N.D. Ill. 2001); Auto Channel, Inc. v. Speedvision Network, LLC, 144 F.Supp.2d 784 (W.D. Ky. 2001).

[108] See, e.g., Penalty Kick Management Ltd. v. Coco Cola Co., 318 F.3d 1284 (11th Cir. 2003); Thermodyn Corp. v. 3M Co., 593 F.Supp.2d 972 (N.D. Ohio 2008); Digital Envoy, Inc. v. Google, Inc., 370 F.Supp.2d 1025 (N.D. Cal. 2005); Web Communications Group, Inc. v. Gateway 2000, Inc., 889 F.Supp. 316 (N.D. Ill. 1995).

[109] See, e.g., *Thermodyn Corp.*, 593 F.Supp.2d at 972 (unfair competition claim 'rests on the alleged misappropriation of [plaintiff's] trade secrets'); *Bliss Clearing Niagara, Inc.*, 270 F.Supp.2d at 950 (unfair competition claim pre-empted to the extent it 'is based upon the theft or misuse of trade secrets', but not as to alleged trademark infringement); Labor Ready, Inc. v. Williams Staffing, LLC, 149 F.Supp.2d 398 (N.D. Ill. 2001) (unfair competition pre-empted as to allegations involving the use of trade secrets but not as to other conduct); *Auto Channel, Inc.*, 144 F.Supp.2d at 784; *Thomas & Betts Corp.*, 108 F.Supp.2d at 968. See also On-Line Tech., Inc. v. Bodenseewerk Perkin-Elmer GMBH, 386 F.3d 1133 (Fed. Cir. 2004) (claim under the Connecticut Unfair Trade Practices Act pre-empted since the allegations relate to the misappropriation of trade secrets); *cf. Thomas & Betts Corp.*, *supra*, also applying the pre-emption provision to a state statutory claim.

empted to the extent that the conspiracy involves the misappropriation of confidential commercial information.[110]

Plaintiffs sometimes assert a claim for breach of confidence or breach of fiduciary duty in addition to or in lieu of a claim under the Uniform Act. However, the right to prevent disclosure or use of a trade secret in breach of 'a duty to maintain its secrecy or limit its use' is an interest that the Act specifically protects through its definition of 'misappropriation'. Thus, when the breach of confidence or fiduciary duty claim alleges only a disclosure or use of commercial information acquired in confidence, it should be pre-empted.[111] A distinction should be drawn, however, between disclosure or use of commercial information by former employees or third parties and disclosure or use by current employees. The latter owe a general duty of loyalty to their employer,[112] including a duty not to

---

[110] See, e.g., *Thermodyn Corp.*, 593 F.Supp.2d at 972; *AutoMed Tech., Inc.*, 160 F.Supp.2d at 915 (conspiracy claim pre-empted to the extent that it relates to confidential information but not with respect to other matter); *Thomas & Betts Corp.*, 108 F.Supp.2d at 968; *R.K. Enter., LLC*, 158 S.W.3d at 685 (Ark. 2004). But see Powell Prods., Inc. v. Marks, 948 F.Supp. 1469 (D. Colo. 1996) (conspiracy claim not pre-empted because 'an agreement' is not an element of a claim under the Uniform Act); Amvac Chemical Corp. v. Termilind, Ltd., 1999 WL 1279664 (D. Or. 1999) (conspiracy claim not pre-empted because 'civil conspiracy is not a separate tort; rather, it extends liability to those who conspired with the tortfeasor'), although the definition of 'misappropriation' in the Uniform Act specifically identifies the persons subject to liability under the Act. On the latter issue, *compare* Infinity Prod., Inc. v. Quandt, 810 N.E.2d 1028 (Ind. 2004) (new employer not liable for misappropriation by the plaintiff's former employee under *respondeat superior* since such a result would conflict with the Act's requirement that the defendant 'knows or has reason to know' of the misappropriation) *with* Newport News Industrial v. Dynamic Testing, Inc., 130 F.Supp.2d 745, 751 (E.D. Va. 2001) ('*Respondeat superior* is not an independent conflicting tort, civil claim or remedy' and hence the pre-emption provision has no bearing on the plaintiff's attempt to impose liability even if the defendants did not know of the misappropriation).

[111] See, e.g., *Penalty Kick Management Ltd.*, 318 F.3d at 1284; Grief, Inc. v. MacDonald, 2007 WL 679040 (W.D. Ky. 2007) (breach of fiduciary claim would be pre-empted as to the disclosure of confidential information, but not as to other alleged misconduct); *Thomas & Betts Corp.*, 108 F.Supp.2d at 968; K.C. Multimedia, Inc. v. Bank of America Tech. & Operations, Inc., 90 Cal. Rptr. 3d 247 (2009); Mortgage Specialists, Inc. v. Davey, 904 A.2d 652 (N.H. 2006). See also RESTATEMENT (THIRD) UNFAIR COMPETITION § 41, cmt. c (subsuming 'breach of confidence' claims within the scope of trade secret law). But see Editions Play Bac S.A. v. Western Pub. Co., 31 U.S.P.Q.2d 1338 (S.D.N.Y. 1993) ('breach of a duty of confidentiality' claim not pre-empted under the Wisconsin Act); Boeing Co. v. Sierracin Corp., 738 P.2d 665 (Wash. 1987) (breach of 'confidential relationship' claim not pre-empted).

[112] RESTATEMENT (SECOND) OF AGENCY § 387 (1958).

compete with the employer.[113] A current employee who uses information obtained from the employer to compete or to assist others to compete with the employer breaches a legal duty that does not depend upon the recognition of any proprietary interest in the information. Although the employee's conduct may also constitute trade secret misappropriation, the breach of loyalty claim arguably protects a distinct interest. As the comment to the pre-emption provision of the Uniform Act states, 'The Act does not apply to a duty imposed by law that is not dependent upon the existence of competitively significant secret information, like an agent's duty of loyalty to his or her principal'.[114] Thus, a claim based on conduct undertaken while the defendant was still employed by the plaintiff should not be pre-empted even if the form of disloyalty involves the use of commercial information.[115] For the same reason, common law actions for misuse of information by corporate officers or directors should also remain available.[116]

Another cause of action sometimes raised in connection with the misuse of confidential commercial information is tortious interference with business relations. As with a claim for breach of loyalty by a current employee, it is possible to argue that this cause of action protects an interest distinct from the interests protected by the Uniform Act – an interest in preserving the economic relationships that a business has formed with its customers. However, the law does not recognize a general right to protect customer relationships. If I open a bakery across the street from an existing one, I am perfectly free to divert that business's customers (even long-standing

---

113 *Id.* § 393.

114 Uniform Act § 7, cmt.

115 E.g., Hecny Transportation, Inc. v. Chu, 430 F.3d 402, 405 (7th Cir. 2005) ('An assertion of claims in a customer list does not wipe out claims of . . . breach of the duty of loyalty that would sound even if the customer list were a public record'); Del Monte Fresh Produce, Inc. v. Chiquita Brands Int'l Inc., 2009 WL 743215 (N.D. Ill. 2009); Coulter Corp. v. Leinert, 869 F.Supp. 732 (E.D. Mo. 1994); *Mortgage Specialists. Inc.*, 904 A.2d at 666 (N.H. 2006) (distinguishing former from current employees); Paint Brush Corp. v. Neu, 599 N.W.2d 384 (S.D. 1999). See also RESTATEMENT (THIRD) UNFAIR COMPETITION § 42, cmt. b (liability of current employees for use of information is actionable either under trade secret law or breach of loyalty).

116 AutoMed Tech., Inc. v. Eller, 160 F.Supp.2d 915, 922 (N.D. Ill. 2001) (claim for breach of fiduciary duty by corporate officer 'states an independent claim, completely distinct from any trade secrets'); Virtual Cloud Serv., Inc. v. CH2M Hill, Inc., 2006 WL 446077 (D. Colo. 2006) (joint venturer). But see Thermodyne Food Serv. Prod., Inc. v. McDonald's Corp., 940 F.Supp. 1300 (N.D. Ill. 1996) (breach of fiduciary duty claim against officer and director held pre-empted since the alleged misconduct was a misappropriation of trade secrets).

ones) to my own business.[117] Interference with such prospective business relations is actionable only if the interference is 'improper',[118] and in the case of a competitor, the propriety or impropriety of the interference turns on whether the competitor has employed 'wrongful means' to accomplish the interference.[119] When the only 'wrongful means' that a plaintiff alleges is a misuse of confidential information, the interest protected by the tortious interference claim becomes identical with the interest protected by the Uniform Act and the propriety of the defendant's conduct should be resolved solely under the rules in the Uniform Act.[120] However, when the relationship between the plaintiff and its customer takes the form of an enforceable contract, the law does indeed recognize an independent interest in preserving the relationship. Improperly interfering with the performance of a contract is a tort,[121] and unlike interference with mere business expectancies, competition even by proper means does not justify the interference.[122] Thus, an allegation that the defendant has interfered with the plaintiff's contractual relations with its customers invokes an interest that is independent of any interest protected under the Uniform Act and should not be pre-empted even if the interference is accomplished through an alleged misuse of information. On the other hand, interference with a

---

117 Restatement (Second) Torts § 768 (1979).

118 *Id.* § 766B ('intentionally and improperly interferes').

119 *Id.* § 768.

120 E.g., Patriot Homes, Inc. v. Forest River Housing, Inc., 489 F.Supp.2d 865, 873 (N.D. Ind. 2007) ('[plaintiff's] tortious interference claims depend solely upon [defendant's] misappropriation of trade secrets, and therefore, to this extent the claims are preempted'); Thomas & Betts Corp. v. Panduit Corp., 108 F.Supp.2d 968 (N.D. Ill. 2000); see Bliss Clearing Niagara, Inc. v. Midwest Brake Bond Co., 270 F.Supp.2d 943 (W.D. Mich 2003) (tortious interference claim would be pre-empted if based solely on trade secret misappropriation); *Mortgage Specialists. Inc.*, 904 A.2d at 667 ('Thus, to the extent that the tortious interference claim is supported by more than the mere misuse of [plaintiff's] customer information, it is not preempted'). See also C. Graves, *Nonpublic Information and California Tort Law: A Proposal for Harmonizing California's Employee Mobility and Intellectual Property Regimes under the Uniform Trade Secrets Act,* 2006 UCLA J.L. & Tech. 1, 83–6 ('If the sole basis for the existence of the [tort claim whose validity depends on a distinct underlying wrong] is an underlying USTA allegation, the rights and remedies should be determined according to the USTA'). But see Smithfield Ham and Prod. Co. v. Portion Pac, Inc., 905 F.Supp. 346 (E.D. Va. 1995) (allowing a tortious interference claim to stand despite its reliance on allegations of information misuse).

121 Restatement (Second) Torts § 766 (1979).

122 *Id.* § 768(2). 'The rule that competition is not an improper interference with prospective contractual relations as stated in Subsection (1) does not apply to inducement of breach of contract.' *Id.*, cmt. h.

non-disclosure or confidentiality agreement between the plaintiff and a recipient of confidential information is different. The Uniform Act specifically deals with 'inducement of a breach of a duty to maintain secrecy'.[123] A claim for tortious interference with a non-disclosure or confidentiality contract relates precisely to an interest protected by the Act and should be pre-empted.[124]

The pre-emption provision of the Uniform Act deserves close attention. Otherwise, the carefully balanced structure of the Act, its contribution to uniformity, and the public interest in competition are all too easily undone.

IV. CHARTING THE FUTURE

Trade secret law is now largely statutory law, but despite the widespread adoption of the Uniform Trade Secrets Act, the subject retains the basic character of its common law roots. In a statutory compendium used in many intellectual property courses, the Copyright Act takes up 223 pages; the Patent Act is only somewhat more modest at 110 pages; the Lanham Act on trademarks seems refreshingly brief at 59 pages. Each statute is supported by hundreds of pages of federal administrative regulations.[125] The Uniform Trade Secrets Act in contrast offers its codification of the law of trade secrets in three pages. Trade secret law, resting on a handful of fundamental concepts whose development is left to the judicial process, offers a potential for academic influence unmatched by its more statutorily constrained cousins. Almost every significant proposal for copyright and patent reform (and many for trademark) require substantial statutory revision. Changes in the federal intellectual property statutes, however, typically reflect the interests of major industry players rather than the academic merits of specific proposals. Volumes of economic analysis,

---

123 Uniform Act § 1(1).

124 E.g., Grief, Inc. v. MacDonald, 2007 WL 679040 (W.D. Ky. 2007); SL Montevideo Tech., Inc. v. Eaton Aerospace, LLC, 292 F.Supp.2d 1173 (D. Minn. 2003); Labor Ready, Inc. v. Williams Staffing, LLC, 149 F.Supp.2d 398, 409 (N.D. Ill. 2001) (interference with contract claim pre-empted 'to the extent the claim is based on misappropriation of trade secrets'); *Thomas & Betts Corp.*, 108 F.Supp.2d at 968; K.C. Multimedia, Inc. v. Bank of America Tech. & Operations, Inc., 90 Cal. Rptr. 3d 247 (2009). But see IDX Sys. Corp. v. Epic Sys. Corp., 285 F.3d 581 (7th Cir. 2002) (concluding that the tort of inducing breach of a non-disclosure contract is not based upon misappropriation of a trade secret).

125 Volume 37 of the Code of Federal Regulations, entitled *Patents, Trademarks, and Copyrights*, exceeds 800 pages in length. 37 C.F.R. (2010).

for example, are unlikely to outweigh the political influence of a Disney Company determined to obtain a copyright term extension that keeps Mickey Mouse from falling into the public domain. Less constricted by rigid and pervasive statutory commands, trade secret law seems more hospitable to good ideas. Litigants and judges seeking to give context and content to the general principles of trade secret law have considerable room to invoke the public interest, thus inviting consideration of the Restatement (Third) of Unfair Competition and other scholarly analyses. Unfortunately, there is as yet comparatively little to consider. A title search in the LexisNexis 'US Law Reviews and Journals' database for 'patent!' recently yielded 2,973 entries. In contrast, a title search for 'trade secret!' produced only 279 results. As the other contributions in this volume illustrate, increased scholarly attention to this overlooked subject can produce noteworthy dividends.

3 Trade secrecy, innovation and the requirement of reasonable secrecy precautions

*Robert G. Bone**

Trade secret law is the ugly duckling of intellectual property. It relies on secrecy to promote innovation even though secrecy impedes sequential creativity. It allows reverse engineering to facilitate dissemination even though the risk of reverse engineering prods trade secret owners to conceal information more aggressively and to shift their research from products to processes that can be kept from public view. This chapter focuses on one of these puzzling features, the requirement that a trade secret owner implement reasonable secrecy precautions to protect its secret (the RSP requirement). By making it more costly for a trade secret owner to sue, the RSP requirement limits trade secret rights and bolsters access. But it also creates incentives to strengthen secrecy safeguards, which makes access more difficult.

The RSP requirement is codified in the Uniform Trade Secrets Act (UTSA), which most states have adopted in one form or another.[1] The UTSA recognizes two requirements for information to qualify as a protectable trade secret: (1) the information must be secret in fact and have economic value as a result; and (2) the information must be 'the subject of efforts that are reasonable under the circumstances to maintain its secrecy'.[2] The puzzle lies with the second requirement. Why should the law force a trade secret owner to invest in access restrictions, fences, signs,

---

* G. Rollie White Excellence in Teaching Professor, University of Texas School of Law. I would like to thank Oren Bracha, Rochelle Dreyfuss and the participants in the NYU Trade Secret Roundtable for very helpful comments, and Dan Devoe and Christy Renworth for their excellent research assistance.

1 Uniform Trade Secrets Act, 14 U.L.A. 433 (1985). Forty-five states have currently adopted some version of the UTSA and all 45 include the reasonable secrecy precautions requirement in the definition of a 'trade secret'. See 1 Roger M. Milgrim and Eric E. Bensen, Milgrim on Trade Secrets § 1.01[2][b] (2008) (hereinafter Milgrim on Trade Secrets) (listing adopting jurisdictions).

2 UTSA § 1(4).

confidentiality agreements, exit interviews, encryption, and the like when the information in question is otherwise valuable and secret-in-fact?[3]

The puzzle of the RSP requirement has two aspects. First, the requirement is unusual in intellectual property law and in property law more generally. For example, a copyright owner can sue for infringement without first encrypting a website that displays her work or insisting that a concert hall search the audience for hidden recorders.[4] Similarly, patent law does not require, as a condition for enforcing patent rights, that a patent owner take reasonable steps to deter others from making, using, selling or importing the patented invention.[5]

The second aspect of the puzzle has to do with the fact that none of the standard justifications for the RSP requirement make sense. Some supporters argue that precautions provide notice that information is meant to be kept secret, but notice can be given without a costly RSP requirement. Some argue that secrecy precautions furnish circumstantial evidence of actual secrecy, value and improper appropriation, but these evidentiary benefits do not justify requiring precautions in all cases, including cases with plenty of other evidence of liability elements.

These justificatory flaws are particularly striking given the adverse impact of an RSP requirement on public access to information. Without such a requirement, a trade secret owner will use self-help up to the point where the marginal private benefits just exceed the marginal costs, and then rely on litigation after that point. Thus, an RSP requirement makes sense only if it forces a trade secret owner to adopt stiffer measures, in effect substituting self-help for litigation at the margin. The problem is that self-help often shields secrets and restricts public access more effectively than litigation. Self-help aims to prevent disclosures before they occur. Litigation, by contrast, usually aims to contain disclosures only after they occur, and this fact limits its efficacy. For example, a secret once disclosed can be difficult to trace, which complicates proof of liability and

---

[3] See 1 Melvin F. Jager, Trade Secrets Law § 5:16–5:26 (2008) (hereinafter Jager, Trade Secrets) (discussing measures that courts have considered relevant, including confidentiality agreements, exit interviews, security badges, security guards and computer passwords).

[4] The 1909 Copyright Act required copyright notice, but the 1976 Act eased the requirement, and in 1989 the notice requirement was eliminated altogether. 2 Melville B. Nimmer and David Nimmer, Nimmer on Copyright § 7.02[C] (Matthew Bender, 2009).

[5] To be sure, a trademark owner must police its mark against infringements at the risk of being held to have abandoned rights in the mark. However, these policing efforts involve diligently pursuing legal remedies rather than preventing infringing uses in advance.

reduces the effectiveness of litigation as a shield.[6] One disclosure also risks further disclosures, spreading the information in a way that is difficult for the trade secret owner to monitor and thus control through litigation. As a secret spreads, moreover, the ideas embodied in it can inspire socially valuable downstream innovations that are virtually impossible to link back to the misappropriated trade secret. Thus, litigation is likely to be more porous than self-help, so substituting self-help for litigation at the margin is likely to reduce information access and impede further innovation.

We are left then with two questions, one descriptive and one normative. As a descriptive matter, why does the law require a trade secret owner to take reasonable steps to maintain information's secrecy? As a normative matter, does this requirement make sense in view of its adverse effect on sequential and cumulative innovation?

It is particularly important to address these questions for three reasons. First, trade secret law is an increasingly significant body of intellectual property (IP) law, and the precautions requirement is a centerpiece of many trade secret cases.[7] Second, the history of the RSP requirement sheds light on the normative tensions plaguing American trade secret law. Third, as I have explained elsewhere, trade secret law has relatively few limiting doctrines to promote information diffusion.[8] While the RSP requirement compounds this problem by shielding secrets more effectively, it also facilitates discovery and dissemination by deterring anti-competitive strike suits and signaling competitors.

The remainder of this chapter is divided into five parts. Part I traces the history of the reasonable precautions requirement, why it was originally

---

6 Trade secret lawsuits are highly imperfect instruments for protecting secrets. They are expensive, plagued by risks and uncertainties, and difficult to win. See Robert G. Bone, *A New Look at Trade Secret Law: Doctrine in Search of Justification*, 86 CALIF. L. REV. 241, 278–9 (1998).

7 See, e.g., Enter. Leasing Co. v. Ehmke, 197 Ariz. 144, 150 (1999) ('Indeed, the most important factor in gaining trade-secret protection is demonstrating that the owner has taken such precautions as are reasonable under the circumstances to preserve the secrecy of the information'); Patrick J. Whalen, *Protecting Trade Secrets in Licenses*, 960 PRACTICING LAW INSTITUTE 67, 78 (2009) ('The efforts of the trade secret owner in maintaining the secrecy of its confidential information are frequently litigated in as much detail as the defendant's actions in misappropriating the information. In defending against a trade secret claim, defendants will search and pounce upon any shortcoming in the plaintiff's efforts to keep its information secret').

8 See Robert G. Bone, *Exploring the Boundaries of Competitive Secrecy: An Essay on the Limits of Trade Secret Law* in LAW, INFORMATION AND INFORMATION TECHNOLOGY 99 (E. Lederman and R. Shapira eds., 2001).

adopted and how it has evolved. Part II critically examines modern efforts to justify the doctrine. Part III returns to basics and shows that the RSP requirement draws little support from the policies usually advanced to justify trade secret law. Parts I, II and III taken together make a strong, almost conclusive, case for eliminating the requirement. Part IV then weakens that case. It identifies enforcement cost and signaling benefits that should be included in any cost-benefit evaluation. Even with these benefits, it might still be optimal to jettison the RSP requirement, but the case against the requirement must be developed more carefully. Part V concludes.

I. A BRIEF HISTORY

Trade secret law developed as a distinct body of law in the United States during the latter half of the nineteenth century.[9] It has always combined, in uneasy tension, a property-based theory aimed at protecting exclusive rights in valuable information and a tort-based theory aimed at preventing or punishing unfair methods of competition. The history of the RSP requirement must be understood against this background.

A. 1860 to 1920: The Dominance of the Property Theory

During the late nineteenth and early twentieth century, a trade secret owner's efforts to protect its secrets were relevant to liability in three general ways: as a condition for implying a confidentiality duty; as a safeguard against publication that forfeited trade secret rights; and as a requirement for common law property rights to attach to information in the first place.

1. Precautions as notice and as safeguard against publication

Nineteenth century judges were willing to impose implied duties of confidentiality on employees, but only if the employees had reason to know that the information was supposed to be kept confidential. One way the employer signaled its expectation was to adopt special safeguards to protect the secret.[10]

---

[9] See Bone, *supra* note 6, at 251–9.

[10] Hamilton Mfg. Co. v. Tubbs Mfg. Co., 216 F. 401, 404, 407 (W.D. Mich. 1908); James Love Hopkins, The Law of Trademarks, Tradenames, and Unfair Competition §§ 109, 111 (3d ed. 1917); Harry D. Nims, The Law of Unfair Business Competition § 215, at 431 (1909).

In addition, precautions that limited public access prevented the sort of 'publication' that forfeited trade secret rights.[11] For example, in one leading case, the court held that the plaintiff, by selling its pump without getting a patent, published any secrets that could be readily ascertained by inspecting the pump and thus lost its right to those secrets.[12]

2. Precautions as necessary to trade secret rights in all cases

There are strong indications in late nineteenth and early twentieth century case law and commentary that precautions played a more central role in trade secret law, serving as a requirement that had to be satisfied in *all* cases before property rights could attach to secret information. The connection between precautions and common law property rights made sense within the natural-law-based theory that dominated much thinking about property in the late nineteenth century.[13] This theory assumed that possession was necessary to common law property rights in a thing and that possession required control or dominion over the thing possessed.[14] Controlling information, however, was extremely difficult because information had a tendency to escape and spread easily. As one court put it, 'conceptions are as free as the birds of the air or the wild beasts of the forest, but they belong to him who first reduces them to captivity'.[15] A person reduced information to 'captivity' by keeping it secret and implementing precautions to protect against disclosure and diffusion.[16]

---

[11] See Tabor v. Hoffman, 118 N.Y. 30, 34, 36 (1889) (noting that 'independent of copyright or letters patent, an inventor or author, has, by the common law, an exclusive property [right] in his invention or composition, until by publication it becomes the property of the general public' and equating publication with abandonment of the secret); Nims, *supra* note 10, § 208; William B. Barton, *A Study in the Law of Trade Secrets*, 13 U. Cin. L. Rev. 507, 556 (1939).

[12] Tabor v. Hoffman, 118 N.Y. 30, 34, 36 (1889); *accord* Rees v. Peltzer, 75 Ill. 475, 478 (1874); Stewart v. Hook, 118 Ga. 445, 446–7 (1903).

[13] See Barton, *supra* note 11, at 530, 535 (noting that 'the property concept is more resorted to by the courts than any other').

[14] See Bone, *supra* note 6, at 254–5. To have ownership of a wild animal, for example, a person must first obtain possession by killing, trapping, caging or otherwise controlling it.

[15] Werckmeister v. American Lithographic Co., 134 Fed. 321, 324 (2d Cir. 1904). The *Werckmeister* court went on to say: 'the common-law protection continues only so long as the captives or creations are kept in confinement or controlled'. *Id.*

[16] See Bristol v. Equitable Life Ass. Soc'y, 132 N.Y. 264, 267 (1892) ('Without denying that there may be property in an idea, or trade secret or system, it is obvious that its originator or proprietor must himself protect it from escape or disclosure'); Haskins v. Ryan, 71 N.J. Eq. 575, 579–80 (1906) (noting with respect to property

This property theory placed precautions at the core of trade secret law.[17] A putative trade secret owner who took no special precautions to preserve the secrecy of its information failed to exercise control or dominion over that information and therefore did not possess it. Without possession, he had no common law property rights in the information and thus no trade secret rights to protect.

McClary v. Hubbard is a good example.[18] The plaintiff in that case sought to protect, as his trade secrets, the components of a machine used to manufacture diamond-shaped glazier's points. The plaintiff took no special precautions,[19] but instead relied on the difficulty of discovering the secrets and 'the improbability that anybody would care to copy [them]'.[20] This strategy worked for many years until the mechanically trained son of the plaintiff's deceased partner studied a disassembled machine that had been stored for some time in his father's barn. The court held that the defendant (son) was not liable because the plaintiff and his deceased partner (the defendant's father) 'took inadequate measures to protect themselves in the control of the secrets',[21] and as a result had no protectable trade secret in the machine components.[22]

---

in ideas 'that can hardly be styled "property", over which there is not some sort of dominion'); Kroegher v. McConway & Torley Co., 149 Pa. 444, 457 (1892) ('So long as the inventor holds the secret in his own possession . . . it is property, or a thing of value for the transfer of which he may demand a price'). The lower court in *Bristol v. Equitable Life Ass. Soc'y*, 52 Hun. 161 (1892) expressed the principles in the following way: 'So long as the originator or possessor of the naked idea . . . keeps it to himself, it is his property, but it ceases to be his own when he permits it to pass from him . . . Ideas of this sort, in their relation to property may be likened to the interest which a person may obtain in bees and birds and fish in running streams, which are conspicuous instances of *ferae naturae*. If the claimant keeps them on his own premises, they become his qualified property, and absolutely his so long as they do not escape. But if he permits them to go he cannot follow them'.

[17] See Christopher Columbus Langdell, *Patent Rights and Copy Rights*, 12 Harv. L. Rev. 553, 553–4 (1898) ('The only means an inventor has, on any principle yet indicated, of preventing the use and enjoyment of his invention by others is that of keeping it secret').

[18] McClary v. Hubbard, 97 Vt. 222 (1923).

[19] *Id.* at 230 ('the precautions taken were such as might be expected in any machine shop where the presence of strangers might tend to reduce the efficiency of the help and where the danger from accident about the machines is ever present').

[20] *Id.* at 231–2.

[21] *Id.* at 234–5: 'it is certain that the findings . . . show a lack of such precaution or care as was sufficient to prevent the alleged secret process from becoming known to other people'. *Id.* at 235.

[22] The court took note that the defendant had not breached any contract, trust or confidence. *Id.* at 234. But it did not stop there, as a modern court

Thus, the requirement of secrecy precautions had both functional and formal roots in the late nineteenth and early twentieth century. On the functional side, the use of precautions served to place employees and third parties on notice that information was meant to be kept confidential and also helped to assure that the information was not published. On the formal side, precautions functioned as the exercise of control necessary to possession and thus to the existence of common law property rights.

B. 1920 to 1940: The Decline of the Property Theory and the Rise of Unfair Competition

Throughout the nineteenth and early twentieth century, the unfair competition strand of trade secret law, with its focus on the unfairness of the defendant's conduct, exerted some influence even as judges relied mainly on a property theory.[23] However, in the 1920s and 1930s, the rise of legal realism and the attack on late nineteenth century formalism spelled the demise of the natural law property theory. [24] In its place, unfair competition emerged as the dominant approach and shifted attention from issues of property ownership to questions of unfair appropriation.[25]

---

probably would have. Instead, it proceeded to determine whether the plaintiff had 'a common law right of property in the process' that the defendant might have infringed. *Id.* The court's answer was no, because the plaintiff had not used precautions specifically aimed at protecting secrecy and thus had not exercised the control necessary to acquire rights. See also Hamilton Mfg. Co. v. Tubbs Mfg. Co., 216 Fed. 401, 404–5 (W.D. Mich. 1908) (holding that the plaintiff failed to prove that the machines and methods were trade secrets, in part because of the absence of precautions ordinarily used to maintain secrecy); Peerless Roll Leaf Co., Inc. v. Lange, 20 F.2d 801, 801–2 (3d Cir. 1927) (holding that the method was not a trade secret because the plaintiff did not use any special secrecy safeguards beyond 'that which normally exists in the average manufacturing business').

[23] See, e.g., Radium Remedies Co. v. Weiss, 173 Minn. 342, 347–8 (1928) (focusing on breach of a confidential relationship); Vulcan Detinning Co. v. American Can Co., 72 N.J. Eq. 387, 395–6 (1906) (focusing on the 'inequitable character of the defendant's conduct').

[24] See, e.g., Bone, *supra* note 6, at 259–60; Note, *Equitable Protection of Trade Secrets*, 23 Colum. L. Rev. 164 (1923) (noting the conflicting theories of trade secret law, but rejecting the property theory and concluding that '[a] trade secret is property only if the court decides to protect it').

[25] In a famous passage from a 1917 U.S. Supreme Court opinion, a passage frequently quoted in later cases and commentary, Justice Holmes rejected the notion that trade secret rules could be derived from an abstract concept of property. E.I. duPont de Nemours Powder Co. v. Masland, 244 U.S. 100, 102 (1917). See also

These developments came to a head with the publication of the First Restatement of Torts in 1939.[26] Sections 757 and 758 of the Restatement synthesized a confusing body of trade secret precedent in an attempt to formulate a succinct statement of the doctrine. In so doing, the Restatement drafters chose unfair competition as the organizing framework.[27] Liability depended on whether the defendant acquired or disclosed the secret by 'improper means', and improper means were defined generally as 'means that fall below the generally accepted standards of commercial morality and reasonable conduct'.[28]

The triumph of the unfair competition theory left the precautions requirement without a clear foundation. The concepts of control and possession, critical to a property theory, were irrelevant to an unfair competition theory that focused on the nature of the defendant's conduct. To be sure, information had to be secret, but there was no apparent reason to require secrecy precautions as well.

The Restatement drafters could have simply eliminated all reference to precautions in the doctrine, but this would have required ignoring well-established precedents like *McClary v. Hubbard*.[29] Instead, they kept the precautions element in the doctrinal mix, but demoted it to a secondary consideration, just one of six factors relevant to determining whether information qualified as a trade secret.[30] The Explanatory Notes

---

International News Service v. Associated Press, 248 U.S. 215, 252–3, 257–8 (1918) (Brandeis, J., dissenting) (observing that earlier property-rights-based decisions actually rest on the manner by which the trade secret was acquired). I should be clear that the phrase 'unfair competition' did not refer to a general theory of trade secret law, but rather to a loose collection of legal wrongs which had in common that they were instances of competitive conduct that a critical mass of judges thought were unfair and should be banned.

26 Restatement (First) of Torts (1939).

27 *Id.* §757, cmt. a: 'The suggestion that one has a right to exclude others from the use of his trade secret because he has a right of property in the idea has been frequently advanced and rejected. The theory that has prevailed is that the protection is afforded only by a general duty of good faith and that the liability rests upon breach of this duty; that is, breach of contract, and abuse of confidence or impropriety in the method of ascertaining the secret'.

28 *Id.* § 757, cmt. f.

29 See supra notes 18–22 and accompanying text.

30 Restatement (First) of Torts §757 cmt. b (1939). The relevant text from Comment b is as follows: 'An exact definition of a trade secret is not possible. Some factors to be considered in determining whether given information is one's trade secret are: (1) the extent to which the information is known outside of his business; (2) the extent to which it is known by employees and others involved in his business; (3) the extent of measures taken by him to guard the secrecy of the information; (4) the value of the information to him and to his competitors; (5)

accompanying the Preliminary Drafts indicate that the drafters distilled the six factors from cases like *McClary*.[31]

The Restatement's multifactor test in effect converted a precautions *requirement* into a precautions *factor*, and one capable, in theory at least, of being outweighed. Moreover, it did so without explaining what a precautions factor contributed that other factors did not already cover.[32]

It appears that the Restatement drafters simply collected an assortment of nineteenth and early twentieth century precedents like *McClary* and grouped them together under the heading of 'substantial secrecy'. Because the precedents were shaped by a formalistic property theory, however, the factors derived from those precedents did not cohere well. It was up to future judges to work out the functional implications of the factors through case-by-case adjudication.

---

the amount of effort or money expended by him in developing the information; (6) the ease or difficulty with which the information could be properly acquired or duplicated by others'.

[31] The Explanatory Notes are available from the HeinOnLine database at www.heinonline.org.ezproxy.bu.edu/HOL/Index?index=ali/aliguide_38&collection=ali. An early set of Notes cites McClary v. Hubbard for the 'necessity of plaintiff's taking adequate measures to keep his device a secret'. *Group 3, Explanatory Notes to Preliminary Draft No. 6* (July 13, 1938). Later versions omit the quoted passage and offer a string cite that relies on *McClary* and other cases to support the proposition that 'substantial secrecy is necessary'. *Group 3, Explanatory Notes to Preliminary Draft 8* (November 14, 1938); *Group 3, Explanatory Notes to Preliminary Draft Nos. 10 & 11* (February 6, 1939).

[32] The first two factors dealt with the extent to which the information was known inside and outside the business and the sixth factor dealt with the ease of acquiring or duplicating the information by proper means. See RESTATEMENT (FIRST) OF TORTS §757 cmt. b (1939). These three factors together would appear to cover everything conceivably relevant to evaluating the degree of secrecy. The multifactor test also suffered from another problem. The fourth and fifth factors – the value of the secret and the amount invested in developing it – made sense within the nineteenth century property theory since substantial value and significant investment were reasons to treat information as property, but it is not clear what they had to do with determining 'substantial secrecy' under the Restatement approach. Conceivably, less secrecy might be required when investment or value was more substantial, either on the theory that broader protection is necessary to promote incentives to create when creation requires greater ex ante investment or on the theory that broader protection is warranted to condemn free-riding when the free rider takes something of greater value. Nevertheless, the Restatement drafters did not mention incentives or free riding when discussing the basis of trade secret law, but rested liability instead on the breach of 'a general duty of good faith'. See id. §757, cmt. a.

C. 1940 to 1980: The Dominance of the Unfair Competition Theory

Although some courts and commentators continued to refer to 'property' or 'property rights' at least for a brief period,[33] most eventually followed the Restatement's lead, eschewed the property label, and focused on the wrongful nature of the defendant's conduct.[34] Some courts insisted on strict secrecy requirements.[35] Others skimmed over potential secrecy problems in an obvious effort to provide relief for egregious breaches of trust.[36] And the more liberal courts tended to treat secrecy precautions in a relatively cursory way.

---

33 See, e.g., National Starch Products, Inc. v. Polymer Industries, Inc., 273 App. Div. 732, 735 (1948) (emphasizing the need for secrecy, noting that '[i]t is well established in the law of this subject that in order that a property right may inhere in a secret process or formula, it must be kept secret').

34 See Joan Stedman, *Trade Secrets*, 23 OHIO ST. L.J. 4, 21, 24 (1963) (noting that 'a third concept that is rarely invoked in support of trade secret law is the concept of "property"' and explaining that 'the most common basis upon which trade secret proceedings rest is "unfair competition"'); Note, *Theft of Trade Secrets*, 120 U. PA. L. REV. 378, 383 (1972) (observing that 'the great majority of American legal scholars and courts have whenever possible deemphasized the question of plaintiff's property interest'). See also 1 RUDOLF CALLMANN, THE LAW OF UNFAIR COMPETITION AND TRADE-MARKS § 51, at 674 (1945) (noting that in most cases 'it is the nature of the defendant's wrong, rather than the nature of the plaintiff's right, which determines the scope and nature of the relief').

35 See, e.g., J.T. Healey & Son, Inc. v. James A. Murphy & Son, Inc., 357 Mass. 728, 737–9 (1970): '[I]f the person entitled to a trade secret wishes to have its exclusive use in his own business, he must not fail to take all proper and reasonable steps to keep it secret . . . As a nationally known member of the patent bar has written, one who claims that he has a trade secret must exercise eternal vigilance. This calls for constant warnings to all persons to whom the trade secret has become known and obtaining from each an agreement, preferably in writing, acknowledging its secrecy and promising to respect it. To exclude the public from the manufacturing area is not enough'. *Id.* at 738–9. See also Wheelabrator Corp. v. Fogle, 317 F.Supp. 633, 637–8 (W.D. La. 1970) (requiring precautions that manifest an intent to keep its process and equipment secret); Jet Spray Cooler, Inc. v. Crampton, 361 Mass. 835, 841 (1972) ('one seeking to prevent the disclosure or use of trade secrets or information must demonstrate that he pursued an active course of conduct designed to inform his employees that such secrets and information were to remain confidential'); Amoco Production Co. v. Lindley, 609 P.2d 733, 743 (Okla. 1980) ('trade secret status is difficult to establish and often entails establishing that affirmative and elaborate steps were taken to insure that the secret claimed would remain so').

36 A particularly striking example is the Second Circuit's 1953 decision in Franke v. Wiltschek, 209 F.2d 493 (2d Cir. 1953). Judge Charles Clark, the author of the majority opinion and a noted legal realist, focused on the defendant's breach of confidence and rejected out-of-hand an argument that the process was not

In *Junker v. Plummer*,[37] for example, the plaintiff used no confidentiality agreements or access restrictions and even allowed the friends of employees to observe the secret machine in operation.[38] The court nevertheless breezed by these lax precautions, eager to reach what it obviously felt was an egregious breach of the employer's trust.[39] *Junker* is characteristic of many cases decided in the decades following adoption of the Restatement, although not all such cases involved precautions as weak as those in *Junker*.[40]

Thus, judicial approaches to precautions varied widely between 1940 and 1980, partly due to uncertainty about how a precautions factor fits into a body of trade secret law based on unfair competition rather than property rights.

---

sufficiently secret, dismissing it as 'totally misconceiv[ing] the nature of the plaintiff's right'. *Id.* at 495. In a very broad passage often quoted by later courts inclined toward a similarly strong conduct-focused approach, Clark all but swept aside the secrecy requirement: 'Plaintiffs do not assert, indeed cannot assert, a property right in their development such as would entitle them to exclusive enjoyment against the world. Theirs is not a patent, but a trade secret. The essence of their action is not infringement, but breach of faith. It matters not that defendants could have gained their knowledge from a study of the expired patent and plaintiffs' publicly marketed product. The fact is that they did not. Instead they gained it from plaintiffs via their confidential relationship, and in so doing incurred a duty not to use it to plaintiffs' detriment. This duty they have breached'. *Id.* at 495.

[37] 320 Mass. 76 (1946).

[38] *Id.* at 78, 80–1.

[39] *Id.* at 79–80. It is revealing to compare *Junker* with McClary v. Hubbard, 97 Vt. 222 (1923) decided 23 years earlier. See *supra* notes 18–22 and accompanying text. The *Junker* court excused the plaintiff's lax precautions by noting that none of the visitors who observed the machine took the trouble to inspect it closely and that no one other than the defendants had succeeded in building a similar machine. *Junker*, *supra* note 37, at 78–9. It is notable that the *McClary* court rejected these very same points in holding that there was no trade secret because the plaintiff failed to employ precautions *aimed specifically* at maintaining secrecy. *McClary*, *supra* note 18, at 231–2. The difference in reasoning reflects a difference in theory. *McClary* worked within a property theory and demanded precautions as a prerequisite to control and possession, while *Junker* worked within an unfair competition theory and ignored lax precautions in order to reach bad conduct.

[40] See, e.g., Space Aero Products Co., Inc. v. R.E. Darling Co., Inc., 238 Md. 93, 111–13 (1965); Allen Mf. Co. v. Loika, 145 Conn. 509, 515 (1958); and Sun Dial Corp. v. Rideout, 29 N.J. Super. 361, 368–71 (1954). See also Ungar Electric Tools, Inc. v. Sid Ungar Col, Inc., 192 Cal. App.2d 398, 404 (1961) (notes secrecy issues, but relies on Franke v. Wiltschek and stresses breach of confidence and the need to encourage commercial morality).

D. 1980 to the Present: Uniform Trade Secrets Act and the Focus on Reasonable Precautions

The adoption of the Uniform Trade Secrets Act (UTSA) in 1980 was a watershed event in the history of trade secret law.[41] Section 1(4) of the UTSA defines 'trade secret' to include RSP and thus makes the reasonableness of precautions an essential inquiry in every trade secret case:

(4) 'Trade secret' means information . . . that:
 (i) derives independent economic value, actual or potential, from not being generally known to, and not being readily ascertainable by proper means by, other persons who can obtain economic value from its disclosure or use, and
 (ii) is the subject of efforts that are reasonable under the circumstances to maintain its secrecy.

The courts have interpreted this provision to create two distinct requirements for information to qualify as a trade secret – actual secrecy and reasonable precautions – and each requirement must be satisfied separately.[42] This is a major change from the multifactor approach of the First Restatement of Torts.[43] And it is also different from the Third Restatement of the Law of Unfair Competition, published in 1995, which treats precautions as mere evidence of secrecy, value and improper appropriation.[44]

The UTSA drafters, however, did not explain why they made RSP a requirement.[45] Moreover, while many states have adopted trade secret

---

[41] The National Conference of Commissioners on Uniform State Laws (NCCUSL) adopted the Uniform Trade Secrets Act (UTSA) in 1979, and the American Bar Association gave its approval in 1980. See 1 MILGRIM ON TRADE SECRETS, *supra* note 1, § 1.01[2]. See also Uniform Trade Secrets Act with 1985 Amendments, Prefatory Note, at 1–4, available at www.law.upenn.edu/bll/archives/ulc/fnact99/1980s/utsa85.htm.

[42] See, e.g., Learning Curve Toys, Inc. v. Playwood Toys, Inc., 342 F.3d 714, 721–2 (7th Cir. 2003).

[43] See *supra* notes 29–32 and accompanying text.

[44] RESTATEMENT (THIRD) OF UNFAIR COMPETITION § 39, cmt. g (1995).

[45] An article written shortly after the UTSA's adoption describes the inclusion of RSP as an unremarkable codification of well-established common law precedent, although one that 'formalizes the requirement of secrecy to a much greater extent than did the *Restatement [of Torts]*'. Ramon A. Klitzke, *The Uniform Trade Secrets Act*, 64 MARQ. L. REV. 277, 292 (1980). Professor Sharon Sandeen, a contributor to this volume, informed me that the RSP requirement was added to the UTSA shortly after removal of a provision requiring trade secrets to be in tangible form. This suggests that the drafters might have meant RSP to serve a

statutes modeled on the UTSA and judges have worked with the RSP requirement for almost 30 years, no one has yet managed to develop a convincing rationale. The following section reviews this post-UTSA history.

II. A CRITICAL REVIEW OF MODERN THEORIES

Before proceeding, it is important to distinguish a relatively obvious use of precautions that is not directly relevant to our inquiry. To illustrate, consider *E.I. duPont de Nemours v. Christopher*,[46] a famous misappropriation case. The defendants in *Christopher* flew over one of DuPont's plants while it was under construction and took photographs of the area housing a secret process while it was uncovered and exposed to view from above. The defendants had no pre-existing relationship with DuPont to support a duty; nor did the flight constitute a trespass, violate FAA regulations, or transgress any other laws. The court nevertheless held that the defendants could be liable for trade secret misappropriation because their 'espionage' offended 'generally accepted standards of commercial morality and reasonable conduct'.[47] In reaching this conclusion, the court had to address the adequacy of DuPont's precautions and in particular determine whether the company should have covered the plant during the entire construction period. It answered the latter question in the negative, emphasizing the high cost of a cover and the morally reprehensible nature of the defendants' conduct.

It is perfectly sensible that an RSP issue should arise in this context. Obviously, the policy arguments for condemning an appropriation are weaker when the plaintiff fails to take steps that it should take to prevent the disclosure.[48] But the cases that interest us are different. In these cases, RSP operates as a separate legal requirement, not just one consideration in the policy analysis for misappropriation. The question is why RSP should have such a prominent role.

Most judges simply apply the RSP requirement without making any

---

function similar to fixation in copyright: to circumscribe the information subject to protection and assist in defining its scope.

[46] 431 F.2d 1012 (5th Cir. 1070). *Christopher* was decided about a decade before adoption of the UTSA, at a time when the extent of precautions was a factor rather than a definitional requirement.

[47] *Id.* at 1016 (citing RESTATEMENT (FIRST) OF TORTS § 757 cmt. f (1939)).

[48] It is worth mentioning, however, that the Comment to the UTSA treats *Christopher* as an RSP case and uses it to support the principle that precautions need only be reasonable. See Prefatory Note, *supra* note 41.

effort to justify it on general grounds.[49] Those who do make an effort usually focus on evidentiary and notice benefits. For example, in *Rockwell Graphics Systems, Inc.*, a well-known precautions case, Judge Posner explained that precautions can support a finding of misappropriation because they make lawful acquisition more difficult, and can also support an inference of substantial value because an owner would not invest to protect a secret with little value.[50] And in *BondPro Corp.*, a later opinion, he explained how precautions can create notice benefits by informing third parties that the owner wishes to preserve secrecy.[51]

The problem, however, is that neither evidentiary nor notice benefits justify requiring precautions in *all* cases.[52] The fact that a particular type of evidence helps prove a point is no reason to require that evidence when the point can be proved in other ways.[53] The same is true for notice. Notice can be given without many (if any) precautions.[54] For example, employees can be notified by the simple act of delivering a piece of paper. Moreover, third parties who take trade secrets by fraud, burglary, or the like show

---

[49] See, e.g., Elm City Cheese Co., Inc. v. Frederico, 251 Conn. 59, 80–6 (1999) (emphasizing the 'highly fact-specific' nature of the precautions inquiry and finding extremely thin and informal precautions to be reasonable).

[50] Rockwell Graphics Systems, Inc. v. DEV Industries, Inc., 925 F.2d 174, 178–9 (7th Cir. 1991). See also *id.* at 179 (suggesting that precautions help to assure that the plaintiff actually suffered loss *as a result of* the defendant's misappropriation); Metallurgical Industries, Inc. v. Fourtek, Inc., 790 F.2d 1195, 1199 (5th Cir. 1986) (relying on precautions as evidence of secrecy itself). Moreover, precautions sometimes make it easier to trace the misappropriation back to the responsible party.

[51] BondPro Corp. v. Siemens Power Gen., Inc., 463 F.3d 702, 708 (7th Cir. 2006) (arguing that a failure to take precautions 'forfeits protection' because it 'sets a trap, since a company that ferrets out information that the originator does not think special enough to be worth incurring any costs to conceal will have no reason to believe that it *is* a trade secret'). See also Omega Optical, Inc. v. Chroma Technology Corp., 174 Vt. 10, 14–16 (2002) (employee notice); Edmund W. Kitch, *The Law and Economics of Rights in Valuable Information*, 9 J. LEG. STUD. 683, 698–9 (1980) (same).

[52] Reasonableness is to be evaluated by comparing the costs of precautions with the benefits. Rockwell Graphics Systems, Inc., 925 F.2d at 179–80.

[53] Professor Kitch argues that the plaintiff's willingness to file a lawsuit and incur the cost of litigation, by itself, should be ample evidence that the trade secret has substantial value. See Kitch, *supra* note 51, at 698. See also Vincent Chiappetta, *Myth, Chameleon, or Intellectual Property Olympian?: A Normative Framework Supporting Trade Secret Law*, 8 GEO. MASON L. REV. 69, 120 (1999) (arguing for filing as sufficient evidence of value).

[54] Moreover, if employees do not have sufficient notice under the existing precautions to justify imposing a confidentiality duty, the judicial response should be to deny the duty rather than deny that the information qualifies as a trade secret.

clearly by their conduct that they already know the information should be kept confidential.[55]

In *Rockwell Graphics*, for instance, the trade secrets (piece part drawings for printing press replacement parts) were clearly valuable to the plaintiff without any need to rely on evidence of precautions to verify that fact. Moreover, the evidence, while disputed, strongly suggested that the defendant obtained the information improperly, and there were also plenty of indications that Rockwell expected the piece part drawings to be kept confidential. [56] In cases like this (and there are many)[57] an RSP requirement must be justified by something other than its evidentiary and notice benefits.

Judges sometimes hint at other justifications, but only in a cursory way. One court explained that a trade secret owner who 'disregards caution' is denied relief 'on the theory that he courted his own disaster', perhaps suggesting an assumption of risk rationale.[58] Another drew a connection to the clean hands doctrine in equity: 'To put it another way, the employer must come into court with clean hands; the employer cannot complain of the employee's use of information if the employer has never treated the

---

[55] See Chiappetta, *supra* note 53, at 116. And there is no need for explicit notice from the trade secret owner when the nature of the relationship or industry custom by itself supports an understanding of confidentiality. See Flotec, Inc. v. Southern Research, Inc., 16 F.Supp.2d 992, 1006–7 (S.D. Ind. 1998).

[56] For example, pre-trial discovery revealed 100 Rockwell piece part drawings in the defendant DEV's possession; DEV was organized by a former Rockwell employee who had access to the piece part drawings while at Rockwell; and DEV hired as its president another Rockwell employee who had been fired by Rockwell for removing piece part drawings from the company. *Rockwell Graphics*, 925 F.2d at 176. Also, while Rockwell was sloppy about retrieving drawings, it did keep them in a vault with limited access and required employees to sign non-disclosure agreements. *Id.* at 177. See Playwood Toys, Inc. v. Learning Curve Toys, L.P., 2002 U.S. Dist. LEXIS 4298 *15–*16 (N.D. Ill. 2002) (noting that there was evidence in *Rockwell Graphics* that the plaintiff 'exercised great caution'). Perhaps it is unfair to expect employees to keep secrets when the employer is somewhat lax about secrecy itself, but the reason has nothing to do with giving employees adequate notice.

[57] See, e.g., J.T. Healey & Son, Inc. v. James A. Murphy & Son, Inc., 357 Mass. 728 (1970) (information was clearly valuable to the plaintiff's jewelry business and the defendant acquired it from plaintiff's employees, yet defendant was not liable because plaintiff failed to use reasonable precautions).

[58] RTE Corp. v. Coatings, Inc., 267 N.W.2d 226, 233 (Wis. 1978) (quoting 1 Rudolf Callmann, The Law of Unfair Competition and Trade-Marks § 55, at 451–3 (1968)).

information as secret'.[59] And yet another court simply asserted without additional argument, but perhaps with the idea in mind that self-help might be less costly than litigation, that 'it would be anomalous for the courts to prohibit the use of information that the rightful owner did not undertake to protect'.[60]

Judges also offer fragmentary clues when remarking on features that do or do not qualify as reasonable. One can find pronouncements to the effect that RSP requires 'affirmative measures'[61] or an 'active course of conduct',[62] even when the trade secret owner believes doing nothing is the best strategy,[63] and that these measures must be aimed specifically at protecting the secret itself.[64] Also, some courts insist that the trade secret owner be the one who implements the safeguards; it is not enough to rely on safeguards adopted by others.[65] Moreover, there are statements in a few cases to the effect that the efforts must involve a 'continuing course of conduct' and 'eternal vigilance' beyond the signing of a confidentiality

---

[59] Electro-Craft Corp. v. Controlled Motion, Inc., 332 N.W.2d 890, 901 (Minn. 1983). Although this point could be about notice, it seems to focus on the nature of the employer's conduct rather than the information available to the employee.

[60] Dicks v. Jensen, 172 Vt. 43, 50 (2001). See also Gallowhur Chem. Corp. v. Schwerdle, 37 N.J. Super. 385, 397 (1955) ('[O]ne may not venture on liberties with his own secret, may not lightly or voluntarily hazard its leakage or escape, and at the same time hold others to be completely obligated to observe it'); Alan J. Tracey, *The Contract in the Trade Secret Ballroom: A Forgotten Dance Partner*, 16 TEX. INTELL. PROP. L.J. 47, 61 (2007) (noting that the RSP requirement 'is based on the rationale that if the owner of the information does not treat it as a trade secret, then the courts should not as well').

[61] Learning Curve Toys, Inc. v. Playwood Toys, Inc., 342 F.3d 714, 722 (7th Cir. 2003); Amoco Production Co. v. Lindley, 609 P.2d 733, 743 (Okla. 1980); JAGER, TRADE SECRETS, *supra* note 3, § 5.16, at 5-105 ('Affirmative steps should be taken to guard secrecy').

[62] *Dicks*, 172 Vt., *supra* note 60, at 50 (quoting Jet Spray Cooler, Inc. v. Crampton, 361 Mass. 835, 841 (1972)).

[63] See JAGER, TRADE SECRETS, *supra* note 3, § 5.16, at 5-106 ('A conscious plan to do nothing to protect secrecy, to avoid arousing interest in the information, is on its face inadequate security precautions').

[64] See Wheelabrator Corp. v. Fogle, 317 F.Supp. 633, 637–8 (W.D. La. 1970); *cf.* Mortgage Specialists, Inc. v. Davey, 153 N.H. 764, 772 (2006) (holding that the precautions 'could have been found by the jury only to demonstrate a need to protect customers . . . rather than an intent to prevent [the plaintiff's] employees from misappropriating customer information').

[65] See Niemi v. American Axle Mfg. & Holding, Inc., 2007 WL 29383 *2 (Mich. App. 2007) (holding RSP requirement not satisfied because the confidentiality safeguards 'do not reflect any effort by plaintiffs to impose confidentiality').

agreement.[66] And finally, courts at times seem to care whether the trade secret owner objectively manifested an intent to keep the information secret.[67]

Reading all these remarks together, one can easily get the impression that many judges simply assume that taking precautions is inherent to the concept of a 'secret'. This assumption fits common usage to some extent. There is a difference, after all, between information not being generally known and information being 'secret'. For example, notes kept in an office are not necessarily secret just because no one has ever seen them; they must ordinarily be treated as secret.[68]

Whatever its merits on semantic grounds, this argument is too formalistic to justify an RSP requirement. It makes no sense to incorporate common meanings of terms unless those meanings fit the policies trade secret law is meant to serve.[69] Thus, whether to require RSP as well as actual secrecy is a policy decision and must be justified on policy not semantic grounds.

Trade secret scholars provide a bit more insight, but not much.[70] Professor Chiappetta, for example, views precautions strictly in notice

---

[66] See Electro-Craft Corp. v. Controlled Motion, Inc., 332 N.W.2d 890, 901 (Minn. 1983); J.T. Healey & Son, Inc. v. James A. Murphy & Son, Inc., 357 Mass. 728 (1970).

[67] See Mortgage Specialists, Inc. v. Davey, 153 N.H. 764, 772 (2006); Electro-Craft Corp. v. Controlled Motion, Inc., 332 N.W.2d 890, 901 (Minn. 1983). See generally David W. Slaby *et al.*, *Trade Secret Protection: An Analysis of the Concept 'Efforts Reasonable under the Circumstances to Maintain Secrecy'*, 5 Santa Clara Computer & High Tech. L.J. 321, 327 (1989): 'It is clear that the efforts must be actual, affirmative measures. Mere intent to maintain secrecy is not enough. The trade secret claimant must manifest its intent by making some effort to keep the information secret. The law also requires such efforts to be a continuing course of conduct, signaling to all concerned that the information is secret'.

[68] See 1 Callmann, *supra* note 34, § 53.1 (arguing that intent to keep secret is an essential element of a trade secret claim and treating precautions as implicit evidence of intent). It is important to be clear that this semantic argument is not about notice. It is about the meaning of the term 'secret', as that concept is generally understood. Satisfying the essential characteristics of a secret might (or might not) also furnish the notice necessary to support a duty of confidentiality, and if it does, it is only as a byproduct of meeting the definitional requirements.

[69] If an example is helpful, one need only consider the Third Restatement of Unfair Competition, which defines a trade secret without reference to precautions. See *supra* note 44 and accompanying text.

[70] Two leading treatises on the subject make no attempt to justify the RSP requirement. See 1 Milgrim on Trade Secrets, *supra* note 1, §§ 1.03–1.04; James Pooley and Charles Tait Graves, Trade Secrets § 2.03[2][e] (2008). Melvin Jager focuses on the evidentiary function, endorsing the approach of the Third

terms,[71] but he also recognizes, correctly, that notice does not always require precautions and that when it does, the necessary precautions need not be as extensive as courts often demand today.[72] Professor Kitch also focuses on notice, but unlike Chiappetta, he fails to appreciate its relatively weak implications.[73] Professor Risch refers to a mix of justifications, including evidentiary and notice benefits.[74] He also alludes briefly, but without elaboration, to a promising analogy with 'the law of contributory negligence, moral hazard, and insurance', where it is optimal for the plaintiff or the insured to take precautionary steps.[75] Finally, a particularly insightful student Note defends the requirement as a tool for minimizing enforcement costs.[76] I shall return to Risch's analogy and the enforcement cost argument later in this chapter.[77]

To recap the discussion so far, we have seen that the RSP requirement made sense in the formalistic world of late nineteenth century property theory, but lost its way when legal realism forced a shift from formalism to

---

Restatement of Torts that makes RSP probative of value and secrecy. JAGER, TRADE SECRETS, *supra* note 3, § 5.16.

[71] Chiappetta, *supra* note 53, at 101–2, 115–16.

[72] *Id.* at 100, 116, 162. Chiappetta proposes stiffer notice requirements for '[w]ide-spread offerings', such as mass-distributed, clickwrap-protected secret information. *Id.* at 127.

[73] Kitch, *supra* note 51, at 699. It appears that Kitch is more concerned about promoting the 'free movement of employees' by preventing employer abuse of trade secret law than he is about furnishing adequate notice, although he seems to equate the two goals. *Id.* One thing is clear: a notice policy cannot justify the rather robust precautions he demands. *See id.* (requiring employers to have a 'consistent and meaningful desire to protect' and 'a consistent policy of overt protection').

[74] Michael Risch, *Why Do We Have Trade Secrets?*, 11 MARQ. INTELL. PROP. L. REV. 1, 44–7 (2007); see Note, *The Law of Trade Secrets: Toward a More Efficient Approach*, 57 VAND. L. REV. 1269, 1294 (2004) (focusing on the evidentiary function but noting that it leaves little work for the RSP doctrine to do).

[75] Risch, *supra* note 74, at 47.

[76] Note, *Trade Secret Misappropriation: A Cost-Benefit Response to the Fourth Amendment Analogy*, 106 HARV. L. REV. 461, 474 (1992).

[77] In a recent article, Charles Tait Graves argues for a property theory of trade secret law largely on the basis of its practical and strategic advantages in protecting the interests of departing employees, and he defends a reasonable precautions requirement as a tool that employees can use to check abusive overreaching by former employers. Charles Tait Graves, *Trade Secrets as Property: Theory and Consequences*, 15 J. INTELL. PROP. L. 39, 67–8 (2007). Helping employees avoid employer abuse is certainly a benefit, but that benefit must be balanced against the costs of the RSP requirement, including the cost of scuttling an employer's non-abusive enforcement of trade secret rights in a meritorious case. In other words, Graves must do more work to fit his practical argument into a normative account of trade secret law.

functionalism. From 1940 to 1980, courts divided on whether reasonable precautions were necessary to liability, and they applied the RSP standard with varying degrees of strictness. In 1980, the UTSA placed precautions at the center of trade secret litigation by including an RSP requirement in the definition of a trade secret. Efforts since then to justify the requirement mostly focus on evidentiary and notice benefits, but these do not support a general requirement or one that operates as a threshold liability element. The case law and commentary contain hints of more persuasive rationales, but none of these are developed rigorously.

III. THE NORMATIVE CASE REVISITED

This section returns to basics and considers whether the RSP requirement can be justified by the deeper policies supporting trade secret law. I have argued in previous writing that there is no distinctive set of trade secret policies and that liability should be governed mainly (though not exclusively) by contract principles.[78] For purposes of this section, I shall assume to the contrary, that trade secret law can be justified by one or more of the conventional economic, moral or contractarian theories advanced to support it. My goal here is to explore whether any of these theories is capable of supporting an RSP requirement.[79]

A. Economic Theories

There are three standard economic arguments for trade secret law: (1) that it promotes incentives to create and does so at low enough cost to yield a net benefit; (2) that it discourages costly and wasteful expenditures on self-help, and (3) that it encourages information transfers by the use of licensing rather than theft.[80]

Even if the first argument works for trade secret law in general (a premise that I question in other writing) it does not justify an RSP

---

[78] Bone, *supra* note 6, at 245, 296–304. Since publication of my article, a number of scholars have offered defenses of trade secret law. This is not the place to review these arguments. While they furnish useful insights, I do not believe they undermine my basic points.

[79] It is worth mentioning that pre-emption should be no obstacle to deleting the RSP requirement from trade secret law, at least if reverse engineering remains lawful. See Kewanee Oil Co. v. Bicron Corp., 416 U.S. 470 (1974).

[80] I have criticized all these arguments as justifications for trade secret law in my previous writing. Bone, *supra* note 6, at 264–70.

requirement. Quite the contrary, requiring precautions dampens incentives to create by making innovation more costly and enforcement of trade secret rights more difficult.[81] To be sure, an RSP requirement also promotes information diffusion by making it more difficult for trade secret owners to enforce their rights, but it also restricts diffusion by encouraging trade secret owners to bolster their self-help measures. Even if the first effect dominates the second – and it is not apparent that it does – it is still an open question whether the requirement reduces costs in a sensible way given the cost-benefit balance trade secret law seeks to achieve. I shall return to this point in Part IV.

The second argument – that trade secret law discourages costly and wasteful investment in self-help – does not readily fit an RSP requirement. The assumption behind the argument is that without the deterrent effect of trade secret law, firms would invest in extremely costly precautions in order to ward off aggressive efforts by competitors to steal secrets, and the resulting arms race of escalating measures and countermeasures would generate substantial social waste.[82] At first glance, this argument seems incompatible with an RSP requirement that forces firms to invest more rather than less in self-help. Part IV, however, explores a more complex version of the argument that seeks to justify the requirement as a doctrinal device to minimize the expected social cost of protecting secrets through a mix of litigation and self-help.

The third argument – that trade secret law encourages parties to obtain secrets through licensing rather than theft – clearly fails as a justification for the RSP requirement. Trade secret law would still encourage licensing without an RSP requirement, and it might do so more effectively by encouraging licensing of all secret information not just information protected by reasonable secrecy precautions. It is possible that precautions help prospective licensees identify the specific secret available for licensing, but this can be done in many other ways.

B. Moral Theories

Lockean labor/desert and unjust enrichment are the usual moral theories used to justify intellectual property rights, but as I have explained

---

[81] Moreover, making the RSP determination hostage to a jury's fact-specific evaluation adds uncertainty costs at the enforcement stage. And an RSP requirement can divert research investment at the margin to innovations that are easier to contain and control, such as physical processes that can be contained in an enclosed area and protected by fencing and other safeguards.

[82] See Bone, *supra* note 6, at 272–81.

elsewhere, neither theory fits American trade secret law and its core doctrines.[83] This leaves arguments from privacy rights and contractarianism.[84]

A privacy rights argument supposes that firms have a moral right to privacy in their secret information. If this argument is viable, it might justify some form of RSP requirement as a way to mark information as private. But there are at least three problems. First, privacy does not always require precautions. If it did, home-owners might have to install locks or burglar alarms before claiming a right of privacy in their homes. Second, the privacy argument cannot explain why judges insist that precautions be directed specifically at the trade secret itself and not just the facility housing the secret.[85] For example, most things inside a home are considered private simply because the home itself is a private space without any need to mark the privacy of individual items. It is not clear then why secret information housed inside a facility is not also private whenever a firm treats the facility itself as private, say, by taking the customary steps to guard against intrusions. Third, and most serious, the privacy rights argument simply does not work as a justification for trade secret law in general. Even if there is such a thing as a moral right to privacy, it is difficult to see how corporations qualify as right holders and how the typical information in trade secret cases falls within the ambit of rights protection.[86]

The second moral argument for trade secret law is contractarian. It asks what rules firms would agree to in a hypothetical bargaining situation designed to give their agreement moral force.[87] Assuming that some form of contractarian argument is capable of justifying trade secret law in general,[88] the question remains why parties in a suitably defined bargaining situation would ever choose to be bound by a reasonable precautions requirement. They might agree to rules that require secrecy and maybe to notice as a condition for a duty of confidence, but it is not evident why they would agree to costly precautions beyond what a firm would find cost-justified on its own.[89]

---

83 See *id.* at 283–4.

84 James Hill has proposed a moral justification for trade secret law based on a personhood theory. James W. Hill, *Trade Secrets, Unjust Enrichment, and the Classification of Obligations*, 4 VA. J. L. & TECH. 2 (1999). I am skeptical. Personhood values do not seem to apply to much of the useful information that trade secret law protects. Moreover, it is not clear how a personhood theory can explain the doctrinal specifics of American trade secret law, and in particular the RSP requirement.

85 See *supra* note 64 and accompanying text.

86 See Bone, *supra* note 6, at 284–9 (discussing these flaws in some detail).

87 *Id.* at 290–1.

88 I argue elsewhere that it is not. See *id.* at 290–4.

89 It might be possible to cast some of the arguments I develop in Part IV in contractarian form, but in that case, the real justificatory work is done by the

IV. THE NORMATIVE CASE FOR AN RSP REQUIREMENT RECONSIDERED

One might conclude from the foregoing analysis that there really is no such thing as a defensible RSP requirement. The doctrine's original rationale is not persuasive now that the property theory has been rejected; conventional justifications based on notice and evidence all have serious shortcomings, and the standard policies cited to justify trade secret law seem to offer little support. This strongly suggests that the RSP requirement should be eliminated, and I am inclined to support this reform.[90] Before implementing it, however, we must be sure we understand all the social benefits of the doctrine. Toward that end, this section describes in a general way three potential benefits that have been largely overlooked and that need more careful study. Two have to do with minimizing enforcement costs, and the third has to do with using precautions as a signal to channel innovation in efficient ways.

A. Enforcement Costs

There are two ways that an RSP requirement can reduce enforcement costs: by reducing process costs or by reducing error costs.

1. Process costs

The key to understanding the process cost argument is to recognize that precautions and litigation are substitute methods for protecting a secret. A rational firm with recourse to a trade secret claim will use precautions to protect its secret up to the point where the marginal cost of additional precaution just exceeds the marginal cost of a trade secret lawsuit and then switch to litigation beyond that point. If all these costs are internalized, the firm's private choice will reflect the efficient social choice.

The problem, of course, is that not all these costs are internalized. For example, adding precautions chills further innovation at the margin by shielding secrets more effectively, and this chilling cost is not borne by the trade secret owner. A trade secret lawsuit does the same, but it also adds

argument itself without the contractarian gloss. One more point. Trade secret law is sometimes defended as a means to enforce informal industry norms. But even assuming this argument makes sense (see *id.* at 294–6), I am not aware of any generally accepted customary norm that requires a trade secret owner to implement precautions.

[90] Assuming, of course, that trade secret law is retained in roughly its current form rather than cut back in the way I have recommended in my other writing.

other externalities in the form of litigation costs borne by the defendant and costs borne by the public in subsidizing the court system.

Because of these externalities, a rational trade secret owner will not invest optimally in precautions. To see why, assume for simplicity that litigation and precautions generate the same chilling costs, so the externalities relevant to the precautions-litigation decision are limited to litigation costs. Under these circumstances, a rational firm will over-utilize litigation and under-utilize precautions because it does not have to pay the full expense of the litigation alternative, including the defendant's litigation costs and the relevant portion of the public subsidy. The RSP requirement forces an additional investment in precaution, which nudges the firm closer to the social optimum.

This argument seems relatively straightforward, but it has two serious difficulties. First, it cannot distinguish other property cases that do not require self-help measures. Commercial firms, for example, can sue in trespass without installing fences or anti-burglary devices, and copyright owners can sue without first encrypting websites or screening audience members. Admittedly, trespass and copyright litigation is likely to be less costly than trade secret litigation insofar as the boundaries of the property right in land and the copyright right in a protected work are more clearly defined. Still, it seems reasonable to suppose that in many cases simple protective measures, such as installing a burglar alarm or encrypting a website, would be much less costly than prosecuting a lawsuit. Yet even these simple measures are not required.

Second, and more important, it is not clear how a judge is supposed to determine the optimal level of precaution. The problem is that the choice of precaution level affects the cost-benefit trade-off, which in turn affects the original choice. The reason is easy to understand. Adding a fact-specific RSP requirement to trade secret law will increase litigation cost externalities because it opens up new issues and makes success a possibility for the defendant in every case. An increase in litigation cost, in turn, calls for a marginal increase in the level of precaution because the purpose of the precautions requirement is to reduce litigation cost externalities. The resulting interaction between choice of precaution level and resulting litigation cost greatly complicates implementation of an open-ended RSP standard.[91]

---

[91] Consider the following simple numerical example. Suppose that a firm can choose among three levels of precaution costing 200, 300 and 400 respectively. Investing 200 in precaution produces a 30% probability of losing the secret. Investing 300 reduces the probability to 25%, and investing 400 reduces it further to 22%. Assume that the law recognizes a trade secret claim but no RSP

In fact, the problem is even more serious than this. When a firm is forced to protect its secret more aggressively, competitors might respond by using more sophisticated measures to obtain it. This response increases the total social cost of additional precautions by adding into the mix the extra cost competitors incur in trying to get the secret. The rational trade secret owner will ignore this extra cost because it does not have to bear it. Nevertheless, the cost is still relevant to determining the socially optimal level of precaution, and pushes toward a lower optimum.

Two important points emerge from this analysis. First, an RSP requirement might not be appropriate for all, or even for any, cases depending on how the countervailing factors work out and how costly it is to determine the optimal precaution level. Second, the task of resolving intricate interaction effects and determining the social optimum is too complex to conduct effectively on a case-by-case basis.[92] This means that if the process

---

requirement, and suppose that the firm's litigation costs are 1,000 and total litigation costs (the plaintiff's plus the defendant's plus the public court subsidy) are 3,000. Assume that meritorious trade secret claims always succeed and that the secret is valuable enough so the firm will sue in each of the scenarios below. (I could assume a litigation error risk but it would complicate the analysis without much benefit for this example.)

A rational firm in this situation will choose a precaution level of 200. Investing 200 yields an expected cost of 200 + 0.3 × 1,000 = 500. Compare this to an expected cost of 550 when the firm invests 300 (i.e., 300 + 0.25 × 1,000 = 550) and 620 when the firm invests 400 (i.e., 400 + 0.22 × 1,000 = 620). From a social perspective, however, the optimal choice is 300. The expected social cost is 1,050 at an investment of 300 (i.e., 300 + 0.25 × 3,000 = 1,050). Compare this to a social cost of 1,100 at an investment of 200 (i.e., 200 + 0.3 × 3,000 = 1,100) and a social cost of 1,060 at an investment of 400 (i.e., 400 + 0.22 × 3,000 = 1,060). Thus, our firm will invest at 200 when 300 is the optimal investment from a social point of view. Adding an RSP requirement and setting it at 300 will force firms to invest at the socially optimal level.

There is a catch, however. Adding the RSP requirement changes the litigation cost assumptions by increasing the firm's private litigation costs as well as the total of private plus public litigation costs of a trade secret lawsuit. Suppose the firm's private litigation costs increase from 1,000 to 1,500 and suppose total litigation costs increase from 3,000 to 4,500. Performing the same calculations as above, it is easy to see that now the firm's optimal expenditure is 300 (since the RSP requirement is satisfied only with an investment of 300), but the optimal choice from a social perspective is 400. Thus, we should set the RSP requirement at 400, not 300 as previously thought.

[92] This distinguishes trade secret law from other areas such as negligence law where judges have used the common law process to develop doctrines like contributory fault that require plaintiffs to take precautions. In contributory fault, the question is whether the plaintiff could have avoided the accident more cheaply than the defendant. Thus, the focus is on comparing the defendant's and the

cost argument is persuasive, the RSP requirement it supports should be implemented by a general rule rather than an open-ended standard. Moreover, the general rule should be formulated in advance by a legislature or advisory body that can take account of global incentive effects and collect and process all the relevant empirical information.[93]

2. Error costs

The error cost argument uses the RSP requirement to screen frivolous trade secret suits and thereby reduce the chilling effect of erroneous recoveries. The RSP requirement does this by using the level of precaution as an easily verifiable proxy for actual secrecy and improper appropriation. Thus, the error cost argument exploits the evidentiary value of an RSP requirement discussed earlier in this chapter, but it does so in order to screen frivolous suits rather than simplify proof in meritorious cases.

The extent of the frivolous suit problem in trade secret law is unclear, but it is easy to see how firms can benefit from filing frivolous suits for strategic gain.[94] In the case of start-ups by former employees, for example, a trade secret lawsuit can create costs and risks that impede the start-up's access to capital markets. Moreover, meritless suits against third parties who have acquired the information lawfully can result in settlements that license or even prevent use of the secret. If these problems are serious enough, they can significantly chill further innovation.

A properly designed RSP requirement can reduce this chilling effect. Verifying precautions is likely to be much easier than verifying secrecy and misappropriation by more direct means. Thus, assuming that precautions correlate positively with likelihood of secrecy and unlawful appropriation, forcing plaintiffs to plead and prove reasonable precautions as part of their *prima facie* case should help screen meritless strike suits.

---

plaintiff's expected precaution costs. In trade secret law's RSP doctrine, however, the analysis is much more complicated because the judge must take account of the dynamic interaction between *two* types of cost: precaution costs *and* litigation costs.

[93] Giving specific content to an RSP requirement by general rule is likely to be difficult, but it is still feasible. Since firms adopt precautions *ex ante* based on expectations about what might happen on average for their type of business, a rule specifying minimum precautions according to the needs of the average case might work reasonably well – such as a rule requiring at a minimum confidentiality agreements and facility access restrictions. If the distribution of firms is too heterogeneous, different rules could be formulated for different categories of cases. Alternatively, one could design the minimum as a strong presumption and allow defendants to rebut it with a clear and compelling showing of inadequacy.

[94] See Bone, *supra* note 6, at 279, nn.172, 173.

This argument is certainly plausible, but it needs further development. The RSP requirement not only screens frivolous suits; it screens some meritorious suits as well. The type of meritorious suit triggering concern is one in which the plaintiff clearly has a valuable secret but does not use reasonable precautions and the defendant actually takes the secret by a breach of confidence or some other improper means. In an ideal system, the plaintiff should win this suit despite its lack of precaution because RSP is merely a proxy for secrecy and wrongful appropriation, both of which are assumed to be present. The fact is, however, that the plaintiff loses with an RSP requirement in place because the plaintiff cannot prove RSP. It follows that the RSP requirement can be justified on error cost grounds only if the reduction in expected error cost as a result of screening frivolous suits exceeds the increase in expected error cost as a result of screening meritorious suits.[95] Whether the error cost balance comes out in this way depends on empirical information about the relative risks and costs of error.[96]

One point stands out clearly, however. The RSP requirement is not likely to screen frivolous suits effectively unless it is designed in a way that supports early summary judgment. If a frivolous plaintiff can avoid summary judgment, it can use the credible threat of trial to leverage a favorable settlement, and this result undermines the screening benefits of the rule. The current version of the RSP requirement suffers from this defect. It is so fact-specific that it makes summary judgment difficult to obtain.[97] One way to empower summary judgment is to define reasonable precautions with some clarity in advance and codify minimum requirements by general rule. Thus, the error cost analysis points in the same direction as the process cost analysis: toward a relatively clear rule formulated in advance.[98]

---

95 In formal terms, expected error cost is the probability of the particular type of error (a successful meritless suit or an improperly screened meritorious suit) *multiplied by* the social cost of that type of error when it occurs.

96 It is certainly possible that a properly designed RSP requirement could yield a net benefit. If the frivolous suit problem is as serious as some of the anecdotal evidence suggests, an RSP requirement could create a significant deterrence benefit. Moreover, it should not screen too many meritorious suits if it is expressed in relatively clear terms so that firms can comply with the requirement in advance. Finally, there is no reason to believe that the social cost of false negatives (in terms, for example, of dampened incentives to create) exceeds the social cost of false positives (in terms of chilling further innovation) – and it is very possible that the relationship is the reverse.

97 See, e.g., Rockwell Graphics Systems, Inc. v. DEV Industries, Inc., 925 F.2d 174, 179–80 (7th Cir. 1991).

98 Indeed, the rule-based approach has the same benefits for error costs as it does for process costs. The higher the level of required precaution, the more difficult it will be for firms to comply and the more false negatives the rule will

B. Signaling

The signaling argument treats precautions as a signal that reduces informational asymmetries between trade secret owners and their competitors. Precautions do this by conveying information about the value of a secret and the aggressiveness of its owner. Armed with this information, competitors will invest more efficiently in learning trade secrets.

To explain how the signaling argument works, consider a firm that believes the best way to protect its secret is to do nothing special to alert competitors to its existence. In the absence of an RSP requirement, this firm would adopt only those precautions ordinarily used to protect facilities like its own. In particular, it would refrain from any secret-specific precautions, or at most use only internal precautions, such as confidentiality agreements, that are unlikely to come to the attention of competitors. Now suppose we add an RSP requirement, and suppose it mandates measures specifically targeting the secret itself, including external precautions such as fences, signs, and the like that competitors can easily observe. With this RSP requirement in place, our firm will have to implement secret-specific and externally visible precautions if it wishes to rely on trade secret law to protect its secret. But if it does that, it signals competitors that it has a secret.

Suppose the firm complies with the RSP requirement and reveals the existence of its trade secret. The incentives of the firm then change markedly, as do the incentives of its competitors. The firm will now expect competitors to go after its secret, so it will beef up precautions to the privately cost-justified level when competitors know that a secret exists. These enhanced precautions in turn signal competitors about the value of the secret, since a firm will take more precautions the more valuable it believes its secret is. Armed with that information, competitors will invest more in trying to obtain the more valuable secrets. In turn, the trade secret owner, anticipating this response from competitors, will invest even more in precautions to counteract competitor efforts and also to signal that it will aggressively enforce its trade secret rights. Thus, competitors can use the level of precaution to learn something about the value of the secret and also something about the aggressiveness of the trade secret owner.

This strategic interaction reaps social benefits. A competitor who knows the trade secret owner is aggressive will be less inclined to steal the secret

---

generate. But the lower the level of required precaution, the less effective the rule will be in screening false positives. The optimal balance can be determined only if incentive effects are considered globally and with the benefit of as much reliable empirical information as possible.

and more inclined to invest in discovering it lawfully – by reverse engineering if possible or independent research if not. These incentives avoid the waste that results from obtaining the secret unlawfully only to be sued and enjoined from using it. Furthermore, armed with information about the secret's value, competitors will direct their research efforts toward the more valuable trade secrets, and doing so should yield larger social benefits in terms of further innovation and deadweight loss reduction.[99]

Signaling by means of an RSP requirement is socially beneficial in another way. One reason trade secret law has such a potentially serious impact on further innovation is that the legal rights it confers last indefinitely, for as long as the information remains secret. By prompting competitors to search for the secret, the RSP requirement accelerates the process of lawful discovery. When enough firms lawfully discover a secret, the information is no longer treated as secret and trade secret rights end. Thus, the RSP requirement in effect shortens the expected length of trade secret protection.

This signaling argument has implications for the optimal form of an RSP rule. The rule it supports, unlike the rules associated with the enforcement cost arguments, should not specify particular precautions in advance. If all firms are required to implement a particular set of precautions, those precautions cannot signal differences among firms. Furthermore, the main function of an RSP requirement in the signaling argument is to discourage a strategy of concealment, so the rule need only force revelation of the secret's existence. Once competitors know that a secret exists and the firm knows competitors know, the firm's strategic interaction with competitors does the rest of the work.

Therefore, the RSP rule need only require that firms implement affirmative measures that are aimed at protecting the secret itself and that are reasonably transparent to be observable by competitors. This means, for example, that purely intra-firm precautions, such as employee confidentiality agreements, should normally be inadequate. Moreover, the rule should require continuing precautions that maintain the strength of the signal over time. And it should apply across the board to all cases, just as it does in the UTSA.[100]

---

[99] In the best of all possible worlds, we would want to avoid duplicative research altogether, but trade secret law rules out that option. The second best alternative is to encourage greater investment in duplicating the more valuable information, because the sharing of more valuable information is likely to produce greater social gains.

[100] It is worth noting that many of these features are already embodied in current RSP law. See *supra* notes 61–7 and accompanying text.

Nevertheless, there are at least four problems with the signaling argument. First, precautions do not guarantee signaling benefits. Those benefits depend on a number of factors, including the proportion of secrets that have high value, the fraction of firms that are aggressive, the cost of taking precautions, and the cost of discovering secrets lawfully and unlawfully. Depending on how these factors come out, there is a chance that all firms will behave the same way in equilibrium, scuttling any possibility of a signaling benefit.[101]

Second, any signal is bound to be noisy when competitors do not know the precise nature of the secret. Some types of information require more stringent security measures than others in order to achieve the same level of protection. This can make it difficult to infer a secret's value from observing the precaution level when the type of secret is not known, and this uncertainty reduces the signaling benefit.

Third, precautions are not the only way to achieve signaling benefits. Trade secret law, for example, could just require a trade secret owner to notify competitors of the secret's existence by whatever means it chooses. However, there are some advantages to an RSP requirement. Precautions are easily verifiable and they avoid the need to evaluate the adequacy of alternative forms of notice. Precautions also create a continuous signal, as well as one that is transparent enough to be accessible to all interested parties.[102]

---

[101] In game theory, this result is known as a pure pooling equilibrium. One can construct a simple model of the signaling game by assuming two types of trade secret owners, those who aggressively enforce trade secret rights (the aggressive type) and those who do not (the passive type), as well as two types of trade secrets, a high value type and a low value type. Only the trade secret owner knows whether it is an aggressive type and what kind of trade secret it has. Trade secret owners choose a level of precaution and their choice signals competitors about firm type and secret type. In turn, competitors choose whether to use lawful or unlawful means to obtain the information and how much effort to invest. As with any signaling game, there is an incentive to pool: passive firms sometimes act as if they are aggressive, and firms with high value secrets sometimes act as if their secrets are low value. Competitors try to force separation by sometimes stealing from firms that appear to be aggressive and sometimes investing a lot in obtaining secrets with low value signals. There are three possible equilibria of this game: pure pooling, partial pooling and pure separating. If the result is a pure pooling equilibrium, then all firms behave the same way and there is no signaling benefit and thus no reason to impose an RSP requirement. If the result, however, is a partial pooling or pure separating equilibrium (and I tend to think partial pooling is likely) imposing an RSP requirement does create signaling benefits. Of course, one would still have to determine whether those benefits justify the costs.

[102] These advantages can also be achieved by setting up a public registration system and requiring all trade secret owners to register the existence of their trade secrets as a condition to using trade secret law (but, of course, not the content of

The fourth problem has to do with the need for signaling. Because signaling works by forcing firms to reveal the existence of their secrets, its value depends on the extent to which firms would use a concealment strategy based on not alerting competitors. We know that some firms have used this strategy.[103] But it is not clear how many would use it in the absence of an RSP requirement. In any event, this is an empirical question, which cannot be answered without more empirical information.[104]

V. CONCLUSION

The RSP requirement is an odd feature of trade secret law with a rocky but revealing history. It first emerged as a sensible element of a formalistic property rights theory based on natural law and the idea of possession. With the demise of this theory, trade secret law became a branch of unfair competition, which shifted the focus from property in the secret to the wrongfulness of the method of appropriation. This shift left the RSP requirement without any obvious normative support, stripped it of independent doctrinal significance, and relegated it to notice and evidentiary functions. The UTSA restored RSP to an independent requirement, but without providing a convincing rationale. The result is a doctrine without a clear foundation and RSP decisions made without meaningful guidance.

On the most general level, the story of the RSP requirement is the story of trade secret law writ small. Since the demise of the formalistic property rights theory, trade secret law, like the RSP requirement, has operated without convincing support. At the beginning of this chapter, I referred to trade secret law as the ugly duckling of intellectual property, but this ugly duckling has yet to turn into a swan.

This chapter bracketed the more general justificatory problem, however, and asked the narrower question whether an RSP requirement makes sense assuming trade secret law makes sense. The answer to that question is not clear. The standard arguments for the requirement do not work, and it is difficult to see how the doctrine follows from the standard economic

---

the trade secret itself). A registration system, however, creates administrative costs, which must be balanced against the benefits. I am indebted to Oren Bracha for alerting me to this possibility.

103 We know this because they tried to rely on it to satisfy the RSP requirement in subsequent trade secret cases. See *supra* notes 61–4 and accompanying text.

104 And it is an empirical question that is very difficult to answer. We cannot rely on the choices of firms under current trade secret law because current law already makes RSP relevant to liability.

and moral theories used to justify trade secret law more generally. The only credible justifications rely on enforcement cost and signaling benefits, but without more careful analysis, we cannot be sure that these benefits are strong enough to justify a general rule applicable to all cases. In the end, if the RSP requirement makes sense, it is likely to be because of a counter-intuitive insight. Secrecy precautions, rather than shielding a secret more effectively, actually serve to enhance its public dissemination and enrich the public domain supporting further innovation.

4 Trade secrecy and common law confidentiality: the problem of multiple regimes

*Charles Tait Graves**

I. INTRODUCTION

Scholars and practitioners interested in analysing trade secret law at the level of theory – that is, exploring its economic, social and philosophical underpinnings in order to recommend policy objectives – face a serious obstacle. Unlike patent or copyright law, which are unitary regimes governed by statutes and, ultimately, the Supreme Court, what we call 'trade secret law' is much more amorphous. As a result, it is sometimes difficult to speak of trade secret law as a single body of law when analysing its effects or offering policy proposals for reform.

The most important example is the definition of secrecy itself. Secrecy is interpreted differently under different tort and contract claims, and regulated differently under non-competition covenants. In some cases, courts have recognized quasi-trade secret claims encompassing non-secret information said to fall within some lesser, but still protectable, category of information. In recent years, this question has come to the forefront as courts have struggled to decide whether the Uniform Trade Secrets Act pre-empts alternative tort formulations in favor of a single definition of protectable information.

This chapter will explore how the theoretical discussion of trade secret law is frustrated by the multiple regimes of confidentiality available in most jurisdictions. Whether one's interest in trade secret law touches on innovation policy, employee interests, or merely describing trade secret law as a body of law subject to predictable results and internal consistency, it is important to understand the confusion among courts and practicing attorneys in everyday litigation. Policy proposals that fail to take account of the workaday landscape of trade secret practice may prove ineffective or even misleading.

* Partner, Wilson Sonsini Goodrich & Rosati, San Francisco; Adjunct faculty, University of California, Hastings College of the Law, San Francisco.

The purpose of this chapter is not to offer a theory for one or another aspect of trade secret law, then, but to offer commentary on the shape of trade secret practice as it exists today for companies, mobile employees and venture capital investors.[1] The goal is to promote a more precise theorization by offering a high-level, structural layout of the different regimes of trade secret regulation that often exist side by side in jurisdictions across the country.

To recognize that trade secret law includes different definitions of secrecy is to recognize that trade secret law can serve inconsistent, even conflicting policy objectives. Subtle differences in the way trade secret law is argued, presented and decided can lead to widely divergent rules being applied. Asking what type of trade secret law applies is thus a question of whose interests will be served, and whose will be less favored, by the choice. It is difficult to pursue policy recommendations for promoting innovation without a blunt assessment of who benefits from different iterations of a trade secret system.

This chapter proposes that the existence of multiple regimes of trade secret regulation implicitly favors interests hostile to entrepreneurship and the diffusion of nimble, small-scale ventures. A multi-tier trade secret regime makes litigation more lengthy, ambiguous and difficult. It makes counseling departing employees and venture investors less certain and predicable. And in litigation, it may save questionable claims over information that is not really secret, or make it easier to file a weak lawsuit. The structure of trade secret law, and the definition of secrecy in particular, has everyday consequences for the risks entrepreneurs take, the degree to which parties are willing to launch litigation over flimsy claims, and the freedom departing employees have to build new companies using public domain information.

To explore these problems, we will focus on four conflicting regimes of trade secret regulation: the official regime of trade secret law under the Uniform Act and Restatement formulations, non-competition covenants, the employee confidentiality contract, and the alternative torts said to govern broader categories of protectable information. For each, we will explore the different interests each favors and the different policy objectives each seems to reflect.

---

[1] This chapter is thus distinct from the ongoing philosophical debate in the law reviews whether trade secret law is best premised on property, contract or some other free-standing rationale. For two contributions that helped sharpen the debate over the past decade, see Robert G. Bone, *A New Look at Trade Secret Law: Doctrine in Search of Justification*, 86 CAL. L. REV. 241 (1998); Miguel Deutch, *The Property Concept of Trade Secrets in Anglo-American Law: An Ongoing Debate*, 31 U. RICH. L. REV. 313 (1997).

We will also explore possible explanations for the confusion in trade secret law, including the general lack of attention trade secret law receives from bench and bar. We will also consider a number of potential solutions for the better organization and better theorization of trade secret jurisprudence, from federalizing trade secret law to better organization among trade secret practitioners and intellectual property scholars.

II. THE PROBLEM: THE MANY VARIATIONS OF TRADE SECRET REGULATION

Trade secret law in everyday practice is not a single regime based on common and widely-understood policy goals, but a hodge-podge of inconsistent doctrines, rules and practices. This disorganization exists in part because legal scholars, judges and practitioners interested in intellectual property have neglected trade secret law, often in favor of the federal intellectual property statutes.

To suggest that trade secret practice is disorganized is an understatement. There is no single body of trade secret regulation within each state. Instead, the states to varying degrees permit a set of inconsistent and overlapping legal regimes, each of which ostensibly regulates the same types of non-public commercial information. Upon close analysis, these multiple regimes employ different standards in order to pursue different, and even conflicting, policy objectives. Yet few if any courts addressing trade secret cases seem to recognize the problem and, worse, some issue rulings that make use of inconsistent common law theories within the same decision.

There is no other area of intellectual property law where the main body of law is supplemented by such a confusing, inconsistent host of alternative possibilities. There may be inconsistent decisions or ambiguous doctrines in patent and copyright, but nothing there approaches the indeterminacy of trade secrecy law. In trade secret law, it is not merely a question of conflicting decisions by different courts on similar points. And it is not a matter of one state applying different rules to peripheral issues such as the statute of limitations. Rather, the very definition of secrecy itself is applied in an inconsistent manner. As a result, restrictions on similarly-situated departing employees may differ depending on which judge hears the case, the titles of the causes of action at issue, or the state in which the lawsuit is filed.

Trade secret law in everyday practice is much more than the law-on-the-books of the Uniform Trade Secrets Act or the Restatement (Third) of Unfair Competition. As we shall see, these formulations do not always provide the final word on what courts will deem protectable. We might define the primary question of trade secret law as what information protected by state law a departing employee can reuse – a definition that focuses on the vast majority of disputes, and the area where the most confusion arises.[2] If that is the proper definition, trade secret law also includes the law of non-disclosure contracts, the law of non-competition covenants, and the host of vague, ill-defined tort claims that many courts have allowed as a sort of adjunct to trade secret misappropriation claims.

If we were starting anew, and if the problem were defined as how best to regulate use of information by departing employees, it seems unlikely that conflicting, parallel approaches would exist. This chapter will explore possible explanations for this inconsistency, from historical leftovers in state common law, to distortions introduced by attorneys, to the lack of serious attention from the judiciary and legal scholars. Although intellectual property scholars produce sophisticated analyses to promote innovation and creativity in patent and copyright law, very few law review articles or symposia are dedicated to problems of trade secret law.[3] Still less have commentators sought to debate what type of trade secret regime might best serve goals of promoting innovation, protecting employee mobility, supporting regional economic growth and ensuring consistent results driven by clear rules and remedies.

If critical attention is to be paid to trade secret law, there is no more important place to start than these multiple, inconsistent layers. In this spirit, we will review the four overlapping regimes of trade secret law, ask what policy objectives each seems to serve, ask who benefits from each. Most important, we will review how each regime defines protectable information. By clarifying these multiple regimes of confidentiality, the hope is to help transform trade secret law from a neglected corner of intellectual property jurisprudence to a body of law that is consistent, that best

---

2 The other two areas of conflict in trade secret law – disputes between two businesses over a non-disclosure agreement and espionage-like activities under civil or criminal law – are rare in comparison to departing employee disputes. Moreover, and for reasons explained in part below, courts apply a much more consistent body of rules in such disputes.

3 Innovation policy as a field of inquiry encompassing the whole of intellectual property law has received some major treatments in recent years, but still remains a nascent field. See generally SUZANNE SCOTCHMER, INNOVATION AND INCENTIVES (MIT Press, 2004) (general survey of innovation regulation in the United States, with a special focus on research institutions; some mention of trade secret law, though patent regulation is the major focus); WILLIAM M. LANDES AND RICHARD A. POSNER, THE ECONOMIC STRUCTURE OF INTELLECTUAL PROPERTY LAW (Harvard University Press, 2003) (analysis of different fields of intellectual property law, including trade secret, from a law and economics perspective).

promotes innovation, and that attracts greater theoretical interest from scholarly commentators.

III. FOUR REGIMES OF CONFIDENTIALITY

A. Official Trade Secret Law

The first of the four regimes of confidentiality is what we might call 'official' trade secret law: the systems of rules governed by the various enactments of the Uniform Trade Secrets Act, other state trade secret statutes, and the handful of states following the Restatement systems.[4] Official trade secret law is what most commentators mean when they discuss 'trade secrecy': the concept that a departing employee is free to use any information generally known to the trade, and is restricted only from using discrete, secret, valuable information. Official trade secret law represents a reasonably objective test that looks to what information was known in the industry at the time of the alleged misappropriation.

This is the system under which, for example, secret elements of a software program or items on a customer list may or may not be protected.[5] Plaintiffs who cannot prove that they protected the information or who released the information in a product susceptible to reverse engineering have no rights to enforce against others in the information.[6]

Official trade secret law is also the system that most commentators seem to be talking about when they are doing theory or analysis. The rules of trade secret presented in textbooks for law students reflect the official

---

[4] More than 40 states and the District of Columbia have enacted versions of the Uniform Act. South Carolina, North Carolina and Alabama have enacted their own comprehensive trade secret statutes. New York, Massachusetts, New Jersey and Texas follow common law formulations. See JAMES POOLEY, TRADE SECRETS § 2.03[7][a] (2008).

[5] See, e.g., Naturalawn of Am., Inc. v. West Group, LLC, 484 F.Supp.2d 393, 399 (D. Md. 2007) (customized aspects of otherwise public software protectable under Maryland UTSA); Morlife, Inc. v. Perry, 56 Cal. App. 4th 1514 (1997) (customer list protectable under California law).

[6] See, e.g., LinkCo, Inc. v. Fujitsu Ltd., 230 F.Supp.2d 492, 498 (S.D.N.Y. 2002) ('courts have held that there can be no trade secret protection, as a matter of law, if the secrecy is necessarily lost when the design or product is placed on the market'); Stilwell Dev. Inc. v. Chen, 11 U.S.P.Q.2d 1328, 1331 (C.D. Cal. 1989) (sanctioning plaintiff for alleging trade secrets in a product already sold to customers before time of alleged misappropriation); Chicago Lock Co. v. Fanberg, 676 F.2d 400, 405 (9th Cir. 1982) (defendant reverse engineered lock codes; no liability).

Restatement and Uniform Act formulations.[7] The law is presented as being generally unified.

Implicit policy objective Official trade secret law promotes clarity, uniformity across jurisdictions and predictable definitions, remedies, and procedures.[8] It seeks to promote innovation both by protecting certain information and by providing clearly-defined means for others to compete. By allowing states to protect unpatented technical information only by contract[9] or through a trade secret misappropriation claim, official trade secret law promotes harmonization with the federal intellectual property regimes and their relationship with state law under the Supremacy Clause.

Whose interests are served? Official trade secret law reflects a balancing of interests. By protecting non-public, competitively valuable information, it rewards the employers who provide the infrastructure for innovation and deters collateral litigation among employee-inventors over ownership. By recognizing objectively-defined limits to that protection (through rules for non-secrecy, lack of value, reverse engineering and independent derivation), official trade secret law promotes the planning and creation of new technology enterprises by departing employees, venture capital investors, and others.

These well-defined limits to trade secret protection provide a reasonably transparent scheme for individuals whose technology development choices may be affected by trade secret law, and to courts who must adjudicate

---

[7] See generally Robert P. Merges, Peter S. Menell and Mark A. Lemley, Intellectual Property in the New Technological Age 33–116 (Aspen Publishers, 2006) (overview of trade secret law focusing on Restatement and UTSA approaches, with some commentary on contract and non-solicitation issues); William H. Francis and Robert C. Collins, Patent Law 7–69 (West Group, 2002) (overview of trade secret law with excerpts from cases under the Restatement and the UTSA).

[8] Some of these goals are made explicit in the section of the Uniform Trade Secrets Act that directs courts to harmonize UTSA rulings with those from other states. See, e.g., Cal. Civ. Code § 3426.8 ('This title shall be applied and construed to effectuate its general purpose to make uniform the law with respect to the subject of this title among states enacting it').

[9] As discussed below, the UTSA enactments do not bar contract-based claims over trade secrets, which is similar to the Supremacy Clause rule that there is no federal pre-emption of contract-based claims over unpatented technology information. See, e.g., Cal. Civ. Code § 3426.7(b)(1) (UTSA does not affect 'contractual remedies, whether or not based upon misappropriation of a trade secret'); *cf.* Aronson v. Quick Point Pencil Co., 440 U.S. 257 (1979) (holding that federal pre-emption of claims over unpatented, non-secret technology does not apply to contract claims).

disputes between claimants to information developed by technology start-ups. This promotes predictability in litigation, as courts and juries can determine trade secrecy by comparison to public domain information available at the time of the alleged misappropriation.

Perhaps more importantly, official trade secret law also promotes predictability in counseling for mobile employees or newly-founded companies. Attorneys in Silicon Valley and other high-innovation regions spend a great deal of time helping individuals plan what information they may use at the new job or new company balanced against the risks of costly litigation. Official trade secret law allows such parties to perform public domain searches in advance and be fairly certain that non-secret information will be free for use – even if the information was learned from a former employer. Intellectual property counseling of this nature is not often a focus of theorizing about trade secret law, nor in published opinions, but is a significant part of the trade secret landscape in everyday practice. This predictability is absent in other regimes of confidentiality law, especially with alternative tort claims that operate to prohibit use of non-secret information.

B. Non-Competition Covenants

The second form of trade secret law is the non-competition covenant. At first glance, non-competition covenants may not appear to be a form of trade secret regulation. Their immediate goal – preventing employees from joining a competitor for some period of time after departing – is accomplished whether or not the employer has any trade secrets, and whether or not the employee would have misused such information. In everyday practice, however, courts across the country point to the protection of trade secrets as the primary justification for enforcing non-competition covenants. Indeed, although courts often express aversion and even hostility to the concept of the non-competition covenant and its effect on the mobile employee,[10] they just as frequently justify the practice (and thus overcome the supposed aversion) by reference to trade secret protection.[11]

---

[10] Cases expressing the common law hostility to non-competition agreements are numerous. Recent examples include Cook Sign Co. v. Combs, 2008 WL 3898267, *7 (Minn. Ct. App. August 26, 2008) (unpublished) (noting Minnesota's disfavor of non-competition covenants while affirming non-competition covenant); Gleeson v. Preferred Sourcing, LLC, 883 N.E.2d 164, 172 (Ind. Ct. App. 2008) (partially enforcing covenant after noting that such contracts 'are in restraint of trade and are not favored by the law').

[11] Some of the recent non-competition covenant cases citing trade secrets as a basis for such contracts include Certainteed Corp v. Williams, 481 F.3d 528,

Non-competition covenants are likely the oldest and broadest form of trade secret regulation.[12] The non-competition covenant prevents the use of even non-secret information for the duration of the covenant. It encompasses a wide range of information, applies to probably hundreds of thousands of employees around the country (if not more), and does not require initiating a lawsuit or establishing wrongdoing to bar competition.

The non-competition covenant operates by excluding affected individuals from entire fields; that is, it regulates intellectual property not at the level of individual items that may or may not be protectable, but by fields or markets of application.

This is a very different model of regulation than the information-specific regime under official trade secret law. The different focus – on fields of work or product markets rather than precise items of data – might lead one to believe that the non-competition covenant is not primarily concerned with regulating confidential information. But a closer analysis indicates that, by and large, courts justify the enforceability of non-competition covenants on trade secret protection.[13] Litigants seeking to enforce such

---

529–30 (7th Cir. 2007); and SD Protection, Inc. v. Del Rio, 498 F.Supp.2d 576, 585 (E.D.N.Y. 2007). A list of non-competition contract cases citing trade secret protection as the main goal, or at least one of the main goals to be served, would likely encompass hundreds of decisions.

[12] There does not appear to be a comprehensive history of non-competition and related non-solicitation covenants. The direct root of the modern non-competition covenant are post-employment restrictions imposed in England as the traditional guild and apprentice system gradually dissolved. The general concepts, however, likely developed earlier. See generally Harlan M. Blake, *Employee Agreements Not to Compete*, 73 Harv. L. Rev. 625, 632–40 (1960) (describing how English courts moved toward greater acceptance of non-competition covenants from the sixteenth to nineteenth centuries); *cf.* Robert P. Merges, *From Medieval Guilds to Open Source Software: Informal Norms, Appropriability Institutions, and Innovation*, Conference on the Legal History of Intellectual Property, November 13, 2004, at *6 (available at <papers.ssrn.com/sol3/papers.cfm?abstract_id=661543>) (noting that the guild system permitted restrictions on solicitation of workers from other masters as early as the fourteenth century).

[13] It should be noted that, as with the confidentiality contracts and alternative torts discussed later in this chapter, some courts have stated that non-competition covenants can regulate information said to be 'confidential', but not a trade secret. See 225 A.2d 288, 291 (Maryland 1967) (noting that non-competition covenants can protect information said to be confidential but not a trade secret). Either way, the point remains the same: the non-competition agreement is first and foremost a means to regulate employee use of information learned on the job.

covenants often place trade secret protection first and foremost in their reasons for filing suit.[14]

Implicit policy objective Because courts enforcing non-competition covenants often engage in a ritual of denouncing the agreement before affirming it by making reference to trade secret law, the policy objectives served by non-competes generally go unspoken. Above all, the non-competition covenant represents a pre-emptive strike against the risk that an employee might misuse trade secrets in the future, without evidence of wrongdoing, and by restraining a wide class of employees rather than just individual wrongdoers. The underlying concept seems to be that the benefits of preventing some trade secret misuse outweighs all the social gains that might be realized from allowing mobile employees to start new, competitive ventures, join existing competitors, and generally apply their skills and experience within the fields where they are most likely to be effective.

This is a very different mindset than that presented by the Uniform Trade Secret Act or the Restatement formulations, to say the least. There, free competition and use of public information is the default rule, and the implicit policy objective is to balance the needs of trade secret owners, competitors and the interests of employees.

When reviewing the enforceability of a non-competition covenant, courts rarely if ever examine the inconsistent policy choices between protecting trade secrets at the level of individual items of information and individual employees, and precluding competition as a broad prophylactic against trade secret misuse.[15] To the contrary, some courts conflate the two forms of regulation and use the existence of a non-competition covenant together with official trade secret law to justify a case for an inevitable disclosure injunction; that is, to transform official trade secret law into a means to shore up the non-competition contract.[16]

---

[14] For a recent and high-profile example, see John Markoff, *IBM Sues to Block Executive's Move to Apple*, New York Times, October 31, 2008 ('The company said that Mr. Papermaster had been one of its top 300 managers and that he had access to a wide range of the company's intellectual property and trade secrets').

[15] California, which prohibits almost all non-competition covenants, is the exception. California courts have analyzed employee mobility concerns in rejecting trade secret-based 'inevitable disclosure' injunctions as a court-created form of non-competition order. See, e.g., Whyte v. Schlage Lock Co., 101 Cal. App. 4th 1443 (2002) (discussing California's public policy in favor of employee movement and barring non-competition covenants while regulating trade secret misuse).

[16] See *MacDermid, Inc. v. Selle*, 535 F.Supp.2d 308, 316–18 (D. Conn. 2008) (injunction barring new employment based on both non-competition covenant and inevitable disclosure-type reasoning); Ciena Corp. v. Jarrad, 200 F.3d 312,

The concept that non-competition covenants and official trade secret law seek to regulate the same information in a conflicting manner has been obscured in the law reviews, in favor of an alternative view that non-competition covenants are primarily related to employee training. A long-running tradition in the economic literature speculates that non-competition covenants are useful to protect employer investments in employee training. According to this theory, employees enter into non-competition covenants in order to obtain needed training, and agree to post-employment restrictions that benefit the employer as a fair trade for such training.[17] A related theory treats the non-competition covenant as a form of trade secret regulation, but theorizes that such covenants allow employers to efficiently disclose secret information to employees when they otherwise would not have incentive to do so.[18]

Empirical analysis would likely show that the policy reasons courts rest on to enforce non-competition covenants rarely involve employee training. Trade secret regulation is far and away the most common justification courts offer when considering a non-competition covenant. Courts rarely ask whether the affected employee received training or try to calibrate the

---

323–4 (4th Cir. 2000) (same); Lumex, Inc. v. Highsmith, 919 F.Supp. 624, 630–5 (E.D.N.Y. 1996) (same).

[17] See, e.g., Gillian Lester, *Restrictive Covenants, Employee Training, and the Limits of Transaction-Cost Analysis*, 76 IND. L.J. 49, 68–9, 71–6 (2001) (criticizing some economists' willingness to uphold all non-competition covenants, but also promoting a view that such covenants protect employer investments in training without analyzing whether such training takes place); Stewart E. Sterk, *Restraints on Alienation of Human Capital*, 79 VA. L. REV. 383, 391–2, 406–7 (1993) (assuming that protection of employer investment in specialized training is a valid basis for non-competition covenants, without analyzing innovation theory); Paul H. Rubin and Peter Shedd, *Human Capital and Covenants Not to Compete*, 10 J. LEGAL STUD. 93, 99, 102 (1981) (examining purported economic rationale for non-competition covenants based on 'the economic logic underlying the law'; assuming that 'contracts with such covenants occur almost entirely in industries and situations in which training is important'; asserting that 'such contracts are needed to lead to efficient levels of investment in training when the person receiving training is unable to pay for the human capital by accepting reduced wages').

[18] See Edward M. Schulman, *An Economic Analysis of Employee Noncompetition Agreements*, 69 DENV. U. L. REV. 97, 102, 108, 110, 115 (1992) (assuming that benefits to employer outweigh limiting employee mobility without considering effects on innovation and the wider economy, assuming that the absence of non-competition covenants would deter employers from hiring employees because they will fear trade secret theft; failing to consider whether trade secret law itself reasonably allays such assumed concerns; also assuming without evidence that employers provide 'expensive training' when there are such covenants in place).

post-employment restriction to match the training as the common analysis would have it.[19] More fundamentally, at least in this author's experience, technology companies provide little formal training, especially for the most highly-skilled engineers, and instead seek to hire employees with advanced degrees or prior relevant job experience.

It appears that the economic literature is mistaken, and that the non-competition covenant is above all a form of trade secret regulation and not generally a means for the employee to compensate the employer for job training. Abstract Law and Economics reasoning about non-competition agreements has been an impediment to better theoretical analysis of trade secret law, because it obscures a direct comparison between the goals and methods of overlapping regimes of trade secret regulation. The artificial focus on job training strains to justify the covenant without comparing it to other forms of trade secret law or asking whether the covenants properly balance the interests at stake in trade secret disputes.

Whose interests are served? The interests served by non-competition covenants are one-sided. Non-competition covenants serve the interests of established, slow-growth businesses – those less likely to be hiring large numbers of new employees. This includes companies with unpleasant or unproductive working environments where inventive employees are unhappy. It also includes businesses that provide little or no job training, because their covenants will generally be enforced without any examination of additional value.[20] The enforcement of such covenants also serves the interests of attorneys by allowing lawsuits against departing employees even in the absence of trade secret misappropriation.

---

[19] Only the rare case takes employee training into account when determining the validity and scope of a non-competition covenant. See, e.g., 7's Ent., Inc. v. Del Rosario, 143 P.3d 23, 32 (Haw, 2006) (employer's provision of training as well as 'confidential' information to low-level travel industry employee justified three-year non-competition covenant for the Honolulu area). It should be noted that Colorado has a unique statute governing non-competition covenants which, among other things, permits such covenants 'for recovery of the expense of educating and training an employee who has served an employer for a period of less than two years'. See Colo. Rev. Stat. § 8-2-113.

[20] Courts often reject non-competition covenants signed after the job begins, and thus that have no tie to the employee's salary or other consideration. See, e.g., Access Organics, Inc. v. Hernandez, 175 P.3d 899, 903–4 (Montana, 2008) (reversing preliminary injunction in favor of former employer where non-competition agreement was signed four months after employment began and where employer offered no new consideration).

C. Divisions in the Law of Confidentiality Contracts

The third form of trade secret regulation is found in the non-disclosure agreements companies use with their employees, contractors and business partners. Whether one considers such contracts as a separate regime of trade secret law depends on how one defines the information that such contracts can place off-limits to departing employees.

To begin with, and to set the stage for the ways in which state courts differ when interpreting the scope of employee confidentiality contracts, it is important to understand how companies use different confidentiality contract terms in different contexts. When companies enter into confidentiality contracts with other businesses, they almost always include exceptions which expressly state that public domain information, pre-existing information and information released by the other party are not subject to the confidentiality clause.[21] As a result, such contracts mirror official trade secret law, and companies can operate with certainty that they will not be liable for using information disclosed by an opposing party but which can be found in the public domain.[22]

Employee confidentiality contracts, by contrast, are often more broadly worded and less likely to include express exceptions for non-secret information. The reason is that both sides to a business contract have attorneys review the document beforehand, to be sure that each side is protected against overbroad interpretations. This is not the case for employees eager to begin work for the new employer, who generally lack negotiating power or legal advice.

The conflict in the law of confidentiality contracts is this: in the absence of an express public domain exception, does a non-disclosure contract bar a former employee from using information that is not a trade secret? Or, to the contrary, is the contract to be interpreted in conformity with official trade secret law, even if there is no express public domain limitation? If the former is the case, the law of employee confidentiality contracts forms a third, separate form of regulation, distinct from the rules governing the Restatement and Uniform Act formulations.

---

[21] I am unaware of any empirical study on the prevalence of such terms in business-to-business and business-to-employee contracts, but many years of experience examining such contracts tells me that, at least in the technology sector, express public domain exceptions are ubiquitous in the former, and much less common in the latter.

[22] Non-employee trade secret cases between business partners exist, but are relatively rare. See generally South East Auto Dealers Rental Assoc., Inc. v. Ez Rent to Own, Inc., 980 So.2d 89, 100–1 (La. Ct. App. 2008) (trade secret claim against licensee for extra-contractual use of licensed secrets).

Some courts have indicated that employee confidentiality contracts should be interpreted in a manner like official trade secret law, where information is protectable only if it is a trade secret.[23] Others have embraced an expansive view of the information encompassed by employee confidentiality contracts, and have held that such contracts can cover an additional, poorly-defined body of 'confidential' information that is not a trade secret.[24]

Some courts seem to condition such rulings on whether the departing employees consulted public domain sources or instead relied on non-secret information learned on the job without first consulting outside materials. In a 1973 Texas case, for example, the court rejected a defense argument that the information at issue was in the public domain by asserting that 'It does not matter that [defendants] could have gained their knowledge from a study of books and magazines. The fact is that they did not do so'.[25] In another case, a court reconciled a seemingly inconsistent jury verdict (denying liability on an UTSA claim while finding liability of breach of an employee confidentiality contract) by drawing a questionable distinction between the definition of secrecy under official trade secret law and under contract law.[26] The court noted that an UTSA law requires a showing

---

[23] See, e.g., American Paper & Packaging Prod., Inc. v. Kirgan, 183 Cal. App. 3d 1318, 1325 (1986) ('An agreement between employer and employee defining a trade secret may not be decisive in determining whether the court will so regard it'); International Settlement Design, Inc. v. Hickey, 1995 WL 864463, *5 (Penn. Ct. Comm. Pleas June 29, 1995) (unpublished) ('Since we have already concluded that the information here does not rise to the level of a "trade secret" as defined in Pennsylvania law, it cannot be contractually protected').

[24] See, e.g., Engineering Excellence, Inc. v. Meola, 2002 WL 31248192, *5 (Ohio Ct. App. October 8, 2002) (unpublished) ('Appellant correctly asserts that confidential information does not have to rise to the level of a trade secret in order to be the subject of a valid non-disclosure agreement between employer and employee'); Berneir v. Merreill Air Engineers, 770 A.2d 97, 103 (Maine, 2001) ('The confidential knowledge or information protected by a restrictive covenant need not be limited to information that is protected as a trade secret by the UTSA'); Allen v. Creative Serv., Inc., 1992 WL 813643, *2 (R.I. Sup. Ct. July 6, 1992) (unpublished) ('While every business interest is not worthy of protection through a restrictive covenant, a business interest worthy of such protection need not rise to the level of a "trade secret"').

[25] See Elcor Chem. Co. v. Agri-Sul, Inc., 494 S.W.2d 204, 213 (Tex. Ct. App. 1973) (emphasizing the defendants' confidentiality contracts).

[26] See Hauck Mfg. Co. v. Astec Industries, Inc., 376 F.Supp.2d 808, 814 (E.D. Tenn. 2005) (seeking to harmonize jury verdict that rejected trade secret claim but found confidentiality contract breached; questionable logic held that trade secret requirements of independent value and reasonable measures distinguished trade secret information from that protected by confidentiality contract).

of reasonable measures to protect the secret and independent economic value, and suggested that no such evidence was required to support a claim for breach of non-disclosure contract.[27]

Implicit policy objective If confidentiality contracts are co-extensive with official trade secret law, then the policy objective is the same balanced regime discussed above for the Uniform Act and Restatement approaches to trade secret law. On the other hand, if confidentiality contracts are interpreted to allow protection of an additional class of information, the implicit policy goals are different. In that case, the view appears to be that it is unethical to take advantage of information and training learned on the job to compete against a former employer, even if the information is not a trade secret. Or, in a stronger version, the view might be that the interests of former employers in preventing employee competition are so worthy that employers should be allowed to subjectively label non-secret information as 'confidential' under a contract in order to prevent reuse by the departing employee.

Along the same lines, at least one commentator has argued that it may be more efficient to base trade secret regulation on confidentiality contracts and do away with a separate trade secrecy requirement, because parties would not have to spend time in court litigating the departing employee's secrecy defense.[28] This theory downplays real-world litigation where parties do not share a pre-lawsuit common understanding of what information should be off-limits, where employers often overreach and file suit over public domain information (whether intentionally or merely by failing to research the public domain ahead of time), and where employers sometimes file suit for anticompetitive purposes.[29] But this type

---

27 The jury did not award damages for the breach, but the real question is the potential for confusion in Tennessee trade secret law introduced by the court's strained reasoning. See 376 F.Supp.2d at 815.

28 See Bone, *supra* note 1, at 302.

29 Another, more far-reaching proposal to limit the employer's need to establish secrecy also asserts that companies do not litigate over non-secret information. See Jonathan R. Chally, Note, *The Law of Trade Secrets: Toward a More Efficient Approach*, 57 VAND. L. REV. 1269, 1291 (2004) ('Moreover, rational commercial entities will not incur litigation costs attempting to protect generally known information because competitive forces preclude those entities from recouping these litigation costs. Therefore, courts would rarely be faced with an attempt to assert exclusive ownership over information that is generally known'). Recognizing that both employers and employees sometimes engage in aggressive and self-centered conduct seems a necessary precondition for effective discussion of employer and employee interests.

of viewpoint is consistent with the implicit policy objectives served when confidentiality contracts are not co-extensive with official trade secret law.

Whose interests are served? To the extent that employee non-disclosure agreements do not overlap with official trade secret law, the contracts clearly favor employers (who include public domain exceptions in their contracts with other companies, but do not always do so in their employment agreements) over their departing employees. Much like a non-competition covenant, an employee may face a form contract and have little bargaining power. Worse, the average employee may not understand the subtleties of a confidentiality contract that does not contain a public domain exception, and indeed may not learn until litigation that the former employer interprets the agreement to protect non-secret information learned on the job.

It is important to note that the Uniform Act did not displace the law of confidentiality contracts.[30] The organization that drafted the model statute did not take a stand one way or the other on interpretation of confidentiality contracts.[31] At the same time, it is unclear whether the statute's drafters intended to give a green light for an additional, alternative system, or believed that such contracts would be interpreted in line with official trade secret law. The lack of discussion in the UTSA commentary may reflect a failure to recognize the problem, a wait-and-see approach, or a general reluctance to limit freedom of contract. As we shall see, the uncertainty in contract interpretation dovetails with the uncertain boundaries of the alternative confidentiality torts available in many jurisdictions, which also can be used to protect information said to be 'confidential' but not secret.

D. Unofficial Trade Secret Law: The Confidentiality Torts

The fourth and most problematic regime of trade secret law is not an organized system of rules, but instead a set of exceptions and minority rulings that recur with sufficient frequency to undermine official trade secret law. This regime consists of cases holding that plaintiffs may pursue a failed trade

---

[30] See, e.g., Cal. Civ. Code § 3426.7(b(1)) ('This title does not affect (1) contractual remedies, whether or not based upon misappropriation of a trade secret').

[31] See National Conference of Commissioners of Uniform State Laws, Uniform Trade Secret Act, Commissioners' Comment to Section 7 (1979) (UTSA 'does not apply to duties voluntarily assumed through an express or an implied-in-fact contract. The enforceability of covenants not to disclose trade secrets and covenants not to compete that are intended to protect trade secrets, for example, are governed by other law').

secret claim, even when the information is not secret, under tort labels such as conversion, unfair competition, breach of duty, and the like. A common formulation is that such torts protect 'confidential information not rising to the level of a trade secret'. In other cases, employers use phrases such as 'proprietary' or 'know-how' to argue for an alternative, fallback category of protectable information distinct from official trade secret law.[32]

Before the Uniform Trade Secrets Act was promulgated in the late 1970s and gradually enacted by more than 40 states, state courts entertained a host of tort claims over the use of information by former employees under a variety of labels.[33] Standards were unclear, and courts split on how secrecy – or protectability – should be defined. A minority of cases found former employees liable for reusing information for a new employer even though the information was in the public domain.[34] The reasoning seemed to be premised on a concept that reuse of non-secret information learned on the job to compete against the former employer was morally wrong, even if the information was publicly available elsewhere.

In some cases, the courts highlighted that the former employees had not gone to the public domain sources to reobtain the information. In perhaps the most well-known example, the Second Circuit rejected an argument that the alleged trade secrets were available in an expired patent, and held the former employees liable for trade secret misappropriation:

---

[32] See Genzyme Corp v. Bishop, 460 F.Supp.2d 939, 951 (W.D. Wisc. 2006) (plaintiff pleaded alternative claims described as 'confidential, non-secret information').

[33] As an English treatise noted in the early 1970s, trade secret law 'is rather confused', and had been pursued under theories of 'property, contract, bailment, trust, fiduciary relationship, good faith, [and] unjust enrichment'. See G.W. Paton and David P. Derham, JURISPRUDENCE § 118(a) (Oxford University Press. 1972) (citation omitted). California saw a similarly wide variety of labels attached to trade secret claims between 1916 and the enactment of the UTSA in 1985. See generally Charles T. Graves, *Nonpublic Information and California Tort Law: A Proposal for Harmonizing California's Employee Mobility and Intellectual Property Regimes under the Uniform Trade Secrets Act*, 2006 UCLA J. L. & TECH. 1 (2006).

[34] See Imax Corp. v. Cinema Techs., Inc., 152 F.3d 1161 (9th Cir. 1998) (allowing a tort claim for unfair competition over non-secret information; ruling based on a Ninth Circuit misreading of California law); Kamin v. Kuhnau, 374 P.2d 912, 916–18 (Oregon 1962) (finding former employees liable for unfair competition even if plaintiff sold products disclosing the information at issue and even if information could have been located elsewhere); Franke v. Wiltscheck, 209 F.2d 493, 495–6 (2d Cir. 1953) (former employees liable even though claimed secrets revealed in marketed product and expired patent). For a detailed summary of such cases under both tort and contract causes of action, *see* Charles T. Graves, *Trade Secrets as Property: Theory and Consequences*, 15 GEORGIA J. INTELL. PROP. L. 39, 51 (2007).

> Defendants argue that the heart of plaintiffs' process was revealed by an expired patent, and that the improvements thereon were unpatentable applications of mechanical skill. This totally misconceives the nature of plaintiffs' rights . . . The essence of their action is not infringement, but breach of faith. It matters not that defendants could have gained their knowledge from a study of the expired patent and plaintiffs' publicly marketed product. The fact is that they did not. Instead they gained it from plaintiffs via their confidential relationship, and in so doing incurred a duty not to use it to plaintiffs' detriment. This duty they have breached.[35]

Although such cases are mostly decades old, the problem of alternative confidentiality torts has arisen with surprising vitality in recent years. The Uniform Trade Secrets Act, discussed above, contains a displacement clause that operates to preclude non-statutory trade secret tort claims.[36] Disputes over UTSA pre-emption have became a frequent issue in trade secret cases during the past decade. Most such disputes occur before busy trial courts on a motion to dismiss or a motion for summary judgment, and the parties rarely engage in complex treatment of the issue.

The UTSA's displacement clause would seemingly extinguish alternative tort claims premised on non-secret information.[37] The UTSA commentary addressed problems of alternative torts based on the historical labels for trade secret claims by noting that the statute substituted a single remedy for trade secret misappropriation in place of the common law's multiplicity of claims.[38] In most jurisdictions, this is indeed the case.[39]

---

[35] See *Franke*, 209 F.2d at 495 (stating that its holding was valid under New York, New Jersey or Massachusetts law).

[36] California's version states: 'This title does not affect (1) contractual remedies, whether or not based upon misappropriation of a trade secret, (2) other civil remedies that are not based upon misappropriation of a trade secret, or (3) criminal remedies, whether or not based upon misappropriation of a trade secret'. See Cal. Civ. Code § 3426.7(b).

[37] See National Conference of Commissioners on Uniform State Laws, Uniform Trade Secrets Act § 7 (1979) ('Effect on Other Law. (a) This Act displaces conflicting tort, restitutionary, and other law of this State pertaining to civil liability for misappropriation of a trade secret [with exceptions for contract, criminal law, and "other civil liability or relief that is not based on misappropriation of a trade secret"]').

[38] See *id.*, Commissioner's Prefatory Note ('The contribution of the Uniform Act is substitution of unitary definitions of trade secret and trade secret misappropriation, and a single statute of limitations for the various property, quasi-contractual, and violation of fiduciary relationship theories of noncontractual liability utilized at common law').

[39] Five state Supreme Courts, for example, have issued rulings in favor of UTSA pre-emption over common law trade secret-type claims. See Mortgage Specialists, Inc. v. Davey, 904 A.2d 652, 665 (N.H. 2006) (criticizing Wisconsin

The UTSA's drafters did not foresee the artful pleading and creative arguments lawyers would use to convince many courts that the UTSA is just one of many state law intellectual property tort claims against a departing employee. The most common method to plead around the UTSA is to label the information at issue in the complaint with synonyms for trade secrecy (such as confidential, proprietary, or know-how) and to raise causes of action under labels such as unjust enrichment, conversion, breach of trust, and the like.

A significant minority of courts ruling on UTSA pre-emption have allowed such alternative tort claims to go forward, often on the argument that the statute does not displace tort claims that seek to protect information deemed 'confidential but not secret'. Whether a product of creative lawyering, a lack of understanding by the judiciary, or a failure of defense lawyers to adequately explain the issues at stake, these rulings implicitly create a second, fallback tier of protectable information in some UTSA jurisdictions.[40]

In some such cases, the courts construe the Uniform Act narrowly such that it applies only when the plaintiff establishes that the information at issue is, in fact, a trade secret. By such reasoning, the UTSA no longer applies if the defendant succeeds in showing that the information is not a trade secret. The defendant's reward for defeating the statutory claim is to face an amorphous secondary claim with no secrecy requirement. Instead of a statutory scheme that encompasses both winning and losing trade secret claims, as the UTSA seemingly does, with its definition of certain

ruling in *Burbank Grease*); RK Enterprise, LLC v. Pro-Comp Management, Inc., 158 S.W.3d 685, 689–90 (Ark. 2004); Savor, Inc. v. FMR Corp., 812 A.2d 894, 898 (Del. 2002); Frantz v. Johnson, 999 P.2d 351, 357–8 (Nevada 2000); Weins v. Sporleder, 605 N.W.2d 488, 492 (South Dakota 2000).

40 In non-UTSA, Restatement jurisdictions, courts sometimes face similar issues when a plaintiff alleges torts with titles other than 'trade secret misappropriation' and argues that these labels support a broader definition of protectable information. See, e.g., Lamorte Burns & Co., Inc., 770 A.2d 1158, 1166 (N.J. 2001) (holding that employer can bring tort claims against employee for information that does not 'rise to the level of a trade secret', and suggesting that such information 'may otherwise be publicly available'); Continental Dynamics Corp. v. Kanter, 408 N.Y.S.2d 801, 802 (N.Y. Ct. App. 1978) ('[W]here customer lists do not rise to the level of trade secrets, an employee's "physical taking" or "studied copying" may, nevertheless, form the basis for a cause of action for unfair competition'); *cf.* Triple Tee Golf, Inc. v. Nike, Inc., 485 F.3d 253, 267 (5th Cir. 2007) (applying Texas trade secret law and limiting plaintiff to trade secret claim, rather than permitting other tort claims premised on a lower standard of protectable information).

defenses and a special remedy for some prevailing defendants,[41] the minority position moves the losing claim out of the UTSA's realm and into an alternative category of protection.

In one case, for example, the Wisconsin Supreme Court chose to depart from the majority of rulings on UTSA pre-emption.[42] The court's logic was not entirely clear (it did not consider policy interests such as employee mobility or innovation policy on the record) but seemed premised on a formalistic conclusion that the UTSA's text should narrowly be construed to exclude information that the plaintiff does not expressly label with the phrase 'trade secret'.[43] So long as the plaintiff remembers to use synonyms such as 'confidential', the Wisconsin UTSA has no application. The Northern District of Illinois employed similar logic when ruling against UTSA pre-emption of common law claims said to be based on 'valuable and proprietary' information.[44] Although the defense argued on a motion to dismiss that the plaintiff's phrases were 'generally consistent' with the information protected by the Illinois UTSA, the court disagreed, holding that 'the ITSA's definition of "trade secret" does not use the language "valuable and proprietary"'.[45] Other courts taking the minority view at the pleading stage have ruled that they cannot dismiss alternative claims, because the plaintiff might have recourse to them if the information were to prove non-secret.[46] Some trial court rulings side with the minority with

---

41 California's UTSA, for example, contains provisions indicating that the statute operates to govern both winning and losing claims. Most important, the statute provides for an award of attorneys' fees and costs to a defendant where a claim is brought in 'bad faith'. See Cal. Civ. Code § 3426.4.

42 See Burbank Grease Serv., LLC v. Sokolowski, 717 N.W.2d 781, 789–94 (Wisc. 2006) (ruling, over strong dissent, against pre-emption of alternative tort claims despite pre-emption clause in Wisconsin UTSA).

43 See *id.* at 789. The ruling did not address any policy concerns, including the effects of permitting alternative confidentiality claims on employee mobility and innovation policy.

44 See Abanco Int'l, Inc. v. Guestlogix, Inc., 486 F.Supp.2d 779, 781–2 (N.D. Ill. 2007).

45 See *id.* at 782. Further highlighting the court's formalistic, word based approach to pre-emption, the court dismissed the plaintiffs' conspiracy claim as pre-empted by the UTSA because the plaintiff used the triggering phrase 'trade secrets' when pleading that cause of action.

46 See Cenveo Corp. v. Slater, 2007 WL 527720, *1 (E.D. Pa. February 12, 2007) (holding that Pennsylvania UTSA does not displace alternative claims unless a trade secret is established); Stone Castle Financial, Inc. v. Friedman, Billings, Ramsey & Co., 191 F.Supp.2d 652, 659 (E.D. Va. 2002) (ruling that UTSA pre-emption applies only if 'it can be clearly discerned that the information in question constitutes a trade secret').

no examination of the policy issues involved and without explaining the court's reasoning.[47]

Even in courts taking the majority position in favor of pre-emption, few courts seem to have understood the primary issue at stake; that is, whether state courts in UTSA jurisdictions can permit a fallback category of protectable but non-secret information.[48] The possibility that a trial court will do this promotes litigation and expansive claims. Attorneys and their clients are sometimes willing to aggressively claim as much as possible, knowing that in the absence of clear rules any given judge may be persuaded and will not engage in critical analysis.

In what is probably an unintended outcome, these rulings leave the plaintiff with a potentially stronger claim than would have existed had the information been found secret. The plaintiff seemingly does not have to establish secrecy, can seek punitive damages under common law instead of facing the UTSA's treble damages cap, and need not fear a ruling that the claim was brought in 'bad faith'. It is unclear what defenses can be raised against 'confidential' information claims. The minority position on UTSA pre-emption, then, not only creates a second regime of protectable information, but maximizes protection for weaker information that is not a trade secret. To date, none of the courts taking the minority position seem to have recognized the consequences of this questionable logic. It is not clear whether trial court judges simply believe attorneys who assert that alternative categories of protectable information exist, or if they are actively nullifying legislative intent to further unstated policy or moral judgments regarding mobile employees.

---

47 See, e.g., ClearOne Comm., Inc. v. Chiang, 2008 WL 4153767, *2 (D. Utah September 3, 2008) (holding, without analysis, that 'The court is persuaded by the minority view as explained in such cases as *Burbank Grease* . . . Accordingly, ClearOne's state law claims based on the unauthorized use of the Honeybee Code are preserved if the Honeybee Code is not found to be a trade secret').

48 Two of the very few courts to engage in a lengthy analysis and recognize that the alternative confidentiality torts would create a back-up layer of protection for non-secret information were Diamond Power Int'l, Inc. v. Davidson, 540 F.Supp.2d 1322, 1345–6 (N.D. Ga. 2007) (considering conflicting case law, weighing public policies, and finding conversion claim pre-empted because it was based on 'the taking of supposedly proprietary information'; 'it would make little sense to go through the rigmarole of proving information was truly a trade secret if a plaintiff could alternatively plead claims with less burdensome requirements of proof'); Hauck Mfg. Co. v. Astec Indus., Inc., 375 F.Supp.2d 649, 661 (E.D. Tenn. 2004) ('If the information is a trade secret, the plaintiff's claim is pre-empted; if not, the plaintiff has no legal interest upon which to base his claim. Either way, the claim is not cognizable').

Moreover, by creating what amounts to state law tort protection for unpatented, non-secret information, the minority logic may give rise to Supremacy Clause concerns when the information at issue involves technology concepts. The Supreme Court and a host of rulings by state and federal courts have invalidated state tort claims seeking ownership and control of unpatented, non-secret technology ideas.[49] It remains to be seen whether the alternative confidentiality torts will pass constitutional muster.

Of the four regimes we have reviewed, the alternative confidentiality torts pose the greatest conflict with official trade secret law. Unlike a non-competition covenant or non-disclosure contract, the alternative torts seek to create liability beyond the parties' contractual obligations or, potentially, the employee's reasonable expectations. They are a product of aggressive and creative lawyering rather than a pre-employment bargain struck between the employer and the employee. They undermine the employee's expected bargain by transforming unpredictable categories of non-secret information into information that is off-limits at the new job.

Implicit policy objectives The rationale of the courts legitimizing alternative confidentiality torts seems to be that the Uniform Trade Secrets Act is an obstacle to the needs of employers and should be construed as narrowly as possible, to avoid protecting employees who have used non-secret information learned on the job. The view may be a covert morality judgment that reuse of information learned on the job is a social wrong (a betrayal, perhaps) that employers should be permitted to remedy through non-contractual, alternative torts such as 'common law unfair competition'. This view may also hold that the social gains from stopping competition by former employees using non-secret information, gains which need not be identified or explicitly weighed in a court ruling, outweigh the losses from reduced competition, formation of fewer start-up enterprises, and interference with the livelihood of employees who decide to change

---

49 Some of the cases in this under-analysed area of law include Bonito Boats, Inc. v. Thunder Craft Boats, Inc., 489 U.S. 141, 157–60 (1989) (voiding state statute that prohibited the use of unpatented, public technology information under the Supremacy Clause); Confold Pacific, Inc. v. Polaris Indus., Inc., 433 F.3d 952, 959–60 (7th Cir. 2006) (unjust enrichment claim based on non-secret product design information pre-empted); Ultra-Precision Mfg., Ltd. v. Ford Mtr. Co., 411 F.3d 1369, 1380 (Fed. Cir. 2005) (same holding as to state law unjust enrichment claim where technology information was not alleged to be a trade secret); Joyce v. GM Corp., 551 N.E.2d 172, 175 (Ohio 1990) (conversion claim based on non-secret technology ideas pre-empted).

jobs. Under this logic as well, the Supremacy Clause should be narrowly interpreted, and states should have the power to regulate employee use of non-secret, unpatented technology concepts through tort law.

As a separate point of statutory construction, the thinking appears to be that state legislatures intended that statutes can be avoided by using synonyms for words found in statutory text, such as 'confidential' instead of 'trade secret'. Likewise, the logic behind the alternative torts suggests that disputes over information learned on the job should not be governed by clear rules, and that concepts such as 'confidential information' should be elastic.

Whose interests are served? The primary beneficiaries of the alternative confidentiality torts are parties who would have losing trade secret or contract claims under official trade secret law and contract law, and who do not have non-competition covenants. Parties with weaker claims gain when there are alternatives available if the first-choice claim fails. Another, perhaps overlapping set of beneficiaries consists of former employers who use the lawsuit process to disable new, competitive ventures founded by former employees. If a court allows a lawsuit to proceed under an alternative theory, this more easily allows anticompetitive lawsuits to survive early motions to limit or dispose of the case, because the plaintiff has greater latitude to label information protectable without having to prove trade secrecy. Finally, intellectual property attorneys stand to benefit when an additional class of weaker claims can be pursued. Discovery, summary judgment, trial and settlement can be more difficult and time-consuming when vague alternative claims are at issue, and this increases attorneys' fees.

E. Results of the Confusion in Trade Secret Law

We have seen that trade secret law is a collection of as many as four different regimes for regulating confidential business information, each with different methods and policy goals. Depending on which regime is applied, different interests are served. Table 4.1 highlights in summary fashion the results generated by these conflicting regimes of confidentiality.[50]

---

[50] It is important to reiterate that these regimes are not the same in every state. California rejects most non-competition covenants, and North Dakota has a similar prohibition. See Edwards v. Arthur Andersen LLP, 44 Cal.4th 937, 948–50 (Cal. 2008) (reaffirming state's statutory ban on non-competition contracts); North Dakota Century Code § 9-08-06 (2008) (statute barring most non-competition covenants). Other jurisdictions, as noted above, have clear precedent rejecting the alternative confidentiality torts.

Table 4.1 Conflicting regimes of confidentiality

	Applies narrowly only to non-public information	Liability only upon misuse of non-public information	Allows for predictable planning for new ventures	Provides reasonably clear rules and remedies for reviewing courts
Official trade secret law	Yes	Yes	Yes	Yes
Non-competition covenants	No	No	Yes	Yes
Confidentiality contracts	Depends on interpre-tation	Depends on Interpre-tation	Depends on interpre-tation	Depends on Interpre-tation
Alternative confidentiality torts	No	No	No	No

If the goal of intellectual property law is to promote innovation, the cumulative effect of having different regimes in the same jurisdiction is almost certainly negative, for several reasons.

The first reason is a simple one: the law lacks consistency and clarity. Trade secret law may or may not be the only area of law in which an alternative regime with different rules about the basic object of the law – what information is protectable – can override a statute with clear rules and definitions. But this is surely unusual, and trade secret law is an area where a lack of clarity can have substantial public policy implications. In turn, it is difficult for commentators to offer theory-based proposals for trade secret law, because the law on the ground is not unitary. Scholarly arguments, for example, that courts should balance this or that interest when considering a request for injunctive relief or considering a case involving employee bloggers may come to nothing if, in the court system, litigants can simply shift their claims and arguments to a different confidentiality regime.

This lack of certainty creates real-world problems. Although discussion about trade secret law tends to focus on case law, a significant percentage of trade secret practice consists of counseling for newly-departed employees changing jobs or founding a start-up venture. Attorneys must guide such individuals by advising them as to what information they can use without meaningful lawsuit risk. Under official trade secret law, departing employees have the clear guideline of the public domain to answer that question. When the definition of secrecy itself is unclear, it is difficult to predict what information might be the subject of a lawsuit, and what information a judge might deem protectable even if non-secret.

Protecting information so broadly – making useful information learned on the job protectable even if not a trade secret – may also inhibit innovation by departing employees. If the result of the unofficial confidentiality torts is to make a planned technology too difficult, or to force a former employee into a different field that is not her specialty, the courts may be incrementally inhibiting innovation through an unspoken morality judgment in favor of former employers.

Uncertain rules and the potential that non-secret information will be found protectable also invites pre-litigation threats and anticompetitive litigation. New technology start-ups are fragile. They must seek funding from venture capitalists who conduct due diligence for threats received from former employers and who ask detailed questions to determine whether the planned development faces potential trade secret problems. Once funded, expensive trade secret litigation can divert financial resources to fend off the lawsuit rather than research and development. Start-ups often must pay a settlement to a former employer because the costs of litigation are too high to continue. In jurisdictions that permit the alternative confidentiality torts, employers can more freely make threats, and can more freely launch litigation for anticompetitive purposes without facing a secrecy requirement.

As discussed above, the confusion in trade secret law also gives rise to potential Supremacy Clause problems, as courts allow state law tort claims seeking ownership and control of unpatented, non-secret technology ideas.

Another potential problem is that concepts of less-than-secret protectable information, once legitimized, may migrate into other areas of law, multiplying uncertainty. In New Jersey, for example, the state Supreme Court held that a post-employment 'holdover' clause for employee inventions might extend to information that is 'not a trade secret or proprietary information'.[51] The ripple effects of the alternative confidentiality torts into related areas of intellectual property law are unpredictable.

A coherent, predicable regime of trade secret law would appear better situated to balance interests between employers and employees, promote

---

51 See Ingersoll-Rand Co. v. Ciavatta, 542 A.2d 879, 894 (N.J. 1988). Although the court held that such a concept should be narrowly construed in the post-employment 'holdover' context, the court nonetheless expanded the reach of unofficial trade secret law into inventions that a former employee creates after leaving that are not based on former employer trade secrets.

innovation by allowing use of non-secret information and deterring anti-competitive threats and lawsuits, and harmonize trade secret law with the policies the federal courts protect under patent law. In the next section, we will consider why this fragmented system arose, and why little has been done thus far to seriously discuss reform.

F. Sources of the Problem

How did we find ourselves in a situation where trade secret law is subject to multiple, inconsistent regimes? Do we have rules because they reflect considered policy goals, or do we have rules because attorneys made winning arguments on a case-by-case basis with nobody asking how it all fits together? The following list of reasons is necessarily speculative, but may be the most likely possibilities.

History In large part, the inconsistent regimes are a historical accident. Different doctrines arose at different times, for different reasons, and were never harmonized by the diffuse common law courts. Old English concepts can linger in contemporary state common law without anyone but specialists noticing. Unrelated, flexible common law concepts like conversion and unjust enrichment can be harnessed for new purposes. Ideas about the balance between employers and employees can change over time, but ideas generated during different thought-paradigms remain embedded in the common law.[52]

Confusion over the goal of trade secret law Another factor may be confusion among courts, practitioners, and litigants over the goals trade secret law should serve. Some may view trade secret law as the regulation of

---

[52] The question whether historical forms of employee mobility restrictions were premised on economic goals, social control or other factors is a fruitful area for research for the scholar with time and resources. Some historical regulation of employee mobility may have been strictly for economic ends. See, e.g., Fernand Braudel, Civilization and Capitalism: The Wheels of Commerce 308–9 (University of California Press, 1982) (describing eighteenth century competition for skilled weavers between Flanders and England and the 'draconian measures' sometimes employed to limit mobility and thus prevent industrial decline). Other regulations may have had an ethical or other non-economic premise. See, e.g., 1 William Blackstone, Commentaries on the Laws of England 417 (University of Chicago Press, 1979 (1769)) (in a seeming judgment of commercial morality, explaining the basis of restrictions on soliciting another's employees by describing the employee's labor as the 'property' of the employer). I am unaware of any historical study in this area.

commercial morality, a viewpoint under which employee use of information learned on the job is potentially unethical. Others view trade secret law as the regulation of employer abuses, in the same manner as wrongful termination law. Still others, probably the majority, view trade secret law as an amoral system that should be calibrated to promote innovation and overall economic growth. Courts may confuse set-in-stone ideas about ethics with the objective, abstract balancing of interests demanded by the innovation policy approach.

Absence of a centralized court system Unlike the federal intellectual property regimes, there is no final arbiter of law in trade secret cases. There are 51 jurisdictions, and federal courts sometimes interpret state law differently than do courts in the state at issue.[53] State Supreme Courts may sometimes look to one another or delve into the history of conflicting strands of law on important questions,[54] but few trade secret cases make it that far.

Crowded state court dockets Most trade secret litigation takes place in state courts. State trial courts, especially in pre-trial motion practice, are crowded, with little time for each particular motion. State court judges are often ill-equipped and sometimes even unwilling to address trade secret cases involving technology. Expecting a lower court judge to understand the policy issues at play in trade secret litigation is unrealistic, and the penalty for making arguments that are too complex may be a loss. In trial courts as in politics, simplistic and emotional rhetoric may too often carry the day. A general practice of permissiveness, especially at the early stages of a lawsuit, may allow anticompetitive lawsuits to continue long enough to destabilize a newly-founded rival.

---

[53] To cite one example, the Ninth Circuit has applied California non-competition and trade secret law in a manner less favorable to employees than rulings in California state courts. See *Arthur Anderson*, 44 Cal.4th at 949–50 (noting and rejecting the Ninth Circuit's line of cases interpreting California's prohibition on non-competition covenants to allow 'narrow restraints' on competition); Self Directed Placement Corp. v. Control Data Corp., 908 F.2d 462, 467 (9th Cir. 1990) (allowing claim for 'common law misappropriation' over seemingly generic training materials that were not trade secrets).

[54] See, e.g., Mortgage Specialists, Inc. v. Davey, 904 A.2d 652, 667 (N.H. 2006) (on UTSA pre-emption issue, reviewing majority and minority positions in other states and siding with majority); Cadence Design Sys., Inc. v. Avant! Corp., 29 Cal.4th 215, 225 (2002) (in deciding whether the California UTSA treats misappropriation as a continuing tort for purposes of the statute of limitations, surveying law in other jurisdictions).

Absence of scholarly oversight An important contributing factor in the confusing state of contemporary trade secret law is relative inattention paid by law professors. The reasons are many. First, law school culture is heavily weighted towards the centers of federal power – federal courts, the U.S. Supreme Court and Congress. State law receives less academic attention, and perhaps carries less prestige. In intellectual property law, patent and copyright law are the subject of far more law review articles than trade secret law. Another factor is the tendency of some in academia to treat intellectual property issues in too abstract a manner, as a matter for game theory equations or efficiency analyses, rather than study of case law and practical problems.

Problems with the intellectual property bar A final, and perhaps insoluble problem associated with the confusion in trade secret law is the nature of the intellectual property bar. First, intellectual property attorneys tend to more readily represent employers in trade secret disputes, because the defendants are often individuals or newly-formed companies with a lesser ability to pay. Long-established companies present repeat business opportunities for law firms, while smaller start-ups and individuals may not. Anecdotal evidence of this disproportionate focus can be found in the large number of practitioner-written articles and commentaries on trade secret law which take a 'how to protect your trade secrets' angle as their primary focus.

Second, many attorneys who litigate trade secret cases, or who provide trade secret-related diligence and counseling for investment rounds and for new companies, are primarily patent attorneys. There are few specialists in trade secret practice, especially outside major technology areas like Silicon Valley. Non-specialists may be more likely to litigate cases based on quick case law summaries, and may not even be aware of the conflicting regimes and differing definitions of secrecy. Lack of specialization fosters confusion.

Third, and unlike criminal law or securities law (to take two examples), intellectual property practitioners generally do not divide themselves into two bars for plaintiffs and defendants. The same attorneys in the same firm might prosecute and defend patent and trade secret cases at the same time, and take conflicting positions in different cases. The absence of a divided bar reduces opportunities for sharp debate about policy, and may also provide an incentive for practitioners to muddle the trade secret rules. Lack of clarity allows a practitioner to safely take conflicting positions without having to commit to one position or another.

Finally, reform is not in the interest of most law firms. Certainty and predictability reduce litigation and shorten lawsuits. In the absence of alternative regimes, cases may settle sooner, or be resolved more often through summary judgment if the information at issue is in the public domain. A say-anything-to-win culture all too often trumps a commitment to justice and the public good.[55]

IV. POTENTIAL SOLUTIONS FOR THE CONFLICTING REGIMES IN TRADE SECRET LAW

It is difficult to come up with short-term solutions to deeply-ingrained problems – legal confusion which runs deep into history, and which spans all the 50 states in their separate common law. It is probably fair to say that most judges handling trade secret cases, even those in U.S. district courts, are unaware that secrecy is defined differently and regulated differently under different regimes in the same jurisdiction, and unaware of the problems caused by this inconsistency. The question, then, is how to create a greater sense among judges and practitioners that trade secret law needs careful attention, with an eye towards longer-term reform.

Greater scholarly attention One possibility is greater scholarly attention, and not just because better-trained law students will be more aware of these issues when they enter practice. Judges may not consistently read law review articles (and certainly practicing attorneys do not) but scholarly activity can nonetheless indicate to judges that people are paying attention to a given area of law. It would not be surprising to learn that judges in patent-heavy dockets (the Eastern District of Texas or the Northern District of California, for example) are aware that their decisions will be scrutinized by academics in articles and blogs, discussed at legal symposia and practitioner seminars, and the like. They issue rulings, in other words, knowing that there is a wider audience than the parties to the case.

There is probably no sense of a wider audience in trade secret cases. Judges may not have a sense that anyone is watching, or that there is any constituency that cares whether the law being applied is consistent or

---

[55] For a relevant and extensive description of the internal firm pressures and increases in hourly billing at large firms in recent years, see generally Mark Galanter and William Henderson, *The Elastic Tournament: A Second Transformation of the Big Law Firm*, 60 STAN. L. REV. 1867 (2007) (noting that intense pressure to maintain and please clients within large firms leads to diminished attention to issues such as gender and ethnic diversity – and, it could be added, general attention to the policy issues underlying specific cases).

makes policy sense. We might see fewer sloppy, unreasoned and under-analysed rulings if the problems in trade secret law were more widely discussed.

Perhaps greater scholarly attention has already begun. 2007 and 2008 saw an increase in the number of substantive law review articles on trade secret law.[56] Given the heavy attention the law reviews have given to patent and copyright law over the past 10 to 15 years, this is a welcome sign that perhaps the tangled questions of trade secret law are beginning to receive badly-needed attention.

If scholars were to direct their energies in any one direction, beyond paying more attention to trade secret law in general, the best area for reform would be promoting a uniform definition of secrecy. There appears no better area for discussion and debate than the boundaries of what is protectable.

Networks among like-minded attorneys Just as scholars might publish and teach more often on trade secret law, practitioners might form networks to discuss trade secret issues. National intellectual property organizations like the American Intellectual Property Law Association (AIPLA) tend to focus on federal law, and practitioners interested in trade secret law appear to be scattered. One example of practitioner attention to trade secret law is the State Bar of California, which has a special section

---

[56] The list of important articles and notes on trade secret law published in 2007–8 (those that go beyond mere practice guide or case summary) includes Michael Ahrens, Note, *Wisconsin Confidential: The Mystery of the Wisconsin Supreme Court's Decision in Burbank Grease Services v. Sokolowski and its Effect upon the Uniform Trade Secrets Act, Litigation, and Employee Mobility*, 2007 Wisc. L. Rev. 1271 (2007); Sarah Gettings, Note, *Burbank Grease Services, LLC v. Sokolowski: Frustrating Uniformity in Trade Secret Law*, 22 Berkeley Tech. L.J. 423 (2007); Charles T. Graves, *The Law of Negative Knowledge: A Critique*, 15 Tex. Intel. Prop. L.J. 387 (2007); Charles T. Graves, *Trade Secrets as Property: Theory and Consequences*, 15 Georgia J. Intel. Prop. L. 39 (2007); Mark R. Lemley, *The Surprising Virtues of Treating Trade Secrets as IP Rights*, 61 Stan. L. Rev. 311 (2008); David Levine, *Secrecy and Unaccountability: Trade Secrets in Our Public Infrastructure*, 59 Florida L. Rev. 135 (2007); Julie Piper, *Note, I Have a Secret?: Applying the Uniform Trade Secrets Act to Confidential Information that Does Not Rise to the Level of Trade Secret Status*, 12 Marq. Intel. Prop. L. Rev. 359 (2008); Michael Risch, *Why Do We Have Trade Secrets?*, 11 Marq. Intel. Prop. L. Rev. 1 (2007); Pamela Samuelson, *Principles for Resolving Conflicts Between Trade Secrets and the First Amendment*, 58 Hastings L.J. 777 (2007); Sharon K. Sandeen, *Kewanee Revisited: Returning to First Principles of Intellectual Property Law to Determine the Issue of Federal Preemption*, 12 Marq. Intel. Prop. L. Rev. 299 (2008).

devoted to trade secret law, and which recently promulgated template jury instructions.[57]

Legislation Future reform might also come through piecemeal legislative efforts. Interested state bar groups or others might sponsor legislature for better identification of trade secret claims, limits on non-competition covenants, and the like. Lobbying efforts on narrow issues may be more successful than wholesale challenges to long-existing doctrines. For example, a lobbying group representing media employees has enjoyed some success in convincing state legislatures, most notably in New York, to abolish non-competition covenants within their profession.[58]

Federalizing trade secret law One sometimes discussed (if unlikely) solution is to federalize trade secret law, so that there is one single statute and one unified body of case law to govern the field, with the potential for high court review.

A federal solution might, however, be worse than the currently-existing problems described above. To begin with, a federal solution might lead to a less favorable environment for innovation if it overrode the law of jurisdictions that favor employee mobility, California in particular.[59]

Similarly, lobbying efforts by self-described industry groups might distort a federal bill in directions opposed to promoting innovation. Something of this nature may have occurred during the 1996 enactment of the federal Economic Espionage Act. That statute, which regulates criminal trade secret misappropriation with a particular focus on foreign espionage, prohibits forms of reverse engineering that are lawful under

---

[57] The webpage for the California State Bar IP Section and the Trade Secret Standing Committee can be found at www.calbar.ca.gov.

[58] The New York Broadcast Employees Freedom to Work Act, barring non-competition covenants for 'any on-air or off-air employee of a broadcasting industry employer' was signed into law by the governor on August 6, 2008. See Governor Paterson Signs 'Broadcast Employees Freedom to Work Act' Among Package of Bills Signed into Law, www.state.ny.us/governor/press/2008pressarchive.html (last visited January 18, 2011); www.assembly.state.ny.us/leg/?bn=S02393&sh=t (text of statute, last visited January 18, 2011); Gary Ventura, *Just Clause? Trying to Change Channels*, Rochester City Newspaper, February 22, 2006, www.rochestercitynewspaper.com/archives/2006/02/Just-cause-Trying-to-change-channels (article describing lobbying efforts by American Federation of Television and Radio Artists; last visited January 18, 2011).

[59] A federal approach that permitted 'inevitable disclosure' injunctions, for example, would overturn California's prohibition of that form of trade secret litigation.

state trade secret law.[60] The statute also contains vague language that could be interpreted to prohibit otherwise lawful forms of competitive intelligence gathering.[61]

Before federal legislation could even be contemplated, then, there would have to be a period of commentary and the development of sophisticated theoretical and empirical analyses to counter the lobbying by clumsy but powerful 'pro-business' groups who may not realize the wider policy ramifications of their assertions. Industry groups might present Congress with flawed and inflammatory data suggesting widespread and out-of-control trade secret misappropriation.[62] If the only approach presented to Congress were one of trade secret owners needing additional protection from supposedly rampant trade secret theft, the result could do nothing to address the problems discussed in this chapter.[63]

In any event, federalization of trade secret law likely would not affect contract law, including confidentiality contracts and non-competition covenants.[64] As a result, state courts could still have as many as three different approaches to protecting confidential information.

---

[60] See James H.A. Pooley, Mark A. Lemley and Peter J. Toren, *Understanding the Economic Espionage Act of 1996*, 5 TEX. INTELL. PROP. L.J. 177, 194 (1997).

[61] See *id.* at 192–4.

[62] An example of seemingly exaggerated trade secret misappropriation is a 2002 study by PricewaterhouseCoopers, the United States Chamber of Commerce and the ASIS Foundation purporting to show that U.S. companies lost U.S. $50 billion from trade secret theft in 2001. The study suffers from obvious flaws. It apparently relied on self-reporting from companies without requiring identification of the alleged secret, without criteria for public domain testing of the alleged secrets, without criteria for valuation, and without criteria for defining theft. The study also does not consider innovation policy. See generally TRENDS IN PROPRIETARY INFORMATION LOSS: SURVEY REPORT (2002) (purporting to show that in 2001 companies suffered losses of 'proprietary information and intellectual property' worth more than U.S. $50 billion dollars; study relied on self-serving responses to a survey by companies who apparently estimated the degree and economic value of their own losses, with no mention how or whether secrecy was considered).

[63] For proposals for federal trade secret law that do not address the concerns raised in this chapter, see R. Mark Halligan, *Protection of U.S. Trade Secret Assets: Critical Amendments to the Economic Espionage Act of 1996*, 7 J. MARSHALL REV. INTELL. PROP. L. 656 (2008); Christopher Rebel J. Pace, *The Case for a Federal Trade Secrets Act*, 8 HARV. J.L. & TECH. 427 (1995).

[64] See Aronson v. Quick Point Pencil Co., 440 U.S. 257, 262–6 (1979) (federal pre-emption does not apply to a commercial contract for royalty payments after a patent expires); Darling v. Standard Alaska Prod. Co., 818 P.2d 677, 682 (Alaska 1991) (explaining how the federal Supremacy Clause rules do not apply to state law contract and trade secret claims).

In short, federal legislation would only be a solution if it could do away with the alternative confidentiality torts. But such far-reaching reform is for the distant future. The issues in trade secret law are not presently well-developed to allow for the meaningful debate and analysis that would be necessary to rescue federal legislation from lobbying by one-sided industry groups.

V. CONCLUSION

There is no unitary field of trade secret law. Instead, states allow a sometimes contradictory set of regimes to control the dissemination of confidential information. Thus, before we propose theories of trade secret law, we must first grapple with the basic definitions of secrecy that trial courts apply around the country.

Because these conflicting regimes are probably not the product of rational deliberation, and are instead accidents of different historical traditions, self-interested lawyering and judicial and scholarly inattention, the best short-term solution is for interested practitioners and scholars to bring more attention to trade secret law and related doctrines, in order to expose their inconsistencies and the conflicting rationales underlying them.

5 The surprising virtues of treating trade secrets as IP rights

*Mark A. Lemley**

INTRODUCTION

Trade secret law is a puzzle. Courts and scholars have struggled for over a century to figure out why we protect trade secrets. The puzzle is not in understanding what trade secret law covers; there seems to be widespread agreement on the basic contours of the law. Nor is the problem that people object to the *effects* of the law. While scholars periodically disagree over the purposes of the law, and have for almost a century, they seem to agree that misappropriation of trade secrets is a bad thing that the law should punish. Rather, the puzzle is a theoretical one: no one can seem to agree where trade secret law comes from or how to fit it into the broader framework of legal doctrine. Courts, lawyers, scholars and treatise writers argue over whether trade secrets are a creature of contract, of tort, of property, or even of criminal law. None of these different justifications has proven entirely persuasive. Worse, they have contributed to inconsistent treatment of the basic elements of a trade secret cause of action, and uncertainty as to the relationship between trade secret laws and other causes of action. Robert Bone has gone so far as to suggest that this theoretical incoherence indicates that there is no need for trade secret law as a separate doctrine at all. He reasons that whatever purposes are served by trade secret law can be served just as well by the common law doctrines that underlie it, whichever those turn out to be.[1]

In this chapter, I suggest that trade secrets can be justified as a form, not of traditional property, but of *intellectual* property (IP). The incentive justification for encouraging new inventions is straightforward. Granting legal protection for those new inventions not only encourages their creation, but enables an inventor to sell her idea. And while we have other laws

* William H. Neukom Professor, Stanford Law School; partner, Durie Tangri LLP. © 2009 Mark A. Lemley. This is an abridged version of an article of the same name that first appeared at 61 STAN. L. REV. 311 (2008).

[1] Robert G. Bone, *A New Look at Trade Secret Law: Doctrine in Search of Justification*, 86 CAL. L. REV. 241, 243 (1998).

that encourage inventions, notably patent law, trade secrecy offers some significant advantages for inventors over patent protection. It is cheaper and quicker to obtain, since it doesn't require government approval, and it extends to protection of types of business and process information that likely would not be patentable.

It seems odd, though, for the law to encourage secrets, or to encourage only those inventions that are kept secret. I argue that, paradoxically, trade secret law actually encourages disclosure, not secrecy. Without legal protection, companies in certain industries would invest *too much* in keeping secrets. Trade secret law develops as a substitute for the physical and contractual restrictions those companies would otherwise impose in an effort to prevent competitors from acquiring their information.

The puzzle then becomes why the law would require secrecy as an element of the cause of action if its goal is to reduce secrecy. I argue that the secrecy requirement serves a channeling function. Only the developers of some kinds of inventions have the option to over-invest in physical secrecy in the absence of legal protection. For products that are inherently self-disclosing (the wheel, say, or the paper clip), trying to keep the idea secret is a lost cause. We don't need trade secret law to encourage disclosure of inherently self-disclosing products – inventors of such products will get patent protection or nothing. But if trade secret law prevented the use of ideas whether or not they were secret, the result would be less, not more, diffusion of valuable information. The secrecy requirement therefore serves a gatekeeper function, ensuring that the law encourages disclosure of information that would otherwise be kept secret, while channeling inventors of self-disclosing products to the patent system.

My argument has a number of implications for trade secret policy. First, the theory works only if we treat trade secrets as IP rights, requiring proof of secrecy as an element of protection. If we give the protection to things that are public, we defeat the purpose and give windfalls to people who may not be inventors (what we might call 'trade secret trolls'). Courts that think of trade secret law as a common law tort rather than an IP right are apt to overlook the secrecy requirement in their zeal to reach 'bad actors'. But it is the courts that emphasize secrecy, not appropriation, as the key element of the cause of action that have it right. Second, an IP theory of trade secrets also encourages pre-emption of 'unjust enrichment' theories and other common law ways courts are tempted to give private parties legal control over information in the public domain. Thus, an IP theory of trade secrets is in part a 'negative' one: the value of trade secret law lies in part in defining the boundaries of the cause of action and pre-empting others that might reach too far. Analysing trade secret claims as IP claims rather than common law contract or tort claims requires courts to focus on what the law is protecting, how, and why – something the common law did not do. As a result, the unified trade secret approach does not expand, but rather cabins, the overbroad reach of the common law. Understanding trade secrets in this negative way, as imposing a consistent set of standards on claims that would otherwise be based on disparate legal theories and claims of entitlement or free riding, advances the goals of innovation and promotes responsible business conduct without limiting the vigorous competition on which a market economy is based.

Finally, treating trade secrets as IP rights helps secure their place in the pantheon of legal protection for inventions. The traditional conception of the trade-off between patents and trade secrets views the disclosure function of the patent system as one of its great advantages over trade secret law. And indeed the law operates in various ways to encourage inventors to choose patent over trade secret protection where both are possible. But for certain types of inventions we may actually get more useful 'disclosure' at less cost from trade secret than from patent law.

In Part I, I review the origins and contours of trade secret law. Part II discusses the various theories of trade secret law, and how they have split courts and commentators. In Part III, I argue that the virtue of treating trade secrets as IP rights is (or at least should be) that it limits business tort claims to circumstances in which there is really a secret to be protected, and therefore compensates for the lack of clear standards in defining what constitutes misappropriation. Finally, in Part IV I discuss the uneven internalization of this lesson in trade secret cases to date, and some of the implications the IP theory of trade secret law has for trade secret doctrine.

I. TRADE SECRET DOCTRINE

A. History of Trade Secret Law

Trade secret law is a relative latecomer to the IP pantheon. While patent and copyright law were well established in Europe by the founding of the Republic, and trademark law had common law roots in various trade doctrines, trade secret law in its modern form in Anglo-American jurisprudence is a common law creation of the nineteenth century. English and American courts first recognized a cause of action for damages for misappropriation of trade secrets in 1817 and 1837, respectively; injunctive relief against actual or threatened misappropriation came later still. These early decisions concerned issues that are still debated in trade secret cases today: the circumstances in which an employee may continue her business after departing her employer, the circumstances in which a competitor may copy another's publicly sold product, and whether courts will enforce a contract requiring that business information be kept confidential. While there were forms of trade secret protection on the Continent dating perhaps as far back as Roman times, modern trade secret law is primarily an Anglo-American doctrine. Indeed, even today trade secret law is not well established outside of common law countries, notwithstanding treaties that require most countries of the world to implement trade secret protection.

The doctrine of trade secrets evolved out of a series of related common law torts: breach of confidence, breach of confidential relationship, common law misappropriation, unfair competition, unjust enrichment, and torts related to trespass or unauthorized access to a plaintiff's property. It also evolved out of a series of legal rules – contract and common law – governing the employment relationship. In the nineteenth century, courts periodically spoke of trade secrets as property rights, though it is not clear that they meant by that term what we mean today. By the early twentieth century, the paradigm had shifted, and misappropriation of trade secrets was treated as a tort based on the confidential relationship between the parties or the misbehavior of the defendant. The standards for trade secret law were collected in the Restatement of Torts in 1939, and that Restatement was strongly of the view that trade secrets were not property rights but torts based on bad-faith competitive conduct. By the 1980s, a view of trade secrets as based in some combination of contract and property was on the ascendancy, both in the U.S. Supreme Court and in state legislatures, the overwhelming majority of which have adopted the Uniform Trade Secrets Act (UTSA) within the last 25 years.

B. Scope of Trade Secret Law

A trade secret claim can be broken down into three essential elements. First, the subject matter involved must qualify for trade secret protection: it must be the type of knowledge or information that trade secret law was meant to protect, and it must not be generally known to those in the industry. On eligible subject matter, the current trend, exemplified by the UTSA, is to protect *any* valuable information as a trade secret. So long as the information is capable of adding economic value to the plaintiff, it can be protected by trade secret law. The requirement that the information not be generally known follows from the label 'trade *secret*'. The requirement is meant to ensure that no one claims intellectual property protection for information commonly known in a trade or industry.

The second element to be established by the plaintiff in a trade secret case is that the plaintiff, holder of the trade secret, took *reasonable precautions* under the circumstances to prevent its disclosure. Courts have shown some confusion over the rationale for this requirement. Some see in it evidence that the trade secret is valuable enough to bother litigating; others argue that where reasonable precautions are taken, chances are that a defendant acquired the trade secret wrongfully. Whatever the justification, it is clear that no one may let information about products and operations flow freely to competitors at one time and then later claim that competitors have wrongfully acquired valuable trade secrets. To establish the right to sue later, one must be reasonably diligent in protecting information. As always, however, the presence of the term 'reasonable' ensures close cases and difficult line drawing for courts, and it is clear that only some precautions, not completely effective ones, are required.

Finally, a trade secret plaintiff also must prove that the defendant acquired the information wrongfully: in a word, that the defendant *misappropriated* the trade secret. Just because a person's information is valuable does not make it wrong for another to use it or disclose it. But use or disclosure is wrong, in the eyes of trade secret law, when the information is acquired through deception, skullduggery or outright theft. Close cases abound in this area, not simply because of the creativity of competitors in rooting out information about their rivals' businesses and products but because the concept of misappropriation is itself ill-defined.

In many cases a defendant's use or disclosure is wrongful because of a pre-existing obligation to the plaintiff not to disclose or appropriate the trade secret. Such an obligation can arise in either of two ways: explicitly, by contract; or implicitly, because of an *implied duty*. A classic example of an implied duty is the case of an employee. Even in the absence of an explicit contract, most employees are held to have a duty to protect their employers' interests in the employers' secret practices, information, and the like. Even where the duty arises by explicit contract, however, public policy limitations on the scope and duration of the agreement will often come into play, in some cases resulting in substantial judicial modification of the explicit obligations laid out in the contract.

Trade secret cases come up in three basic sets of circumstances: competitive intelligence, business transactions, and departing employees. The intelligence-gathering cases define rights between strangers, usually competitors, when the defendant engages in some conduct designed to learn of information in the possession of the plaintiff. Some amount of competitive intelligence gathering is permissible, but courts have said that if that activity exceeds some (relatively ill-defined) bounds of commercial morality it is misappropriation of trade secrets. Often those cases will involve violations of some other law. But that is not always true. In *E.I. duPont de Nemours & Co. v. Christopher*, for example, the court held that the defendant misappropriated secrets by taking aerial photographs of the plaintiff's chemical engineering plant while it was under construction.[2] There was no law preventing the Christophers from flying where they were, or taking pictures, but in the court's view it was a 'school boy's trick' that trade secret law should not permit.[3] Not surprisingly, the genesis of these cases is in tort (and, to a lesser extent, criminal) law, which traditionally governs relations between strangers.

The business-transaction and departing-employee cases, by contrast, involve parties who have been in a business relationship, or at least a negotiation towards a business relationship. As a result, the trade secret rules in these cases tend to derive from contract law. Sometimes this is express: the question the court considers is whether negotiating parties signed a non-disclosure agreement, or whether an employee signed an employment agreement restricting the use or disclosure of trade secrets. In other cases, courts are willing to imply restrictions on the use of confidential information created or disclosed in such a relationship even in the absence of a contract. In *Smith v. Dravo Corp.*, for example, the court implied a confidentiality restriction when the plaintiff disclosed confidential information to the defendant, who was considering buying the plaintiff's company.[4] The departing-employee cases take the same form, though in the modern world it is rare for such employees not to have an employment contract. As with the competitive-intelligence cases, trade secret law takes a basic common law principle (there tort, here contract) and supplements it in certain cases in the interest of fairness.

Misappropriation of trade secrets, then, does not simply require use of a trade secret, but acquisition, use or disclosure of a secret in a way that runs afoul of the prohibitions of trade secret law. Further, some conduct will be protected even if it discloses a trade secret. For example, a defendant who acquires a trade secret by developing it on her own or by reverse engineering it is free to do what she wants with the secret.

Proof of trade secret misappropriation gives rise to a panoply of remedies whose origin is as diverse as the original sources of trade secret law. Depending on the circumstances, trade secret owners can obtain criminal penalties (a remedy based in criminal law), an injunction (a remedy that sounds in property law), damages measured by the greater of the owner's loss or the defendant's gain (a remedy based in tort law), or a limited 'head start' injunction designed to put the parties back in the same situation they

---

2 431 F.2d 1012, 1017 (5th Cir. 1970).

3 *Id.* at 1016.

4 203 F.2d 369, 376 (7th Cir. 1953).

would have been in had the misappropriation not occurred (a remedy that sounds in the expectation-damages rule of contract law).

II. EFFORTS TO UNDERSTAND TRADE SECRET THEORY

Legal protection for trade secrets has been premised primarily on two theories that are only partly complementary. The first is utilitarian. Under this view, protecting against the theft of proprietary information encourages investment in such information. This idea is sometimes associated with the view that trade secrets are a form of property. The second theory emphasizes deterrence of wrongful acts and is therefore sometimes described as a tort theory. Here the aim of trade secret law is to punish and prevent illicit behavior, and even to uphold reasonable standards of commercial behavior. Although under the tort theory trade secret protection is not explicitly about encouraging investments, it is plain that one consequence of deterring wrongful behavior would be to encourage investment in trade secrets. Hence, despite their conceptual differences, the tort and property/incentive approaches to trade secrets may well push in the same direction in many respects. These primary theories co-exist with other explanations. In this Part, I discuss the strengths and weaknesses of each existing theory of trade secret protection.

A. Tort Law

A primary explanation for trade secret law throughout the twentieth century is what might be described as a 'duty-based' theory, or what Melvin Jager calls '[t]he maintenance of commercial morality'.[5] The U.S. Supreme Court adopted this view in *E.I. duPont de Nemours Powder Co. v. Masland*, a famous early decision, albeit one that bore only a tangential relationship to trade secret law:

> The word 'property' as applied to trademarks and trade secrets is an unanalyzed expression of certain secondary consequences of the primary fact that the law makes some rudimentary requirements of good faith. Whether the plaintiffs have any valuable secret or not the defendant knows the facts, whatever they are, through a special confidence that he accepted. The property may be denied, but the confidence cannot be. Therefore the starting point for the present

---

5 1 MELVIN JAGER, TRADE SECRETS § 1:3, 1-4.

> matter is not property or due process of law, but that the defendant stood in confidential relations with the plaintiffs.[6]

This tort-based view gained significant currency at the beginning of the twentieth century, in part because of *Masland* but also because of changing conceptions of property. By 1939, the American Law Institute firmly classed trade secret misappropriation as a tort, including it in the Restatement of Torts. The tort-based view is also frequently invoked today by scholars seeking to justify trade secret law, and sometimes by those who believe the tort approach will help limit that law. The ultimate expression of the tort view would replace trade secrets entirely with a general tort of wrongful misappropriation of information.

The problem with the tort view is that it is ultimately empty. It presupposes a wrong without offering any substantive definition of what that wrong is. In *Masland*, it appears to be the breach of a confidential relationship that is the problem. *Masland* is not alone: many trade secret cases arise out of a 'duty' explicitly stated in a contract, such as a technology license or an employment agreement. But if that is the wrong, trade secret law is nothing more than contract law. The tort-based theory of breach of duty merges in those cases with a standard common law action for breach of contract, express or implied. Calling this breach a trade secret claim merely adds a stronger panoply of remedies for what is in essence a breach of contract claim. And if the gravamen of trade secret misappropriation is nothing more than contract, why would we want to make breach of that contract a crime?

The problem of lack of substantive guidelines becomes more acute with the 'improper means' prong of trade secret law. It is unhelpful for courts to say no more than that people cannot act 'improperly' in acquiring information. If by 'improper means' the law intends nothing more than that acts already illegal (hacking, trespass, theft) are illegal here as well, then it has the same problem as the breach of confidence prong: trade secret law adds nothing to existing doctrine. But most people think improper means encompasses more. In *E.I. duPont de Nemours & Co. v. Christopher*,[7] for example, the aerial photography case discussed above, the court acknowledged that the defendants had broken no law. Nonetheless, the court found that their 'school boy's trick' was improper. The court does not offer a particularly clear standard, however:

> [W]e realize that industrial espionage of the sort here perpetrated has become a popular sport in some segments of our industrial community. However,

---

[6] 244 U.S. 100, 102 (1917).
[7] 431 F.2d 1012 (5th Cir. 1970).

> our devotion to free wheeling industrial competition must not force us into accepting the law of the jungle as the standard of morality expected in our commercial relations. Our tolerance of the espionage game must cease when the protections required to prevent another's spying cost so much that the spirit of inventiveness is dampened. Commercial privacy must be protected from espionage which could not have been reasonably anticipated or prevented . . . Perhaps ordinary fences and roofs must be built to shut out incursive eyes, but we need not require the discoverer of a trade secret to guard against the unanticipated, the undetectable, or the unpreventable methods of espionage now available.
>
> In the instant case DuPont was in the midst of constructing a plant. Although after construction the finished plant would have protected much of the process from view, during the period of construction the trade secret was exposed to view from the air. To require DuPont to put a roof over the unfinished plant to guard its secret would impose an enormous expense to prevent nothing more than a school boy's trick.[8]

While there is a standard here – the court will judge the relative costs of protection and of espionage – it is not one that is predictable or easy to implement.

That vagueness in itself wouldn't necessarily be a problem; we have vague standards in other areas of law where needed to achieve efficient results. And some would argue that the case itself is *sui generis*. But the *Christopher* case begs a larger question: why is it bad to acquire information in this way? We don't always or even often punish efforts to obtain competitive intelligence through legal means. One reading *Christopher*'s standard might reasonably wonder, for example, why reverse engineering a chemical, or learning a competitor's prices by walking through their store during business hours, or attempting to predict a competitor's business strategy based on their market behavior, aren't similarly cheap efforts to acquire knowledge that would be expensive to protect. And yet those activities are clearly legal.

The courts applying the tort standard are effectively defining certain acts as 'unfair competition' or 'free riding'. But there is a growing tendency in the courts to treat the term 'unfair competition' as redundant, using the doctrine to punish aggressive competition in the name of protecting 'fair' business practices. Without some reason to protect a secret, the tort theory of secrecy is likely to devolve into challenges to a variety of competitive information gathering, with courts unable to resolve those challenges on any principled basis, instead making ad hoc judgments based on their perception of the defendant's intent. And that in turn leaves a zone of uncertainty around business behavior that is likely to discourage robust

[8] *Id.* at 1016.

competition by companies who fear that competition may later be deemed unfair. It may also have similar deterrent effects on departing employees: courts are more likely to impose obligations on departing employees and to punish those deemed to have acted unfaithfully if it views 'bad acts' and breach of contract as the central justifications for trade secret law.

B. Contract Law

Courts and commentators have periodically suggested that trade secret law is (or more commonly, should be) co-extensive with contract. The problems with contract as a stand-alone explanation for trade secret law are two-fold. First, contract theory cannot explain an important subset of trade secret cases: those determining legal rights between strangers. This includes not only the improper-means cases, but also those in which a trade secret is acquired by accident or mistake, and those in which liability extends not merely to those in privity with the trade secret owner but also to those who deal with one who is in privity. At best, then, contractual relations could be only a partial explanation for trade secret law. Second, even in the subset of cases dealing with parties in a contractual relationship, contract theory cannot explain the various ways in which trade secret law departs from enforcing the bargain those courts have struck. Nor can a contract theory explain the strong remedies afforded trade secret owners. In no other area of contract law do we impose criminal penalties.

C. Property Law

The most significant competing theory of trade secrets is that they are property rights, something owned because possessed by the trade secret plaintiff. This seems to have been a commonly held view in the nineteenth century, though analysis of the early cases is complicated by the fact that the label 'property' at that time meant something rather different than it means to many people today, and often little more than that the right was to be protected by the injunctive power of courts in equity (the 'property rule'). After a period in which the property approach took a back seat to misappropriation theory, the U.S. Supreme Court resurrected the property view of trade secret law in *Ruckelshaus v. Monsanto Co.*[9] There, the Court faced the question of whether a federal law that required Monsanto to publicly disclose its trade secrets was a 'taking of private property' for which the Fifth Amendment required compensation. The Court, in finding

---

9 467 U.S. 986, 1001–4 (1984).

that trade secrets could be 'property' protected by the Constitution, reasoned in part that '[t]rade secrets have many of the characteristics of more tangible forms of property. A trade secret is assignable. A trade secret can form the *res* of a trust, and it passes to a trustee in bankruptcy'.[10] Many have argued that the UTSA ushered in a property view of trade secrets as well.

Treating trade secrets as property begs the question of why the government has created such property, however. After all, these secrets have not been protected since time immemorial. Nor are they rivalrously consumed, so that absent legal protection the information that is the basis of the protection would be 'overused' like a commons might be overgrazed. Courts made a decision to grant protection, something that rarely happens with other forms of property. Further, while secrecy is a requirement of protection, courts make it clear that trade secret owners do not have to maintain perfect secrecy. They are free to market products incorporating the secret, and to disclose the secret itself to others in the service of making money. The 'property', then, is not merely a right to exclude others from something in the sole possession of the plaintiff, but a right to restrict the access, use and disclosure of information that is actually or potentially in the possession of others, often through the action of the secret owner herself.

References to a 'property' right in trade secret law, therefore, seem in fact not to mean that non-public information is similar to real or chattel property, but instead to mean that trade secrets should be treated as IP rights. The trade secret owner is entitled to control certain information even once it has left the owner's possession. Why? 'Because I possess it' cannot be the answer. The answer instead must be instrumental. We grant rights over secret information for the same reason we grant rights in patent and copyright law: to encourage investment in the research and development that produces the information.

Treatment of trade secrets as property rights vested in the trade secret 'owner' is consistent with a view of trade secret law as providing an additional incentive to innovate beyond those provided in patent law. Trade secrets protect types of information that are not eligible for patent protection. They also provide immediate protection, while it takes years to get a patent. The Supreme Court has offered some support for this incentive view in cases such as *Kewanee Oil Co. v. Bicron Corp.*[11] But protecting secrecy seems an odd way of encouraging innovation. As a result, a

---

[10] *Monsanto*, 467 U.S. at 1002–4.
[11] 416 U.S. 470, 481–5 (1974).

number of commentators have suggested that if trade secret law is an IP right, it is a misguided one.

D. Commercial Morality and Other Theories

While the IP and tort theories have predominated in judicial decisions and scholarly commentary, commentators and occasional courts have offered other theories in an attempt to unify and justify trade secret law. Most notable is the oft-quoted justification that trade secret law is designed to maintain 'standards of commercial morality'.[12] This norm-based approach would embed in legal doctrine the common standards of behavior, either across industries or varying the law industry by industry.

Unfortunately, the commercial morality approach doesn't cure the defects of tort-based theories of trade secrecy. 'Commercial morality' has no more substantive content than 'unfair competition' or 'unjust enrichment' – it still requires some external source to determine what behavior is and is not moral. To be sure, the commercial morality approach does at least point us to an external source – the emergent consensus (if there is one) of what constitutes acceptable behavior. But relying on such a vague norm to set legal standards has a number of problems. It is context and time dependent; normal behavior in one industry may end up being illegal in another. Those norms may change over time in ways that make protection unpredictable; flying over a chemical plant to see how it was laid out was improper in 1970, but one might reasonably doubt that looking at satellite photos of the same plant on Google Earth would be illegal today. It requires courts to engage in what Stephen Carter has called 'judicial . . . anthropology',[13] an endeavor at which they may not be particularly skilled. It is likely to lead to inefficient results, retarding rather than enhancing innovation. And its inherent vagueness may create due process problems, particularly when trade secret law is enforced through criminal sanctions. In any event, commercial morality may not do a very good job of explaining the case law: one study found

---

[12] E.I. duPont de Nemours & Co. v. Christopher, 431 F.2d 1012, 1016 (5th Cir. 1970) (refusing to accept 'the law of the jungle as the standard of morality expected in our commercial relations').

[13] Stephen L. Carter, *Custom, Adjudication, and Petrushevsky's Watch: Some Notes from the Intellectual Property Front*, 78 VA. L. REV. 129, 140 (1992); see also Jennifer E. Rothman, *The Questionable Use of Custom in Intellectual Property*, 93 VA. L. REV. 1899, 1905–6 (2007) (challenging judicial efforts to discern and rely upon private customs in IP cases).

no evidence that courts actually took ethics into account in rendering their trade secret decisions.[14]

E. Bone's Challenge: Does Trade Secret Law Serve a Purpose?

Finally, Robert Bone has surveyed this doctrinal morass and decided that the game isn't worth the candle. Bone's argument is that none of the theories of trade secret law work. He claims:

> Those who tout economic efficiency either ignore the broader legal context within which trade secret law operates or fail to take into account all the costs of a trade secret system. Those who argue from rights and fairness are unable to identify a right or a coherent conception of fairness that fits trade secret law. And those who point to conventional norms – so-called 'generally accepted standards of commercial morality and reasonable conduct' – do so without citing empirical support for the conventions they invoke and without explaining why trade secret remedies are needed to enforce these norms.[15]

He argues that most of the positive virtues of trade secret law can be found in other legal doctrines, notably contract and tort law. To the extent that trade secret law goes beyond those doctrines, as in the *Christopher* case, he argues that it is unjustified. The common law, says Bone, can do just fine, and accomplish most of the same ends, without a doctrine of trade secret law.

Bone's criticism has particular bite for those who claim that trade secret law doesn't really have a single theoretical basis, but a multitude of them: that it is part tort, part contract, part property, part commercial morality. Perhaps this is fair enough as a descriptive matter, but it begs Bone's question: if trade secret law is simply a compilation of bits and pieces of other laws, what good is it to speak of trade secret law at all, and how can one justify the parts of that law that *don't* track their common law sources?

In Part III, I suggest that trade secrets are best conceived as IP rights, and that, as IP rights, they work – they serve the basic purposes of IP laws.

III. CONSTRUCTING AN IP THEORY OF TRADE SECRETS

Trade secrets are best understood not as applications or extensions of existing common law principles (warranted or unwarranted), but as IP

---

14 Anita Cava and Don Wiesner, *Stealing Trade Secrets Ethically*, 47 MD. L. REV. 1076, 1127–8 (1988).

15 Bone, *supra* note 1, at 246 (citations omitted).

rights. In this Part, I explain the two critical features trade secrets share with other IP rights: they promote inventive activity and they promote disclosure of those inventions. I then seek to explain the most significant anomaly – the requirement of secrecy.

A. Incentives to Invent

Trade secret law confers an exclusive right on the possessor of valuable information not generally known to or readily ascertainable by competitors. Exclusivity is the hallmark of an IP right. Both patents and copyrights confer similar rights to prevent use by others on the developers of new and valuable information. In so doing, patents and copyrights are generally acknowledged to serve a utilitarian purpose: the grant of that legal control encourages the development of new and valuable information by offering the prospect of supracompetitive returns, returns possible only if the developer does not face competition by others who use the same idea. In this way, patents and copyrights avoid the risk of underinvestment inherent with public goods, which are more costly to invent than to imitate once invented.

Trade secrecy has the same effect. It gives the developer of new and valuable information the right to restrict others from using it, and therefore the prospect of deriving supracompetitive profits from the information. This may be true of business as well as technical secrets, since some protection for business ideas helps ensure a first-mover advantage for those who take risks on untested business models. True, the right of exclusion in trade secret law is not absolute. The trade secret owner cannot sue someone who develops the idea independently, or who reverse engineers a product on the open market to learn the secret. But the same is true of copyright law. A right to exclude does not have to be absolute to be effective in rewarding and therefore encouraging innovation. It need merely provide sufficient advantage in terms of lead time or relative costs to minimize or eliminate the public goods problem.

The Supreme Court has acknowledged that trade secrets give companies incentives to innovate. In *Kewanee Oil Co. v. Bicron Corp.*,[16] the Court refused to hold that patent law pre-empted trade secret law, reasoning in part:

> [T]he patent policy of encouraging invention is not disturbed by the existence of another form of incentive to invention. In this respect the two systems are not and never would be in conflict . . .
>
> Trade secret law will encourage invention in areas where patent law does not

---

16 416 U.S. 470 (1974).

> reach, and will prompt the independent innovator to proceed with the discovery and exploitation of his invention. Competition is fostered and the public is not deprived of the use of valuable, if not quite patentable, invention.[17]

Kewanee's conclusion that two incentive systems can never conflict is too facile; the goal is not simply to maximize legal protection, but to balance it. Nonetheless, the *Kewanee* Court is right in one important respect: the additional incentive provided by trade secret law is important for innovation. Trade secret law reaches into a number of corners patent law cannot. The definition of trade secret (valuable information) is broader than the definition of patentable subject matter, for example, protecting business plans, customer lists and so-called 'negative know-how' against use by others. Patent law cannot protect valuable information of that sort. Further, inventors must apply for patents, publish their applications after 18 months, and then wait perhaps four years for the Patent and Trademark Office to decide whether to grant protection. That significant delay renders patents unavailable as a practical matter in fast-moving industries. Trade secrets, by contrast, are automatically protected upon creation provided the requirements of the statute are met. Finally, patent litigation is as much as three times as expensive as trade secret litigation, with a price tag (a median of U.S. $5 million per side in legal fees for large cases) that puts it out of reach of many small firms. Small wonder, then, that economic literature suggests that some firms, particularly start-ups, rely heavily on the incentive to invent provided by trade secret law. In many cases patents are simply not an adequate substitute.

Trade secret law also reaches where contract alone cannot. Trade secret law precludes acquisition of information by strangers using improper means – computer hacking and other forms of corporate espionage. Further, it extends the reach of the law beyond privity of contract to anyone who comes into contact with a secret knowing that they have acquired it by accident, mistake, or by another's malfeasance.

B. Incentives to Disclose

Patent and copyright law do not exist solely to encourage invention, however. A second purpose – some argue the main one – is to ensure that the public receives the benefit of those inventions. Patent and copyright law address this goal in various ways. Patent law requires that an applicant describe her invention in sufficient detail that a person of ordinary

---

[17] *Id.* at 484–5.

skill in the field can make and use it, and requires that that information be published. As a result, the public is free to read the patent and use the invention once the patent expires 20 years after it is filed, and even before that time scientists can learn from the patent disclosure and use that information to improve on the invention or to design around it. Further, patent law discourages secrecy in a number of ways.[18] It is not clear that patent law serves this disclosure function particularly well, but it seems quite clear that dissemination, not just invention, of new information is one of the goals of the patent system. Copyright similarly encourages disclosure in various ways, originally by conditioning protection on publication of a work and even today by requiring deposit of the work with the Library of Congress, where it is available to others in most circumstances. There is decent evidence to support the idea that at least one function of an IP right is not just to encourage new invention, but to encourage the *dissemination* of those new ideas.

At first blush, trade secret law seems to push in the opposite direction. After all, protection under trade secret laws is conditioned on secrecy, and so it seems to encourage secrecy, or at least the development of inventions that can be kept secret. Paradoxically, however, trade secret law actually encourages broader disclosure and use of information, not secrecy. It does so in two ways. First, the legal protection trade secret law provides serves as a *substitute* for investments in physical secrecy that companies might otherwise make. The facts of *E.I. duPont de Nemours & Co. v. Christopher*[19] once again provide an example. There, the plaintiff was constructing a chemical plant, and during construction it was apparently possible to see the layout of the plant from the air and so to discern the secret process DuPont was using. The court noted that DuPont could have built a temporary roof over the plant during construction, but only at 'enormous expense'.[20] It didn't need to build that roof because the law pro-

---

[18] Section 102(b) requires prompt filing once an inventor begins using an invention in its business, at the risk of losing the right to protection. 35 U.S.C. § 102(b). And § 102(g) provides that those who 'suppress' or 'conceal' an invention lose their claim to be the first inventor, at least until they start down the path to public disclosure. 35 U.S.C. § 102(g); Paulik v. Rizkalla, 760 F.2d 1270 (Fed. Cir. 1985) (*en banc*). As a result, patent law discourages reliance on secrecy, to the point that a first inventor who maintains that invention as a trade secret may not only lose the right to claim patent protection, but may even be sued for patent infringement by a second inventor who did disclose the invention. See, e.g., Gillman v. Stern, 114 F.2d 28 (2d Cir. 1940).

[19] 431 F.2d 1012 (5th Cir. 1970).

[20] *Id.* at 1016. Putting a cover on the large plant during construction might or might not itself be an 'enormous expense'. The better point is that protecting

tected its interest in avoiding (aerial) prying eyes. Had the law not done so, however, it is reasonable to suppose that DuPont might have built the roof rather than risk loss of its trade secrets. That investment in secrecy would have been inefficient; it is cheaper (both for DuPont and for society) for the law to provide that protection. And even if the investment in secrecy were efficient for DuPont in the absence of the law, it would still impose a social cost by restricting the flow of information – a cost DuPont would have no reason to take into account.

There is empirical evidence that over-investment in secrecy is a real problem in the absence of trade secret protection. Examples can be found as far back as the guild system that pervaded Western economies in the Middle Ages. Guilds were places that could and did develop technical knowledge, but in the absence of legal means to protect that knowledge they went to great lengths to prevent others from learning of it, imposing draconian limits on the mobility of employees and the development of competing firms. The same problem remains today in countries that do not provide legal protection for secrets. Robert Sherwood studied business practices in Mexico and Brazil, two countries that do not have strong legal protection for trade secrets and in which resort to the courts may not be viable for a variety of reasons.[21] He found that companies in those countries make business decisions that inefficiently limit the disclosure of information because they fear that they cannot rely on the courts to prevent the use of information they do disclose.[22] For example, they may be less willing to contract production out to third parties if it means giving out information about secret processes, even where the third party could use the process more efficiently. They may take elaborate security measures, building walls and fences and hiring armed guards. And they may hire employees whom they expect to be loyal, such as family members, rather than strangers who would do a better job.[23]

The problem also remains for products or industries that do not qualify for IP protection. Michael Pollan explains that the developers of new breakfast cereals, for example, engage in enormous efforts to protect

oneself against all the possible ways prying eyes could discern the secret would collectively require enormous expense.

[21] Robert M. Sherwood, Intellectual Property and Economic Development 111–17 (1990).

[22] *Id.* at 113–16.

[23] Similarly, Michael Risch recounts the story of a client in China that invested extraordinary amounts to protect its secrets, installing fingerprint scanners, limiting Internet access and filtering outgoing email. Michael Risch, *Why Do We Have Trade Secrets?*, 11 Marq. Intell. Prop. L. Rev. 1, 44 (2007).

the secrecy of their new ideas in order to gain a few months' first-mover advantage. For the same reason, they operate their own machine shops to design the cereals, rather than outsourcing that work to those presumably more specialized in it.[24]

None of this evidence is perfect. One of the problems with social science is that it is hard to run clean tests in the real world. Nonetheless, there are both logical and evidentiary reasons to believe that, without legal protection, companies in certain industries would invest *too much* in keeping secrets. These investments are inefficient, in several senses. In many cases, the problem they address could be avoided by the courts at lower cost than the building of walls and fences. Second, physical investments must be made for each secret, while legal investments need be made only if there is misappropriation. That means that even if a physical investment in secrecy is individually cheap, in the aggregate the cost of having to make that investment for every secret may outweigh the cost of resort to law, which will be necessary only in those few cases in which the secret is actually misappropriated.[25] Finally, and most importantly, restrictions on the flow of information between business partners or to new employees slow the process of commercialization and improvement of the secret inventions, and therefore interfere with both the invention and disclosure functions of IP law. Trade secret law develops as a substitute for the physical and contractual restrictions those companies would otherwise impose in an effort to prevent a competitor from acquiring their information. In so doing, it encourages disclosure of information that companies might otherwise be reluctant to share for fear of losing the competitive advantage it provides.

To be sure, trade secret law still encourages some secrecy. So if the alternative were a world in which companies freely disclosed their inventions, that world might be preferable. But the empirical evidence suggests that is

---

[24] MICHAEL POLLAN, THE OMNIVORE'S DILEMMA: A NATURAL HISTORY OF FOUR MEALS 92 (2006) (quoting one cereal company executive as saying: 'Recipes are not intellectual property; you can't patent a new cereal. All you can hope for is to have the market to yourself for a few months to establish your brand before a competitor knocks off the product. So we're very careful not to show our hand'). To be fair, this example can cut both ways – apparently cereal companies don't trust trade secret law enough to disclose information. But it is consistent with the idea that companies will opt for excessive secrecy in the absence of what they consider adequate legal protection.

[25] The reverse can sometimes be true, however. If a single fence can protect a host of secrets that the owner would have to sue individually to protect in court, fencing might be cheaper than legal protection. But when secrets are released to third parties, as most of the good ones generally must be, that becomes less likely.

unlikely to be the alternative. Rather, a world without trade secret protection is likely to have more, not less, secrecy.

Trade secret laws can encourage disclosure in a second way as well: they serve as a partial solution to Arrow's Information Paradox.[26] The paradox is this: in the absence of any legal protection, the developer of a potentially valuable but secret idea will have a difficult time selling that idea to someone who could make more efficient use of it. In order to sell the idea he will have to disclose it to allow the buyer to evaluate it, but disclosing it destroys the value inherent in its secrecy. To see this, imagine that I tell you I have a great idea, and I'll share it with you for U.S.$1 million. Should you take the deal? You can't know the answer to that question unless I tell you what the idea is. But in the absence of legal protection, if I tell you what my idea is, you no longer need to pay me U.S.$1 million.

Now add trade secret law (or any IP right) to the picture. The existence of a legal right to prevent others from using or disclosing my idea in breach of a confidential relationship allows me to disclose the idea in precontractual negotiations, secure in the knowledge that the other side is not free to take the idea without compensating me. The law, by giving certain rights to the holder of the secret, allows him to disclose information he would otherwise have been unwilling to share, and therefore permits business negotiations that can lead to commercialization of the invention or sale of the idea, serving both the disclosure and incentive functions of IP law. True, the parties could have entered into a contract limiting what could be done with the information, but the putative buyer may be reluctant to sign such a contract without knowing what they might be limiting themselves from using. Both venture capitalists and Hollywood executives, for example, are notoriously unwilling to sign non-disclosure agreements before reading business plans or movie scripts. Trade secret law reaches beyond contract law by allowing courts to infer the existence of a confidential relationship from circumstances in which transactions might be difficult or impossible without that assumption.

The fact that trade secret law reduces rather than increases an innovative firm's investment in secrecy answers many of the objections people have offered to trade secret law, in particular Bone's claim that legally induced secrecy will interfere with rather than promote innovation. Bone's argument is right as far as it goes – companies that keep too much

---

[26] Kenneth J. Arrow, *Economic Welfare and the Allocation of Resources for Invention*, in THE RATE AND DIRECTION OF INVENTIVE ACTIVITY: ECONOMIC AND SOCIAL FACTORS 609, 615 (National Bureau of Economic Research, 1962) (arguing that sellers will not disclose information to buyers absent legal protection, and so buyers will be unable to value that information).

secret may reduce rather than increase aggregate innovation – but for the reasons I outline in this section, that argument is a justification for, not a challenge to, trade secret law.

C. Channeling Protection Between Patents and Trade Secrets

So far, so good. But at this point the reader might object that, if the goal of trade secret law is to give legal rights over an invention while encouraging its disclosure, we don't really need the secrecy requirement at all. In this vein, a number of scholars have suggested that *any* investment in protecting trade secrecy is wasted, since the law is requiring companies to spend money in ways that reduce, not increase, the dissemination of ideas. If the goal of trade secret law is to encourage dissemination by giving the security of a legal right, this argument runs, why not just grant that right to any information, regardless of whether it is secret?

The problem with this argument is that without some basis for defining the legal right, it will sweep too broadly. If I can get ownership rights in any information, no matter how public, the result will be to deter, not promote, the dissemination of that information. Broad legal rights may restrict employee mobility, with negative consequences for the economy. If any idea, no matter how public, is subject to a claim of legal rights, individuals and companies will reasonably worry about using any information they do not themselves develop. If I could sue you for repeating my explanation of trade secret law, the result is not likely to be wide discussion of that explanation, even if I have no intention of actually suing you for discussing my idea.[27] And while we could theoretically substitute a defendant's conduct for proof of secrecy as the basis for entitlement to a legal right, as we saw in Part II, such conduct-based definitions are circular (competition is unfair if it is likely to be defined by courts as unfair) and ultimately empty.

Granted that we need some definition of the entitlement, why secrecy? The answer, I believe, is that the secrecy requirement serves to channel inventors into the appropriate form of IP protection. Consider three different types of inventions: one that is impossible to conceal once it is in widespread use (think of the wheel or the paper clip); one that is impossible to discern by evaluating the product (think of the formula for Coca-Cola); and one that can be discerned by evaluating the product, but only with difficulty (think of software source code, which is not evident from the object code sold to customers but which might be reverse engineered). In a world

27 I don't.

with patent law but no trade secret law, companies with inventions in the first category (those who have developed inherently self-disclosing inventions) will turn to patent law if they can. If not, they will be out of luck. If the paper clip were not patentable,[28] companies wouldn't be able to keep it secret and still make much profit from it. Their best option would likely be to sell the paper clip and hope to make some profit from brand recognition or first-mover advantages.

Companies with inventions in the second category, by contrast (those who develop inventions that are not transparent to the world, such as chemical processes and some formulas) might well decide to keep an invention secret in the absence of legal protection. They may reason that secrecy may give them a greater advantage than patent law, since patents may be held invalid, may be easy to design around, and in any event will expire within 20 years. Indeed, there is some empirical evidence that they do so: that where secrecy is possible, inventors choose it over patent protection. Without trade secret law, the efforts those companies take to protect their secrets may be excessive, as I discussed in the previous Part. That over-investment may be specific (protection of a particular idea) or general (imposing too many restrictions on employees and business partners). Either way, the result is both inefficiency from over-investment in secrecy and the loss of the benefits of public disclosure of information.[29]

A secrecy requirement provides protection to companies in the second category, not in the first. Thus, it ensures that trade secret law provides legal protection in circumstances in which inventors might otherwise choose excessive secrecy, but denies protection to inventions that compa-

---

[28] It was. Indeed, there were many different claimed inventors and even substantial litigation over ownership of the exclusive rights to the paper clip. See, e.g., Cushman & Denison Mfg. Co. v. Denny, 147 F. 734, 734–5 (S.D.N.Y. 1906). And more modern variants are still patented today. See Plastic Paper Clip, U.S. Patent No. 5,179,765 (filed January 8, 1992).

[29] The same can be said (with some adaptations) of business rather than technical trade secrets. Consider customer information, some of which is readily accessible to the public (phone numbers) and some of which is not (purchasing budget for each customer, likes and dislikes, etc.). In a world without trade secret protection, companies might put too much effort into protecting the latter category of information from disclosure. Unlike technical information disclosed in products, these efforts are likely to take the form of compartmentalization of information within the company or of efforts to prevent salespeople from leaving the company through non-competition agreements, and the like. Trade secret law may substitute for some of those efforts, as it does in California, which forbids restrictions on employee mobility, see California Business and Professional Code § 16600 (West 2008), but allows enforcement of claims to information that is in fact secret. See Edwards v. Arthur Andersen LLP, 189 P.3d 285 (Cal. 2008).

nies would not keep secret in the absence of patent protection. By drawing this line, even the secrecy requirement of trade secret law has the surprising effect of reducing, not increasing, the secrecy of inventions.

What, then, of inventions in the intermediate category? Companies with inventions in this third category might or might not rely on secrecy rather than patent law. Both approaches have risks. As noted above, patents might be invalid, or easy to evade, and in any event will expire in a set period of time. On the other hand, reliance on secrecy provides only tenuous protection, since the secret could be discerned by reverse engineering or independent development or disclosed by an employee or business partner in the absence of trade secret law. In this case, the effects of introducing trade secret law are ambiguous. If companies in this third category would have opted for secrecy, then the introduction of trade secret law reduces the negative effects of that secrecy for the same reasons it did in the second category. But if they would have opted for patent protection rather than secrecy without law, adding trade secret law might encourage them to keep secret information they would otherwise have patented (and therefore disclosed).

To avoid inadvertently encouraging secrecy rather than disclosure, trade secret law incorporates limits on the scope of the right, notably the defenses of independent development and reverse engineering. As the Supreme Court suggested in *Kewanee Oil Co. v. Bicron Corp.*, and as commentators have suggested, these defenses weaken the trade secret right sufficiently that it does not entice inventors to choose secrecy over patent protection. That isn't always true, of course; the inventors of Coca-Cola could have chosen to patent it but didn't. But importantly, weakening trade secrets means that those in the intermediate category are unlikely to choose secrecy over patenting. Taken together, the secrecy requirement and the relative weakness of the trade secret law help ensure that the law protects those who would otherwise rely on secrecy without law, and encourages disclosure in those cases, while not displacing patent law as the means of protection for self-disclosing inventions. Put another way, the secrecy requirement channels particular inventors to the form of IP protection that best achieves the goals of society.

Trade secret law may or may not get this judgment right. The enforcement of trade secrets has costs as well as benefits, and as with all IP rights, it is hard to know whether we are getting the balance right. Further, as I suggest below, not every trade secret case fits this framework neatly. But the theory of trade secrets as IP rights coheres, in the sense both that the fundamental features of trade secret law fit quite nicely within the goals and framework of IP law more generally and that the same arguments and concerns that arise in other areas of IP arise in trade secret law. Further, as I will argue, thinking about trade secrets as IP rights can help us to improve the doctrine itself. Resolving those arguments, and striking that balance, is the subject of Part IV.

IV. IMPLICATIONS FOR TRADE SECRET LAW

How does this understanding of trade secret law translate into policy? As a preliminary matter, the articulation of a solid theoretical basis for trade secret law helps defuse Robert Bone's criticism of the doctrine. Trade secret laws promote the goals of IP rights more generally, and it is the doctrines specific to trade secret law rather than those borrowed from contract or tort that help it do so.

Beyond justifying the entire endeavor, the IP theory of trade secret rights has several implications for the development of trade secret doctrine. In this Part, I discuss two primary implications and some other possible lessons theory can provide for practice.

A. The Centrality of Secrecy

One implication of the theory I articulated in Part III is that the requirement of secrecy is not an accident or a mistake. It is a central part of what makes trade secret law work. A significant benefit of thinking of trade secrets as IP rights rather than as unfair competition torts is that it puts the focus of the legal inquiry first and foremost on whether the plaintiff has an IP right at all. The UTSA, for example, defines the legal rights of trade secret owners by requiring the existence of a secret and defining what constitutes a secret. Doing so prevents plaintiffs from ignoring or glossing over proof of the existence of a trade secret in their effort to prevent what they see as improper use of their information.

This point may seem obvious: *of course* winning a trade secret case requires the plaintiff to prove the existence of a trade secret. But in fact a number of cases and commentators that have applied the tort theory of trade secrecy have minimized or even ignored that requirement.[30]

---

[30] That their doing so stems from the tort theory of trade secrets is evident from Kamin v. Kuhnau, 374 P.2d 912, 918 (Or. 1962), which said that '[t]he cases adopting the higher standard of "commercial morality" emphasize the breach of confidence reposed in the defendant, rather than the existence of the trade secret.' See also FMC Corp. v. Varco Int'l, Inc., 677 F.2d 500, 503 (5th Cir. 1982) ('The fact that a trade secret is of such a nature that it can be discovered by experimentation or other fair and lawful means does not deprive its owner of the right to protection

The Supreme Court itself led courts astray in *E.I. duPont de Nemours Powder Co. v. Masland*, where it said that '[w]hether the plaintiffs have any valuable secret or not, the defendant knows the facts, whatever they are, through a special confidence that he accepted. The property may be denied, but the confidence cannot be'.[31] A number of courts applying the Restatement of Torts have followed the lead of the *Masland* dictum, holding that defendants misappropriated trade secrets by acquiring or using a secret by improper means or in breach of a confidential relationship without determining that the information was itself a secret at all. An example is *Smith v. Dravo Corp.*, in which the defendant had clearly made use of information obtained from the plaintiff during acquisition negotiations in later entering the market in competition with the plaintiff.[32] The court found liability on the basis of the defendant's admittedly troubling business behavior. But in doing so, the court elided the distinction between the use of information that was truly secret, such as the plaintiff's confidential patent applications, and information that was readily accessible to the public, such as the dimensions of plaintiff's shipping containers that were already on the market.

There are a number of other examples. In *United States Sporting Products, Inc. v. Johnny Stewart Game Calls, Inc.*,[33] for example, the court held that publicly sold, uncopyrightable recordings of bird calls were protectable. The court focused on the labor the plaintiff had put into collecting them, but ignored the fact that they were not secret. In *Rohm & Haas Co. v. Adco Chemical Co.*,[34] the court ignored the fact that the defendant's alleged secret process was in fact disclosed in a number of industry publications because it found that the defendant did not in fact learn the information from those publications, but instead from the plaintiff. And in *Franke v. Wiltschek*, the Second Circuit elevated this idea to a general rule based on *Masland*:

> It matters not that defendants could have gained their knowledge from a study of the expired patent and plaintiffs' publicly marketed product. The fact is that they did not. Instead they gained it from plaintiffs via their confidential relationship, and in so doing incurred a duty not to use it to plaintiffs' detriment. This duty they have breached.[35]

---

from those who would secure possession of it by unfair means', quoting K & G Oil Tool & Serv. Co. v. G & G Fishing Tool Serv., 314 S.W.2d 782, 788 (Tex. 1958)).

31 244 U.S. 100, 102 (1917).

32 203 F.2d 369 (7th Cir. 1953).

33 865 S.W.2d 214 (Tex. Ct. App. 1993).

34 689 F.2d 424 (3d Cir. 1982).

35 209 F.2d 493, 495 (2d Cir. 1953).

These courts have departed from the principle of trade secrets as IP rights. Perhaps they are blinded by the defendant's suspicious conduct, or perhaps they view employee mobility itself as suspect. Whatever the reason, they ignore the critical limit on the scope of that IP right. Doing so risks turning trade secrets from a well-defined legal right that serves the broader purposes of IP law into a standardless, free-roaming right to sue competitors for business conduct that courts or juries might be persuaded to deem objectionable. Secrecy is critical to ensuring that trade secret law does not interfere with robust competition or with the dissemination of new ideas. Courts that ignore that requirement undermine the purpose of trade secret law. The dictum of *Masland* should not only be disregarded but reversed: 'The starting point in every case of this sort is not whether there was a confidential relationship, but whether, in fact, there was a trade secret to be misappropriated'.[36] Understanding trade secrets as IP rights, and therefore as premised first and foremost on the existence of such a legal right, will help restore the centrality of the secrecy inquiry. And as a corollary, it may help ensure that the plaintiff clearly defines what it claims to own, rather than (as happens all too often in practice) falling back on vague hand waving.

B. Relationship Between Trade Secret Law and Other Torts

The importance of secrecy in channeling inventors between patent and non-patent IP protection has a second implication as well. Requiring trade secret plaintiffs to prove that they own real secrets will do little good if those same plaintiffs can turn to other legal doctrines to provide equivalent protection without the requirement of secrecy. Unfortunately, there are a number of state common law doctrines that offer just that prospect. The common law doctrine of breach of confidence, for example, required only proof that something was offered to the defendant in confidence, and that the defendant disclosed that information. Other common law doctrines, including misappropriation, unfair competition and unjust enrichment (at least in those states in which it is an independent cause of action), similarly have no elements other than a loose definition of improper conduct. And still other torts, such as interference with contract or 'idea submission', may well overlap almost completely with trade secret claims in particular cases.

---

[36] Den-Tal-Ez, Inc. v. Siemens Capital Corp., 566 A.2d 1214, 1228 (Pa. Super. Ct. 1989) (citing *Van Prods. Co.*, 213 A.2d at 780); *accord* Patriot Homes, Inc. v. Forest River Hous., Inc., 512 F.3d 412, 415 (7th Cir. 2008).

Trade secret law should pre-empt these torts when they are applied to protect information that would, if secret, have been protected by trade secret law.[37] That is, a plaintiff who complains of the defendant's use of its information, but who cannot prove that the information is secret, should not be able to rely on one of these torts (or any other common law variants) to bypass the requirement that it prove secrecy. If trade secret law does not pre-empt these torts, the point of the secrecy requirement will be lost, and with it the benefits of dissemination of new inventions. Companies will be unable to rely on the presence of ideas in the public domain; any information might potentially be subject to one of these torts. As a result, companies will be less willing to compete vigorously on the merits. Departing employees will be less willing to rely on information in the public domain to start new companies, and as a result more reluctant at the margins to start those companies. As Jim Pooley notes, 'there is arguably little social utility' in allowing state claims based on misappropriation of trade secrets to go forward if the plaintiff cannot prove the elements of a trade secret claim.[38]

Trade secret law should not, however, pre-empt state laws that have as an object something other than the protection of information. A defendant who breaks into an office to steal information has committed a tort (and indeed a crime) regardless of whether the information in question was secret. Trade secret law should pre-empt laws within the same general scope as trade secrecy, but not laws that serve fundamentally different purposes.

Once again, conceiving of trade secrets as IP rights helps achieve the goal of pre-emption of conflicting common law torts. If trade secret law is one tort among many common law torts, there is no reason to privilege it over other torts when the two conflict.[39] But we have a well-established

---

[37] And indeed the UTSA does pre-empt state torts, with the notable exception of contract law. Uniform Trade Secrets Act § 7, 14 U.L.A. 433 (1985).

[38] James H.A. Pooley, Trade Secrets § 3.04[4], 3-43–3-44. This is why I believe Bone has it backwards to suggest that a world without trade secret law, but with common law torts, would give greater freedom to reverse engineering, independent development and employee mobility. See Robert G. Bone, *Exploring the Boundaries of Competitive Secrecy: An Essay on the Limits of Trade Secret Law*, in Law, Information and Information Technology 99, 121–3 (Eli Lederman and Ron Shapira eds., 2001). Trade secret law has limits, and can supplant the application of common law torts that lack those limits.

[39] Indeed, some courts applying the tort theory have allowed claims for misappropriation to proceed where trade secret claims failed, even in jurisdictions in which the UTSA seems clearly to foreclose application of those torts. See, e.g., Imax Corp. v. Cinema Techs., Inc., 152 F.3d 1161, 1169 (9th Cir. 1998); City

set of principles by which IP rights pre-empt state common law rules that interfere with those rights. We have those pre-emption principles because we recognize IP rights as utilitarian rules created by government to address public goods problems, and the policy decisions implicit in those rules will at a minimum be complicated and may even be overridden by layering on additional causes of action not designed with public goods problems in mind. The *Compco* and *Sears* cases provide IP examples of how this can work.[40] While those cases involved federal Supremacy Clause pre-emption of state laws, there are state-level examples as well. Most notably, the California Supreme Court held that California's unfair competition statute could not be applied to undo the limits of the Cartwright Act, the state's antitrust law.[41] The rationale was the same as it is here: applying a general, open-ended tort to override the specific limits of a statutory policy defeats the purpose of that policy. Treating trade secret law as an IP right dependent on proof of secrecy highlights the policy stakes, and will encourage courts to pre-empt common law claims that threaten to undermine the balance trade secret law strikes. In so doing, it may further advance the trade secret policy of disclosure by removing state laws that block the flow of non-trade secret information.

C. Other Implications for Trade Secret Doctrine

Besides the centrality of secrecy to trade secret law, and the attendant need to pre-empt torts that undermine that requirement, an IP theory of trade secret law may have other implications for trade secret doctrine as well. The implications I discuss in this section are more speculative; they represent not necessary implications of the IP theory of trade secrets, but legal doctrines that seem to fit uneasily with the IP theory or that are likely to draw greater sustenance for that theory.

1. Reasonable efforts to protect secrecy

First, while proof that the plaintiff's information is secret serves a critical role in channeling towards trade secret protection only those inventions

---

Solutions, Inc. v. Clear Channel Commc'ns, Inc., 242 F.Supp.2d 720, 735 (N.D. Cal. 2003), *aff'd in relevant part*, 365 F.3d 835, 842 (9th Cir. 2004); Burbank Grease Servs., Inc. v. Sokolowski, 717 N.W.2d 781 (Wis. 2006). But see Mortgage Specialists, Inc. v. Davey, 904 A.2d 652 (N.H. 2006) (rejecting *Burbank Grease*).

40 *Compco Corp.*, 376 U.S. at 234; *Sears, Roebuck & Co.*, 376 U.S. at 229.

41 Cel-Tech Commc'ns v. L.A. Cellular Tel. Co., 973 P.2d 527 (Cal. 1999) (holding that state antitrust law pre-empts allegations of unfair competition between competitors unless those allegations are sufficient to state an antitrust claim).

that are best served by trade secret law, the same is not necessarily true of the parallel requirement that trade secret owners take reasonable efforts to protect their secrets. That requirement seems to stem from traditional tort notions of contributory negligence, under which plaintiffs were barred from relief if they themselves contributed to the tort. The explanation I have offered for trade secret law (and for the secrecy requirement) is not one that values secrecy as an end in itself; far from it. The benefit of trade secret law is that it *reduces* investment in secrecy compared to what would happen absent that law. So there is no reason we should want to establish a minimum investment level as an end in itself. And it may have negative consequences in particular circumstances.

The question then becomes whether reasonable efforts serve some other end. For example, some courts suggest that efforts to protect information as a secret are a sufficiently strong proxy for the secrecy of the invention that we should rely on them as evidence in support of the existence of a secret. But they are surely not perfect evidence; any litigator will tell you that companies regularly label as secret lots of things that clearly are not secret. Even assuming that reasonable efforts at secrecy do provide such evidence, that doesn't justify the imposition of reasonable efforts as a separate requirement, just the consideration of that evidence in the overall secrecy inquiry. Alternatively, it may be that efforts to protect secrecy serve to put potential defendants on notice of the claim of secrecy, and therefore prevent inadvertent misappropriation. This may be true of some, but not all, efforts at secrecy, so again, it seems to justify reasonable efforts only as evidence, not as a separate requirement. More to the point, it will be true only as to some defendants; others may be aware of the secrecy of the information they take whether or not those secrets were reasonably protected. It seems more logical to cabin the risk of liability for inadvertent misappropriation by imposing some kind of *scienter* requirement than through this kind of constructive notice through enforcement efforts.[42]

Reasonable efforts to protect secrecy, then, may make sense as evidence of secrecy or even as evidence of *scienter*, but they probably don't make

---

[42] Trade secret law does have such a requirement, though it rarely becomes an issue, probably because the requirement of misappropriation by improper means limits the number of cases in which defendants act in good faith but still meet the test for infringement. See Rohm & Haas Co. v. Adco Chem. Co., 689 F.2d 424, 433 n.9 (3d Cir. 1982) (imposing a negligence requirement as to whether the information taken constituted a secret and concluding that '[a] good faith belief, even if credited, is no defense to an action for misappropriation of trade secrets'); James Pooley, Trade Secrets § 6.04[1], 6-30 (2008) ('Knowledge on the part of the defendant is an element of liability for misappropriation').

sense as a separate requirement. In this case it is the Restatements that have it right and the UTSA that has it wrong; both the Restatement of Torts and the Restatement of Unfair Competition treat reasonable efforts solely as evidence of secrecy, while the UTSA treats them as a separate condition for protection.

2. Contracting around trade secret law

A second possible implication of an IP theory of trade secret rights involves efforts to contract around those rights. Just as treating trade secrets as IP rights makes pre-emption of conflicting tort laws more feasible by highlighting the policy purposes trade secret laws serve, it raises the question of whether trade secret rules are merely default rules that the parties can contract around, or whether they are policy judgments that courts should not allow the parties to undermine. There is a similar debate in copyright law, where courts have split on the question of whether parties can contract to prevent reverse engineering of software despite copyright rules that make reverse engineering legal under most circumstances. In trade secret law, this comes up in three significant contexts: efforts to contract around the requirement of secrecy itself, whether in business disputes or in restrictive employee covenants; efforts to ban reverse engineering by contract; and the question of whether a confidential relationship can be implied absent a contract. In each case, there are substantial policy interests that underlie the choice of trade secret rules. Indeed, in the case of secrecy itself, they are fundamental to the point of trade secret law. Accordingly, my inclination is to prevent parties from opting out of particular rules of trade secret law, at least to the extent they rely on trade secret rather than contract remedies. This limits the power of trade secret owners in some cases – reverse engineering and secrecy – but strengthens their power in others – implied confidential relationships. Understanding trade secrets as IP rights won't resolve this debate, any more than it has in the copyright context. But it will make it clear that there must be a debate, and that it must be conducted with trade secret policy in mind. And it may strengthen the hand of those who argue that there is more at stake here than just the agreement of two private parties.

3. IP, property and 'absolute dominion'

Third, the theoretical underpinnings of trade secret law bear on the relationship between the IP conception of trade secrets and the freedom of others to use information to compete. A number of scholars suggest that conceiving of trade secrets as property rights will lead to stronger protection for trade secrets, at the expense of employee mobility and robust competition, and perhaps even of free speech. Conceiving of trade secrets as IP rights may affect the way that other laws, such as antitrust, interact with trade secret law. Others worry that a property conception of trade secrets – and perhaps therefore an IP conception – will cause courts to gloss over the First Amendment and afford less protection to journalists or whistleblowers. In fact, however, I suggest in this chapter that conceiving of trade secrets as IP rights has the opposite effect: it encourages courts to focus on the requirements and limits of trade secret law, particularly when compared to the standardless theories of unfair competition and unjust enrichment that seem the most obvious alternatives. In doing so, it is more likely to promote economic efficiency than any competing approach. Nor does conceiving of trade secrets as IP rights mean that they are unlimited, or that the First Amendment must give way; I have explained elsewhere why the First Amendment cannot give way merely because 'property' is at stake.

4. How long does secrecy last?

The final implication is also the most speculative: it may be that an IP theory of trade secrets suggests that there should be a term limit on trade secret protection. Patents and (at least until recently) copyrights expire after a set term of years. Trade secrets, by contrast, are protected for an indefinite term, until they are no longer secret. The theory is that the possibility of publication of the secret, whether by malfeasance or by independent development or reverse engineering, means that the secret is fragile, and that over time it is likely to be revealed to the world. But it is not clear that this indefinite term properly strikes the balance between providing incentives to invent and ensuring that the world benefits from the new invention. It may be that after a certain period of time the additional incentive from the prospect of secrecy is marginal, while the costs of maintaining secrecy are not. Coca-Cola, for example, surely did not count on over a century of trade secret protection when it made the choice between patent and trade secret law. One possible implication of treating trade secrets as IP rights, then, is that the law should provide that trade secrets 'expire' after a certain period. Certainly, an IP view of trade secret rights requires us to give thought to striking the right balance between encouraging innovation and unduly limiting disclosure, a question that, whatever its proper resolution, might not arise at all under a different conception of trade secrecy. That doesn't mean we should define a term for trade secrets. It may be too hard to decide on a start date, and therefore an end date, and compelling disclosure of information at the end of the term may also prove problematic. But thinking of trade secrets as IP rights at least gives us a perspective from which to think about the question.

CONCLUSION

Trade secrets are IP rights. They serve the same purposes as patent and copyright law: they encourage innovation and the disclosure and dissemination of that innovation, though they sometimes serve those purposes in surprising ways. Trade secret law reduces investments in secrecy and encourages the dissemination of the secret to more people who can make productive use of it. Indeed, trade secret rights may serve the purposes of IP law better than more traditional IP rights, at least for certain classes of inventions. The public disclosure function of the patent system doesn't work very well in most industries, and doesn't work at all if inventors opt out of the patent system.

Understanding trade secrets as IP rights allows them to take their proper place in the pantheon of social policy designed to encourage innovation. It also gives us a way to think about how those rights are designed, a way that has significant implications for how trade secret law looks and how it interacts with other laws. Most surprisingly, those implications are ones that offer greater, not lesser, latitude for competitors and departing employees than the unfair competition rationale most commonly articulated as an alternative.

6 Trade secrets as intellectual property rights: a disgraceful upgrading – Notes on an Italian 'reform'*

*Gustavo Ghidini*** and Valeria Falce****

Since Italy's enactment of a new Code of Industrial Property in 2005, trade secrets have gained the status of an intellectual property right. Because the request for stronger non-patent protection for trade secrets is growing across jurisdictions, the Italian experiment should be of interest to foreign observers, who would be well advised to prevent this untoward development becoming part of their own legislation.

I. THE TRADITIONAL LEGAL FRAMEWORK

As in many legal systems, both civil and common law, the protection of industrial and trade secrets (that is, any information which has an economic value by reason of being confidential, is subject to reasonable measures to keep it as secret, and is in fact not in the public knowledge nor easily accessible or inferable by an average expert in the relevant field) has been traditionally ensured in Italy within the framework, and according to the limits, of unfair competition law. Thus, protection was granted only against acts of 'misappropriation', meaning only if either the acquisition was made on behalf, or in the interest of, a competitor and in 'a manner contrary to honest commercial practises'. Since misappropriation generally required a breach of contract, a breach of confidence, or an inducement to breach, competitors were liable for infringement only when they

---

* The present Article refers to the Italian rules on trade secret protection introduced in the original text (2005) of the Italian Code on Industrial Property. Subsequently, in 2010, those rules have been marginally and formally changed, leaving the original perspective criticized in the Article substantially unmodified.

** Full Professor of Intellectual Property and Competition Law, Università degli Studi of Milan; Director of the Intellectual Property and Competition Observatory, LUISS, Guido Carli University, Rome.

*** Ph.D., LL.M., Associate Professor of Intellectual Property and Competition Law, Università Europea di Roma.

knew, or were grossly negligent in failing to know, that improper practices were involved when they acquired and used such information.

The same systemic perspective is evident in Article 39 of the TRIPS Agreement, which grants protection to 'undisclosed information' 'as part of the unfair competition regime laid out in Article 10*bis* of the Paris Convention'.[1] According to Article 10*bis*(2), this includes 'act[s] of competition contrary to honest practices in industrial or commercial matters'.[2] In other words, the TRIPS Agreement, as with the vast majority of national legislation, does not acknowledge trade secrets as the object of a genuine intellectual property right: no 'absolute' (*erga omnes*) exclusive right is granted; rather, protection is 'relative' (in the aforesaid sense of limited to) and solely enforceable against unfair acts of appropriation.

Conversely, in the absence of a breach of confidentiality or other competitive misbehaviour, no liability arises from the acquisition and use, even for competitive purposes, of previously confidential information. Thus, the use thereof cannot be enjoined.[3] Freedom to utilize the information

---

[1] According to Note 10 to Article 39(2) (such Note being part of the official text of the TRIPS Agreement), 'a manner contrary to honest commercial practices' means 'at least practices such as breach of contract, breach of confidence and inducement to breach, and includes the acquisition of undisclosed information by third parties who knew, or were grossly negligent in failing to know, that such practices were involved in the acquisition'. See also MODEL PROVISIONS ON PROTECTION AGAINST UNFAIR COMPETITION art. 6 (World Intellectual Property Organisation 1996) (indicating the circumstances under which use of trade secret constitutes an act of unfair competition); Surinder Kaur Verma, *Intellectual Property Protection of Trade Secrets and Confidential Information*, in INTELLECTUAL PROPERTY AND MARKET POWER: ATRIP PAPERS 2006–2007, 771–86 (Gustavo Ghidini and Luis Mariano Genovesi eds., 2008).

[2] For an historical overview, see G. Ghidini, *La concorrenza sleale dalle corporazioni al corporativismo*, 5 POLITICA DEL DIRITTO 64 (1974). As specifically concerns trade secrets, see also K. Jorda, *Patent and Trade Secret Complementariness: An Unsuspected Synergy*, 48 WASHBURN L.J. 1, 8 (2008).

[3] For a critical analysis, see Pamela Samuelson and Suzanne Scotchmer, *The Law and Economics of Reverse Engineering*, 111 YALE L.J. 1575, 1582–4 (2002). The authors note that: 'Courts have treated reverse engineering as an important factor in maintaining balance in intellectual property law. Federal patent law allows innovators up to twenty years of exclusive rights to make, use, and sell an invention, but only in exchange for disclosure of significant details about their invention to the public. This deal is attractive in part because if an innovator chooses to protect its invention as a trade secret, such protection may be short-lived if it can be reverse-engineered. If state legislatures tried to make trade secrets immune from reverse engineering, this would undermine federal patent policy because it would "convert the . . . trade secret into a state-conferred monopoly akin to the absolute protection that a federal patent affords". Reverse engineering, then, is an important part of the balance implicit in trade secret law' (citations omitted).

occurs, in particular, when the secret is acquired by means of independent development, reverse engineering, lawful 'decompilation' of a product or a process openly marketed, and, *a fortiori*, when the secret becomes known thanks to accidental disclosure.[4] In other words, the 'owner' of a trade secret can only enjoy a precarious 'head start,' that is, an uncertain period of natural lead time during which the innovator can recoup its investments.[5]

II. THE NEW ITALIAN REGIME

In 2005, the clear borderline between the enforcement of unfair competition and the protection of intellectual property was obscured. As hinted by its title, the Codice della proprietà industriale (Italian Code on Industrial Property) (the 'Code'), the new legislation overturned the traditional approach embodied in article 6*bis* of the previous Patent Law, which had adopted the principle of TRIPS Article 39. First, the Code now includes confidential commercial and technical information in the general definition of 'intellectual property'.[6] Second, the new Code provides for 'absolute' protection for such information, expressly distinguished from – and added to – that stemming from the rules against unfair competition.[7]

In particular, the concept of a (protectable) secret encompasses any information which has an economic value by reason of being confidential, is submitted to reasonable measures to keep it as confidential, and is in fact not in the public knowledge nor easily accessible or inferable by an average

---

See also W.R. Cornish, and David Llewelyn, Intellectual Property: Patents, Copyright, Trade Marks and Allied Rights 313, 314 (5th ed. 2003); Rudolf Krasser, The Protection of Know-How in 13 Countries 27 (1972).

[4] In this respect, trade secret rights may be defined as 'disappearing rights' that become vulnerable to discovery and disclosure by others. See J. C. Stedman, *Trade Secrets*, 23 Ohio St. L.J. 4, 21 (1962).

[5] See Jerome H. Reichman, *Legal Hybrids Between the Patent and Copyright Paradigms*, 94 Colum. L. Rev. 1994, 2521 (1994); Jerome H. Reichman and Pamela Samuelson, *Intellectual Property Rights In Data?*, 50 Vand. L. Rev. 51, 60 (1997). Both the original innovator and subsequent innovators will be able to recoup development costs until the information protected as a trade secret is generally known throughout the industry. Once this happens, the information can no longer be priced above the market rate, so consumers pay the lower prices associated with a thoroughly competitive market. See also Jonathan R. Chally, Note, *The Law of Trade Secrets: Toward a More Efficient Approach*, 57 Vand. L. Rev. 1269, 1281 (2004).

[6] Code, arts. 1 and 2.

[7] *Id.* arts. 98 and 99.

expert of the field.[8] Thus, the new Italian Code designs the protection of trade secrets as an exclusive and absolute (*erga omnes*) proprietary regime, thereby 'upgrading' confidential information to the status of an object of a genuine intellectual property right.

Specifically, the owner of the trade secret is allowed to prevent anybody from acquiring and using it, independently of the breach of explicit or implied secrecy obligations and, more broadly, of the performance of acts of unfair competition. The Code makes secrecy obligations a requisite of the legal notion of confidential information, but not a condition for protection.[9] Further, the provision clearly depicts 'unfair competition' as a possibly concurring circumstance, which does not at all condition, or modify, the aforesaid new regime of absolute protection.[10] Under the new rules, then, a party may be charged with infringement of a secret even if the confidential information was acquired by lawful means, such as through the acquiror's own activities, or by accident, or through bona fide purchase without knowledge of the unlawful conduct.[11] As a result, the traditional dichotomy that characterized access to trade secrets as lawful or unlawful conduct disappears; any attempts to learn a rival's firm trade secret is now an infringement of a property right.

III. A CRITICAL ASSESSMENT

The new regime and its economic motivations can be criticized for its basic, irreconcilable contradiction with the pro-competitive features of

---

[8] *Id.* art. 98. The condition about 'reasonable measures' is similar to U.S. law. See Mark A. Lemley, *The Surprising Virtues of Treating Trade Secrets as IP Rights*, 61 STAN. L. REV. 311 (2008) (suggesting that the reasonable measures requirement is functional, as it discourages firms from engaging in costly and inefficient self-help, substituting it with a legal system); see also Edmund W. Kitch, *The Law and Economics of Rights in Valuable Information*, 9 J. LEGAL STUD. 683, 698 (1980) (noting that the reasonable precautions requirement allows courts to identify what secrets are sufficiently secret and demands that employers provide notice to employees of those ideas considered trade secrets); see Robert G. Bone, Chapter 3.

[9] P. Auteri, *Commento al nuovo art. 6bis l. invenzioni, nel Commentario al d.lgs. 19 marzo 1996, n. 198*, in LE NUOVE LEGGI CIV. COMM. 124 (1998).

[10] Code, art. 99 clearly states that its regime applies 'save the application of the unfair competition regime . . .'.

[11] For an analysis of independent discovery in trade secret law, see Surinder Kaur Verma, *Protection of Trade Secrets under the TRIPS Agreement, and Developing Countries*, 1 J. WORLD INTELL. PROP. 723 (1998).

the patent paradigm,[12] especially as embodied in the national laws enacting the European Patent Convention (EPC). These laws are traditionally construed so as to favour dynamic innovation; that is, the process whereby innovation fosters competition and competition is presumed to lead to more innovation.[13] In particular, our concerns focus on three intersecting norms of the current innovation system:

(a) limitations on the reach of the patent right;[14]
(b) the belief that a proprietary right should be secured only when

---

[12] The fundamental bases of this argument are questioned by Michael Abramowicz and John F. Duffy, *Intellectual Property for Market Experimentation*, 83 N.Y.U. L. Rev. 337 (2008). According to the authors: 'One of the common justifications for trade secret law is that it serves a purpose similar to the patent system: protection of secrets encourages firms to invest in the production of valuable secrets and thus in technical and scientific advances. Yet this theory has some important difficulties. First, one of the main policies of the patent system is to ensure that nonobvious technical information is made public and is not kept as a trade secret. A firm can pay a heavy price for maintaining nonobvious technological information as a trade secret – including the possibility that another firm may patent that information and enjoin the original creator's use. Second, it seems puzzling that the law should seek to protect technical advances that are so minimal that they would not qualify for patent protection, presumably because they are obvious. A partial answer to this puzzle is that trade secret protection avoids the transaction costs associated with attempts to secure patents, but this answer purports to reduce trade secret law to a kind of second-class intellectual property protection for relatively unimportant innovations'.

[13] Prof. Steven D. Anderman has pointed out that 'within each legal system, the different means used by intellectual property rights legislation and competition law operate in many ways in conjunction rather than in conflict with each other'. Steven D. Anderman, *International Competition Law/IP 'Interface'*, in The Interface Between Intellectual Property Rights and Competition Policy 5 (Steven D. Anderman ed., 2007) ('Interface'). On the intersection between intellectual property and competition, see Mark A. Lemley, *A New Balance Between IP and Antitrust*, 13 SW. J. L. & TRADE AM. 237 (2007); R. Pitofsky, Antitrust and Intellectual Property: Unresolved Issues at the Heart of the New Economy, paper presented at the Conference on Antitrust, Technology and Intellectual Property, University of Berkeley, California, March 2, 2001, available at www.ftc.gov/speeches/pitofsky/ipf301.shtm; see also Gustavo Ghidini, Profili Evolutivi del diritto Industriale-Innovazione (2008); V. Falce, Profili pro-Concorrenziali Dell'istituto Brevettuale (2008).

[14] See e.g., Bilski v. Kappos, No. 08-964, slip op. at 43 (2010) ('[Sometimes] *too much* patent protection can impede rather than "promote the Progress of Science and the useful Arts"', quoting Laboratory Corp. v. Metabolite Laboratories, Inc., 548 U.S. 124, 126 (2006) (Breyer, J., dissenting from the dismissal of certiorari)). The dysfunctions deriving from such trends are pointed out by Adam B. Jaffe and Josh Lerner, Innovation and Its Discontents: How Our Broken Patent

the overall benefits for innovation surpass the social costs arising from the subtraction of the *quid inventum* from the public domain; and

(c) the preference for a regulation which, from its prerequisites, might guarantee a cautious balancing between the need to promote innovation and the acknowledgement that even imitation and improvement through imitation are necessary to foster innovation and a well functioning market economy.[15]

These norms, as embodied in most jurisdictions, extend the competitive arena to all the firms that participate in the overall innovative process, thus allowing them to obtain patents of their own, if or when they realize non-trivial substitutes or improvements on the first mover's technology. All three are violated by the Italian 2005 'reform'.

Thus, the new regime allows in principle that all sorts of commercial information, including customer lists and sales figures, marketing, professional and managerial procedures, to benefit from the exclusive right (*ius excludendi alios*).[16] In contrast to patent law, the trade secrecy regime

---

SYSTEM IS ENDANGERING INNOVATION AND PROGRESS, AND WHAT TO DO ABOUT IT (2004).

[15] See Bonito Boats, Inc. v. Thunder Craft Boats, Inc., 489 U.S. 141, 146 (1989). Or, as Ghidini has put it: 'Third parties paying a reasonable royalty to the IP right holder in order to obtain access to a certain technology cannot be equated to free riders. The latter do not pay anything, of course. Moreover, . . . licensing can be a valuable source of revenues, of profits even equal or superior to the ones deriving from direct sales by the IP right holder. At the same time, paying access based on a truly competitive compensation preserves for the IP holder its competitive advantage'. Gustavo Ghidini, Panel Discussion, *To What Extent Does IP Require/Justify a Special Treatment under Competitive Rules?*, in EUROPEAN COMPETITION LAW ANNUAL 2005: THE INTERACTION BETWEEN COMPETITION LAW AND INTELLECTUAL PROPERTY LAW 10 (Claus Dieter Ehlermann and Isabela Atanasiu eds., 2007).

[16] See Abramowicz, *supra* note 12, at 391: 'justifying trade secret law as an appropriate social subsidy to encourage market experimentation makes for a more solid foundation. This view accounts for why trade secret law protects information such as customer lists and other data that would naturally be produced during the ordinary course of business. In our view, then, the goal of trade secret law is not to encourage the production of that information so much as the production of the business. Sometimes, of course, a business's success will be difficult to disguise, but even then there might be uncertainty about whether the business is so successful as to justify entry by a competitor. The law protects whatever business data can be hidden, thus discouraging subsequent entry, increasing a first entrant's expected share of rents, and creating stronger incentives for the market experiments that produce the data. On our theory, trade secret law may be overinclusive – it protects

utilizes a functional definition for determining what is a protectable subject, with the consequence that virtually anything maintained in secret by a business enterprise that affords it a competitive advantage is eligible for the new and absolute trade secret protection.[17] In this regard, the new legislation circumvents the boundaries of the patent system as set up by the EPC, which clearly keeps presentations of information and business methods, and *a fortiori* simple bits of information, outside the arena of patentability.[18]

Even within the realm of strictly technical information, the new regime circumvents basic principles of the patent system. The inventor can secure absolute protection regardless of the possible lack of novelty and inventive character of the undisclosed information.[19] As a result, the ambit of protected subject matter is much wider than that envisioned by the TRIPS

---

copycat businesses too – but in general, innovators are the businesses that have the most information worth protecting'.

17 See Andrew Beckerman-Rodau, *The Choice Between Patent Protection and Trade Secret Protection: A Legal and Business Decision*, 84 J. PAT. & TRADEMARK SOC'Y 371 (2002). The benefits for the trade secret owner in comparison to those of the public are analysed by Michael P. Simpson, Note, *The Future of Innovation: Trade Secrets, Property Rights, and Protectionism – An Age-Old Tale*, 70 BROOK. L. REV. 1121, 1149–55 (2005). On the issue, see also S.J. Soltysinski, *Are Trade Secrets Property?* 17 INT'L REV. INDUS. PROP. & COPYRIGHT L. 331 (1986). The extension of trade secret protection to the realm of commercial information has been questioned by Prof. Robert G. Bone, who has queried: 'It is unclear . . . whether trade secret law is needed to encourage the production of non-technological information. After all, a firm must have a marketing plan and must compile financial data in any event, if it is to compete effectively. The anticipated profit from product sales is itself an inducement to create this information, and firms can use trademarks to capture at least some of the benefit of a marketing plan. Conceivably, a firm might invest more if it knew it could protect the results through trade secret law, but it is not evident that the additional investment would enhance competition or product quality enough to justify the social costs'. Robert G. Bone, *A New Look at Trade Secret Law: Doctrine in Search of Justification*, 86 CAL. L. REV. 241, 282 (1998).

18 Convention on the Grant of European Patents, October 5, 1973, 13 I.L.M. 270 (as amended by Revision Act of November 29, 2009) (EPC), art. 52.

19 See Vincent Chiappetta, *Myth, Chameleon or Intellectual Property Olympian? A Normative Framework Supporting Trade Secret Law*, 8 GEO. MASON L. REV. 69, 77 (1999). Prof. Rudolf J.R. Peritz has noted that 'the incentive to invent is better understood as merely coincidental to trade secret protection because claimants are not required to prove innovation . . . In contrast to copyright and patent protection, courts and policy makers are not called upon to determine a level of protection that optimizes ex ante incentives to invent. Rather, they are asked to make an ethical determination whether an accused party is a free rider in the extreme case – someone who has engaged in conduct akin to theft, fraud, or abuse of

Agreement or provided for by the EPC, which requires (or grants) protection only to advances that involve an inventive step.[20] The end result of failing to filter out non-inventive technologies is that the trade secret owner can propertize the patent-free zone and thus diminish the ambit of the public domain.

Furthermore, by across-the-board relocation of a misconduct-grounded liability rule into the property right realm, the new regime strongly reduces the incentive to patent. This is especially true in those cases (typically concerning processes) where the innovative features cannot be easily perceived by an average expert through an examination of the patented advance. Indeed, since the trade secret comes to enjoy the same proprietary protection as a patent, why should anyone patent if that person can get an exclusive right in another manner? Why incur the high (and sunk) costs of patent examination and registration when the new intellectual property right is offered at no cost? Why accept a fixed term of exclusive exploitation when, in the absence of easy duplication,[21] a much longer, indefinite monopoly is possible? And, most importantly, why disclose the innovation to the vast public of actual and potential competitors?[22] With overly generous trade secrecy protection, it could well be that even pioneer inventions become known quite late, slowing down the overall pace of subsequent (derivative and substitutive) innovation and depressing dynamic competition. By reducing the incentive to patent, the new protection of trade secrets will also allow inventors to avoid national working requirements. Further it will enable them to pursue strategies of programmed obsolescence: in the absence of potential competition, they could undermine the

---

trust'. *Competition Policy and its Implications for Intellectual Property Rights in the United States*, in INTERFACE, *supra* note 13, at 155.

[20] Agreement on Trade-Related Aspects of Intellectual Property Rights art. 27, April 15, 1994, 33 I.L.M. 81 (1994) (TRIPS), art. 27; EPC, arts. 52 and 56.

[21] On the issue, see generally Vincenzo Denicolò and Luigi Alberto Franzoni, *Innovation, Duplication and Contract Theory of Patents*, in THE ECONOMICS OF INNOVATION: INCENTIVES, COOPERATION, AND R&D POLICY (Roberto Cellini and Luca Lambertini eds., 2006).

[22] 'The tension is greatest in the relationship between trade secrets and patents because encouraging concealment of potentially patentable inventions conflicts directly with patent policy's principal goal of encouraging dissemination of knowledge. The upshot is a patent law that disfavours trade secrets'. Peritz, *supra* note 19, at 155. See also James R. Chiappetta, *Of Mice and Machine: A Paradigmatic Challenge to Interpretation of the Patent Statute*, 20 WM. MITCHELL L. REV. 155, 168 (1994); GHIDINI, *supra* note 13; FALCE, *supra* note 13; PROFILI PRO-CONCORRENZIALI DELL'ISTITUTO BREVETTUALE 101–22.

interests of consumers and innovation alike by delaying market entry of improved products as long as the earlier versions keep selling.

In short, upgrading of trade secrets to the upper circle of intellectual property rights frustrates the informative function linked to the mandatory public disclosure of the patented invention. It is all too evident that the balance that the patent paradigm expresses between private and public interests – privatizing the exploitation, publicizing the teachings[23] – would easily be disrupted by the ability to obtain full protection for undisclosed information; the more so if the latter does not require the right holder to meet either the 'merit' conditions or the 'type' limitations required of patents. And because the exclusive right granted to the trade secret owner is conditioned on non-disclosure and continued secrecy, the criticized new regime can negatively affect the process of technology transfer. Most troubling, if the Italian approach were to become the international norm, the impact on developing countries, where progress depends on learning technological know-how from the developed world, would be severe.[24]

---

[23] *See* Fritz Machlup and Edith Penrose, *The Patent Controversy in the Nineteenth Century*, in 10 J. ECON. HIST. 1, 10 (1950): 'To secure [industrial progress] at a sustained rate it is necessary that new inventions become generally known as parts of the technology of society. In the absence of protection against immediate imitation of novel technological ideas, an inventor will keep his invention secret . . . Hence it is in the interest of society to induce the inventor to disclose his secret for the use of future generations. This can best be done by granting exclusive patent rights to the inventor in return for public disclosure of his invention'. See also Robert G. Bone, *Secondary Liability for Trade Secret Misappropriation: A Comment*, 22 SANTA CLARA COMPUTER & HIGH TECH. L.J. 529, 535 (2006): 'By rewarding secrecy, trade secret law encourages firms to keep secrets, and secrecy impedes the diffusion of information. When one firm's stronger trade secrecy prevents other firms from building on the information, the pace of innovation is likely to slow with negative effects on economic productivity'.

On the contrary, in Prof. Lemley's original opinion, trade secret law actually encourages broader disclosure and use of information, not secrecy. In fact, trade secret law develops as a substitute for the physical and contractual restrictions those companies would otherwise impose in an effort to prevent a competitor from acquiring information. In so doing, it encourages disclosure of information that companies might otherwise be reluctant to share for fear of losing the competitive advantage it provides. Besides, trade secret law reaches beyond contract law by allowing courts to infer the existence of a confidential relationship from circumstances in which transactions might be difficult or impossible without that assumption. *See* Mark A. Lemley, *The Surprising Virtues of Treating Trade Secrets as IP Rights*, Stanford Law School John M. Olin Program in Law and Econ., Working Paper No. 358 (2008), available at http://papers.ssrn.com/sol3/papers.cfm?abstract_id=1155167.

[24] See J.H. Reichman, *From Free Traders to Fair Followers: Global Competition under the TRIPS Agreement*, 29 N.Y.U.J. INT'L L. & POL. 11 (1997).

To put this another way, the traditional framework essentially uses trade secrecy to fill the gaps left by the patent system. Innovators who were unsure whether they met the patentability requirements (or knew they did not), firms that needed secrecy to maximize returns, and inventors who wanted to avoid the costs of patent filings could utilize the trade secrecy system to obtain some level of protection.[25] Under the new regime, trade secrecy no longer performs this function. Rather, it could easily replace the patent system across-the-board. This in turn annuls the legal policy line grounded on the complementarity between the two legal regimes that the classical paradigm had secured, namely providing different patterns of protection, respectively, for lower grade innovation of short-term market value and qualified invention that requires a longer and time-certain lead-time to recoup investments and ensure profits.

IV. THE ECONOMIC DRIVERS OF THE NEW REGIME

As usual in contemporary intellectual property law-making, strong corporate interests lobbied in favour of the criticized 'reform'. The bulk of the Italian economy is made up of medium and small-to-medium firms (some of the bigger ones live on monopoly- or incumbency-related rent seeking, or upon variously disguised public aids). Such firms' financial structure is often fragile, and can be strongly cost-strained. This means that they are rarely committed to high-level, long-term oriented research and development. Instead, they often concentrate their competitive efforts in low-level incremental (and subpatentable) innovation,[26] or on design, marketing, branding, pricing strategies, and the like. Also, as an intertwined consequence, they have not developed (with some exceptions) an 'intellectual asset management' culture in the modern sense.

This category of firm typically perceives patenting as a cost rather than as an opportunity. And this is especially the case because the Italian system has traditionally granted patent protection without any in-depth

---

[25] See J.H. Reichman, *Beyond the Historical Lines of Demarcation: Competition Law, Intellectual Property Rights, and International Trade After the GATT's Uruguay Round*, 20 BROOK. J. INT'L L. 75, 77 (1993) (discussing the role of trade secrets law as well as other intellectual property law in the economy); see also Katarzyna A. Czapracka, *Antitrust and Trade Secrets: The U.S. and the EU Approach*, 24 SANTA CLARA COMPUTER & HIGH TECH. L.J. 207, 216–18 (2008) (clarifying that 'trade secrets supplement [patent protection]').

[26] See Reichman, *supra* note 25, at 86.

prior examination of novelty and inventiveness.[27] Thus, it has tended to produce 'uncertified' patents, basically incapable of attracting venture capital or representing a guarantee for financing.[28] Moreover, the lack of serious certification has translated into uncertainty as well as frequent and burdensome judicial challenges. This, in turn, has led to the widespread business sentiment that it is useless to patent, since even trifling modifications will bypass the right.[29] The result could well be that businesses with a greater capacity for innovation will benefit – again with negative effects on competition – from the protection offered by the reform. This would not only be in terms of the patent-related costs that would be saved, but also in terms of the competitive advantage they could gain from secrecy. Without the disclosure mandated by patent law, competitors would be less able to develop their own subsequent (derivative or substitutive) innovation. In short, the dominant position enjoyed by the owner of the secret would be strengthened.

Thus, it can be easily understood how this context of economic motivations, actual experience and perceptions has nurtured a diffuse quest for protection that is 'off-patent'.

V. CONCLUSION

Of course, the sentiments underlying Italy's reformed trade secrecy regime are understandable expressions of legitimate business interests that might be shared even in other countries with similar industrial structure. However, a far-sighted legislator should look above sectorial, though legitimate, *short-term* interests, and refuse to strike such a major blow to the innovation and competition-enhancing logic underlying the patent paradigm and its inherent trade-off of exclusivity for disclosure. As previously suggested, while that paradigm publicizes knowledge while privatizing

---

27 However, this has changed. Effective July 2008, the Italian Patent Office issues a prior art report made by the European Patent Office. See Italy: A Guide to Prior Art Searches – Managing Intellectual Property, available at www.managingip.com/Article/2004553/Italy-A-guide-to-prior-art-searches.html (last visited January 5, 2011).

28 *Cf.* Clarisa Long, *Patent Signals*, 69 U. Chi. L. Rev. 625 (2002) (describing many functions of U.S. patents).

29 See generally David D. Friedman *et al.*, *Some Economics of Trade Secret Law*, 5 J. Econ. Persp. 62 (1991); Robert P. Merges and others share the view that '[T]rade secrets, though important to all firms, are absolutely crucial for the small companies that drive innovation in many developing fields'. Robert P. Merges *et al.*, Intellectual Property in the New Technological Age 29 (2003).

exploitation, granting intellectual property protection to secrets privatizes both. The 'reform' also contradicts the general principle that in absence of patents or passing-off and other unfair conduct, imitation is a legitimate expression of the general freedom of competition.

Hence, we call for radical rethinking[30] of the 'reform' and restoration of the unfair competition perspective on trade secrecy protection in accordance with the dominant international framework, including the TRIPS Agreement. This would not necessarily amount to neglecting the interests of small and medium-size businesses, for their interests could be dealt with in other ways. For instance, the cost of obtaining patents could be reduced, and research and development projects, as well as innovation-oriented joint ventures, could be supported in other ways, such as through government grants or tax credits.

---

30 See note 1.

7 Trade secret law and information development incentives

*Michael Risch**

I. INTRODUCTION

Trade secrets differ from other forms of intellectual property in many subtle ways that affect incentives to invest in information development. These differences relate not only to the types of information protected, but also to the requirements one must meet to protect each type of information. The various divergences from and intersections between trade secret law and other intellectual property laws result in 'differential incentives', leading to differences in the amount and types of investments companies make in developing information. This chapter explores five types of differential incentives associated with trade secret law:

(a) trade secret law versus no trade secret law;
(b) trade secret law versus patent law;
(c) trade secret law versus copyright law;
(d) trade secret law versus trademark law;
(e) trade secret law versus right to privacy.

As discussed in more detail throughout the chapter, these comparisons flow directly from differences in the underlying theories for providing protection to different types of information.

The theoretical framework for incentives provided by non-secret intellectual property protection is fairly well established. Copyright law and patent law are based in part on the theory that creativity and innovation, respectively, are incentivized by rewarding creators with limited governmental protection that facilitates recovery of investments in creation. Furthermore, the policies of copyright and patent law favor building on

* Associate Professor of Law, Villanova University School of Law. The author thanks Alan Hyde, Mark Lemley, Anne Lofaso, Sharon Sandeen, David Schwartz, Katherine Strandburg, and participants of the NYU Workshop on Trade Secrecy. Valuable research assistance was provided by Gabriele Wohl, Nate Griffith and Tommy Huycke.

prior work, as well as freedom for all to use subject matter that is outside the scope of protection.[1] The result is a consistent tension about the proper balance of protected versus public domain material.

On the other hand, trade secrets are treated in exactly the opposite way: the trade secret owner is rewarded for keeping information that may be neither new nor original away from the public for as long as possible. Thus, information that could not be copyrighted or patented is still protected for as long as the owner can keep the information secret. But trade secret law does not stop there; the overlap between regimes is such that information about some things that can be copyrighted or patented (indeed some that *are* already covered by copyright or patent) may also be held as a trade secret. For example, a computer software program may be simultaneously protected by copyright, patent and trade secret law. Its source code, a particular expression of the program's functionality, is protected as a literary work. Its functionality, the process by which it achieves a result, may be protected by patent law through the use of flowcharts without disclosure of all or even any source code. Finally, most of the source code can be maintained secretly; copyright registration does not require the disclosure of trade secrets and it is possible to register the copyright by submitting a redacted form that is virtually indecipherable.

Thus, the usual tension is skewed. All trade secret information is protected and none is in the public domain, but if any information ceases to be a trade secret, it may still not be part of the public domain if it is patented or copyrighted.

The overlap of trade secrets and other IP regimes leads to two criticisms of trade secret law. First, critics argue that the law does not provide a social benefit when secret information is hidden from the public domain. Second, critics argue that trade secret law provides little or no incentive to innovate because trade secrets are already privatized, and thus should not be treated as public goods. This chapter primarily addresses the second of these criticisms.[2]

---

[1] William M. Landes and Richard A. Posner, The Economic Structure of Intellectual Property 11, 115–23 (2003) (noting that the 'incentive' versus 'access' paradigm is important in intellectual property, but that it should not be the only analysis to consider); see *id.* at 115–23 (discussing public benefits of the fair use doctrine in copyright law). Note, however, that copyrighted works need not be published to be protected, but there is little doubt that the public benefits more when such works are published and when others can fairly use portions of them in new works.

[2] For a discussion of public benefits, see Mark A. Lemley, Chapter 5; Michael Risch, *Why Do We Have Trade Secrets?*, 11 Marq. Intell. Prop. L. Rev. 1 (2007).

The incentive criticism is right for the most part: trade secret law provides little incentive to innovate as compared to a world without trade secret law, for two possible reasons. First, the law provides little incentive because companies will create secret information even in the absence of the legal protection – trade secret law provides little protection that self-help protection does not. Second, the value of shared information (for example, in creating complementary products) means that often companies would rather share nominal secrets than spend money protecting them, such that trade secret laws are routinely disregarded in investment decisions. This chapter explores each of these alternate theories, as well as limits and exceptions to each.

Trade secret law does, however, provide some incentives to innovate *vis-á-vis* other types of intellectual property, although the incentives are not always obvious, intuitive or necessarily great. This chapter considers how trade secret law differs from other types of intellectual property laws, and uses those distinctions to show that trade secret law will have some effect on incentives to innovate when compared to other forms of protection. The goal is not to quantify such incentives, but rather to point out where the differential incentives exist so that future data gathering and empirical research can study just how much effect trade secrets have on innovation.

II. INCENTIVES: TRADE SECRET LAW VERSUS NO PROTECTION

One economic theory of trade secret law[3] is that trade secrets provide an incentive to create secret information by granting protection for that information, in much the same way that copyrights and patents protect certain intangible goods.[4] As discussed below, the protection of secret information that the law provides does incentivize the generation of information, but in a world without protection of trade secrets innovation would not be impacted as much as one might expect. It turns out that creating incentives to innovate is a very minor justification for trade secret law.[5]

---

[3] For discussion of non-economic theories, see Risch, *supra* note 2.

[4] A second, better, theory is that the availability of trade secret remedies provides a disincentive to spend money protecting secret information, which counterintuitively makes it cheaper to misappropriate information. This unusual use of moral hazard seeks to avoid an 'arms race' of protection. For further discussion, see Mark A. Lemley, Chapter 5; Risch, *supra* note 2.

[5] For further discussion of trade secrecy and incentives to innovate, see Robert G. Bone, *A New Look at Trade Secret Law: Doctrine in Search of Justification*,

There are two potential explanations for the law's lack of impact on incentives. First, because secret information can be protected through self-help, companies will create information whether or not there is a law to protect that information. The only question is how much companies will spend to protect the information.[6] Second, because some information is more valuable when shared, information secrecy may not necessarily maximize firm profit. As a result, in such cases, trade secret law would not incentivize the creation of information because companies would not choose to keep the information secret.[7] To be sure, each explanation has exceptions, which is why the incentive created by trade secret law is minimal, and not zero.

A. Inherent Secrecy Incentives

Patents and copyrights foster an incentive to create by allowing for a period of exclusive use. The exclusivity is granted because of the 'public good' nature of inventions and original works: once information is published, anyone can use it without diminishing the creator's ability to do so. If others could freely use inventions and original works, then the creator might not be able to recover the cost of creation. Thus, creators are allowed exclusive use for a period of time so they can more readily recoup costs of creation. In industries where there is no extra-legal ability to enforce exclusive use (such as book publishing), patent and copyright may be the only source of protection to encourage innovation.

Trade secrets do not fall into the 'public good' category like patents and copyrights because the disclosure of secret information for public use negates both secrecy and most of the value that could come from that secrecy. Thus, in the absence of forced disclosure,[8] the marginal incentive to innovate provided by trade secret law is small because companies would still protect secret information by, obviously enough, keeping such information secret. This is true even of patentable and copyright-

---

86 Cal. L. Rev. 241, 266–70 (1998); Vincent Chiappetta, *Myth, Chameleon or Intellectual Property Olympian? A Normative Framework Supporting Trade Secret Law*, 8 Geo. Mason L. Rev. 69 (1999).

6 See Mark A. Lemley, Chapter 5; Risch, *supra* note 2.

7 *See generally* Eric von Hippel and Georg von Krogh, Chapter 9.

8 One would expect a forced disclosure rule to hinder incentives for innovation. The extent of such an effect would depend on the mix of potentially patentable innovations versus unpatentable innovations. For a detailed discussion of forced disclosure, see Risch, *supra* note 2.

able information that is not publicly disclosed or easily discernable by competitors.[9]

Secret information need not be an invention: even the earliest trade secret law protected customer information.[10] However, secret information must be exploited non-publicly, or it cannot be exploited at all – at least not to competitive advantage. As a result, companies can and will use self-help mechanisms (such as locked doors and non-disclosure agreements) to keep information a secret, private good whether or not trade secret law provides a remedy for misappropriation. Even if an owner of secret information could not use it for internal purposes, then underlying contract law, and not trade secret law, would create an incentive to innovate by providing a mechanism to license secret information.[11]

Thus, if information can be kept secret through self-help, then owners will spend money to do so, even in the absence of the law.[12] For example, Robert Sherwood describes the costly efforts that businesses in Brazil and Mexico exert in an attempt to keep information secret in the absence of meaningful trade secret remedies.[13] Additional anecdotal evidence suggests that companies with offices in multiple countries will spend more money protecting secrets in those countries without trade secret remedies.[14] These examples provide evidence that it is not the law that drives generation of information, but rather that information will be generated in any event, and then protected by whatever methods are available.

Because secret information can be protected and exploited without law, the 'base level' of such information in a 'zero-IP' society – the level of

---

[9] Katherine J. Strandburg, *What Does the Public Get? Experimental Use and the Patent Bargain*, 2004 WIS. L. REV. 81, 106 (companies will develop secret inventions whenever there is a market for them, regardless of patent protection).

[10] Empire Steam Laundry v. Lozier, 130 P. 1180 (Cal. 1913). Further, a primary economic question is whether a company should divulge its information in a patent application. For a thorough discussion, see LANDES AND POSNER, *supra* note 1, at 294–333, 354–71.

[11] Rochelle Cooper Dreyfuss, *Dethroning Lear: Licensee Estoppel and the Incentive to Innovate*, 72 VA. L. REV. 677, 696–7 (1986); Luigi Franzoni and Vincenzo Denicolo, *Innovation, Duplication, and the Contract Theory of Patents*, in THE ECONOMICS OF INNOVATION: INCENTIVES, COOPERATION, AND R&D POLICY (R. Cellini and L. Lambertini eds., 2008).

[12] Bone, *supra* note 5, at 264–8; Michael P. Simpson, *The Future of Innovation: Trade Secrets, Property Rights, and Protectionism – An Age-Old Tale*, 70 BROOK. L. REV. 1121, 1144 (2005); Thomas Rønde, *Trade Secrets and Information Sharing*, 10 J. ECON. & MGMT. STRATEGY 391 (2001).

[13] ROBERT M. SHERWOOD, INTELLECTUAL PROPERTY AND ECONOMIC DEVELOPMENT 117–19 (1990).

[14] Risch, *supra* note 2.

secret information we would expect without protection – would remain high.[15]

Further, if a company cannot keep its secrets confidential through self-help, then trade secret protection will not add new ways to keep the information secret; the law requires reasonable efforts to maintain secrecy and then provides a remedy only for certain types of misappropriation. Unlike copyright and patent law, trade secret law does not privatize what would otherwise be freely accessible and usable information. Thus, trade secret law provides no incentive to create non-secret information.

1. No extraordinary monopoly rents

Another reason that trade secret law does not necessarily create an incentive to innovate is that the law (and even secrecy without the law) does not necessarily confer an opportunity for the owner to charge more for its products or services than would be available on the open market. Further, to the extent that trade secrets allow for some price control, it is the secrecy, not the law, that creates the incentive.

Many markets are slightly imperfect, such that product differentiation and barriers to entry can allow for higher prices. Thus, a trade secret might have competitive value as a product differentiator, but every company has information with competitive value. Trade secrets make it harder to copy the differentiator, but competitors can develop different secret differentiators.[16] Take customer lists, for example: knowing who to contact will reduce costs of sales vis-à-vis a company's competitors. This fact, however, does not mean that a company can extract monopoly pricing; while the company may have some advantage and even the ability to increase price for a short period, competitors eventually join the market and develop their own customer lists.

Even a secret process for making goods will not necessarily allow for monopolistic pricing. For example, assume there is a secret process for making food taste better or making a widget more cheaply. Producers compete with other food and widget makers, and they still have some price competition. Competitors will have their own methods for taste enhancement and cost reduction. As a result, development of the secret process will not be motivated very substantially by the law or any exclusionary rules. Instead the benefits are based primarily on the ability to keep the

---

[15] Bruce Abramson, *Promoting Innovation in the Software Industry: A First Principles Approach to Intellectual Property Reform*, 8 B.U. Sci. & Tech. L. 75, 94–5 (2002).

[16] G.B. Ramello, *Intellectual Property and the Markets of Ideas*, 4 R. Network Econ. 161 (2005).

secret. Selling food to slightly more people or at a slightly higher price provides sufficient incentives for most innovations. Unless the secret creates a unique product with no substitutes, it will not allow for pure monopoly rents.

One concrete example of both the incentive to create absent law and the lack of monopoly rents is the tax preparation software market: TurboTax and TaxCut. Each has source code that is a trade secret; having that source code gives each an advantage over the other to the extent that the code includes differentiating features, and both have an advantage over those who do not have a product and face the high cost of development as a barrier to entry. Yet, each product costs approximately the same amount; the two are in stiff competition with each other and with other tax preparation options (both software and non-software), implying somewhat competitive pricing.

Now, if an employee of Intuit, the maker of TurboTax, wants to enter the market cheaply, he or she might take the Intuit source code and call the new product 'SuperTax'. That employee will save development time, and can undercut the price the other two companies charge because of lower investment requirements.[17] That lower price does not mean that the original pricing was monopolistic, though market imperfections mean that the software was likely selling for more than its marginal cost, which is very low for software.[18]

Thus, even if trade secret law did not exist, Intuit would likely create a tax program if it saw market demand. Further, it would want to keep the TurboTax source code secret even in the absence of a law doing so. Finally, even if trade secret law gives Intuit a remedy against the misappropriating employee, that remedy does not provide monopoly rents from its secret source code. Instead, damages based on somewhat competitive pricing would have to suffice as the incentive to develop secret source code.

Note that copyrights and patents share similar pricing features where the invention is not a significant differentiator. While an invention might

---

[17] In theory, the price of the product would be the marginal cost of production because Intuit's development costs are sunk. However, return on development investment would be considered part of the marginal cost – an opportunity cost, but a cost nonetheless. This is obviously true in reality, because the cost of software is not zero, even in highly competitive markets (such as the tax market).

[18] This is similar to copyright protection in the same code. The copyright gives the developer a private good to sell; without protection, the code could be copied, driving the price to zero. Software is often described as a potential natural monopoly due to the high ratio between development costs, which are substantial in some cases, and virtually zero reproduction costs.

be incorporated into a device such as a DVD player, one cannot say that monopoly profits are available to the maker of the DVD player unless the invention creates a new product category. Indeed, in many areas innovation may occur despite the ability of others to freely imitate, precisely because of some competitive product differentiation.[19]

There are times that patents and copyrights will make a difference, primarily for inventions that are easily viewed and copied.[20] Unlike trade secrets, copyrighted and patented information may be publicly disclosed, so that the costs of creation may not be recouped. Thus, copyrights and patents provide protected product differentiators such that pricing may be slightly elevated in a mostly competitive market. Of course, competitors may create their own product differentiators, but they must do so without the benefit of the copyrighted or patented information, creating a slight barrier to entry. Furthermore, if the copyright or patent creates a new product without substitutes, pure monopoly pricing will be available.

2. Policy effects

The revelation that trade secret law per se does not provide an incentive to innovate could have an effect on how trade secret law and its remedies are analysed. Particularly, analysis that assumes trade secret law will create an incentive to innovate in all cases may not reach justified or complete conclusions. For example, Roger Blair and Thomas Cotter lump trade secret damages in with copyright law when considering the amount of damages to award in order to preserve the incentive to create works.[21] Cotter and Blair likely reach mostly sound conclusions because their analysis is based on deterrence of misappropriation/infringement, which is similar to the protection cost minimization theory of trade secrets.[22] Even so, their analysis could be enhanced by more explicit attention to the differences between the incentives created by trade secret and copyright law.

3. When does the law create an incentive?

There are a few areas, however, in which trade secret law will spur creation of secret information where such information might not have been developed in the absence of legal remedies. The following are some areas

---

[19] Michele Boldrin and David K. Levine, *Perfectly Competitive Innovation*, 55 J. MONETARY ECON. 435 (2008); Stephen N.S. Cheung, *Property Rights and Trade Secrets*, 20 ECON. INQUIRY 40 (1982).

[20] Strandburg, *supra* note 9.

[21] Roger D. Blair and Thomas F. Cotter, *An Economic Analysis of Damages Rules in Intellectual Property Law*, 39 WM. & MARY L. REV. 1585, 1642 (1998).

[22] Risch, *supra* note 2, at 59.

where neither self-help nor existing legal remedies would be sufficient to incentivize creation of the information.

a. Lack of absolute secrecy Where absolute secrecy would be too costly (or even impossible) through self-help, trade secret law will incentivize expenditures in innovation because it provides a remedy for misappropriation even if the owner only used 'reasonable means' instead of 'every means' to protect information.[23] The prototypical case is *E.I. duPont de Nemours & Co. v. Christopher*, in which the Fifth Circuit held that it was trade secret misappropriation to fly a plane over a construction site in order to learn about the new building's manufacturing facilities, even where such flight did not violate any other laws.[24]

Trade secret law incentivized construction of the building because it would have been extremely costly (and perhaps too costly for the builder) to protect the construction site from airplane surveillance. Money spent on protection would have reduced the money available to spend on the actual building and its secret manufacturing facility.

While some have called this decision an outlier,[25] this type of incentive will become more important as surveillance technology improves[26] – if all buildings required Pentagon-like construction in order to protect commercial secrets, incentives to create secret information would be much reduced.

b. Government regulation Where companies deal with government agencies for product approval or for other regulatory purposes, trade secret law will provide a separate incentive for innovation. It is unlikely that government agencies will negotiate separate non-disclosure agreements with each affected constituent, but many regulatory laws require state agencies to maintain the secrecy of information that qualifies as a trade secret without the need for an agreement to do so. Without trade secret laws, such information either would not be created or would have low value due to public availability, reducing the incentive for its creation. Of course, without trade secret laws, the government might be more willing to protect information by contract, but even then the costs of doing so may

---

23 Cheung, *supra* note 19, at 44.

24 431 F.2d 1012 (5th Cir. 1970).

25 Landes and Posner, *supra* note 1.

26 Rochelle Cooper Dreyfuss, *Trade Secrets: How Well Should We be Allowed to Hide Them? The Economic Espionage Act of 1996*, 9 Fordham Intell. Prop. Media & Ent. L.J. 1, 37 (1998).

be prohibitive. David S. Levine in Chapter 16 discusses trade secrets in government regulation in more detail.

c. Multi-stage manufacturing Where products are manufactured by multiple companies in a multi-stage process, each link in the manufacturing chain may have a non-disclosure agreement with the links directly on each side, but there will be no privity of contract between links that are more than once removed from earlier or later stages. Also, in some industries information sharing agreements are rare due to custom or transactions costs.[27] Non-privity and informal transactions might not pass contractual muster, but trade secret law still imposes a duty of secrecy on the entire chain, such that each link that seeks a non-disclosure agreement would be able to enforce its rights even without a contract.[28] This makes it less costly to enter into such contracts, and thus enhances the desire to innovate.[29] Without trade secret law, parties might be more likely to obtain iron-clad contracts with all parties; here trade secret law creates incentives by reducing a particular type of protection cost.

d. Employer-owned information In industries where information is typically owned by the employer by operation of law rather than by contract[30] and in occupations where information is typically owned by the employer without an assignment agreement (such as sales contact information), trade secret law will provide an incentive to develop information separately from any contractual obligations. Because norms would militate against non-disclosure contracts, companies might not create or share the information as readily to avoid information loss.

This incentive is likely quite low. First, to the extent that such information is necessary for doing business, it might be created even without trade secret law.[31] Second, if the information were valuable enough, lack of trade secrecy protection might lead to new norms of contractual protection.

Similarly, the notion of a 'company' keeping information secret

---

[27] Dan L. Burk and Brett H. McDonnell, *The Goldilocks Hypothesis: Balancing Intellectual Property Rights at the Boundary of the Firm*, 2007 U. ILL. L. REV. 575, 601–2.

[28] Dan L. Burk, *Intellectual Property and the Firm*, 71 U. CHI. L. REV. 3, 8–9 (2004).

[29] *Id.* at 615; Robert P. Merges, *A Transactional View of Property Rights*, 20 BERKELEY TECH. L.J. 1477, 1507 (2005); Cheung, *supra* note 19, at 44.

[30] California Labor Code § 2860 (West 2003); Nathan Newman, *Trade Secrets and Collective Bargaining: A Solution to Resolving Tensions in the Economics of Innovation*, 6 EMP. RTS. & EMP. POL'Y J. 1, 43 (2002).

[31] Bone, *supra* note 5, at 272.

simplifies the complexities associated with multi-employee development and portable work experience. Information is often developed by multiple employees and it is difficult to manage any given employee's ownership claims on information. Contract law cannot fully compensate for multi-employee development because some states bar non-competition agreements and most states frown on employers keeping employees from using their general knowledge and skills for new employers. Separating general knowledge from specific trade secrets can be difficult.

However, trade secret law will give employers an incentive to invest in innovation because even if each employee claims that his or her own knowledge comprises personal skills and experience that can be transported from job to job, the employee cannot claim to own the information developed by others.[32] Trade secret law thus creates a framework for companies to protect shared innovation as against individual employees who might claim to own pieces of the whole as general knowledge.[33]

This incentive should not be overstated. Multiple departing employees who form a competing company might claim that their combined general skills are the same as what their previous employer viewed as a trade secret. Further, employee incentives to innovate for an employer will be reduced if trade secrets cannot be separated from general experience.[34] As a result, the employer must strike a delicate balance between general knowledge and specific secrets, to jointly maximize employer investments in development of information and employee incentives to create valuable secrets for the employer. Doing so may mean relinquishing some potential trade secrets to employees.

e. Non-disclosure agreements In states where non-disclosure agreements are only enforced if the information to be protected is a trade secret, then trade secret law creates an incentive that is co-extensive with contract law. This incentive, however, is illusory; in a world without trade secret law (which pre-empts other laws under the Uniform Trade Secrets Act in any event), courts would likely enforce secrecy contracts because no law would stop them from doing so.

The above differential incentives are all related. First, they appear in the gaps created by contract, tort and self-help. These gaps may be due to

---

32 Burk and McDonnell, *supra* note 27, at 618.

33 *Id.* at 614; Newman, *supra* note 30, at 35–6.

34 Burk and McDonnell, *supra* note 27, at 608–9; Newman, *supra* note 30, at 33–4; Dreyfuss, *supra* note 26, at 38–9.

the type of information, the type of self-help available, or even the background law.

In addition to the above categories, to the extent that trade secret laws eliminate wasteful spending or otherwise reduce the cost (or increase the value) of research, then companies may spend more on generating certain types of intellectual assets.[35] Such shifting of expenditures, however, is not the type of incentive envisioned by this chapter because the shift need not necessarily be toward information development. Indeed, *any* cost constraint or subsidization will give incentives to shift limited expenditures among different ways to make money, including information development; this chapter primarily addresses whether or not the protection enhances innovation by creating a greater return on intellectual property investments.[36]

The distinction is an area of potential further research. For example, it would be interesting to know whether barring the use of high-tech surveillance creates an incentive to create information where no incentive might otherwise exist or whether barring such surveillance simply decreases the cost of hiding information that would have been created anyway. The answer likely differs by industry and information type.

B. The Value of Shared Information

An alternative reason why trade secret laws might provide little incentive to create information is that companies do not necessarily value the secrecy of information, but instead maximize profit by sharing information.[37] Alan Hyde, for example, argues that areas of high worker mobility have greater innovation due to the value of shared information.[38] Further,

---

[35] Dreyfuss, *supra* note 26, at 39.

[36] See, e.g., Petra Moser, *How do Patent Laws Influence Innovation? Evidence from Nineteenth-Century World's Fairs*, 95 Am. Econ. Rev. 1214, 1231 (2005) (in countries without patent laws, innovation shifted toward industries in which secrecy was available).

[37] See von Hippel and Krogh, *supra* note 7.

[38] Alan Hyde, Working in Silicon Valley: Economic and Legal Analysis of a High-Velocity Labor Market (2003); Lawrence Lessig, The Future of Ideas: The Fate of the Commons in a Connected World 70–1 (2001); Paul Almeida and Bruce Kogut, *Localization of Knowledge and the Mobility of Engineers in Regional Networks*, 45(7) Mgmt. Sci. 905 (1999); John Dubiansky, *The Role of Patents in Fostering Open Innovation*, 11 Va. J.L. & Tech. 7 (2006), 14; Ronald J. Gilson, *The Legal Infrastructure of High Technology Industrial Districts: Silicon Valley, Route 128, and Covenants not to Compete*, 74 N.Y.U. L. Rev. 575, 600–1 (1999).

unclear definitions of what specific information employers consider to be trade secrets[39] increase the likelihood of knowledge sharing.[40] Ben-Atar goes so far as to argue that America's early economic development was founded on the emigration of skilled labor from Europe to the United States and the ensuing knowledge transfer.[41] Knowledge now flows from the United States to other countries as well.

Patent citations illustrate this point. Patent citation studies show that inventors are more likely to cite patents of local companies than distant companies.[42] This implies that information disseminates more readily in local regions as employees move from company to company, and by extrapolation secret information is similarly being shared. Further studies show that patent citation knowledge is shared most readily in Silicon Valley, where worker mobility is highest.[43] Also, 'connectedness' may be a key factor in innovation,[44] implying that the value of shared information is strongest where there is direct sharing between people.

Assuming that sharing secret information is widespread, companies in theory do not consider the availability of trade secret laws when generating information; they either assume that they will not enforce their rights or that the law will not provide a remedy for most information leakage.[45] Studies that show high levels of innovation in spite of unused trade secret protection imply that trade secret laws do not provide any additional incentive to innovate.[46] Gilson, for example, posits that companies unhappy with information spillovers in Silicon Valley due to weak trade secret law would move out of the state, but in fact they have not done so.[47]

Whether Professor Hyde's findings in Silicon Valley can be extrapolated to all geographic regions and all trade secrets is questionable. Citation

---

[39] James Pooley, *The Top Ten Issues in Trade Secret Law*, 70 TEMP. L. REV. 1181, 1182 (1997).

[40] Newman, *supra* note 30, at 39; Almeida and Kogut, *supra* note 38.

[41] DORON S. BEN-ATAR, TRADE SECRETS 99–101 (Yale University Press, New Haven, 2004).

[42] ADAM B. JAFFE AND MANUEL TRAJTENBERG, PATENTS, CITATIONS AND INNOVATIONS 174–5 (2002).

[43] Almeida and Kogut, *supra* note 38.

[44] Lee Fleming, Charles King III and Adam I. Juda, *Small Worlds and Regional Innovation*, 18 ORG. SCI. 938 (2007).

[45] Yuval Feldman, *Experimental Approach to the Study of Normative Failures: Divulging of Secrets by Silicon Valley Employees*, 2003 U. ILL. J.L. TECH. & POL'Y 105, 119.

[46] Robert P. Merges, *The Law and Economics of Employee Inventions*, 13 HARV. J.L. TECH & POL'Y 1, 51 (1999); LESSIG, *supra* note 38.

[47] Gilson, *supra* note 38, at 620–2.

studies may push shared information theory beyond its limit; patents that are cited in other patents are necessarily public, and reliance on patent citations to make the argument assumes that secret as well as public information is shared in the regional network. It is also unclear whether sharing increases value everywhere. For example, Sherwood's study of research parks in Brazil and Mexico shows the type of free-flowing information that Hyde posits in Silicon Valley, yet innovation in the former areas hardly mirrors that of the latter.[48]

Newman argues that extensive sharing is not desirable, even in Silicon Valley, and theorizes that free mobility of information merely transfers knowledge from lower-skilled workers to 'opportunistic skilled workers' at a cost of profitability among large companies, who can no longer provide job security to lower-skilled workers.[49] Similarly, high turnover rates may hurt innovation by decreasing the incentives of companies to invest in their employees' human capital.[50] Newman argues that a better solution is governmental encouragement and mandates that facilitate protected technology collaboration, as seen in Japan, rather than relying on ex-employees and low job security to create positive network effects of information.[51]

III. INCENTIVES TO INNOVATE AMONG DIFFERENT IP FRAMEWORKS

While trade secret law does not in and of itself always provide large incentives to innovate, it does provide protection different from that provided by other forms of intellectual property, and as such may provide differential incentives to create different types of intangible assets. These differences allow trade secret laws to avoid significant conflict with other intellectual property laws. That lack of conflict can shift resources toward certain types of investment in intangible assets, which leads to differential incentives to innovate depending on the type of protection available and selected by the innovator.

---

48 SHERWOOD, *supra* note 13, at 119–22.

49 Newman, *supra* note 30, at 46–7.

50 Bruce Fallick, Charles A. Fleischman and James B. Rebitzer, *Job-hopping in Silicon Valley: Some Evidence Concerining the Microfoundations of a High-Technology Cluster*, 88 R ECON. & STAT. 472 (2006). The reduction in investment may be outweighed by benefits of high mobility, especially in the computer industry.

51 Newman, *supra* note 30, at 36.

Understanding these differential incentives first requires examination of the differential protection available. Trade secrets are both similar to and dissimilar from other areas of intellectual property in a variety of ways:

(1) Unlike patented inventions, trade secret information need not be unique, novel or non-obvious to be protected.[52]
(2) In fact, trade secret information need not even be original, allowing for protection of information like names and phone numbers in a client list that would not be protected by copyright.[53]
(3) Unlike patent and trademark law, but like copyright, trade secret laws allow protection of identical information[54] if two parties independently discover it.[55] Two companies can own the same trade secret, though they arguably would never know it.
(4) Unlike all other forms of intellectual property, the trade secret right to exclude applies only when information is obtained by improper means, such as theft, breach of duty or confidence, or costly surveillance. This rule is arguably most like copyright's distinction between 'illicit copying' and fair use, reverse engineering, or independent development;[56] however, the analogy is weak because copyright does not require any wrongdoing other than the copying itself, whereas trade secret misappropriation requires improper means in addition to the 'copying'.
(5) Trade secret requirements resemble the patent requirement for usefulness[57] and the trademark requirement for actual use[58] because the trade secrets must have some independent economic value by being unknown to others. This threshold is relatively low, however, and minimal 'sweat of the brow' is usually sufficient

[52] 35 U.S.C. §§ 101–3 (2006).

[53] Feist Publications, Inc. v. Rural Telephone Service Co., 499 U.S. 340, 349 (1991); ABBA Rubber Co. v. Seaquist, 286 Cal. Rptr. 518 (Cal. Ct. App. 1991).

[54] Two parties can own the same trademark, so long as the mark protects different goods and services, or if they exclusively serve different geographic regions. Such overlap is not really 'identical' information as that term is used here because they actually designate different origination sources for different types of goods.

[55] California Civil Code § 3426.1(a) (West 1997) ('Reverse engineering or independent derivation alone shall not be considered improper means'). The Uniform Trade Secrets Act (UTSA) does not include this sentence, though reverse engineering is commonly accepted as an exception to improper means. Uniform Trade Secrets Act § 1 (amended 1985), 14 U.L.A. 437 (West Supp. 2006).

[56] 17 U.S.C. § 107 (2006).

[57] 35 U.S.C. § 101 (2006).

[58] 15 U.S.C. § 1051(a) (2006).

for protection.[59] Trade secrets only require potential value, while trademarks require actual use in commerce, which implies actual value.[60]

(6) With respect to registration, trade secrets are most like unregistered common law trademarks and unregistered copyrights. Unlike copyrights, there is no registration requirement prior to filing suit,[61] and unlike patents and trademarks, there is no examination.[62] The lack of registration means that trade secrets are often not clearly defined. This may justify weaker protection[63] and will certainly affect the types of innovations that are kept secret rather than copyrighted or patented.

(7) Finally, unlike a patent, which must meet strict novelty requirements, or a copyright, which must meet strict originality requirements, a trade secret need not meet strict secrecy requirements. All that is required are reasonable efforts to maintain secrecy, and information that is publicly available but obscure might still be secret, such as a posting on a single server on the Internet where no index points to the information.[64]

These differences and overlaps in protection can lead to differential incentives not only to create information, but also to create certain types of information. The following discussion compares the effect of trade secret law on such incentives in light of the laws of patents, copyrights, trademarks and privacy.

A. Trade Secret Law versus Patent Law

The differences in protection between patents and trade secrets will lead to different incentives to develop inventive information. Patent law and trade

---

59 Alex Foods, Inc. v. Metcalfe, 290 P.2d 646, 654 (Cal. Ct. App. 1955) (finding that peculiar 'likes and fancies' of customers are protectable).

60 But see 15 U.S.C. § 1051(b) (2006) (registration for intent to use).

61 17 U.S.C. § 411 (2006).

62 35 U.S.C. § 111 (2006); but see California Code of Civil Procedure § 2019.210 (West 2005) (requiring a plaintiff to identify the trade secrets at issue prior to discovery). Section 2019.210 is formerly and better known as § 2019(d).

63 Burk and McDonnell, *supra* note 27, at 608–9.

64 DVD Copy Control Ass'n v. Bunner, 10 Cal. Rptr. 3d 185, 192–3 (Cal. Ct. App. 2004) ('Publication on the Internet does not necessarily destroy the secret if the publication is sufficiently obscure or transient or otherwise limited so that it does not become generally known to the relevant people, i.e., potential competitors or other persons to whom the information would have some economic value').

secret law cannot be co-extensive because trade secrets must be secret and patents must be publicly disclosed. This dichotomy can lead to differing investments in different types of information, but the choices are more complex than that. As discussed below, there are potentially patentable inventions that an inventor might keep secret; there are inventions that are patentable but for which related information might be kept secret; and there are inventions that can never be patentable. These and other combinations lead to complex effects on incentives to innovate.

1. Limited terms

One of the primary differences between trade secrets and patents is the protection term. U.S. patents expire 20 years after the patent application is filed, and applications are generally published 18 months after they are filed, giving competitors a head start in developing non-infringing alternatives even before the patent issues.[65] Trade secrets, however, may be protected for as long as the owner can keep the information a secret.

As a result, businesses must decide whether exclusive rights for a relatively short period (offset by the commensurate disclosure) are more valuable than secrecy rights potentially exercised over the long term (offset by the risk of disclosure and independent development).[66]

A gating factor is the ability to keep the invention secret in the first place; inventions that can be easily studied make poor trade secret candidates.[67] Other factors affecting this differential incentive include the likelihood of obtaining a patent (and the commensurate loss associated with public disclosure but no patent) as well as the likelihood that others will independently develop the same innovation in the future, which would shorten the life of the trade secret.[68] Additionally, the desire to license the innovation is a concern – it is much less costly (and more common)

---

[65] Nisvan Erkal, *The Decision to Patent, Cumulative Innovation, and Optimal Policy*, 23 INT'L J. INDUS. ORG. 535 (2005); Sharon K. Sandeen, *Kewanee Revisited: Returning to First Principles of Intellectual Property Law to Determine the Issue of Federal Preemption*, 12 MARQ. INTELL. PROP. L. REV. 301, 344 (2008).

[66] Jared Earl Grusd, *Internet Business Methods: What Role Does and Should Patent Law Play?*, 4 VA. J.L. & TECH. 9, 47–9 (1999); Erkal, *supra* note 65; BRIAN C. REID, CONFIDENTIALITY AND THE LAW 62 (1986).

[67] Petra Moser, *Why Don't Inventors Patent?*, National Bureau of Economic Research, Cambridge, Working Paper No. 13294 (June 30, 2009) (inventors are less likely to patent where their inventions are more easily kept secret), available at http://ssrn.com/abstract=930241; Cheung, *supra* note 19; REID, *supra* note 66. Some have argued that in the limiting case patents and trade secrets are perfect substitutes where there is no risk of reverse engineering. Franzoni and Denicolo, *supra* note 11.

[68] Erkal, *supra* note 65. Strandburg, *supra* note 9, at 107–8 calls this the

to license patented inventions.[69] It appears that many innovations can be kept secret long enough to dissuade inventors not to file a patent; one study shows that approximately 15 percent of important innovations were patented, and that the patenting rate depends on secrecy.[70]

A final factor is whether part of the innovation can be patented and part can be kept secret. Firms will, if possible, choose an optimal mix of patenting conjoined with undisclosed know-how and improvements that are maintained as trade secrets.[71] U.S. patent law currently gives inventors a year to make this determination; commercial exploitation of secret inventions will nullify any patent filed more than a year after such exploitation.

2. Non-patentable subject matter

Some inventive information cannot be patented, such as newly discovered mathematical algorithms and natural phenomena. To the extent that businesses can make money from such non-patentable ideas (and keep them secret), then trade secret law would provide a differential incentive to develop such ideas.[72] Thus, this category might be a good way to measure what the incentive effect of trade secret law might be in the absence of patent law, because patent law might as well not exist for unpatentable subject matter.

For example, in *In Re Schrader*, the patent applicant developed a purportedly new way to calculate the winners of a particular type of auction.[73] The Federal Circuit Court of Appeals ruled that such an invention, no matter how novel, could not be patented because it was essentially a mathematical algorithm. Armed with this ruling, future developers of such mathematical methods will instead rely on trade secret law to protect innovative algorithms that have no application in a broader physical process.[74]

Included in this category is the tacit know-how that trade secret law can protect but that cannot be made concrete enough to patent. Also included are incentives for market experimentation, where only trade

---

'expected trade secret return', the amount that the inventor expects to earn before the secret information is discovered.

[69] Cheung, *supra* note 19, at 46; ASHISH ARORA, ANDREA FOSFURI AND ALFONSO GAMBARDELLA, MARKETS FOR TECHNOLOGY: THE ECONOMICS OF INNOVATION AND CORPORATE STRATEGY 262 (2001).

[70] See generally, Moser, *supra* note 67.

[71] Elisabetta Ottoz and Franco Cugno, *Patent-Secret Mix in Complex Product Firms*, 10 AM. L. & ECON. R. 142 (2008); REID, *supra* note 66, at 64–5.

[72] REID, *supra* note 66, at 62.

[73] 22 F.3d 290 (Fed. Cir. 1994).

[74] Moser, *supra* note 36 (in countries without patent laws, innovation shifted toward industries that provided effective secrecy).

secrets can protect information about whether a certain business plan will be successful.[75]

Like know-how, information developed by consultants might be incentivized by trade secret laws. Such knowledge providers sell pure ideas to their clients (sometimes applying such ideas to a particular problem), but they keep the storehouse of general knowledge a secret in order to offer a service that clients are willing to pay for. Trade secret law gives consultants a differential incentive to develop this knowledge because patent law provides no incentive whatsoever.

This incentive arguably applies only when the information would not have been created anyway. Indeed, one argument against patenting certain subject matter is that no incentive is needed to create such inventions in the first place,[76] and trade secret law should not be wrongly credited with creating an incentive either. The difficulty is determining whether it is trade secret law that encourages an incentive, rather than the underlying availability of secrecy through self-help mechanisms. One would expect the differential to be greatest in areas where self-help cannot fully protect secrecy but where trade secret law provides a remedy, such as where absolute secrecy cannot be assured at a reasonable cost.

On the other hand, the existence of a patent (or other intangible or even physical technology asset) may create an additional incentive to create or improve know-how on the part of manufacturers and consultants. Because patents and other technology often require additional information to be useful to the licensee (whether intended by the creator or not) a desire to license or sell the underlying asset will incentivize the creation or improvement of know-how that can be licensed as well. First, the know-how may become more valuable if it is coupled with complementary technology, such as a patent.[77] Second, including know-how in a license may allow patentees to receive royalties even if the patent is invalidated. Third, patents can make it cheaper to apply specific knowledge to 'a much broader array of applications' creating an additional incentive to create know-how in different areas.[78]

Note, though, that while trade secret law may provide an incentive

---

[75] Michael Abramowicz and John F. Duffy, *Intellectual Property for Market Experimentation*, 83 N.Y.U. L. Rev. 337, 390–1 (2008); but see Lessig, *supra* note 38 (arguing that market experimentation need not be (and often is not) secret in order to provide an incentive to experiment).

[76] Katherine J. Strandburg, *Users as Innovators: Implications for Patent Doctrine*, 79 U. Colo. L. Rev. 467, 476–7 (2008).

[77] Arora, Fosfuri, and Gambardella, *supra* note 69, at 116.

[78] *Id.* at 262.

to create non-patentable inventions, the result may be a suboptimal incentive. It might be that allowing inventors to patent currently unpatentable subject matter would provide more returns to them than are available through trade secrecy As a result, inventors currently might not have as much incentive to invest in development as they might if patents were available.

Also, inventors may not know which investments will yield inventions that fall outside current patentable subject matter. As a result, overall investment in development might be less than it could be because of the risk that investment will lead to non-patentable subject matter. This effect is exacerbated where the information is self-revealing and the inventor is unable to keep the resulting invention secret by contract or other means; because developers may not know whether the information will be self-revealing *ex ante*, investment may be even further depressed by the inability to patent certain subject matter.

These trade-offs are empirical questions, likely tied to particular industries, but even if some inventions might be developed without trade secrecy law, many potential inventions might never be pursued.

3. Obvious innovations

Somewhere between easily patentable innovations and unpatentable or clearly old ideas lie marginally patentable innovations: patentable subject matter that may or may not be obvious. Here, patent law and trade secrecy offer similar incentives to innovate. First, to the extent that an innovation is obvious due to the requirement of little research and development, then there will likely be little need for incentive in the first place – the improvement will happen in the ordinary course of business. Second, if an innovation is obvious, then it would likely be invented by others as well, eliminating the chance for obtaining a patent and significantly diminishing the value of secrecy.

This is not to say that there is no incentive to invest in the creation of obvious innovations. In the absence of costly research projects, such innovations would almost always be driven by business needs in the ordinary course of business. Thus, neither patent nor trade secret law would provide much additional push to develop 'necessary' inventions. Where the discovery is wholly unexpected, the differences between legal regimes would have almost no incentive effect as the discovery will have been complete at the time the company decides whether to file a patent or rely on trade secrecy.

If, however, *ex ante* investments are made in innovations that are not 'obviously obvious', such that patentability is uncertain, the choice between trade secret protection and patentability might very well create differential incentives. The calculus will depend on the type of innovation and the timing of the investment decision.

At the point of the research investment decision, trade secret law may encourage expenditures in areas that might not yield patents because trade secrecy will still preserve some value for 'obvious' discoveries.[79] The amount of investment will still vary, however. Where a research program is expected to yield at least some unlikely (that is, non-obvious) results, the amount spent on that program will depend on the perceived likelihood of patentability as well as the perceived value of any discovery in the competing protection schemes.[80] Perhaps counterintuitively, the ease of getting a patent may offset its value; as patents become easier to obtain their values may decrease.[81] Even if the patent route is selected, secrecy might be important for protecting intermediate results pending patent application and grant.[82]

In the pharmaceutical industry, for example, the availability of trade secret law will have little effect on drug incentives since the value of a secret pharmaceutical is near zero. However, where the data associated with pharmaceuticals may be kept secret, there may be an incentive to develop such complementary information. Indeed, 'data exclusivity' is an important policy issue precisely because such data cannot always be kept secret.[83]

With respect to business processes, however, trade secrecy may provide a valuable alternative to an otherwise risky patent application because a rejected patent will still be published, effectively destroying the trade secret.[84] Even so, patent law penalizes the choice not to patent: if someone else patents the same invention the secret first inventor can be sued for infringement despite being the first inventor.[85] Thus, the end effect on

---

79 Dreyfuss, *supra* note 11, at 732; REID, *supra* note 66, at 62–3.

80 Erkal, *supra* note 65.

81 Robert M. Hunt, *Nonobviousness and the Incentive to Innovate: An Economic Analysis of Intellectual Property Reform*, Federal Reserve Bank of Philadelphia, Working Paper No. 99-3 (April 1999), available at http://papers.ssrn.com/sol3/papers.cfm?abstract_id=160674.

82 Bone, *supra* note 5, at 271–2; Cheung, *supra* note 19, at 49; Hunt, *supra* note 81, at 11; Suzanne Scotchmer and Jerry Green, *Novelty and Disclosure in Patent Law*, 21 RAND J. ECON. 131 (1990).

83 See Rebecca S. Eisenberg, Chapter 18 for a further discussion of data exclusivity.

84 Christopher R. Balzan, *Mandatory Publication of Patent Applications Prior to Issuance of Patents: A Desirable Change in U.S. Policy?*, 18 LOY. L.A. INT'L & COMP. L. REV. 143, 147–50 (1995).

85 Burk and McDonnell, *supra* note 27, at 609. The law in other countries may not penalize prior secret users in the same way. REID, *supra* note 66, at 64. In the

innovation is ambiguous and situation specific; the likelihood that one will attempt to patent a marginal invention is not the same as the likelihood that one will expend resources to develop the invention in the first place.

4. Application costs

More practically, the cost of obtaining protection will cause differential incentives to innovate. Trade secrets are usable immediately, while the right to exclude a patented invention can take much longer to secure. The information covered by the patent application may be used immediately, but not for more than one year before filing. After that, the patent right is lost unless a filing is made. Filing an application, in turn, usually leads to a destruction of the trade secret 18 months later when the application is published. If, at the end of the process, no patent issues then the mere attempt at a patent will have left the owner with nothing. Thus, the application process places constraints on how and when information can be used and how long it will retain value as a secret. In most cases, the one year limit will not delay usage of an invention, but in those cases of costly delay, trade secret protection may be preferred because it allows immediate commercial use of the information.

For example, a company may develop a secret manufacturing process that requires extensive tweaking before the end product is available for mass production. The one year patent clock will begin to run as soon as the first test unit is produced and sold, but it might take two years of market testing before the end product is widely released. Even if the patent application were filed at the last possible moment, it would become public six months after mass production begins. The company would have to decide whether six months' lead time is sufficient. If so, then patent protection will be favored over secrecy. If not, then secrecy will be favored.

Even when patents issue, they can be costly to obtain,[86] and as such may not be used for relatively low value innovations, nor will they be used for innovations that take time to generate revenue when a firm has low cash flow and is unable to obtain significant financing.[87] By implication,

---

United States, secret users of business methods cannot be sued. 35 U.S.C. § 273 (2006).

[86] Applications can cost from U.S.$2,500 to U.S.$250,000 or more depending on the nature of the application and any challenges to it on appeal or during patent interferences. Even U.S.$2,500 will be cost prohibitive for many individual or small company inventors.

[87] Josh Lerner, *Patenting in the Shadow of Competitors*, 38 J.L. & ECON. 463 (1995).

smaller firms might focus more on trade secrecy and focused licensing, whereas large firms can develop a diversified portfolio of research and development.[88]

Further, the ease with which a development can be described will lead to differential incentives. Patent law requires an applicant to describe how a peer can make and use the invention at issue and to definitely claim the scope of the invention. If the innovator 'knows' a method of manufacturing but cannot describe it without expending significant costs, then trade secrets will provide a positive differential incentive to create such new methods.

This is not a far-fetched consideration given the role of apprenticeships throughout history. Methods that are taught through practice rather than through 'book learning' might be too costly or even impossible to translate into the language of a patent. Law practice is one example: firms develop information about how particular judges rule on particular matters. This information is usually a 'gut feel', learned through experience and not specific or definite enough to satisfy patent claim requirements. Such information is likely not even concrete or replicable enough to write down in an instruction manual. Nonetheless, law firms would be more likely to invest in the development and oral dissemination of such information throughout the firm if they could keep it secret, even though the information is too amorphous to be patentable.

B. Trade Secret Law versus Copyright Law

At first blush, one would not expect too many differential incentives to innovate between copyright law and trade secret law. In theory, the two regimes are co-extensive. For example, one might protect computer software source code as a copyrighted work as well as a trade secret because copyright registration does not require disclosure of trade secret source code.[89] Thus, whatever incentives copyright law provides should operate independently of any incentives that trade secret law provides. Closer examination, however, reveals that there are a few exceptions.

---

[88] Dreyfuss, *supra* note 11, at 680; Josh Lerner, *The Importance of Trade Secrecy: Evidence from Civil Litigation*, Harvard Business School, Working Paper No. 95-043 (2006), available at http://papers.ssrn.com/sol3/papers.cfm?abstract_id=6089.

[89] There is no requirement that a registration be filed at all in order to secure a copyright, though in the United States one must file a registration in order to pursue an infringement claim.

1. Uncopyrightable information

Certain types of information, such as ideas, facts, and processes, are uncopyrightable.[90] Abstract ideas and facts are not copyrightable because they are not written down; only expression is protected by copyright, and even then the underlying idea or fact is free for all to use. Further, non-creative expression, no matter how much 'sweat of the brow' was expended gathering the information, is afforded no copyright protection. For example, unwritten business plans, written product ideas, and customer names and telephone lists may be copied without infringement liability.[91]

Trade secret law, on the other hand, is precisely designed to protect unwritten business plans, written product ideas, customer lists and other non-creative and 'sweat of the brow' information. Trade secret law requires that information have some independent economic value, and that value is often expressed in terms of cost of creation. Thus, trade secret law is designed to protect certain types of information that copyright law expressly disclaims.

As such, trade secret law provides a clear differential incentive to create uncopyrightable information because alternative protection is unavailable. The lack of cross-correlation with copyright incentives means that in most cases the incentive would be no different than the incentives to create the information in a world without copyright law.

2. Copyright's effect on trade secret

There are also times when the incentive to develop secret uncopyrightable information does depend on the existence of copyright law. Copyright law provides an incentive to express or simply organize secret information in a creative way. In a world without copyright law, authors would still attempt to keep secret information secret; the existence of copyright law would not necessarily change the nature of that secret information.

However, because otherwise uncopyrightable information can gain copyright protection by being organized in a particular creative way, copyright law can create an incentive for trade secret owners to organize secret information in a particular way. For example, a secret pricing methodology might produce copyrightable price lists if the methodology is creative. For example, in *CDN Inc. v. Capes*,[92] the court affirmed copyrightability of individual coin prices where the prices were selected by a secret but creative examination of information in the public domain. It held that its

---

[90] 17 U.S.C. § 102 (2006).

[91] *Feist*, 499 U.S. 340, at 349.

[92] 197 F.3d 1256 (9th Cir. 1999).

prices were 'compilations of data that represent its best estimate of the value of the coins'.[93]

Similarly, because copyright law does not protect ideas or functionality, copyright law gives software authors an incentive to express those ideas in creative ways, such as creative variable names, creative 'pseudo-code' in comments, and creative source code organization.[94] The practical effect of such an incentive is to make it easier to identify identical copying by someone with access to the source code, which aids in detection and proof of both copyright infringement and trade secret misappropriation.

3. Trade secret's effect on copyright

Trade secret law might affect the type of copyrighted works that are created and how they are protected. Imagine a world without trade secret law: such a world would only allow for the protection of source code so long as a company can actually keep it secret. Furthermore, registration of the source code with the copyright office – a requirement to sue for infringement – would require disclosure of that source code because no legal regime would be available for authors to request a secret registration.[95]

What might software authors do to maximize profits in such a world? First, the author may choose to forego registration. It is true that copyright is created at the time the work is written down, but in the United State a registration is required to enforce the copyright. Without an enforcement mechanism, copyright law would create little or no independent incentive to create secret works,[96] or at the very least to distribute such works in a format that might be copyable. To be sure, this will not always be the case because publication of copyrighted material ironically makes it easier to

---

93 *Id.* at 1260. This ruling applied to *each* price, not the organization of the list of prices. *Id.* at 1259.

94 Pseudo-code is a non-functional representation of computer code written in plain English rather than in a computer language. For example, the computer code $c := a+b$ might be expressed in pseudo-code as 'add the values of variables a and b and assign the result to c'.

95 The discussion above explains how trade secrets might provide an independent incentive to create source code where the law provides protection from disclosure by a regulatory agency (here, the Copyright Office). Diane Zimmerman in Chapter 13 further discusses issues associated with copyright registration of trade secrets.

96 Of course, the Copyright Office might allow 'secret' registrations without trade secret law, but in a world where trade secrets are not recognized by law, there is no reason to expect governmental agencies to protect information just because a company wants to keep it secret. In that sense, the existence of the law shifts the mindset toward protection.

prove that someone else copied the work.[97] However, this might not prove to be enough of a benefit to induce authors to publish their source code – if it were, then they would already be doing so even with the benefit of trade secret law.

Second, if the author desired copyright registration, it might use a computer language that is not easily discernable or a format that is not easily copyable,[98] if the use of such a language or format would cost less than the potential loss due to copying, whether by undetected copying, inactionable fair use or copying of ideas only. For example, rather than using an easily readable high level language (such as the C programming language), a company might use machine language. Similarly, a company might fragment its code, such that only a small portion is registered; this would protect against wholesale copying (by a departing employee, for example) but would not protect against partial copying of those portions that are not registered.

The above scenarios have been borne out in a related context, namely access control measures and penalties for bypassing such measures under the Digital Millennium Copyright Act (DMCA). Where content providers were unable to limit access to materials, they took steps to make those materials less readable. For example, DVDs are encrypted to make movies more difficult to copy because the movie industry was hesitant to allow for DVD distribution without copy protection. Further, Congress's passage of the DMCA makes it illegal to bypass access controls such as encryption to effectuate copyright protection where high quality copying might go easily undetected. This law does not necessarily create an incentive for the creation of more copyrighted work, but it certainly has an effect on the types of work created as well as the types and scope of distribution.[99]

In sum, trade secret law is similar to the DMCA with respect to incentives to innovate. Trade secret law provides additional remedies for the unauthorized use of secret copyrighted information and provides methods for making access to such information more difficult. This allows authors

---

97 Burk and McDonnell, *supra* note 27, at 607–8.

98 Software becomes less copyable if it is distributed with a 'dongle', a physical device that must be connected to the computer before the software will operate.

99 Robert A. Kreiss, *Accessibility and Commercialization in Copyright Theory*, 43 UCLA L. REV. 1, 54–6 (1995). The DMCA is similar to trade secret law with respect to spending on protection; without the DMCA, more money would be spent on technology, such as better encryption or more fragmented data, which would better limit access to copyrighted work in the absence of a remedy for bypassing the control. The DMCA creates an incentive for information producers to limit overspending on access control technology.

to use lower cost development methods and avoid lost revenues, making the copyrighted material more valuable. As such, trade secret law increases the incentive to create secret copyrighted material.

C. Trade Secret Law versus Trademark Law

The types of information represented by trade secrets and trademarks cannot overlap. Trade secret information has value due to its secrecy, while trademarks have value if they effectively communicate information to the public. Even so, there are times when trademarks and trade secrets will interact in order to create additional incentives to create one or the other.

As discussed above, trademarks must be used in commerce in order to be protected. Similarly, under older law, one must have used information for it to be considered a trade secret. Even under the newer Uniform Trade Secrets Act, information must provide some competitive economic value. The combination of trademark and trade secret use provides an additional incentive to create each type of information. When trade secrets are given specific names, they can convey information to the world even if the secret itself is never revealed.[100]

Such trademarks show up in everyday life; indeed, the 'special sauce' on a particular hamburger is so commonly associated with trade secrets[101] the two have become synonymous: trade secret defendants often attempt to discern what the plaintiffs' alleged 'secret sauce' might be.[102] The Kentucky Fried Chicken Original Recipe® is an example of a registered trademark covering a trade secret.

Measuring this incentive may be more difficult, however. The question is whether (a) such 'secret formulas' and other trade secrets would have

---

[100] Grusd, *supra* note 66, at 47–9.

[101] Despite its fame, the 'special sauce' mark is not a registered trademark. The only registered mark associated with the 'special sauce' is Twoallbeefpattiesspecialsaucelettucecheesepicklesonionsonasesameseedbun® to McDonald's Corp. Even unregistered, however, the 'special sauce' mark has trademark value, as a different company attempted to obtain 'special sauce' as a trademark covering a sandwich dressing and had the mark cancelled.

[102] Quite often the secret sauce claimed by trade secrets plaintiffs ends up looking a lot like Thousand Island dressing. Indeed, the trade secret status of the 'special sauce' is dubious since it can be reverse engineered. One such attempt is available at www.topsecretrecipes.com/recipedetail.asp?id=65. Even so, the actual recipe is so closely guarded that McDonald's itself lost the recipe for a time. Wallet Pop, Closely-Guarded Trade Secrets, www.walletpop.com/specials/closely-guarded-trade-secrets?photo=2.

been created in the absence of the ability to obtain trademark protection; and/or (b) whether additional money was spent to improve the formulas because of the importance of distinguishing the 'secret' through trademark law. It is unclear whether either of these propositions is true in general; the answer will likely vary by industry and even by company.

Conversely, another consideration is whether a company would invest as much time and money commercializing a secret if it could not identify the secret separately as a trademark. Here, it is quite likely that companies would attempt to exploit the secret, even if not by name. Simply having a better formula, whether or not named (or even whether or not secret) is something that might be advertised even in the absence of trademark protection for the secret.

This last point also sheds some light on how trademarks and advertising in general might affect the creation of information in the absence of trade secret law. If trade secret law did not exist, potential secret products would have two states: actually unknown to others, or actually known to others. Regardless of how those two states might affect incentives to invest in the creation of such information, the ability to protect a 'secret' formula by name would likely increase the incentive to create such formulas whether or not the formula was actually kept secret. Trademarks are used to protect many products that are otherwise fungible commodities (e.g. bleach), even though the product itself is easily and cheaply reproducible. Thus, strong trademark protection can substitute for trade secrecy to some extent. If trade secret law is available, stronger trademark protection will add even more incentive to create secret formulas than weaker trademark protection. Thus, the protection of both types of laws may maximize incentives.

D. Trade Secret Law versus Right to Privacy

While copyrights, patents and trademarks all require registration in the United States for maximum protection, developers of such information may want to keep the work in progress private pending publication or registration. The 'Harry Potter' books, for example, were kept under very strict secrecy prior to their general availability. That secrecy no doubt enhanced interest in the book and likely enhanced early (and overall) sales of the book.

The value of keeping intellectual property private until published was recognized at least as early as 1890 by Warren and Brandeis:

> In every case, the individual is entitled to decide whether that which is his shall be given to the public. No other has the right to publish his productions without his consent . . . It may exist independently of any corporeal being, as in words

> spoken, a song sung, a drama acted . . . The right is lost only when the author himself communicates his production to the public . . . The statutory right [provided for the private material] is of no value, *unless* there is a publication; the common-law right is lost *as soon as* there is a publication.[103]

Indeed, privacy protects not just the work itself, but also publication of a list of the private works,[104] such as the disclosure of a secret project even if the details are not disclosed. One would therefore expect the right to privacy to incentivize development of intellectual property that is not immediately published.

However, the right of privacy provides little protection for a variety of reasons. First, it does not protect information that is of public interest.[105] Second, the right is individualistic; corporate entities receive little consideration.[106] Third, the individual right disappears if the private information is disclosed to a third party.[107] Fourth, the right to privacy applies to publication, and not use.[108] Finally, in states that follow the UTSA, the right to privacy may be pre-empted in the economic value context.[109] Of course, in the absence of trade secret law, privacy law might have evolved differently.

The limitations of privacy law mean that the availability of trade secret protection provides a differential incentive to spend more time and money developing commercial works in progress before such intellectual property becomes publicly known.[110] Measuring the effect of trade secret law may be difficult, however, because in many cases companies would keep IP development information secret in any event, so much of such development would undoubtedly occur without trade secret laws.

---

[103] Samuel D. Warren and Louis D. Brandeis, *The Right to Privacy*, 4 HARV. L. REV. 193, 199–200 (1890) (emphasis in original).

[104] *Id.* at 202.

[105] *Id.* at 214.

[106] *Id.* at 216, Neil M. Richards and Daniel J. Solove, *Privacy's Other Path: Recovering the Law of Confidentiality*, 96 GEO. L.J. 123, 180–1 (2007).

[107] Richards and Solove, *supra* note 106, at 180–1; Sharon K. Sandeen, *Relative Privacy: What Privacy Advocates Can Learn from Trade Secret Law*, 2006 MICH. ST. L. REV. 667, 696–8 (2006).

[108] Sandeen, *supra* note 107, at 702–3.

[109] Uniform Trade Secrets Act §7 ('except as provided in subsection (b), this [Act] displaces conflicting tort, restitutionary, and other law of this State providing civil remedies for misappropriation of a trade secret'). Of course, private information may be excluded from the pre-emption if the information does not fall under the definition of trade secret. Charles Tait Graves in Chapter 4 further discusses pre-emption.

[110] Warren and Brandeis, *supra* note 103, at 212 (comparing trade secret laws to the right of privacy).

Even so, there may be areas where remedies afforded by law provide additional incentives. First, incentives provided by trade secret law generally (such as where contract law fails or where protection is extremely costly) will apply to IP under development like any other secret information. For example, where works in progress can be fully protected only by extraordinary means, trade secret law will protect the secret even if only 'reasonable' methods are used. This reduces the cost of development, encouraging more investment.

Second, trade secret law provides an additional incentive where the underlying IP protection does not allow for protection prior to publication. For example, if someone misappropriates an idea and patents it, the patent is void,[111] but the original inventor cannot claim the patent because the information is now public.[112] Similarly, the Copyright Act makes clear that the unpublished nature of a work is not necessarily a bar to a finding of fair use copying.[113] In cases like these, trade secret law provides the only remedy to protect the inchoate IP right, and that remedy may provide an additional incentive to fully develop ideas rather than rush to patent inventions or publish writings before they are complete.

Thus, trade secret law will provide a differential incentive to create other forms of IP where unpublished work in progress cannot otherwise be kept absolutely secret and where such work is not otherwise protected by law.

IV. CONCLUSION

There are two competing traditional notions of trade secret law and its effect on innovation. The first is that the law provides an important incentive to create information. The second is that trade secret law harms society and should not protect much, if any, information. The truth, of course, lies somewhere in between. This chapter has identified several ways that trade secrets can provide additional incentives to innovate, but also has identified many areas where there are no such additional incentives.

Additionally, this chapter has identified areas in which the incentives to create secret information are intertwined with other types of intellectual property, and how the absence of protection in any area might affect the other areas.

---

[111] 35 U.S.C. § 116 (2006).

[112] 35 U.S.C. § 102 (2006).

[113] 17 U.S.C. § 107 (2006).

This analysis is by no means complete, and much of it can be further explored by gathering evidence. However, the chapter provides several paths that empirical research might follow to determine just how much of an incentive to innovate trade secret law provides vis-à-vis other types of intellectual property.

PART II

SECRECY AND SHARING

8 How trade secrecy law generates a natural semicommons of innovative know-how

*Jerome H. Reichman**

It is both disappointing and exhilarating to re-examine the functions of trade secrecy law for this volume. The disappointment stems from encountering many of the same old questions that Reichman, Samuelson and Scotchmer have addressed over a 20-year period.[1] The exhilaration comes from rereading that brilliant article by Samuelson and Scotchmer on reverse engineering at some distance, and realizing how many questions these collective efforts managed to answer. So let me try to set the record straight in a few short pages, beginning with the question of whether or not it is better to treat trade secrecy law as a form of intellectual property law rather than as a business tort under unfair competition law.[2]

I. TRADE SECRETS AS A FORM OF INTELLECTUAL PROPERTY

The logical point of departure is to observe that 'intellectual property' has never been just about exclusive rights in intangible, non-rivalrous creations. It has always included conduct-based liability rules found in some *sui generis* regimes, as well as absolute liability rules that confer only a

---

* Bunyan S. Womble Professor of Law, Duke University School of Law, Durham, North Carolina.

The author gratefully acknowledges the support of the National Human Genome Research Institute and the Department of Energy (CEER Grant P50 HG003391, Duke University, Center of Excellence for ELSI Research).

[1] J.H. Reichman, *Charting the Collapse of the Patent–Copyright Dichotomy: Premises for a Restructured International Intellectual Property System*, 13 CARDOZO ARTS & ENT. L.J. 475, 504–17 (1995); J.H. Reichman, *Legal Hybrids Between the Patent and Copyright Paradigms*, 94 COLUM. L. REV. 2432, 2504–57 (1994); Pamela Samuelson and Susan Scotchmer, *The Law and Economics of Reverse Engineering*, 888 YALE L.J. 1575 (2002).

[2] Mark A. Lemley, The *Surprising Virtues of Treating Trade Secrets as Intellectual Property Rights*, 61 STAN. L. REV. 311, 315–53 (2008) (discussing the origins of trade secrecy law in torts, then constructing an IP theory of trade secrets); see also Gustavo Ghidini and Valeria Falce, Chapter 6.

'license of right' yielding reasonable royalties, as occurs with mechanical recordings under copyright law and, in most countries, with public performances of sound recordings under neighboring rights laws.[3] All of these are 'intellectual property', which the classical tradition subdivides into 'industrial property' and 'literary and artistic property' (including neighboring rights laws).[4]

Formally, when international intellectual property law first recognized trade secrets under Article 39 of the TRIPS Agreement, the drafters deliberately inserted it into Article 10*bis* of the Paris Convention, which regulates unfair competition norms as a subset of industrial property law.[5] The purpose of this move was to emphasize that Article 39 of the TRIPS Agreement had, in and of itself, not created any exclusive rights. Rather, it had recognized trade secret protection as a specification of the obligations to avoid unfair competition in international trade already set out in the Paris Convention. Unfortunately, the drafters of Article 39, which tracked the Uniform Trade Secrets Act (UTSA) in the United States,[6] failed expressly to mention lawful reverse engineering. Yet, the understanding that reverse engineering is privileged perfects and operationalizes trade secret protection in the United States; its very purpose is to generate more innovation than would otherwise occur.[7]

If we think of intellectual property rights only as comprising exclusive rights, labeling trade secrets as 'intellectual property' deforms the entire history of trade secrecy law. But if we broaden our understanding of intellectual property to include all forms of property rights in intangible, non-rivalrous creations, including *ex ante* and *ex post* liability rules, then

---

[3] See 17 U.S.C. §115 (2006); International Convention for the Protection of Performers, Producers of Phonograms and Broadcasting Organizations, Rome, Italy, October 26, 1961, 496 U.N.T.S. 43 ('Rome Convention'), Art. 12.

[4] See Berne Convention for the Protection of Literary and Artistic Works, September 9, 1886, as last revised at Paris, July 24, 1971, 828 U.N.T.S. 221 ('Berne Convention'), Arts. 1, 2; Paris Convention for the Protection of Industrial Property, March 29, 1883, as revised at Stockholm, July 14, 1967, U.S.T. 1583 ('Paris Convention'), Art. 1(1), (3); Rome Convention, Arts. 4–6.

[5] Agreement on Trade-Related Aspects of Intellectual Property Rights, April 15, 1994, 33 I.L.M. 81 (1994) ('TRIPS Agreement'), Art. 39.1; Paris Convention, Art. 10*bis*. See generally Jerome H. Reichman, *Rethinking the Role of Clinical Trial Data in International Intellectual Property Law: The Case for a Public Goods Approach*, 13 MARQ. INTELL. PROP. L. REV. 1, 17–22 (2009).

[6] *Compare* Uniform Trade Secrets Act, §1(2) 14 U.L.A. 438 (1985) *with* TRIPS Agreement, Art. 39.2.

[7] See generally Samuelson and Scotchmer, *supra* note 1; RESTATEMENT (THIRD) OF TORTS §43 (1995) ('Independent discovery and analysis of publicly available products or information are not improper means of acquisition').

we may say that there is a property right in trade secrets in the form of an entitlement to either lead time or compensation for lost lead time due to a wrongful appropriation. While there may or may not be an injunction to enforce that entitlement, the compensation is properly measured only in terms of the loss of lead time that it would have taken a routine engineer to reverse engineer the trade secret by honest means.

The modality of enforcement via an injunction in such cases does not convert trade secrecy law into a regime of exclusive property rights. It remains a conduct-based liability rule, but no less a property right, in the sense of an *ex ante* entitlement. It is, however, a peculiar property right, in that a third party's reverse engineering by honest means will truncate its existence without more. As the late Professor John C. Stedman accurately observed in 1962, it is 'a disappearing property right', unlike any other in that respect.[8]

It follows that treating trade secrets as an 'intellectual property right' does little in itself to advance our understanding. We must push on to consider what exactly trade secrecy law protects, and what its true normative function really is.

II. TRADE SECRECY LAW PROTECTS INVESTMENT IN INNOVATION AS SUCH

Viewed as a subset of intellectual property law, the distinctive characteristic of trade secrecy law is that it *protects investment in innovation as such*. Until the 1990s, when Switzerland tried to codify a misappropriation law for this very purpose (as Owen Paepke long ago desired),[9] this distinctive aspect of trade secrecy law was virtually unique.[10] By their nature, virtually all other so-called intellectual property rights (disregarding trademarks and the like) provide exclusive, non-exclusive or semi-exclusive rights to some predefined *product of intellectual creativity*, such as 'inventions' in patent

---

[8] See John C. Stedman, *Trade Secrets*, 23 OHIO STATE L.J. 4, 8 (1962).

[9] See Federal Law on Unfair Competition of December 1986, art. 5(c) (effective March 1, 1988) (Switz); Reichman, *Legal Hybrids*, *supra* note 1, at 2474–6; C. Owen Paepke, *An Economic Interpretation of the Misappropriation Doctrine: Common Law Protection for Investments in Innovation*, 2 HIGH TECH. L.J. 65 (1987); see also Douglas Gary Lichtman, *The Economics of Innovation: Protecting Unpatentable Goods*, 81 MINN. L. REV. 693 (1997).

[10] But see Reichman, *Legal Hybrids*, *supra* note 1, at 2477–8 (describing the protection of construction project designs by means of an *ex ante* liability rule under art. 99 of the Italian Copyright Law).

law, 'literary and artistic works' in copyright law, 'ornamental designs' (appearance designs) in design protection laws, or 'distinctive varieties' in plant variety protection law.[11] These intellectual property rights, in turn, typically depend on the attainment of a specified level of creativity, as manifested in a specified type of intellectual creation, which will last for a specified period of time. The end result is to enable the creator to recoup his or her investment and turn a profit in the intangible, non-rivalrous creation, which might otherwise be duplicated rapidly (despite potentially high front-end costs, including R&D costs, where applicable) and disseminated at relatively low marginal costs of reproduction.

As Stephen Ladas once explained, what trade secrecy law protects is an entrepreneur's investment in applications of know-how to industry, which may or may not rise to the level of a non-obvious invention.[12] In this context:

> know-how consists of information about how to achieve some technical or commercial advantage over competitors, typically by means of novel methods or processes of production. Such information may or may not be secret. If secret, it may be held only under actual, but not legal, secrecy, which in turn affects the degree of protection the law affords.[13]

This concept of know-how applied to industry has been successfully invoked to address the appropriation problems of innovations as diverse as applications interfaces in platform information technologies,[14] traditional knowledge generated by indigenous communities,[15] and clinical trial data.[16] It therefore seems pointless to try to define the subject matter of trade secrecy laws in any other terms, although we must recognize that this same know-how may sometimes also qualify for protection as confidential information on other grounds and with different policies in mind.[17]

---

[11] See generally *id.* at 2448–72.

[12] STEPHEN P. LADAS, PATENTS, TRADEMARKS AND RELATED RIGHTS: NATIONAL AND INTERNATIONAL PROTECTION 1616 (1975).

[13] *Id.* at 1617.

[14] Samuelson and Scotchmer, *supra* note 1.

[15] Jerome H. Reichman and Tracy Lewis, *Using Liability Rules to Stimulate Innovation in Developing Countries: Application to Traditional Knowledge*, in INTERNATIONAL PUBLIC GOODS AND TRANSFER OF TECHNOLOGY UNDER A GLOBALIZED INTELLECTUAL PROPERTY REGIME 321 (Keith E. Maskus and Jerome H. Reichman eds., Cambridge University Press, 2005).

[16] Reichman, *Role of Clinical Trial Data*, *supra* note 5.

[17] See generally J.H. Reichman, *Overlapping Proprietary Rights in University-Generated Research Products: The Case of Computer Programs*, 17 COLUM. J.L. & ARTS 51 (1992).

Precisely because we are dealing with investments in know-how applied to industry as such, and not specified levels of creative achievement, classical trade secrecy law confers no exclusive property rights whatsoever. Rather, it provides a legal entitlement to a period of what I have earlier called 'natural lead time', during which a second comer may reverse engineer the originator's know-how from publicly available exemplars by honest means.[18] Even for products of ordinary manufacture, this period of lead time could have been relatively long when the industrial revolution first got underway, although lead times today tend to be relatively short on the whole.[19]

Short or long, lead time conceptually enables a first comer to recoup investment in R&D and to establish distinguishing trademarks that help to preserve profits against second comers who successfully reverse engineer the otherwise unprotected know-how.[20] More importantly, the process of reverse engineering itself, by methodically extracting the innovator's know-how from a given application, tends to generate technical improvements over time, including cost-saving modes of manufacture that reduce prices to consumers.[21] For example, the ballpoint pen, which entered the market through jewelry stores at U.S.$70 per piece, is now available to everyone at 7¢ a piece.

In so doing, trade secrecy law promotes healthy competition by securing investors in innovative applications of know-how to industry against market-destructive forms of free riding, while simultaneously stimulating these same third-party competitors to contribute to the technical community's aggregate costs of research and development:

> In all cases, liability rules govern in the sense that, without permission, second-comers may extract and improve preexisting industrial applications of know-how as long as, in the absence of any contractual agreement to the contrary, they either defray the costs of reverse engineering or pay the equivalent costs of having usurped lead-time advantages by improper means.[22]

---

[18] Reichman, *Legal Hybrids, supra* note 1, at 2439, and n.25.

[19] See J.H. Reichman, *Of Green Tulips and Legal Kudzu: Repackaging Rights in Subpatentable Innovation*, 53 VAND. L. REV. 1743, 1750–1 (2000).

[20] Of course, the second comer may prefer to purchase a license from the originator when the costs and/or the difficulties of reverse engineering appear formidable. See Samuelson and Scotchmer, *supra* note 1.

[21] See, e.g., Leo J. Raskind, *The Misappropriation Doctrine as a Competitive Norm of Intellectual Property Law*, 75 MINN. L. REV. 875 (1991); Leo J. Raskind, *The Semiconductor Chip Protection Act of 1984 and Its Lessons: Reverse Engineering, Unfair Competition, and Fair Use*, 70 MINN. L. REV. 385 (1985).

[22] J. H. Reichman, *Saving the Patent Law from Itself*, in PERSPECTIVES ON PROPERTIES OF THE HUMAN GENOME PROJECT 289, 293 (F. Scott Kieff ed., Elsevier Press, 2003).

From these observations, two important conclusions follow that merit further attention. First, the conduct-based liability rules of trade secrecy law were the primary vehicle for stimulating investment in innovative enterprise after the industrial revolution. This conclusion follows because most innovation consists of cumulative and sequential applications of know-how to industry by routine engineers at work on common technical trajectories. Given relatively high standards of non-obviousness in patent law, as well as the possibilities for inventing around patents once issued, most commercial ventures depended on the conduct-based liability rules of trade secrecy law (and other unfair competition laws, as well as trademark law) for opportunities to recoup their investments in R&D.[23] In this sense, trade secrecy laws mediated between the strong protection of patents, when available, and the risk of wholesale duplication (that is, the risk of zero lead time) in a totally unregulated environment of unbridled copying, as occurred in many developing countries before the TRIPS Agreement entered into force.

The second and more far-reaching conclusion is that this classical system of innovation gave rise to a naturally occurring pool of technological resources that was openly available to all routine engineers who played by the rules. Because this proposition has attracted insufficient study, it deserves a closer look here.

III. A NATURAL OPEN-SOURCE TECHNOLOGY POOL

The exclusive rights of classical intellectual property law may be viewed as operating in the space left free by two other regimes that intersect with them but which are governed by totally different principles. The three regimes taken together provide a rough map or outline of the classical system of innovation inherited from the industrial revolution. This scheme is represented in Figure 8.1.[24] At the top of the diagram, lies the 'upstream' dimension, as it would be called today, in which scientific and technical knowledge is generated by the public science community, typically working at universities or other research centers. This basic research is often funded by government entities (in the United States,

[23] See Reichman, *Legal Hybrids*, *supra* note 1; Reichman, *Green Tulips*, *supra* note 19. Hence the old saying that intellectual property law provided only 'islands of protection in a sea of free competition', which is no longer in vogue today.

[24] Reproduced and modified from Reichman, *Saving the Patent System*, *supra* note 22, at 292.

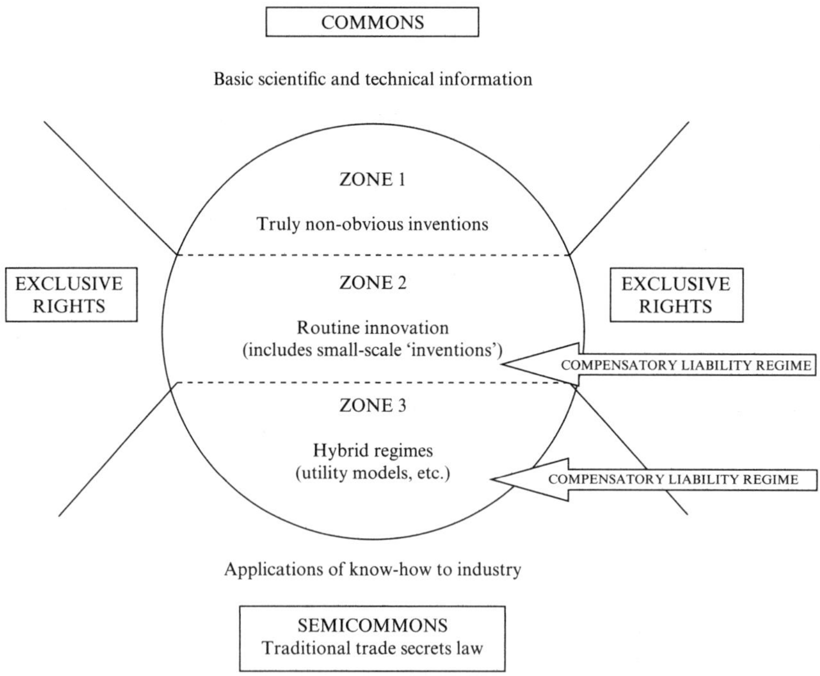

Figure 8.1 Expansion of exclusive rights in lieu of actual or legal secrecy

this would include the National Science Foundation (NSF), the National Institutes of Health (NIH), or the Department of Energy (DOE)), as well as by universities themselves, foundations, and even private industry, in support of basic research that can lead to downstream applications.[25] In its most enlightened embodiment, this sphere of activity is one in which scientific and technical information flow freely as a relatively unregulated input, governed by the norms of science.[26] Subject to growing pressures of a legal, technical and economic nature, the scientific and technical data and information generated here are, in principle, destined to become freely available to other scientists in what ideally approximates a true

---

[25] See, e.g., Arti K. Rai and Rebecca S. Eisenberg, *Bayh-Dole and the Progress of Biomedicine*, 66 LAW & CONTEMP. PROBS. 289 (2003); Anthony So *et al.*, *Is Bayh-Dole Good for Developing Countries? Lessons from the U.S. Experience*, 6 PLOS BIOLOGY 2078 (2008), available at www.plosbiology.org/article/info:doi/10.1371/journal.pbio.0060262.

[26] Arti K. Rai, *Regulating Scientific Research: Intellectual Property Rights and the Norms of Science*, 94 NW. U. L. REV. 77 (1999).

commons, one that has played a fundamental role in our national system of innovation.[27]

It is, however, in the lesser-known domain, deep in the bowels of the free enterprise economy, where scientific and technical know-how are applied to industry, that we must focus primary attention in this chapter. In Figure 8.1, this space is represented as lying under the sphere in which the exclusive rights of intellectual property law otherwise predominate (Zones 2 and 3). In this vast space, trade secrecy laws traditionally govern the productions of routine engineers who develop applications of know-how to industry without securing patent protection.[28]

Within this space, the reverse engineering clause built into the trade secret paradigm operates as an open invitation to third parties to make use of the first comer's innovative know-how for certain purposes, especially for devising improvements, or in exchange for compensation. The routine engineers working on common technical trajectories thus basically constitute an interrelated group that operates under a de facto sharing ethos. As explained in an earlier article:

> [t]hey form a natural, open-source community built around the practice of reverse engineering and the availability of adequate lead time under the liability rules governing trade secrets and confidential information. In this endeavor, routine engineers depend on the reciprocal insights and contributions that the relevant technical communities derive from the [pooled] domain – the shared body of knowledge that underlies the common technical trajectories – and on their inability to remove novel insights and cumulative contributions to know-how from [that domain].[29]

However, unlike the scientific commons depicted 'upstream', the newest technical knowledge emerging in real time under the aegis of trade secrecy laws is typically available to routine engineers only on condition either

---

[27] See, e.g., Paul David, *The Economic Logic of 'Open Science' and the Balance Between Private Property Rights and the Public Domain in Scientific Data and Information: A Primer*, in The Role of Scientific and Technical Data and Information in the Public Domain 19 (Julie M. Esanu and Paul F. Uhlir eds., NAS Press, 2003); J. H. Reichman and Paul F. Uhlir, *A Contractually Reconstructed Research Commons for Scientific Data in a Highly Protectionist Intellectual Property Environment*, 66 Law & Contemp. Stud. 315 (2003); see also Michael J. Madison, Brett M. Frischmann and Katherine J. Strandburg, *Constructing Commons in the Cultural Environment*, 95 Cornell L. Rev. 657 (2010).

[28] Reichman, *Collapse of the Patent–Copyright Dichotomy*, *supra* note 1; Reichman, *Legal Hybrids*, *supra* note 1.

[29] Reichman, *Saving the Patent System*, *supra* note 22, at 294.

that they invest time, money and effort to reverse engineer the first comer's know-how from publicly available embodiments by honest means, or that they negotiate upfront licensing agreements and pay directly to acquire such unpublished, up-to-date know-how. In this respect, the technical knowledge generated by routine engineers under trade secrecy laws also differs from that generated by patent laws, which enters the public domain by virtue of disclosure and publication rules. Because the up-to-date, unpublished knowledge generated by routine engineers is only available to those willing to defray either the costs of recreating it from scratch, or the costs of reverse engineering it by honest means, or the costs of licensing it, we are constrained to depict the vast space emerging from their collective efforts as a 'semi-commons', operating on pay-to-play principles, rather than as a true commons or public domain in which everything is freely available to all comers:

> The collective knowledge available from [this semi-commons] . . . advances by dint of the small-scale contributions of single innovators. These contributions are statistically predictable in the sense that they [usually] inhere in what was already known about existing technical paradigms . . . The progressive development of know-how is thus a community project that benefits from the countless small-scale contributions to the prior art by individuals who draw from [both] the public domain [and the semi-commons] to make improvements, and who thereby enrich the [semi-commons] by generating new information that others in the technical community may exploit to their own advantage. [30]

Historically, the legal protection of trade secrets was accordingly organized around a distinctive class of liability rules that stimulated competition in subpatentable improvements by discouraging market-destructive conduct harmful to the relevant technical community as a whole. This regime did not endow single innovators with any power to remove their subpatentable or otherwise unpatented contributions from the semicommons, as exclusive rights would otherwise allow. On the contrary, trade secrecy law's traditional role was to avoid market failure by enabling entrepreneurs to recoup their investments in small-scale innovation without creating barriers to entry and without impeding qualified second comers from making follow-on applications of others' routine innovations.

---

[30] *Id.* Here we must concede the possibility that an innovator whose creation rises to the level of a patentable invention may prefer to remain in trade secrecy law if the risks and costs of reverse engineering appear very high. See Lemley, *supra* note 2; Samuelson and Scotchmer, *supra* note 1.

IV. PROBLEMS OF SELF-REVEALING KNOW-HOW AND SMALL-SCALE INNOVATION GENERALLY

From Figure 8.1, it becomes evident that the space available for both common use of public scientific and technical information at the top, and the space available for applications of know-how at the bottom, will either shrink or expand according to the amount of room occupied by the exclusive rights regimes on both sides of the circle. Within the circle, in Zone 1, are innovations that qualify for patent protection as non-obvious inventions. The size of this space varies with the judicial rigor of the non-obviousness standard, which, until recently, had become relatively low.

In Zones 2 and 3, one finds all the subpatentable innovations that could not qualify for patent protection under the extant non-obviousness standard but which could conceivably qualify for trade secrecy protection if kept legally secret within the conditions set by the UTSA.[31] Because, however, lots of valuable know-how is borne on or near the face of products distributed in the open market, investors often obtain little or no lead time because second comers can rapidly duplicate the visible know-how without spending time or money to reverse engineer it from scratch. Legislators increasingly respond to this risk of market failure by enacting *sui generis* exclusive property rights in small-scale innovations, such as industrial designs, utility models, plant breeders' varieties, compilations of data, and the like. As these 'legal hybrid' regimes proliferate in Zone 3, the natural semicommons available to all competitors below the circle correspondingly contracts.

No one familiar with my previous work will be surprised to learn that, owing to a proliferation of hybrid intellectual property regimes, coupled with an expansion of both the domestic and international patent and copyright laws,[32] both the science commons and the routine engineers' technology pool have lately shrunk in a striking and, many would say, a most alarming fashion.[33] Professor James Boyle has felicitously called this and related phenomena 'The Second Enclosure Movement'.[34]

---

[31] See, e.g., Robert Denicola, Chapter 2. Robert G. Bone, Chapter 3.

[32] See, e.g., Keith E. Maskus and Jerome H. Reichman, *The Globalization of Private Knowledge Goods and the Privatization of Global Public Goods*, in INTERNATIONAL PUBLIC GOODS AND TRANSFER OF TECHNOLOGY, *supra* note 15, ch. 1.

[33] Reichman, *Collapse of the Patent – Copyright Dichotomy*, *supra* note 1; Reichman, *Legal Hybrids, supra* note 1; Pamela Samuelson *et al.*, *A Manifesto Concerning the Legal Protection of Computer Programs*, 94 COLUM. L. REV. 2308 (1994).

[34] James Boyle, *The Second Enclosure Movement and the Construction of the Public Domain*, 66 LAW & CONTEMP. PROBS. 33 (2003); see also David Lange,

V. PRESERVING THE COMMONS IN A HYPER-PROTECTIONIST LEGAL ENVIRONMENT

In his article proclaiming the virtues of trade secrecy law as an intellectual property right, Professor Lemley rightly points out that a positive economic effect of this law is to discourage excessive or wasteful investment in maintaining actual secrecy, which would be necessary in the absence of the protection guaranteed by the tenets of trade secrecy law itself.[35] At the same time, Professor Lemley dismisses self-revealing innovation that can be copied without reverse engineering as of little or no consequence, for the logical reason that, lacking secrecy, it cannot be covered by a law dedicated to the legal protection of secrets.

In reality, that proposition, despite its apparent logic, remains empirically anachronistic in the sense that worldwide intellectual property law has rejected it by refusing to condemn what I have called 'incremental innovation bearing know-how on its face'[36] to the public domain, where Lemley believes it belongs. Disregarding the United States, the rest of the world tends to protect such small-scale, self-revealing know-how under utility model laws (petty patent law), design protection laws, plant variety protection laws (also available in the United States), database protection laws, codified misappropriation laws, and numerous other hybrid legal regimes.[37] The common denominator of such regimes is that they protect small-scale innovations that lack sufficient novelty to qualify for patent protection and that cannot realistically trigger the secrecy requirement of trade secrecy law either.

Because such innovation tends to bear its investor's know-how on or near its face, second comers (not otherwise legally impeded) can simply extract that know-how by duplicating the products that embody it, without any corresponding costs or time inherent in the process of reverse engineering. In the raw state of affairs, the innovator thus obtains zero lead time in which to recoup his investment in R&D, and the second comer free rides on the first comer's investment, while avoiding any similar cost

---

Recognizing the Public Domain, 44 LAW & CONTEMP. PROBS. 147 (1981); Jessica Litman, *The Public Domain*, 39 EMORY L.J. 965 (1996).

[35] Lemley, *supra* note 2.

[36] See J.H. Reichman, *Computer Programs as Applied Scientific Know-How: Implications of Copyright Protection for Commercialized University Research*, 452 VAND. L. REV. 639 (1989).

[37] Reichman, *Legal Hybrids*, *supra* note 1, at 2453–504; Reichman, *Green Tulips*, *supra* note 19, at 1753–6; see also Mark Janis, *Second Tier Patent Protection*, 40 HARV. INT'L L.J. 151 (1999).

structure of his own.[38] The hybrid *sui generis* regimes seek to rectify these disincentives to invest by substituting copyright-like or patent-like regimes of exclusive property rights for the absence of lead time protection under trade secrecy law.[39]

In the United States, instead, where there is officially no utility model law, the patent authorities periodically lower the non-obviousness standard to the point where the patent law itself absorbs an increasingly larger share of the small-scale innovations elsewhere covered by hybrid legal regimes. Thus U.S. patent law protected the paper clip,[40] which is the quintessential type of self-revealing functional design that utility model laws protect in other countries. Indeed, the low non-obviousness standard practiced in the United States until recently means that U.S. patent law periodically operates as a *de facto* utility model law in many industrial sectors.

However, a low non-obviousness standard generates high social costs of its own. It blurs the boundaries between inventions, generating litigation and other high transaction costs.[41] More important, it shrinks both the domain of upstream basic research results freely available to scientists and the downstream domain of small-scale innovation available to routine engineers.[42] In response, the U.S. Supreme Court periodically elevates the standard of non-obviousness, as it recently did in the *KSR* decision of 2008,[43] in an effort to promote the granting of 'quality patents'.

An inevitable consequence of these decisions is that a large swath of small-scale innovations, which can readily be duplicated, will fall out of patent protection, only to receive little or no protection in trade secrecy law because they will tend to bear their know-how on or near the face of the products that embody them. Given the predictable outbreak of free riding likely to ensue, and the corresponding disincentives to invest it fosters, one should expect both state and federal courts to push back by invoking various and often questionable doctrines of unfair competition law, as well as trademark or trade dress laws, which can become even more anticompetitive than the proliferating hybrid intellectual property rights under foreign laws. Whether recent U.S. Supreme Court decisions limiting

---

38 Raskind, *Misappropriation*, *supra* note 21; Samuelson and Scotchmer, *supra* note 1.

39 Reichman, *Legal Hybrids*, *supra* note 1.

40 See Lemley, *supra* note 2.

41 See Jerome H. Reichman and Rochelle Cooper Dreyfuss, *Harmonization Without Consensus: Critical Reflections on Drafting a Substantive Patent Law Treaty*, 57 DUKE L.J. 85 (2007) (citing authorities).

42 *Cf.* Boyle, *supra* note 34.

43 KSR Int'l Co. v. Teleflex Inc., 550 U.S. 398 (2007).

the use of such ancillary doctrines to supply artificial lead time where otherwise unavailable would hold up against this tide,[44] should it emerge, remains to be seen.

In *Of Green Tulips and Legal Kudzu*, which appeared in 2000,[45] I argued that, while it was unsustainable to cast the bulk of present-day small-scale innovations, with their high front-end costs and ease of duplication, into a world of zero lead time, it was also wrongheaded to address the chronic failure of secrecy under trade secrecy law by means of an expanding set of exclusive property rights that generate overlapping legal entitlements, high transaction costs, and barriers to entry, all of which seriously diminish both innovation and the pace of competition. Above all, the greatest long-term social costs of this flawed strategy are a reduction of upstream inputs into public science (most dramatically under database protection cum copyright laws) and of downstream inputs into applications of know-how to industry.

The correct solution to this problem, in my view, is to replace the failing liability rule of domestic trade secrecy laws, where secrecy keeps diminishing even as the value of vulnerable technical outputs keeps rising, with a general purpose liability rule that would directly address the market failure to which incremental innovation bearing know-how on its face is otherwise susceptible. It is this premise that underlies the 'compensatory liability regime', first developed in *Green Tulips*.[46] Ideally, its adoption would render the hybrid regimes of exclusive rights in Zone 3 of Figure 8.1 superfluous and lead to their repeal over time.

Under a compensatory liability regime, a small-scale innovator who operates in Zone 2 would obtain protection against wholesale duplication for a specified period of time. However, that innovator would also labor under an obligation to allow second comers to use his or her know-how for purposes of making improvements, in exchange for a reasonable royalty to be paid over a specified, but relatively short, period of time. Under this regime, there is an *ex ante* entitlement, in the form of an automatic license, for compensation from follow-on innovators; but there is no possibility of excluding the second comer from making those improvements. If many improvers emerge, the first comer may experience lottery effects from the

---

[44] Traffix Devices, Inc. v. Marketing Displays, Inc., 532 U.S. 23 (2001); Wal-Mart Stores, Inc. v. Samara Brothers, Inc. 529 U.S. 205 (2000); Bonito Boats, Inc. v. Thunder Craft Boats, Inc., 489 U.S. 141 (1989).

[45] Reichman, *Green Tulips*, *supra* note 19; see also Jerome H. Reichman, *Of Green Tulips and Legal Kudzu: Repackaging Rights in Subpatentable Innovation*, in Expanding the Boundaries of Intellectual Property 23 (Rochelle Dreyfuss *et al.* eds., Oxford University Press, 2001).

[46] See Reichman, *Green Tulips*, *supra* note 19, at 177–97.

contributions of his *de facto* partners, and that same first comer may also utilize some of their improvements to advance his or her own competitive position by paying a corresponding reasonable tithe in exchange.[47]

I will not delve more deeply into the intricacies of a 'compensatory liability regime' within the confines of this short chapter on the legal logic of trade secrecy law. Suffice it to say, this proposed regime attempts to address the biggest problem facing trade secrecy law today, which is not its lack of systemic logic, but its growing inability to function in a world without significant secrecy in important sectors of technological innovation. Absent such an alternative regime, we may expect to witness a continuing unraveling of the trade secrecy paradigm, with mounting aberrations, such as the criminalization of trade secrecy law in the United States[48] and the adoption of an exclusive right to trade secrets in Italy.[49] To the extent that these and other aberrations cumulatively exert a chilling effect on innovation, we end up more or less where market failures from too much free riding would otherwise have carried us in the raw state of affairs.

In contrast, the compensatory liability model seeks to replace a time-tested liability rule rooted in secrecy with a portable liability rule covering applications of know-how to industry that is detached from the requirement of secrecy (but not that of a modicum of novelty). It can thus co-exist with trade secrecy law and allow small-scale innovators two different, but pro-competitive options. If the innovator chooses the compensatory liability regime, it will provide him or her with more or less the same remedies as trade secrecy law. It would inhibit wholesale duplication as a dishonest form of reverse engineering,[50] and allow second comers to 'pay' for lessened lead time advantages by investing in improvements of their own and then sharing some of the resulting profits with the first comer.

CONCLUSION

I will end by noting four additional benefits likely to flow from adoption of a compensatory liability regime for small-scale innovation. First, such a second-tier regime would actually reinforce the courts' willingness to

---

47 For details, see generally Reichman, *Green Tulips*, *supra* note 19, at 177–90.

48 Rochelle Cooper Dreyfuss, *Trade Secrets: How Well Should We be Allowed to Hide Them? The Economic Espionage Act of 1996*, 9 FORDHAM INTELL. PROP. MEDIA & ENT. L.J. 1 (1998).

49 See Ghidini & Falce, Chapter 6.

50 See Samuelson and Scotchmer, *supra* note 1 (analysis of plug mold statutes in this regard).

maintain a stiff non-obviousness standard, and thus remove the clutter that accumulates both upstream and downstream when weak patents are issued. The existence of a second-tier liability rule would reinforce the judges' scrutiny of obviousness, by assuring them that those innovations that fail the test will nonetheless be rescued from wholesale duplication and free riding forms of market failure (without fostering corresponding barriers to entry). This could prove to be of particular benefit to the information technology sector, which has been suffocating under the weight of too many patents, but which seems ever more comfortable with existing uses of liability rules.

Second, resort to a compensatory liability rule for small-scale innovation should obviate the need for adding more hybrid regimes of exclusive property rights to Zone 3, where the cumulative social costs are becoming unsustainable. Third, once set in place, a compensatory liability model can be adapted to the needs of different industries without damage to its basic mechanisms Just as the semiconductor chip industry had some particular understanding about the boundaries of reverse engineering in the Semiconductor Chip Protection Act of 1984,[51] so different sectors can contractually adjust the liability model to their own needs, within outer limits set by legislators, relevant regulators or industry governance boards (when an industry voluntarily adopts a liability rule for itself).

Finally, once a compensatory liability regime becomes a more familiar alternative intellectual property model, it can be adapted to address numerous problems at the margins that may otherwise seem intractable. For example, in previous articles, I have tried to show how such a liability rule could resolve hard problems encountered with respect to traditional knowledge,[52] clinical trial data,[53] and the quest for an acceptable form of database protection.[54] This regime also has a promising future in supporting the formation of pooled inputs for scientific research where the possibility of downstream applications might otherwise undermine the sharing norms of science.[55]

---

[51] Semiconductor Chip Protection Act of 1984 (SCPA), title III of Pub. L. No. 98-620, 98 Stat. 3335, 3347 (November 8, 1984) codified at 17 U.S.C. §§ 901–14 (§906 expressly permits reverse engineering); see also Raskind, *Semiconductor Chip Act*, *supra* note 21.

[52] Reichman and Lewis, *supra* note 15.

[53] Reichman, *Role of Clinical Trial Data*, *supra* note 5.

[54] Jerome H. Reichman and Pamela Samuelson, *Intellectual Property Rights in Data?*, 50 VAND. L. REV. 51, 145–51 (1997); Reichman and Uhlir, *supra* note 27.

[55] Arti K. Rai *et al.*, *Pathways Across the Valley of Death: Novel Intellectual Property Strategies for Accelerated Drug Discovery*, 8 YALE J. HEALTH POL'Y L. & ETHICS 1, 25–8 (2008); see also Jerome H. Reichman, Tom Dedeurwaerdere and

In this regard, at least one important international treaty concerning plant genetic resources for food and agriculture has actually embodied a rudimentary model of such a compensatory liability regime.[56] Efforts are underway to develop a more refined application of such a regime to microbial science in order to mediate between the demands of developing countries for control of their local genetic resources and the needs of the worldwide scientific community.[57] It also seems likely that liability rules could play an important role in enabling developing countries to accommodate patented climate-change technologies to their own needs over time.[58]

Paul F. Uhlir, Designing the Microbial Research Commons: Global Intellectual Property Strategies for Accessing, and Using Essential Public Knowledge Assets, ch. 2 (Draft version, February 2, 2011) (unpublished manuscript, on file with authors).

[56] International Treaty on Plant Genetic Resources for Food and Agriculture, November 3, 2001, available at www.fao.org/legal/treaties/033f-e.htm; Laurence R. Helfer, *Using Intellectual Property Rights to Preserve the Global Genetic Commons: The International Treaty on Plant Genetic Resources for Food and Agriculture*, in INTERNATIONAL PUBLIC GOODS AND TRANSFER OF TECHNOLOGY, *supra* note 15, at 217–24.

[57] Reichman, Dedeurwaerdere and Uhlir, *supra* note 55, chs. 2 and 6.

[58] See, e.g., Jerome Reichman, Arti K. Rai, Richard G. Newell and Jonathan B. Wiener, *Intellectual Property and Alternatives: Strategies for Green Innovation*, Chatham House Energy, Environment and Development Programme, Paper No. 08/03 (2008), available at www.chathamhouse.org.uk/files/13097_1208eedp_duke.pdf.

9 Open innovation and the private-collective model for innovation incentives

*Eric von Hippel and Georg von Krogh**

I. INTRODUCTION

We define an innovation as 'open' when design information about that innovation, as well as contextual information others would need to understand, reproduce, modify and improve that design, are offered on equal terms to all at no charge.[1] Open revealing is the feature of open innovation that makes it possible to have collaborative design processes in which all can participate, as is famously the case in open source software projects.[2] Open revealing of findings, discoveries and knowledge is also a defining characteristic of what Paul David and colleagues call open science.[3]

Discussions of intellectual property law often assume that if patents are not available, inventors will resort to trade secrecy if they are able to do so. Empirical research findings and theoretical considerations we will discuss in this chapter show that this need not be, and often is not, the case.

In this chapter, we begin by reviewing the empirical evidence on open

* Eric von Hippel is T. Wilson Professor of Innovation Management and Professor of Engineering Systems at MIT. Georg von Krogh is Professor of Strategic Management and Innovation at ETH Zurich. We greatly appreciate assistance received from Florian Bertram. This chapter is based on Eric von Hippel and Georg von Krogh, *Free Revealing and the Private-Collective Model for Innovation Incentives*, 36 R&D MGMT. 3 (2006).

[1] Definitions of 'open innovation' are not uniform among scholars today. Notably, some define open innovation in terms of *organizational* 'openness' to (e.g., willingness to engage in) the purchase, sale and exchange of protected intellectual property. See, e.g., Henry Chesbrough, *The Era of Open Innovation*, 44 MIT SLOAN MGMT. REV. 35, 35–41 (2003). Clearly a very different matter.

[2] ERIC S. RAYMOND, THE CATHEDRAL AND THE BAZAAR: MUSINGS ON LINUX AND OPEN SOURCE BY AN ACCIDENTAL REVOLUTIONARY (1999).

[3] Partha Dasgupta and Paul A. David, *Towards a New Economics of Science*, 23 RES. POL'Y 487 (1994); Paul A. David, *Knowledge, Property, and the System Dynamics of Technological Change*, in PROCEEDINGS OF THE WORLD BANK ANNUAL CONFERENCE ON DEVELOPMENT ECONOMICS 1992, 215 (1992); Paul A. David, *Knowledge Spillovers, Technology Transfers, and the Economic Rationale for Public Support of Exploratory Research in Science*, BACKGROUND PAPER FOR EUR. COMM. FOR FUTURE ACCELERATORS (1998).

revealing of innovation-related information by innovating firms. Next, we discuss the case for open revealing from an innovators' perspective, and argue that it often can be the best *practical* route for innovators to increase profit from their innovations. Finally, we discuss the implications of open revealing for innovation theory. We show that open revealing can be understood in terms of a 'private-collective' model of innovation incentives.[4] This model occupies a fertile middle ground between the traditional private and collective action models of innovation incentive.

When we say that an innovator, be it an individual or a firm, 'openly' or 'freely' reveals proprietary information, we mean that all intellectual property rights to that information are voluntarily given up by that innovator and all parties are given equal access to it: the information becomes a public good.[5] A public good is characterized by non-excludability and non-rivalry: if anyone consumes it, it cannot feasibly be withheld from others.[6] Intellectual property may be openly revealed whether or not it is first protected by patents or copyrights. All that is required is that the owners of the protected information elect to do this. For example, in the case of copyrighted software 'writings', authors may openly reveal their code by placing it under a software license that conveys all rights granted to the author under copyright law to all parties without charge and on a non-discriminatory basis. Of course, authors that openly reveal information are not necessarily able to convey legal rights to others to freely *use* the information they have revealed. Property rights held by others (for example, rights to other patents also needed to 'practice' an innovation that has been openly revealed) may still stand in the way.

Open revealing as we define it does not mean that recipients necessarily acquire and utilize the revealed information at no cost to themselves. Nor does it mean that the benefits of acquiring and applying openly-revealed information will necessarily outweigh the costs. Recipients may, for example, have to pay for a subscription to a journal or a website and/or cover the expenses for a field trip to an innovation site to acquire the information being openly revealed. Also, in order to understand or make use of openly revealed information to solve problems, the recipient must already

---

4 Eric von Hippel and Georg von Krogh, *Open Source Software and the 'Private-Collective' Innovation Model: Issues for Organization Science*, 14 ORG. SCI. 209, 213, 217–18 (2003).

5 Dietmar Harhoff, *Strategic Spillovers and Incentives for Research and Development*, 42 MGMT. SCI. 907 (1996).

6 MANCUR OLSON, THE LOGIC OF COLLECTIVE ACTION 14 (1967). Cf. Michael J. Madison, Chapter 10, who argues that trade secrecy can be used to facilitate sharing within a closed group.

possess or create necessary complementary knowledge.[7] However, if the possessor of the information does not profit from any such expenditures made by the information adopters, the information itself is still openly revealed, according to our definition. This definition of open revealing is rather extreme in that revealing with some small constraints, as is sometimes done, would achieve largely the same economic outcome. Still, it is useful to discover that innovations are often openly revealed even in terms of this stringent definition.

II. EVIDENCE OF OPEN REVEALING

Intentional and routine open revealing among profit-seeking firms was first reported by Allen.[8] He noticed the phenomenon, which he called 'collective invention', in historical records from the nineteenth-century English iron industry. In that industry, ore was processed into iron by means of large furnaces heated to very high temperatures. Two attributes of the furnaces used had been steadily improved during the period 1850–75: chimney height had been increased and the temperature of the combustion air pumped into the furnace during operation had been raised. These two technical changes significantly and progressively improved the energy efficiency of iron production, a very important matter for producers. Allen noted the surprising fact that employees of competing firms publicly revealed information on their furnace design improvements and related performance data in meetings of professional societies and in published material.

After Allen's initial observation, a number of other authors searched for open revealing among profit-seeking firms and frequently found it. Nuvolari studied a historical period akin to that studied by Allen and found a similar pattern of open revealing in the case of improvements made to steam engines used to pump out mines in the 1800s.[9] At that time, mining activities were severely hampered by water that tended to flood into mines of any depth, and so an early and important

---

[7] Wesley M. Cohen and Daniel A. Levinthal, *Absorptive Capacity: A New Perspective on Learning and Innovation*, 35 ADMIN. SCI. Q. 128 (1990); Donald MacKenzie and Graham Spinardi, *Tacit Knowledge, Weapons Design, and the Uninvention of Nuclear Weapons*, 101 AM. J. SOC. 44 (1995).

[8] Robert C. Allen, *Collective Invention*, 4 J. ECON. BEHAV. & ORG. 1 (1983).

[9] Allesandro Nuvolari, *Collective Invention During the British Industrial Revolution: The Case of the Cornish Pumping Engine*, 23 CAMBRIDGE J. ECON. 347 (2004).

application of steam engines was for the removal of water from mines. Nuvolari explored the technical history of steam engines used to drain copper and tin mines in Cornwall, England. Here, patented steam engines developed by James Watt were widely deployed in the 1700s. After the expiration of the Watt patent, an engineer named Richard Trevithick developed a new type of high-pressure engine in 1812. Instead of patenting his invention, he made his design available to all for use without charge. The engine soon became the basic design used in Cornwall. Many mine engineers improved Trevithick's design further and published what they had done in a monthly journal, *Lean's Engine Reporter*. This journal had been founded by a group of mine managers with the explicit intention of aiding the rapid diffusion of best practices among these competing firms.

Open revealing has also been documented in the case of more recent industrial equipment innovations developed by equipment users. Thus, Lim reports that IBM was first to develop a process to manufacture semiconductors that incorporated copper interconnections among circuit elements instead of the traditionally used aluminum ones.[10] After some delay, IBM revealed increasing amounts of proprietary information about the manufacturing process to rival users and to equipment suppliers.

Open revealing was widespread in the case of innovations developed by users for use on automated clinical chemistry analysers manufactured by the Technicon Corporation for use in medical diagnosis. After commercial introduction of the basic analyser, many users developed major improvements to both the analyser and to the clinical tests processed on that equipment. These users, generally medical personnel, openly revealed their improvements via publication, and at company-sponsored seminars.[11] Mishina found open, or at least selective no-cost revealing in the lithographic equipment industry.[12] He reported that innovating equipment users would sometimes reveal what they had done to machine manufacturers. In a study of library IT search software, Morrison, Roberts and von Hippel found that innovating users openly revealed 56 percent

---

[10] Kwanghui Lim, *The Many Faces of Absorptive Capacity: Spillovers of Copper Interconnect Technology for Semiconductor Chips*, 18 Indus. & Corp. Change 1249 (2009).

[11] Eric von Hippel and Stan N. Finkelstein, *Analysis of Innovation in Automated Clinical Chemistry Analyzers*, 6 Science & Public Policy 24 (1979).

[12] Kazuhiro Mishina, Essays on Technological Evolution (unpublished Ph.D. dissertation, Harvard University, 1989).

of the software modifications they had developed.[13] Reasons given for not revealing the remainder had nothing to do with considerations of intellectual property protection. Rather, users said they had no convenient users' group forum for doing so, and/or they thought their innovation was too specialized to be of interest to others.

Innovating users of sports equipment also have been found to openly reveal their new products and product modifications. Franke and Shah, in their study of four communities of serious sports enthusiasts found that innovating users uniformly agreed with the statement that they openly revealed their innovation to their entire community free of charge – and strongly disagreed with the statement that they sold their innovations ($p < 0.001$, t-test for dependent samples).[14] Interestingly, two of the four communities they studied engaged in activities involving significant competition among community members. Innovators in these two communities reported high but significantly less willingness to openly reveal, as one might expect in view of the potentially higher level of competitive loss such conduct would entail.

Contributors to the many open source software projects extant (more than 150,000 were listed on SourceForge.net in 2009) routinely make the new code they have written public under a license granted by authors based upon their rights in copyright law. Many copyright owners decide to license their work under terms prescribed by the GNU General Public License (GPL).[15] Basic rights transferred to those possessing a copy of software licensed under the GPL include the right to use it at no cost, the right to study its source code, the right to modify it, and the right to distribute modified or unmodified versions to others at no cost. Open source software licenses do not grant downloaders the full rights associated with open revealing as that term was defined earlier. For example, the GPL license prohibits anyone from incorporating software covered by that license into proprietary software that they then sell.

While it may seem reasonable that open revealing is practiced among innovators that face low rivalry, at first glance it would seem less likely that direct competitors would openly reveal much information and share knowledge. Interestingly, Henkel showed that open revealing is sometimes

---

13 Pamela D. Morrison, John H. Roberts and Eric von Hippel, *Determinants of User Innovation and Innovation Sharing in a Local Market*, 46 MGMT. SCI. 1513 (2000).

14 Nikolaus Franke and Sonali Shah, *How Communities Support Innovative Activities: An Exploration of Assistance and Sharing Among End-Users*, 32 RES. POL'Y 157 (2003).

15 GNU General Public License, available at www.gnu.org/licenses/gpl.html.

practiced by directly competing manufacturers.[16] He studied manufacturers that were competitors and that had all built improvements and extensions to a type of software known as embedded Linux. (Such software is 'embedded in' and used to operate equipment ranging from cameras to chemical plants.) These manufacturers openly revealed improvements to the common software platform that they all shared and, with a lag, also revealed much of the equipment-specific code they had written. Even under adverse competitive conditions, there may be practical reasons why innovators want to openly reveal information. Next, we explore some of these reasons.

III. THE PRACTICAL CASE FOR OPEN REVEALING

The 'private investment model' of innovation incentives assumes that innovation will be supported by private investment if and as innovators can incur profits from doing so. In this model, any open revealing or uncompensated spillovers of proprietary knowledge developed by private investment directly reduce the innovator's profits. It is therefore assumed that innovators will strive to avoid spillovers of innovation-related information. From the perspective of this model, then, open revealing is an enigma: it seems to make no sense that innovators would intentionally give away information and knowledge for free that they had invested money to develop.[17] In this section we offer an explanation by pointing out that open revealing is often the *best practical* option available to innovators.

Harhoff *et al.* found that it is in practice very difficult for most innovators to protect their innovations from direct or approximate imitation.[18] This means that the practical choice is typically *not* the one posited by the private investment model of innovation incentives: should innovators voluntarily openly reveal their innovations, or should they protect them? Instead, the real choice facing innovators is often whether to voluntarily

---

[16] Joachim Henkel, *Software Development in Embedded Linux: Informal Collaboration of Competing Firms*, in PROCEEDINGS DER 6. INTERNATIONALEN TAGUNG WIRTSCHAFTSINFORMATIK 2003 (W. Uhr, W. Esswein and W. Schoop eds., 2003).

[17] Eric von Hippel and Georg von Krogh, *Open Source Software Development and the Private-Collective Innovation Model: Issues for Organization Science*, 14 ORG. SCI. 208 (2003).

[18] Dietmar Harhoff *et. al.*, *Profiting from Voluntary Information Spillovers: How Users Benefit by Openly Revealing their Innovations*, 32 RES. POL'Y 1753 (2003).

openly reveal or to arrive at the same end state, perhaps with a bit of a lag, via involuntary spillovers. The practical case for voluntary open revealing is further strengthened because it can often be accomplished at low cost, and often yields significant private benefits to the innovators. When benefits from open revealing exceed the benefits that are *practically* obtainable from holding an innovation secret or licensing it, open revealing should be the preferred course of action for a profit-seeking firm or individual.

A. When Others Know Something Close to 'Your' Secret

Innovators seeking to protect innovations they have developed as their intellectual property must establish monopoly control over the innovation-related information and knowledge.[19] In practice, this can be done either by intentionally and effectively hiding the information or knowledge as a trade secret, or by obtaining effective legal protection by patents or copyrights.[20] (Trademarks also fall under the heading of intellectual property, but we do not consider those here.) In addition, however, for exclusive rights to be effective at preserving profits, information must be unequally distributed amongst innovators, and it must be the case that *others* do not hold substitute information and knowledge that skirt these protections and that they *are* willing to reveal. If multiple individuals or firms have substitutable information or knowledge for which usage is not blocked by existing patents, they are likely to vary with respect to the competitive circumstances they face. A specific innovator's ability to protect 'its' innovation as proprietary will then be determined for all holders of such information or knowledge by the decision of the one having the *least* to lose by open revealing. If one or more information holders expect no loss or even a gain from a decision to openly reveal, then the secret will probably be revealed despite other innovators' best efforts to avoid this fate.[21] For those innovators whose preference is to keep information private, the challenge then becomes how to compete with free.[22]

---

19 Kenneth J. Arrow, *Economic Welfare and the Allocation of Resources for Inventions*, in THE RATE AND DIRECTION OF INVENTIVE ACTIVITY 609–25 (Richard R. Nelson ed., 1962); OVE GRANSTRAND, THE ECONOMICS OF MANAGEMENT OF INTELLECTUAL PROPERTY (1999).

20 Julia P. Liebeskind, *Knowledge, Strategy, and the Theory of the Firm*, 17 STRATEGIC MGMT. J. 93 (1996).

21 ERIC VON HIPPEL, DEMOCRATIZING INNOVATION (2005).

22 Richard C. Levin and Georg von Krogh, *How Can You Compete with Free?*, in INFO. TECHS. & TELECOMMS. INDUS. MONITOR, World Economic Forum, January 22, 2004.

Commonly, many firms and individuals have information that would be valuable to firms or individuals seeking to imitate a particular innovation. This is because innovators and imitators seldom need complete access to a specific version of an innovation. Indeed, engineers seldom even want to see a solution exactly as their competitors have designed it: specific circumstances differ even among close competitors, and solutions must in any case be adapted to each adopter's precise circumstances. The cost of doing so may offset the rewards from imitation. Therefore, what an engineer often wants to extract from the work of others is the algorithms, principles and the general outline of a possible improvement, rather than the details, which are often easy to redevelop. Interestingly, this information is likely to be available from many sources, because a single innovation type is likely to be applied to many different problems and markets.

For example, suppose you are a system developer at a bank and you are tasked with improving in-house software for checking customers' credit online. On the face of it, it might seem that you would gain most by studying the details of the systems that competing banks have developed to handle that same task. It is certainly true that competing banks may face market conditions very similar to those facing your bank, and they may well not want to reveal the valuable innovations they have developed to a competitor. However, the situation is still by no means bleak for an imitator. There are also many non-bank users of online credit checking systems in the world – probably hundreds of thousands. Some will have innovated and have the information you need. Of this group, in turn, some may be willing to reveal. The likelihood that the information you seek will be openly revealed by some individual or firm is further enhanced by the fact that your search for novel basic improvements may profitably extend far beyond the specific application of online credit checking. Other fields will also have information on *aspects* of the solution you need. For example, many applications in addition to online credit checking use software designed to determine whether persons seeking information are authorized to receive it. Any can potentially be a provider of information for this element of your improved system.

A finding by Lakhani and von Hippel illustrates the possibility that many firms and individuals may have similar information.[23] They studied Apache help-line websites, sites that enable those having problems with Apache software to post questions, and others to respond with answers. The authors asked those who provided answers how many other help-

---

[23] Karim Lakhani and Eric von Hippel, *How Open Source Software Works: 'Free' User-to-User Assistance*, 32 Res. Pol'y 923 (2003).

Table 9.1 Others may also know 'your' information

How many others do you think knew the answer to the question you answered?	*Frequent providers (n = 21)*	*Other providers (n = 67)*
Many	38%	61%
A few with good Apache knowledge	38%	18%
A few with specific problem experience	24%	21%

Source: Lakhani and von Hippel, table 10, at 935.

line participants they thought also knew a solution to specific and often obscure problems they had answered on the Apache online forum. Information providers generally were of the opinion that some or many other help-line participants also knew a solution, and could have provided an answer if they themselves had not done so (see Table 9.1).

Even in the unlikely event that a secret is held by one individual, that information holder will not find it easy to keep a secret for long. Mansfield studied 100 American firms and found that 'information concerning development decisions is generally in the hands of rivals within about 12 to 18 months, on the average, and information concerning the detailed nature and operation of a new product or process generally leaks out within about a year'.[24] This observation is supported by Allen's analysis of open revealing in the nineteenth-century English iron industry.[25] Allen notes that developers of improved blast furnace designs were unlikely to be able to keep their valuable innovations secret because 'in the case of blast furnaces and steelworks, the construction would have been done by contractors who would know the design'.[26] Also, 'the designs themselves were often created by consulting engineers who shifted from firm to firm'.[27]

B. When Profits from Patenting are Low

Next, suppose that a single innovator *is* the only holder of a particular innovation-related information, and that for some reason there are no easy substitutes for that information. Under these conditions an information holder actually does have a real choice with respect to disposing of its

---

[24] Edwin Mansfield, *How Rapidly Does New Industrial Technology Leak Out?*, 34 J. Indus. Econ. 217 (1985).

[25] Allen, *supra* note 9.

[26] *Id.* at 17.

[27] *Id.*

intellectual property: it can keep the innovation secret and profit from in-house use only, it can license it, or it can choose to openly reveal the innovation. We have just seen that the practical likelihood of keeping a secret is low, especially when there are multiple potential providers of very similar secrets. But if one legally protects an innovation by means of a patent or a copyright, one need not keep an innovation secret in order to control it. Thus, a firm or an individual that openly reveals is forgoing any chance to get a profit via licensing of intellectual property for a fee. What, in practical terms, is the likelihood of succeeding at this and so of forgoing profit by choosing to openly reveal?

In most subject matters, the relevant form of legal protection for intellectual property is the patent, generally the 'utility' patent. (The notable exception is the software industry, where material to be licensed is generally protected by copyright and sometimes also protected by patent.) In the United States, a utility patent may be granted for a 'new and useful process, machine, manufacture, or composition of matter, or any new and useful improvement thereof'.[28] They may not be granted for ideas per se, mathematical formulas, and laws of nature, and have at times been denied on the grounds that a particular invention was repugnant to morals and public policy.[29] Within subject matters possible to protect by patent, protection will be granted only when the intellectual property claimed meets additional criteria of utility, novelty and non-obviousness to those skilled in the relevant art.[30]

The real-world value of patent protection has been studied for more than 40 years. Various researchers have found that, with a few exceptions, innovators do *not* believe that patents are very useful either for excluding imitators or for capturing royalties in most industries.[31] (Fields generally cited as exceptions include pharmaceuticals, chemicals and chemical processes, where patents do enable markets for technical information.)[32] Moreover, a majority of respondents state that the availability of patent

---

[28] 35 U.S.C. § 101 (2006).

[29] Diamond v. Diehr, 450 U.S. 175, 185 (1981) (listing exclusions from patentable subject matter, including laws of nature, natural phenomena and abstract ideas); Gottschalk v. Benson, 409 U.S. 63 (1972); Funk Bros. See Co. v. Kalo Inoculant Co., 333 U.S. 127, 130 (1948) (excluding laws of nature from patentability); Juicy Whip, Inc. v. Orange Bang, Inc., 185 F.3d 1364, 1366–7 (Fed. Cir. 1999) (discussing prior history of denying patent protection for inventions offensive to public policy or morality).

[30] 35 U.S.C. §§ 101, 102, 103, 112 (2006).

[31] James Bessen and Michael J. Meurer, Patent Failure (2008).

[32] Ashish Arora, Andrea Fosfuri and Alfonso Gambardella, Markets for Technology (2001).

protection does not induce them to invest more in research and development than they would if patent protection did not exist. Taylor and Silberston reported that for 24 of 32 firms, only 5 percent or less of the R&D expenditures were dependent on the availability of patent protection.[33] Levin *et al.* surveyed 650 R&D executives in 130 different industries and found that all except respondents from the chemical and pharmaceutical industries judged patents to be 'relatively ineffective' compared to other measures such as secrecy or lead time advantages.[34]

Obtaining a patent typically costs thousands of dollars, and it can take years to get the necessary approval.[35] This makes patents especially impractical for many individual innovators, and also for small and medium-size firms of limited means. As a stark example, it is hard to imagine that an individual who has developed an innovation in sports equipment would find it appealing to invest in a patent and in follow-on efforts to find and prosecute imitators and/or find a licensee and enforce payment. Indeed, in a study of sports equipment innovations developed mostly by individuals, Shah found that few patented their inventions, and that those who did seldom gained any return from licensees as payment for their time and expenditures.[36]

Copyright is a low-cost and immediate form of legal protection that applies to original writings and images ranging from software code to music and movies. Authors do not have to apply for copyright protection; it 'follows the author's pen across the page'. Licensing of copyrighted

---

[33] CHRISTOPHER T. TAYLOR AND Z.A. SILBERSTON, THE ECONOMIC IMPACT OF THE PATENT SYSTEM (1973).

[34] Richard C. Levin *et al.*, *Appropriating the Returns from Industrial Research and Development*, 3 BROOKINGS PAPERS ON ECON. ACTIVITY 783, 794–5, 811 (1987). Others have also reported similar findings. See EDWIN MANSFIELD, INDUSTRIAL RESEARCH AND TECHNOLOGICAL INNOVATION (1968); Anthony Arundel, *The Relative Effectiveness of Patents and Secrecy for Appropriation*, 30 RES. POL'Y 611 (2001); Wesley M. Cohen *et al.*, *Protecting their Intellectual Assets: Appropriability Conditions and Why U.S. Manufacturing Firms Patent (or Not)*, NBER Working Paper Series, Paper No. 7552 (February 2000); Wesley M. Cohen *et al.*, *R&D Spillovers, Patents, and the Incentives to Innovate in Japan and the United States*, 31 RES. POL'Y 1349 (2002); Edwin Mansfield, *How Rapidly Does New Industrial Technology Leak Out?*, 34 J. INDUS. ECON. 217 (1985); Henrik Sattler, *Appropriability of Product Innovations: An Empirical Analysis for Germany*, 26 INT'L J. TECH. MGMT. 502 (2003).

[35] See, e.g., Harhoff *et al.*, *supra* note 19.

[36] Sonali Shah, *Sources and Patterns of Innovation in a Consumer Products Field: Innovations in Sporting Equipment*, MIT Sloan School of Management, Working Paper No. 4105 (2000), available at http://opensource.mit.edu/papers/shahsportspaper.pdf.

works is common, and it is widely practiced by commercial software firms. When one buys a copy of a non-custom software product, one is typically buying only a license to use the software for a certain period of time, not buying the intellectual property itself. However, in the case of intellectual property protected by copyright only the specific original writing itself is protected, not the underlying invention or ideas. As a consequence, those who wish to imitate the *function* of a copyrighted software program can do so by writing new software code to implement that same function. As seen in the case of the operating system GNU/Linux, innovators will do so if copyrighted software programs are too costly to license or if they lack the appropriate quality.

To summarize, in many practical situations little profit is being sacrificed by firms or individuals that choose to forgo the possibility of legally protecting their innovations in favor of open revealing.

C. When Incentives for Open Revealing are Positive

As was noted earlier, when we say that an innovator 'openly reveals' proprietary information we mean that all existing and potential intellectual property rights to that information are voluntarily given up by that innovator and that all interested parties are given access to it – the information becomes a public good. These conditions can often be met at a very low cost. For example, an innovator can simply post information about the innovation on a website without publicity, so those potentially interested must discover it. Or a firm that has developed a novel process machine can agree to give a factory tour to any firm or individual that thinks to ask for one, without attempting to publicize the invention or the availability of such tours in any way. However, it is clear that many innovators go beyond such basic, low-cost forms of open revealing. Often, innovators spend significant money and time to ensure that their innovations are seen in a favorable light, and that information about them is effectively and widely diffused. Writers of computer code may work hard to eliminate all bugs in the code they contribute to an open source community, and perhaps strive to document it in a way that is very easy for potential adopters to understand before openly revealing it. Plant owners may repaint their plants, announce the availability of tours at a general industry meeting, and then provide free lunches for their visitors.

Innovators' *active* efforts to create awareness about their openly revealed innovations suggest that there are positive, private rewards to be obtained from open revealing. A number of authors have considered what these might be. Foray discusses implications of the distributed nature of knowledge production among users and others, and notes that the increased capabilities of the computing and communication technologies tend to reduce innovators' ability to control the knowledge they create.[37] He proposes that the most effective knowledge-management policies and practices will be biased toward knowledge sharing. Allen and Nuvolari both suggest that an important private reward is that open revealing of new designs and their performances may significantly increase the rate of collective learning, leading to a more rapid development of better performing designs.[38] This has also been modeled and shown to be an important factor rewarding the formation of innovation communities within which innovations are openly revealed.[39]

Allen also proposed that reputation gained for a firm or for its managers might offset a reduction in profits for the firm caused by open revealing.[40] Both Raymond and Lerner and Tirole elaborated on this idea when explaining motivations of those making contributions to open source software development projects.[41] Sharing of high-quality code, they noted, can increase a programmer's reputation with his peers. This benefit can lead to other benefits, such as an increase in the programmer's value on the job market.[42]

Open revealing may also increase an innovator's profit in other ways. When an innovator openly reveals an innovation, the direct result is to increase the extent and pace of diffusion of that innovation relative to what it would be if the innovation were either licensed at a fee or held secret. The innovator may then benefit from the increase in diffusion via a number of effects. Among these are network effects. (The classic

---

37 Dominique Foray, Economics of Knowledge (2004).

38 Allen, *supra* note 9; Nuvolari, *supra* note 10.

39 Carliss Y. Baldwin *et al.*, *The Migration of Products from Lead-Innovators to Manufacturers*, Working Paper MIT Sloan School of Management, Working Paper No. 4554-05 (September 2005); Carliss Y. Baldwin and Kim B. Clark, *The Architecture of Participation: Does Code Architecture Mitigate Free Riding in the Open Source Development Model?*, 52(7) Mgmt. Sci. 1116–27 (2006).

40 Allen, *supra* note 9.

41 Raymond, *supra* note 3; Josh Lerner and Jean Tirole, *Some Simple Economics of Open Source*, 50 J. Indus. Econ. 197 (2002).

42 Free and open source software licenses do not grant users the full rights associated with free revealing as that term was defined earlier. Those who obtain the software under a license such as the General Public License (GPL) are restricted from certain practices. For example, they cannot incorporate GPL software into proprietary software that they then sell. Indeed, contributors of code to open source software projects are very concerned with enforcing such restrictions in order to ensure that their code remains accessible to all. Siobhan O'Mahoney, *Guarding the Commons: How Open Source Contributors Protect their Work*, 32 Res. Pol'y 1179 (2003).

illustration of a network effect is that the value of each telephone goes up as more are sold, because the value of a phone is strongly affected by the number of others who can be contacted in the network.) In addition, and very importantly, an innovation that is openly revealed and adopted by others can quickly become a 'dominant design' or even an 'open standard' that may pre-empt the development and/or commercialization of other versions of the innovation. If, as Allen has suggested, the innovation that is revealed is designed in a way that is especially appropriate to conditions unique to the innovator, this may result in creating a permanent source of competitive advantage for that innovator.

Being first to reveal a certain type of innovation increases a firm's chances of having its innovation widely adopted, other things being equal. This may induce innovators to race to reveal first. Firms engaged in a patent race may disclose information voluntarily if the profits from success do not go only to the winner of the race. If being second to the market quickly is preferable to being first to the market relatively late, there will be an incentive for voluntary revealing in order to accelerate the race.[43]

Positive incentives to openly reveal have been most deeply explored in the context of open source software projects. Research on the open source software development process reports that innovators have a number of motives for openly revealing their code. If they openly reveal, others can debug and improve upon the modules they have contributed, to everyone's benefit. Code that is openly revealed in open source projects has been found to be extensively reused. Von Krogh *et al.* studied software reuse in 15 open source software projects.[44] They report that *most* of the lines of software code in the majority of open source projects investigated were taken from the commons of other open source software projects and software libraries and reused. In addition, the developers interviewed stated that they were motivated by 'giving back' to those whose openly revealed code has been of value to them. Many developers therefore developed software specifically for others to reuse. They also enjoyed being part of a community of developers where learning through feedback from peers is very effective. The latter finding supports the earlier work by Hertel *et al.*[45]

---

[43] Giovanni de Fraja, *Strategic Spillovers in Patent Races*, 11 INT'L J. INDUS. ORG. 139 (1993).

[44] Georg von Krogh *et al.*, *Knowledge Reuse in Open Source Software: An Exploratory Study of 15 Open Source Projects*, 7 PROCEEDINGS OF 38TH ANNUAL HAWAII INT'L CONF. ON SYSTEM SCIS. (2005).

[45] Guido Hertel *et al.*, *Motivation of Software Developers in Open Source Projects: An Internet-Based Survey of Contributions to the Linux Kernel*, 32 RES. POL'Y 1159 (2003).

Software code developers are also motivated to have their improvement incorporated into the standard version of the open source software that is generally distributed by the volunteer open source organization because it will then be updated and maintained without further effort on the innovator's part. It must be noted that an improvement will be assured of inclusion in new 'official' software releases only if it is approved and adopted by the coordinating group of the software project, sometimes called 'core developers'. To become a core developer on a software project, a software project participant must expend considerable resources to identify and fix bugs or competently perform other tasks useful to the community.[46]

By openly revealing information about an innovative product or process, a user makes it possible for manufacturers to learn about that innovation. Manufacturers may then improve upon it and/or, assuming economies of scale in production, offer it at a price lower than users' in-house production costs.[47] When the improved version is offered for sale to the general market, the original 'user-innovator' (and others) can buy it and gain from in-house use of the improvements. For example, consider that manufacturers often convert user-developed innovations ('home-builts') into a much more robust and reliable form when preparing them for sale on the commercial market. Also, manufacturers may offer related services, such as field maintenance and repair programs, that innovating users must otherwise provide for themselves.

A variation of this argument applies to the open revealing among competing manufacturers documented by Henkel.[48] Competing developers of embedded Linux systems were creating software that was specifically designed to run the hardware products of their specific clients. Each manufacturer could openly reveal this equipment-specific code without fear of direct competitive repercussions: it was applicable mainly to specific products made by a manufacturer's client, and it was less valuable to others. At the same time, all would jointly benefit from open revealing of improvements to the underlying embedded Linux code base, upon which they all build their proprietary products. After all, the competitive advantages of all their products depended on this code base's being equal to or better than the proprietary software code used by other manufacturers of similar products. Additionally, Linux software was a complement to the

[46] Georg von Krogh *et al.*, *Community, Joining, and Specialization in Open Source Software Innovation: A Case Study*, 32 Res. Pol'y 1217 (2003).

[47] Georg von Krogh *et al.*, Enabling Knowledge Creation (2000); Suresh Kotha, *Mass Customization: Implementing the Emerging Paradigm for Competitive Advantage*, 16 Strategic Mgmt. J. 21 (1995); Harhoff *et al.*, *supra* note 19.

[48] Henkel, *supra* note 17.

computer hardware that many of the manufacturers in Henkel's sample also sold. Improved Linux software would likely increase sales of their complementary hardware products. (Complementary suppliers' incentives to innovate have been modeled by Harhoff.)[49]

To summarize, we have shown that open revealing is often the best practical option available to innovators in different contexts.

IV. THE PRIVATE-COLLECTIVE MODEL FOR INNOVATION INCENTIVES

We have seen that open revealing of innovation-related information developed at private cost may often be the most practical – and most profitable – course of action for innovators. How can we tie these observations back to theory, and perhaps improve theory as a result? Recall that at present there are two major models that characterize how innovation gets rewarded in industry and society.[50] The private investment model, discussed earlier, is based on the assumption that innovation will be supported by private investors expecting to make a profit. To encourage private investment in innovation, society grants innovators some limited rights to the innovations they generate via patents, copyrights and trade secrecy laws. These rights assist innovators in getting private returns from their innovation-related investments. At the same time, the monopoly control that society grants to innovators create a loss to society relative to the free and unfettered use by all of the knowledge that the innovators have created. Traditionally, society elects to suffer this social loss in order to increase innovators' incentives to invest in the creation of new knowledge.[51]

The second major model for inducing innovation is the collective action model for innovation incentives. This model is applied to the provision of public goods, where a public good is defined by its non-excludability and non-rivalry, as explained above.[52] The collective action model assumes that innovators relinquish control of knowledge or other assets they have developed to a project and so make them a public good. This requirement

---

49 Harhoff, *supra* note 6.

50 Eric von Hippel and Georg von Krogh, *Open Source Software Development and the Private-Collective Innovation Model: Issues for Organization Science*, 14 Org. Sci. 208, 208–23 (2003).

51 Arrow, *supra* note 20; Kenneth W. Dam, *Some Economic Considerations in the Intellectual Property Protection of Software*, 24 J. Legal Stud. 321 (1995).

52 See Olson, *supra* note 7.

enables collective action projects to avoid the social loss associated with the restricted access to knowledge of the private investment model. At the same time, it creates problems with respect to recruiting and motivating potential contributors. Since contributions to a collective action project are a public good, those who will benefit from that good have the option of waiting for others to contribute and then free riding on what they have done.[53]

The literature on collective action deals with the problem of recruiting contributors to a task in a number of ways. Oliver and Marwell as well as Taylor and Singleton predict that the description of a project's goals and the nature of recruiting efforts should matter a great deal.[54] Researchers also argue that the creation and deployment of selective incentives punishing or rewarding contributors for their contributions is essential to the success of collective action projects. However, the importance of selective incentives suggests that small groups will be most successful at executing collective action projects.[55] In small groups, selective incentives can be carefully tailored for each group member and the individual contributions can be more effectively monitored.[56] Science is often mentioned as an example of the collective action model. Incentives to create good science include targeted funding of research, and reputation awarded to those who make significant and recognized contributions to the field.[57] However, additional incentives in the form of public subsidies may also be required to generate adequate contributions. Thus, it is common to provide university scientists with research grants from public funds to induce them to create and openly reveal scientific research findings.[58]

Open source projects create a public good and so would seem to naturally fall within the province of the collective action model. Interestingly,

---

[53] *Id.*

[54] Pamela E. Oliver and Gerald Marwell, *The Paradox of Group Size in Collective Action: A Theory of the Critical Mass II*, 53 AM. SOC. REV. 1 (1988); Michael Taylor and Sara Singleton, *The Communal Resource: Transaction Costs and the Solution of Collective Action Problems*, 21 POL. & SOC. 195 (1993).

[55] Debra Friedman and Doug McAdam, *Collective Identity and Activism: Networks, Choices and the Life of a Social Movement*, in FRONTIERS IN SOCIAL MOVEMENT THEORY (Aldon Morris and Carol McClurg eds., 1992); Pamela E. Oliver, *Rewards and Punishment as Selective Incentives for Collective Action: Theoretical Investigations*, 85 AM. J. SOC. 1356 (1980).

[56] OLSON, *supra* note 7; Elinor Ostrom, *A Behavioral Approach to the Rational Choice Theory of Collective Action*, 92 AM. POL. SCI. REV. 1 (1998).

[57] Paula Stephan, *The Economics of Science*, 34 J. ECON. LITERATURE 1199 (1996).

[58] See sources cited *supra* note 4.

however, open source software projects deviate significantly from the guidelines for successful collective action projects just described. With respect to project recruitment, goal statements provided by successful innovation projects vary from technical and narrow to ideological and broad, and from precise to vague and emergent. For examples of goal statements in open source projects, see the websites of projects hosted on Sourceforge.net. Further, such projects may engage in no active recruiting beyond simply posting their intended goals and access addresses on a general public repository, such as a website customarily used for this purpose (for examples, see the Freshmeat.net website). Also, projects have shown by example that they can be successful even if large groups (perhaps thousands) of contributors are involved. Finally, projects that thrive on open revealing such as open source software projects seem to expend no effort to discourage free riding. In open source software, anyone is free to download code or seek help from project websites, and no apparent form of moral pressure is applied to make a compensating contribution (e.g., 'If you benefit from this code, please also contribute . . .').

What can explain these deviations from expected practice? In other words, what can explain open revealing of privately funded innovations and enthusiastic participation in projects to produce a public good? From the theoretical perspective, we think the answer involves revisiting some of the basic assumptions and easing some of the constraints conventionally applied to the private investment and collective action models for innovation incentives. Both, in an effort to offer 'clean' and simple models for research, have excluded from consideration a very rich and fertile middle ground where incentives for private investment and collective action can co-exist, and where a 'private-collective' model for innovation incentives can flourish. More specifically, a private-collective model occupies the middle ground between the private investment model and the collective action model in two ways. First, based on the empirical evidence discussed above regarding the private rewards associated with open revealing, we must reject the assumption in private investment models that open revealing of innovations developed with private funds necessarily involves a loss of private profit for the innovator. Indeed, the private-collective model of innovation incentives incorporates quite a different assumption: under common conditions, open revealing of proprietary innovations will increase rather than decrease innovators' private profit.

Second, a private-collective innovation incentive model modifies the assumption in collective action models that a free rider obtains benefits from the public good that are equal to those a contributor obtains. Instead, it assumes that private benefit to innovators from innovations openly contributed as a public good will yield *higher* private benefits to innovators than to free riders. This is realistic because contributors to a public good can obtain private rewards tied to the *development* of that good. Consider that the problem solving process and effort used to produce the public good yield private benefits that innovators have been shown to value, such as learning, enjoyment and a sense of ownership of the user's work product. (In open source software and other software projects the technical learning opportunities have been found to be substantial.[59] Previous coding and learning, in turn, can increase the user's returns on learning in future activity.)[60]

In addition, individual benefits in open source software projects have been tied to *participation* in communities surrounding the projects as opposed to simple free riding.[61] Hertel *et al.* support this view in a test of two extant models in the social psychology and sociology literatures.[62] The first model is by Klandermans and explains the incentives for people to participate in social movements.[63] The second model deals with motivational processes in small work teams, particularly 'virtual teams' with members working in different places and coordinating their work mainly via electronic media.[64] The researchers found a good fit between both models and data derived from a survey of 141 contributors to the Linux kernel, that is, they found that contributors' identify with the Linux developer community. They are also motivated by pragmatic motives to improve their own software, and by group-related factors such as their perceived indispensability for the team with which they were working.

Finally, it seems reasonable that if the cooperation among innovators is intense and sustainable, the rewards to innovators from social interactions might even outweigh individual rewards from the collective

---

59 Hertel *et al.*, *supra* note 46.

60 W. Brian Arthur, *Path-dependence, Self-reinforcement, and Human Learning*, in INCREASING RETURNS AND PATH DEPENDENCE IN THE ECONOMY 133 (W. Brian Arthur ed., 1997).

61 Jae Yun Moon and Lee Sproull, *Essence of Distributed Work: The Case of the Linux Kernel*, FIRST MONDAY, November 5, 2000, http://firstmonday.org/htbin/cgiwrap/bin/ojs/index.php/fm/article/view/801/710; PETER WAYNER, FREE FOR ALL (2000); O'Mahoney, *supra* note 43; von Krogh *et al.*, *supra* note 45; RAYMOND, *supra* note 3.

62 Hertel *et al.*, *supra* note 46.

63 BERT KLANDERMANS, THE SOCIAL PSYCHOLOGY OF PROTEST (1997).

64 Guido Hertel, *Management Virtueller Teams auf der Basis Sozialpsychologischer Modelle*, in SOZIALPSYCHOLOGIE WIRTHSCHAFTLICHER PROZESSE 172 (Erich H. Witte ed., 2002); Guido Hertel *et al.*, *Managing Distance by Interdependence: Goal Setting, Task Interdependence, and Team-based Rewards in Virtual Teams*, 13 EUR. J. WORK & ORG. PSYCHOL. 1 (2004).

Table 9.2 Three models of innovation incentives

Private investment model	***Collective action model***	***Private-collective model***
Applies to: Provision of private goods **Key assumption:** Innovators will gain higher profits than free riders only if innovations *are not* openly revealed as public goods **Impact on social welfare:** Monopoly control granted to innovators represents a loss to society relative to free use by all of knowledge created	**Applies to:** Provision of public goods **Key assumption:** Innovators and free riders profit equally from innovations contributed as public goods **Impact on social welfare:** Open revealing by participants in collective action projects avoids social loss problem, but public subsidy may be required to reward contributors	**Applies to:** Provision of public goods **Key assumption:** Innovators gain higher profits than free riders from openly-revealed innovations because some sources of profit remain private **Impact on social welfare:** 'Best of both worlds': Public goods are produced at private expense. Innovators relinquish control of knowledge produced, but at the same time gain private profits, so public subsidy not required

good being jointly developed. Typically, innovators that expend considerable resources in a cooperative project develop feelings of solidarity, fairness and altruism. Interestingly, such 'transformation of individual psychology' can make the innovator voluntarily contribute to the project beyond a level that would correspond to the individual benefits derived from the public good and its production.[65] Therefore, the analysis of the nature of the community of cooperating innovators must complement the analysis of individual rewards in the open revealing of innovation: many rewards are tied to entry into, contribution to and exit from the community.

Table 9.2 summarizes the line of argumentation in this section by distinguishing and comparing the private investment, collective action and private-collective model with respect to incentives to innovate, and the social implications of each model. The private-collective model of innovation incentives explains conditions under which an innovation created by private funding may be offered openly to all.

---

[65] Jon Elster, An Introduction to Karl Marx 132 (1986).

When these conditions are met, society appears to have the best of both worlds: new knowledge is created by private funding and then openly offered to all.

V. CONCLUSION

We have argued that open revealing of the detailed workings of novel products and services is a central feature of 'open innovation'. We have also shown that innovators frequently openly reveal proprietary information and knowledge regarding both the information-based products and the physical products they have developed. Such open revealing can make good economic sense for innovators and for society as well, and there are several incentives, some weak and others strong, that promote this behavior. The phenomenon of open revealing suggests that an alternative exists to the private and collective action models of innovation incentives. A 'private-collective' model of innovation incentives combines elements of the private model with elements of the collective action model. It occupies a middle ground that appears to offer society 'the best of both worlds': public goods created by private funding.

We suggest further research to develop a better understanding of this intriguing middle ground. In particular, research should investigate how the incentives proposed in the private-collective model interact to produce or prevent open revealing as an outcome of innovation. In addition, future empirical research is needed on open revealing as a competitive strategy. As mentioned above, innovators often reveal information and knowledge with a time lag. There is a need to better understand the nature of this lag, and the associated costs or benefits for both innovation developers and innovation adopters.

10 Open secrets

*Michael J. Madison**

I. INTRODUCTION

Both inside and outside the thing that the law calls a 'trade *secret*' lie domains of *open* information exchange. Trade secrecy demands a corresponding openness precisely by virtue of the law's requirement that the information may be protected as a trade secret provided that its secret status supplies its owner with economic value or a commercial advantage.[1] That advantage necessarily comes via exchange with others. Perhaps the most famous and commercially successful trade secret in history, Coca-Cola's formula for its classic soft drink, is the foundation of millions of dollars in sales to consumers worldwide. The commercial software industry likewise distributes products containing its trade secrets to millions of end-users annually.

This Janus-like or two-faced character of trade secrets has long been an implicit feature of accounts of the law of trade secrets. The open character of trade secrets appears in accounts that analyse the doctrine in relational terms, when those accounts note that trade secrecy's scope is usually limited to certain commercial or technical contexts. Information may be secret for purposes of interactions that are subject to special duties, such as those between employers and employees, and between business partners, but that same information may be accessible for other purposes, such as relations between a supplier and consumers, and between competitors. The latter groups ordinarily are entitled to access the secret, at least so long as they use 'legitimate' means.

Openness also appears in accounts that focus on the thing-like character of the trade 'information' that is held in secret,[2] in arguments that the law

---

* Professor of Law and Associate Dean for Research, University of Pittsburgh School of Law. My thanks to participants in a Workshop on the Law of Trade Secrets held at the New York University School of Law in February 2009 for helpful comments on a preliminary version of this chapter.

1 I focus here on trade secrecy rather than on the related but distinct concept of technical know-how.

2 See Michael J. Madison, *Law as Design: Objects, Concepts, and Digital Things,* 56 CASE W. RES. L. REV. 381, 440–1 (2005).

of trade secrets should be assimilated to other regimes of managed openness, such as patent and copyright law,[3] or that trade secrecy is founded on the idea of possession and use that distinguish owned things from nature.[4] Openness appears in accounts that emphasize the complementary nature of trade secret law and patent law. In that sense, disclosure via the latter mechanism and secrecy via the former are simply alternative mechanisms for appropriating value from technological innovation when those innovations are exploited commercially. Openness appears in accounts that note the transactions costs that burden licenses of secret information, known as Arrow's Information Paradox.[5] The prospective licensor is unlikely to disclose the secret information in the absence of a promise by the prospective licensee not to use the secret information; the prospective licensee is unlikely to make the promise before the secret is disclosed. [6] Both parties are navigating the boundary between what is secret and what is open.

This dialectical relationship between secrecy and openness distinguishes *trade* secrecy from other broader social uses of secrecy. Secrecy may be essential to the constitution of certain social groups. Some indigenous peoples want to preserve the secrecy of their sacred rituals not because they care to exploit them commercially but precisely and solely because the rituals are theirs and theirs alone.[7] The same dialectic distinguishes trade *secrecy* from the types of open and public property that we more typically associate with commerce.[8] This chapter explores a more explicit and general version of this point. Trade secrets and the law that defines and enforces them can be understood jointly in essentially structural terms, as

---

3 See Mark A. Lemley, *The Surprising Virtues of Treating Trade Secrets as IP Rights*, 61 STAN. L. REV. 311 (2008).

4 See Adam Mossoff, *What is Property? Putting the Pieces Back Together*, 45 ARIZ. L. REV. 371, 418 (2003) (describing the core of property as 'rights to acquire, use, and dispose of things'); Carol M. Rose, *Possession as the Origin of Property*, 52 U. CHI. L. REV. 73, 79–85 (1985). A 'commonly understood and shared set of symbols . . . gives significance and form to what might seem the quintessentially individualistic act: the claim that one has, by "possession", separated for oneself property from the great commons of unowned things'. Rose, *supra*, at 88.

5 See Lemley, *supra* note 3, at 336.

6 See Robert G. Bone, *A New Look at Trade Secret Law: Doctrine in Search of Justification*, 86 CAL. L. REV. 241, 280 (1998).

7 See MICHAEL F. BROWN, WHO OWNS NATIVE CULTURE? 13–14 (2003), reviewed in Carol M. Rose, *Property in All the Wrong Places?*, 114 YALE L.J. 991 (2005) (book review). In this context, generally there is no need to balance openness and secrecy.

8 See Carol Rose, *The Comedy of the Commons: Custom, Commerce, and Inherently Public Property*, 53 U. CHI. L. REV. 711, 769 (1986); Brett Frischmann, *An Economic Theory of Infrastructure and Commons Management*, 89 MINN. L. REV. 917 (2006).

managing boundaries between what is legally secret and what is legally public as part of broader social processes that construct and manage knowledge-related boundaries between groups. Quite aside from its possible role in promoting innovation,[9] trade secret law manages the creation and existence of social groups, firms and institutions, and manages interfaces between groups and outsiders generally.[10]

The chapter is organized in the following way. Part II explores one model for that structural relationship, the idea of the information or knowledge commons, and it briefly describes how the major formal features of trade secret law map onto the idea of commons. The part presents the central observation of this chapter, the apparent paradox that trade secrecy might offer structural support for the concept of an institution designed primarily to support sharing of information. Part III supplies several brief illustrations of the commons/trade secrecy intersection. The structural dialectic between openness and secrecy exists in numerous different patterns, rather than in a single form. The examples in this Part illustrate but do not define the universe of all possible cases. Part IV concludes.

II. TRADE SECRETS AND COMMONS

The relational secrecy that protects the commercial interests of a trade secret's owner may simultaneously promote broad social interests in access to, conservation and use of information. The process of protecting and defining a trade secret may simultaneously protect and define social activity inside a group, shield that activity from interference by others, and structure the interface between group insiders and those outside the group. Each of these features, and all of them in combination, support the proposition that secrets and the law of trade secrets may be used to create and protect commons.

---

9 See Lemley, *supra* note 3.

10 The purposes of boundary management are varied. I leave further exploration of the relationship between boundary management and the purposes of boundary management for another time. *Cf.* Dan L. Burk, *The Role of Patent Law in Knowledge Codification,* 23 BERKELEY TECH. L.J. 1009, 1018 (2008) (noting that apart from its role in constructing incentives to innovate, 'intellectual property may have important effects on the structure of firms and of industries').

Others have postulated that rival firms and communities of practitioners may rationally share technical know-how, both in order to optimize processes of innovation and in order to reinforce existing communities themselves. See Stephen R. Munzer, *Commons, Anticommons, and Community in Biotechnological Assets*, 10 THEORETICAL INQUIRIES L. 271 (2009); ERIC VON HIPPEL, THE SOURCES OF INNOVATION 76–92 (1988).

A. What is Commons?

I use the phrase information or knowledge *commons* to describe collections of knowledge and knowledge resources that are contributed to and available for use in a limited, managed, legally-, technologically- and socially-constructed institution, organization or structure. A public library is a kind of knowledge commons that consists of books and other objects maintained in its collections. A patent pool is a kind of knowledge commons constructed by owners of patents to related technologies, who contribute those patents to the pool and make them available to members of the pool on standardized terms. An open source computer program is a kind of commons constructed by software developers who contribute code to that program and make that code available to others. The open Internet itself is a kind of knowledge commons, which consists of webpages and other data that are posted by Internet users to openly-accessible hosts and made available to all other Internet users.

Commons in this account are important and essential structures for managing the production, conservation and exploitation of knowledge in ways that are complementary to but distinct from markets, that is, from structures defined legally by individual entitlements and private ordering, and complementary to but distinct from custom and social norms. By design, commons are *open* institutions, but they are not open in a raw, chaotic sense ('open to all comers, who can take whatever they want so long as they pay the going rate') or open in a public domain sense ('free from legal restriction, and free for the taking and use'). Commons are open in the sense that law and related social institutions design and manage the resources in the commons so that commons members, and individuals and institutions organized in adjacent places, can produce, sustain and consume commons resources in a sensible way. The boundaries of the commons and governance by commons members guard against the threat of corruption, pollution or privatization of commons resources.

Commons resources may be more or less open and accessible; likewise, the membership of the community or collective that contributes to and manages those resources may be more or less open and changeable. This idea of an information or knowledge commons is borrowed from the work of Elinor Ostrom and her colleagues, who have developed a rich literature studying commons for natural resources – trees, fish, pastures, water, and so forth.[11]

[11] See Elinor Ostrom, Governing the Commons: The Evolution of Institutions for Collective Action (1990); Elinor Ostrom and Charlotte Hess, *A Framework for Analyzing the Knowledge Commons*, in Understanding

Madison, Frischmann, and Strandburg have incorporated Ostrom's commons framework into a modified platform for analysing knowledge commons.[12] They argue that knowledge commons share many features with natural resource commons, with two major exceptions.

First, the resources that form the pool at the center of a natural resource commons are mostly given by nature's design. No law needs to create the lobsters that form the core of the Maine lobster fishery, which is the object of a major recent book on natural resource commons.[13] By contrast, knowledge commons consist primarily of intangible knowledge resources, such as copyrightable works of authorship, patentable inventions, and even unowned or unownable facts and ideas, that are defined and given shape by relevant bodies of law, often, but not exclusively, bodies of intellectual property law. The construction and function of a knowledge commons is correspondingly more complex, but also potentially more flexible. As I argue below, the law of trade secrets is one of those sources of commons construction.

Second, the social benefits offered by commons accrue not solely or even primarily to the parties to the commons relationship. In the natural resources context, commons institutions govern relations between commons members, primarily for the benefit of commons members. The Maine lobster fishery thrives as a natural commons because a complex set of informal and formal rules ensures that local fishermen harvest just so many lobsters each season as will lead to a viable fishery in the next season. Lobster live to breed another generation; lobstermen sustain their livelihoods.

In the context of knowledge commons, there is the possibility of knowledge being produced and shared not only within commons, but also via parties and institutions that are adjacent to commons but are not inside it. The commons institution governs not only what happens inside the commons but also the relationships (including benefits and costs) between the commons and other groups and outsiders. What happens in commons does *not* stay in commons. For example, the Associated Press (AP) cooperative wire service is a kind of knowledge commons constructed by member media enterprises. The AP pool consists of news items generated by the AP itself (funded by member contributions) and by AP members, who both contribute news to the commons and rely on the contents of the

---

KNOWLEDGE AS A COMMONS: FROM THEORY TO PRACTICE (Charlotte Hess and Elinor Ostrom eds., 2007).

[12] See Michael J. Madison, Brett M. Frischmann and Katherine J. Strandburg, *Constructing Commons in the Cultural Environment*, 95 CORNELL L. REV. 657 (2010).

[13] See generally JAMES M. ACHESON, CAPTURING THE COMMONS: DEVISING INSTITUTIONS TO MANAGE THE MAINE LOBSTER INDUSTRY (2003).

commons to build and operate their own, distinct newspapers, magazines and other media outlets *for the intended benefit of their audiences*, whose access to information depends heavily on operation of the AP and similar wire operations. Frischmann and Lemley generalize the intended third party benefits of knowledge institutions, or the positive welfare effects of openness, as 'spillovers'.[14] While commons arise and exist for a wide array of reasons, this 'spillovers' feature suggests that commons can serve important roles in solving production and sustainability problems associated with the public goods nature of knowledge resources.[15]

B. Trade Secrecy as a Feature of Commons

Recognizing and understanding the mechanics and purposes of a particular commons requires identifying and describing the mechanics of two essential elements: the knowledge or knowledge resources that constitute the commons, and the boundaries and boundary conditions that define what and who lie inside the commons, and what and who lie outside it. Commons is defined by what lies within, who has access to that material, and the rules and standards by which commons is governed.

Trade secret law, by virtue of its focus on secrecy, the legal requirement that the owner of a trade secret take reasonable precautions to maintain its secrecy, and liability standards that focus on breach of a duty of confidence or other use of improper means, can supply precisely the knowledge resources, boundary conditions and governance rules that commons requires. The two leading sources of the law of trade secrets, the Uniform Trade Secrets Act and the Restatement (First) of Torts, both can be deconstructed into three principal elements. Both begin with the proposition that some specific 'information' lies at the heart of the trade secret owner's claim. That information often consists of technical know-how, but it need not; non-technical information may constitute a trade secret. A successful claim of trade secret misappropriation requires proof that (1) the trade secret owner has exercised reasonable efforts to maintain the secrecy of the subject information;[16] (2) the information derives actual or potential economic value or some business or competitive value from its secrecy,[17] and (3) the defendant misappropriated the information via

[14] See Brett M. Frischmann and Mark A. Lemley, *Spillovers*, 107 Colum. L. Rev. 257 (2007).

[15] See Madison, Frischmann and Strandburg, *supra* note 12.

[16] See Uniform Trade Secrets Act § 1, 14 U.L.A. 437 (1986).

[17] See *id.* The Restatement definition, found in § 757, comment b is: 'A trade secret may consist of any formula, pattern, device or compilation of information

an act or disclosure that constitutes 'improper means', such as breach of an express or implied duty of confidentiality or industrial espionage.[18] The Uniform Trade Secrets Act (UTSA), by design, captures a broader range of information as potential 'trade secrets' and a broader range of conduct as improper conduct, than the Restatement does.[19] For present purposes, the differences are not significant.

The three basic elements of trade secrecy, when viewed in the context of a knowledge commons, can be mapped onto means for defining and maintaining commons, resources, membership and governance. Secrecy, which in some accounts of trade secret law amounts to a puzzling 'bug' to be explained,[20] may instead be a 'feature' of certain commons. Misappropriating a trade *secret* may be regarded as unlawful because of the harm that the misappropriation does to the operation of a commons.

---

which is used in one's business, and which gives him an opportunity to obtain an advantage over competitors who do not know or use it . . . [i]t is not simply information as to single or ephemeral events in the conduct of the business . . . A trade secret is a process or device for continuous use in the operation of the business'. Restatement (First) of Torts § 757 cmt. b (1939). The Restatement supplied six factors to consider in determining whether or not a trade secret exists: (1) the extent to which the information is known outside [the employer's] business; (2) the extent to which it is known by employees and others involved in his business; (3) the extent of measures taken by him to guard the secrecy of the information; (4) the value of the information to him and to his competitors; (5) the amount of effort or money expended by him in developing the information; (6) the ease or difficulty with which the information could be properly acquired or duplicated by others. Though these factors were not brought forward into the UTSA, they are commonly used by courts in applying the UTSA. See, e.g., Learning Curve Toys, Inc. v. Playwood Toys, Inc., 342 F.3d 714 (7th Cir. 2003) (applying Illinois version of the UTSA).

The extent to which the secret must create economic value varies from state to state. California's version of the UTSA, for example, requires that the trade secret must provide a 'substantial' business advantage over the competitors of the trade secret owner. See 2007 California Bar Model Jury Instructions, available at www.calbar.ca.gov/calbar/pdfs/sections/ipsection/tradesecrets/2007-12_caci-trade-secret-jury-instructions.pdf.

This discussion elides the possible distinction between the proposition that the subject information must constitute 'a secret', on the one hand, and the alternative construction that the information need not be 'a secret' but rather should be the subject of efforts to maintain its secrecy, even if the information is not, on all readings, 'a secret'.

18 See Uniform Trade Secrets Act § 1.

19 See Lemley, *supra* note 3; Michael Risch, *Why Do We Have Trade Secrets?*, 11 Marq. Intell. Prop. L. Rev. 1 (2007).

20 See Dan L. Burk, *Muddy Rules for Cyberspace*, 21 Cardozo L. Rev. 121, 173 (1999).

The fact that the secret relates to *trade* (or business or commerce) is part of the social motor that drives the open/secret commons in the first place. In other words, trade secrets may constitute the resources that are conserved and managed in a knowledge commons, allowing the community of members in the commons to flourish and structuring the interface between development and conservation of secret information inside the commons, on the one hand, and commercial exploitation of the secret information beyond the commons, on the other hand. Conduct that undermines that institutional arrangement is punished by the law as misappropriation.

The following sections describe the mapping between the doctrinal elements of a claim of trade secret misappropriation and the structural elements of a knowledge commons, especially with regard to resource definition, commons membership and boundary management issues, in greater detail. Part III then shifts from formal argument to illustrations taken from real world commons that are built wholly or partly from trade secret resources.

1. Trade secret definition and commons resources

The first and most elemental attribute both of a trade secrets lawsuit and of a knowledge commons is a definition of those informational things that comprise it. A trade secret plaintiff is expected to identify and describe the information that it seeks to protect.[21] The 'item' may be a process, formula, method or list; it may be the product of technological research or the subject matter of a confidentiality agreement between actual or prospective business partners. The secret is something that may be constructed as part of business operations, as part of business negotiations, or even (often, in fact) as part of the process of prosecuting a lawsuit.[22] The knowledge resources that constitute a commons are likewise constituted in any number of different ways: via the practices of an individual actor or firm as part of an industry or discipline; as part and parcel of legal processes that recognize intellectual property assets (patent law, copyright law); or in other ways.

In trade secrets and commons contexts, these paired questions – 'what is the thing?' and 'how did it come to be part of a complex business or commercial relationship?' – are close cousins. Answering them with regard to any particular trade secrets lawsuit (and with regard to a possible commons) requires answering more specific subsidiary questions, including how much

---

[21] See, e.g., MAI Sys. Corp. v. Peak Computer, Inc., 991 F.2d 511 (9th Cir. 1993).

[22] See Risch, *supra* note 19.

time, money and effort has gone into creation of the information (that is, is the information squarely part of the commons) and who does and who does not have authorized access to the information (who is a commons 'insider' and who is on the outside). Defining the trade secret defines what is in the commons, who has access to it and on what terms.

Importantly, the 'reasonable measures' requirement with respect to secrecy signals that secrecy (and its counterpart, openness) is both a legal and a cultural construct, not an innate characteristic of the information. The requirement provides a doctrinal and policy tool for adjusting the line between what is secret and what is 'open', or the degree to which 'openness' is permitted or required. To a sizable degree, the law of trade secrets demands that trade secret information be 'open' for others to appropriate lawfully. The U.S. Supreme Court held in *Kewanee Oil Co. v. Bicron Corp.*[23] that trade secret law must permit 'reverse engineering' of the trade secret by non-owners in order to maintain its consistency with federal patent law. Openness can be achieved in more than one way.

Consider the famous case of *E.I. duPont deNemours & Co. v. Christopher*,[24] in which the owner of trade secrets in a partially completed methanol plant was able to obtain relief against photographers who flew over the plant, likely at the request of a competitor who wished to learn the plant's secrets. Given the fact that the plant was readily observable from above, the court gave an entirely constructed meaning to the line between what was secret, in that case, and what was 'open'.

2. Business advantage and commons membership

As suggested by the paired questions above – 'what is the thing?' and 'how did it become part of the relationship in question?' – the definition of membership is closely aligned with the definition of the trade secret. Membership in the trade secret context is defined partly prospectively and positively, by virtue of an employment relationship, business partnership arrangement or other express duty of confidentiality. Membership is defined partly retrospectively, by virtue of a judicially-imposed duty of proper competitive behavior. This combination of formal and informal (or positive and normative) membership standards mirrors the positive and normative standards that define who is entitled to contribute to and take resources from a commons.

In any commons context, there is necessarily an interface between what and who exists inside the commons, on the one hand, and those

---

23 416 U.S. 470 (1974).

24 431 F.2d 1012 (5th Cir. 1970).

institutions and individuals who operate outside that commons and deal with it, with its members, and with its resources at arms' length or on other non-member terms, on the other hand. That interface is captured by what Frischmann and Lemley called 'spillovers', as resources in the commons are managed and leveraged in ways that provide benefits to people outside the commons. The commons is, as noted earlier, at least partly open, on terms defined in the context of each particular example.

In trade secret law, the interface between what is secret and what is open is also governed by the requirement that information to be protected as a trade secret offer its owner some (actual or potential) business or competitive advantage by virtue of its secrecy. The business/commercial requirement mandates that what is secret be of value in relation to what is part of the (open) marketplace. Purely personal, social or religious information rarely has actual or potential commercial value; such information may be intended to erect a boundary between inside and outside but is rarely designed or intended to govern an interface between who and what is part of the institution that controls its secrecy, on the one hand, and other, unrelated interests, on the other hand. Coca-Cola and Microsoft rely on trade secrecy to govern their relationships with consumers; a church guards secret doctrines to ensure the integrity of its rituals.

3. Misappropriation and commons governance

The details of the interface between the trade secret owner and its customers, and between commons and outside interests, matter intensely, of course. In the trade secrets context, the interface is governed by the requirement that a defendant is liable only for having used improper means to obtain the secret, either by breaching a duty of confidentiality or, as in the case of the aerial spy in *Christopher*, otherwise breaching some obligation of fair competition. The best known example of proper means in trade secret law, the well-known exception for competitors who engage in reverse engineering of an object or process that embodies a trade secret, illustrates the proposition perfectly. The exception for reverse engineering exists in large part to ensure that trade secrets owners cannot control information through secrecy that public policy deems significant to (fair) open market competition or (open) technological progress, or both.[25]

Governance of a knowledge commons requires a comparably detailed inquiry into what is proper conduct with regard to contributing resources to the commons, extracting resources from the commons, and otherwise

[25] See Pamela Samuelson and Suzanne Scotchmer, *The Law and Economics of Reverse Engineering*, 111 Yale L.J. 1575 (2002).

exploiting or conserving commons resources. Trade secrets cannot be appropriated via 'improper means', a standard that reflects a combination of formal and informal normative guides reflected in contracts, duties implied by law, and courts' sense of commercial morality. Commons resources are likewise governed by formal and informal rules that dictate 'appropriate' management. Governance in the commons context includes formal rules embodied in agreements, statutes and other formal sets of rules, and informal rules reflected in community norms, all establishing and monitoring membership and resource consumption and setting and enforcing sanctions for violations.[26]

In both situations, the point of governance is partly to ensure that the resources and people governed can accomplish their purpose, that is, to ensure the successful conveyance of knowledge from secret status to open status, in modified form. Preserving the secrecy of Coca-Cola's secret formula assures the company that it can produce and sell soft drinks in the open commercial marketplace. A famous early patent pool, a species of knowledge commons, was organized among the producers of airplanes, each of whom owned patents necessary to aircraft production, so that cross-licensing could be implemented and planes could fill the skies above World War I.[27]

The point of governance also may be to ensure the continuing stability and evolution of the trade secret-owning or commons-inhabiting social group or institution itself. One of the persistent puzzles of the law of trade secrets is what organizing principle makes that body of law comprehensible.[28] Some parts of the law are grounded in property law, others in tort; some seem aligned with innovation policy, others with competition and fair dealing. The suggestion here is that if an organizing principle is needed (and it may not be), that principle may be found not in the things that trade secret law produces but in the social arrangements that it enables.

---

[26] The discussion in this Part does not exhaust the possible mappings of trade secrets and trade secret law onto a framework for analysing a knowledge commons. For example, a central question in commons analysis is the composition of the community that has access to commons resources. That community is usually characterized by a degree of openness that is governed by community members themselves, who decide who is and who is not permitted to access commons resources. The law of trade secrecy imposes a counterpart requirement that the trade secret owner exercise 'reasonable measures' to maintain the secrecy of the protected information, rather than that the trade secret owner maintain the information in absolute secrecy.

[27] See Robert P. Merges, *Contracting into Liability Rules: Intellectual Property Rights and Collective Rights Organizations*, 84 CAL. L. REV. 1293, 1343–6 (1996).

[28] See Bone, *supra* note 6.

Trade secrets, the institutions that create and control them, and the rules those institutions create and use to govern the secrets, are interlinked devices that sustain distinct and legitimate forms of social organization.

A knowledge commons is far from the only social organization that this body of law may support. Indeed, trade secrecy is perhaps most closely associated with industrial firms. It is important to recognize, however, that trade secret law supports a variety of institutions, not only industrial firms, and that what those institutions share is a managed or governed boundary, policed by the law and other things, between what is secret, on the one hand, and what is open, on the other hand.[29] Among those institutions are those that are designed with the sharing of information as one of their core objectives. Trade secret law may support a knowledge commons; a knowledge commons may consist in part of trade secret information. The legitimacy of the institution emerges from its structure, not only from its output.[30]

Understanding not only why and how trade secret law feeds industrial firms much of the time, but also that it can be understood in the context of other social structures, such as knowledge commons, requires sensitive case-by-case analysis. The next part offers some brief examples.

III. CREATING AND PROTECTING COMMONS THROUGH SECRECY

The claim here is not that trade secrets are always necessary to the creation and maintenance of a knowledge commons. The general purpose personal computer and its operating system/application software environment

---

[29] On 'law' defined as a mechanism for communication among social actors and as a system for stabilizing the normative expectations of participants in those systems by recursively selecting norms to protect, which interacts with other systems of social communication, see NIKLAS LUHMANN, LAW AS A SOCIAL SYSTEM 93 (2004); *cf.* ANTHONY GIDDENS, THE CONSTITUTION OF SOCIETY: OUTLINE OF THE THEORY OF STRUCTURATION 162 (1984) (describing structuration as the mutually constituting interaction of individuals (actions) and groups (rules)); Jack M. Balkin, *Respect-Worthy: Frank Michelman and the Legitimate Constitution*, 39 TULSA L. REV. 485 (2004) (identifying a 'feedback effect' between popular interpretations and institutional effects as a necessary feature of certain theories of constitutional legitimacy).

[30] Secrecy in institutional settings designed for sharing knowledge can be contrasted with secrecy in traditional knowledge settings referred to earlier, *see supra* note 7 and accompanying text, in which the point of governance is to keep knowledge from migrating beyond the group.

formed a kind of knowledge commons for the benefit of consumers and software developers that was maintained, in part, by the trade secret status of certain relevant Microsoft technology.[31] It is possible, and some might say even likely, that an equivalent commons might have emerged in the absence of Microsoft's market position and trade secret strategy, and/or that the modern Internet represents the demise of the personal computing 'commons' and its replacement by something different. The high-velocity labor market that characterizes the Silicon Valley's high technology industries is a sort of trade secret-based knowledge commons[32] that might have emerged for different reasons.

Nor do I argue that commons defined in part by trade secret law are necessarily welfare-enhancing or even, speaking anecdotally, good things. Normative assessment of any commons requires developing and applying normative criteria. Whether any given institution or practice is a good thing, and why a trade secret-based institution might be chosen over some alternative, are important and interesting questions that await further analysis.[33] The discussion here focuses principally on description.

The claim instead is that trade secrets and the law of trade secrets can serve a structural function, that is, can be integral to the management of a knowledge-related institution, such as a commons. This part highlights several different ways in which trade secret law intersects with knowledge commons, as a complement to other, related commons-reinforcing mechanisms: physical boundaries, the definition of boundary resources, social norms and customs, traditions and histories, and subsidies and privileges

---

[31] See JONATHAN ZITTRAIN, THE FUTURE OF THE INTERNET – AND HOW TO STOP IT (2008).

[32] See Alan Hyde, The Wealth of Shared Information: Silicon Valley's High-Velocity Labor Market, Endogenous Economic Growth, and the Law of Trade Secrets (September 1998) (unpublished paper, available at http://andromeda.rutgers.edu/~hyde/); ALAN HYDE, WORKING IN SILICON VALLEY: ECONOMIC AND LEGAL ANALYSIS OF A HIGH-VELOCITY LABOR MARKET (2003); ANNALEE SAXENIAN, REGIONAL ADVANTAGE: CULTURE AND COMPETITION IN SILICON VALLEY AND ROUTE 128 (1996); Ronald J. Gilson, *The Legal Infrastructure of High Technology Industrial Districts: Silicon Valley, Route 128, and Covenants Not to Compete*, 74 N.Y.U. L. REV. 575 (1999). Mark Lemley's claim that software companies routinely ignore patents offers indirect support for the claim. See Mark A. Lemley, *Ignoring Patents*, 2008 MICH. ST. L. REV. 19.

[33] As an example of an alternative strategy, Von Hippel and von Krogh explore the possibility that innovators may intentionally choose a strategy of 'free revealing' of the workings of novel products and services. See Eric von Hippel and Georg von Krogh, *Free Revealing and the Private-Collective Model for Innovation Incentives,* 36 R&D MANAGEMENT 295 (2006).

reflected in the law. Neither trade secret law, trade secrecy, nor secrecy is sufficient, alone, to sustain a commons.

The point in each example below is that trade secrecy is not only or not necessarily a means of promoting innovation and creativity by or among those who are part of the commons itself. In the examples below, the boundaries and managed openness supplied by trade secrecy serve as means of ensuring that commons resources remain available not only to commons participants but also to those who interact with the commons via spillovers. Through trade secrecy, commons resources are available for use in processes of innovation and creativity, or are preserved and sustained against possible corruption, pollution or unintended privatization, or both.

A. Secrets as Commons Resources

A knowledge commons requires commons resources, knowledge objects or things that are produced in the commons, contributed to the commons and/or appropriated from the commons. Trade secrets can be those things.

An example of a trade secret commons in this sense is the BioForge project organized under the auspices of the CAMBIA BiOS initiative.[34] The BiOS initiative aims to support open source biotechnology, using an open, shared model of research results that mirrors the successful model used by open source software communities (which are themselves examples of knowledge commons, grounded in copyright law and software licenses).

---

[34] See BioForge, www.cambia.org/daisy/cambia/4292 (last visited February 1, 2010). CAMBIA stands for Center for Application of Molecular Biology to International Agriculture, an Australian non-profit organization. BiOS is CAMBIA's Biological Innovation for Open Society initiative. Emerging cousins of the BioForge initiative, attempting to use patent rights to build managed commons of research in synthetic biology, include the BioBricks Foundation and the MIT Registry of Standard Biological Parts. See the BioBricks Foundation, http://bbf.openwetware.org/ (last visited February 1, 2010); Registry of Standard Biological Parts, http://partsregistry.org/Main_Page (last visited February 1, 2010). These represent efforts to map concepts from the Free and Open Source Software movement onto biological research, by using strong (patent) rights to avoid rather than reinforce the potentially stifling 'thicket' of abundant patent claims on complementary technologies. One leading commentary on the design of commons institutions for synthetic biology recognizes that the mapping is awkward, but it does not mention trade secret law. See Arti K. Rai and James Boyle, *Synthetic Biology: Caught Between Property Rights, the Public Domain, and the Commons,* 5 PLoS Biology e58 (2007), available at www.plosbiology.org/article/info%3Adoi%2F10.1371%2Fjournal.pbio.0050058.

By contrast to open source software initiatives, the biotechnology domain is governed in the first place by patent law, and a difference between patent law and copyright law drives a key feature of the BioForge framework. In copyright law, public disclosure of a copyrighted work of authorship does not affect the scope of the copyright owner's exclusive right. Instead, even after publishing the work, the copyright owner retains the exclusive right to republish and distribute copies. An open source software license acts, in part, to place conditions on the authorized exercise of that right by an authorized user or modifier of the licensed work of authorship.[35] In patent law, open disclosure of an invention prior to patenting may invalidate the patent and undermine incentives to commercialize new technologies that are supplied by the patent system. On the whole, therefore, the patent system is designed to discourage early publication of inventions but encourage publication that accompanies patenting. In the context of scientific research, however, this 'pull of patents', to use Frischmann's phrase,[36] may lead to a reluctance or even unwillingness of researchers to share research results, because of the fear that they might jeopardize later commercialization opportunities. The insight of the promoters of BioForge is that open sharing of research results may co-exist with an institutional structure that accommodates the desire to commercialize.

Thus, participants in BioForge projects coordinate research communities via websites for publication and sharing of biotechnology inventions, including not only potentially patentable information but also related business and technical know-how, including trade secrets.[37] The temporal sequence here involves first constructing a commons via legal instruments that define membership, governance rules and the relevant resource types, then contributing research results and techniques, including trade secrets. Within the defined commons, community members are entitled to free use and free distribution of those inventions and know-how among members of the group. (Technology developed in the commons may be transferred outside for commercial development.) Importantly, the commons consists not only of the shared portfolio of research and (bio)technology, but also a constructed space within which commons participants can discuss their work *in confidence*.[38] So long as discussions take place inside the commons, or what the BiOS initiative refers to as a non-public 'protected'

---

[35] See Jacobsen v. Katzer, 535 F.3d 1373 (Fed. Cir. 2008).

[36] See Brett M. Frischmann, *The Pull of Patents*, 77 FORDHAM L. REV. 2143 (2009).

[37] See BioForge, *supra* note 34.

[38] See *id.*

commons, then they are (according to BiOS) non-public and therefore not subject to claims that later patents are invalid on prior disclosure grounds.[39] Assuming that the institutional structure works as intended, both in the sense that the legal forms are regarded as legitimate and in the sense that BioForge attracts members who participate according to its intended set of norms, then BioForge members can preserve the benefits of both secrecy, from a patent law perspective (where loss of secrecy via publication would defeat potential patent rights), and openness, from a shared research perspective. Recursive development, contribution and use of both secret and public commons resources according to the terms of the BioForge Charter is the engine that may sustain the commons.

Neither trade secrets nor trade secret law create this particular commons, but there is a specific relationship between trade secrets and commons in this case. The BioForge commons both exists despite trade secret law, because of the need to accommodate the demands of patent law in this scientific research context, and relies on trade secret law. The impact of trade secret law on the commons structure is specific: it supplies a legal standard – 'reasonable measures' to ensure secrecy – by which BioForge promoters and members hope to preserve the 'secret' status of shared research. Patent law pressures researchers not to publish their results before patenting. The BioForge construct enables researchers to retain the benefits of pre-patenting secrecy, while enjoying the science-related benefits of openness.

B. Secrets and Boundary Conditions

The BioForge project is novel. The claim that a 'protected commons' shields internal discussions of inventions from characterization as 'public' for patent law purposes is untested.[40] And it is not clear that the project

---

[39] For discussions of the BioForge project, see Robin Feldman, *Open Source, and Open Transfer: Market Approaches to Research Bottlenecks,* 7 Nw. J. Tech. & Intell. Prop. 14 (2008); Joseph Eng, Jr., *From Software to Life Sciences: The Spreading of the Open Source Production to New Technological Areas,* 24 Temp. J. Sci. Tech. & Envtl. L. 419 (2005); Stephen M. Maurer, *Open Source Drug Discovery: Finding a Niche (or Maybe Several),* 76 UMKC L. Rev. 405 (2007). The mechanics of BioForge are not fairly characterized as an open source software commons might be, as constructed from so many different property claims that it constitutes a 'comedy of the anticommons', or so fragmented in property terms that it is effectively immunized from privatization by any one party.

[40] A related proposal by Keith Aoki offers a 'limited commons' over secret information as a mechanism for protecting classes of traditional knowledge. See Keith Aoki, *Weeds, Seeds and Deeds: Recent Skirmishes in the Seed Wars,* 11 Cardozo J. Int'l & Comp. L. 247 (2003) (arguing for a 'limited commons'

has attracted or will attract a mass of researchers that is large enough to sustain a meaningful amount of innovation under the BioForge umbrella.

Two far less technologically chic examples illustrate a related but distinct use of trade secrecy to define and protect a commons. Both examples were developed originally as case studies of social norms that offer appropriation mechanisms that are equal or superior to copyright or patent rights in promoting innovation and creativity. Both, however, indirectly shed light on norm-based commons defined by trade secrecy, with trade secrets serving partly as commons resources but more importantly as boundary objects.[41] Access to trade secrets defines who is part of the commons and has access to its resources (and who is therefore subject to a normative duty to protect its secrets) and define measures of fair behavior in participating in and competing with the commons, that is, proper and improper 'means' of accessing trade secret information.

Fauchart and von Hippel describe the community of French chefs and the measures that they take to protect the distinct techniques and recipes that define their discipline.[42] The rules governing the community of chefs are recognized and enforced as informal but regular norms that mirror the law of trade secrets in some respects. Fauchart and von Hippel summarize a key finding of their research as follows:

> The community acknowledges the right of a recipe inventor to exclude others from practicing his invention, even if all the information required to do so is publicly available. A second norm mandates that, if a chef reveals recipe-related secret information to a colleague, that chef must not pass the information on to others without permission. This norm gives a chef a property right similar to that attainable via a contract under trade secrecy law. That is, protected by this norm, a chef can *selectively* reveal his secret information to another without fearing that as a result, the information will become generally known.[43]

---

approach to address problems presented by intellectual property protection of traditional knowledge); Gelvina Rodriguez Stevenson, *Trade Secrets: The Secret to Protecting Indigenous Ethnobiological (Medicinal) Knowledge* , 32 N.Y.U. J. INT'L L. & POL. 1119 (2000).

[41] See Shubha Ghosh, *Patent Law and the Assurance Game: Refitting Intellectual Property in the Box of Regulation*, 18 CAN. J. L. & JURISPRUDENCE 307, 318–19 (2005) (comparing Mertonian scientific commons to the commercial market and describing trade secrecy as barriers to entry in both); Steven Wilf, *Trade Secrets, Property, and Social Relations*, 34 CONN. L. REV. 787, 796 (2002) (describing property boundaries as two sides of a common coin, involving both a duty to police and a right to exclude).

[42] See Emmanuelle Fauchart and Eric von Hippel, *Norms-Based Intellectual Property Systems: The Case of French Chefs*, 19 ORG. SCI. 187 (2008).

[43] *Id.*

Related norms dealt with what the authors call 'honorable' (or a trade secrets lawyer might call 'proper') behavior. A chef receiving a recipe in confidence from another chef is honor-bound not to perform the recipe exactly, and to acknowledge the source of the recipe in contexts, such as cookbooks or cooking shows, where disclosing the source might be contextually appropriate.[44] Finally, there is a disciplinary norm:

> As one accomplished chef said: 'If another chef copies a recipe exactly we are very furious; we will not talk to this chef anymore, and we won't communicate information to him in the future'.[45]

Importantly for purposes of assimilating trade secrets to boundary objects in the commons, the discipline applied to violators of the chefs' code is, in effect, banishment from the community. The commons consists of recipes as trade secrets; trade secrecy simultaneously defines the community. In contrast to the BioForge example, the temporal sequence in this description involves secrecy and commons community co-evolving, simultaneously.

In a similar spirit, Loshin describes social norms that govern development of, access to and use of magic tricks by the community of practicing magicians.[46] In many respects, magicians and chefs use trade secrecy to similar effect. But there are important differences. Loshin describes three types of 'secret' tricks, what he characterizes as 'popular' magic (which is hardly secret at all), 'common' magic shared widely among magicians, and 'proprietary' magic shared selectively among practicing professionals. These levels of secrecy both constitute and are reinforced by commons and community boundaries. He describes the chief risk to the magicians' commons (a term that I ascribe to his framework, rather than a term that he invokes) not as unacknowledged copying, as in the cooking context, but exposure of the secret itself to the world beyond the magicians' community.

---

44 Serving a meal based on the recipe does not necessarily imply sharing the recipe itself; even reciting the formal recipe might not constitute disclosure of secret disciplinary techniques needed to execute the recipe properly. In both senses, the secrets are maintained in the corps of chefs while gastronomes can enjoy French restaurants and cookbooks. Strandburg develops the related distinction between self-disclosing and non-self-disclosing inventions in her analysis of the experimental use defense in patent law. See Katherine J. Strandburg, *What Does the Public Get? Experimental Use and the Patent Bargain,* 2004 WIS. L. REV. 81, 104–18.

45 See Fauchart and von Hippel, *supra* note 42.

46 See Jacob Loshin, *Secrets Revealed: How Magicians Protect Intellectual Property Without Law*, in LAW AND MAGIC: A COLLECTION OF ESSAYS (Christine A. Corcos ed., 2009), available at http://ssrn.com/abstract=1005564.

In these two examples, trade secrecy serves related but different roles in guarding the interface between insiders and outsiders, and between what is secret and what is open, when compared with the BioForge example. First, the law of trade secrets is doing relatively little work in defining and managing the chefs' and magicians' commons and the resources within it. Instead, communal norms define what is secret and what is not and the obligations that accompany each status. What is noteworthy, however, is not the relative unimportance of formal law but how the commons is constructed via social structures that echo formal law so closely. (In a different sense, the relative unimportance of formal intellectual property law in these 'creative' domains was part of the point of the original research. It is possible, in fact, to consider recipes for *haute cuisine* not to be trade secrets in the legal sense at all, precisely because the risk of misappropriation by non-chefs is so low. These recipes may be known to non-chefs, yet protected from misappropriation by them because non-chefs lack the expertise to execute the recipes.) Second, whereas BioForge members structured their commons to ensure secrecy on the inside and openness (and commercial marketability) with respect to the outside, French chefs necessarily share certain features of their secrets with the marketplace (those who eat at fine French restaurants). Any particular dish necessarily embodies openness and secrecy all at once, both inside and outside the commons. Magicians, by contrast, expect graded openness on the inside and absolute secrecy with respect to the outside marketplace.

The point is that in the commons context, secrets and trade secrets do not come in a single flavor. Openness of the resource and openness of the community are measured relative to context. Making magicians' secrets accessible to lay audiences would disrupt the magicians' commons; magicians care both about the secrecy of the content and access by non-magicians. Serving food prepared using chefs' secrets not only would not disrupt the chefs' commons but might even reinforce it, to the extent that the restaurant experience ratifies the distinctive status of the chefs; French chefs care differently (and perhaps less) about the content of the 'secret recipes' but care very much about who, precisely, has access to them.

C. Secret Methods and Constructing a Commons

A final example of commons structured via trade secrets is Google's search engine results. In this instance, the results themselves constitute the commons, which are open and available for use by anyone with access to Google's service. The relevant trade secrets are Google's secret methods for compiling results in response to a given search query.

The fact that Google's search algorithms are largely secret, like those of most Internet search engines, is indisputable.[47] Google and other firms have patent portfolios related to their search technologies, which expose certain aspects of search and its methods to public view via the disclosures associated with patenting. But maintaining the secrecy of search methods, including the mechanics of Google's PageRank algorithm, is necessary, according to Google, both to ensure that Google maintains its competitive advantage relative to other search engines and to prevent third parties from 'gaming' search results in their favor.[48] Google has been subject to claims by firms that allege that their status in Google's search results has been diminished unfairly. Google has largely prevailed on those claims, partly on the ground that Google is deemed to have a free speech interest in its search results as 'speech'[49] and, more important for present purposes, on the ground that Google's use of secret methods to compile search results does not amount to anticompetitive conduct.[50] Even more significantly, Google has successfully resisted enforcement of a government subpoena for search-related data on trade secret grounds.[51]

What does trade secrecy buy in this example, not only from Google's perspective, but in light of the commons framework? Here, trade secrecy offers a direction to the spillovers that are important parts of a knowledge commons. As Frischmann writes, not only is the World Wide Web or the Internet an open information commons,[52] but the search landscape provided by private firms is a structured commons nested inside the Internet's broader commons framework.[53] The fact that this latter commons is managed by a private firm raises questions of degree but not character. Google is not akin to Coca-Cola, simply selling a product (or service) that is constructed via secret methods. Search results and the information to

---

47 See James Grimmelmann, *The Structure of Search Engine Law,* 93 Iowa L. Rev. 1, 48–50 (2007).

48 Google argues that 'trust' in search is a vital part of the user experience. See Gonzales v. Google, 234 F.R.D. 674, 683–4 (N.D. Cal. 2006).

49 See Search King, Inc. v. Google Tech., Inc., No. CIV-02-1457-M, 2003 WL 21464568, at *2–5 (W.D. Okla. May 27, 2003); Kinderstart.com LLC v. Google, Inc., No. C 06-2057 JF (RS), 2006 WL 3246596, at *4–7 (N.D. Cal. July 13, 2006).

50 See *Kinderstart.com*, 2007 WL 831806.

51 See Gonzales v. Google, 234 F.R.D. at 686.

52 See Michael A. Carrier and Greg Lastowka, *Against Cyberproperty,* 22 Berkeley Tech. L.J. 1485, 1506–7 (2007).

53 See Brett M. Frischmann, *Cultural Environment and* The Wealth of Networks*,* 74 U. Chi. L. Rev. 1083, 1112 (2007) (reviewing Yochai Benkler, The Wealth of Networks: How Social Production Transforms Markets and Freedom (2006)).

which they link are commons resources in the sense that they are produced and supplied in a political and technological environment that is open by design for use by anyone, for any purpose. Any user of the World Wide Web can create a resource that will be searched by Google; any user who searches the Web via Google can use its search results. Search results and the information to which they link offer precisely the kind of spillover benefits to users that often define knowledge commons. The beneficiaries of the commons governed in part by Google's search technologies may not be the users for whom Internet resources were designed or intended. Yet those search results, as managed by Google, are the products of largely secret processes. Google asserts that Google users 'trust' its results and that the secrecy of Google's algorithms is necessary to maintain the integrity of those results. Trust, protected by Google's claims of trade secrecy, helps to assure that the spillover mechanism operates as Internet users expect and intend.[54]

It should be noted that the structural relationship between trade secrecy and commons does not necessarily promote social welfare. The fact that Google's secret methods contribute substantially to the construction of a search results commons is precisely the point at which Google's critics engage with the company. Bracha and Pasquale argue forcefully that harmful information asymmetries exist between search firms and consumers, which they trace largely to the secrecy of search engine algorithms.[55] Instead, the openness and salience of search results in the contemporary knowledge economy, and the information that is linked to in those results – the commons role of search, in other words – means that government supervision of search results is both appropriate and consistent with search engines' interests in protecting their trade secrets.[56]

Reasonable people may disagree about the possibility that 'neutral' search results are possible under any scenario, let alone under the guidance of government regulators,[57] but the role of secrecy in constructing this commons seems uncontested. Equally important and distinctive is the

---

[54] There is a parallel here between the role of trade secrecy in structuring a search commons and the role of trade secrecy in Microsoft's provision of certain technology that enabled the development of the open architecture of the personal computer. See note 31 *supra* and accompanying text.

[55] See Oren Bracha and Frank Pasquale, *Federal Search Commission? Access, Fairness, and Accountability in the Law of Search*, 93 CORNELL L. REV. 1149 (2008).

[56] See *id.* at 1201–7.

[57] In the closely related case of allocation of telecommunications spectrum, a knowledge commons that historically has been tightly regulated under arguably transparent government regulation, some critics now argue that technological secrecy (encryption technology) is a viable tool for managing possible electromag-

role of the law of trade secrets in defining the scope of what is secret, and what is not, about Google's search technologies. Like French chefs, whose meals do not disclose secret recipes and techniques, Google's search results do not disclose its secret search algorithms. In Google's case, however, unlike the chefs', the firm relies explicitly on formal trade secret law to define its own interests and the scope of what is open and what is not in the commons of search results.

IV. CONCLUSION

This chapter has argued that trade secrets and trade secret law can serve a structural function in the organization of groups, practices and firms in the knowledge economy. Central to this structural role is the dual nature of a trade secret, as hidden from view on one side but as necessarily open on the other. The flexibility inherent in each of the several doctrinal elements that comprise a claim of misappropriation of trade secrets allow parties and courts to use the law to construct and manage what is secret, and what is open, as part of that structural role. A trade secret is never inherently secret or open. The secrecy and openness of the secret depends on how the secret is embedded in relationships among secrets and among those who develop or use the secret information.[58] To illustrate the point, the chapter reviews a series of examples of knowledge commons and explores the various roles played by trade secret law in each of them.

Like firms, markets, social norms and informal rules, commons are neither inherently productive nor inherently efficient. Like each of those things, commons offer the prospect of distinctly valuable forms of social ordering as platforms for novel and collaborative uses of knowledge, but also offer risks of socially stifling, anticompetitive and inefficient outcomes. The fact that trade secrets can be used to construct and protect

---

netic interference. See, e.g., Susan P. Crawford, *The Radio and the Internet,* 23 BERKELEY TECH. L.J. 933 (2008).

The availability of secrecy thus justifies far broader *de*regulation of private firms that supply commons resources than law or incumbent industry has been willing to accept.

[58] *Cf.* Michael J. Madison, *Complexity and Copyright in Contradiction,* 18 CARDOZO ARTS & ENT. L.J. 125, 154, n.107 (2000) (noting that normatively attractive 'open', heterogeneous urban communities like Berkeley and Greenwich Village may depend on their proximity to comparatively 'closed', homogeneous communities – much of San Francisco and New York). Secret status depends on its contrast with openness.

commons does not mean that their structural role always promotes social welfare.

While an analysis of the structural role of trade secrets is far from complete, this preliminary review does suggest some implications.

The first implication is that a conception of trade secret law that relies exclusively or primarily on a single policy objective is likely to be under-inclusive with respect to the possibly welfare-enhancing roles that trade secrets may play in the economy and society. Whether that single metric focuses on innovation incentives, commercial morality or unfair competition, there is a risk that the law might concern itself too much solely with private, bilateral interests and pay insufficient attention to collective or social institutions that offer the possibility of welfare gains by third parties, i.e., spillovers.

The second and broader implication is linked to the possibility offered previously by others, including Burk, that intellectual property rights in addition to trade secrets may serve structural or social functions that relate indirectly, if at all, to their purpose in promoting innovation and creativity.[59] Further investigation is necessary to understand what might be called the structural mechanics of intellectual property, including the relative strengths and weaknesses of all forms of intellectual property rights as structural devices, and the relative significance of intellectual property rights and other structural elements. Further investigation is also necessary to better understand the impact of specific elements of IP doctrines in constructing and managing the resources and boundaries that are essential to IP institutions, especially commons. Some commons related to trade secrets are connected to formal trade secrets doctrines; some are connected to secrecy norms. Compared to copyrights and patents, trade secrets are comparatively unfixed. Thus, as secret status evolves, both in practice and in response to legal doctrine, how do commons dynamics change?

A third and final broad implication is that given the possibility that a given commons or other institution might develop around information resources other than secrets, knowledge commons that do form around trade secrets depend not only on trade secrets rights alone and the norms and technologies to which they relate. Knowledge commons constructed by French chefs, magicians, bioscientists and Google engineers depend not only on their respective secrets. They depend as well on normative

---

[59] See Burk, *supra* note 10. See also Stephen R. Munzer, *Commons, Anticommons, and Community in Biotechnological Assets*, 10 Theoretical Inq. L. 217, 295–7 (2009) (considering possible symbioses between open and proprietary models of innovation in synthetic biology).

evaluations of magic-based entertainment, French food, synthetic biology and access to online information. The further investigation suggested by this chapter is both narrow, in the sense that further case studies that focus on specific intellectual property rights are warranted, and broad, in the sense that legal entitlements alone cannot be the sole focus of study.

11 Uncorking trade secrets: sparking the interaction between trade secrecy and open biotechnology

*Geertrui Van Overwalle**

INTRODUCTION

'Three may keep a secret, if two of them are dead.' This quote from Benjamin Franklin reflects well the delicate, if not impossible attempt to share a secret. Sharing secrets, however, is of vital importance. Translated in legal parlance, the exchange of trade secrets may be essential to the operation and further development of patented inventions. Beyond the information disclosed in patents, users might need to acquire complementary know-how in order to make the patented technology function optimally.[1]

The exchange of patented inventions and related know-how often takes place through bilateral or cross-licenses. Our previous research examined the role of collaborative licensing models in streamlining access and use of patents, specifically in the field of genetics.[2] The present chapter examines the potential role of collaborative licensing models in facilitating the transfer of related trade secrets. The central question, around which the chapter

* Professor of Intellectual Property Law, University of Leuven, Belgium; Professor of Patent Law and New Technologies, University of Tilburg, the Netherlands. The present research was supported by the Sixth Framework Programme of the European Union (Eurogentest) and the Vancraesbeeck Fund (K.U. Leuven, Belgium). Special thanks go to Pamela Samuelson and Robert Bone for helpful discussions, and Rochelle Dreyfuss and Esther van Zimmeren for comments on an earlier draft of this chapter.

1 See Ashish Arora, *Contracting for Tacit Knowledge: The Provision of Technical Services in Technology Licensing Contracts*, 50 J. DEV. ECON. 233, 246 (1996).

2 GENE PATENTS AND COLLABORATIVE LICENSING MODELS: PATENT POOLS, CLEARINGHOUSES, OPEN SOURCE MODELS AND LIABILITY REGIMES 477 (Geertrui Van Overwalle ed., Cambridge University Press, 2009); Geertrui Van Overwalle *et al.*, *Models for Facilitating Access to Patents on Genetic Inventions*, 7 NATURE REV. GENETICS 143 (2006); Birgit Verbeure *et al.*, *Patent Pools and Diagnostic Testing*, 24 TRENDS IN BIOTECHNOLOGY 115 (2006); Esther van Zimmeren *et al.*, *A Clearinghouse for Diagnostic Testing: the Solution to Ensure Access to and Use of Patented Genetic Inventions?*, 84 BULL. WORLD HEALTH ORG. 352 (2006).

revolves, is whether the transfer of know-how, incident to a patent, might be accelerated by the use of collaborative licensing strategies. In other words, can collaborative institutions fuel the sharing of trade secrets and reshape them into 'open secrets',[3] thereby fostering the construction of 'open biotechnology' projects and infrastructures? This question is explored from a conceptual-theoretical and empirical perspective, rather than from a normative point of view.

The present chapter will conclude that, in principle, collaborative license mechanisms, in particular patent pools and open source regimes, may facilitate the transfer of know-how complementary to patented inventions, and thus assist in uncorking know-how and fostering 'open secrets'. Clearinghouses seem somewhat less fit to assist in the transfer of confidential technical information incidental to patented inventions, but they may be useful for the exchange of confidential business information. In practice, however, knowledge producers have been somewhat reluctant to make use of collaborative licensing models in the life sciences in order to engage in hybrid licensing agreements involving the exchange of both patents and trade secrets. The absence of a personal relation of trust and Europe's lack of a well established codification of trade secrecy law modeled along the lines of the Uniform Trade Secrets Act (UTSA)[4] may well account for some hesitation about participating in such collaborative rights platforms.

Part I focuses on the first core element of the twin concept of 'open secret', namely trade secrecy. The section briefly introduces prevailing legal protection regimes for trade secrets, and points to the emergence of trade secrecy regimes in biotechnology. Part II discusses the second component of the twin concept, namely openness. The section looks into the disclosure effect of trade secrecy law and provides a succinct overview of other projects and initiatives fostering openness, such as 'open access', 'open patent' and 'open biotechnology'. Part III then examines the key question of the present inquiry and explores the role of collaborative licensing models, such as patent pools, clearinghouses and open source regimes, in assisting the fluid transaction of trade secrets and in building 'open biotechnology' infrastructures, both from theoretical and practical perspectives. Part IV closes by examining some perceived obstacles in using these models for the exchange of hybrid licensing agreements and suggests some avenues for further research.

---

[3] Courtesy of OpenSecrets.org, www.opensecrets.org/index.php.

[4] Uniform Trade Secrets Act, § 1(2) 14 U.L.A. 438 (1985). The Act was approved in August 1979 and recommended for enactment in all the states, and amended in August 1985.

I. RISE OF TRADE SECRECY PROTECTION IN BIOTECHNOLOGY

The Agreement on Trade-Related Aspects of Intellectual Property Rights ('TRIPS Agreement') prescribes that in the course of ensuring effective protection against unfair competition, members shall protect undisclosed information and requires all signatories to ensure that trade secrets are regarded as protectable subject matter, without specifying a particular legal regime for achieving trade secret protection.[5] The inclusion of trade secrets under the TRIPS Agreement was considered a major achievement[6] in that it represented the first multilateral acknowledgement of the essential role that trade secrets play in industry.[7]

In the United States, most states provide fully fledged codified trade secrecy laws. In the years since 1979, when it was first promulgated by the National Conference of Commissioners on Uniform Laws, and particularly since its amendment in 1985, the UTSA has been adopted by a majority of the states in the United States.[8] Eminent scholars suggest that trade secrecy law is best seen as an intellectual property (IP) right.[9] In most states, the UTSA displaces conflicting tort, restitutionary and other law, but does not affect contractual and criminal remedies.[10]

In most European countries, no all-embracing legal protection regime exists for undisclosed know-how.[11] In the absence of the establishment of

---

[5] TRIPS Agreement, April 15, 1994, 33 I.L.M. 81 (1994), Art. 39(1).

[6] Thomas Cottier, *The Prospects for Intellectual Property in GATT*, in COMMON MKT. L. REV. 404 (1991); see also Sharon K. Sandeen, Chapter 20.

[7] François Dessemontet, *Protection of Trade Secrets and Confidential Information*, in INTELLECTUAL PROPERTY AND INTERNATIONAL TRADE: THE TRIPS AGREEMENT 239 (Carlos M. Correa and Abdulqawi A. Yusuf eds., Kluwer Law International, 1998).

[8] See Robert Denicola, Chapter 2. See also Gregory M. Wasson, Annotation, *Misappropriation of Trade Secrets under the Restatement of Torts*, 14 AM. JUR. PROOF FACTS 619, 629 (1991).

[9] Mark A. Lemley, *The Surprising Virtues of Treating Trade Secrets as IP Rights*, 61 STAN. L. REV. 103, 118 (2008). Trade secret rights have two critical features in common with IP rights: they should be viewed as (non-absolute) exclusionary rights promoting (a) inventive activity, and (b) disclosure. See also Mark A. Lemley, Chapter 5.

[10] For more details, see UTSA § 7.

[11] With the exception of Italy, where a trade secrecy protection regime has been introduced which has gained the status of a full intellectual property right. See Gustavo Ghidini and Valeria Falce, Chapter 6.

a 'legal monopoly'[12] on undisclosed know-how, it is, however, possible to obtain a monopoly as a practical matter.[13] Such a monopoly is based on the physical control of information complemented with confidentiality agreements – often referred to in legal doctrine as protection through 'self-help'.[14] Unauthorized use of undisclosed know-how may be further deterred by a variety of fragmented legal measures established in criminal law, labor law or competition law.

Trade secrecy protection may be chosen for a variety of reasons. In some situations, trade secrecy protection may be the *only* form of protection at hand. Trade secrecy may be the only available protection for unpatentable advances such as (new) algorithms, or inventions that are neither novel, inventive/non-obvious or industrially applicable/useful.[15] In other cases, trade secrecy is the *preferred* mode of protection.[16] Sometimes an inventor prefers secrecy because it is cheaper than patenting, less often leads to litigation, and can sometimes last for longer than the 20-year term of patents. In yet other instances, trade secrecy is opted for to protect technical know-how which is complementary to patented inventions.

In the biotechnology sector, trade secrecy has become a vital form of protection,[17] even though to date patents have been the premier form of protection.[18] In some circumstances, trade secrecy may be the *preferred*

---

[12] BERNARD REMICHE AND VINCENT CASSIERS, DROITS DES BREVETS D'INVENTION ET DU SAVOIR FAIRE 636, 642 (Larcier, 2010); see also Fernand De Visscher, *Brevets et savoir-faire*, in LES DROITS INTELLECTUELS 283 (Dominique Kaesmacher ed., Larcier, 2007) ('La protection des informations confidentielles diffère fondamentalement de celle qui résulte d'un droit de propriété intellectuelle en ce sens que la loi ne prévoit aucun monopole, aucun droit exclusif d'exploitation; au cas où un tiers reproduit ou utilise des informations qu'une entreprise juge lui appartenir à titre d'informations confidentielles, il ne suffira pas à celle-ci de s'en prévaloir pour arrêter cette activité du tiers') ('The protection of confidential information fundamentally differs from the protection resulting from intellectual property rights, in the sense that the legislator does not foresee a monopoly, nor an exclusive exploitation right. Whenever a third party reproduces or uses the information an enterprise considers to be its own on the basis of confidentiality, it will not suffice to refer to the confidential status to stop the activity of that third party').

[13] REMICHE AND CASSIERS, *supra* note 12, at 642.

[14] The term 'self-help' can mainly be found in U.S. literature, see Michael Risch, Chapter 7. Self-help includes locked doors and non-disclosure agreements. See *id.*

[15] Risch, *supra* note 14.

[16] *Id.*

[17] Robert W. Payne, *The Emergence of Trade Secret Protection in Biotechnology*, 6 NAT. BIOTECHNOL. 130 (1988).

[18] Dan L. Burk, *Misappropriation of Trade Secrets in Biotechnology Licensing,* 4 ALB. L.J. SCI. & TECH. 121, 139 (1994).

mode of protection. Industrial processes may often be best maintained as trade secrets.[19] Given that process inventions are hard to police[20] and that the end-product rarely reveals the method used,[21] in other words is not available for public scrutiny or reverse engineering,[22] it may be preferable to preserve secrecy. Particular examples of such methods include separation and purification processes,[23] or culturing techniques to grow organisms that produce biotechnology products.[24] When only the end-product is sold in the marketplace, intermediary products may also be better off with a trade secret status.[25] Specific examples encompass organisms and expression vectors for the manufacture of valuable end-products, such as monoclonal antibodies,[26] or organisms involved in the production of recombinant proteins, such as recombinant plasmids or transgenic host cells.[27]

In other situations, trade secrecy may be the *only* form of protection in biotechnology available. Inventions which are not patent eligible may only be shielded by trade secrecy. Examples include 'negative information',[28] which is not eligible for patent protection,[29] and inventions which do not meet the patentability requirements of novelty and inventive step/non-obviousness. Illustrative examples include recombinant versions of products that have already been isolated from nature and thus no longer considered novel, and the use of recombinant DNA to produce biological substances, which is often considered routine and obvious once the technique is well-established.[30]

---

19 *Id.* at 140.

20 *Id.*

21 Payne, *supra* note 17, at 130.

22 Burk, *supra* note 18, at 138. See also ROMAN SALIWANCHIK, LEGAL PROTECTION FOR MICROBIOLOGICAL AND GENETIC ENGINEERING INVENTIONS 10 (1982); Charles E. Lipsey *et al.*, *Protecting Trade Secrets in Biotechnology*, 2 TRADE SECRET L. REP. 42, 44 (1986).

23 Payne, *supra* note 17, at 130. See also Burk, *supra* note 18, at 139.

24 Burk, *supra* note 18, at 138–9.

25 Payne, *supra* note 17, at 130.

26 *Id.*

27 Robert W. Payne, *Trade Secret Litigation in the Biotechnology Industry: The Coming Storm*, in BIOTECH USA, 127, 128–31 (1988).

28 The definition of trade secret includes information that has commercial value from a negative point of view, for example, the results of lengthy and expensive research which proves that a certain process will *not* work could be of great value to a competitor, see UTSA § 1 cmt.

29 Knowing where not to look and what techniques are ineffectual may give biotechnology firms a market advantage, see Burk, *supra* note 18, at 139–40. *Cf.* Denicola, *supra* note 8.

30 *Cf.* Donna Smith, Comment, *Copyright Protection for the Intellectual Property Rights to Recombinant Deoxyribonucleic Acid: A Proposal*, 19 ST. MARY'S L.J. 1083, 1093–5 (1988); see also Dan L. Burk, *Biotechnology and Patent Law:*

II. EMERGENCE OF OPEN INFRASTRUCTURES

At first sight, trade secrecy law appears to encourage concealment, rather than openness. Trade secrecy regimes seem to shield information rather than to disseminate it.[31] As trade secrets are less susceptible to exposure, they reduce the possibility the trade secret holder's contribution will enter the public domain.[32] Such a view calls for some nuance. As eminent scholars have argued, trade secrecy law, paradoxically, also encourages disclosure.[33] Without trade secrecy law, companies in certain industries would invest too much in keeping secrets through self-help: trade secrecy law can therefore be seen as a substitute for the physical and contractual restrictions those companies would otherwise impose in an effort to prevent competitors from acquiring their information.[34] By making it more costly for a trade secret owner to litigate and prove secrecy, the requirement of reasonable secrecy precautions limits the scope of trade secret rights, bolsters access, and facilitates public dissemination.[35] In contrast to self-help, trade secrecy law tolerates some amount of information diffusion and fosters disclosure.[36] The counterintuitive impression thus is that secrecy precautions serve to enhance public dissemination, rather than shielding a secret more effectively.[37]

Starting from the recognition that trade secrecy law encourages disclosure, it must be admitted, however, that trade secrecy law fosters disclosure on a rather limited scale (*inter partes*), compared to patent law, where abso-

---

Fitting Innovation to the Procrustean Bed, 17 RUTGERS COMPUTER & TECH. L.J. 1, 42–3 (1990). An interesting example of the mix of patent protection and trade secret protection, and the resulting dispute (*Genentech v. Eli Lilly* over recombinant insulin), is discussed in Burk, *supra* note 18, at 143. See also Bertram I. Rowland, *Legal Implications of Letter Licenses for Biotechnology*, 1 HIGH TECH. L.J. 99, 121 (1986).

[31] *Cf.* Rochelle C. Dreyfuss, *Dethroning Lear: Licensee Estoppel and the Incentive to Innovate*, 72 VA. L. REV. 677 (1986).

[32] This is a concern expressed, for example, in Rochelle Dreyfuss, *Trade Secrets: How Well Should We be Allowed to Hide Them? The Economic Espionage Act of 1996*, 9 FORDHAM INTELL. PROP. MEDIA & ENT. L.J. 1, 2 (1998).

[33] Lemley, *supra* note 9, at 123.

[34] *Id.* Trade secrecy law reaches beyond contract law by allowing courts to infer the existence of a confidential relationship from circumstances in which transactions might be difficult or impossible without that assumption.

[35] See Robert G. Bone, *Trade Secrecy, Innovation and the Requirement of Reasonable Secrecy Precautions*, Boston University School of Law, Working Paper No. 09-40 (2009), available at http://papers.ssrn.com/sol3/papers.cfm?abstract_id=1467723.

[36] *Id.*

[37] *Id.*

lute disclosure is enforced (*erga omnes*).[38] Nonetheless, trade secrecy laws promote the sharing of knowledge by facilitating licenses under agreements of confidentiality.[39] If a trade secret owner could only rely on actual secrecy, he might be less inclined to license out the information because licensing could create an opportunity for his information to become generally known or misappropriated. Trade secrecy laws penalize misuse of licensed proprietary knowledge, thus providing extra assurance to a potential licensor.[40] Besides, in practice, initially restrictively shared trade secrets, will 'leak' out and diffuse to the public at large in the long run. Imagine that secret and substantial knowledge about a certain production process possessed by a trade secret holder is shared with his employees;[41] later on, this knowledge is passed on to a licensee in the form of training of the licensee's employees; gradually, the circle of those possessing the trade secret will expand, and ultimately everyone will know. Once the materials and information are widely disseminated, the protection fades as no one can seriously claim that the information remains a secret or that the whole world is bound by letters of confidentiality.[42] Bearing this in mind, trade secrets mainly confer a head start, an uncertain period of natural lead time, during which originators seek to recoup their investment in research and development.[43]

Furthermore, in comparison to patents, trade secrecy law extends to an extremely wide variety of information. The effect of this broad scope is that more, and not less information, can be protected under trade secrecy

---

38 Cf. Ghidini and Falce, Chapter 6 (describing the fully fledged Italian trade secrecy regime).

39 Cf. Edmund W. Kitch, *The Nature and Function of the Patent System,* 20 J.L. & ECON. 265, 277–8 (1977).

40 *Id.* at 278.

41 In U.S. trade secrecy law, the holder must take reasonable precautions to keep the secret information from becoming generally known, but may reveal the secret as necessary to employees, licensees or others under an agreement of confidentiality. RESTATEMENT OF TORTS § 757 cmt. b (1939).

42 Rowland, *supra* note 30, at 120.

43 Jerome H. Reichman and Pamela Samuelson, *Intellectual Property Rights Data?*, 50 VAND. L. REV. 51, 60 (1997); see also Pamela Samuelson and Suzanne Scotchmer, *The Law and Economics of Reverse Engineering,* 111 YALE L.J. 1575, 1582 (2002) ('We argue that legal rules favoring the reverse engineering of manufactured products have been economically sound because an innovator is nevertheless protected in two ways: by the costliness of reverse engineering and by lead time due to difficulties of reverse engineering.'). *Cf.* UTSA § 2 cmt. ('The general principle of Section 2 (a) and (b) is that an injunction should last for as long as necessary, but no longer than is necessary *to eliminate the commercial advantage or "lead time"* with respect to good faith competitors that a person has obtained through misappropriation' (emphasis added)).

law and thus barred from unfettered and easy public disclosure.[44] Yet an unfavorable effect is that the prevailing non-disclosure approach in trade secrecy law may run counter to public interests in information, and in particular, risk assessment procedures.[45]

The (limited) disclosure in trade secrecy law results from an initiative from the *legislature*, facilitating openness through the creation of formal legal rules.[46] Openness in other fields of IP also stems from initiatives from private actors, such as *knowledge holders*. Examples include 'open access',[47] 'open source', or 'open patent'.[48] Recently, the term 'open biotechnology' has popped up. Scholars have employed the term 'open

---

44 See Vincent Chiappetta, *Myth, Chameleon or Intellectual Property Olympian? A Normative Framework Supporting Trade Secret Law*, 8 GEO. MASON L. REV. 69, 89 (1999); David S. Levine, Chapter 16.

45 Mary L. Lyndon, *Secrecy and Access in an Innovation Intensive Economy: Reordering Information Privileges in Environmental, Health, and Safety Law*, 78 U. COLO. L. REV. 465 (2007). The author takes the view that disclosure and transparency for environmental, health and safety (EHS) risk assessment should prevail over non-disclosure principles in trade secrecy law.

46 For the distinction between formal *legal* rules and formal rules of *contract,* see Tom Dedeurwaerdere, *The Role of Law, Institutions and Governance in Facilitating Access to the Scientific Research Commons*, in GENE PATENTS AND COLLABORATIVE LICENSING MODELS, *supra* note 2, at 365. Some authors speak of 'forced disclosure' in this regard, see Risch, *supra* note 14.

47 Open access refers to the free and unrestricted online availability of peer reviewed literature, to all scientists, scholars, teachers, students and other curious minds, permitting them to read, download, copy, distribute, print, search or link to the full texts of these articles, crawl them for indexing, pass them as data to software, or use them for any other lawful purpose, without financial, legal or technical barriers other than those inseparable from gaining access to the Internet itself. (Definition applied in the Budapest Open Access Initiative, www.soros.org/openaccess/read.shtml.) The basis of open access is the willingness of the (individual) copyright holder to allow access.

48 'Open patent' is a translation of the open source principles to patented software technology. The basic idea is to change the rules in such a way that they are beneficial to participants in solving the problems of software patents (see www.openpatents.org/). Stated differently, the open patent movement seeks to build a portfolio of patented inventions that can freely be distributed under a copyleft-like license (see Wikipedia, Open Patent, http://en.wikipedia.org/wiki/Open_patent). The open patent movement should not be confused with the open patents initiative, (www.openpatents.net/), an interface for those looking for new free ideas to patent, or to deposit ideas which are never going to be patented. The latter is a platform where 'bright and good people from around the world donated their free ideas for you to patent, and many entrepreneurs are waiting for your ideas, right now!'. Open source principles are currently being tested in technical areas other than software, such as genetics, to optimize access to knowledge, see below.

biotechnology' to refer to different types of projects, including open journals,[49] new bioinformatic tools,[50] databases,[51] big science projects,[52] projects to facilitate access to biotech research tools,[53] or combinations of these.[54] 'Open biotechnology' seems to be used as an umbrella term for all kinds of projects and approaches fostering open and collaborative research in the biotechnology sector.

Openness in all of these open projects is usually achieved either by deliberately renouncing IP protection, or by willingly sharing IP entitlements through the design of formal rules of contract.[55] A pivotal prerequisite for many innovative and successful open infrastructures is indeed the power of the knowledge and/or technology owners to force users to behave in a certain (sharing) way. Copyrights and patents invest knowledge and/or technology owners with such authority. Exclusive or proprietary rights, through the shaping of their license policies, can be used to leverage access, to promote dissemination and to safeguard downstream use rights. The notion of promoting access through rights that exclude is indeed the underlying paradox of IP law and policy.[56]

III. TRADE SECRECY AND OPEN BIOTECHNOLOGY

An overview of current trends in the field of IP and biotechnology reveals two (opposing) tendencies. On the one hand, there seems to be an increasing trend to use trade secret protection – witness IP practices as

---

49 See, e.g., Public Library of Science, www.plos.org/.

50 For instance, the BioMoby messaging standard, for interoperability between biological data hosts and analytical services. The Moby-S system defines an ontology-based messaging standard through which a client will be able to automatically discover and interact with task-appropriate biological data and analytical service providers, without requiring manual manipulation of data formats as data flows from one provider to the next. See BioMoby, http://biomoby.open-bio.org/.

51 See, e.g., NIH db GaP, a database of genome wide association studies, see www.ncbi.nlm.nih.gov/projects/gap/cgi-bin/about.html.

52 For example, HapMap or the Human Genome Project, http://hapmap.ncbi.nlm.nih.gov/.

53 For example, Cambia BiOS, www.cambia.org/daisy/cambia/home.html.

54 Yann Joly, *Open Biotechnology: Licenses Needed,* 28 NATURE BIOTECHNOLOGY 417–19 (2010).

55 For the distinction between formal *legal* rules and formal rules of *contract,* see Dedeurwaerdere, *supra* note 46.

56 Antony Taubman, *Several Kinds of 'Should': The Ethics of Open Source in Life Sciences Innovation*, in GENE PATENTS AND COLLABORATIVE LICENSING MODELS, *supra* note 2.

documented in scholarly writings.[57] On the other hand, there is a clear call for attenuating the grip of IP – witness the rise of 'open biotechnology' initiatives. If the objective is to maintain trade secrecy protection, while fostering fluid exchange of know-how (ultimately leading to large-scale openness), models of collaborative licensing might be helpful. Under a trade secret regime, the exchange or sharing of patented knowledge and related undisclosed know-how usually takes the form of *bilateral* or *cross*-licenses. Hybrid agreements combining patent licenses and know-how are popular.[58] Limited openness (indirectly) results from the disclosure effect of trade secrecy law, in contrast to self-help regimes. If the goal is to maintain the trade secrecy regime, while at the same time creating more openness, facilitating the conclusion of hybrid agreements through the establishment of *collaborative* licensing platforms may be an interesting option.

The central question around which the present chapter revolves is whether the transfer of know-how incident to a patent might expand by the use of collaborative licensing. In other words, can collaborative institutions fuel the sharing of hybrid or mixed agreements?[59] The intriguing issue is thus whether collaborative models can assist in reshaping trade secrets as 'open secrets' and in fostering the construction of 'open biotechnology' projects and infrastructures. Facilitating the conclusion of agreements, does not (necessarily) mean *accelerating* or fastening transactions, as the major net advantage of trade secrecy protection seems to be lead time, which should

---

[57] See Burk, *supra* note 18; Payne, *supra* note 17; Payne, *supra* note 27.

[58] Rochelle Dreyfuss' reports on a survey of 150 randomly selected corporations, although too limited to yield statistically significant conclusions, revealed that a majority of all licenses contained both patent and know-how components. In the chemical, mechanical and pharmaceutical industries royalties were lower for know-how licenses than patent licenses, whereas in the electrical, petroleum and transportation industries, royalty percentages for know-how and patent licenses were almost identical. See Dreyfuss, *supra* note 31, at n.66 (citing Rostoker, *PTC Research Report: A Survey of Corporate Licensing*, 24 IDEA 59 (1983); J.M. Lightman, *Comparative Income Roles of US Industrial Property Rights Licensed Abroad*, 14 IDEA 352, 359 (1970), J.M. Lightman, *Compensation Patterns in US Foreign Licensing,* 14 IDEA 1, 3 (1970)). It remains to be examined to what extent the same pattern emerges in Europe. Interesting data might emerge from ALFONSO GAMBARDELLA *ET AL.*, THE VALUE OF EUROPEAN PATENTS, EVIDENCE FROM A SURVEY OF EUROPEAN INVENTORS: FINAL REPORT OF THE PATVAL EU PROJECT (2005).

[59] 'Mixed' is the term used in European Commission Regulation 240/96 on the Application of Article 85(3) of the EU Treaty to Certain Categories of Technology Transfer Agreements [1996] O.J. L31/2–13.

not be snatched away.[60] Facilitating here rather means offering opportunities to conclude transactions in a *fluid* manner, and keeping costs to a minimum, thanks to the existence of (a variety of) preconfigured standard license conditions, or other measures with a similar effect.

Our previous research focused on the role of collaborative rights organizations, such as pools and clearinghouses, in mediating access and use of patents in genetics and, hence, fostering open biotechnology.[61] Indeed, patent pools, requiring as a matter of competition law an open and non-discriminatory licensing policy *vis-à-vis* interested third parties, convert the exclusivity principle of patent protection into a liability regime – essentially, a take-and-pay rule. Patent pools turn exclusive patent rights into commonly shared assets.[62] In other words, patent pools reshape the patent and exclusive ownership regime into a 'reconstructed commons' or 'positive commons', and thus contribute to the establishment of open biotechnology.[63]

This paradoxical effect of collaborative mechanisms on private entitlements was suggested by Robert Merges as early as 1996,[64] but the approach was not explored in depth or put into operation in genetics, which is where our research stepped in. Recent scholarship has taken the debate further

---

60 Reichman and Samuelson, *supra* note 43.

61 Van Overwalle *et al.*, *supra* note 2; van Zimmeren *et al.*, *supra* note 2; Verbeure *et al.*, *supra* note 2; GENE PATENTS AND COLLABORATIVE LICENSING MODELS, *supra* note 2.

62 Geertrui Van Overwalle, *Of Thickets, Blocks and Gaps: Designing Tools to Resolve Obstacles in the Gene Patents Landscape*, in GENE PATENTS AND COLLABORATIVE LICENSING MODELS, *supra* note 2, at 381.

63 The term 'reconstructed commons' is drawn from JEROME H. REICHMAN AND PAUL UHLIR, A CONTRACTUALLY RECONSTRUCTED RESEARCH COMMONS FOR SCIENTIFIC DATA IN A HIGHLY PROTECTIONIST INTELLECTUAL PROPERTY ENVIRONMENT 315 (2003); see also Geertrui Van Overwalle, *Octrooien op Maat? Naar een Evenwicht Tussen Publieke Opdracht en Privaat Goed* (*Patents Fit All? Towards an Equilibrium Between Public Mission and Private Good*), in TUSSEN MARKT EN AGORA: OVER HET STATUUT VAN UNIVERSITAIRE KENNIS (BETWEEN MARKET AND AGORA: ABOUT THE STATUS OF ACADEMIC KNOWLEDGE) 181 (Bart Pattyn and Geertrui Van Overwalle eds., Peeters, 2006). The closely related term 'positive commons' is taken from Peter Drahos, *A Defence of the Intellectual Commons*, 16 CONSUMER POL'Y REV. 3 (2006). A positive commons is 'a common in which resources are jointly owned and so use of those resources by any one commoner depends on all the commoners having consented'. See Geertrui Van Overwalle, *L'intérêt général, le domaine public, les commons et le droit des brevets d'invention*, in L'INTÉRÊT GÉNÉRAL ET L'ACCÈS À L'INFORMATION EN PROPRIÉTÉ INTELLECTUELLE 149 (Séverine Dussolier and Mireille Buydens eds., Emile Bruylant, 2008).

64 Robert P. Merges, *Contracting into Liability Rules: Intellectual Property Rights and Collective Rights Organizations*, 84 CAL. L. REV. 1293 (1996).

and has tried to develop a theoretical framework to systematize a series of current managed-access property initiatives ranging from patent pools and open source to Wikipedia.[65] Building on the work of Elinor Oström, these scholars take up the challenge of better understanding the governance of environments where the resources to be produced are pieces of information – cultural and scientific knowledge – that are distributed through institutions supporting pooling and sharing of knowledge, thus leading to a 'constructed cultural commons'. They anticipate that social ordering both depends on and generates a wide variety of formal and informal institutional arrangements and that the logical and normative priority assigned to proprietary rights and government intervention may turn out to be misplaced.

Let us now return to the central question whether the transfer of know-how incident to a patent might expand by the use of collaborative licensing, such as patent pools, clearinghouses or open source infrastructures.

A. Patent Pools

A first model that may make proprietary inventions and related know-how more easily accessible for further use is the patent pool model. The term 'patent pool' has acquired different meanings. In its widest sense, a patent pool refers to a loose collection of patents held by different patent owners. In a more narrow sense, a patent pool points to an agreement between two or more patent owners to license one or more of their patents to one another, and to license them as a package to third parties who are willing to pay the royalties that are associated with the license.[66] Licenses are provided to the licensees either directly by the patentee or indirectly through a new entity that is specifically set up for the administration of the pool.[67]

---

[65] Michael J. Madison, Brett M. Frischmann and Katherine J. Strandburg, *Constructing Commons in the Cultural Environment*, 95 CORNELL L. REV. 657 (2010).

[66] JEANNE CLARK *ET AL.*, PATENT POOLS: A SOLUTION TO THE PROBLEM OF ACCESS IN BIOTECHNOLOGY PATENTS? (2000), www.uspto.gov/web/offices/pac/dapp/opla/patentpool.pdf; see also Robert P. Merges, *Institutions for Intellectual Property Transactions: The Case of Patent Pools*, in EXPANDING THE BOUNDARIES OF INTELLECTUAL PROPERTY 123 (Rochelle Dreyfuss, Diane L. Zimmerman and Harry First eds., Oxford University Press, 2001); Letter from Joel I. Klein, Antitrust Division, U.S. Department of Justice, to Gerrard R. Beeney (June 26, 1997) (on file with author).

[67] Van Overwalle *et al.*, *supra* note 2; van Zimmeren *et al.*, *supra* note 2; Verbeure *et al.*, *supra* note 2.

Thoughtful observers have suggested that a patent pool leads to the institutionalized exchange of patented knowledge, as well as technical information not covered by patents through a mechanism for sharing technical information relating to the patented technology, which would otherwise be kept secret. This is reflected by an exchange of know-how brought along by the set-up of a patent pool, thereby further facilitating innovation and efficient use of resources.[68] However, companies should be aware that the exchange of sensitive business information may violate competition law. They should be extremely careful where the information concerns prices or business strategies, in particular if their partners are competitors.[69]

A recent European survey we carried out on licensing in the medical biotechnology sector indicates that in practice, participating in collaborative licensing infrastructures is seen as somewhat cumbersome, in part due to fear of loss of secrecy.[70] Almost 50 percent of the respondents in our sample were aware of patent pools. Notwithstanding their knowledge, only 23 percent of respondents indicated that their organization was actually involved in patent pools, whereas 70 percent of them had no experience with patent pools at all. Most respondents explained that the complexity of patent pools and the loss of secrecy and control were important reasons not to form a pool.[71] There do not seem to be significant differences between the different types of organizations who refuse to participate in a pool.[72] A co-pendant Australian survey revealed the same attitude. Dominant concerns not to participate in a pool included lack of opportunity and unequal bargaining power, with loss of secrecy, lack of need, and time as additional factors.[73]

B. Clearinghouses

Somewhat lesser attention has been paid to another licensing arrangement, the clearinghouse. The term 'clearinghouse' is derived from banking

---

[68] Birgit Verbeure, *Patent Pooling for Gene-Based Diagnostic Testing: Conceptual Framework*, in GENE PATENTS AND COLLABORATIVE LICENSING MODELS, *supra* note 2, at 3.

[69] Personal comment Esther van Zimmeren, September 13, 2010.

[70] ESTHER VAN ZIMMEREN, SVEN VANNESTE AND GEERTRUI VAN OVERWALLE, PATENT LICENSING IN MEDICAL BIOTECHNOLOGY 5 (ACCO in press).

[71] *Id.* at 84, 119.

[72] *Id.* at 76.

[73] See Dianne Nicol, *Patent Licensing in Medical Biotechnology in Australia: A Role for Collaborative Licensing Strategies?*, Centre for Law and Genetics Occasional Paper No. 7, 49, fig. 7 (2010), available at www.lawgenecentre.org/occpaper_7.pdf.

institutions and refers to the mechanism by which checks and bills are exchanged among member banks to transfer only the net balances in cash. Nowadays the concept has acquired a broader meaning that refers to any mechanism by which providers and users of goods, services and/or information are matched.[74] Based on the various functions a clearinghouse may fulfill, different types can be distinguished.[75] Two models merely provide access to (protected) information: the information clearinghouse and the technology exchange clearinghouse. The information clearinghouse provides a mechanism for exchanging simple information related to technology or patents.[76] Examples vary from general search engines such as Google or PubMed, to Espacenet or Google Patent Search. Access to know-how is usually not furnished by the information clearinghouse.

The technology exchange clearinghouse is inspired by the Internet-based business-to-business (B2B) model and provides an information service listing the available technologies, thus allowing technology owners and/or buyers to initiate negotiations for a license. Examples include yet2.com and Pharmalicensing. Actual access to the patented inventions and related know-how is not usually granted by the technology exchange clearinghouse, but rather by the individual patent holder after one-to-one licensing negotiations have taken place with the licensee.[77] The clearinghouse does not provide a one-stop licensing access to patented inventions and related tacit technical knowledge. The user still has to enter into negotiations with the patent holder and develop a relation of trust and understanding.[78] The clearinghouse may well provide more comprehensive mediating and managing facilities,[79] and assist during the one-to-one negotiation process by evaluating the most pertinent options for buying or licensing technology and know-how.[80] The usefulness of information

---

[74] Anatole Krattiger, *Financing the Bioindustry and Facilitating Biotechnology Transfer*, 8 IP Strategy Today 1 (2004); van Zimmeren *et al.*, *supra* note 2.

[75] For a more extensive description of the different types of clearinghouses and their respective pros and cons, see E. van Zimmeren, *Clearinghouse Mechanisms in Genetic Diagnostics: Conceptual Framework*, in Gene Patents and Collaborative Licensing Models, *supra* note 2, at 63; see also van Zimmeren *et al.*, *supra* note 2.

[76] Van Zimmeren, *supra* note 75, at 69.

[77] Van Zimmeren *et al.*, *supra* note 2.

[78] Van Zimmeren, *supra* note 75.

[79] Krattiger, *supra* note 74; Gregory Graff and David Zilberman, *Towards an Intellectual Property Clearinghouse for Agribiotechnology*, 3 IP Tech. Today 1 (2001); van Zimmeren *et al.*, *supra* note 2.

[80] This is the case, e.g., for the BirchBob platform, www.birchbob.com. See Esther van Zimmeren and Dirk Avau, *Case 4. BirchBob: An Example of a*

and technology exchange clearinghouses for the exchange of confidential information are thus rather limited, as they usually do not guarantee the authorized use of patented inventions and related know-how, and they still require one-to-one licensing negotiations.

Two more elaborate models not only provide access, but also standardize the use of the protected inventions: the standardized licenses clearinghouse and the royalty collection clearinghouse. The standardized licenses clearinghouse provides access to and offers standardized licenses for the use of patented inventions. Standard does not mean a one-size-fits-all license, but a preset license scheme with options that have been established in negotiations between the right holder and the clearinghouse. Such a licensing regime can operate via an Internet portal through which licensors and licensees can, with drop-down menus and standard questions, choose a patent license.[81] A well-known example of a standard clearinghouse for copyrighted material is Creative Commons,[82] which was recently extended to the patent realm with the Science Commons project.[83] Such a standard licenses clearinghouse may provide assistance with critical areas of technology transfer, such as the licensing of know-how. Helpful in this regard may be the working relationships some clearinghouses have with the owners of the covered technologies.[84]

The royalty collection clearinghouse comprises all the functions of the information clearinghouse, the technology exchange clearinghouse and the standardized licenses scheme,[85] with a mechanism to cash license fees from users on behalf of the patent holders in return for access to and use of the inventions.[86] The patent holder is reimbursed by the clearinghouse pursuant to a set allocation formula, which has been negotiated beforehand.[87] These are, in effect, similar to copyright collection societies. Although this mechanism is in many ways an ideal vehicle for the exchange of genetic and biological information, at present no clear-cut examples exist of royalty collection clearinghouses for patents in this area.

Technology Exchange Clearing House, in GENE PATENTS AND COLLABORATIVE LICENSING MODELS, *supra* note 2, at 125.

[81] van Zimmeren, *supra* note 75, at 76–7.

[82] See Creative Commons, http://creativecommons.org/.

[83] See Science Commons, http://sciencecommons.org/.

[84] This is the case for the PIPRA platform, www.pipra.org/, see Alan Bennett and Sara Boettiger, *The Public Intellectual Property Resource for Agriculture (PIPRA): A Standard License Public Sector Clearinghouse for Agricultural IP*, in GENE PATENTS AND COLLABORATIVE LICENSING MODELS, *supra* note 2, at 135–42.

[85] van Zimmeren *et al.*, *supra* note 2.

[86] Merges, *supra* note 64.

[87] van Zimmeren *et al.*, *supra* note 2.

More elaborated platforms, such as the standardized licenses and the royalty collecting clearinghouse, may have limited capacity to foster wide-scale exchange of know-how. Even though these models may provide authorized and standardized use of patented inventions, the exchange of complementary know-how may be difficult to organize.[88] These platforms may not be able to guarantee the exchange of know-how to all non-exclusive licensees, and at the same time, maintain the requisite degree of secrecy. Furthermore, because the deals are so different, the licensing of know-how can hardly be standardized *ex ante*. Thus, with respect to complex technologies, direct negotiations between the licensor and the licensee on the secret know-how may still be required, and that may well do away with the advantages of standardized and patent royalty collection clearinghouses.[89] The usefulness of such clearinghouses may therefore be limited to 'simple' inventions which do not necessitate the exchange of complementary know-how.[90] A clearinghouse for DNA sequences would be a good example of the latter.

Our European survey on licensing in the medical biotechnology sector reveals that the reasons most relevant to the decision not to participate in clearinghouses are the unequal bargaining position between the negotiating parties, the absence of need (bilateral licenses are usually sufficient), the lack of opportunities when the organization has nothing to offer in return and, to a lesser extent, the fear of loss of secrecy.[91] Pharmaceutical companies find loss of secrecy significantly more important than universities, research institutes and biotechnology companies.[92] The suggestion that the value of a secret is near to zero in the pharmaceutical industry, and that trade secrecy law will have little effect,[93] should be reconsidered in view of the responses we received in our survey.

A positive feature of clearinghouses noted by respondents is that clearinghouses may serve as a firewall preventing contamination of confidential *business* information. The patent owner and licensee will provide the clearinghouse with the necessary

---

88 van Zimmeren, *supra* note 75; Michael Spence, *Comment on the Conceptual Framework for a Clearing House Mechanism*, in GENE PATENTS AND COLLABORATIVE LICENSING MODELS, *supra* note 2, at 161.

89 van Zimmeren, *supra* note 75, at 63–119.

90 *Id.*

91 See *Table 5.5 Reasons no experience with cross-licensing by type of organisation (ANOVA)* in van Zimmeren *et al.*, *supra* note 70, at 62.

92 *See* van Zimmeren et al., *supra* note 70, at 62.

93 Risch, *supra* note 15.

information about their conditions, needs and interests. This might be confidential information. The clearinghouse will use this information to match the appropriate partners without transferring the confidential information.[94]

C. Open Source Regimes

Another model for facilitating large-scale access to patented inventions and complementary know-how is open source. Open source is characterized by three elements, namely credible commitment, competition and, optionally, copyleft.[95] All three features are designed to encourage follow-on innovators to contribute to cumulative development of open source technologies.[96] Credible commitment means that to be open source, a technology must be protected by IP or other proprietary rights and distributed on terms that are perceived to be legally enforceable.[97] As various observers have remarked, this is by far the most striking – and unexpected – feature of the open source model: open source is *based* on IP because protection is needed in order to ensure adherence to the terms of the license.[98] A technology that is made available under the open source model is not in the public domain,[99] but rather owned by the licensor, who makes a legally enforceable promise via the license agreement not to interfere with others' freedom to use, improve or circulate the technology,[100] and thus not to lock them in a web of IP. Copyleft imposes an obligation on the licensee to make any downstream innovations that it chooses to distribute beyond the boundaries of its own organization

---

94 *See* VAN ZIMMEREN *ET AL.*, *supra* note 70, at 94.

95 Janet Hope, *Open Source Genetics: A Conceptual Framework*, in GENE PATENTS AND COLLABORATIVE LICENSING MODELS, *supra* note 2.

96 *Id.*

97 *Id.*

98 See Yochai Benkler, *Coase's Penguin, or, Linux and the Nature of the Firm*, 112 YALE L.J. 369 (2002); Arti Rai, *'Open and Collaborative' Research: A New Model for Biomedicine*, in INTELLECTUAL PROPERTY RIGHTS IN FRONTIER INDUSTRIES: SOFTWARE AND BIOTECHNOLOGY 131, 137 (Robert W. Hahn ed., AEI Press 2005). Absent an IP right, restrictions must be imposed entirely through contract, which might do more damage than good, as the HapMap project has shown. See also Arti Rai, *Critical Commentary on 'Open Source' in the Life Sciences*, in GENE PATENTS AND COLLABORATIVE LICENSING MODELS, *supra* note 2.

99 Similarly, Richard Jefferson, *Science as a Social Enterprise: The CAMBIA, BiOS Initiative*, 1 ECON. PAPERS 13 (2006).

100 Hope, *supra* note 95.

available under the same terms as the original technology.[101] The archetypal example of an open source license is the General Public License (GPL).[102]

The open source philosophy has also found its way to the biotechnology realm through the field of patented inventions.[103] Some working examples of open source have emerged, mainly in the field of agricultural biotechnology. A prominent case is the Biological Open Source (BiOS) License from the Centre for Applications of Molecular Biology in International Agriculture (CAMBIA), a private non-profit research institute located in Canberra.[104] The open source philosophy of BiOS requires that all BioForge portfolios and related know-how are available for use by anyone who agrees to the terms of the BiOS License.[105] Cornerstones are the BiOS License and associated support and material transfer agreements covering both patented and unpatented enabling technology, as well as know-how, materials, biosafety data, and data needed for regulatory approvals.[106] Another working example is the open source style license policy promoted by Diversity Arrays Technology (DArT) Proprietary Ltd.[107] Under this arrangement, CAMBIA offers DArT through its BIOS initiative while DArT PL offers a license to practice the technology in the context of a complete technology package, including software tools, know-how, training and libraries of markers.[108]

---

101 *Id.*

102 See the GNU Operating System, www.gnu.org/.

103 The phrase 'open source' as applied to patents results in a kind of misnomer, as an essential function of the patent system is to ensure openness in the sense that the information about the invention (*cf.* the 'source code') is made available through disclosure or deposit. Sara Boettiger and Dan Burk, *Open Source Patenting*, 1 J. Int'l Biotechnology L. 221 (2004); Taubman, *supra* note 56. Rather, the term 'open source' in a patent context refers to a certain philosophy of access, improvement, production and public use.

104 See BiOS Home Page, www.bios.net; see also Nele Berthels, *CAMBIA's Biological Open Source Initiative (BiOS)*, in Gene Patents and Collaborative Licensing Models, *supra* note 2, at 194.

105 Berthels, *supra* note 104.

106 For more details on BiOS (Biological Open Source) Licenses and MTAs, see www.bios.net; see also Berthels, *supra* note 104. However, as with all patent licenses, freedom to operate cannot be ensured as dominating patents may exist or arise.

107 See Andrzej Kilian, *Case 9. Diversity Arrays Technology Pty Ltd.: Applying the Open Source Philosophy in Agriculture*, in Gene Patents and Collaborative Licensing Models, *supra* note 2, at 204.

108 *Id.*

IV. CLOSING OBSERVATIONS

Although collaborative license models may be promising for the exchange of patented information and complementary know-how, these models actually do not as yet maximize access and use of patented inventions and related confidential information. Various reasons come to the fore that may explain this reserve.

First and foremost, the absence of a personal relation of trust between the patent/trade secret holder and the patent/trade secret user may account for some hesitation. It has been repeatedly suggested that the licensing of trade secrets is based on trust. An intimate, deeply-felt trust towards the know-how worker is much more of a prerequisite in the licensing of trade secrets than it is in the licensing of patented inventions.[109] Know-how users must enter into negotiations with the patent holder and develop a relation of trust and understanding.[110] To prevent information leaks, the inventor may decide to forgo licensing opportunities in order to keep know-how confined to those he trusts or those whose security precautions he can monitor.[111] Putting a patent into a collaborative rights platform implies the willingness to license complementary know-how to unknown users with whom a relationship of trust has not been established.

Second, the lack of a full-fledged trade secrecy law may explain some of the scepsis. Under current European trade secrecy regimes, the duty not to disclose confidential information generally stems from a contractual relationship between the know-how owner and the person(s) to whom the know-how is communicated.[112] Although it might be sufficient to take the agreement between the parties as the ground for breach of confidentiality,[113] not all contingencies might be foreseen,[114] particularly when a new technology, such as biotechnology, is involved. Furthermore, the contract theory may be difficult to apply when a third party who is not party to the agreement with the know-how owner benefits from unduly working the know-how or from putting it to use. It may well be that, in the framework of a collaborative rights infrastructure, undue divulgation is more adequately dealt with under a genuine and well-elaborated trade secrecy law such as the UTSA.

---

109 Dessemontet, *supra* note 7, at 240.

110 van Zimmeren, *supra* note 75.

111 Dreyfuss, *supra* note 32, at 36.

112 See also Dessemontet, *supra* note 7, at 243.

113 *Id.*

114 Burk, *supra* note 18, at 141.

Third, taking a patent onto a collaborative rights platform implies information disclosure in order to attract licensees: the patent owner is expected to describe his technology and outline possible applications. The side-effect of such disclosure is that (potential) competitors can access and make use of the information, which may trigger competitive research, or even attract new competitors, without any requirement for compensating the inventor. Hence, there are grounds for inventors not to position their most valuable patents at collaborative rights platforms and to engage rather in bilateral cross-licensing negotiations that do not imply large-scale information disclosure.[115]

So, as a matter of principle, collaborative license mechanisms, in particular patent pools and open source regimes, may facilitate the swift transfer of patented inventions and related know-how, thereby fostering open biotechnology initiatives. Clearinghouses seem somewhat less fit to assist in the transfer of confidential technical information complementary to patented inventions, but may nevertheless be useful for the exchange of confidential business information. In practice, knowledge producers have been somewhat reluctant in making use of collaborative licensing models in the life sciences and in setting up hybrid agreements involving the exchange of both patents and trade secrets. The absence of a personal relation of trust and the lack of a well-established UTSA-like trade secrecy law in Europe may well account for some hesitation in participating in such collaborative rights platforms.

Further research is needed on the interplay between trade secrecy protection regimes, collaborative licensing models and open biotechnology. The debate may be widened to include research on the dynamics between patent and trade secrecy legislation, as well as open innovation strategies in general. There is growing evidence that successful innovation depends increasingly on the combination of new ideas and inventions. As a result, firms can no longer confine their efforts to internal R&D, but must adopt the so-called 'open innovation paradigm'[116] in which firms do not develop new technologies independently from other actors in the innovation

---

[115] Geertrui Van Overwalle, *Designing Models to Clear Patent Thickets in Genetics*, in WORKING WITHIN THE BOUNDARIES OF INTELLECTUAL PROPERTY: INNOVATION POLICY FOR THE KNOWLEDGE SOCIETY 305 (Rochelle C. Dreyfuss, Diane L. Zimmerman and Harry First eds., Oxford University Press, 2010).

[116] HENRY WILLIAM CHESBROUGH, OPEN INNOVATION: THE NEW IMPERATIVE FOR CREATING AND PROFITING FROM TECHNOLOGY (Harvard Business School Press, 2003); see also OPEN INNOVATION: RESEARCHING A NEW PARADIGM (Henry Chesbrough, Wim Vanhaverbeke and Joel West eds., Oxford University Press, 2006).

systems, as well as open their innovation strategy towards more collaboration and external sourcing of technical knowledge protected by patents or confidentiality.[117]

[117] The author, Esther van Zimmeren (K.U. Leuven Center for Intellectual Property Rights), Bruno Cassiman, Dirk Czarnitzky and Bart Van Looy (K.U. Leuven Department of Managerial Economics, Strategy and Innovation) have been awarded a research grant from the Research Council of the K.U. Leuven to investigate the dynamics of legal architectures and open innovation in various industries ranging from information, telecommunication and semiconductors over pharmaceutics and biotechnology to green technology. The project will run from October 2010 to 2014 and employ both legal and economic scholars.

PART III

IMPACT ON OTHER PUBLIC POLICY ARENAS

12 First Amendment defenses in trade secrecy cases

*Pamela Samuelson**

Courts often refuse to enjoin the use or disclosure of unlawful information (e.g., defamatory statements) because this would be inconsistent with free speech principles embodied in the First Amendment to the U.S. Constitution.[1] Yet, courts routinely enjoin the use and disclosure of misappropriated trade secrets. This chapter will explain why injunctions in trade secret are generally, but not always, consistent with the First Amendment.

In the typical trade secret case, the misappropriator is an errant licensee, a faithless employee, an abuser of confidences, a trickster who uses deceit or other wrongful means to obtain the secrets, or a knowing recipient of misappropriated information who is free riding on the trade secret developer's investment. Trade secrecy law requires parties to abide by express or implicit agreements they have made, to respect the confidences under which they acquired secrets, and to refrain from wrongful conduct vis-à-vis the secrets.

First Amendment defenses to trade secret claims have been relatively rare; yet they have occasionally been successful.[2] These successes have generated considerable controversy. Some commentators assert that trade secrets are categorically immune (or nearly so) from First Amendment scrutiny, [3] while others argue that the First Amendment

---

* Richard M. Sherman Distinguished Professor of Law and Information, University of California at Berkeley. This chapter is a derivative work of *Principles for Resolving Conflicts Between Trade Secrets and the First Amendment*, 58 HASTINGS L.J. 777 (2007).

[1] See Mark A. Lemley and Eugene Volokh, *Freedom of Speech and Injunctions in Intellectual Property Cases*, 48 DUKE L.J. 147 (1998).

[2] See, e.g., CBS, Inc. v. Davis, 510 U.S. 1315 (1994); Procter & Gamble Co. v. Bankers Trust Co., 78 F.3d 219 (6th Cir. 1996); Ford Motor Co. v. Lane, 67 F.Supp.2d 745 (E.D. Mich. 1999); State ex rel. Sports Management News, Inc. v. Nachtigal, 921 P.2d 1304 (Or. 1996); see also O'Grady v. Superior Court, 44 Cal. Rptr. 3d 72 (Ct. App. 2006).

[3] See Andrew Beckerman-Rodau, *Prior Restraints and Intellectual Property: The Clash Between Intellectual Property and the First Amendment from an Economic Perspective*, 12 FORDHAM INTELL. PROP. MEDIA & ENT. L.J. 1, 5 (2001);

requires significant limits on the issuance of injunctions in trade secrecy cases.[4]

Part I discusses why First Amendment defenses have been rare in trade secrecy cases. It reviews some limiting doctrines of trade secrecy law that generally prevent free speech-related tensions from arising in trade secrecy cases. Part II suggests that tensions between trade secrecy law and the First Amendment may increase in the future insofar as mass market licenses restrict disclosure of information that firms wish to maintain as trade secrets. It illustrates this point by discussing *DVD Copy Control Association v. Bunner*,[5] which involved the posting of information claimed as a trade secret that had been derived from reverse engineering encryption code in violation of an anti-reverse engineering provision of a shrink-wrap license. Part III discusses the California Supreme Court's decision in *Bunner* holding that the First Amendment has no application in trade secret cases because trade secrets are property and property rights trump the First Amendment. This Part refutes the California Supreme Court's First Amendment analysis and argues that other courts should not follow that decision. Part IV argues that although trade secrets are not categorically immune from free speech challenges, First Amendment challenges to trade secret claims will rarely succeed. Especially in need of rigorous First Amendment scrutiny are cases in which third parties have lawfully obtained newsworthy trade secrets which they intend to disclose over the objection of someone who claims the information as a trade secret. Part

---

see also Bruce T. Adkins, *Trading Secrets in the Information Age: Can Trade Secret Law Survive the Internet?*, 1996 U. ILL. L. REV. 1151 (1996); Richard A. Epstein, *Privacy, Publication, and the First Amendment: The Dangers of First Amendment Exceptionalism*, 52 STAN. L. REV. 1003 (2000); Adam W. Johnson, *Injunctive Relief in the Internet Age: The Battle Between Free Speech and Trade Secrets*, 54 FED. COMM. L.J. 517 (2002); Franklin B. Goldberg, Case Note, Ford Motor Co. v. Lane, 16 BERKELEY TECH. L.J. 271 (2001).

4 The strongest proponent of the First Amendment as a significant restraint on trade secrecy injunctions is David Greene, *Trade Secrets, the First Amendment and the Challenges of the Internet Age*, 23 HASTINGS COMM. & ENT. L.J. 537 (2001); see also Lemley and Volokh, *supra* note 1, at 229–31; Eugene Volokh, *Freedom of Speech and Intellectual Property: Some Thoughts After* Eldred, 44 Liquormart, and Bartnicki, 40 HOUSTON L. REV. 697, 739–48 (2003).

5 *See* DVD Copy Control Ass'n v. McLaughlin, No. CV 786804, 2000 WL 48512 (Cal. Super. Ct. 2000), *rev'd sub nom.* DVD Copy Control Ass'n v. Bunner, 113 Cal. Rptr. 2d 338 (Ct. App. 2001), *rev'd* 75 P.3d 1 (Cal. 2003), *remanded to* 10 Cal. Rptr. 3d 185 (Ct. App. 2004). Textual and footnote references to this case will designate the trial court decision as *Bunner I*, the first Court of Appeal decision as *Bunner II*, the California Supreme Court decision as *Bunner III*, and the Court of Appeal on remand as *Bunner IV*.

V discusses several First Amendment due process issues, such as whether appellate courts should engage in *de novo* review of constitutionally relevant facts when First Amendment defenses have been raised in trade secret cases.

I. WHY HAVE THERE BEEN SO FEW TRADE SECRET AND FIRST AMENDMENT CASES?

First Amendment defenses are rarely raised in trade secret cases for at least five reasons. First, many trade secrets are things, such as the molds firms use to cast their products, precision tools for refining products, chemicals, and the like, that typically do not implicate the First Amendment or First Amendment values.

Second, trade secrecy law generally regulates the use of illegal or otherwise wrongful means of acquiring trade secrets, such as wiretapping another firm's phones to obtain trade secrets, going through a competitor's trash bins to obtain discarded documents, or using deception to get a firm's secrets. The First Amendment does not protect those who engage in such wrongful conduct.

Third, enforcing non-disclosure obligations arising from a trade secrecy contract or deriving from confidential receipt of the information is generally consistent with the First Amendment.

Fourth, trade secrecy law mainly focuses on preventing unauthorized *private* uses or disclosures of secrets by commercial firms that undermine incentives to invest in innovation. First Amendment interests are less weighty insofar as the secrets are matters of private, rather than public, concern. Although First Amendment values may be more salient when the defendant's goal is to publicly disclose the secrets, public disclosure of trade secrets is rare because misappropriators generally have the same interest as the secret's developer in maintaining secrecy as against the public and other industry participants. Misappropriators typically want to use their victims' secrets in their own commercial enterprises without paying appropriate license fees or being subject to restrictions that might attend licensed use. Revealing secrets to the public would not only thwart the misappropriator's intent to free ride on the secret; it would also facilitate detection of the misappropriation and increase the likelihood that the trade secret's developer can take effective action against him.

Fifth, several doctrines internal to trade secrecy law mitigate tensions that might otherwise arise between trade secrecy law and the First Amendment. Consider, for example, trade secrecy law's rule that the results of lawful reverse engineering can be published, as in *Chicago Lock*

Co. v. Fanberg.[6] Chicago Lock charged the Fanbergs with misappropriating its trade secret key codes by publishing a book about them. The Fanbergs obtained much of the key code information by reverse engineering locks for their customers, and the rest from fellow locksmiths who performed similar services. Because trade secrecy law considers reverse engineering to be a fair means of acquiring trade secrets, the court refused to enjoin publication of the Fanbergs' book.

The Ninth Circuit found it unnecessary to invoke the First Amendment in *Fanberg*, although enjoining publication of the book would obviously be difficult to justify under the First Amendment. The court did, however, express a constitutional concern about Chicago Lock's claim, saying that if California state trade secrecy law did not allow the Fanbergs to reverse engineer Chicago locks and disclose the results of lawful reverse engineering, it 'would, in effect, convert the Company's trade secret into a state-conferred monopoly akin to the absolute protection that a federal patent affords. Such an extension of [state] trade secrets law would certainly be pre-empted by the federal scheme of patent regulation',[7] invoking the U.S. Supreme Court's decision in *Kewanee Oil Co. v. Bicron Corp.*[8]

Kewanee considered the compatibility of trade secrecy and patent law. Bicron argued that Kewanee's trade secret claim was pre-empted by federal patent law and policy. Its theory was that Kewanee should have gotten a patent for its crystal-making process instead of claiming the process as a trade secret, and courts should not reward Kewanee for neglecting to seek a patent. Trade secrecy law, in Bicron's view, had created a significant obstacle to achieving important patent policy objectives, such as promoting disclosure of significant innovations and limiting the duration of legal protection available to them. Kewanee's process was unpatented and, because Kewanee had been using it for several years without seeking a patent, it had become unpatentable. Yet, trade secrecy law provided Kewanee with protection for a potentially infinite duration without any quid pro quo of disclosure to justify the grant of legal protection. The Sixth Circuit Court of Appeals found Bicron's arguments persuasive; the Supreme Court did not.

In concluding that trade secrecy law was compatible with patent law and policy, the Court focused on the weaknesses of trade secrecy law. Trade secrets can easily be lost, not only by reverse engineering, but also through accidental disclosure, independent creation by another, use of other

6 676 F.2d 400 (9th Cir. 1982).
7 *Id.* at 405.
8 416 U.S. 470 (1974).

proper means to obtain the secret, and all too often by misappropriation. 'Where patent law acts as a barrier', said the Court, 'trade secret law functions relatively as a sieve. The possibility that an inventor who believes his invention meets the standards of patentability will sit back, rely on trade secret law, and after one year of use forfeit any right to patent protection is remote indeed'.[9] Federal courts should, however, be skeptical when state courts try to 'plug' the leakiness of trade secrecy law in order to maintain compatibility with federal intellectual property law.

The leakiness of trade secrecy law is also important to its compatibility with the First Amendment. Consider, for instance, *Religious Technology Center, Inc. v. Lerma*,[10] in which RTC charged the *Washington Post* with trade secrecy misappropriation for publishing excerpts of documents that RTC claimed as trade secrets. The *Post* was able to obtain a copy of the documents from a court clerk, despite RTC's efforts to block access to the records. 'Although The Post was on notice that the RTC made certain proprietary claims about these documents, there was nothing illegal . . . about The Post going to the Clerk's office for a copy of the documents . . . .'[11]

The court in *Lerma* did not need to invoke the First Amendment in support of its ruling because an internal limiting principle (or 'weakness', to use *Kewanee*'s terminology) of trade secrecy law protected the First Amendment interests of the *Washington Post*, its reporters and readers eager to know about Scientology practices.

Another limiting doctrine of trade secrecy law that may mitigate tensions between trade secrecy law and the First Amendment is its secondary liability rule. Recipients of misappropriated secrets can be held secondarily liable only if they knew or had reason to know that the information they received from another was acquired by improper means or was subject to non-disclosure requirements under a contract or confidence. Merely knowing that information is claimed as a trade secret does not, however, give rise to liability if the information leaks out through no fault of the recipient, as in *Lerma*.[12]

A further limiting principle of trade secrecy law is the well-recognized privilege to disclose trade secrets 'in connection with . . . information that

---

9 *Kewanee*, 416 U.S. at 490 (citation omitted).

10 908 F.Supp. 1362 (E.D. Va. 1995).

11 *Id.* at 1369.

12 *Id.* at 1368. This rule of trade secrecy law also limits the potential for conflicts between trade secret law and the First Amendment. But see Gustavo Ghidini and Valeria Falce, Chapter 6 (describing how Italian law changes these rules and removes some of the 'leakiness').

is relevant to public health or safety, or to the commission of a crime or tort, or to other matters of substantial public concern'.[13] Public policy may also limit the enforceability of agreements between a firm and its employees forbidding disclosure of non-public information about the firm when government agents initiate legitimate inquiries into the firm's business.[14] Some state and federal 'whistle-blowing' statutes privilege disclosures that might otherwise be regarded as trade secret misappropriations.[15] Firms also cannot enforce a contract to treat information as a trade secret when it is not, in fact, a secret.[16]

II. TENSIONS BETWEEN TRADE SECRECY LAW AND THE FIRST AMENDMENT MAY INCREASE

Increasingly common in recent years have been efforts by firms to strengthen trade secrecy protection through mass market license terms that, if enforced, would plug some information leakages that trade secrecy law would ordinarily allow. Efforts to thwart reverse engineering through mass market licenses are mainly of concern because of their potential impact on innovation and competition, but they can also have free speech implications. Enforcement of restrictions on disclosure can facilitate what some scholars have characterized as the 'privication' of information that would otherwise be public.[17]

Consider, for instance, the lawsuit brought by the DVD Copy Control Association (DVD CCA) against Andrew Bunner who posted on his website source code of a computer program, DeCSS, that contained information, acquired by third parties, that DVD CCA claimed as trade secrets. DVD CCA alleged this information had been obtained by reverse engineering software in violation of a term of a mass market license agreement.

DVD CCA, which holds intellectual property rights in certain DVD technologies, required all licensed makers of DVD players to install an encryption program, known as the Content Scramble System (CSS), to

---

13 Restatement (Third) of Unfair Competition § 40, cmt. c (1995).

14 See, e.g., Alan E. Garfield, *Promises of Silence: Contract Law and Freedom of Speech*, 83 Cornell L. Rev. 261, 264–6 (1998) (giving examples).

15 See, e.g., 5 U.S.C.A. § 2302(b)(8) (West 2010); N.Y. Lab. Law § 740 (West 2010); see also Mary L. Lyndon, Chapter 17.

16 Restatement (Third) of Unfair Competition § 41, cmt. d (1995).

17 See Jonathan Zittrain, *What the Publisher Can Teach the Patient: Intellectual Property and Privacy in an Era of Trusted Privication*, 52 Stan. L. Rev. 1201 (2000).

protect movies from unauthorized copying. Licensees were also obliged to undertake various security measures to ensure that CSS remained secret and to use mass market licenses that forbid reverse engineering. DVD CCA believed that the web of licensing obligations it created through such agreements gave it trade secret rights in CSS information that were, in effect, good against the world.

Approximately two months after Bunner posted DeCSS on the Web, DVD CCA sued him, 20 other persons and 500 John Does for trade secret misappropriation, alleging that they knew or should have known that DeCSS contained or was derived from DVD CCA's trade secrets. Bunner denied he had misappropriated DVD CCA trade secrets, but also claimed a First Amendment right to post DeCSS source code on the Internet.

The trial judge granted DVD CCA's motion for a preliminary injunction in *Bunner I*, finding that CSS had likely been reverse engineered in violation of a license agreement, that DeCSS embodied or was substantially derived from stolen trade secrets, and that Bunner and his co-defendants were liable as co-misappropriators of CSS secrets because they knew or ought to have known DeCSS contained stolen secrets.[18] The judge also took into account the 'considerable time, effort, and money [that had been spent] in creating the intellectual property at issue in order to protect the copyrighted information contained on DVDs'.[19] Bunner was enjoined from posting DeCSS on the Internet or otherwise disclosing DeCSS or CSS secrets.

The California Court of Appeal ruled in *Bunner II* that Bunner's First Amendment defense had merit and ordered dissolution of the preliminary injunction. The California Supreme Court overturned this ruling in *Bunner III* and remanded the case to the Court of Appeal. In *Bunner IV* the Court of Appeal ruled that DVD CCA's secrets had dissipated because DeCSS was available on hundreds of websites for two months before DVD CCA commenced the lawsuit and three months before the preliminary injunction issued.

Left for another day was the question whether DVD CCA could use mass market licenses to override the reverse engineering privilege of trade secrecy law and to bind the whole world not to reverse engineer globally distributed DVD players through multiple layers of license requirements reaching down to the end-user.

Had the courts in *Bunner* been attentive to federal pre-emption considerations, they might have recognized that upholding DVD CCA's claim

---

18 *Bunner I*, No. CV 786804, 2000 WL 48512, at *2 (Cal. Super. Ct. 2000).

19 *Id.* at *3.

'would, in effect, convert the [plaintiff's] trade secret into a state-conferred monopoly akin to the absolute protection that a federal patent affords'.[20] As the Ninth Circuit said in *Fanberg*, '[s]uch an extension of California trade secrets law would certainly be preempted by the federal scheme of patent regulation'.[21] It would also create tensions between trade secrecy and the First Amendment.

The vulnerability of trade secrets to dissipation by Internet postings has led to some calls for strengthening trade secrecy law. Commentators skeptical of First Amendment defenses in Internet posting cases such as *Bunner* make several points. First, virtually anyone can become a publisher of information on the Internet. Second, information published on the Internet has a potentially global audience. Third, anonymous postings make it difficult to track down misappropriators. Fourth, quantifying losses to trade secret developers may be difficult. And fifth, Internet misappropriators may be judgment-proof. 'With the Internet, significant leverage is gained by the gadfly, who has no editor looking over his shoulder and no professional ethics to constrain him'.[22]

The *Bunner I* decision illustrates the temptation to protect trade secrets against misappropriation on the Internet. The judge worried that unless he enjoined Bunner and others from posting DeCSS, it would 'encourage misappropriators of trade secrets to post the fruits of their wrongdoing on the Internet as quickly as possible and as widely as possible thereby destroying a trade secret forever. Such a holding would not be prudent in this age of the Internet'.[23] He stretched existing trade secrecy law by: (1) treating the anti-reverse engineering clause of DVD CCA's mass market license as enforceable not just against the reverse engineer, but also against Bunner; (2) construing CSS secrets as not having been dissipated notwithstanding considerable Internet-based discussion about DeCSS and almost three months of postings on hundreds of sites; (3) concluding that Bunner and others must have known that DeCSS embodied DVD CCA's trade secrets based on *braggadocio* by a few of them; and (4) neglecting to even mention Bunner's First Amendment defense.

Posting information on the Internet does not automatically dissipate trade secret protection. If the misappropriation is quickly detected, a trade secret developer can generally obtain a court order to require the information to be taken down and to forbid its reposting. Even if information

---

20 Chicago Lock Co. v. Fanberg, 676 F.2d 400, 405 (9th Cir. 1982).

21 *Id.*

22 Ford Motor Co. v. Lane, 67 F.Supp.2d 745, 753 (E.D. Mich. 1999).

23 *Bunner I*, 2000 WL 48512 at *3.

is publicly accessible on the Internet for some period of time, it will not necessarily lose its trade secret status if it is on an obscure site and very few persons have actually seen the information.

Of course, the longer information is available on the Internet, the more sites at which it is available, the larger the number of people who have viewed the information, the farther word has spread about the availability of the information (e.g., through newsgroups or in chatrooms), the greater is the likelihood that its trade secret status will be lost. This is unfortunate, but it is a risk inherent to trade secrecy law that information may leak out, particularly if it is susceptible to reverse engineering.

The dangers of lost secrets via the Internet are, however, somewhat overblown. Firms can take a number of steps to protect trade secrets from Internet misappropriation.[24] There have, in fact, been relatively few publicized instances of trade secret misappropriation via the Internet. A significant deterrent to publication of trade secrets on the Internet is the high probability of detection of the misappropriation, and the consequent risk of substantial financial liability for misappropriation and/or criminal prosecution under state or federal laws. This seems to have substantially deterred trade secret anarchists or vengeful persons from posting valuable trade secrets.

The Internet poses risks for many important societal interests, such as protecting children from pornography, protecting privacy and copyrights, preventing spam, spyware and fraudulent solicitations. As the Supreme Court has observed, such risks are not so grave that courts should distort existing laws or First Amendment principles to make the rules stricter in cyberspace than in other realms.[25]

III. TRADE SECRET CLAIMS AND REMEDIES ARE NOT CATEGORICALLY IMMUNE FROM FIRST AMENDMENT SCRUTINY

Although Bunner eventually won the lawsuit brought by DVD CCA because the firm's secrets had been dissipated by the widespread posting of them, his First Amendment defense to DVD CCA's charges met with mixed success. Although the California Court of Appeal found it

---

[24] See, e.g., Victoria A. Cundiff, *Trade Secrets and the Internet: A Practical Perspective*, 14 Computer Law., no. 8, 1997 at 6.

[25] See, e.g., ACLU v. Reno, 521 U.S. 844, 870 (1997) (rejecting arguments for lessening First Amendment protections for Internet communications).

persuasive, the California Supreme Court did not. In *Bunner III*, that court held that trade secrets are categorically immune from First Amendment protection because trade secrets are 'property', and property rights trump the First Amendment.[26] This Part challenges the view that trade secrets are 'property' akin to copyrights, patents or land. It also shows that even if trade secrets can be properly characterized as property for some purposes, this does not mean that trade secret claims are thereby immunized from First Amendment scrutiny. Finally, it discusses several trade secrecy cases in which First Amendment defenses succeeded. Courts should follow the latter decisions rather than the California Supreme Court decision in *Bunner III*.

The main reason the California Supreme Court went astray in *Bunner III* is because the Court of Appeal in *Bunner II* gave too much credence to Bunner's First Amendment defense. *Bunner II* ruled that the preliminary injunction against posting DeCSS online was 'a prior restraint on Bunner's First Amendment right to publish the DeCSS program',[27] noting that prior restraints 'on pure speech are highly disfavored and presumptively unconstitutional'.[28] To overcome this presumption, the court said that the 'publication must threaten an interest more fundamental than the First Amendment itself'.[29] Because DVD CCA's trade secret interests were not more fundamental than the First Amendment, the Court of Appeal thought no injunction should issue, even if DVD CCA's trade secret claim had merit. *Bunner II* thus called into question the constitutionality of *all* preliminary injunctions in informational trade secrecy cases.

Microsoft, among others, filed an *amicus* brief in support of DVD CCA's appeal saying that if the Court of Appeal's decision was upheld, the consequences would be highly injurious to the American economy, for it would risk making California into 'a haven for intellectual property thieves'.[30] The California Attorney General also argued for reversal of *Bunner II*.

Although the California Supreme Court agreed with the Court of Appeal that DeCSS was First Amendment protected speech, '"that conclusion still leaves for determination the level of scrutiny to be applied in determining the constitutionality of" an injunction prohibiting the

---

26 *Bunner III*, 75 P.3d 1, 11–16 (Cal. 2003).

27 *Bunner II*, 113 Cal. Rptr. 2d 338, 350 (Ct. App. 2001).

28 *Id.* at 351.

29 *Id.*

30 See Brief of Microsoft Corp. *et al.* as *Amici Curiae* Supporting Plaintiff/Respondent at 1–2, *Bunner III*, 75 P.3d 1 (Cal. 2003) (No. S102588), available at www.eff.org/IP/Video/DVDCCA_case/#bunner-pi-case.

dissemination of computer code'.[31] The court concluded that the injunction in *Bunner* was a content-neutral restraint on speech that passed intermediate scrutiny because trade secrecy law itself was neutral; because the lower court found that Bunner had misappropriated a trade secret; because trade secrets were property; because the government had a significant interest in protecting trade secrets; and because the highly technical nature of the secret made it a matter of only private concern.[32]

Bunner III opined that 'the preliminary injunction does not violate the free speech clauses of the United States and California Constitutions, *assuming* the trial court properly issued the injunction under California's trade secret law'.[33] The importance of the trade-secrets-as-property-rights argument as a justification for lowering the level of scrutiny in trade secret/ First Amendment cases is evident from the more than 20 references to property rights in core parts of the court's First Amendment analysis.

It is certainly true that some cases have spoken of trade secrets as property,[34] that some real property cases have rejected First Amendment defenses raised by trespassers engaged in speech or protest activities,[35] and that certain decisions have opined that there is no First Amendment right to infringe intellectual property rights.[36] But each of these propositions is contestable, and contrary rulings exist.

A. Trade Secrets are Not Property Akin to Patents, Copyrights or Land

Trade secrecy law emerged as a common law claim in the nineteenth century to provide remedies for two common forms of unfair competition: the use of improper means, such as bribery or deceit, to obtain another's valuable secret, and abuses of a confidence or contract under which another's valuable secrets had been disclosed. Regulating improper acquisition

---

31 *Bunner III*, 75 P.3d at 11 (quoting Universal City Studios, Inc. v. Reimerdes, 111 F.Supp.2d 294, 327 (S.D.N.Y. 2000)).

32 *Id.* at 11–16.

33 *Id.* at 19.

34 See, e.g., Ruckelshaus v. Monsanto Co., 467 U.S. 986, 1003–4 (1984) (holding that reports and data on safety claimed as trade secrets were property for purposes of Fifth Amendment takings analysis).

35 See, e.g., Lloyd Corp. Ltd. v. Tanner, 407 U.S. 551, 568–70 (1972) (holding that the First Amendment did not require mall owner to allow distribution of antiwar handbills on its premises).

36 See, e.g., Dallas Cowboy Cheerleaders, Inc. v. Scoreboard Posters, Inc., 600 F.2d 1184, 1188 (5th Cir. 1979) (finding no First Amendment right to infringe an owner's intellectual property).

of secrets and enforcing confidential relationships continue to be the core interests protected by trade secrecy law.

Justice Holmes famously criticized the 'property' characterization for trade secrets in *E.I. duPont de Nemours Powder Co. v. Masland*:

> The word 'property' as applied to trademarks and trade secrets is an unanalyzed expression of certain secondary consequences of the primary fact that the law makes some rudimentary requirements of good faith. Whether the plaintiffs have any valuable secret or not the defendant knows the facts, whatever they are, through a special confidence that he accepted. The property may be denied, but the confidence cannot be. Therefore the starting point for the present matter is not property or due process of law, but that the defendant stood in confidential relations with the plaintiff[s] . . .[37]

The American Law Institute took a similar view in its 1939 Restatement of Torts: 'The suggestion that one has a right to exclude others from the use of his trade secret because he has a right of property in the idea has been frequently advanced and rejected. The theory that has prevailed is that the protection is afforded only by a general duty of good faith and that the liability rests upon breach of this duty'.[38]

The more recent Restatement (Third) of Unfair Competition does not take a stand on the trade-secrets-as-property debate, but it observes that '[t]he dispute over the nature of trade secret rights has had little practical effect on the rules governing civil liability for the appropriation of a trade secret'.[39] Courts may characterize trade secrets as property because the secrets have value, but they treat such rights as 'effective only against defendants who used or acquired the information improperly'.[40]

An important respect in which trade secrecy law differs from real property and intellectual property laws is that the former does not grant developers any exclusive rights in their secrets, no matter how costly or time-consuming their development or how valuable they are. Trade secrets are more properly characterized as 'non-exclusive rights'.[41]

Copyrights and patents, by contrast, are more appropriately described as 'property' rights because the Constitution explicitly gives Congress power to grant authors and inventors 'exclusive rights' in their writings and discoveries. Congress has implemented this constitutional power

---

37 244 U.S. 100, 102 (1917).

38 American Law Institute, Restatement of Torts § 757, cmt. a (1939).

39 Restatement (Third) of Unfair Competition § 40, cmt. c (1995).

40 *Id.*

41 2 Roger M. Milgrim, Milgrim on Trade Secrets § 9.02[5][a] at 9-86 (2010).

by explicitly granting qualifying innovators a set of exclusive rights to control certain exploitations of the protected innovations.[42] Patentees and copyright holders can exercise the right to exclude unauthorized persons from trespassing upon their rights, just as owners of real property can exclude unauthorized persons from their lands. However, trade secret developers can only sue those who use improper means to get the secrets or breach contracts or confidences. Trade secrecy law may sometimes be clustered for the sake of convenience under the general rubric of 'intellectual property' rights, but this does not alter the essential nature of trade secrets as a regulation of unfair competition.

B. Even if Trade Secrets are Property for Some Purposes, This Does Not Immunize Trade Secret Claims from First Amendment Challenges

The U.S. Supreme Court observed in *Ruckelshaus v. Monsanto Co.* that trade secrets may be treated as property for purposes of determining whether government use or disclosure of the secrets violates the Fifth Amendment.[43] Monsanto challenged legislation authorizing the Environmental Protection Agency (EPA) to look at and make use of studies that Monsanto had submitted to the agency about the safety, efficacy, and environmental impacts of pesticides to gain approval to sell these chemicals when later considering competitors' applications for approval to sell chemical equivalents. The same law also allowed the EPA to disclose Monsanto's studies to the public if the agency deemed such disclosure necessary to address health, safety, or environmental concerns. Monsanto considered these use and disclosure rules to be unconstitutional takings of its private property.

The Court concluded that the EPA's use and disclosure of this trade secret information would not constitute a taking unless the government had specifically promised not to use or disclose the data submitted to the EPA. The absence of such a promise in the legislation (except for one five-year period) meant that Monsanto did not have an investment-backed expectation that its secrets could not be used or disclosed by the EPA for those purposes. During the five-year period in which the statute promised

---

[42] U.S. Constitution art. I, § 8, cl. 8. See also 17 U.S.C. § 106 (2006) (setting forth exclusive rights of copyright); 35 U.S.C. § 271 (2006) (setting forth exclusive rights of patent owners).

[43] 467 U.S. 986, 1002–4 (1984). But see Pamela Samuelson, *Information as Property: Do* Ruckelshaus *and* Carpenter *Signal a Changing Direction in Intellectual Property Law?*, 38 Cath. U. L. Rev. 365 (1989) (critical of the property ruling in *Ruckelshaus*).

that trade secret data submitted to EPA would not be used in assessing competing applications or disclosed to the public, the Court decided that the EPA could go ahead and use this data in considering competing applications and disclose the data to the public if necessary to respond to health and safety concerns. Such use or disclosure of data submitted in these five years would be a taking, but it was a taking for a public purpose. Hence, the EPA could still use or disclose this data as long as it compensated Monsanto.

Proponents of the trade-secrets-as-property theory invoke *Ruckelshaus* as support,[44] but fail to acknowledge that the Court actually rejected Monsanto's strong property rights arguments and balanced trade secret interests against other societal interests. The Court in *Ruckelshaus* found the public interest in competition and public access to health and safety data more compelling than Monsanto's commercial interests in non-disclosure.

The public interest in access to newsworthy information is among the public policies with which courts must occasionally grapple in trade secret cases. In *O'Grady v. Superior Court*,[45] for instance, Apple Computer claimed that there was no public interest in access to trade secrets that O'Grady published on his website. The court disputed this assertion, saying that sometimes '[t]imely disclosure [of trade secrets] might avert the infliction of unmeasured harm on many thousands of individuals'.[46] O'Grady had not stolen the secrets 'for venal advantage', but wanted only to make 'a journalistic disclosure to . . . "an interested public"'.[47] When both property and free speech interests are in conflict, said the court, 'it is the quasi-property right that must give way, not the deeply rooted constitutional right to share and acquire information'.[48]

As Professor Volokh has insightfully observed, 'calling a speech restriction a "property right", though, doesn't make it any less a speech restriction, and it doesn't make it constitutionally permissible'.[49] The First Amendment has an especially important role to play when the question is not *where* certain speech activities can take place (e.g., on the plaintiff's real property as in the trespass cases), but rather *whether* certain speech

44 See, e.g., Beckerman-Rodau, *supra* note 3, at 21 n.95.
45 44 Cal. Rptr. 3d 72, 112 (Ct. App. 2006).
46 *Id.* at 112
47 *Id.*
48 *Id.*
49 See, e.g., Eugene Volokh, *Freedom of Speech and Information Privacy: The Troubling Implications of a Right to Stop People from Speaking About You*, 52 STAN. L. REV. 1049, 1063 (2000).

activities can take place at all (e.g., disclosing information claimed as a trade secret to the public). First Amendment defenses have, moreover, been successful in many intellectual property cases.[50] In *Eldred v. Ashcroft*,[51] the Supreme Court explicitly criticized the D.C. Circuit for its assertion that copyright law is categorically immune from First Amendment challenges. This suggests the Court would repudiate a similar theory in respect of trade secrets. Indeed, to be consistent with the Court's rejection of categorical immunity in *Eldred*, characterizing information as 'property' merely because it may cover exclusive intellectual property rights should not insulate it from all First Amendment scrutiny.

C. *Bunner III* is Also Inconsistent with Other Precedents

Several courts have held that preliminary injunctions in informational trade secrecy cases may be unconstitutional prior restraints.[52] In *CBS, Inc. v. Davis*,[53] for instance, Justice Blackmun vacated a preliminary injunction that forbade the network from broadcasting or otherwise revealing videotape footage obtained from an employee of a meatpacking firm who filmed it inside the plant during his work shift. After learning of CBS's intent to feature this footage in a television news program, the firm sued to enjoin the broadcast, alleging, among other things, that the tape revealed the firm's 'confidential and proprietary practices and processes' in violation of state trade secrecy law and that broadcast of the tape would cause it irreparable injury.[54] A state court granted the preliminary injunction

---

[50] See, e.g., ETW Corp. v. Jireh Pub'g, Inc., 332 F.3d 915 (6th Cir. 2003) (holding that First Amendment overrides publicity rights claim as to print of Tiger Woods); Mattel, Inc. v. MCA Records, Inc., 296 F.3d 894, 901, 904 (9th Cir. 2002) (holding that the First Amendment limits trademark and dilution law to permit expressive uses of marks such as song about Barbie dolls); Cardtoons L.C. v. Major League Baseball Players Assn, 95 F.3d 959 (10th Cir. 1996) (holding that First Amendment interests of maker of parody baseball cards outweighed players' publicity rights interests).

[51] 537 U.S. 186, 221 (2003).

[52] See CBS, Inc. v. Davis, 510 U.S. 1315 (1994); Procter & Gamble Co. v. Bankers Trust Co., 78 F.3d 219, 224 5 (6th Cir. 1996); Ford Motor Co. v. Lane, 67 F.Supp.2d 745, 750 (E.D. Mich. 1999); Religious Technology Center v. Lerma, 897 F.Supp. 260, 262 (E.D. Va. 1995); State ex rel. Sports Management News, Inc. v. Nachtigal, 921 P.2d 1304 (Or. 1996); Garth v. Staktek Corp., 876 S.W.2d 545, 549–50 (Tex. App. 1994); see also Bridge C.A.T. Scan Assoc. v. Technicare Corp., 710 F.2d 940, 945–6 (2d Cir. 1983).

[53] 510 U.S. 1315 (1994).

[54] *Id.* at 1316. The *CBS* case may be an example of a firm asserting a trade secrecy claim in order to prevent information about its practices from becom-

'because the videotape "was obtained by CBS, at the very least, through calculated misdeeds"', which rendered 'conventional First Amendment prior restraint doctrine . . . inapplicable'.[55]

Justice Blackmun granted CBS's motion for an emergency stay of this preliminary injunction so that the broadcast could take place as scheduled, saying:

> Although the prohibition against prior restraints is by no means absolute, the gagging of publication has been considered acceptable only in 'exceptional cases'. Even where questions of allegedly urgent national security or competing constitutional interests are concerned, we have imposed this 'most extraordinary remedy' only where the evil that would result from the reportage is both great and certain and cannot be mitigated by less intrusive measures.[56]

Even if 'economic harm were sufficient in itself to justify a prior restraint', Justice Blackmun concluded, 'speculative predictions' about harm are insufficient.[57] Even accepting that the court below was 'no doubt . . . correct that broadcast of the videotape "could" result in significant economic harm',[58] Justice Blackmun was not convinced that this proof satisfied constitutional standards.

Nor did CBS's alleged misdeeds render prior restraints doctrine inapplicable. 'Subsequent civil or criminal proceedings, rather than prior restraints, ordinarily are the appropriate sanction for . . . misdeeds in the First Amendment context'.[59] Even if engaging in criminal activity to obtain the videotape 'could justify an exception to the prior restraint doctrine', Justice Blackmun opined, 'the record as developed thus far contains no clear evidence of criminal activity on the part of CBS, and the court below found none'.[60]

These pronouncements about the applicability of the prior restraint doctrine in informational trade secret cases are particularly notable given that Justice Blackmun was among the dissenting justices in *New York Times Co. v. United States* who were amenable to enjoining the ***Times***' publication of the Pentagon Papers.[61] Given this, one might have expected

---

ing public. It is difficult, however, to believe that the firm's rivals would get any competitive advantage from the CBS broadcast.

55 *Id.*

56 *Id.* at 1317 (internal citations omitted).

57 *Id.* at 1318.

58 *Id.*

59 *Id.*

60 *Id.*

61 See New York Times Co. v. United States, 403 U.S. 713, 759–63 (1971) (Blackmun, J., dissenting).

Justice Blackmun to construe prior restraints doctrine more narrowly than his colleagues. Yet, not only did he think the prior restraint doctrine applied, he also suggested that First Amendment considerations required a more rigorous showing of likelihood of success on the merits and of irreparable harm before issuing preliminary injunctions to stop public disclosure of trade secrets.

The *CBS* case also illustrates the risk of court-enforced private censorship that may lurk in the background of some trade secret cases. Viewed in a light favorable to CBS, the plaintiff may have alleged trade secret misappropriation and sought an injunction in order to avoid embarrassment or other harm to the firm's reputation from a news report that was about to reveal unsanitary or brutal conditions inside its meatpacking factory. CBS was, in this view, giving the public access to information in which it had a legitimate interest in knowing, not misappropriating trade secrets.

Although the California Supreme Court in *Bunner III* acknowledged that *CBS* and other decisions had characterized trade secret preliminary injunctions as prior restraints, it believed later decisions by the Court limited the prior restraint doctrine to instances in which the government was attempting to censor speech based on its content. The decisions on which *Bunner III* relied, however, involved time, place, and manner restrictions on speech, not rulings that forbade speech to take place at all, as with the injunction in *Bunner*. Preliminary injunctions have been regarded as prior restraints in many cases involving private litigants.[62] Justice Blackmun in *CBS* may have regarded the meatpacker's evidence of harm as speculative, but he did not challenge the lower court's finding that CBS had used improper means to obtain information the firm claimed as a trade secret. These precedents further suggest that the First Amendment analysis in *Bunner III* is flawed and should not be followed.

---

[62] See e.g., Aguilar v. Avis Rent a Car Sys., Inc., 21 Cal. 4th 121, 142–5 (1999) (upholding permanent injunction forbidding use of racial epithets after trial on the merits, but recognizing that preliminary injunctions in civil litigations may be unconstitutional prior restraints); Wilson v. Superior Court, 13 Cal. 3d 652 (1975) (holding preliminary injunction against distribution of newsletter to be an unconstitutional prior restraint in libel case); see also Organization for a Better Austin v. Keefe, 402 U.S. 415, 419–20 (1971) (holding temporary injunction against leafleting in private litigation for invasion of privacy to be unconstitutional prior restraint); Metropolitan Opera Ass'n, Inc. v. Local 100, Hotel & Restaurant Employees Int'l Union, 239 F.3d 172, 176 (2d Cir. 2001) (treating preliminary injunction against publication as a prior restraint in litigation between private parties); Bridge C.A.T. Scan Assoc. v. Technicare Corp., 710 F.2d 940, 946 (2d Cir. 1983) (holding improperly issued protective order in private litigation to be unconstitutional prior restraint on speech).

IV. RECONSIDERING TRADE SECRET CLAIMS AND THE PRIOR RESTRAINTS DOCTRINE

CBS v. Davis is among the precedents that have treated preliminary injunctions in trade secret cases as prior restraints that are presumptively unconstitutional. While this presumption should not be applied in ordinary trade secrecy cases in order to preserve adequate incentives to invest in innovation and to enforce well-accepted trade secrecy norms, the prior restraints doctrine and its presumption of unconstitutionality have more salience in cases involving those who propose to disclose newsworthy secrets to promote public discourse on matters of public concern.

A. Injunctions in Ordinary Trade Secret Cases

In ordinary trade secret cases, trade secret defendants are (1) private profit-making firms or individuals who work for or with such firms (2) who intend to make private uses or disclosures of another firm's secrets (3) as to information that is neither newsworthy nor a matter of public concern and (4) who have breached an enforceable contract to maintain secrecy, abused the confidence under which they received another's trade secrets, and/or used improper means, such as bribery or fraud, to obtain the secrets (5) under circumstances likely to give rise to substantial and irreparable harm arising from the defendants' competitive uses of the secrets. Preliminary injunctions protect trade secrets from further misuses and/or preserve the status quo pending final adjudication of the dispute between the parties.

Garth v. Staktek Corp. is an example of an ordinary trade secret case in which a First Amendment defense was properly rejected.[63] Garth had participated in a joint venture to develop three-dimensional high-density memory packages for mini- and microcomputer applications. He signed an agreement not to use or disclose information generated or exchanged during the venture unless it entered the public domain. A trial court held that Garth violated the non-disclosure agreement by using and disclosing the joint venture's secrets to his new firm and granted Staktek's motion for a preliminary injunction. On appeal, Garth argued that the preliminary injunction against further use or disclosure of the secrets was an unconstitutional prior restraint on speech.

The Texas court noted that it was well-settled under Texas law that 'injunctive relief may be employed when one breaches his confidential

[63] 876 S.W.2d 545 (Tex. App. 1994).

relationship in order to unfairly use a trade secret'.[64] It also recognized that this rule needed to be consistent with the First Amendment and the Texas Constitution. 'Texas law begins with the presumption that prior restraints on free speech are unconstitutional', said the court, but 'prior restraints may be permitted to prevent an imminent and irreparable harm, so long as no less restrictive alternative form of protection is available'.[65] It added: 'Monetary compensation may not sufficiently protect the creator of a new product from unfair competition by those who improperly appropriate confidential information'.[66]

Because Garth's firm had attempted to sell the protected technology to other firms, the appellate court agreed that there was irreparable harm from the defendants' pattern of improper uses of the secret and there appeared to be no less restrictive way than a preliminary injunction to ensure that the defendants would not continue to misuse the secrets. *Garth* is illustrative of the many ordinary trade secrecy cases in which the presumption of unconstitutionality can be overcome.

B. Can Direct Misappropriators Raise First Amendment Defenses?

CBS v. Davis is a highly unusual trade secrecy case in that: (1) the alleged misappropriator was a news organization; (2) its intent was to broadcast footage containing the alleged secrets; (3) conditions inside meatpacking firms were newsworthy matters of public concern; (4) the harm that might arise from disclosure was speculative; and (5) such harm as occurred would most likely not be attributable to the loss of trade secrets. The *CBS* decision cautions against adoption of a blanket rule that preliminary injunctions are always appropriate against those who obtained trade secrets by wrongful means.

Nor should there necessarily be a blanket rule against First Amendment defenses if a defendant's public disclosure of a secret would breach a contract or confidence. In *Cohen v. Cowles Media Co.*,[67] the plaintiff sued for damages suffered by being fired from his job working for a candidate for governor because Cowles' newspapers disclosed, in breach of a promise of anonymity, that Cohen was a key source for a story Cowles published about charges levied against a candidate for lieutenant governor. The Supreme Court allowed Cohen to proceed with his claims for damages

---

[64] *Id.* at 549.
[65] *Id.*
[66] *Id.* at 550.
[67] 501 U.S. 663 (1991).

suffered as a result of Cowles' breach of this promise. Nothing in the *Cohen* decision suggests that the Court would have upheld a preliminary injunction against Cowles' publication of Cohen's name in breach of a promise not to do so. Because the Court was so deeply split (5–4) on whether Cohen could recover damages for breach of this promise, it is doubtful that the Court would have upheld a prior restraint on publication of this information by the newspapers, had this question been presented.

There may thus be some, albeit rare, circumstances in which a court should be receptive to First Amendment defenses in trade secrecy cases notwithstanding contractual or confidential non-disclosure obligations.

C. First Amendment Defenses as to Third Party Recipients of Newsworthy Secrets

Most of the trade secrecy cases in which First Amendment defenses have been successful have presented a common pattern: a third party journalist (and/or news provider) obtains non-public information from a second party that it later learns a first party claims as a misappropriated trade secret or confidential information. The journalist then decides to publish the information because it is newsworthy. Because the journalist is not bound by any contractual or confidential obligation to the first party (even if the person from whom the third party got the secret may be) and did not act in concert with the second party in any misappropriation of the secret, the journalist feels justified in publicly disclosing the information. The first party then asserts that the journalist knew or ought to have known the information was a misappropriated trade secret. And when the first party seeks a preliminary injunction, the journalist then raises a First Amendment defense.

In *Procter & Gamble Co. v. Bankers Trust Co.*,[68] for example, *Business Week* obtained information about Procter & Gamble's lawsuit against Bankers Trust from documents that had been filed under seal. Upon learning of the magazine's intent to publish a story using this information, the litigants requested a temporary restraining order (TRO) to forbid the magazine from publishing secrets obtained from the documents. The trial court not only granted the TRO, but ruled that the magazine should be permanently enjoined from publishing the information because it had knowingly violated a protective order in getting access to the information.

The Sixth Circuit reversed and criticized the trial court for its insensitivity to First Amendment considerations: '"[P]rohibiting the publication of

---

[68] 78 F.3d 219 (6th Cir. 1996).

a news story . . . is the essence of censorship", and is allowed only under exceptional circumstances'.[69] The trial court 'fail[ed] to conduct any First Amendment inquiry before granting the two TROs' and 'compounded the harm by holding hearings on issues that bore no relation to the right of *Business Week* to disseminate the information in its possession'.[70] Instead of trying to determine the source of the leak, the trial court should have focused on whether the parties had proved exceptional circumstances that would justify a prior restraint on publication.

Similarly, in *State ex rel. Sports Management News, Inc. v. Nachtigal*,[71] the Oregon Supreme Court overturned a preliminary injunction issued by a lower court that forbade Sports Management News (SMN) from publishing reports about a new shoe design that Adidas claimed as a trade secret. The court recognized that the design was a trade secret, that Adidas had only made this information available to select employees who were bound by confidentiality agreements, and that SMN may have known that the information was disclosed in breach of confidence. Yet the court characterized a lower court order that SMN refrain from publishing any information derived from Adidas proprietary information as a classic prior restraint because it required SMN to submit to the court for its approval any reports about Adidas products prior to publication.

A third such case is *Ford Motor Co. v. Lane*,[72] in which a trial court denied the car-maker's motion for a preliminary injunction to stop Lane from posting information on the Internet about unreleased automobile designs and other non-public information that Ford claimed as trade secrets. Ford argued that Lane knew that Ford employees were obliged not to leak such secret information, so Lane knew the information had been misappropriated, and hence, he should be secondarily liable for the misappropriation. Yet, because Lane did not have a contractual or confidential relationship with Ford and did not himself misappropriate the information, the court ruled that 'Lane's alleged improper conduct in obtaining the trade secrets are not grounds for issuing a prior restraint'.[73]

Lane has sometimes been criticized for adopting an overbroad interpretation of the First Amendment in trade secrecy cases. One critic of *Lane* believes that '[a]s between the two immediate parties to the dispute, the full set of efficiency arguments opts strongly for the protection of trade

---

[69] *Id.* at 225 (quoting *In re* Providence Journal Co., 820 F.2d 1342, 1345 (1st Cir. 1986)).
[70] *Id.*
[71] 921 P.2d 1304 (Or. 1996).
[72] 67 F.Supp.2d 745 (E.D. Mich. 1999).
[73] *Id.* at 753.

secrets, given their essential role in modern industry'.[74] Lane knew full well that the persons from whom he got Ford's secrets had misappropriated them, and '[h]e decided to publish the trade secrets on his website to retaliate against Ford after a dispute about Lane's right to attend certain Ford trade shows and to use either the Ford trade name or its Blue Oval trademark on his website'.[75] Lane seemingly 'utilized the power of the Internet to extort concessions or privileges from Ford, by threatening to sell blueprints or other confidential documents'.[76]

Yet, it cuts in Lane's favor that he had been providing news about Ford and its designs on his website for years, and, as of this writing, still does. Lane's knowledge that the information he published had been divulged in breach of a confidence or contract is far from atypical for news organizations. 'Leaks of confidential information are a staple of modern investigative journalism and have helped break many important stories'.[77] Courts should be 'extremely wary' of deciding what news can and cannot be published.[78]

The Supreme Court's prior restraint decisions, especially *New York Times v. United States* (i.e., the Pentagon Papers case)[79] have led some commentators to assert that courts must always presume that preliminary injunctions against third party uses or disclosures of trade secret information are unconstitutional prior restraints on speech. The *Procter & Gamble* decision would seem to concur. In the Pentagon Papers case, the Supreme Court ruled that the First Amendment forbade enjoining newspapers from publishing excerpts of government documents which the newspapers knew had been obtained unlawfully by the person from whom they obtained the documents. However, a closer look at the Pentagon Papers decision suggests that it may not be as much of a shield against injunctions in trade secret cases as some commentators believe.

The facts of the Pentagon Papers case are well-known, but worth briefly restating. Daniel Ellsberg obtained access to a set of documents analysing the Vietnam War prepared for the U.S. Department of Defense while working for the Rand Corporation. Ellsberg communicated with the *New*

---

74 Epstein, *supra* note 3, at 1037.

75 *Id.*

76 Ford Motor Co. v. Lane, 67 F.Supp.2d 745, 753 (E.D. Mich. 1999).

77 Volokh, *supra* note 4, at 741.

78 See, e.g., O'Grady v. Superior Court, 139 Cal. App. 4th 1423, 1477 (Cal. App. 6th 2006).

79 403 U.S. 713 (1971) (per curiam). The Pentagon Papers case was relied upon in CBS v. Davis, 510 U.S. 1315, 1317–18 (1994); Procter & Gamble Co. v. Bankers Trust Co., 78 F.3d 219, 225 (6th Cir. 1996); *Ford*, 67 F.Supp.2d at 751; Religious Tech. Ctr. v. Lerma, 897 F.Supp. 260, 263 (E.D. Va. 1995); and *Bunner II*, 113 Cal. Rptr. 2d 338, 351 (Ct. App. 2001).

York Times and *Washington Post* about the documents and arranged for copies to be delivered to these newspapers. The *Times* and the *Post* spent several months analysing the documents, and then began publishing excerpts in their newspapers. The United States sued to enjoin further publication from them. The Supreme Court ruled (6–3) that the newspapers could continue publishing the Pentagon Papers.

Each member of the Court wrote his own opinion. Justices Black and Douglas were convinced that the press must always be free to publish news without government prior restraint.[80] Justice Brennan accepted that prior restraints were justifiable in 'an extremely narrow class of cases', but thought that the government's case was 'predicated upon surmise or conjecture that untoward consequences may result'.[81] Justices White and Stewart thought that publishing these reports would cause substantial damage to U.S. interests, but believed that the government had not satisfied the 'unusually heavy justification' for a prior restraint, especially 'in the absence of express and appropriately limited congressional authorization for prior restraints in circumstances such as these'.[82] Justice Marshall pointed out that Congress had enacted numerous laws to punish those who wrongfully disclosed secret information, yet had decided not to enact a law to give the Executive Branch authority to proceed against newspapers in situations such as this.[83]

Chief Justice Burger and Justice Harlan, in dissent, were unsympathetic to the newspapers' pleas in large part because the publishers knew that the documents had been stolen.[84] Justice Blackmun objected to the pressure, panic, and sensationalism with which the case had been adjudicated, saying that did not allow for proper judicial consideration. He would have remanded the case for further proceedings after some discovery and an orderly presentation of evidence and argumentation.[85] All three dissenters objected to the haste with which the case had been brought before the Court and thought that the government should have had more of an opportunity to make its case.[86]

Those who take the broadest view of the prior restraints doctrine in trade secrecy cases perceive the Pentagon Papers case to present four

---

[80] New York Times Co. v. United States, 403 U.S. 713, 714–24 (1971) (Black, J., concurring).

[81] *Id.* at 725–6 (Brennan, J., concurring).

[82] *Id.* at 731–3 (White, J., concurring).

[83] *Id.* at 743–7 (Marshall, J., concurring).

[84] *Id.* at 749–51 (Burger, C.J., dissenting); *id.* at 754–5 (Harlan , J., dissenting).

[85] *Id.* at 761–2 (Blackmun, J., dissenting).

[86] *Id.* at 748–62 (Burger, C.J., Harlan & Blackmun, JJ., dissenting).

salient characteristics: (1) the documents about to be published had been misappropriated; (2) although publishers of the documents had not participated in the initial wrongdoing, they knew that the documents to be published had been wrongfully obtained; (3) because of this, the publishers risked criminal and civil liability; and (4) publication of the documents could damage important interests.[87] They argue that the economic interests of trade secret owners are less fundamental than the national security interests at stake in the Pentagon Papers case. 'If a threat to national security was insufficient to warrant a prior restraint in *New York Times Co. v. United States*', said one court, 'the threat to plaintiff's copyrights and trade secrets is woefully inadequate'.[88]

This statement seems overblown, however, given that the Pentagon Papers case involved highly respected traditional news publishers, deliberative exercises of editorial judgment, news having a significant bearing on governmental decisions on matters of considerable public concern, and governmental attempts to assert censorial powers over the publication decisions of major newspapers. First Amendment defenses in trade secrecy cases have not thus far presented a similar confluence of peak First Amendment values.

Peak First Amendment values were also important in a more recent Supreme Court decision, *Bartnicki v. Vopper*,[89] which involved the radio broadcast of an illegally intercepted telephone conversation among union officials who were contemplating violent action against the union's enemies. The *Bartnicki* decision suggests that free speech defenses in trade secrecy cases are more likely to succeed when they involve third party disclosures of newsworthy information or matters of public concern.

The federal wiretap law makes it illegal to 'intentionally disclose[]. . . to any other person the contents of any wire, oral, or electronic communication, knowing or having reason to know that the information was obtained through the [illegal] interception of a wire, oral, or electronic communication'.[90] Vopper did not deny he had reason to know that the person who recorded this conversation had done so illegally, but once the recording came into his hands through no wrongdoing by him, he argued he had a First Amendment right to broadcast the conversation because of its newsworthy qualities. This defense was initially rejected because the

87 See, e.g., Greene, *supra* note 4, at 540, 543–51.
88 See *Lerma*, 897 F.Supp. at 263.
89 532 U.S. 514 (2001).
90 18 U.S.C. § 2511(1)(c) (2006).

lower court regarded the wiretap law as a content-neutral law of general applicability that satisfied intermediate scrutiny standards.

The Supreme Court ruled that it was not consistent with the First Amendment to hold Vopper liable for damages for disclosing the illegally intercepted information. Justice Stevens, writing for a plurality of the Court, distinguished *Bartnicki* from typical wiretap cases on three grounds:

> First, respondents played no part in the illegal interception. Rather, they found out about the interception only after it occurred, and in fact never learned the identity of the person or persons who made the interception. Second, their access to the information on the tapes was obtained lawfully, even though the information itself was intercepted unlawfully by someone else. Third, the subject matter of the conversation was a matter of public concern.[91]

The wiretap law's prohibition on third party disclosure 'is fairly characterized as a regulation of pure speech', and 'if the acts of "disclosing" and "publishing" information do not constitute speech, it is hard to imagine what does fall within that category'.[92]

Justice Stevens invoked several precedents upholding the right of the media to publish lawfully obtained truthful information even when laws forbade its disclosure.[93] However, Justices Breyer and O'Connor were only willing to support Vopper's First Amendment defense because the public's interest in disclosure of Bartnicki's conversation was 'unusually high' and the public interest in non-disclosure as 'unusually low' because of the violent sentiments expressed during the call.[94]

Had the question in *Bartnicki* been whether the First Amendment would shield Vopper from a preliminary injunction against public broadcast of the contents of the tape, the Court would almost certainly have considered that to be an unconstitutional prior restraint on speech. After all, six Justices believed that the First Amendment immunized Vopper from damages claims.

Some critics of *Bartnicki* have argued that the issuance of preliminary injunctions should not turn on whether the information about to be disclosed is a matter of public or private concern, for it calls for 'a highly subjective judgment'.[95] Judicial decisions based on this distinction will

---

91 *Bartnicki*, 532 U.S. at 525 (citation omitted).

92 *Id.* at 526–7 (alteration in original) (quoting *Bartnicki v. Vopper*, 200 F.3d 109, 120 (3d Cir. 1999)).

93 *Id.* at 528.

94 *Id.* at 535, 540 (Breyer, J., concurring).

95 Volokh, *supra* note 4, at 747.

'simply reflect [the courts'] judgments about who should win or lose in this case, rather than more principled judgments about the actual value of the speech to the public'.[96]

There is some merit to this view, as *Bunner* illustrates. Although the California Supreme Court in *Bunner III* noted that the CSS secrets 'may have some link to a public issue',[97] it characterized the secrets as matters of private concern because they 'convey only technical information about the method used by specific private entities to protect their intellectual property' and because Bunner 'did not post them to comment on any public issue or to participate in any public debate'.[98] In that court's view, disclosure of CSS secrets 'adds nothing to the public debate over the use of encryption software or the DVD industry's efforts to limit unauthorized copying of movies on DVDs'.[99]

While the general public may not be able to understand all of the fine details of encryption technologies, nuclear power plant safety systems, or complex chemical processes, scientists who assess the implications of such technologies for the security and safety of the public are engaged in discourse on matters of public concern when they publish information about their safety, security, and the like. The assertion in *Bunner III* that trade secrets only implicate matters of private concern seems wrong. Indeed, on remand, the Court of Appeal gave credence to Bunner's belief that DeCSS would contribute to making Linux-compatible DVDs, and this would make the Linux platform more attractive to consumers and more competitive with Microsoft's platforms.[100] There was also evidence in *Bunner* that computer security experts benefited from access to information about CSS and its vulnerabilities.[101]

Even though the private/public distinction may sometimes be murky, *Bartnicki* and other precedents suggest that it is likely to matter whether about-to-be-disclosed trade secret information is newsworthy or of public concern, as First Amendment interests are strongest in these circumstances.

Courts should not limit the privilege to professional journalists, however, but should consider 'whether the person seeking to invoke the [First

---

96 *Id.*

97 *Bunner III*, 75 P.3d 1, 16 (Cal. 2003).

98 *Id.* at 15.

99 *Id.* at 16.

100 *Bunner IV*, 10 Cal. Rptr. 3d 185, 189–90 (Ct. App. 2004).

101 See Declaration of David Wagner, *Bunner I*, No. CV786804 (Super. Ct. Cal. January 14, 2000), available at www.eff.org/IP/Video/DVDCCA_case/20000107-pi-motion-wagnerdec.html.

Amendment] privilege had "the intent to use material – sought, gathered, or received – to disseminate information to the public and [whether] such intent existed at the inception of the newsgathering process"'.[102] Under such a test, intellectual property anarchists and vengeful former employees could not succeed with First Amendment defenses for Internet posting of trade secrets, although those seeking to promote public awareness and discourse might.

Consistent with *Bartnicki*, third party disclosers of newsworthy trade secrets should also not be held liable for damages attributable to the loss of trade secret status.

V. OTHER FIRST AMENDMENT-BASED DUE PROCESS ISSUES IN TRADE SECRET CASES

The First Amendment has implications in trade secret cases beyond the prior restraints issue discussed in Part IV. First Amendment-based due process issues may also arise as to matters such as how much evidence of success on the merits must be shown in trade secret cases involving plausible First Amendment defenses, whether appellate courts should conduct *de novo* review of trial court findings when plausible First Amendment defenses are raised in trade secret cases, and how injunctions should be tailored to respect First Amendment values in trade secret cases.

In ordinary trade secret cases, as when the trade secrets are not being used or disclosed to contribute to public discourse, but have been misappropriated for private use or disclosure for purposes of commercial exploitation to the plaintiff's detriment, it is proper to use the generally applicable standard for preliminary injunctions, which considers proof of a reasonable probability of success on the merits and a balance of harms to the parties that tips in favor of the plaintiff.

In those rare cases in which a preliminary injunction is being sought to prevent public disclosure of information claimed by the plaintiff to be a trade secret, courts should require a greater showing of probability of success on the merits (e.g., a high probability of success) and a showing that grave and irreparable harm to the trade secret claimant will result from such disclosure, as in the *CBS* and *Procter & Gamble* cases. As Justice Blackmun observed in *CBS*, preliminary injunctions should not issue against public disclosure of trade secret cases, unless 'the evil that

---

[102] Shoen v. Shoen, 5 F.3d 1289, 1293 (9th Cir. 1993) (alteration in original) (quoting *von Bulow v. von Bulow*, 811 F.2d 136, 144 (2d Cir. 1987)).

would result from the [disclosure] is both great and certain and cannot be mitigated by less intrusive measures'.[103] This is also consistent with other Supreme Court decisions that require heightened scrutiny and substantive standards when the law imposes prior restraints on publication.[104]

Appellate courts should also undertake a *de novo* review of the relevant constitutional facts when defendants raise First Amendment defenses to trade secret misappropriation claims, as the California Supreme Court directed in *Bunner III*.[105] Deferential review of a trial court's findings of fact pertinent to the issuance of a preliminary injunction may be appropriate in an ordinary trade secret case, but such deference is not warranted when free speech and press interests are at stake. If the *de novo* examination leads the appellate court to conclude that the evidence is insufficient to support the injunction, it should be vacated.

Conducting independent appellate review of constitutionally relevant facts serves two purposes: to 'prevent . . . prejudiced or erroneous deprivation of constitutional rights by fact finders' and 'to help prevent future mistakes by making the lines in free speech law clearer and more administrable'.[106] Appellate review of the facts in *Bunner IV* served both purposes. The preliminary injunction against posting of DeCSS on trade secrecy grounds was erroneously granted because the secrets had been available for months on the site before the injunction was sought. Future courts might have construed *Bunner I* as a substantial expansion of California trade secrecy law but for the appellate court's *de novo* review of the constitutionally relevant facts in that case.

Trade secret injunctions often provide that if the protected information becomes public or commonly known in an industry by means other than wrongful acts of the defendant, he or she will then be free to disclose the secrets. A trade secrecy injunction that fails to include such a limitation will stifle the free flow of information without adequate justification. To be consistent with First Amendment principles, trade secrecy injunctions ought to allow the defendants to use and disclose previously secret information if it later becomes public or commonly known in an industry. To the extent they do not so provide, courts reviewing such injunctions ought to read such a limiting term into the order to comport with First Amendment principles.

---

103 CBS Inc. v. Davis, 510 U.S. 1315, 1317 (1994).

104 See, e.g., Gertz v. Robert Welch, Inc., 418 U.S. 323, 342 (1974) (clear and convincing evidence needed in public figure libel cases).

105 *Bunner III*, 75 P.3d I, 20 (Cal. 2003).

106 See, e.g., Eugene Volokh and Brett McDonnell, *Freedom of Speech and Independent Judgment Review in Copyright Cases*, 107 YALE L. J. 2431, 2432 (1998).

Finally, trade secret injunctions should be narrowly tailored so that the termination of an unsuccessful collaboration does not result in a former collaborator being foreclosed from continuing to work in the field. Consider *Southwest Research Institute v. Keraplast Technologies, Ltd.*,[107] in which a preliminary injunction unduly restricted the First Amendment interests of researchers. After a falling out between the firms, SWRI undertook research projects in the field in which it had previously done work under contract with Keraplast. Keraplast then sued for trade secrecy misappropriation on the theory that 'all the knowledge [SWRI] obtained is proprietary and confidential to Keraplast'.[108] The injunction forbade SWRI and its researchers from conducting further research, publishing and otherwise communicating information related to the field of keratin-based technology. This included 'without limitation, presentations, interviews, papers, advertisements, electronic or written communication or business inquiries'.[109] The injunction also forbade SWRI from filing patent applications in this field, initiating any tests or research to be performed by third parties, and applying for research grants or submitting contract research proposals to any private enterprise or government.[110] The Texas appellate court found the injunction to be impermissibly overbroad, citing SWRI's free speech interests as a factor. Other courts should follow *Keraplast* when reviewing the breadth of injunctions to ensure that they do not unduly encroach on First Amendment rights.

CONCLUSION

Previous commentary on free speech defenses in trade secrecy cases has tended to adopt one of two extreme positions. One extreme is that trade secret claims are categorically immune from First Amendment scrutiny because trade secrets are 'property' and enforcing these property rights is necessary to provide adequate incentives to invest in innovation. The other extreme is that preliminary injunctions against disclosures of trade secrets are presumptively unconstitutional prior restraints on speech and should rarely if ever issue because trade secrets are not as important societal interests as the national security issues at stake in the Pentagon Papers case.

---

107 103 S.W.3d 478 (Tex. App. 2003).

108 *Id.* at 483.

109 *Id.* at 481.

110 *Id.*

The middle ground explored in this chapter recognizes that the First Amendment is not generally implicated in ordinary trade secret cases. In ordinary cases, courts are merely ensuring that wrongdoers cannot make private use and disclosure of illegally or otherwise wrongfully acquired information. This is generally consistent with the First Amendment because such private uses and disclosures of trade secrets do not contribute in a meaningful way to public discourse. When defendants are under contractual or other obligations not to disclose secrets to others, holding them to their promises is also generally consistent with the First Amendment.

However, when persons or firms seek to promote public discourse on matters of public concern, they may have viable First Amendment privileges to reveal trade secrets. First Amendment defenses are especially likely to succeed when raised by those who did not participate in misappropriating the trade secret and who plan to make public disclosure of newsworthy information to contribute to public discourse.

Despite the dire predictions of some commentators, trade secrets and trade secrecy laws are surviving the challenges of the Internet age. Courts are generally doing a good job in balancing the private interests of trade secret developers who cannot justify investments in innovation if the law does not adequately protect them against the public's interest in having access to information about matters of public concern. Trade secrecy law should not be unwittingly torn from its roots in unfair competition principles just because some think that stronger protection for trade secrets is necessary to protect incentives to invest in innovation. Preserving confidential relationships, respecting contractual obligations, and promoting fair competition should continue to be the mainstay of trade secrecy law. Making trade secrecy law considerably stronger will not only distort free speech and free press principles, but undermine the competition and innovation policies of intellectual property laws.

13 Trade secrets and the 'philosophy' of copyright: a case of culture crash

*Diane Leenheer Zimmerman**

Except for a brief flurry of interest a quarter century ago, the nature of the interface in the United States between trade secrecy and copyright has rarely been thought to merit more than a passing reference in the most thorough of intellectual property casebooks. But both the expansive notion of what can constitute a trade secret and current debates about how best to understand copyright's theoretical and constitutional underpinnings suggest that the subject is worthy of further exploration. Developments in the law over recent decades have pulled these two philosophically distinct forms of intellectual property into one another's orbit, and the result has been what you would expect if two cars were headed toward one another at high speed in the same traffic lane: a 'crash' of cultures.

I. NATURE OF THE PROBLEM

Most commonly, trade secrets[1] involve methods or formulas or know-how that may or may not be eligible for patent protection, but that certainly do not qualify for copyright with its proscription against protecting ideas or factual information.[2] There are, however, instances in which the trade secret inheres in a particularized mode of expression, and in those cases, the secret material does fall within the subject matter of copyright. For example, the source code version of a computer program has been recognized as a kind of literary work that fits within the scope of copyright. At the same time, the elements that 'express' the program also represent a series of design and organizational choices that the owner, anxious to

---

* Samuel Tilden Professor of Law Emerita, New York University School of Law. This research was supported by a grant from the Filomen D'Agostino and Max E. Greenberg Research Fund at New York University School of Law. Able research assistance was provided by Genevieve York-Erwin, J.D., N.Y.U. Law, 2009.

1 For a definition of 'trade secret', see RESTATEMENT (THIRD) OF UNFAIR COMPETITION § 39 (1995).

2 See 17 U.S.C. § 102(b)(2000); Baker v. Selden, 101 U.S. 99 (1879).

protect the product's market share, may well want to keep competitors from understanding. Thus, it is an example of a trade secret. Technical drawings and specifications, too, are copyrightable subject matter that can also potentially embody material that the author or owner wishes to hold as a trade secret. Copyrighted expression and trade secrets overlap in other places as well; for example, in the case of secure tests, such as the Law School Aptitude Tests (LSATs), where the way particular questions are phrased is copyrightable, but where keeping those questions secret is essential in order for them to be reused in subsequent tests. Published manuals, proprietary databases or such compilations as customer lists are also copyrightable but owners often wish to impose access limitations on them by such means as confidentiality agreements. Even written lectures delivered before a limited audience could under some circumstances qualify as trade secrets.

There is nothing new about the possibility that expression eligible for copyright can contain the kind of commercially valuable material that trade secrecy law has traditionally protected. But until three decades ago, the overlap was not a source of concern either to commentators or courts. Owners of expressive works could choose to treat them as trade secrets without ever running across a copyright issue because copyright came into play only on publication. Most expressive works embodying trade secrets were not 'published' in the copyright sense even if they were circulated to others, as long as the distribution was subject to confidentiality agreements.

Several changes occurring in the 1970s, however, altered the intellectual property landscape sufficiently that the historically frictionless interface between copyright and trade secrecy began to rub uncomfortably. One of these changes was technological – the introduction of the personal computer (PC) with its concomitant appetite for widely disseminated software.[3] The second was the thoroughgoing reform of American copyright law represented by passage of the 1976 Copyright Act.[4]

Before the PC, deciding to treat software as a trade secret was quite feasible; specially developed programs designed to be used on particular mainframes did not need to be published to be useful; they could be developed by employees or independent contractors who could be bound by

---

[3] See generally Martin Campbell-Kelly and William Aspray, Computer: A History of the Information Machine 207–53 (2d ed. 2004) (describing rise of personal computer in mid-1970s and early 1980s and the development of the application software market).

[4] Copyright Act of 1976, Pub. L. No. 94-553, § 102(a), 90 Stat. 2541, 2544–5 (codified as amended at 17 U.S.C. § 102(a) (2000)).

promises not to reveal their design. By contrast, the market for software to run PCs was a mass market; multiple copies of programs were produced to be sold directly to end-users, or to be incorporated into computers that would themselves be widely distributed. Either form of distribution clearly involved publication. This change led those in the software industry to see the advantage in trying to take advantage of copyright while retaining the benefits of trade secrecy. The use of copyright would enable them to distribute copies of their works in object code (that is, computer-readable) form to the public backed up by the threat of sanctions for infringement to ward off rampant copying. At the same time, developers wanted to maintain the economic value of their programs and ward off competition by keeping the expression that embodied the design of these programs – their source code – a secret.[5] The objective was achieved by convincing the Copyright Office to accept registration of software under its 'rule of doubt', an approach subsequently affirmed by Congress when it opted expressly to include software as a protected category under the statute.[6] The problem of keeping the copyrighted expression secret was not, however, addressed by Congress; rather, as will be discussed more fully later in this chapter, it came about through a regulatory compromise forged with the Copyright Office.[7]

The second development that led to the uncomfortable face-off between copyright and trade secrecy was the redesign of copyright in the 1976 Act and its remake of the American legal landscape with regard to expressive works. Most significant for purposes of this article was the decision to attach copyright automatically to any original expressive work once fixed in tangible form; also significant was the decision to continue to relax the deposit requirements that served as a mechanism for making the contents of protected works publicly accessible. Both of these changes opened the door to an argument that Congress was abandoning the basic assumptions that had served, historically, as the underpinnings of copyright law. At the same time, the new statute included an express pre-emption provision that suggested to many at the time that Congress was intending to deprive copyright claimants of much of the protections they had

---

5 The other alternative, patenting, did not at the time seem feasible. The U.S. Supreme Court did not approve of a patent involving a computer program until 1981, Diamond v. Diehr, 450 U.S. 175 (1981). Prior to that, the Court was thought to view software as unpatentable. Parker v. Flook, 437 U.S. 584 (1978).

6 See 17 U.S.C. § 117 (1998) (titled 'Limitations on exclusive rights: Computer programs').

7 37 C.F.R. § 202.20(c)(2)(vii) (2008) (describing registration and deposit requirements for computer programs containing trade secrets).

hithertofore enjoyed under state law, in particular coverage under state trade secrecy law.

The idea that copyright could protect secrets threatened to break an almost two hundred year old linkage between the protections offered by statutory copyright and the goal of promoting public access to new works. Prior to 1978, the effective date of the revised Act, copyright in the United States was available only for works that were published,[8] and, even then, only if the owner 'elected' coverage by complying with a series of formal steps, including attaching a copyright notice to each distributed copy.[9]

While the work remained unpublished, however, its protections were a product of state rather than federal law. State law gave authors and their assigns the right to decide when or whether to publish, and whether or not to maintain a mantle of secrecy around the work. The right of first publication was protected in perpetuity by common law copyright, and other state remedies, such as those for misappropriation of trade secrets or invasions of privacy, could also be called upon in appropriate circumstances to remedy unconsented uses. Since, prior to the advent of the PC, proprietors who wanted to maintain the secrecy of the contents of their expressive works were unlikely to publish them, federal copyright law, with its emphasis on public access, and trade secrecy, with its quite opposite focus, could co-exist in essentially independent realms. The 1976 Act upended this simple co-existence on two fronts. First, it caused the issue of pre-emption to rear its unruly head, and second, it made the idea of 'secret' copyrights facially plausible. For the idea of secret copyrights to make sense, however, it was necessary to assume an intent to jettison a

---

[8] The 1909 Copyright Act did, for the first time, make copyright available for a narrow class of unpublished works that were in fact publicly accessible. Section 12 of the Act permitted authors or owners to register specific categories of unpublished materials for federal protection, including sculpture, motion pictures and dramatic works. As one commentator noted, 'This act of grace was accorded these particular classes because they are primarily adapted for performance or exhibition and may achieve their purpose without being reproduced in copies for sale or public distribution'. HERBERT A. HOWELL, THE COPYRIGHT LAW 102 (3d ed. 1952). In addition to providing federal remedies for infringement of these unpublished works, the provision gave owners an opportunity to act pre-emptively to avoid the risk that they might be deemed to have injected their work into the public domain by making it too accessible. See id. at 103; see also The Letter Edged in Black Press, Inc. v. Public Building Comm'n of Chicago, 320 F.Supp. 1303 (N.D. Ill. 1970) (finding Picasso sculpture 'published without notice' and hence injected into public domain).

[9] If the owner either neglected to comply with whatever formal requirements were in place at the time the work was published, or chose for some reason not to do so, the work lost all protection upon publication and entered the public domain.

long and consistent history of treating disclosure and access as core copyright values.[10]

In truth, however, the consequences of the changes in question seem not to have been intended, but instead to have resulted from inadvertence, from changes made with virtually no thought about whether and how federal copyright should take into account protection of materials that were never intended to be disclosed.[11] Legal changes that do not take adequate account of downstream consequences quickly lead to intellectual incoherence, a problem increasingly apparent in copyright. Thus, in addition to the benefits of examining the current interface between copyright and trade secrecy, beginning with the pre-emption problem, and then turning to the tension between secrecy and access, a study of these issues opens a window onto the process which has led, as Professor Graeme Austin has trenchantly put it, to a point in copyright where, today, 'there are few instances where theory dictates the formulation and development of positive law'.[12]

II. THE PROBLEM OF PRE-EMPTION

The possibility that a body of state law, including the law of trade secrecy, could conflict with, and be pre-empted by, federal intellectual property

---

[10] See Boucicault v. Hart, 3 F.Cas. 983, 986 (S.D.N.Y. 1875) (stating that copyright claimant cannot cut off rights of others and at the same time conceal the content of the work).

[11] Some of the initial problems sorted themselves out as the statute continued to evolve. For example, for the first ten years after the new copyright statute became effective, copyright notice continued to be required on works at the time of publication. See Copyright Act of 1976, Pub. L. 94-553, 90 Stat. 2541, 2576, §§ 401(a), 403(a) (amended 1988). Although failure to comply no longer immediately propelled a work into the public domain, if the error was not appropriately cured, copyright could be lost. *Id.* § 405(a). This led some owners of trade secrets to put copyright notices on their work prophylactically to avoid any risk to their rights; only to open themselves up to the argument that, because they had in essence self-declared that their work was now published, they could no longer claim it was a secret. See, e.g., *Compuware, infra* note 33. The notice requirement was abandoned when the United States joined the Berne Convention in 1988 and rewrote several provisions in the statute to eliminate formal requirements for perfecting copyright. See Berne Convention Implementation Act of 1988, Pub. L. 100-568, § 7, 102 Stat. 2853, 2857 (codified at 17 U.S.C. §§ 401–6).

[12] Graeme W. Austin, *Copyright's Modest Ontology: Theory and Pragmatism in Eldred v. Ashcroft*, 16 CAN. J. L. & JURIS. 163 (2003).

law predated the 1976 Act because such laws could always be challenged as violations of the Supremacy Clause.[13] However, the new Act increased the possibility of conflict by including an express pre-emption clause. The section, 17 U.S.C. § 301, displaces state remedies that are 'equivalent to any of the exclusive rights within the general scope of copyright' and that come 'within the scope of copyright' as set out in sections 102, 103 and 106. This provision threw into doubt the continued viability of a wide range of state common law and statutory causes of action relating to unpublished expressive works, including protection for trade secrets. As its possible implications became clear and § 301 pre-emption challenges to trade secrecy law started working their way through the courts,[14] a number of commentators became so concerned that they urged Congress (unsuccessfully) to revise the statute to make clear that trade secrecy protection was not intended to be reduced or even lost in return for expanded copyright coverage.[15] Congress may not have expected the pre-emption provision to threaten the protection of trade secrecy, but, as has often been noted, the language used in the section is open to many interpretations, and its legislative history internally contradictory.[16] The result was confusion and litigation.

On the flip side, however, and assuming that the pre-emption question could somehow be resolved, some proprietors of now-copyrighted works saw potential advantages from a dual system of protection. Not only might they be able to stack copyright's equitable and monetary remedies on top of the state remedies for misappropriation of secrets,[17] but if for any reason the expressive work in question were deemed by a court not to

---

[13] Patent law pre-emption cases made their way to the Supreme Court several times before passage of the 1976 Act. See, e.g., Sears, Roebuck & Co. v. Stiffel Co., 376 U.S. 225 (1964); Compco Corp. v. Day-Brite Lighting, Inc., 376 U.S. 234 (1964); Kewanee Oil Co. v. Bicron Corp., 416 U.S. 470 (1974). Only one Supremacy Clause based pre-emption case, Goldstein v. California, 412 U.S. 546 (1973), involved copyright.

[14] See, e.g., Associated Film Distribution Corp. v. Thornburgh, 520 F.Supp. 971 (E.D. Pa. 1981); Allied Artists Corp. v. Rhodes, 496 F.Supp. 442 (N.D. Ohio 1980).

[15] See, e.g., Proposed Resolution 206-1, 1981 A.B.A. SEC. PATENT, TRADEMARK & COPYRIGHT L. REP. 91 (urging amendment of § 301 to clarify that state trade secrecy law is not pre-empted by federal copyright law).

[16] See MELVILLE B. NIMMER AND DAVID NIMMER, 1 NIMMER ON COPYRIGHT § 1.01[B] (Mathew Bender & Co. ed., 2008) (discussing interpretive difficulties regarding pre-emption provisions in 1976 Act); see generally Joseph P. Bauer, *Addressing the Incoherency of the Preemption Provisions of the Copyright Act of 1976*, 10 VAND. J. ENT. & TECH. L. 1 (2007) (same).

[17] Whether or not this hope will be realized is uncertain. *See infra* note 32.

be sufficiently 'secret', copyright could be counted on to provide a second line of defense against unconsented copying.

At least once prior to the effective date of § 301, in 1974, a case (*Kewanee Oil Co. v. Bicron Corp.*[18]) was litigated under the Supremacy Clause, challenging state trade secrecy law as inconsistent with the federal patent system. The challenge failed even though the arguments in favor of pre-emption had considerably more bite than similar arguments would have had at the time in relation to copyright. Patent law is premised on the notion that 'knowledge monopolies' should be sparingly granted, and explicitly requires prompt public disclosure of any protected underlying art as one condition of gaining such protection.[19] Trade secrecy, in contrast, protects know-how monopolies precisely by avoiding disclosure of the information in question. The U.S. Supreme Court acknowledged that a legal regime offering protection for 'secret' inventions could undercut the philosophy of the patent system, but was not convinced that the numbers of inventors who would choose the common law protection over patenting was sufficiently large to trigger Supremacy Clause pre-emption.[20]

By contrast, copyright in 1974 was only available once the decision was made by the author or owner to grant the public access to her expression by virtue of publishing it. The law did not require authors to publish, and, in fact, both before and after the passage of the 1976 Act, Congress and the federal courts have been extremely deferential toward authorial choice about whether and when to make expression public.[21] For that

---

[18] 416 U.S. 470 (1974).

[19] The law encourages potential patent holders to file for protection quickly, by establishing a legal presumption that favors the first to file in awarding the patent. See 35 U.S.C. § 102(g)(2) (2002) (filing creates presumption of invention by time of filing).

[20] First, the Supreme Court had already held in earlier cases that state laws granting owners exclusive rights to unpatented or unpatentable products and improvements were invalid because they created a conflict with federal patent policy. See, e.g., Sears, Roebuck & Co. v. Stiffel Co., 376 U.S. 225 (1964); Compco Corp. v. Day-Brite Lighting, Inc., 376 U.S. 234 (1964). Trade secrecy protection seemed particularly vulnerable to similar treatment because it seemed inconsistent with the requirement in patent law that, in return for a limited term of exclusivity, owners of new inventions must publicly disclose the underlying art. *Kewanee*, 416 U.S. at 484. The Court refused to find that trade secrecy protection for unpatentable works was impermissible, although the majority acknowledged that, were it likely that very many of the inventors eligible for patents would instead opt for trade secrecy protection, 'we would be compelled to hold that such a system could not constitutionally continue to exist'. *Id.* at 489.

[21] See, e.g., Harper & Row Publishers, Inc. v. Nation Enters., 471 U.S. 539, 551 (1985) ('Publication of an author's expression before he has authorized its

reason, trade secrecy could safely be said to be no threat to copyright policy.

When Congress moved the onset of federal copyright protection in 1976 from the time of publication to the moment of fixation, the existence of a conflict between the two bodies of law as a Supremacy Clause matter seemed more plausible (although no one took up the challenge of convincing the Supreme Court on the matter). But the express pre-emption provision in § 301 was a source of more overt conflict and uncertainty.

At first, some courts tried to justify the survival of an independent cause of action for violation of trade secrecy rights on the dubious ground that the two actions did not involve equivalent subject matter.[22] Because copyright protected only expression, the argument went, the states under § 301 were free to provide complementary protection for the information and ideas that the work contained.[23] If this reasoning had persisted, it would have led to a serious Supremacy Clause conflict.[24] The fact that copyright does not protect facts and ideas is not an omission or an accident,[25] but is

---

dissemination seriously infringes the author's right to decide when and whether it will be made public'); American Tobacco Co. v. Werckmeister, 207 U.S. 284, 299 (1907) (finding under common law that 'the property of the author or painter in his intellectual creation is absolute until he voluntarily parts with the same'). The common law 'limited publication rule' allowed an author to share her unpublished work with a limited audience for particular purposes without the work being considered 'published' as a result. See, e.g., White v. Kimmell, 193 F.2d 744, 747–8 (9th Cir. 1952) (holding publication of manuscripts to be general rather than limited, since circulation was not sufficiently 'restricted both as to persons and purpose'); King v. Mister Maestro, Inc., 224 F.Supp. 101, 107–8 (S.D.N.Y. 1963) (holding distribution of advance copies of Dr. King's famous speech in press kit to be 'limited publication' since they were not offered to the public).

22 See, e.g., M. Bryce & Assocs., Inc. v. Gladstone, 107 Wis. 2d 241, 258–9, 319 N.W.2d 907, 915–16 (1981); Warrington Assocs., Inc. v. Real Time Eng'g Sys., Inc., 522 F.Supp. 367, 368 (N.D. Ill. 1981); *cf.* Technicon Medical Info. Sys. Corp. v. Green Bay Packaging, Inc., 687 F.2d 1032, 1038 (7th Cir. 1982), *cert. denied*, 459 U.S. 1106 (1983) (a pre-1976 Act cause of action in which the court suggested that this division in subject matter meant no pre-emption under Supremacy Clause).

23 *Warrington*, 687 F.2d at 1038.

24 See RESTATEMENT (THIRD) OF UNFAIR COMPETITION § 38 cmt. e (1995) (state protection of facts and ideas would undercut balance struck by copyright and would likely offend Supremacy Clause).

25 See 17 U.S.C. § 102(b)(2000) ('In no case does copyright . . . extend to any idea, procedure, process, system, method of operation, concept, principle, or discovery, regardless of the form in which it is described, explained, illustrated, or embodied in such work'); see also *Baker*, 101 U.S. at 100–1 (explaining principled distinction between copyrightable expression and uncopyrightable facts and ideas).

a fundamental part of the so-calied copyright bargain. Historically, courts and commentators alike have agreed that in return for copyright's grant of exclusive rights to an author's actual expression, the factual content and ideas embodied in the expression are donated to the public domain.[26] Although neither the statute nor the Supreme Court has ever expressly held that state law cannot be used to protect non-patentable ideas and information, strong dicta suggest that the public domain status of ideas and information is fundamental to copyright policy, is of constitutional dimension and is beyond the power of states to change.[27]

This potential source of conflict was avoided by the eventual emergence of a different consensus among courts on why trade secrecy law could apply to expressive works without being pre-empted by § 301. They concluded that actions under trade secrecy law, unlike those for copyright infringement, require proof either of a violation of a confidential relationship or wrongful acquisition of the information.[28] These acts make trade secrecy violations different from copyright infringement, hence providing the necessary 'extra element' that saves state law from § 301 pre-emption.

This approach, however, seems unlikely to save all state trade secrets cases from the reach of § 301. In several instances, what might pass in state court for a breach of confidence or the wrongful acquisition and use of a trade secret, upon analysis, looks remarkably like simple copyright infringement. Consider, for example, a situation where liability for misappropriation of a trade secret rests on a finding of an 'implied' confidential relationship between plaintiff and defendant. As one federal appellate court recently cautioned, these claims must be carefully scrutinized when they involve expressive works, lest an 'implied' relationship may be found that is really 'nothing more than a dressed-up version of a copyright infringement claim'.[29] Similarly, law in many states permits recovery

---

[26] See Feist Publ'ns, Inc. v. Rural Tel. Serv. Co., 499 U.S. 340 (1991).

[27] See, e.g., Eldred v. Ashcroft, 537 U.S. 186, 218–21 (2003) (discussing close historical and theoretical relationship between First Amendment rights and copyright's idea-expression dichotomy); *Harper & Row*, 471 U.S. at 555–60 (recognizing certain 'First Amendment protections already embodied in the Copyright Act's distinction between copyrightable expression and uncopyrightable facts and ideas'). *Harper & Row* in particular suggests that federal copyright policy requires that ideas and facts remain in the public domain, unprotected by state law.

[28] See, e.g., Avtec Sys., Inc. v. Peiffer, 21 F.3d 568, 575 (4th Cir. 1994); Gates Rubber Co. v. Bando Chem. Indus., Ltd., 9 F.3d 823, 847–8 (10th Cir.1993); Computer Assocs. Int'l, Inc. v. Altai, Inc., 982 F.2d 693, 717 (2d Cir. 1992); Expediters Int'l v. Direct Cargo Mgmt. Servs., Inc., 995 F.Supp. 468, 480 (D.N.J. 1998).

[29] Bateman v. Mnemonics, Inc., 79 F.3d 1532, 1549–50 (11th Cir. 1996).

against defendants even in the absence of some pre-existing confidential relationship with the plaintiff and without active engagement in trying to acquire the secret. Liability in such cases has been justified on the ground that the defendant used the information in the face of actual or constructive notice that it was secret and that the third party who provided it was under a duty not to do so.[30] Imposing liability under these circumstances may serve the policy goals of trade secrecy, but from a copyright perspective, again, such a case looks functionally indistinguishable from a simple knowing act of copyright infringement.[31]

Thus, trade secrecy claims that do not rest on a concrete showing of breach of duty in the context of an actual as opposed to a theoretical relationship (for example, violation of an express contractual duty, or of a duty imposed by some generally recognized form of fiduciary or confidential relationship, or on some form of independent wrongdoing such as trespass, industrial espionage, or active inducement of a breach by a third person) seem highly suspect under § 301. Mere receipt and use of secret expressive works without permission, even in cases of clear *scienter*, does not seem to provide the 'extra element' that would allow states to escape the pre-emptive effect of copyright law. This means that, by folding unpublished works into copyright, Congress may on the margins have limited the flexibility of states in developing statutory and common law protections for trade secrets in ways that otherwise might be unobjectionable.

---

[30] As a California court wrote: 'While such a confidential relationship usually exists, trade secret law may bar unauthorized disclosure by strangers to the secret who stumble upon it improperly or with notice of mistake'. Balboa Ins. Co. v. Trans Global Equities, 267 Cal. Rptr. 787, 800 n.30 (Cal. Ct. App. 1990).

[31] The *Altai* decisions nicely illustrate the two sides of this debate. See Computer Assocs. Int'l v. Altai, Inc., 775 F.Supp. 544, 565 (E.D.N.Y.1991) ('The trade secret rights in this case are "equivalent to" the exclusive rights granted to copyright owners under § 106, and are therefore preempted by federal law'), *aff'd in part, vacated in part, and remanded*, 982 F.2d 693, 717 (2d Cir.1992) ('*Altai II*') ('The defendant's breach of duty is the gravamen of such trade secret claims, and supplies the "extra element" that qualitatively distinguishes such trade secret causes of action from claims for copyright infringement that are based solely upon copying'). Like the *Altai* district court, the Ninth Circuit found the federal and state causes of action functionally equivalent in a case regarding an unfair competition claim. See Del Madera Props. v. Rhodes & Gardner Inc., 820 F.2d 973, 987 (9th Cir. 1987) (extra element of breach of fiduciary duty does not exist where defendant is third party who receives and uses documents acquired through another's breach). But see *Balboa Ins.*, 267 Cal. Rptr. at 800–2 (finding clear demarcation between copyright and trade secrecy laws); *Warrington*, 522 F.Supp. at 368 ('The practical distinction between the two [trade secrecy and copyright] interests is manifest').

The interesting question is whether parties with secrets to protect have gotten something valuable in return for the protection they may have lost. To answer that question requires a different discussion: one dealing with the tension between public access and secrecy that was created once the 1976 Act extended automatic copyright to all expressive works from creation onward. Or, to put it differently, it requires a look at the serious *Kewanee* issues created by this massive statutory reform.

Here is the problem. In situations where a trade secrecy cause of action can survive § 301 pre-emption, a party with colorable claims under both federal and state law will now face a potential dilemma in trying to benefit from the protection copyright theoretically offers her.[32] The trade secret owner could certainly go to state court to vindicate her state-granted rights in the expressive work. But the minute she tries to join her dual claims in federal court, she confronts a conundrum. The court will have no authority to hear her copyright claim unless the plaintiff first registers her work and accompanies the registration form with the requisite, publicly accessible, deposit copy required by law. Thus, she faces the immediate risk that enforcing her copyright will result in her valuable secret becoming worthless.[33] And if § 301 bars the trade secrecy claim and leaves the plaintiff only with copyright coverage, she may be unable to pursue relief unless she is willing to disclose the secret by registration. There is no small irony in the possibility that coverage of her work by the Copyright Act will limit the copyright owner's access to trade secrecy remedies in state court without providing any obvious way of benefitting safely from any coverage that copyrights provide.[34]

---

[32] Several courts have said that plaintiffs are entitled to sue for both copyright and trade secrecy violations related to the same expressive work. Whether any hope parties may have had of 'stacking' the remedies from both causes of action will be fulfilled, however, is questionable. The Second Circuit, for example, has sensibly suggested that a plaintiff who is successful on both claims ought not get double recovery. *Altai II*, 982 F.2d at 720.

[33] In *Compuware*, 77 F.Supp. 2d at 822, the District Court struggled visibly in its attempt to justify the conclusion that the deposit of an unredacted copy of the plaintiff's program with the Copyright Office did not destroy its trade secrecy claim on the unconvincing ground that Copyright Office rules made copying of the work onerous. Presumably, however, learning the secrets contained in a work does not depend on the ability to make a copy of it.

[34] Some other problems were faced by trade secrecy owners who also wanted copyright protection, but many of these sorted themselves out as the statute continued to evolve. For example, for the first ten years after the new copyright statute became effective, copyright notice continued to be required on works at the time of publication. See Copyright Act of 1976, Pub. L. 94-553, 90 Stat. 2541, 2576, §§ 401(a), 403(a) (amended 1988). Although failure to comply no longer immediately

III. THE ACCESS PARADIGM AND TRADE SECRECY IN EXPRESSION

A. The Impetus for Secret Copyrights

The attempt to resolve the forced disclosure issue, surprisingly, came not at the behest of holders of trade secrets embodied in unpublished works, but rather from parties who had either clearly, or most probably, published their work. They were the creators and disseminators of mass-marketed software and of so-called secure tests. The mediator was not Congress, but the Copyright Office, relying on its regulatory authority. If the outcome was correct, however, non-disclosure should theoretically be available to owners of unpublished works as well.

The situation faced by the makers of software for PCs, desiring both secrecy and protection from copyists, has already been noted.[35] Success in gaining copyright protection for software would be something of a pyrrhic victory, in their view, if owners had to comply with the deposit requirements of copyright to enjoy these benefits. Since object code was at the time (and even now) not humanly intelligible, the only meaningful form of deposit was in the program's 'literary' mode: its source code.[36] Without seeing that, the Copyright Office could not know what the claimant sought

---

propelled a work into the public domain, if the error was not appropriately cured, copyright could be lost. *Id.* § 405(a). This led some owners of trade secrets to put copyright notices on their work prophylactically to avoid any risk to their rights; but this opened them up to the argument that, because they had in essence self-declared that their work was now published, they could no longer claim it was a secret. See, e.g., *Compuware,* 77 F.Supp.2d at 820. As noted *supra* note 11, notice is no longer required to obtain or retain copyright.

[35] *See supra* text accompanying note 17.

[36] See Pamela Samuelson, *CONTU Revisited: The Case Against Copyright Protection for Computer Programs in Machine-Readable Form*, 1984 DUKE L.J. 663, 715 (1984). Absent great skill, enormous inputs of time (and probably some luck), decompilation – working backward from object code to recreate the underlying source code – is impractical, meaning that for all intents and purposes, especially in the early years of the personal computer, the program in object code successfully hid most of its secrets. See Andrew Johnson-Laird, *Reverse-Engineering of Software: Separating Legal Mythology from Actual Technology*, 5 SOFTWARE L.J. 331, 342–5 (1992) (explaining 'reverse engineering' in detail, and noting that '[d]eciphering computer-executable programs is extremely tedious and error prone; it can take up to a minute or so for each computer instruction (a typical program might contain 500,000 instructions – 347 days' worth of deciphering'); see also Apple Computer, Inc. v. Franklin Computer Corp., 714 F.2d 1240, 1245 (3d Cir. 1983) (noting defendant decided to copy plaintiff's operating system because replicating program through reverse engineering was too difficult).

to protect with copyright; source code thus was the only workable form in which to deposit the work. But if the source code were deposited, it would become a public record, and would reveal to potential competitors the design of the program and its developers' solutions to programming problems.

Software designers had another concern as well. Although they could have opted to rely only on trade secrecy and forego the protections of copyright, that strategy had its own problems. In addition to any worries they may have had about § 301 pre-emption, pursuing remedies under trade secrecy was a risky strategy for a product that was in fact mass-marketed. By securing the source code behind a wall of secrecy, owners could get remedies for breach where access to the product was granted only sparingly and conditionally. But designers of software for PCs could not be sure that courts would treat their programming devices and choices as 'secrets' once thousands, even millions, of copies of the programs embodying them were being sold (albeit in the impenetrable form of object code). Being able to claim copyright was a kind of legal insurance policy against the risk that a court might refuse to recognize the existence of trade secrets in software distributed to the public at large.

The other group that also wanted both secrecy and copyright protection were the standardized test preparers. They wanted to be able to reuse questions in successive years without running the risk that the questions would become publicly known. Secrecy both reduced the costs of production and, more importantly, allowed test givers to identify the questions that worked well and then be able to reuse them. They also worried about relying solely on trade secrecy because thousands of copies of the tests are made and then administered to people each year. Although the testing agencies take what steps they can to secure the actual questions on the tests, the information is widely circulated and therefore prone to 'escape'. A copyright infringement action can be a useful legal tool because, even if particular questions no longer qualify as secrets,[37] a suit for copyright infringement would be a useful way to discourage people from future revelations. But, again, these owners too needed to comply with the registration and deposit requirements if they hoped effectively to pursue infringers.

The statute simply did not address these issues. Rather, it was the Copyright Office that came to the rescue of software and secure test owners

---

[37] See, e.g., Nat'l Conference of Bar Exam'rs v. Multistate Legal Studies, Inc., 692 F.2d 478, 486 n.8 (7th Cir. 1982) (finding that secure tests are 'probably' unpublished); Assoc. of Am. Med. Colls. v. Carey, 728 F.Supp.873, 885 (N.D.N.Y. 1990) (noting that the claim that these tests are 'secret' and unpublished is open to serious question in spite of efforts to retain their confidentiality).

with a regulatory fix that allowed the benefits of copyright to flow to owners without actually requiring them to let the public at large know all or most of what was being protected. These regulations permitted owners of secure tests to submit deposit copies to the Copyright Office with the assurance that the full copies would be returned 'promptly' after the work was examined for copyrightability.[38] Computer software designers were allowed to deposit only portions of their source code, carefully structured to ensure that nothing the owner considered a valuable secret would be revealed.[39] And where those regulations did not solve a copyright owner's problem, that party could petition the office for 'special relief'[40] tailored to its particular needs. Thus, the 'secret' copyright was given formal recognition.

Subsequently, the Seventh Circuit, in *National Conference of Bar Examiners v. Multistate Legal Studies, Inc.* (the most significant judicial opinion on the subject to date),[41] upheld the Copyright Office's special deposit rules for secure tests, concluding that the statute's deposit requirements did not require public disclosure of the content protected by copyright.[42] In the court's view, the statute gave the Copyright Office sufficient discretion to allow it to set deposit requirements in a way that would simultaneously allow claimants to keep their secrets and protect their copyrights. In a moment of candor, the court acknowledged its concern that, were it to strike down the compromise forged by the challenged regulations, the Copyright Act would be 'unavailable for protecting a secure test' and, presumably, other secret information as well. Such a holding would violate, the court said, 'the presumption that acts of Congress are passed for beneficial purposes, not their frustration'.[43]

B. Consequences of Legislative Inadvertence, Part I: The Deposit Requirement

How the court reached the profoundly counterintuitive conclusion that the law is consistent with 'secret copyrights' can only be understood by examining the effects of inadvertence in the process of copyright legislative reform. Both the changes to the deposit provisions and the decision to have copyright from fixation rather than publication were made for reasons having nothing to do with a Congressional desire to promote

38 37 C.F.R. § 202.20(c)(vi) (2008).
39 *Id.* § 202.20(c)(vii).
40 *Id.* § 202.20(d).
41 692 F.2d 478 (7th Cir. 1982).
42 *Id.* at 485.
43 *Id.* at 484 n.6.

secret copyrights, but had the unexpected consequence of opening the door to just that result.

Prior to the copyright revision of 1909, deposit of a work for which protection was sought had to occur by the date of publication or the copyright would not issue at all.[44] In other words, deposit was a formal prerequisite for protection. Furthermore, the government was required to keep all deposit copies on permanent file, available for consultation by members of the public. That long-standing policy was altered in 1909. Deposit ceased to be a prerequisite for protection, and the Library of Congress and the Copyright Office were for the first time offered some freedom to modify the deposit requirements downward and even to dispose of some deposits once made. On the surface, one could interpret this evidence as suggesting that Congress had begun as early as the 1909 Act to move away from a commitment to the idea that copyright protection existed to ensure the public's access to new works. Certainly this was a view that the Seventh Circuit in *National Conference of Bar Examiners* seemed to endorse.

But the reasons for loosening the deposit requirements in the 1909 Act had nothing to do with a lessening interest in access; rather the purpose was to find a solution to two specific practical problems that had arisen under prior law. One objective was to prevent inadvertent failure to obtain copyright simply by virtue of not getting the deposit copy to Washington in a timely way. As the House report noted, 'the failure of a shipping clerk to see that the copies go promptly forward to Washington may destroy a copyright of great value, and many copyrights have been lost because by some accident or mistake this requirement was not complied with'.[45]

The second goal, and the explanation for why the Copyright Office and the Library of Congress were no longer required to retain all deposits, was to provide these entities with respite from a pressing practical difficulty: sheer lack of space. Up to then, all deposit copies had to be kept, even if they were of no particular interest to Library patrons, with the result that many were simply put into storage at some considerable government expense.[46]

---

[44] The first Copyright Act required deposit with the clerk of the district court by the date of publication as a condition of protection. Copyright Act of 1790, ch 15, § 3, 1 Stat. 124, 125. That pattern was maintained for the next 120 years. See Elizabeth K. Dunne, *Study No. 20: Deposit of Copyrighted Works*, in 1 STUDIES ON COPYRIGHT 409, 411 (Arthur Fisher Memorial ed., 1963). Originally, deposits were collected by the Secretary of State, but when the Library of Congress was created in the nineteenth century, provision was made for deposit copies to be turned over to it to build a national public collection. *Id.* at 421–2.

[45] *Washingtonian*, 306 U.S. at 36 n.2 (quoting H.R. Rep. No. 2222 (1909)).

[46] *Id.*

George Putnam, who was the Librarian of Congress at the time, testified at hearings preceding the passage of the 1909 Act:

> There are now on file in the Copyright Office, irrespective of the contents of the Library proper, a million and a half articles. That represents the accumulation since 1870. They have invaded practically half of the lowest stack of the Library building. . . . Now, how long, considering that it is a practical question, is the United States government going to be called upon to provide accommodation for that tremendous mass of material?[47]

In reading Putnam's various statements on the space issue, one can sense a growing feeling of desperation as the number of deposits piled up – 200,000 alone in 1905.[48] The solution – permitting the Copyright Office and the Library to dispose of some deposits by giving them to other libraries, returning them to the copyright owner, or destroying them[49] – was driven by the physical impossibility of doing otherwise. To assuage the concerns of publishers, who wanted all deposit copies to be kept for evidentiary purposes, the Copyright Office was given the authority to issue a certificate of registration to serve as *prima facie* evidence of copyright in the work and was also required to keep a catalogue of all entries.[50] The practices of the Copyright Office at the time suggest that it did not understand these changes to represent a devaluation by Congress of the evidentiary and public access functions of deposit; rather, it simply saw the new law as providing give in a situation that was fast becoming untenable. Support for this claim can be found in the fact that the Copyright Office voluntarily kept virtually all copies of the works that would be hardest for the public to find in other ways: unpublished but registered works,[51] including dramas, photographs and music.[52]

---

47 Statement of George Putnam, New York City, November 2, 1905 in 2 LEGISLATIVE HISTORY OF THE 1909 COPYRIGHT ACT 137 (E. Fulton Brylawski and Abe Goldman eds., 1976) ('LEGISLATIVE HISTORY').

48 See Arguments Before Joint Comm. on Patents, June 609, 1906, in 4 LEGISLATIVE HISTORY 14.

49 Act of March 4, 1909, ch. 320, §§ 59–60, 35 Stat. 1075, superseded by Copyright Act of 1976, Pub. L. No. 94-553, 90 Stat. 2541, available at www.copyright.gov/history/1909act.pdf ('Copyright Act of 1909').

50 *Id.* §§ 54, 55.

51 The 1909 Act permitted, for the first time, registration and copyright of a class of unpublished works that were nonetheless commonly exploited by performance or display rather than by reproduction. William S. Strauss, *Study No. 29: Protection of Unpublished Works in Studies on Copyright*, in 1 STUDIES ON COPYRIGHT 189, 196 (Arthur Fisher Memorial ed., 1963). These included dramatic and musical works, motion pictures and works of art. *Id.* at 197.

52 See Dunne, *supra* note 44, at 433.

Also, Congress continued to treat deposit of publicly-accessible copies of protected works as central to copyright.[53] The new Act continued to require beneficiaries of copyright to deposit copies of their works with the Copyright Office for its own uses and to enrich the collection of the Library of Congress, only now the requirement kicked in at publication and not before. And, significantly, the 1909 Act provided that failure to comply with post-publication deposit requirements could result in forfeiture of the copyright.[54]

When Congress next made major revisions in the copyright law in the 1976 Act, deposit requirements were again loosened. Now deposit was neither a prerequisite to obtaining copyright or to retaining it. Nevertheless, the statute continued to treat deposit as mandatory for published works. Failure to supply the requisite deposit copies to the Library of Congress can result in a variety of fines.[55] A separate deposit requirement for purposes of registration with the Copyright Office is also set out in the 1976 Act,[56] although in practice the same deposit can be used to satisfy both provisions.[57]

For most trade secret owners, the requirement to deposit the work with the Library of Congress poses no difficulties because it does not arise until publication, and they have no intention of publishing their work. What does make deposit so uncomfortable to trade secrecy claimants is the second deposit requirement. In drafting the 1976 law, Congress carried over a carrot (or a stick, depending on one's perspective) from the 1909 Act:[58] no suit for infringement can be brought until the allegedly infringed work, published or not, is first registered.[59] And for added punch, two of the most important remedies offered by the law, statutory damages and attorneys fees, were made unavailable for infringing acts occurring prior to registration.[60] This means that, to have any hope of effective enforcement of a copyright in any work, published or unpublished, the owner must

---

53 That the deposit was for the benefit of the public was made clear in Wheaton v. Peters, 33 U.S. (8 Pet.) 591, 665 (1834). The requirement that records, including deposits, be publicly available is explicit in the 1976 Act, 17 U.S.C. § 705(b), as it was in the 1909 Act that preceded it, Copyright Act of 1909, § 212. See also 37 C.F.R. § 201.2(b)(1)(2008). Public library collections are by definition intended to be utilized by members of the public.

54 Copyright Act of 1909 § 14.

55 17 U.S.C. § 407(d)(1997).

56 *Id.* § 408.

57 *Id.* § 408(b).

58 Copyright Act of 1909 § 13.

59 17 U.S.C. § 411(a) (1998).

60 *Id.* § 412.

deposit it with the Copyright Office[61] and accede to the fact that it is thenceforth part of the public record.[62] This is why trade secret owners wanted the Copyright Office to craft special deposit rules on their behalf.

In passing on the legitimacy of such regulations, the Seventh Circuit in *National Association of Bar Examiners* relied on the changes over the years in the deposit requirements to conclude that the 'beneficial purposes' copyright law was intended by Congress and by the copyright clause to serve did not include public access. The Seventh Circuit reached that conclusion based largely on a literal reading of the 1976 Act deposit provisions without considering the history that underlay them. The court observed in particular that, under the statute, neither the Copyright Office nor the Library of Congress is required to keep copies of everything they receive. It used this to substantiate its view that deposit is neither a mechanism for public disclosure[63] nor a quid pro quo extracted in return for protection. The court relied heavily for support on dicta from a rather obscure Supreme Court decision, *Washingtonian Publishing Co. v. Pearson*.[64]

In *Washingtonian*, the plaintiff failed to deposit copies of its work product with the Copyright Office for 14 months after publication. The defendant argued that, because the plaintiff had not deposited 'promptly', as the statute required, its copyright was forfeit.[65] The majority rejected that argument, concluding that accepting it would undercut the very reforms that prompted Congress to rewrite the Act in 1909 in the first place.[66] The defendant's interpretation would continue to leave failure to deposit 'promptly' as a way to lose copyright through inadvertence. This kind of unfortunate result, the majority opined, was exactly what the 1909 Act was trying to avoid.[67] Merely switching the prompt deposit requirement from before publication to after it, as the defendant urged, would simply continue 'the uncertainty and confusion'.[68]

---

[61] Deposit copies are intended for enrichment of the collection of the Library of Congress and use of the Copyright Office. Deposit requirements have existed as part of the registration process since the first Copyright Act in 1790. See Dunne, *supra* note 44, at 411.

[62] See *supra* note 53.

[63] In actual fact, the Copyright Office is required to keep all deposit copies of unpublished registered works, 17 U.S.C. § 704(d)(1976), something the court noted but to which it attached no significance. 692 F.2d at 481, 483.

[64] 306 U.S. 30 (1939).

[65] *Id.* at 36.

[66] *Id.* at 36 n.2.

[67] *Id.* at 36 n.2.

[68] The effect of the majority's reading of the statute was to make registration and deposit in the first term of the copyright essentially voluntary unless either

The majority went further down this road than it needed to decide the case, opening in the process the escape hatch the Seventh Circuit later used to approve secret deposits. Relying on the fact that the 1909 Act no longer legally required the Librarian of Congress and the Copyright Office to retain all deposit copies and indeed gave them the discretion to destroy or give away deposit copies they did not want to keep,[69] the Supreme Court rejected outright any assertion that deposit served a public access function.[70] What the Court did not attempt to explain was why, if that were the case, the statute nevertheless continued to mandate deposits and to make the failure to respond to a demand for deposit grounds for voiding a copyright; to the majority, whatever deposit might once have been intended to do, it was reduced by the 1909 Act to no more than a means for enriching the Library of Congress's collection.[71]

The majority opinion prompted a sharp dissent by Justice Black. Black was convinced that a plaintiff who ignored a crucial requirement of the Copyright Act ought not be entitled to retain protection. Although his interpretation of the statute seems less well-supported than the majority's, Justice Black's take on the role and importance of access in American copyright nevertheless seems closer to the mark than the majority's. He pointed out that deposit had long been understood as serving two important disclosure functions: first, it ensured that 'owners of patent or copyright monopolies [would] disclose upon the public records the extent of their claimed monopolies',[72] and second, it provided a mechanism 'for the diffusion of public knowledge'.[73] It was highly unlikely, he concluded, that Congress would abandon its long-standing commitment to deposit as a tool to promote access without making its intention to do so explicit.[74]

Considerable evidence exists in support of Black's assertion that Congress remained committed to the public availability of copyrighted

---

the plaintiff wanted to sue to enforce his rights, see Copyright Act of 1909 § 12, or the Copyright Office made a demand for the deposit, *id.* § 13. For a discussion of the case, see Robert Wedgeworth and Barbara Ringer, *The Library of Congress Advisory Committee on Copyright Registration and Deposit (ACCORD)*, September 15, 1993, in No. 186 Copyright L. Reps., September 27, 1993, at 30–1 (Phase I report).

[69] Dunne, *supra* note 44, at 425.

[70] It rejected the argument that 'copies are now required in order that the subject matter of protected works may always be available for information and to prevent unconscious infringement'. *Washingtonian*, 306 U.S. at 38–9.

[71] *Id.* at 41.

[72] *Id.* at 48.

[73] *Id.* at 49.

[74] *Id.* at 47.

works. First was the retention, as already mentioned, of forfeiture of the copyright as a consequence of non-compliance with deposit. If the requirement was not met following publication, the law permitted the Register of Copyrights to issue a demand for the missing deposit; failure to cure within a specified time would result in a fine and the termination of copyright protection.[75] If Congress had merely been thinking of deposit as a convenient way to enrich the collection of the Library of Congress, so harsh a penalty would not seem appropriate. The legislative history cited by the *Washingtonian* majority itself makes clear, however, that the strictness of the deposit requirement was not a product of inadvertence. 'It was suggested', said the House Report, 'that the forfeiture of copyright for failure to deposit copies was too drastic a remedy, but your committee feel that in many cases, it will be the only effective remedy'.[76] Second, deposit was a prerequisite for filing an infringement action.[77] Although the changes made in the deposit requirement inevitably lessened its role as a tool of disclosure, nothing in the history leading up to the statutory reform indicates a fundamental shift in copyright philosophy was intended.

The 1976 Act once again watered down the deposit requirements: failure to comply now would result in a possible fine rather than forfeiture of the copyright. But Congress continued the tradition of treating deposit as mandatory.[78] Like the 1909 Act, the 1976 version also continued to treat deposit as a prerequisite for the filing of an infringement action, but with an added stick to encourage compliance: the law now made important statutory remedies unavailable to plaintiffs for infringements that occurred prior to registration.

In the spirit of the 1909 Act, Congress also continued to increase the flexibility of both the Library and the Copyright Office by amplifying their authority to accept substitute forms of deposit under appropriate circumstances and to dispose of deposits when necessary. Nevertheless, the law specifically required the Registrar of Copyrights to retain all deposits not required by the Library of Congress in government storage 'for the longest period considered practicable and desirable' and to retain all deposits of unpublished work.[79] In discussing the reasons for giving the Copyright

---

[75] Copyright Act of 1909 § 13.

[76] *Washingtonian*, 306 U.S. at 36 n.2 (quoting H.R. Rep. No. 2222 (1909)).

[77] Copyright Act of 1909 § 12.

[78] The new version of the statute actually contains two deposit requirements: one to benefit of the Library of Congress (set out in 17 U.S.C. § 407 (1997)) and one as a required part of registering a protected work with the Copyright Office (set out in § 408).

[79] 17 U.S.C. § 704(d) (1976).

Office and the Library even greater opportunities to prescribe alternative forms of deposits, and to dispose of some, the relevant Congressional committee reports again cited reasons of space and the practical problems that arise from trying to deposit and preserve works of unusual size or physical composition. The House Judiciary Committee, for example, mentioned the need for flexibility under section 408 so that special arrangements could be made where the works in question are 'bulky, unwieldy, easily broken, or otherwise impractical to file',[80] or are 'rare or extremely valuable copies which would be burdensome or impossible to deposit'.[81] Nowhere in the legislative history is there any indication that Congress intended the relaxation of deposit requirements as a rejection of the public access principle, or that it expected the Copyright Office to exercise the discretion it was given explicitly for the purpose of rendering the contents of a work or classes of works publicly inaccessible.

Nonetheless, when faced with the demand that something be done to protect economically valuable secrets from disclosure, the Copyright Office in fact did use that flexibility in just that way. Subsequently, the courts, too, contributed to the effort to smooth out the misfit between the two quite different legal 'cultures' of copyright and trade secrecy, even if in doing so they had to rely on arguments that were less than wholly convincing.[82] The result has been to give copyright one more small push along a trajectory at the end-point of which all claim of the copyright system to internal consistency would simply vanish.

Judge Posner, in *Chicago Board of Education v. Substance, Inc.*,[83] admitted that, with regard to the secure test rules, 'It may seem paradoxical to allow copyright to be obtained in secret documents'.[84] Although the judge went on to explain why, in his view, good reason existed for the practice, the question that begs to be explored in depth is why copyright for secrets so predictably strikes the average informed person as oxymoronic. How that question is answered may in turn help us evaluate whether, even if the *National Conference of Bar Examiners* opinion[85] was right that the deposit

---

[80] Judiciary Committee, Copyright Law Revision, H.R. Rep. No. 94-1476, 154 (1976), *as reprinted in* 1976 U.S.C.C.A.N. 5659, 5746. See also S. Comm. on Judiciary, S. Rep. No. 94-473, 136 (1975).

[81] H.R. Rep. No. 94-1476 at 154.

[82] See, e.g., Chicago Bd. of Educ. v. Substance, Inc., 354 F.3d 624 (7th Cir. 2003); *Nat'l Council of Bar Exam'rs*, 692 F.2d at 482–8 (finding that 1976 Act deposit provisions were aimed exclusively at preservation and that copyright does not require public disclosure).

[83] 354 F.3d 624.

[84] *Id.* at 627.

[85] 692 F.2d 478.

requirements of the 1976 Act do not mandate the maintenance of a full, publicly available archive of copyrighted works, the Court was wrong in the inferences it drew from that fact.

C. Consequences of Legislative Inadvertence, Part II: The Role of Access

To the extent that any clear agreement exists about a central animating principle of American copyright, it is that copyright is intended to convey a public benefit.[86] While there is room for disagreement about the nature of the benefit that copyright is supposed to convey,[87] most copyright scholars, and the judiciary as well, have understood that language as meaning the promotion of public access to the content of protected works.[88] The possibility that copyright might become a vehicle for protecting the secrecy of information, as the ensuing discussion will show, was one that Congress, from the available evidence, certainly did not contemplate and certainly did not intend when it retooled the deposit requirements and changed the point at which copyright attaches to expressive works.

The idea of extending statutory copyright to secret materials sits uneasily both with the history of Anglo-American copyright and with our deepest intuitions about the nature and purpose of this form of intellectual property.[89] The model for American copyright, the British Statute of Anne, did not come with a coherent philosophical, jurisprudential framework attached.[90] But in the decades following its passage, a theoretical gloss was added to the law as judges were asked to interpret and enforce it. The British courts noted that the Statute of Anne was denominated an Act to promote learning.[91] From this frail reed, they developed the understanding that copyright was limited to giving authors rights to the precise expression they had used; the content of the works, in contrast, was what

[86] See, e.g., Fogerty v. Fantasy, Inc., 510 U.S. 517, 527 (1994) (stating that copyright is for the benefit of the public, not to reward authors).

[87] See *infra* text accompanying nn. 95 to 123.

[88] See Boucicault v. Hart, 3 F. Cas. 983, 986 (S.D.N.Y. 1875) (stating that a copyright claimant cannot cut off rights of others and at the same time conceal the content of the work).

[89] In Chicago Board of Education v. Substance, Inc., 354 F.3d at 627, Judge Posner comments on the seemingly 'paradoxical' nature of copyright protection for secrets even though he then goes on to attempt to justify it.

[90] See generally Diane Leenheer Zimmerman, *It's An Original! (?): In Pursuit of Copyright's Elusive Essence*, 28 COLUM. J.L. & ARTS 187 (2005).

[91] The Act was entitled one 'for the encouragement of learning'. Statute of Anne, 1710, 8 Ann., c. 19 (Eng.).

promoted learning and that part, once published, belonged to the world. As Justice Yates wrote in his influential dissent in *Millar v. Taylor*:[92]

> But how can an author, after publishing his work, confinc it to himself? If he had kept the manuscript from publication, he might have excluded all the world from participating with him, or knowing the sentiments it contained; but by publishing the work, the whole was laid open; every sentiment in it made public, for ever; and the author can never recall them to himself, never more confine them to himself, and keep them subject to his own dominion.[93]

Yates took the position that, by publishing, the author made an irrevocable gift of the work to the public,[94] in return for which he was given, for a limited time, the sole right to reproduce the work in copies for sale.

This understanding of copyright was highly influential with the Framers, and is reflected in the public benefit theory that is the core of American copyright law. The purpose given in the Constitution for granting Congress the power to offer copyright protection is 'To promote the progress of science and useful arts'.[95] This has been understood to mean that authors obtain protection against the copying of their expression in return for giving the public access to a steady stream of new ideas and information, or at least ideas and information in new expressive form.[96] To carry the access paradigm even further, all protected works of authorship must eventually fall into the public domain, at which time, the public can copy or otherwise utilize the author's expression free from further legal restraint.[97]

---

92 (1769) 98 Eng. Rep. 201, 233 (KB), overruled by Donaldson v. Beckett (1774) 1 Eng. Rep. 837 (HL). Although Yates dissented in *Millar*, his views were quite influential in leading the House of Lords later to refute *Millar*'s holding that common law copyright remained perpetual, surviving the end of the statutory copyright term. See *Donaldson*, 1 Eng. Rep. at 847.

93 98 Eng. Rep. at 233.

94 *Id.* at 234.

95 U.S. Const. art. I, § 8, cl. 8.

96 Lyman Ray Patterson, Copyright in Historical Perspective 190 (1968). The history of the copyrights and patents clause reinforces the argument that public access was the benefit that the Framers saw as the justification for copyright. See Zimmerman, *supra* note 90, at 197–200.

97 The Constitution expressly states that protection can only be for a limited time. At the end of that time, the work must enter the public domain. See Eldred v. Ashcroft, 537 U.S. 186, 223 (2003) ('the requirement that those exclusive grants be for "limited Times" serves the ultimate purpose of promoting the "Progress of Science and useful Arts" by guaranteeing that those innovations will enter the public domain as soon as the period of exclusivity expires'); *Wheaton*, 33 U.S. at 660–2 (recognizing that the Constitution establishes durational limits on

The importance of access has been reiterated time and again in Supreme Court copyright jurisprudence. The Court has expressly identified public access to new works as the public benefit that flows from the grant of a limited monopoly to authors.[98] And both it and the lower federal courts[99] claim that they rely on the importance of access as the fundamental public benefit underlying copyright as a touchstone for resolving unclear cases.[100] The Ninth Circuit, for example, has permitted defendants to copy programs in object code to reverse engineer them. The court, in one of its decisions on the issue, reasoned that allowing a defendant to uncover the content hidden in the object code was justifiable because that result supports public access to the 'ideas and functional concepts' which is the 'fundamental purpose of the copyright law'.[101]

Scholars, too, have quite consistently over time accepted the idea that

---

copyright). Other bodies of law, federal or state, cannot be used to extend the monopoly beyond the period mandated by the copyright statute. See Dastar Corp. v. Twentieth Century Fox Film Corp., 539 U.S. 23, 33–5 (2003) (rejecting interpretation of Lanham Act that would limit public's right to copy and use works whose copyrights have expired).

[98] See, e.g., *Eldred*, 537 U.S. at 190 (referring to disclosure as objective of party seeking copyright); *id.* at 219 ('copyright's purpose is to *promote* the creation and publication of free expression') (emphasis in original); New York Times Co. Inc. v. Tasini, 533 U.S. 483, 520 (2001) (Stevens, J., dissenting), quoting Twentieth Century Music Corp. v. Aiken, 422 U.S. 151, 156 (1975) ('copyright law demands that "private motivation must ultimately serve the cause of promoting *broad public availability* of literature, music, and the other arts"'); (emphasis in original); *Fogerty*, 510 U.S. at 527 ('copyright law ultimately serves the purpose of enriching the general public through access to creative works'); Twentieth Century Music Corp. v. Aiken, 422 U.S. at 156 (purpose of copyright to promote access).

[99] See, e.g., Suntrust Bank v. Houghton Mifflin Co., 268 F.3d 1257, 1261–2 (11th Cir. 2006) (emphasizing the importance of public access in copyright); Video Pipeline, Inc. v. Buena Vista Home Entm't, Inc., 342 F.3d 191, 205–6 (3d Cir. 2003) (same).

[100] The U.S. Supreme Court itself has on numerous occasions made use of general theory to 'explain' its copyright decisions. For instance, in Twentieth Century Music Corp. v. Aiken, 422 U.S. 151, 156 (1975), the Court justified its decision to allow music to be played on a radio in a small restaurant in part as follows: 'The immediate effect of our copyright law is to secure a fair return for an "author's" creative labor. But the ultimate aim is, by this incentive, to stimulate artistic creativity for the general public good. "The sole interest of the United States and the primary object in conferring the monopoly", this Court has said, "lie in the general benefits derived by the public from the labors of authors" . . . When technological change has rendered its literal terms ambiguous, the Copyright Act must be construed in light of this basic purpose'.

[101] Sega Enterprises v. Accolade, Inc., 977 F.2d 1510, 1527 (9th Cir. 1992). For a discussion of reverse engineering of software, see Pamela Samuelson and

the public benefit intended to be conferred by copyright is inextricably linked to public access.[102] In the nineteenth century, one prominent scholar explained copyright as the specific response to technological developments that permitted broad dissemination of works for profit.[103] Another commentator, Augustine Birrell, wrote that '[the author's] desire is to make his book known and by publication he gives it to the world'.[104] Twentieth century authors, too, continued to echo similar ideas.[105] According to the late historian of copyright, L. Ray Patterson, access to copyrighted works was a logical outgrowth of the 'dominant idea [behind the copyright clause] in the minds of the framers of the Constitution', 'the promotion of learning'.[106] Copyright, he wrote, was designed as a system of incentives to encourage authors to make their work publicly available.[107]

This logic was muddied by the decision in the 1976 Act to extend copyright to unpublished works, but did Congress, in folding published and unpublished works into one package, actually mean to denigrate the importance of the access principle, or even think about the implications of offering the benefits of copyright to works that were intended to be kept

---

Suzanne Scotchmer, *The Law and Economics of Reverse Engineering*, 111 Yale L. J. 1575 (2002).

[102] See, e.g., Stacey L. Dogan and Joseph P. Liu, *Copyright Law and Subject Matter Specificity: The Case of Computer Software*, 61 N.Y.U. Ann. Surv. Am. L. 203, 216–17 (2005) (identifying access as a key concern of copyright); Robert A. Kreiss, *Copyright Fair Use of Standardized Tests*, 48 Rutgers L. Rev. 1043, 1059 (1996) (same).

[103] See Brander Matthews, *The Evolution of Copyright*, in The Question of Copyright 324, 329 (George H. Putnam ed., 2d ed. 1896).

[104] Augustine Birrell, Seven Lectures on the Law and History of Copyright in Books 18 (1899). If an author, contrary to Birrell's assumptions, did not want to 'make his book known', he did not publish it and hence, historically, conflicts with the access theory would not arise.

[105] See, e.g., Howard B. Abrams, *The Historic Foundation of American Copyright Law: Exploding the Myth of Common Law Copyright*, 29 Wayne L. Rev. 1119, 1120 (1983) (noting that society gives authors incentives to create works so they will make them accessible to the public); Kreiss, *supra* note 103, at 1046. ('Generally, copyright owners seek an economic return sufficient to justify the time and effort expended in creating a copyrighted work. By contrast, the public seeks access to the ideas and expression in copyrighted works, so that public learning and knowledge – the "Progress of Science" – can advance'). In his classic work, An Unhurried View of Copyright, Kaplan, too, emphasized the important role of access, and even speculated at one point that, should authors ever grow unreasonable about providing adequate access, the law ought to step in and protect the public's right. Benjamin Kaplan, An Unhurried View of Copyright 120 (1967).

[106] Patterson, *supra* note 96, at 193.

[107] *Id.* at 190.

secret?[108] And whether or not it did, is there any way that secret copyrights can be made to mesh philosophically and constitutionally with the purpose behind American copyright?

In point of fact, the decision to have copyright protect works from the point of fixation rather than publication seems to have occurred with absolutely no thought to the fact that much of the material now folded into copyright was undisclosed and might never voluntarily be revealed. Certainly, federal law did affirmatively take on the job of protecting the right of first publication, which implicitly acknowledges a right within copyright not to publish,[109] but much of the new law's thrust was in the direction of further promoting public access. New provisions, for example, created incentives to publish previously unpublished work[110] and, at a minimum, to end the perpetual protection of what remained unpublished.[111] Copyrighted works were also subjected to an express fair use provision that seemed on its face to apply to unpublished as well as published work.[112]

---

[108] In cases where infringement of an unpublished work has been at issue, typically the work is registered, and its contents quite freely discussed in both the parties' briefs and the judicial opinions. 'Unpublished' does not generally translate as 'secret'. See, e.g., Salinger v. Random House, Inc., 811 F.2d 90, 93, 98–9 (2d Cir. 1987) (where subject of suit is unpublished letters).

[109] The 1976 Act folded this right into the general bundle of rights protected by copyright. See 17 U.S.C. § 106(1) (2002) (right to reproduce work in copies or phonorecords); see also *Harper & Row*, 471 U.S. at 552 ('[The 1976 Act] extend[ed] statutory protection to all works from the time of their creation'). The 1909 Act before it contained a separate provision preserving the rights of authors and owners of unpublished works. See Copyright Act of 1909 § 2.

[110] 17 U.S.C. § 303 (1998) (extending copyright term for works formerly covered by common law copyright that were published before end of 2002).

[111] JUDICIARY COMMITTEE, COPYRIGHT LAW REVISION, H.R. Rep. No. 94-1476, at 130 (1976), *as reprinted in* 1976 U.S.C.C.A.N. 5659, 5746. Though even unpublished works now eventually enter the public domain, the public has no guarantee that it will ever have access to them. See R. Anthony Reese, *Public But Private: Copyright's New Unpublished Domain*, 85 TEX. L. R. 585, 613–33 (2007) (discussing ways in which owners of unpublished works in public domain can continue to limit public access).

[112] Fair use claims were regularly raised by defendants to justify copying material that the plaintiff considered a trade secret. See, e.g., *Chicago Bd. of Educ.*, 354 F.3d 624 (recognizing claim of fair use where six secure tests are copied). After several years of confusion in the courts about how to reconcile fair use with the previously absolute control that authors enjoyed over their unpublished works, see, e.g., *Harper & Row*, 471 U.S. at 552–5 ('Under ordinary circumstances, the author's right to control the first public appearance of his undisseminated expression will outweigh a claim of fair use'), Congress amended the fair use provision, 17 U.S.C. § 107, to make clear that a work's unpublished status did not immunize

Nevertheless, the decision to move to a system of universal coverage for all fixed, original works without regard to their publication status does fairly raise the question of how certain it is that access remains a fundamental goal of copyright. The question can best be resolved by attempting to understand why copyright was altered to include unpublished works.

There were several reasons for moving to the new baseline and none them involved a rejection of the public access goal. One was a desire to end the doctrinal confusion around the question of what did and what did not constitute 'publication'.[113] On one hand, the advent of new means for communicating content meant that authors no longer needed to rely solely on print and the mass dissemination of physical copies to exploit their works, making 'publication' less useful as a device for determining when copyright kicked in.[114] Because, historically, mere performance of a work was not enough to 'publish' it, courts refused to find that dissemination by a variety of new means implicated statutory copyright. For example, music captured on a phonorecord was held to be 'performed' but not 'published',[115] which meant that, if the owner dispensed with the distribution of sheet music in favor of a sound recording, the proprietor could exploit the economic value of the music in perpetuity under the umbrella of common law rather than statutory copyright. Congress wanted to eliminate the published/unpublished divide to end this possibility, which it believed was an offense against the limited times provision of the copyright and patent clause.[116]

Another reason to move away from publication as the relevant dividing

---

it from fair use – arguably making the situation of trade secrecy owners more tenuous. By that time, however, members of Congress seem to have been made aware at least of the concerns of one class of claimants. Accordingly, the Senate Report accompanying the amendment stated that the bill was 'not intended to reduce the protection of secure tests, the utility of which is especially vulnerable to unauthorized disclosure'. S. Rep. No. 102–41, at 6 (1991); see also Nat'l Conference of Bar Exam'rs v. Saccuzzo, No. 03-CV-00737, 2003 WL 21467772, at *8–9 (S.D. Cal. June 10, 2003) (citing several similar public statements by lawmakers and Register of Copyrights).

113 Senate Committee on the Judiciary, Copyright Law Revision Report, S. Rep. No. 94-473, at 113 (1975).

114 House Judiciary Committee, Copyright Law Revision Report, H.R. Rep. No. 94-146, at 129–30 (1976).

115 White-Smith Music Publ'g Co. v. Apollo Co., 209 U.S. 1 (1908) (holding music captured on a piano roll not published).

116 Judiciary Committee, Copyright Law Revision, H.R. Rep. No. 94-1476, at 130 (1976), *as reprinted in* 1976 U.S.C.C.A.N. 5659, 5746 ('Enactment of [state pre-emption] section 301 would also implement the "limited times" provision of the Constitution . . . Common law protection in "unpublished" works is now

point was the muddle courts had made of the definition of publication in the process of trying to prevent parties from accidentally casting their works into the public domain by publishing them without the requisite copyright notice. The effort to save owners from themselves resulted in additional, serious confusion over what counted as publication for purposes of statutory copyright and what forms of distribution did not. In some cases, authors were permitted to share their work with hordes of people while courts continued to say they had not published,[117] whereas, on similar facts, authors in other cases might find their work unceremoniously injected into the public domain because a court would conclude that what they had done did constitute publication.[118]

Solving these last two problems assuredly did not require elimination of common law protection for genuinely unpublished works, including works that contained trade secrets which, although commercially exploited, were never publicly disseminated. Early in the discussions that preceded the 1976 Act, the Register of Copyrights proposed that statutory copyright kick in not at publication, but at the moment of 'public dissemination'. This was an eminently sensible way to cure the increasingly messy problems caused by using 'publication' as the dividing line, and adopting it would have retained the hitherto unbroken connection in American law between statutory copyright and public access.

It would not, however, have furthered the most pressing objective of Congress in writing the 1976 Act – making possible future adherence to the Berne Convention for the Protection of Literary and Artistic Works – and for that reason it was abandoned.[119] By moving to a new model that measured copyright from fixation to the author's death plus 50 years, U.S. copyright laws now tracked international copyright norms sufficiently that it would not take another major rewrite of the law to make eventual acces-

---

perpetual . . . the bill would place a time limit on the duration of exclusive rights in them').

[117] See, e.g., *King*, 224 F.Supp. 101 (enjoining sale of recordings of speech as infringing common law copyright); *see also* Estate of Martin Luther King, Jr., Inc. v. CBS, Inc., 194 F.3d 1211 (11th Cir. 1999) (reversing summary judgment for defendant and remanding to determine at trial if 'general publication' had occurred).

[118] Public Affairs Assocs. v. Rickover, 284 F.2d 262 (D.C. Cir. 1960), *judgment vacated*, 369 U.S. 111 (1962), *on remand*, 268 F.Supp. 444 (D.D.C. 1967).

[119] *Copyright Law Revision, Serial No. 36, Pt. I: Hearing on H.R. 2232 Before the Subcomm. on Courts, Civil Liberties, and the Admin. of Justice of the H. Comm. on the Judiciary*, 94th Cong. 97 (1975) (statement of Barbara Ringer, Register of Copyrights).

sion to the Convention feasible.[120] However desirable conformity with Berne norms might have been for practical and political reasons (views, it must be said, vary on this point), the fact is that those norms flow from a view of the goals and purposes of copyright not necessarily in sync with those which have historically animated American copyright law, and the attempt to meld the two has not been entirely successful. A considerable amount of duct tape has been needed to paste together the theoretical understanding of copyright that animated the pre-1976 law, and the shape imposed on copyright after the 1976 Act. The fate of secrecy claims is just a small example of how these problems have played out.

Having given the preceding explanation for the changes in the law bearing on access, the question remains whether or not public access is really constitutionally required in copyright, or whether Congress might simply have adopted, *de facto*, a different but permissible interpretation of the term 'public benefit' in moving to the 1976 Act formulation. One way to understand what is meant by the public benefit theory of American copyright law is to say that the public benefits from whatever is good for the economic and artistic welfare of authors and disseminators of works – or to put it differently, that the interests of authors and the public are essentially congruent.[121]

If one were to take that position, then arguably, it would be possible to conclude that the public benefits from 'secret' copyrights and copyrights in secrets so long as such protection incentivizes authors to invest in the creation of new works. Copyright would benefit the public even if the public never learns the nature of the expression copyright is protecting. A colorable claim could certainly be made that copyright for secure tests or for computer programs incorporating trade secrets encourages production of these works, and that their production is beneficial to the public whether or not the public ever learns the content of these kinds of works. Furthermore, one could argue that the public may also benefit by sharing in positive spillovers generated from the economic success of companies permitted to copyright their secrets.

---

[120] The United States joined the Berne Convention in 1988. See Berne Convention Implementation Act of 1988, Pub. L. No. 100-568, 102 Stat. 2853 (1988) (codified in scattered sections of 17 U.S.C.).

[121] See James Madison in THE FEDERALIST NO. 43, 270–1 (Rossier ed., 1961) ('The public good fully coincides in both [copyright and patent] cases with the claims of individuals'); David Ladd, *The Harm of the Concept of Harm in Copyright: The Thirteenth Donald C. Brace Memorial Lecture*, 30 J. COPYRIGHT SOC'Y 421, 431 (1983) (arguing that both authors and public benefit when copyright is left to market forces).

Falling back on this vague formulation of public benefit would certainly give a kind of coherence to copyright's bits and pieces. But it does not explain why we need copyright to do these jobs when a trade secrets doctrine capable of carrying most of the load already exists. As the Supreme Court observed in *Kewanee* in the context of the patent/trade secrecy interface, the function of trade secret law is to provide an alternative to patents to 'encourage invention in areas where patent law does not reach, and will prompt the independent innovator to proceed with the discovery and exploitation of his invention'.[122] Nor does it explain why Congress would jettison what was and continues to be the best and historically the most widely accepted interpretation of public benefit as public access without ever explicitly raising the issue or flagging the change. Indeed, it is not clear that, if the arguments in favor of the access paradigm are truly of constitutional dimensions, as seems quite plausible, Congress could adopt another approach.

The most reasonable conclusion is that, while Congress may have done things that fit poorly with the access piece of copyright theory, it did not intend to repudiate it. Indeed, and ironically, the Final Report of the National Commission on New Technology Uses of Copyrighted Works (CONTU) (the closest thing to legislative history that exists for section 117 on computer programs) certainly did not expect program code to enjoy secret copyright. The Report made clear that it considered copyright superior to trade secrecy for protecting programs because it is less burdensome for program designers, better for consumers, and avoids the wasted effort caused when 'people do for themselves that which others have already done but are keeping secret'.[123]

IV. CONCLUSION

In sum, neither the decision to fold unpublished works into copyright or to protect computer software suggest Congress has (if indeed it could) abandoned the longstanding link between protecting expression and public access. The requirement that the owner make a public record of what is protected remains, despite an admitted level of incoherence, much as it

---

[122] *Kewanee*, 416 U.S. at 485.

[123] Nat'l Comm. on New Tech. Uses of Copyrighted Works (CONTU) ch. 3: *Copyright and Other Methods Compared*, in Final Report 18 (1978), available at http://digital-law-online.info/CONTU/PDF/Chapter3.pdf. For a full discussion of CONTU and its approach to disclosure issues with regard to software, see Samuelson, *supra* note 36, at 719–27.

has always been: something that comes into play if the copyright owner chooses to publish or desires to avail himself of the remedial provisions of the statute. Had Congress intended to copyright secrets and abandon the access paradigm, it could have done so by eliminating the requirement of deposits as a prerequisite to filing suits involving unpublished works – a move that was in fact considered and ultimately rejected.[124]

Simply put, copyright law is not all things to all kinds of intellectual property. Implicit in copyright for the last two centuries has been the importance of providing conditions that promote the availability of original works of authorship to the citizenry. This commitment does not mean that copyright has no role to play in protecting writings that contain secrets, but the protection it can offer them can in no sense be deep.

If access is a central value of copyright, then a strong argument can be made that the Copyright Office, whatever freedom it may have to solve its own pragmatic space and materials problems, cannot also use its regulatory discretion to promulgate rules solely for the purpose of undercutting access to, and preserving the secrecy of, selected forms of content. If non-disclosure is appropriate for owners of trade secrets in copyright cases, then it would seem that similar solicitude should be due a wide range of owners with other motives to keep their content under wraps. Many unpublished works involve an author's private affairs or represent incomplete drafts or contain embarrassing information.[125] But if all of these were given a pass from the normal registration and deposit requirements,

---

[124] The application of deposit to unpublished works cannot be viewed as an accident. At one point, post-1976 and following U.S. adherence to Berne, Congress thoroughly considered, and then rejected, a proposal to repeal sections 411 and 412. Despite arguments in favor of the change, the provisions have continued to be in effect. Among the objections raised for repealing the sections were concerns that allowing infringement actions for unregistered, unpublished works would increase problems with rights clearance and would also be an impediment to news reporting by subjecting the press to litigation for using unpublished documents in reportage without permission. See John B. Koegel, *Bamboozlement: The Repeal of Copyright Registration Incentives*, 13 CARDOZO ARTS & ENT. L.J. 529, 538–9 (1995); Pamela Samuelson, *Will the Copyright Office be Obsolete in the Twenty-first Century?*, 3 CARDOZO ARTS & ENT. L.J. 55, 57 n.11 (1994); Emio F. Zizza, Note, *Eliminating the Preferential Treatment of Foreign Works under United States Copyright Law: Possible Impacts of the Copyright Reform Bill of 1993*, 19 SETON HALL LEGIS. J. 681, 704–9 (1995). For a defense of repeal, see Shira Perlmutter, *Freeing Copyright from Formalities*, 13 CARDOZO ARTS & ENT. L.J. 565 (1995).

[125] See, e.g., *Salinger*, 811 F.2d 90. In this case, private letters had to be registered before a suit could be brought, although, as the district court noted, 'Salinger for some 30 years had maintained a reclusive privacy, avoiding all publicity. He replied that he would regard any biography written during his lifetime as

the Copyright Office would come close to rewriting those sections of the law that Congress itself refused, after due consideration, to amend or repeal.[126] And it would tacitly be affirming what, to this author, seems an unfortunate and inaccurate conclusion: that gradual modifications in copyright law have actually been made with the purpose and intent of severing copyright's historical and philosophical ties to access.

Of course, in the eyes of some observers of the copyright scene today, worrying about theoretical coherence already seems almost quaint because, as previously noted, they see scant evidence to support a claim that the law embodies any coherent, shaping theory. What seems to explain the shape of copyright, however, is not conscious choice to abandon organizing principles, but inadvertence. Piecemeal corrections over the years, coupled with the radical reforms of the 1976 Act (including extending copyright to unpublished works), have eroded the 'sense' of copyright in that they have undercut both predictability and reasonable consistency. Attempts to cure discrete problems[127] or to achieve political goals[128] or satisfy the economic demands of owners[129] have exacted a cost to the basic focus of the Framers[130] on copyright as a device to promote public knowledge. Access as a core value has absorbed many an accidental blow.

Where does this leave parties with valuable secret expression to protect? I would argue that it should leave them with an election to make between two important but internally incompatible forms of intellectual property protection. If disclosure is a problem, then trade secrecy should be the sole cause of action; if the cost of disclosure is tolerable, then copyright might be the vehicle of choice. But having both just does not work. Despite the fact that some courts have so held, the claim that a party can make a public deposit of a work containing trade secrets with the Copyright Office

---

an invasion of privacy', and for this reason objected strenuously to the use of his unpublished letters. 650 F.Supp. at 416.

[126] Following accession to Berne, Congress debated eliminating registration as a prerequisite to a suit and to the recovery of attorneys' fees and statutory damages. After lengthy consideration, the proposed legislation did not pass. See Copyright Reform Act of 1993, H.R. 897, S. 373, 103d Cong. (1993).

[127] See, e.g., *supra* notes 43–54 and accompanying text (describing reasons for 1909 Act's changes to deposit and registration requirements).

[128] See, e.g., Vessel Hull Design Protection Act of 1998, Pub. L. No. 105-304, 112 Stat. 2860 (codified as amended at 17 U.S.C. § 1301 (2000)) (creating narrow new copyright in boat hull designs).

[129] See, e.g., Sonny Bono Copyright Term Extension Act of 1998, Pub. L. No. 105-298, 112 Stat. 2827 (codified as amended in scattered sections of 17 U.S.C.) (extending copyright renewal term by additional 20 years).

[130] Zimmerman, *supra* note 90, at 197–8.

without being said to have disclosed those secrets is simply untenable. And the *National Conference of Bar Examiners* decision not only gets its legislative history wrong, but seems to grant the Copyright Office a kind of flexibility in rule-making that the statute was never intended to provide.

The cleanest solution to the problem of how to smooth the copyright and secrecy interface would be to introduce a clear rule separating the two domains. That way a party would not expect to shelter under copyright unless it accepted the reality that doing so requires at least the possibility that the public will see what the work contains. Separation would have the added benefit of not clipping the corners off trade secrecy law by partial pre-emption for no valid policy reason. What we have instead is something considerably messier. Cleaning up the mess, however, is not best achieved by bending copyright even further out of shape than it already is by trying to shoehorn into it parties who want benefits that copyright, for good reason, has not traditionally supplied.

14 Trade secrets and antitrust law

*Harry First**

I. INTRODUCTION

The antitrust treatment of trade secrets has remained largely hidden. There has been little separate focus on the competition problems that trade secrets may present, even though trade secret protection was raised as a defense in early antitrust litigation. The U.S. federal antitrust agencies' Intellectual Property Licensing Guidelines treat trade secrecy the same way they treat other forms of intellectual property.[1] Antitrust commentary focused on trade secrets is scarce.[2] In a sense, the antitrust metes

---

* Charles L. Denison Professor of Law, New York University School of Law. I thank Tomas Nilsson and Anthony Badaracco for their excellent research assistance. A research grant from the Filomen D'Agostino and Max E. Greenberg Research Fund at New York University School of Law provided financial assistance for this chapter.

1 See U.S. Dep't of Justice and Fed. Trade Comm'n, Antitrust Guidelines for the Licensing of Intellectual Property § 2.1 (1995), available at www.usdoj.gov/atr/public/guidelines/0558.pdf ('IP Guidelines'). A more recent report issued by the federal enforcement agencies similarly treats trade secrets the same as other forms of intellectual property. See U.S. Dep't of Justice and Fed. Trade Comm'n, Antitrust Enforcement and Intellectual Property Rights: Promoting Innovation and Competition (2007), available at www.usdoj.gov/atr/public/hearings/ip/222655.pdf ('Promoting Innovation'). The IP Guidelines are discussed *infra* notes 25–6 and accompanying text.

2 See, e.g., A.B.A. Section of Antitrust Law, Antitrust Law Developments 1156–7 (6th ed. 2007) ('ALD 6') (briefly noting various antitrust doctrines implicated by trade secrets law); Jerry Cohen and Alan S. Gutterman, Trade Secrets Protection and Exploitation 379–95 (BNS Books 1998) (stating that most trade secret licenses are upheld by antitrust courts); Herbert Hovenkamp, Mark D. Janis and Mark A. Lemley, IP and Antitrust: An Analysis of Antitrust Principles Applied to Intellectual Property Law § 33.8c (Aspen Publishers, 2007) (noting that 'several' courts have upheld horizontal geographical restrictions involving trade secret licenses on the ground that each restriction was 'ancillary' to a technology-sharing joint venture); 2 Melvin F. Jager, Trade Secrets Law §§ 11:1–6 (West, 2009); Rudolph Peritz, *Competition Policy and its Implications for Intellectual Property Rights in the United States*, in The Interface Between Intellectual Property Rights and Competition Policy 190–3 (Steven D. Anderman ed., Cambridge University Press, 2007) (stating that trade secret protection generally does not cause antitrust problems).

and bounds circumscribing the use of trade secrets are as elusive as trade secrets themselves.

There is no inherent reason for trade secrets to have escaped antitrust scrutiny. The core of a trade secret is the competitive significance of undisclosed information, so the possession and use of trade secrets would seem bound to raise antitrust questions. For example, can dominant firms be forced to disclose trade secret information to rivals? Those who have such information frequently license its use to others. What restrictions can be placed on a licensee's use of such information, particularly when the licensee is a competitor of the licensor, or on the licensee's sales of products that embody trade secrets?

The purpose of this chapter is to reveal the competition issues that trade secrecy protection raises. This inquiry shows that although the antitrust treatment of trade secrets fits generally into the debate over the proper antitrust treatment of intellectual property rights, the arguments for according deference to the use of confidential trade secret information are somewhat different, and far weaker, than the arguments for according such deference to the holders of either patents or copyrights.

The chapter begins with the fundamental issues for antitrust analysis of trade secrets: What is a trade secret and what consequence should flow from a firm's decision to choose the trade secret regime when it wants to protect information? The next section maps the state of the law dealing with antitrust and trade secrets, beginning with the early history (which predates the Sherman Act), and then discusses how the courts have dealt with licensing issues under Section 1 of the Sherman Act and with exclusionary conduct under Section 2. The final section sets out and applies a more general framework for antitrust analysis of trade secrets, proposing three guiding principles: (1) trade secrets should receive no deference or presumptions when raised as a defense to anticompetitive conduct; (2) antitrust courts, when assessing the economic consequences of trade secret protections, should be mindful of the legal properties of trade secrets; (3) antitrust courts should respect – but not expand – the bargain that trade secret protection provides to its holders to incentivize investment in the production of information.

II. ANALYTICAL FUNDAMENTALS

A. What is A Trade Secret?

Definitional issues loom large in understanding trade secrets, beginning with the question of what sort of right a trade secret is. Some argue that a trade secret is a property right; some argue that it is an *intellectual* property right.[3] Trade secrecy protection can claim state common law tort roots, for it provides an *ex post* cause of action for misappropriation by an agent or a knowing third party, but trade secrecy protection can also be the product of contract, whether express or implied.[4] Trade secrets now also find some definition in state statutory law (primarily the Uniform Trade Secrets Act),[5] in federal law (the Economic Espionage Act of 1996)[6] and, to a degree, in international treaties (TRIPS Article 39).[7]

Related to the question of the mixed legal basis for trade secrets is the question of what sort of information can qualify as a trade secret. The problem here is that 'information' has no conceptual boundary and the three usual qualifications on what information trade secrecy protects – the information must be used in business, provide a competitive advantage

---

[3] See, e.g., Richard Epstein, *The Constitutional Protection of Trade Secrets under the Takings Clause*, 71 U. Chi. L. Rev. 57, 60 (2004) (arguing that the protection of trade secrets is closely analogous to physical property rights); Mark A. Lemley, Chapter 5.

[4] See Restatement (First) of Torts § 757 (1939) (recognizing a cause of action for using or disclosing another's trade secret); Restatement (Third) of Unfair Competition § 39 cmt. h (1995) (acknowledging the analogy between trade secrecy and 'claims in tort alleging the appropriation of ideas', while pointing out that plaintiffs often 'rely on contract claims alleging an express or implied-in-fact promise by the recipient'); Katarzyna A. Czapracka, *Antitrust and Trade Secrets: The U.S. and the EU Approach*, 24 Santa Clara Computer & High Tech. L.J. 207, 213–15 (2008) (discussing the roots of trade secrecy protection in contract theory).

[5] Uniform Trade Secrets Act § 1 (1985) (defining trade secrets as 'information [that] derives independent economic value, actual or potential, from not being generally known to, and not being readily ascertainable by proper means by, other persons who can obtain economic value from its disclosure or use, and . . . is the subject of efforts that are reasonable under the circumstances to maintain its secrecy').

[6] Economic Espionage Act of 1996, 18 U.S.C. § 1839 (2006) (defining trade secrets as 'all forms and types of financial, business, scientific, technical, economic, or engineering information [if] the owner thereof has taken reasonable measures to keep such information secret; and . . . the information derives independent economic value, actual or potential, from not being generally known to, and not being readily ascertainable through proper means by, the public').

[7] Agreement on Trade-Related Aspects of Intellectual Property Rights, December 15, 1993, 33 I.L.M. 81, 98 (1994), Art. 39 (defining trade secrets as information that 'is secret in the sense that it is not . . . generally known among or readily accessible to persons within the circles that normally deal with the kind of information in question . . . has commercial value because it is secret [and] has been subject to reasonable steps . . . to keep it secret').

and be secret – are similarly broad.[8] To further complicate things, trade secrets are sometimes lumped in with 'know-how', an even less precise type of information that seems to have no legal definition whatsoever.[9] The result is that calling something a 'trade secret' tells us very little about the type of information that we are being asked to protect.

There is one important way in which trade secrets have *not* been characterized, however. Courts have generally not called a trade secret a 'monopoly'.[10] This is unlike other intellectual property rights, particularly patent and copyright, which have a long history of being seen in monopoly terms. For some time the monopoly label led courts to restrict patent and copyright holders in their sales of products protected by these rights, particularly in their ability to tie together complementary products.[11] Although the U.S. Supreme Court has long recognized that patents do not necessarily confer monopoly power, it was not until 2007 that the Court finally rejected the economic equation of patent rights and monopoly.[12]

From the point of view of antitrust analysis, the fact that trade secrets

---

[8] See Kewanee Oil Co. v. Bicron Corp., 416 U.S. 470, 474–5, 493 (1974) (finding that Ohio law, which adopted this three-part test, was valid and not pre-empted by federal patent law).

[9] Antitrust commentators often use the terms interchangeably. See ALD 6, *supra* note 2, at 1156 n.570; S. Chesterfield, *The Patent-Antitrust Spectrum of Patent and Know-How License Limitations: Accommodation? Conflict? Or Antitrust Supremacy?*, 15 PAT. TRADEMARK & COPY. J. RES. & ED. 1, 18 (1971) ('In my discussion I use the terms 'trade secret' and 'secret know-how' as virtually interchangeable'). Economists refer generally to the difficulties of exchanging non-codified knowledge, without regard to legal characterization. See, e.g., Eric Brousseau, Natalia Lyarskaya and Carlos Muniz, *Complementarities Among Governance Mechanisms: An Empirical and Theoretical Assessment of Cooperative Technology Agreements*, in WORKING WITHIN THE BOUNDARIES OF INTELLECTUAL PROPERTY 229, 233 (Rochelle C. Dreyfuss, Harry First and Diane L. Zimmerman eds., 2010) ('the impossibility of fully codifying knowledge leads to a weaker protection of intellectual property rights').

[10] That is, other than the Federal Circuit. See Dow Chem. Co. v. Exxon Corp., 139 F.3d 1470, 1474 (Fed. Cir. 1998) (describing Ohio's law of trade secrets as having 'granted monopoly protection to processes and manufacturing techniques').

[11] See, e.g., United States v. Glaxo Group Ltd., 410 U.S. 52, 61–2 (1973).

[12] See Illinois Tool Works Inc. v. Indep. Ink, Inc., 547 U.S. 28, 46 (2007) (holding that 'a patent does not necessarily confer market power upon the patentee'). For an earlier case recognizing that patents do not by themselves confer an economic monopoly, see Standard Oil Co. of Indiana v. United States, 283 U.S. 163, 175 (1931) (recognizing competing patented processes for producing 'cracked' gasoline and finding that 'no monopoly' resulted from cross-licensing the patents in question, per Brandeis, J.).

do not come freighted with the monopoly tag is paradoxically liberating, because it helps us see how trade secrets do and do not function:

(1) Trade secrets are about appropriability. They provide protection for confidential firm-specific information so as to allow those who have access to the information to appropriate the economic benefits that the information can provide. Trade secrets do not come with the legislative assumption that monopoly profits are needed to incentivize the production of this information. On the contrary, trade secrecy protection simply recognizes that businesses create all sorts of information and would have trouble competing effectively were their operations simply on view to their competitors.

(2) Trade secrets come with no legislative assumption about the innovative quality of the information being protected. Unlike patents, for example, there is no economic policy to give the holders of trade secrets additional profits so that they will produce the optimal level of secret information. If a mattress seller provides 'secret' instructions to its sales people on how best to sell a mattress, we might protect those secrets from being misappropriated by a faithless employee, but that does not make the sales method innovative, nor would there be any sound reason to protect this sales method through the grant of a patent, thereby excluding others from selling mattresses in a similar way.[13]

(3) Firms have the option of exploiting secret information in whatever way they think will maximize profits, whether it is through keeping the information within the firm or sharing the secrets with others outside the firm in a cooperative working relationship.[14] Whatever competitive significance the confidential information has comes from the economic benefits the information confers on those who use it, rather than being directly connected to a specific product that embodies that information. In contrast to patented products or copyrighted products, there are no 'trade secreted' products.

B. Regime Choice

Parties often have a choice of legal regime for protecting information. For example, under federal law, trade secrets can include 'patterns, plans . . . programs, or codes',[15] any of which could be protected under copyright

---

[13] This does not mean that the mattress seller might not want such a patent, or even that the Patent Office might not (outrageously) grant such a patent. See Harry First, *Controlling the Intellectual Property Grab: Protect Innovation, Not Innovators*, 38 RUTGERS L. J. 365, 378–9 (2007) (discussing a patent on 'Methods of Promoting Sleep Systems').

[14] See Brousseau *et al.*, *supra* note 9, at 233.

[15] 18 U.S.C. § 1839(3) (2006).

law. Similarly, federal law includes as trade secrets 'prototypes, methods, techniques, processes, [and] procedures', any of which might be eligible for patent protection. Taking just one industry as an example, developers of software interfaces have shifted their protective regime from trade secrets, to copyright, then to patent, and finally back to trade secrets in an effort to find the legal regime that gives them the most protection for this type of information.[16] Each regime has its legal advantages and disadvantages.

When invention is involved, the closest potential legal substitute for trade secrecy is the patent system. Economists suggest that firms will have the greatest incentive to patent where inventions are self-revealing in use, because those inventions cannot be kept secret once the product that embodies them is publicly sold.[17] Conversely, firms have incentives to use trade secrecy for inventions that can be kept secret for longer than the patent term. Firms may choose to rely on trade secret protection for other types of inventions as well, particularly because of the time and expense associated with obtaining a patent.[18]

The two regimes are not perfect legal substitutes, however. Patents provide a clearer property right, because of the registration and specification requirements, but they also come with a fixed, limited term. Trade secrets are undefined until it is time to litigate, and they last as long as the firm can keep a secret – long for Coca-Cola, shorter for many high-technology companies that cannot delete all knowledge from ex-employees' brains.[19] For an invention to qualify for a patent it must be useful and non-obvious, and it is tested by government examination before being accorded protection.[20] For a writing to qualify for copyright,

---

[16] See Pamela Samuelson, *The Strange Odyssey of Software Interfaces and Intellectual Property Law*, U.C. Berkeley Public Law Research Paper No. 1323818 (2008), available at http://papers.ssrn.com/sol3/papers.cfm?abstract_id=1323818.

[17] See Mark A. Lemley, *The Surprising Virtues of Treating Trade Secrets as IP Rights*, 61 Stanford L. Rev. 311, 338–9 (2008) (giving the paper clip as an example of an invention that could easily be analysed and reproduced without the protection of a patent); Katherine J. Strandburg, *What Does the Public Get? Experimental Use and the Patent Bargain*, 2004 Wis. L. Rev. 81, 104–7 (2004) (discussing self-revealing and non-self-revealing inventions vis-à-vis trade secrecy and patenting).

[18] See James Bessen and Michael J. Meurer, Patent Failure: How Judges, Bureaucrats, and Lawyers Put Innovators at Risk 218, 289 n.3 (2008).

[19] See Edwin Mansfield, *How Rapidly Does New Industrial Technology Leak Out?*, 34 J. Indus. Econ. 217, 219–21 (1985) (explaining that information about the detailed nature and operations of a new product or process is in the hands of at least some rival firms within a year, on the average, after a new product is developed, and sometimes within six months).

[20] 35 U.S.C. §§ 101–3, 131 (2006).

it must be original.[21] Trade secrets may be valuable because they are secret, but there is no threshold of originality for protection except in cases where the public availability of the secret information undercuts the claim that it had been kept secret.[22] So, for example, information in a database may be protected by trade secrecy, while at the same time, the database will be unprotected by copyright because it lacks originality.[23]

It is fair to assume that when firms choose one regime over another to protect information, they have made a rational cost-benefit decision. Each legal regime will have varying incidents depending on its statutory bases and purposes. Private parties cannot combine regimes to get all the protection they would like. They must take the bitter with the sweet.

How should this strategic choice affect antitrust analysis? At present, neither antitrust courts nor antitrust enforcement agencies appear to be paying any sustained attention to regime choice. The current federal antitrust enforcement agency guidelines relating to licensing intellectual property, issued in 1995, analyse trade secrets as but one form of intellectual property. Although these guidelines recognize that there are 'clear and important differences' among the 'intellectual property regimes of patent, copyright, and trade secret', the guidelines state that 'the governing antitrust principles are the same'.[24] Indeed, despite the acknowledged legal differences among these regimes, nowhere in the guidelines do these distinctions make a difference.

The guidelines do not distinguish among the various forms of intellectual property protection because they see these forms as all performing the same economic function; that is, providing 'incentives for innovation and its dissemination and commercialization by establishing enforceable property rights for the creators of new and useful products, more efficient processes, and original works of expression'.[25] Certainly, some trade secrets do protect innovative products or processes, but, as we have seen, trade secrecy protects 'information' that may have nothing to do with innovation (a database, for example, or a customer list).

Antitrust enforcers have not always taken the position that antitrust analysis should be the same without regard to whether a patent or a trade secret is involved. Justice Department enforcement guidelines issued

21 17 U.S.C. § 102(a) (2006).

22 See, e.g., CVD, Inc. v. Raytheon Co., 769 F.2d. 842 (1st Cir. 1985) ('Once a trade secret enters the public domain, the possessor's exclusive rights to the secret are lost').

23 See Feist Publ'ns, Inc. v. Rural Tel. Serv. Co., Inc., 499 U.S. 340, 364 (1991).

24 IP Guidelines, *supra* note 1, § 2.1.

25 *Id.* § 1.0.

in 1977 made some effort to give lesser scope to the licensing of trade secrets than to the licensing of patents, stressing the lack of Congressional mandate for trade secrets and the lack of patent law's disclosure quid pro quo for legal protection.[26] But these distinctions have been lost under the current guidelines, with antitrust analysis focusing more on economic effects than on legal categories and ignoring the different legal properties of the trade secrets regime.

Regime choice should matter to antitrust analysis, however, because the nature of the legal protection granted the right holder is related to the economic reasons for that protection. Parties that choose trade secrets over patent are making a decision that may very well reflect what they feel needs protecting the most, as well as accepting the trade-offs that such a decision entails. Parties that choose trade secrecy do not make public disclosure, but they do gain protection from misappropriation, even when 'free' appropriation might advance competition in the short run. By not taking the 'patents for disclosure' bargain they also lose the ability to keep others from developing the same invention through reverse engineering, a significant risk associated with trade secret protection.[27] In assessing the economic effects of restrictive agreements or exclusionary conduct related to trade secrets, good economic analysis will pay attention to these legal choices that the parties have made.

III. ANTITRUST TREATMENT OF TRADE SECRETS: THE STATE OF THE LAW

A. Historical Background

1. Pre-Sherman Act

Courts began considering the potential anticompetitive effects of protecting trade secrets long before passage of the Sherman Act in 1890. They did so in the context of the common law rule that contracts 'in

---

[26] See U.S. Dep't of Justice, Antitrust Guide for International Operations, Cases E, F, 32–3 (1977). See also Richard H. Stern, *The Antitrust Status of Territorial Limitations in International Licensing*, 14 Pat. Trademark & Copy. J. Res. & Ed. 580, 589–94 (1970–1) (discussing the analogy between patent and trade secret licensing) (author was chief of the Patent Section of the Antitrust Division).

[27] See Bonito Boats, Inc. v. Thunder Craft Boats, Inc., 489 U.S. 141, 150–1 (1989) (discussing the bargain of legal protection and disclosure faced by patent recipients).

restraint of trade' were considered void, but that some types of contracts could be enforceable so long as the restraint in the agreement was 'not unreasonable'.[28] Four important pre-Sherman Act cases show the difficulties in applying this reasonableness test when trade secrets are involved.

The first is *Vickery v. Welch*,[29] the first reported trade secrets case in the United States, which was decided by the Massachusetts Supreme Court in 1837.[30] Welch sold his chocolate manufacturing plant to Vickery 'together with his exclusive right and art or secret manner of making chocolate, and all information pertaining to his said manner of making chocolate'.[31] Welch subsequently refused to convey this alleged exclusive right or 'art', stating 'that I have no patent or other exclusive right or arts except what I have gained by my skill and experience . . . and do not hereby even impliedly covenant not to communicate the results of my experience to others'.[32] In fact, it appeared that 'two or three others' knew this 'secret art' but had agreed not to divulge it so long as Welch was still manufacturing chocolate.[33]

Vickery sued on Welch's bond. The court gave judgment on the bond for Vickery.[34] The court had no trouble finding Welch's claim inconsistent with his contractual obligation, rejecting the argument that the contract was void because it was in restraint of trade.[35] The court reasoned that if the secret art were worth anything, 'the defendant would use the art and keep it secret, and it is of no consequence to the public whether the secret art be used by the plaintiff or by the defendant'.[36] The court assumed that the value of the transaction was affected by the covenant to convey the exclusive right to the secret, but it did not explore the question whether the public would have been better off had the price been lower, the secret non-exclusive, and the defendant left free, 'for love or money, to communicate the secret to all other people'.[37]

---

[28] See Oregon Steam Navigation Co. v. Winsor, 87 U.S. 64, 66–7 (1874) ('It is a well-settled rule of law that an agreement in general restraint of trade is illegal and void; but an agreement which operates merely in partial restraint of trade is good, provided it be not unreasonable and there be a consideration to support it') (upholding a territorial division of markets).

[29] 36 Mass. 523 (1837).

[30] See Melvin F. Jager, 2 Trade Secrets Law § 11:3 (2008).

[31] 36 Mass. at 523.

[32] *Id.* at 523–4.

[33] *Id.* at 524.

[34] *Id.* at 527.

[35] *Id.*

[36] *Id.*

[37] *Id.*

The second case is *Taylor v. Blanchard*,[38] decided by the Massachusetts Supreme Court nearly 30 years later. Taylor manufactured shoe-cutters, the manufacture of which the court described as 'an art' known only to the plaintiff and three other business firms.[39] Blanchard, who was 'wholly ignorant of the business', became Taylor's partner, agreeing that if the partnership ended, he would not divulge 'any of the secrets' relating to the business nor establish any shoe-cutter business in Massachusetts.[40] Three years later the business dissolved, Blanchard opened a competing business in Boston, and Taylor sued to collect liquidated damages.[41]

Competition concerns won out in this case. The court began its opinion by pointing out that '[t]he law has always regarded monopolies as hostile to the rights and interests of the public'.[42] One exception to this policy is for grants to use a new invention for a limited period, 'indulged for the encouragement of ingenuity'; patent and copyright laws 'rest on this ground'.[43] Another exception is for 'contracts for the partial restraint of trade', which might be upheld 'to a reasonable extent'.[44] Citing *Vickery v. Welch*, the court noted that a party might lawfully bind himself not to carry on a 'secret trade' or not to divulge the secret.[45] But the court in this case rejected the argument that Taylor's art was 'secret'.[46] The method for manufacturing shoe-cutters might not be 'generally known to the public', but it was carried on 'in three different towns in the Commonwealth, by three different parties, who had no connection in business with the parties to this contract'.[47] Whether there was anything unusual (or innovative) about Taylor's process that might favor protection was of no apparent concern to the court; nor was the court much concerned about assessing how much competition there was among the various shoe-cutters or whether excluding Blanchard would affect that competition. It was enough for the court that '[c]ombinations of men in business . . . often succeed in obtaining exorbitant profits from the public'.[48]

---

38 95 Mass. 370 (1866).
39 *Id.* at 370
40 *Id.* at 371.
41 *Id.*
42 *Id.* at 372.
43 *Id.*
44 *Id.* at 373.
45 *Id.* at 374.
46 *Id.*
47 *Id.* at 373–4.
48 *Id.* at 375.

The third case, *Peabody v. Norfolk*,[49] was decided by the Massachusetts Supreme Court only two years after *Taylor v. Blanchard*. Peabody had for many years engaged in 'inventing and adapting machinery, and originating and perfecting a process, to manufacture gunny cloth from jute butts'.[50] Once successful, he built a 'large factory' and hired Norfolk, a machinist, to be the engineer of the factory, requiring him to sign a contract to consider the machinery 'sacred' and to prevent others from learning how to use it.[51] Less than two years later, Norfolk left Peabody's employ, with models and drawings, and was helping others to set up a competing plant. Peabody sought to enjoin Norfolk from communicating the secrets to others.[52]

The court's approach was now more like the approach in *Vickery* than the approach in *Taylor v. Blanchard*. The court easily rejected a defense argument that the contract should be void as in restraint of trade but it made no mention of the evils of monopoly. Instead, the court wrote somewhat expansively about what we would today consider the economic justifications for upholding such contracts: 'It is the policy of the law, for the advantage of the public, to encourage and protect invention and commercial enterprise'.[53] This encouragement could be done through protecting goodwill, trade marks, patents on 'new and useful' inventions, and secret processes of manufacture 'whether a proper subject for a patent or not'.[54] The court recognized that secret processes are protected differently than patents – there is no 'exclusive right to it as against the public, or against those who in good faith acquire knowledge of it'.[55] But the court also recognized that such secrets are protected for a somewhat different purpose – 'to prevent . . . a breach of trust'[56] – and noted that Justice Story had stated the policy for protecting trade secrets 'in the broadest terms', as follows: courts will restrain a party from disclosing secrets 'communicated to him in the course of a confidential employment; and it matters not, in such cases, whether the secrets be secrets of trade or secrets of title, or any other secrets of the party important to his interests'.[57]

---

[49] 98 Mass. 452 (1868). *Peabody* is credited with 'crystallizing the law of trade secrets in the United States'. See Robert G. Bone, *A New Look at Trade Secret Law: Doctrine in Search of Justification*, 86 CAL. L. REV. 241, 252 (1998).

[50] 98 Mass. at 453.

[51] *Id.*

[52] *Id.* at 454.

[53] *Id.*

[54] *Id.* at 457–8.

[55] *Id.* at 458.

[56] *Id.* at 458.

[57] *Id.* at 459.

These three early cases look surprisingly familiar. The economic problems entrepreneurs faced in the 1800s are the same as entrepreneurs face today. Inventors need capital and labor for manufacturing; the manufacturing process takes skill and knowledge; skill and knowledge are hard to convey and hard to protect, at least to the degree necessary to appropriate their benefits. Courts seek to protect relations of trust and contracts that enable knowledge and skill to be transferred, recognizing that such arrangements can incentivize invention. At the same time, the courts recognize that such agreements can harm the public by restraining competition. Somehow a balance must be struck, as the court said in *Taylor v. Blanchard*, 'for the sake of the public, and not for the sake of the parties'.[58]

The fourth significant case, however, shows how trade secrets can easily go beyond the paradigmatic examples (inventor/investor or employer/faithless employee) and be used to create much broader anticompetitive arrangements. This case also shows the tendency of common law courts to weight the interests of secrecy and invention over the interests of the public in competition.

The case is *Fowle v. Park*,[59] decided by the U.S. Supreme Court in 1889, one year before passage of the Sherman Act. *Fowle* involved 'Wistar's Balsam of Wild Cherry', a 'medicinal preparation' good for 'certain complaints and diseases'.[60] In 1844 its original inventor had conveyed the formula and manufacturing rights in enumerated states to one Butts, who then conveyed his rights to Fowle. At the same time the inventor conveyed the rights in other states to Park. In the conveyances, both Fowle and Park agreed not to sell the elixir below a set price.[61] Between 1849 and 1864 both Fowle and Park were selling small amounts of the product west of the Rockies 'in competition'.[62] As this area became more populated, Fowle paid Park to agree not to sell in the West. Over time, however, Park began selling in Fowle's territories, at prices below those specified in the original agreements. In 1884, Fowle sued for an injunction and damages.[63]

The Supreme Court was 'unable to perceive' how the contract could be regarded as 'so unreasonable' as to be unenforceable.[64] The Court's reasoning combined the policies of protecting trust and protecting incentives.

58 Taylor v. Blanchard, 95 Mass. at 373.
59 131 U.S. 88 (1889).
60 *Id.* at 88.
61 *Id.*
62 *Id.*
63 *Id.*
64 *Id.* at 97.

The inventor, the Court wrote, had 'property' in the 'secret process of manufacturing the article he had discovered', so his grantees 'could claim relief as against breaches of trust in respect to it'.[65] Further, the policy of the law 'is to encourage useful discoveries by securing their fruits to those who make them'.[66] Harking back to the reasoning in *Vickery v. Welch*, the Court wrote that '[i]f the public found the balsam efficacious, they were interested in not being deprived of its use, but by whom it was sold was unimportant'.[67]

Lost in the Supreme Court's analysis was any concern for competition or for assessing how innovative the formula for 'Wistar's Balsam of Wild Cherry' was. The public was not quite indifferent as to who was selling the medication; presumably consumers preferred to buy it at Park's lower price. Similarly, the law might want to incentivize invention, but how confident could the Court be that this 'secret' process, discovered and conveyed 40 years before Fowle ever brought suit, was still even secret, let alone (in the Court's words) a 'useful discovery'?

2. Early Sherman Act decisions

Fowle v. Park played a minor role in the legislative history of the Sherman Act. In the debate in the House of Representatives, Representative Morse placed the Supreme Court's decision into the Congressional Record.[68] Morse's concern was not the protection of trade secrets or innovation, but the protection of what he called the 'contract system' of specifying minimum resale prices as a way to prevent 'cutthroat competition' and 'insure quality'.[69] Although Morse approved 'suppress[ing] great combinations that oppress the people', he wanted manufacturers and merchants to be able to control resale prices, a result which the Supreme Court had allowed under the common law by upholding the agreements in *Fowle*.[70] No one took up Morse's argument, however, and the Sherman Act passed with its deliberately ambiguous language outlawing 'restraints of trade or commerce'.[71] As Representative Culberson explained, when reporting the bill on behalf of the House Judiciary Committee: 'Now, just what contracts . . . will be in restraint of the trade or commerce mentioned in

---

65 *Id.*
66 *Id.*
67 *Id.*
68 See 21 Cong. Rec. 5,954–5 (June 11, 1890).
69 *Id.* at 5,954.
70 See *id.*
71 15 U.S.C. § 1.

the bill will not be known until the courts have construed and interpreted this provision'.[72]

Courts were soon presented with cases raising the question whether the type of agreements used in *Fowle* would be lawful under the new Act. In two important decisions the courts tilted the rule of reason balance back towards competition, a result more traceable to the courts' careful reasoning than to the change in the legal regime. Interestingly enough, both cases involved the same price-cutter whom Fowle had successfully sued, John D. Park.[73]

The first case is *John D. Park & Sons Co. v. Hartman*,[74] decided by the Sixth Circuit in 1907. Hartman manufactured 'Peruna', then the most popular 'patent medicine' on the market (although there was no patent, of course).[75] Peruna was manufactured under a secret formula 'known only to him and his trusted employees'.[76] Hartman sold Peruna to distributors with a required minimum resale price. Park managed to get supplies of Peruna which it then sold to retailers below the fixed minimum price.[77]

Judge Lurton's opinion addressed two critical issues. The first was whether trade secrets deserved the same legal exemption from competition rules as patents and copyrights. The second was whether the price restraints that Hartman placed on its wholesale and retail distributors were reasonable, either at common law or under the new Sherman Act. The former involved what we would think of today as the conflict between antitrust and intellectual property; the latter involved the proper analytical approach for applying the rule of reason.

Lurton firmly rejected equivalent treatment for trade secrets and patents

---

72 21 CONG. REC. 4,089 (May 1, 1890).

73 See *Patent Medicine Trade; Efforts to Secure a New Plan for Distributing Articles: Cutters Still Defy Wholesalers*, NEW YORK TIMES, November 29, 1895, at 8; *18 Years Getting a Suit to Trial; Action of John D. Park & Sons Co. Against Alleged Drug Trust Almost Ready*, NEW YORK TIMES, June 7, 1915, at 7; Rudolph J.R. Peritz, *'Nervine' and Knavery: The Life and Times of Dr. Miles Medical Company*, in ANTITRUST STORIES 74–90 (Eleanor M. Fox and Daniel A. Crane eds., 2007) (discussing the wide scope of contemporaneous litigation involving assertions of exclusionary rights by intellectual property holders).

74 153 F. 24 (6th Cir. 1907).

75 See Peritz, *supra* note 73, at 80.

76 Hartman v. John D. Park & Sons Co., 145 F. 358, 359 (C.C.E.D. Ky. 1906). It turned out that 'Peruna' was in fact a mixture of 72.5 percent water, 27.07 percent alcohol, and nearly all the rest burnt sugar; numerous 'chemists and doctors' agreed that 'the stuff had absolutely no medical value'. E.E. Munger, *Education as an Adjuvant*, in THE MEDICO-PHARMACEUTICAL CRITIC AND GUIDE 138 (William J. Robinson ed., 1907).

77 145 F. at 359.

and copyrights. As he understood the law at the time, patentees and copyright holders could impose resale price restraints on their buyers or licensees.[78] Lurton pointed out, however, that trade secrets were different, both legally and economically. The holder of a trade secret 'cannot appeal to the protection of any statute creating a monopoly in his product' or giving him any 'special property' interest.[79] The economic value of a trade secret comes from keeping the information secret, so the law will protect the transfer of the secret information under a promise of confidentiality, just as the law protects the transfer of other types of information upon similar promises.[80] Were it otherwise, 'there could be no sale of secret processes of manufacture'.[81] But the public remains free to discover the process, if it can, and, once discovered, 'anyone has the right to use it'.[82]

Lurton also rejected the argument, implicit in the earlier trade secrets cases from *Vickery v. Welch* to *Fowle*, that because trade secret owners have the right to keep the process secret and not share it with others, or even to not make the product at all, it should not matter to the public whether the product is produced and sold by the trade secret holder or by others.[83] Lurton pointed out, however, that the only thing that trade secret law protects is the secret itself, not the product manufactured under the secret.[84] Distribution of the product would not reveal that secret (except to the extent that the buyer might lawfully figure it out) so there was no economic reason to allow the trade secret owner to control further trade in the product. The manufacturer of a product produced under secret process should be treated just the same as 'the man who grows potatoes'.[85] Neither product's 'commercial value' will 'vanish' if subjected to the normal principles that govern restraints of trade.[86]

---

78 153 F. at 27. This would soon change, as the Supreme Court would come to hold that resale price restraints were not within the statutory rights of patentees or copyright holders and violated the Sherman Act. See, e.g., Bobbs-Merrill Co. v. Straus, 210 U.S. 339, 351 (1908); Straus v. Victor Talking Mach. Co., 243 U.S. 490, 501 (1917); United States v. Gen. Elec. Co., 272 U.S. 476, 489 (1926) ('It is well settled . . . that where a patentee makes the patented article, and sells it, he can exercise no future control over what the purchaser may wish to do with the article after his purchase. It has passed beyond the scope of the patentee's rights').

79 153 F. at 29.

80 See *id.* at 31 (discussing the examples of stock quotations and news).

81 *Id.* (quoting Ammunition Co. v. Nordenfeldt, L.R. 1 Ch. Div. 630 (1894)).

82 *Id.* at 29.

83 See *id.* at 30.

84 See *id.* at 29.

85 *Id.* at 33.

86 *Id.*

Lurton then went on to the second issue, applying common law principles to Hartman's contracts. The legal test was the 'ancillary restraints' doctrine, developed by then-Judge Taft nine years earlier in the already-famous *Addyston Pipe* case:[87] Are the covenants 'ancillary to a principal contract' and 'no more than necessary to afford a fair protection to the business of the complainant and not so large as to interfere with the interests of the public'?[88] Lurton saw the 'prime object' of this agreement as the suppression of competition among wholesalers and retailers (in other words, this was primarily a dealers' cartel), with only an incidental benefit to the manufacturer that was not intended to protect its 'retained business' from the buyer's competition, as would be the case in the sale of a business with a covenant not to compete.[89] The economic effects, though, were large. This was a 'general system' of contracts: 'The single covenant might in no way affect the public interest, when a large number might'.[90] Further, there were no competing manufacturers to supply the product – there was only one 'Peruna'. Thus, retailers not bound by the agreement could not supply the public with a substitute. The result of the agreement, then, would be sales 'at a higher price to the consumer than would otherwise have been paid'.[91] This was not in the interests of the public. Allowing the parties to suppress allegedly 'demoralizing' low prices would 'whittle away broad economic principles lying at the bottom of our public policy'.[92]

The reasoning and result in *Hartman* were echoed in the second important case, the Supreme Court's 1911 decision in *Dr. Miles Medical Co. v. John D. Park & Sons Co.*[93] *Dr. Miles* later became enshrined in antitrust jurisprudence as the case holding that vertical resale price agreements are illegal per se (although the Court did not use such terms then), a precedent that lasted 96 years before being overruled in 2007.[94] At the time of its decision, however, the case was more a reprise of Judge Lurton's decision

---

87 See United States v. Addyston Pipe Co., 85 Fed. 271 (6th Cir. 1898).

88 153 F. at 41, 43 (*citing Addyston Pipe*, 85 Fed. at 281, 282).

89 153 F. at 45.

90 *Id.* at 41, 43. Lurton began his opinion by noting that this type of agreement had 'generally been adopted' by retail and wholesale druggists in the United States, 'a business which amounts to more than $60,000,000 annually' *Id.* at 26.

91 *Id.* at 45.

92 *Id.* at 46. Included in the price-cutters about which Hartman complained were 'department stores'. *Cf.* Bobbs-Merrill Co. v. Straus, 210 U.S. 339, 351 (1908) (invalidating a minimum price restriction imposed on Macy's for the sale of a copyrighted book).

93 220 U.S. 373 (1911).

94 See Leegin Creative Leather Prods., Inc. v. PSKS, Inc., 551 U.S. 877, 907 (2007).

in *Hartman*. Indeed, *Dr. Miles* was argued by the same lawyers on both sides who had argued *Hartman*, and it was decided below by Judge Lurton for the same Sixth Circuit panel (his opinion began by noting that there was 'no substantial difference' between the contracts or products in the two cases).[95] By the time *Dr. Miles* reached the Supreme Court, Lurton had been appointed an Associate Justice. Although he recused himself from the case, the Court's opinion closely followed his views.

The first issue was whether price-restrictive agreements involving trade secrets should be treated the same as price-restrictive agreements involving patents.[96] As in *Hartman*, the Court carefully distinguished the two rights. Patents are given to an inventor for a fixed time 'to stimulate invention'.[97] Dr. Miles, however, 'has no statutory grant' and 'has not seen fit to make the disclosure required by the statute'.[98] As in *Hartman*, the Court also distinguished between communicating the secret and selling the manufactured product: 'It is said that the [medicinal] remedies "embody" the secret. It would be more correct to say that they are manufactured according to the secret process and do not constitute a communication of it'.[99]

The second issue was whether the agreements unreasonably restrained

---

95 See Dr. Miles Med. Co. v. John D. Park & Sons Co., 164 F. 803, 809 (6th Cir. 1908) ('We see no substantial difference between the systems of contracts under which the Dr. Miles Medical Company is now conducting its business and that under which Dr. Hartman carried on his business as a manufacturer of Peruna, considered by this court at length in the case of John D. Park & Sons v. Hartman'). The legal difference was that Dr. Miles recast the relationship between it and its wholesalers and retailers as one of 'agency' and the transfers of the product as 'consignments'. 220 U.S. 373, 397–8. While Lurton found this to be subterfuge, see 164 F. 804–5, the Supreme Court in *Dr. Miles* avoided the issue by finding that the system was intended to bind wholesalers or retailers even if they purchased the products from parties other than Dr. Miles. See 220 U.S. at 399. See also Peritz, *supra* note 73, at 86–9.

96 Note that the Court had previously held that the grant of a copyright does not include the right to set resale prices. See *Bobbs-Merrill*, 210 U.S. at 350–1. The law remained otherwise for patents. See, e.g., E. Bement & Sons v. Nat'l Harrow Co., 186 U.S. 70, 92 (1902) ('[The Sherman Act] clearly does not refer to that kind of a restraint of interstate commerce which may arise from reasonable and legal conditions imposed upon the assignee or licensee of a patent by the owner thereof, restricting the terms upon which the article may be used and the price to be demanded therefore. Such a construction of the act, we have no doubt, was never contemplated by its framers'); United States v. Gen. Elec. Co., 272 U.S. 476, 494 (1926) (upholding a limit on selling prices imposed in a license to manufacture and vend).

97 *Dr. Miles*, 220 U.S. at 401.

98 *Id.* at 402.

99 *Id.* at 403.

trade. The Court here did not invoke the 'ancillary restraints' doctrine discussed in *Hartman*, but its articulation of the proper test was quite similar. The restraint, the Court wrote, must be reasonable 'both with respect to the public and to the parties' and must be 'limited to what is fairly necessary' to protect the covenantee.[100] This was not a case of a sale of a business or goodwill or the 'right to use a process of manufacture', nor was it a single transaction 'conceivably unrelated to the public interest'.[101] Rather, the agreements were intended to 'maintain prices' primarily for the benefit of the dealers, leading the Court to treat the agreement 'no better . . . [than if] the dealers themselves . . . formed a combination'.[102] Dr. Miles having sold its product at prices satisfactory to itself, 'the public is entitled to whatever advantage may be derived from competition in the subsequent traffic'.[103]

To twenty-first century eyes, the two *Park* cases may look a little quaint, or even humorous. The 'medicines', after all, were widely known to be composed mostly of alcohol, and their claims for efficacy strain credulity.[104] But the economic interests involved were substantial. As Lurton pointed out at the very beginning of his opinion in *Hartman*, the annual revenues of the proprietary medicine business were more than U.S.$60 million.[105] We cannot know whether Lurton or the Justices on the *Dr. Miles* Court were skeptical of the companies' secret formulae, unlike the *Fowle* Court's uncritical view of 'Wistar's Balsam of Wild Cherry'. But they were less willing to give broad immunity to trade secret claims where the innovation had never been tested by public examination, where the inventor did not disclose its invention for later public use, and where the protection could last far longer than the term of a patent.

Both cases are also important for their key analytical points. On the

---

[100] *Id.* at 406.

[101] *Id.* at 407.

[102] *Id.* at 407–8.

[103] *Id.* at 409. *See* Thomas C. Arthur, *The Core of Antitrust and the Slow Death of* Dr. Miles, 62 SMU L. Rev. 437, 456–62 (2009) (discussing the *Dr. Miles* case). See also *id.* at 446 (noting the nearly complete absence of any discussion of resale price maintenance in the legislative history of the Sherman Act) (*citing* Joseph E. Fortenberry, *A History of the Antitrust Law of Vertical Practices*, 11 Research in Law and Economics 133, 209 n.161 (Richard O. Zerbe, Jr. ed., 1988)).

[104] See Munger, *supra* note 76.

[105] See John D. Park & Sons Co. v. Hartman, 153 F. 24, 26 (6th Cir. 1907). Another indication of the economic interests involved is that counsel for the drug companies was Alton Parker, former Chief Judge of the New York Court of Appeals and the Democratic presidential candidate in 1904 (he was defeated by Theodore Roosevelt). See Albert H. Walker, History of the Sherman Law of the United States 249 (1910).

intellectual property side, the courts recognize that the economic value of trade secrets lies in being able to keep information secret but still transact around it. This means enforcing promises not to disclose secrets that transferees make to transferors, but it does not imply that trade secrets are the equivalent of patents. Rather, the products made through secret processes can be subject to the same competition rules as any other product (whatever those rules might be) – they are to be treated no differently than potatoes. On the competition side, both courts condemned agreements that raise price; and both courts sought to keep competitive restrictions as narrow as possible in light of whatever permissible objectives the parties might have.

Neither case, however, disturbed a key point in *Fowle v. Park*. In *Fowle*, Park had been given the right to use the secret process as a manufacturer, subject to territorial and pricing limitations on sales of the product.[106] The courts in *Hartman* and *Dr. Miles* were able to distinguish *Fowle*, pointing out that in *Hartman* and *Dr. Miles*, Park was only a purchaser of the product, not a sharer of a secret.[107] This is certainly an important distinction, but it allowed the courts to avoid passing on the question whether price and territorial restrictions in a trade secret manufacturing license might be unreasonable restraints of trade, particularly when they clearly limit price competition between two direct manufacturing competitors. The question left open, to use Judge Lurton's words, was whether such restrictions were 'no more than necessary to afford a fair protection to the business of the complainant and not so large as to interfere with the interests of the public'.[108]

B. Current Law: Restraints of Trade

1. Price restraints

Antitrust law has traditionally condemned price fixing agreements, whether between competitors (horizontal) or between buyers and sellers fixing resale prices (vertical). The general view, which has its roots in the early cases such as *Addyston Pipe* and *Dr. Miles*, is that such agreements are per se unlawful.

Whether the per se rule would be applied to price restraints in trade secret licensing today, however, is unclear. As an historical matter, there has not been a legal challenge to *Dr. Miles*' apparent approval of such

---

106 See Fowle v. Park, 131 U.S. 88 (1889).

107 See *Hartman*, 153 F. at 32–3; *Dr. Miles*, 220 U.S. at 402.

108 *Hartman*, 153 F. at 43.

restraints in the context of licensing a trade secret to manufacturers that are competitors, and the Supreme Court later approved such licensing in the patent context.[109] Nevertheless, subsequent twentieth-century commentators have taken the view that the courts would no longer approve such price restrictions,[110] and the federal agencies' 1995 IP Guidelines treat price restrictions as per se illegal, even when the manufacturer is the licensee and first seller of the product.[111]

The view that price restraints are per se unlawful has been taken in light of the background antitrust rule that all price fixing agreements are per se unlawful, whether between competitors (horizontal) or between a manufacturer and its distributor (vertical). In 2007, however, in *Leegin v. PSKS*,[112] the Supreme Court overruled *Dr. Miles*' per se ban on vertical resale price agreements.[113] Although the Court did not consider the application of its decision in the trade secrets or intellectual property context (indeed, no one raised the issue), it is difficult to avoid the conclusion that vertical resale price agreements when a trade secret license is involved would today be considered under the rule of reason.

Leegin raises two questions for trade secret licensing that courts have not yet faced. Suppose that a trade secret licensor (TS) licenses a manufacturer (M) to produce a product (P) using the trade secret. Setting the price at which M can sell P would appear to fall squarely within *Leegin*'s rule of reason holding. But suppose that TS is also a manufacturer of P. Is the price restraint now between competitors, and therefore subject to a per se rule? Or suppose that TS does not itself manufacture P, but licenses M1, M2 . . . Mn to manufacture P and then sets their selling prices. Is TS now orchestrating a horizontal cartel of Ms, making the agreements per se unlawful? There is precedent for viewing such cases as horizontal,[114] but whether the courts will do so in a trade secret licensing case is hard to predict.

The second question is how to do the rule of reason analysis. *Leegin*

---

109 See United States v. General Electric Co., 272 U.S. 476, 493 (1926) ('price fixing is usually the essence of that which secures proper reward to the patentee').

110 See, e.g., David R. Macdonald, *Know-How Licensing and the Antitrust Laws*, 62 MICH. L. REV. 351, 363 (1964) (arguing that 'reliance upon *Dr. Miles* or *General Electric* seems ill-advised, even with respect to patent licenses', and more so with respect to 'know-how').

111 See IP Guidelines, *supra* note 1, § 5.2, n.34.

112 Leegin Creative Leather Prods., Inc. v. PSKS, Inc., 551 U.S. 877 (2007).

113 See *id.* at 907.

114 See United States v. Gen. Motors Corp., 384 U.S. 127 (1966) (finding a price agreement between General Motors and three associations of GM automobile dealers to be per se unlawful).

gives precious little guidance, even with respect to its own situation, that is, the distribution of branded goods where the seller has no apparent market power and the product is subject to interbrand competition (Leegin made handbags and belts, presumably selling them in competitive markets).[115] In the trade secrets context, however, the facts may be quite different. Depending on the quality of the trade secret, TS may have sufficient market power to price above the competitive level. Arguably, this could shift the burden to TS to show a plausible efficiency justification for the price restraint, ultimately requiring the court to balance this justification against the anticompetitive effect of the higher selling prices. Again, it remains to be seen whether this will be the result after *Leegin*.

2. Territorial and use restraints

Although the per se illegality of territorial restraints, whether horizontal or vertical, has a somewhat checkered antitrust history,[116] courts in trade secrets cases have applied a rule of reason analysis and have almost always upheld the restraints. This result is consistent with *Fowle* and the dictum *in Dr. Miles* approving such restrictions.[117]

Two cases well illustrate the courts' approach. One involved a 1934 agreement between an English company that owned 'certain secret processes, recipes and formulae' for making flux (no patents were involved) and a U.S. company to which it gave the exclusive license to manufacture and sell the fluxes in the United States and Canada.[118] The English company agreed not to sell in the United States and Canada, and the U.S. company agreed not to export to any other countries.[119] Seventeen years later the U.S. company sold U.S.$4.00 worth of flux to a buyer in

---

115 See *Leegin*, 551 U.S. at 882, 883 (discussing the relevant market).

116 *Compare* White Motor Co. v. United States, 372 U.S. 253, 261 (1963) (holding that vertical territorial restrictions are not per se violations of the Sherman Act), *with* United States v. Arnold, Schwinn & Co., 388 U.S. 365, 379 (1967) (holding that it is 'unreasonable without more for a manufacturer to seek to restrict and confine areas or persons with whom an article may be traded after the manufacturer has parted with dominion over it'), *with* Continental T.V., Inc. v. GTE Sylvania Inc., 433 U.S. 36, 58 (1977) (overruling *Schwinn* and returning to the *White Motor* approach of applying the rule of reason to vertical non-price restraints). See also United States v. Topco Assocs., Inc., 405 U.S. 596 (1972) (holding that a territorial sales restriction imposed by a cooperative association of supermarket chains was a per se unlawful horizontal restraint).

117 See *supra* text accompanying notes 59–67, 97–9.

118 See Foundry Servs., Inc. v. Beneflux Corp., 110 F.Supp. 857, 857–8 (S.D.N.Y. 1953).

119 See *id.* at 858.

Mexico. The English company declared the U.S. company in breach of the agreement and began making flux in the United States.[120] When the U.S. company sued to enforce the territorial restriction, the English company defended by arguing that the parties had entered into 'an "international cartel agreement" which violates our [U.S.] antitrust laws by dividing the world's markets'.[121]

Not surprisingly, the court was unimpressed with the English company's change of heart. Echoing *Vickery v. Welch*, the court wrote that the English company 'could make disclosures or not; sell or not; as it pleased and the public had no legal interest whatever in that choice'.[122] The court also pointed out that this was a single contract, the two firms were not competitors at the time, there was no price agreement, and that although the fluxes 'are no doubt good and valuable', they were not 'the only ones available or in use in the manufacture of metal castings'.[123] The court concluded that the license restraint was 'only ancillary to a valid primary purpose' and was not 'unreasonable'.[124]

The second case tells a more complicated industrial story, this time involving the monopolization of cellophane.[125] Cellophane was first produced commercially in France in 1917 by La Cellophane S.A. DuPont, which produced synthetic fabrics, heard of La Cellophane's success and entered the business. La Cellophane, however, had a distinct competitive advantage because of the 'secret, novel' process for manufacturing cellophane that it had developed through operational experimentation.[126] In 1923 DuPont and La Cellophane formed the DuPont Cellophane Company, and La Cellophane granted DuPont Cellophane the exclusive right to make and sell cellophane in North and Central America under La Cellophane's secret processes; La Cellophane was given the rest of the world.[127] It was estimated at the time that it would have taken DuPont several years to develop a competitive production technique.[128]

---

120 See *id.*

121 *Id.* at 860.

122 *Id.*

123 *Id.*

124 See *id.* at 860–1.

125 See United States v. E.I. duPont de Nemours & Co., 118 F.Supp. 41 (D. Del. 1953), *aff'd*, 351 U.S. 377 (1956).

126 See 118 F.Supp. at 218.

127 See *id.* at 57–8.

128 The district court and the Supreme Court did not quite agree on just how long it would have taken DuPont. *Compare* 118 F.Supp. at 59 ('Evidence shows DuPont could not have developed a successful process for cellophane manufacture in less than five to eight years and then only at very substantial cost') *with* 351 U.S. at

In 1947 the Justice Department brought suit against DuPont for monopolizing the cellophane market. One of the Department's arguments was that DuPont had acquired its monopoly illegally by engaging in a per se unlawful division of world markets, effected through the creation of DuPont Cellophane and the licensing of La Cellophane's trade secrets.[129] The district court disagreed with the Department's view of the agreements. Stressing DuPont's weak competitive position when the deal was struck, the high value of the trade secrets that La Cellophane licensed, and the riskiness of the cellophane venture even with La Cellophane's help, the court held the agreements lawful.[130] Citing both *Fowle* and *Dr. Miles*, the court wrote: 'Among the ancillary restraints which are considered reasonable, both under common law and the Sherman Act, are those which limit territory in which the contracting parties may use the trade secret'.[131]

The Justice Department's litigating posture in *DuPont*, however, led the district court away from some difficult issues. For one, the court was not asked to do a full rule of reason analysis because the Department presented the trade secret licensing as a per se violation. The court's rule of reason analysis is thus more like the rough balancing done in the earlier common law cases, taking account of the economic benefits of the agreement to the parties and the utility of La Cellophane's innovations but not focusing on the consumer welfare loss from the territorial allocations, nor on the question whether the incentives for innovation would have been equally well served by a more limited agreement. For another, the Department's argument focused on the legality of the agreements when made in 1923, rather than on the question whether the agreements had an unreasonable effect on competition in 1947, when suit was brought. Had the case been framed differently, the court would have been required to consider whether trade secret territorial restraints, unlike patent territorial restraints, can be of unlimited duration.

An opportunity to advance the analysis on these two issues was presented in 1994 when the Justice Department brought suit against Pilkington, an English company.[132] In the late 1950s Pilkington developed a new commercially successful method for producing flat glass, called the

382 n.4 ('It was estimated that in 1923 it would have taken four or five years of experimentation by a new producer of cellophane to attain this production technique').

[129] See 118 F.Supp. at 218–20.

[130] See id. at 220.

[131] *Id.* at 219. The Justice Department did not appeal the court's ruling on this point. See 351 U.S. at 379.

[132] Complaint, United States v. Pilkington PLC, Civ. A. No. CV 94-345 (D. Ariz. May 25, 1994), available at www.usdoj.gov/atr/cases/f0000/0014.pdf.

float process. In 1962 Pilkington entered into patent and know-how licensing agreements with all its principal glass making competitors (which were still producing flat glass through other methods).[133] The licensees were permitted to use the patents and know-how only in a specified country or countries; they could not export their glass, build new plants outside their assigned territories, or sublicense the technology.[134] By the time the Department brought suit, Pilkington's principal patents had expired and all royalty obligations had been concluded. Yet Pilkington continued to enforce the territorial restrictions regarding its know-how, unless the licensee could prove that all the float glass technology it was using had become public.[135] A 'substantial part' had, but not all.[136]

The Justice Department alleged that Pilkington's agreements had created a worldwide cartel preventing U.S. firms not only from exporting flat glass, but also from exporting their services in building float glass plants in foreign countries, where there was strong demand for new plants.[137] These territorial restraints, the Department alleged, were not justified by any intellectual property rights 'of substantial value', given the expiration of the patents and the disclosure of much of the technology.[138] Because Pilkington had no intellectual property rights of substantial value, the restraints were 'neither ancillary nor reasonably necessary' to any legitimate transaction and were, therefore, 'unreasonable restraints of trade'.[139]

The Justice Department settled its suit against Pilkington with a

---

133 See *id.* at 8.

134 See *id.* at 8–9.

135 See *id.* at 10.

136 *Id.* at 11.

137 See *id.*

138 See *id.* at 10.

139 See Competitive Impact Statement at 10, United States v. Pilkington PLC, Civ. A. No. CV 94-345 (D. Ariz. May 25, 1994), available at www.usdoj.gov/atr/cases/f220800/220861.pdf. For other cases where courts have weighed the value of the licensed information, although at the date when the license agreements were made, see United States v. Timken Roller Bearing Co., 83 F.Supp. 284, 313 (N.D. Ohio 1949) (holding that the defendant's know-how was not a 'secret process', but consisted of 'designs, data showing how defendant manufactured its product, the advice of defendant's employees and help of like nature'), *aff'd*, 341 U.S. 593 (1951); United States v. Imperial Chemical Indus., 100 F.Supp. 504, 592 (S.D.N.Y. 1951) (finding that the defendants' license agreements served to accomplish a 'world-wide allocation of markets'); United States v. General Electric Co., 82 F.Supp. 753, 846 (D.N.J. 1949) (no clear evidence what the trade secrets were). See also A. & E. Plastik Pak Co. v. Monsanto Co., 396 F.2d 710, 715 (9th Cir. 1968) (characterizing the trade secret agreements in these cases as 'subterfuges' for market division and price fixing).

consent order, so the Department's legal theory was never tested in court. Nevertheless, the case is a good example of government enforcers paying closer attention to the actual economic value of the apparently secret technology involved and, implicitly, taking account of the change in circumstances from when the original license agreements were entered into. A trade secret license, even if permissible under the antitrust laws when made, can become unreasonable over time, preventing competition among the licensees and with the licensor, and lasting longer than is necessary to provide incentives for innovation.

3. Tying

There is a long history of litigation over tying the sale of intellectual property right-protected products to the sale of products that are not protected. The issue arose first in the patent area, leading Congress to pass Section 3 of the Clayton Act in 1914, condemning the practice.[140] Over time the Supreme Court came to hold that ties involving patents were per se violations of Section 1 of the Sherman Act, an approach subsequently extended to copyrights.[141] Commentators later pointed out, however, that although patents and copyrights give their owners certain rights to exclude others from using an invention or copying a work, these legal rights did not necessarily confer economic power (or 'market power') on the seller.[142] In the 1995 Intellectual Property Guidelines, the federal enforcement agencies accepted this critique and disavowed the view that intellectual property

---

[140] Clayton Antitrust Act, 15 U.S.C. § 14 (2006). The Supreme Court had originally approved the practice as a matter of patent law, see Henry v. A.B. Dick Co., 224 U.S. 1, 17–19 (1912), but reversed its view after the passage of section 3. See Motion Picture Patents Co. v. Universal Film Mfg. Co., 243 U.S. 502, 516–17 (1917) (overruling *A.B. Dick*).

[141] See United States v. Loew's, Inc., 371 U.S. 38, 49 (1962) (holding that tying arrangements, of both patented and copyrighted products, 'both by their inherent nature and by their effect injuriously restrained trade') (internal citations omitted).

[142] See, e.g.,10 PHILIP AREEDA, HERBERT HOVENKAMP AND EINER ELHAUGE, ANTITRUST LAW ¶ 1737a (2d ed. 2004) ('[T]here is no economic basis for inferring any amount of market power from the mere fact that the defendant holds a valid patent'); WILLIAM LANDES AND RICHARD POSNER, THE ECONOMIC STRUCTURE OF INTELLECTUAL PROPERTY LAW 374 (2003); Kenneth J. Burchfiel, *Patent Misuse and Antitrust Reform: 'Blessed be the Tie?'*, 4 HARV. J.L. & TECH. 1, 57, n.340 (1991) (noting that the existence of a market power presumption had been extensively criticized); 1 HOVENKAMP, JANIS AND LEMLEY, *supra* note 2, § 4.2a ('coverage of one's product with an intellectual property right does not confer a monopoly').

rights, in themselves, conferred market power.[143] In 2006, in *Illinois Tool Works v. Independent Ink*,[144] the Supreme Court agreed as well, overruling its prior case law and holding that market power in a tying case could not be presumed merely from the fact that the tying product was protected by a patent.[145]

Trade secrets did not go through the same legal development as patents and copyrights. In fact, the courts have specifically rejected the argument that trade secrets should be treated like other intellectual property rights in tying cases.[146] Given the variability of the quality of the information that can be protected by trade secrets, as well as the permissibility of lawful discovery through reverse engineering, a non-presumption approach to trade secret ties made good sense even when patent and copyright ties were per se unlawful. It is certainly correct today, when patent and copyright ties are not considered per se unlawful.

This does not mean that ties involving trade secrets are per se lawful under Section 1. Unlike trade secret licensing restrictions on price or territory, tying arrangements involving products produced under trade secrecy do not come freighted with the ancillary restraints doctrine – there is nothing to which the tying arrangement is 'ancillary'. Rather, the questions they raise would be those involved in any tying analysis: (1) does the seller's trade secret confer market power; (2) what are the anticompetitive effects of the tying sale; and (3) are there any efficiency justifications for the tie.

It is certainly possible that a trade secret could be sufficiently strong to confer market power on its possessor. Indeed, trade secret litigation abounds with allegations of the novelty and essentiality of the trade secret that its possessor is trying to protect. In previous tying litigation, where products have often been protected by other intellectual property rights as well as by trade secrets, legal doctrine led the parties away from focusing on the economic advantages conferred by trade secrets as opposed to patent or copyright protection.[147] Post-*Illinois Tool*, however, this may

---

143 See IP Guidelines, *supra* note 1, § 2.2. The agencies included trade secrets as well as patents and copyrights. See *id.*

144 Illinois Tool Works, Inc. v. Independent Ink, Inc., 547 U.S. 28 (2007).

145 See *id.* at 33–43 (canvassing legal history and commentators' critiques).

146 See, e.g., In re Data General Corp. Antitrust Litigation, 490 F.Supp. 1089, 1113–14 (N.D. Cal. 1980) ('Unlike the copyright issue, it has never been held that trade secrets protection is sufficient to create a presumption of economic power'), *rv'sd on other grounds*, Digidyne Corp. v. Data General Corp., 734 F.2d 1336 (9th Cir. 1984).

147 In *Digidyne*, for example, the software plaintiffs argued that the defendant's copyright and trade secret protection in its software, when combined, should

change, leading litigants to examine more carefully the quality of the trade secrets a seller claims.

C. Current Law: Monopolization

1. Refusal to supply

A critical assumption in the trade secrets restraint of trade cases, whether at common law or under Section 1 of the Sherman Act, has been that the holder of the trade secret can always keep the secret to itself rather than disclose it to others, whether to a partner or to an employee. Because the trade secret holder had this option, the law could be indifferent as to which option the holder chose, or what restrictions the holder, as licensor, put on the licensee to whom it disclosed. The public is in the same position whether the secret is kept by the secret's originator or kept, with restrictions, by the secret's licensee.

Does this argument change if a monopolist controls the trade secret? Courts have often pointed out that a monopolist, 'as a general matter', can 'freely . . . exercise his own independent discretion as to parties with whom he will deal'.[148] There can be exceptions, of course, but, as the Court notes in *Trinko*, the courts have been 'very cautious in recognizing such exceptions',[149] something which has been true without regard to whether the monopolist's product is protected by an intellectual property right or not. The reason for this caution, *Trinko* points out, is the 'uncertain virtue' of forced sharing and the difficulty courts can have in 'identifying and remedying' the monopolizing conduct.[150]

The trade secrets case that best illustrates this cautious approach is *Berkey Photo, Inc. v. Eastman Kodak, Inc.*,[151] a private treble-damages

---

give rise to a presumption of market power; the court of appeals held for the plaintiffs on the ground that the copyright in the software could be presumed to confer market power to impose the tie. See 734 F.2d at 1344. One of the plaintiffs, however, was a hardware maker that argued that Data General's CPU was protected through trade secrecy. The district court had found that the plaintiff made 'an impressive factual showing that Data General actually possesses economic power by virtue of its trade secrets', relying, in part, on Data General's president's statement doubting that anyone could design a Data General 'emulator' without infringing on Data General's trade secrets. See *Data General*, 490 F.Supp. at 1115.

[148] See Verizon Comm'ns Inc. v. Law Offices of Curtis V. Trinko, LLP, 540 U.S. 398, 408 (2004) (*quoting* United States v. Colgate & Co., 250 U.S. 300, 307 (1919) (internal quotations omitted)).

[149] See *id.*

[150] See *id.*

[151] 603 F.2d 263 (2d Cir. 1979).

action involving Kodak's introduction of a new small camera and film. Kodak had a monopoly position in the camera and film markets; Berkey was a competitor in the camera market.[152] Camera makers' abilities to innovate were limited by the fact that they could not introduce a new camera unless there was film that fitted. This left Kodak free to design new cameras with new film formats at its own pace. Indeed, competitors like Berkey could not even begin to design a competing new camera until they knew the size of the new film's cartridge and its format.[153]

Less than two months before Kodak introduced the new small camera and film that led to the litigation, it provided Berkey, at a charge of U.S.$60,000, 11 pages of specifications and notes relating to the new film format.[154] These disclosures, however, were inadequate to allow Berkey to be present 'at the starting line' when Kodak introduced its new camera, so Berkey sued for the profits it lost over the 18 months it took to catch up.[155]

The court of appeals rejected, as a matter of law, Berkey's claim that Kodak's failure timely to disclose the specifications was monopolizing conduct in violation of Section 2.[156] Although technically Kodak did not claim legally protectable trade secrets in this information, there was little doubt that Kodak had kept this information confidential, and the court treated it as such. Relying on an earlier Supreme Court trade secrets case,[157] the court pointed out that 'a firm may normally keep its innovations secret from its rivals as long as it wishes'.[158] Were the rule otherwise, the incentives to innovate would be lessened: 'The first firm, even a monopolist . . . has a right to the lead time that follows from its success'.[159] Further, a liability rule for failure to predisclose secret information would be difficult to apply and enforce. How would a monopoly firm or a court figure out how detailed the information must be, and when would the information be sufficiently '"ripe" for disclosure?' These uncertainties, the court felt, would have 'an inevitable chilling effect on innovation'.[160]

The court thus appeared to shut the door on a monopolization claim for a refusal to supply confidential information prior to a product's

---

152 See *Id.* at 267.
153 See *id.* at 279–84.
154 See *id.* at 280–1.
155 See *id.* at 281.
156 See *id.*
157 See Kewanee Oil Co. v. Bicron Corp., 416 U.S. 470 (1974).
158 603 F.2d at 281.
159 *Id.* at 283.
160 *Id.* at 282.

introduction. Nevertheless, one should be cautious in taking the position that all failures to predisclose confidential information are per se lawful. For example, in 1998 the Federal Trade Commission issued a complaint against Intel for changing its policy of sharing prerelease technical information with three customers that designed and sold products using Intel chips.[161] Intel did so in apparent retaliation for patent infringement suits that the customers had filed against either Intel or Intel's customers, which alleged that Intel technology was infringing patents on their microprocessor technology.[162] The FTC alleged that because most firms that develop microprocessor-related technologies were 'dependent on Intel' and 'vulnerable to retaliation', Intel's conduct could diminish incentives those firms had to innovate in the microprocessor market that Intel monopolized.[163] The FTC settled the case shortly before trial, so its theories were never tested in court. Nevertheless, the fact-pattern is a reminder of how trade secret information may be used strategically to maintain monopoly power.[164]

The most significant decision requiring a monopolist to disclose trade secret information, however, comes not from a U.S. court, but from Europe. At issue was a request that Sun Microsystems made to Microsoft in 1998 to provide it with 'the complete information' that would allow Sun's server operating systems to be fully interoperable with networks of servers and PCs running Microsoft's Windows operating system.[165] When Microsoft refused, Sun petitioned the European Commission to

---

[161] See Complaint, In the Matter of Intel Corp., No. 9288 (Fed. Trade Comm'n June 8, 1998), available at www.ftc.gov/os/1998/06/intelfin.cmp.htm.

[162] See *id.* paras. 13, 18.

[163] See *id.* paras. 14, 39.

[164] See *FTC Staff, Intel Withdraw Case from ALJ in Anticipation of Reaching Settlement*, 76 Antitrust & Trade Reg. Rep. (BNA) 237 (March 11, 1999) (describing arguments made in the parties' pretrial briefs before an FTC Administrative Law Judge). The settlement order is available at www.ftc.gov/os/1999/08/intel.do.htm. Intergraph's related antitrust suit was ultimately unsuccessful because it did not allege that the refusal to supply the information harmed competition in any market in which it and Intel competed. See Intergraph Corp. v. Intel Corp., 195 F.3d 1346, 1357 (Fed. Cir. 1999). Nevertheless, the Federal Circuit's opinion showed great skepticism toward Intergraph's argument that failure to disclose the information violated Section 2. *See id.* at 1357–8 ('The notion that withholding of technical information and samples of pre-release chips violates the Sherman Act, based on essential facility jurisprudence, is an unwarranted extension of precedent and can not be supported on the premises presented').

[165] See Case COMP/C-3/37.792 – Microsoft Corp., Comm'n Decision, [2007] O.J. L32/23, para. 185 (March 24, 2004), available at http://ec.europa.eu/competition/antitrust/cases/decisions/37792/en.pdf.

initiate proceedings against Microsoft for abuse of dominant position in violation of Article 82 of the EC Treaty (the rough analogue to Section 2 of the Sherman Act). As the Commission subsequently pointed out, Sun's request for interoperability information, to be implemented in Sun's products, might reveal 'innovations that are currently not disclosed' and which are 'protected by trade secrecy'.[166] Indeed, Microsoft pointed out that although some of the requested information was protected by patent, and therefore publicly disclosed, the communications protocols that Sun sought for interoperability 'remain highly proprietary and confidential'.[167]

In 2004 the Commission determined that Microsoft's refusal to supply the requested information violated Article 82.[168] The Commission concluded that Microsoft had followed a 'leveraging strategy' to extend its dominant position in the PC operating systems market into the adjacent work group server operating system market.[169] By withholding interoperability information, Microsoft had deprived competitors in the work group server operating systems market of information that was 'indispensable' for viable competition, thereby allowing the company to exploit 'a range of privileged connections' between its Windows operating system and its work group server operating system.[170]

The Commission never decided, however, whether Microsoft's proprietary information actually qualified as protected trade secrets, or whether Microsoft actually had the patent and copyright protection it claimed, because Microsoft never made the relevant specifications available for review.[171] Rather, the Commission assumed the information was protected in some way, but concluded that these protections were not, in themselves, sufficient justification for failing to supply the requested information, in light of the competitors' need for the information and the positive effect that supplying the information would have on their incentives to innovate.

On review, the European Court of First Instance upheld the Commission's decision, agreeing that the refusal to supply the requested information was likely to eliminate effective competition in the work group server operating system market.[172] In its argument before the Court,

---

[166] *Id.* para. 190.
[167] *Id.* para. 190 n.249.
[168] *Id.* para. 784.
[169] *Id.* para. 1063.
[170] See *id.* paras. 1063–5.
[171] See *id.* para. 190.
[172] See Case T-201/04, Microsoft Corp. v. Comm'n [2007] E.C.R. II-3601, para. 620 (Ct. First Instance), available at http://curia.europa.eu/jurisp/cgi-bin/

the Commission raised the possibility that trade secrets should be treated differently – and less favorably – than either patents or copyrights in terms of any 'presumption of legitimacy' of a refusal to supply, because 'the protection that such secrets enjoy under national law is normally more limited than that given to copyright or patents'.[173] The Commission also argued, however, that there was no need to decide this issue, and the Court agreed.[174] The Court noted that the Commission's decision had assumed the legal validity of Microsoft's patent, copyright and trade secret claims and then judged Microsoft's behavior under the test which was 'most favorable' to Microsoft.[175] Similarly, the Court decided to treat trade secrets as 'equivalent' to the other intellectual property rights, finding no need to treat them any less favorably.[176]

The Court also considered Microsoft's argument that forced disclosure of its protected interoperability information would diminish its incentives to innovate. The Court determined that once the Commission had proved the adverse competitive impact of the failure to disclose, Microsoft then had the burden of showing how its incentives to innovate would be adversely affected. The Court wrote that Microsoft had not carried its burden, instead merely putting forward 'vague, general and theoretical arguments'.[177] The Commission, by contrast, had examined the widespread industry practice of commonly disclosing interoperability information and had pointed out that Microsoft's fear that Sun, or other competitors, might simply copy ('clone') its products was exaggerated.[178]

The decision in the European *Microsoft* case has been highly controversial and was much criticized by U.S. Justice Department officials at the time, who took the view that a refusal to license intellectual property should never be a violation of Section 2 of the Sherman Act.[179] This view,

---

gettext.pl?lang=en&num=79929082T19040201&doc=T&ouvert=T&seance=ARRET ('CFI *Microsoft* Decision').

173 *Id.* para. 280.

174 See *id.* para. 283.

175 See *id.* paras. 284, 289, 313.

176 See *id.* para. 289.

177 *Id.* para. 698.

178 See *id.* para. 710.

179 See Harry First, *Netscape is Dead: Remedy Lessons from the* Microsoft *Litigation*, NYU Law and Economics Research Paper No. 08-49, 20–1 (2008) available at http://ssrn.com/abstract=1260803 (describing the U.S. Department of Justice's immediately critical reaction to the European judgment); Bo Vesterdorf, *Article 82 EC: Where Do We Stand after the* Microsoft *Judgment?*, 1 ICC Global Antitrust Rev. 1, 14 (2008) (arguing that the CFI's judgment 'may have what some might call negative consequences for holders of IPRs, which perhaps might deter

however, did not differentiate among the different types of intellectual property protection, and it was articulated in the context of a broader policy view that unilateral refusals to deal in general should not be found to violate Section 2.[180] In 2009, moreover, the Obama administration Justice Department withdrew the Report embodying this general policy view, bringing into question how current enforcement officials would evaluate refusals to license intellectual property rights by monopoly firms like Microsoft.[181]

2. Bad faith litigation

A familiar problem in antitrust law is the alleged bad faith assertion of an intellectual property right as part of an effort to exclude competitors. If the intellectual property right holder has sufficient market power, such efforts can give rise to a violation of Section 2, either as monopolization or attempted monopolization. Most of these cases involve patents, but some have involved trade secrets.

The leading trade secrets case is *CVD v. Raytheon*.[182] Raytheon manufactured two chemical-based materials that were the only ones suitable for certain government defense uses, such as windows on missiles and jet

---

investments that otherwise would be made and in turn have negative consequences for competition') (author was President of the CFI and participated in the court's *Microsoft* decision), available at www.icc.qmul.ac.uk/GAR/GAR2008/Vesterdorf.pdf. See also Promoting Innovation, *supra* note 1, at 32 ('The Agencies also conclude that antitrust liability for mere unilateral, unconditional refusals to license patents will not play a meaningful part in the interface between patent rights and antitrust protections'); Gerald F. Masoudi, Deputy Assistant Attorney General, U.S. Department of Justice, Intellectual Property and Competition: Four Principles for Encouraging Innovation, Address before the Digital Americas 2006 Meeting (April 11, 2006), at 5, available at www.usdoj.gov/atr/public/speeches/215645.pdf (arguing that although 'outside the intellectual property realm' parties are sometimes liable for refusing to deal with others, that does not mean that 'there must also be some circumstance in which the unilateral, unconditional refusal to license a patent must constitute an antitrust violation', and suggesting that liability for such a refusal to license 'has not found support in U.S. legal decisions').

[180] See U.S. Dep't of Justice, Competition and Monopoly: Single-Firm Conduct under Section 2 of the Sherman Act 127 (2008), available at www.usdoj.gov/atr/public/reports/236681.pdf ('Section 2 Report') ('The Department thus concludes that antitrust liability for unilateral, unconditional refusals to deal with competitors should not play a meaningful part in Section 2 enforcement').

[181] For the statement withdrawing the Report, see Christine Varney, Assistant Attorney General U.S. Department of Justice, Vigorous Antitrust Enforcement in this Challenging Era, Remarks as Prepared for the Center for American Progress (May 11, 2009), available at www.usdoj.gov/atr/public/speeches/245711.pdf.

[182] CVD, Inc. v. Raytheon Co., 769 F.2d. 842 (1st Cir. 1985).

aircraft. Raytheon manufactured these materials under the 'cvd process', which no other firm in the world used.[183] In 1979 an engineer who had worked at Raytheon for 20 years told Raytheon that he was leaving to form a competing company to manufacture the materials using the cvd process. Raytheon told him that he could not do so without infringing Raytheon's trade secrets.[184] Their dispute eventually became a Section 2 case in which the plaintiff-competitor showed both the invalidity of the trade secrets claim and Raytheon's bad faith in asserting it. For the former, the plaintiff proved the extent to which Raytheon had made details of the cvd process public (including reports to the federal government and papers published in scientific journals). To show bad faith, plaintiff proved that Raytheon had never followed any of its usual internal procedures for demarcating trade secret-protected matters.[185]

The court of appeals upheld the jury's verdict for the plaintiff-competitor, finding that '[t]he assertion of trade secret claims in bad faith . . . is a predatory practice' that can violate Section 2 of the Sherman Act, so long as the plaintiff can show monopoly power or an attempt to monopolize.[186] The court analogized the case to antitrust liability for bad faith patent infringement suits. The court pointed out that the rationale behind both types of legal protection is similar – 'to encourage invention' – even while recognizing that the 'cornerstone' of trade secret protection is secrecy and the scope of rights is narrower, affording no protection against independent development.[187] Perhaps because trade secret law allows more room for independent competition, the court allowed the plaintiff's suit even though the defendant had only threatened trade secret litigation but had never actually brought it.[188]

Raytheon is somewhat unusual in that it does not involve patents at all. Other cases involve the more familiar combination of patents and trade secrets to protect technology. For example, in *A. & E. Plastik Pak v.*

---

183 See *id.* at 847–8.

184 See *id.* at 848.

185 See *id.*

186 *Id.* at 855.

187 See *id.* at 850.

188 See *id.* at 848. This was in contrast to the case law at the time on bad faith patent litigation, which required an infringement suit to have been brought. See *id.* at 851. Subsequent cases have been more liberal, allowing a Sherman Act claim where there is a reasonable expectation that an infringement suit would be filed. See Hydril Co. LP v. Grant Prideco LP, 474 F.3d 1344, 1350 (Fed. Cir. 2007). *Cf.* Christopher R. Leslie, *The Anticompetitive Effects of Unenforced Invalid Patents*, 91 MINN. L. REV. 101, 125–6 (2006) ('No actual enforcement, or even a direct threat of litigation, is required to create anticompetitive effects').

Monsanto,[189] the plaintiff alleged that Monsanto acted in bad faith when it claimed trade secret protection for a manufacturing process after its patent expired, in an effort to stop the plaintiff from manufacturing a competing product (with the assistance of a former Monsanto engineer).[190] Similarly, in *International Technologies Consultants, Inc. v Pilkington PLC*,[191] a private suit involving the technology for making float glass, the plaintiff alleged a multi-year effort to exclude it from the market for designing float glass plants by filing numerous lawsuits baselessly asserting trade secret protection for the float glass technology after the relevant patents had expired.[192]

The court of appeals in *Pilkington* was appropriately appalled at the effort to use a bogus trade secrets claim to protect technology that should have been in the public domain:

> Alistair Pilkington invented an ingenious new method of making high quality flat glass at high speed, much less expensively than by grinding and polishing it, in the 1950's. He thereby made a great contribution to cheap, good plate glass for everyone. There was no way to exploit his invention while keeping it a close secret, as with the formula for Coca-Cola, because the weight and fragility of glass required that the method be used in factories around the world. The patent enabled the Pilkington company to take exclusive benefit of the idea for a limited period of time, even though numerous other people necessarily knew the method almost immediately. . . . We do not know whether [the defendants] have conspired to prevent others from using the ideas in Pilkington's expired patents, in violation of the antitrust laws, by means of unjustified litigation and threats of litigation. But if they have, as the complaint alleges, then the world is being deprived of the economic value of Alistair Pilkington's great invention. Indeed, in poorer areas of the world, doubtless people lack windows to let in the sun and keep out the rain, wind, cold, and insects, because of improper exploitation of monopoly pricing.[193]

IV. AN ANALYTICAL FRAMEWORK FOR ANTITRUST AND TRADE SECRETS

---

189 A. & E. Plastik Pak Co., Inc. v. Monsanto Co., 396 F.2d 710 (9th Cir. 1968).

190 The court, in dictum, indicated that such conduct could be a violation of the antitrust laws. See *id.* at 715.

191 137 F.3d 1382 (9th Cir. 1998).

192 See *id.* at 1388. ITC's allegations involve conduct similar to that alleged in the Justice Department's 1994 complaint, see *supra* text accompanying notes 132–9. Although ITC's complaint was filed in 1993 in the same district court as the Justice Department's, there is no mention of ITC's allegations in either the Department's complaint or settlement.

193 *Id.* at 1392–3.

A. General Principles

I would like to suggest three general principles for analysing antitrust cases involving trade secrets. First, trade secrets should not be treated as the equivalent of other intellectual property rights. This means that there should be no presumption that the restrictions that trade secret holders impose are welfare-enhancing and therefore pro-competitive. Second, antitrust economic analysis of trade secrets should take account of their essential legal properties: trade secrets are not necessarily innovative, and their legal protection can last far longer than might be necessary to incentivize their production, but this legal protection will be lost once the secret is out. Third, in assessing the competitive effects of protecting trade secrets, trade secret holders should get the benefits of their bargain but no more – a time-unlimited right to appropriate the value of whatever can be kept secret, but no right to monopoly profits and no right to restrict others from independent discovery.

1. Trade secret distinctiveness: no deference, no presumptions

It is fair to say that the current approach to applying antitrust law where intellectual property rights are involved has been one of deference. That is, courts and enforcers have generally been willing to defer to the decisions that intellectual property rights holders have made when attempting to maximize the rents they can get from their inventions or writings. This policy of deference is rooted in a simple Schumpeterian view of the incentives for innovation: monopoly profits are 'the baits that lure capital on to untried trails'.[194] Antitrust enforcers and courts should therefore be quite careful in restricting the profits that intellectual property owners can obtain, lest they diminish the incentives for innovation.

Courts have recognized that trade secret protection also serves the goal of incentivizing innovation.[195] Particularly when it comes to manufacturing processes, the ability to maintain proprietary control over information allows innovators to get returns from their efforts. Courts recognize that getting an invention, even a patentable one, from idea to production is a complex process. Experimentation is necessary and it is often difficult to reduce every aspect of production to writing. This is the lesson of

---

194 Joseph A. Schumpeter, Capitalism, Socialism, and Democracy 90 (3d ed. 1950).

195 See Kewanee Oil Co. v. Bicron Corp., 416 U.S. 470, 471 (1974) (noting that 'trade secret law will encourage invention and prompt the innovator to proceed with the discovery and exploitation of his invention, and to license others to exploit secret processes').

chocolate making, gunny cloth manufacture and cellophane, to take just a few examples from the case law discussed above.

The courts have also recognized another important purpose of trade secret protection – the preservation of confidential relationships. Much of trade secret law is shaped in the context of faithless agents or partners. The law's desire to protect these relationships may have many roots, whether located in notions of 'commercial ethics and fair dealing';[196] or an instinct about the importance of maintaining social networks of trust for organizing enterprises efficiently; or a realization that innovation may require the enforcement of legal norms relating to the sharing of information.[197]

Although these ideas have often led the courts to defer to trade secrets claims, there are some cases that take what I will call a neutrality approach toward trade secrecy. In these cases, courts have not assumed that trade secret holders should be permitted to maximize their returns like other intellectual property rights holders. Rather, these courts have paid attention to three key interrelated differences between trade secrets and other forms of intellectual property protection, particularly patents: (1) duration; (2) absence of a federal right; and (3) lack of a disclosure bargain.

(1) Duration Patents have a fixed term (now 20 years); trade secrets have no fixed term.[198] A policy of deference to patents thus has some natural limitation: at some time the protection will run out. A policy of deference to trade secrets is not limited in this way. Protection runs out when the secret is out, something that clever reverse engineering can help along. Courts have paid most attention to the length of protection in those cases when trade secrets are being used to avoid the patent's fixed term.[199]

---

[196] See CVD, Inc. v. Raytheon Co., 769 F.2d 842, 850 (1st Cir. 1985).

[197] See Katherine J. Strandburg, *Norms and the Sharing of Research Materials and Tacit Knowledge*, in WORKING WITHIN THE BOUNDARIES OF INTELLECTUAL PROPERTY 85–110 (Rochelle C. Dreyfuss, Harry First and Diane L. Zimmerman eds., 2010).

[198] Copyrights are now effectively unlimited in duration. See Eldred v. Ashcroft, 537 U.S. 186, 208 (2003) (approving Congress' extension of copyright protection until 70 years after the author's death through the Sonny Bono Copyright Term Extension Act, Pub. L. No. 105-298, 11 Stat. 2827 (1998)).

[199] See, e.g., Christianson v. Colt Indus. Operating Corp., 486 U.S. 800, 805–6 (1988) (rejecting a defendant's trade secret claim that was filed only after an expired patent was found to be invalid). But see Aronson v. Quick Point Pencil Co., 440 U.S. 257 (1979) (holding that a contract to pay royalties for the defendant's product, signed alongside an application to patent the product, should be enforced even when the patent application is denied and the defendant's trade secrets become public in the process).

(2) Absence of a federal statutory right Beginning with Judge Lurton's opinion in *Hartman*, courts have seen a distinction between the 'monopoly' given by federal patent law and the lesser protection afforded under state trade secret law.[200] Although the courts have put this argument in somewhat formal legalistic terms, a better way of looking at it is that federal patent law is intended to provide the patent holder with the profits that are 'reasonably within the reward' of the patent grant, that is, the profits from whatever monopoly power the patent allows the patentee to exercise.[201] There is no such maximizing policy in trade secret law. Rather, the policy is to protect the secret from being misappropriated by others, in part to advance the law's interest in protecting fiduciary relationships and in part to advance innovation. The goal is not necessarily to maximize the return the secret's holder can get.

(3) Lack of a disclosure bargain Beginning with the Supreme Court's 1911 decision in *Dr. Miles*, courts have paid attention to the fundamentally different bargain that is struck under the patent and trade secret regimes.[202] Patentees get exclusive use of the invention (that is, protection against independent invention) in return for disclosing their information to the public. Trade secret holders get no such right and make no such disclosure. Courts generally keep the parties to their bargain lest trade secrets become like patents but without the disclosure bargain and without any time limit.[203]

There is a fourth key difference between patents and trade secrets, but it is one to which the courts have not paid attention – the lack of any *ex ante* or *ex post* review of the quality of the innovation protected as a trade secret. This difference, however, is another important reason not to give deference to trade secrets in antitrust litigation.

A strong policy of deference to patent holders reflects a maximalist view of intellectual property, resting on an economic argument that suboptimal innovation will occur unless inventors are able to appropriate the full monopoly returns from their inventions. Critics of expansive

---

[200] See John D. Park & Sons Co. v. Hartman, 153 F. 24, 32–3 (6th Cir. 1907). The federal Economic Espionage Act, 18 U.S.C. §§ 1831–9, makes it a crime to steal or misappropriate a trade secret, but provides no private rights for the trade secret holder and is not directed at providing incentives for innovation. See Roger Milgrim, Milgrim on Trade Secrets § 12.6(3) (discussing the exclusively criminal provisions of the Act).

[201] United States v. Gen. Elec. Co., 272 U.S. 476, 489 (1926).

[202] See Dr. Miles Medical Co. v. John D. Park & Sons Co., 220 U.S. 373, 401–3 (1911).

[203] See, e.g., *id.*

intellectual property rights, on the other hand, argue for parsimony in rewarding intellectual property rights holders: intellectual property rights holders should be given just enough to incentivize innovation, but no more.[204]

Whatever one thinks about these two positions, however, both sides advance their positions in the context of a system where a government agency screens inventions before a patent can issue and where the invention must meet statutory standards of patentability (novelty, utility and non-obviousness).[205] In recent years critics on both sides of the presumption debate have become concerned about the quality of *ex ante* review and the lowering of standards for patent grants. This has led to proposals for improving the Patent and Trademark Office,[206] as well as to judicial decisions making it harder to get patents.[207]

Trade secrets go through no such *ex ante* review, nor are they subject to any quality review *ex post*. This is yet another reason why trade secrets should come to the courts with no presumptions, either legal or factual, about their innovativeness.[208] For all the courts know, an 'invention' protected by a trade secret could be the equivalent of the patent medicines of yore – just alcohol, bitters and water. If we are skeptical about the quality of reviewed inventions, shouldn't we be even more skeptical about the quality of unreviewed inventions?

2. Trade secrets' legal properties and their economic effects

Modern economic analysis in antitrust cases applies a rule of reason balance – an effort to balance the anticompetitive effects of particular arrangements (harm to consumer welfare or the competitive process)

---

204 The debate is discussed in First, *supra* note 13, at 376.

205 See 35 U.S.C. § 101 (2000) (utility and novelty); *id.* § 103 (amended in 2004) (non-obviousness).

206 See, e.g., Mark A. Lemley and Carl Shapiro, *Probabilistic Patents*, 19 J. Econ. Persp. 75 (2005); Robert P. Merges, *As Many as Six Impossible Patents Before Breakfast: Property Rights for Business Concepts and Patent System Reform*, 14 Berkeley Tech. L.J. 577 (1999).

207 See, e.g., KSR Intern. Co. v. Teleflex Inc., 550 U.S. 398, 419 (2007) (rejecting the Federal Circuit's test for obviousness for having become a 'rigid and mandatory' formula and writing that '[g]ranting patent protection to advances that would occur in the ordinary course without real innovation retards progress').

208 *Compare* 35 U.S.C. § 282 (2002) ('A patent shall be presumed valid'), *with* 17 U.S.C. § 410(c) ('In any judicial proceedings the certificate of a registration made before or within five years after first publication of the work shall constitute prima facie evidence of the validity of the copyright and of the facts stated in the certificate. The evidentiary weight to be accorded the certificate of a registration made thereafter shall be within the discretion of the court').

against any pro-competitive (efficiency) justifications. Although courts in Section 1 trade secrets cases have often used the language of 'ancillary restraints' to structure this rule of reason balancing, this doctrine has never been fully embraced by the Supreme Court and its exact meaning is unclear.[209] Better analysis avoids this categorizing effort, looking directly at economic effects. This is true in Section 2 cases as well, where, despite much controversy over various phrasings of the 'test' for finding monopolizing conduct, in the end the courts are most likely to assess a monopolist's conduct using a rule of reason balance.[210]

Analysing the competitive effects of a restraint involving a trade secret requires assessing the economic value of the trade secret. This is not the same as requiring the trade secret holder to prove that it has confidential information that would be protectable under state law as a 'trade secret'. Rather, it involves an assessment of the secret information itself in light of the market effect of the practice under consideration (whether a license or a refusal to supply) and the efficiency justification for the practice.

Each of the legal properties of trade secrets discussed above – no requirement of innovation, maintenance of secrecy and indefinite duration – can affect this competitive analysis, because these legal properties relate to the efficiency justification a trade secret holder might advance to support a restrictive or exclusionary practice. To take one example, courts assessing the pro-competitive effect of a restriction involving a trade secret should require some proof of innovation before finding that the restriction is a necessary incentive for innovation. Another example

---

209 *Cf.* Texaco Inc. v. Dagher, 547 U.S. 1, 7 (2006) (although stating that ancillary restraints are 'valid' while 'naked restraints' are not, the Court also noted that the ancillary restraints doctrine had 'no application here' because the business practice involved 'the core activity of the joint venture itself', namely, the pricing of its goods).

210 See, e.g., United States v. Microsoft Corp., 253 F.3d 34 (D.C. Cir. 2001), *cert. denied*, 534 U.S. 952 (2001); Varney, *supra* note 181 (arguing that, 'following . . . *Microsoft*', the Department of Justice should 'look closely at both the perceived procompetitive and anticompetitive aspects of a dominant firm's conduct, weigh these factors, and determine whether on balance the net effect of this conduct harms competition and consumers'). For a discussion of the possible tests, see, e.g., Section 2 Report, *supra* note 180; Antitrust Modernization Commission, Report and Recommendations 81–3 (2007), available at http://govinfo.library.unt.edu/amc/report_recommendation/amc_final_report.pdf (reaffirming the appropriateness of the rule of reason in Section 2 cases). The Commission did call for greater judicial clarity in refusal to deal cases. See id. at 83 (advocating a clearer declaration that '[i]n general, firms have no duty to deal with a rival in the same market').

would be to recognize that as a secret leaks out, so too does the efficiency gain in restricting a licensee's use of it. This means that even if a trade secret license might have been justified when entered into, as a way to allow innovators to share their technology and thereby diffuse innovation, this efficiency justification may diminish over time. Finally, even though trade secret protection can theoretically last forever, at some point society will have paid the innovator the full social value of the invention. At that point the trade secret holder might still be able to prevent misappropriation of its secret but should not be able to use the secret to continue to reap monopoly profits.

3. Respect the bargain

All intellectual property regimes have internal balances that moderate the scope of protection and help balance the trade-off between exclusion and access. In patent law, for example, the exhaustion doctrine ends the power of the patentee to control use of a product after the first lawful sale.[211] In copyright, there is a statutory exemption for fair use.[212]

Courts are often called upon to interpret these balancing doctrines within the context of the relevant intellectual property regime. There are occasions, however, when an intellectual property right holder attempts to tilt the internal balance in a way that also restricts competition, and the case gets framed as an antitrust violation rather than as an intellectual property right violation. A patent holder, for example, might transfer its product under a single use license, trying to avoid the first sale doctrine so as to have an enforceable patent right. If the conduct also gives rise to an antitrust claim, however, courts will be required to decide how to interpret the scope of the intellectual property right, so as to determine whether the purported license is really a subterfuge for anticompetitive conduct.[213]

---

[211] See Quanta Computer, Inc. v. LG Elecs., Inc., 128 S.Ct. 2109, 2117–18 (2008); Adams v. Burke, 84 U.S. 453, 455 (1873).

[212] 17 U.S.C. § 107. See Sony Corp. of America v. Universal City Studios, Inc., 464 U.S. 417, 432–3 (1984).

[213] See Mallinckrodt, Inc. v. Medipart, Inc., 976 F.2d 700, 701 (Fed. Cir. 1992) (holding that the single-use only restriction could be enforced through a patent infringement suit, the restriction being neither patent misuse nor a per se antitrust violation); First, *supra* note 13, at 386–90 (criticizing *Mallincrodt* and subsequent cases). *Compare* Straus v. Victor Talking Mach. Co., 243 U.S. 490, 501 (1917) (rejecting enforcement of 'license notice' attached to phonograph machines: 'real and poorly-concealed purpose is to restrict the [resale] price'); *Dr. Miles Med. Co.*, *supra* note 95 (describing as 'subterfuge' defendant's effort to characterize product transfers as 'consignments' rather than sales).

For trade secrets, the internal balance is spelled out in the bargain that trade secrets holders make in choosing trade secrecy over some other form of intellectual property protection. They get to exclude others from gaining unauthorized access to the protected information, and they are not required to make any showing of the innovative quality of that information, but they can't keep others from figuring out the information on their own, whether by reverse engineering or by independent invention.

As in other areas of intellectual property, courts can be required to take account of this internal balance in the context of antitrust litigation.[214] Respecting that balance, and the trade secret owner's original bargain, means that the courts should be particularly concerned about the ways in which trade secret holders try to restrict information from becoming more widely known. For example, post-employment restrictions with substantial anticompetitive effect could be narrowly confined to cases of clear breaches of fiduciary duty, thereby respecting trade secrets' internal balance of exclusion while not unduly burdening access and adversely affecting competition. Similarly, efforts to keep licensees from reverse engineering could be narrowly construed so as to be sure that the legal limitations on the scope of trade secrecy protection are maintained.

B. Applying the General Principles

1. Price and territorial license restrictions

It is time to lay to rest the dictum from *Hartman* and *Dr. Miles* that restrictions on price and territory in licenses to manufacture using a trade secret are lawful under the Sherman Act.[215] The dictum is a holdover from *Fowle v. Park* and the pre-Sherman Act days, when the question was whether such agreements were unenforceable as general restraints of trade. Later courts, however, have not closely analysed the competitive effect of these restraints, usually preferring to take refuge in the 'ancillary restraints' label rather than doing a full rule of reason analysis.[216]

Although a doctrinal argument can be made for treating these restraints as per se unlawful when they can be characterized as horizontal,[217] for

---

214 See, e.g., Bonito Boats, Inc. v. Thunder Craft Boats, Inc., 489 U.S. 141, 160 (1989) (reaffirming the right of third parties to reverse engineer products to discern their composition, even when protected by a trade secret).

215 See *supra* text accompanying notes 106–8.

216 See, e.g., Foundry Servs., Inc. v. Beneflux Corp., 110 F.Supp. 857, 857–8 (S.D.N.Y. 1953).

217 See *supra* notes 109–11and accompanying text.

illustrative purposes it is more helpful to see how these restraints might be analysed under a rule of reason approach that takes proper account of trade secrecy protection.[218] Thus, our analysis would begin with an assessment of likely anticompetitive effects and then consider the efficiency justifications that trade secret protection might raise.

Looking first at the anticompetitive effects, in many of the price and territorial licensing cases discussed above it is quite likely that the restrictive agreements raised prices. First, a number of the cases involved competitors or potential competitors, either at the time the license was first entered into (e.g., the cellophane makers in *DuPont* and the glass makers in *Pilkington*) or, at least, by the time litigation occurred (the flux makers in *Beneflux*). Second, in *Fowle v. Park*, although the original trade secret licensor was the inventor of the formula and apparently not a manufacturer, the national system of price and territorial restraints that his licensing created was designed to prevent competition between his two licensees.[219] The licensees themselves strengthened this anticompetitive outcome by making a later agreement not to compete in the West, an area to which the original agreement apparently did not extend.[220] The case thus went beyond a simple inventor/manufacturer license, which might have no impact on price competition, to involve a much broader system whose effect on price was apparent (after all, Fowle was complaining of Park's price competition).

When we examine the efficiency justifications, the analysis should start with a 'no presumption' principle for trade secrets. This means placing the burden on the trade secret holder to demonstrate efficiency justifications, rather than just relying on a presumption that the confidential information actually described the sort of innovation whose creation we might want to incentivize with monopoly profits.

The strongest of our cases for the innovativeness of the secret information appears to be *DuPont* cellophane, where the trade secrets for the manufacturing process gave La Cellophane a strong competitive

---

218 Use of a rule of reason also recognizes that trade secret licenses are often complex and raise at least a facial claim of an efficiency justification. *Cf.* Broadcast Music, Inc. v. Columbia Broad. Sys., Inc., 441 U.S. 1, 19–20 (1979) (finding that a blanket performing rights license offered by collective organizations of composers, authors, publishers and broadcasters should be viewed under the rule of reason because the blanket license 'facially' appeared to be 'designed to increase economic efficiency and render markets more, rather than less, competitive') (internal quotation marks omitted).

219 131 U.S. 88 (1889).

220 See *id.*

advantage over a struggling DuPont.[221] Weaker is *Pilkington*, a case where the patents, rather than trade secrets, were critical and where most aspects of the 'secret' process became known fairly quickly once a licensee began to manufacture float glass. Once the patents expired in *Pilkington* it was apparently difficult to make out a case for the innovativeness of the trade secrets standing alone.[222] The weakest is the formula for Wistar's Balsam of Wild Cherry in *Fowle v. Park*. The 'secret' there is the least innovative – more akin to the bartender's mix of a cocktail than to a new or non-obvious invention.[223]

The two other legal properties of trade secrets – continued secrecy and length of protection – interact in a way that will likely make the efficiency justification weaker as time goes on. That is, the longer the restriction is in place, the more likely it is that the secret has worn thin, and the less necessary it is to continue rewarding the innovator with a monopoly.

It is hard to tell from the facts of most of the cases examined above how thin the secrecy had become (*Pilkington* being the exception), but in all of the cases the competitive restrictions on price or territory had been in effect for a substantial period of time prior to being challenged. Particularly dubious in this regard is *Fowle v. Park*, where the restraints had been in effect for 40 years before Fowle brought suit.[224] Surely the need 'to encourage useful discoveries by securing their fruits to those who make them', as the Court put it in *Fowle*, had been fully satisfied by then.[225] *Beneflux* is closer to the line. The territorial restraints had been in force for 17 years when suit was brought to enforce them, coincidentally the length of the patent term at the time – a good, even if not perfect, reference point.[226] Of course, it is impossible to calibrate accurately how much reward is enough. The challenge in a rule of reason analysis will be to weigh time against innovative quality and secrecy to determine whether the justification for a

---

221 See United States v. E.I. DuPont de Nemours & Co., 118 F.Supp. 41, 53 (1951).

222 See *supra* text accompanying notes 138–9.

223 For a discussion of protecting cocktails through trade secrets, see Czapracka, *supra* note 4, at 221, nn.71–80 (discussing Mason v. Jack Daniel Distillery, 518 So. 2d 130 (Ala Civ. App. 1987) (finding that a cocktail recipe comprised of Jack Daniel's whiskey, Triple Sec, sweet and sour mix, and 7-Up was a valid trade secret)). See also KFC Corp. v. Marion-Kay Co., Inc., 620 F.Supp. 1160, 1170 (D. Ind. 1985) (finding that KFC may impose restrictions on its licensees' reproduction of its seasoning blend, protected by a trade secret).

224 See 131 U.S. at 88.

225 *Id.* at 97.

226 See Foundry Servs., Inc. v. Beneflux Corp., 110 F.Supp. 857, 857–8 (S.D.N.Y. 1953).

territorial restriction still holds, particularly when there is the less restrictive alternative of royalties without territorial allocation.[227]

The *DuPont* cellophane case presents the most interesting fact-pattern.[228] The territorial restraints in question had been in effect for 24 years at the time the Justice Department brought suit. The facts indicate that La Cellophane's process was likely innovative at the time it was licensed to DuPont; indeed, it was critical for making commercially successful cellophane. On the other hand, evidence in the record also indicates that DuPont could have figured out how to make cellophane successfully within, at most, eight years (presumably by independent invention).[229] Thus, at least for this eight-year period (in effect, La Cellophane's lead time) La Cellophane would arguably be entitled to supra-competitive returns on its process, assuming, of course, that the process was innovative. It is hard to see, however, why the parties should be allowed to continue to divide world markets beyond that time, particularly where the restraint ends up being in effect even beyond the patent term.[230]

2. Monopoly firm conduct

One of the most contested areas of antitrust law in recent years has been the question whether a monopoly firm has any duty to license to a competitor its patent or copyright in circumstances where the refusal to license would maintain a monopoly. The first chapter of the federal antitrust enforcement agencies' 2007 Intellectual Property Report, for example, was devoted to this issue, ultimately concluding that antitrust liability for 'mere unilateral, unconditional refusals to license' would not play a 'meaningful part' in antitrust enforcement regarding patent rights.[231] This view reflected the Justice Department's contemporaneous condemnation of an earlier Ninth Circuit case, which had upheld a jury verdict arising out of a

---

227 See Aronson v. Quick Point Pencil Co., 440 U.S. 257, 264–6 (1979) (allowing time-unlimited royalties for trade secrets even where the patent on the invention did not issue).

228 See *supra* notes 125–31 and accompanying text.

229 See *supra* note 128.

230 This argument is consistent with the position taken by the Justice Department in its 1977 guidelines for international operations. See GUIDE FROM THE U.S. DEPARTMENT OF JUSTICE, ANTITRUST AND INTERNATIONAL OPERATIONS 31 (1977) (parties to a territorial restraint in a know-how license that extends beyond the time that the licensee would need to develop the technology on its own 'bear the burden of proving the necessity of the restraint').

231 See Promoting Innovation, *supra* note 1, at 32.

monopolist's refusal to sell patented replacement parts to competitors in the service aftermarket.[232]

Critical to the courts' and enforcers' views in this area has been the presumption that the dominant firm's refusal to license its intellectual property right is justifiable, both as a matter of statutory construction of the Patent Act (or Copyright Act) and because of the economics of innovation.[233] In the area of trade secrets, however, there should be no such legal or economic presumption.

With regard to the legal claim, as the courts recognized in the early Sherman Act cases, there is no statutory right in the trade secrets area similar to the patentee's exclusive right to 'make, use, or sell' the patented invention.[234] The only legal right a trade secret owner has is the right to prevent others from misappropriating the secret.

Without a legal presumption that the refusal to license a trade secret is justifiable, a court would be required to examine the case for a monopolist trade secret holder's claim that the failure to supply otherwise secret information is economically efficient. Using the general principles proposed above, the analysis would first examine the innovativeness of the withheld information and then consider the duration of protection and the question of how secret the withheld information might be.

Although there have not been many antitrust cases involving a refusal to supply secret information, one area in which this issue has arisen is the refusal to disclose interface information. As a general matter, interfaces will likely have a weak claim to innovativeness. Interface information is usually critical simply because the maker of a complementary product needs to know the specifications of the interface. Whether the interface

---

232 See Image Technical Servs., Inc. v. Eastman Kodak Co., 125 F.3d 1195, 1200 (9th Cir. 1997). For enforcement views, see, e.g., R. Hewitt Pate, Assistant Attorney General U.S. Department of Justice, Competition and Intellectual Property in the U.S.: Licensing Freedom and the Limits of Antitrust, Address at the 2005 EU Competition Workshop (June 3, 2005), at 4, available at www.usdoj.gov/atr/public/speeches/209359.pdf ('the argument is that there must . . . be *some* circumstance in which the unilateral, unconditional refusal to license a patent must constitute an antitrust violation. With a single much-criticized exception [*Kodak*], this is an argument that has never found support in any U.S. legal decision. At this point in the development of U.S. law, it is safe to say that this argument is without merit').

233 See, e.g., Pate, *supra* note 232, at 4 ('A unilateral, unconditional refusal to license a valid patent cannot, by itself, result in antitrust liability under U.S. law').

234 35 U.S.C. § 271(a) (2000). It is debatable, however, whether the statutory right to exclude use precludes antitrust liability for failure to sell the product made under a patent. See Harry First, Microsoft *and the Evolution of the Intellectual Property Concept*, 2006 Wis. L. Rev. 1369, 1426.

represents some new or non-obvious invention is not what matters most, although, of course, there can be innovation in designing interfaces. The critical issue is how to plug into the monopolist's product, something that becomes important to competition by virtue of the complementary product manufacturer's dependence on the monopoly producer.

The European *Microsoft* case is a good example of a case where the interface information was important because of the dominant firm's market position rather than the innovative quality of the interface itself. In that case Microsoft's monopoly was in the PC operating system market.[235] Sun, its competitor in network server operating systems, needed interoperability information so that its work-stations could operate in a network of Microsoft PCs and servers and communicate with both.[236] In the Court of First Instance (CFI), the European Commission disputed the innovativeness of the communications protocols that Sun sought, arguing that the secret information's value 'lies not in the fact that it involves innovation but in the fact that it belongs to a dominant undertaking'.[237]

The CFI ultimately did not decide whether the interface information was innovative, choosing to uphold the Commission's decision on the assumption that it was, but the Commission faced the issue head-on in its subsequent decision involving Microsoft's lack of compliance with its order to license the information at a reasonable royalty rate.[238] The Commission determined that if the fees were to be more than nominal, the information had to be innovative in the sense that it was not 'obvious to persons skilled in the art'.[239] To make this assessment, the Commission hired technical experts to review each of the 173 non-patented protocols that Microsoft had not disclosed. The experts ultimately concluded that only seven of the protocol technologies were innovative.[240]

---

[235] See CFI *Microsoft* Decision, *supra* note 172, paras. 30–1.

[236] *Id.* paras. 2, 36.

[237] *Id.* paras. 276, 280.

[238] See *id.* para. 620.

[239] See Commission Decision of November 10, 2005, Case COMP/C-3/37.792, imposing a periodic penalty payment pursuant to Article 24(1) of Regulation 1/2003 on Microsoft Corporation (*Microsoft*) para. 105, available at http://ec.europa.eu/comm/competition/antitrust/cases/decisions/37792/art24_1_decision.pdf.

[240] See Commission Decision of February 27, 2008, Case COMP/C-3/37.792 (*Microsoft*) para. 175, n.201, available at http://ec.europa.eu/comm/competition/antitrust/cases/decisions/37792/decision2008.pdf. The Commission determined that the protocols that were patented were presumptively innovative. See *id.* para. 132. See also *id.* para. 151 (concluding that Microsoft's expert witness 'confirms the Commission's assessment that Microsoft in order to meet its product design

Similarly, in *Berkey v. Kodak* the withheld interface information would appear to have lacked much of an innovative quality.[241] Although Kodak disclosed 11 pages of specifications to Berkey relating to interoperability, the specifications only involved the size of the film cartridge and the fit in the new camera.[242] Kodak's innovation was in making a small camera with film that would produce acceptable-quality images, not in engineering the fit between the two.[243]

The fact that an interface lacks innovation, however, does not end the antitrust analysis. Two more issues remain relating to trade secrecy – time and the amount of secrecy involved. In interface cases, these issues can be difficult to assess when there is a trade-off between competition and innovation. Interfaces may not be that difficult to reverse engineer once the product is on the market (it took Berkey 18 months to do so, for example). This means that they will not stay secret for long. A modest amount of lead time may give the innovator a modest return on a modest invention, but even incremental advances can increase consumer welfare.

The optimal approach from a competition and innovation perspective would be for the monopolist to license the interface sufficiently in advance of introduction to allow the complementary producer to adapt its product. In this way the innovator would get a return on its innovation without skewing competition in the complementary product market. Given the potential administrative problems in assessing the timeliness of disclosure and reviewing the price at which it is made, however, courts are no doubt warranted in being cautious about finding liability for the failure to license interface information. Nevertheless, a per se rule of *legality* is unwarranted as well. This is particularly true in cases such as *Berkey*, where the monopolist had disclosed interfaces in the past and had even done so in the case that gave rise to the litigation, albeit in an untimely way. Further, the concern for administrability is likely overdrawn. In the settlement of the monopolization litigation against Microsoft in the United States, Microsoft has been required to license application programming interfaces ('APIs') and communications protocols.[244] The court's experience in admin-

---

goals largely relies on combinations of existing solutions and slight improvements to known approaches, which are dictated by ordinary engineering skills and common sense, rather than on innovative protocol technology').

241 603 F.2d 263 (2d Cir. 1979).

242 *Id.* at 281.

243 *Id.* at 270.

244 See Harry First and Andrew I. Gavil, *Re-Framing Windows: The Durable Meaning of the* Microsoft *Antitrust Litigation*, 2006 UTAH L. REV. 641, 693–5 (analysing the settlement decree's forward-looking requirements that Microsoft

istering the decree has been mixed; API disclosure has gone smoothly, but technical problems have plagued the protocol disclosure.[245] The *Microsoft* experience at least shows, however, that courts are unwarranted in giving carte blanche to monopolists to keep interface information secret, out of fear that remedy will prove impossible to administer.

Rule of reason analysis, especially when considered alongside our experience with administering decrees requiring disclosure, indicates that there may very well be times when a monopolist's refusal to license trade secret information should be found to violate Section 2 of the Sherman Act. Maintaining monopoly may cause serious consumer injury and retard innovation in an industry. A weakly-innovative trade secret should not be used as a justification for withholding information in such circumstances.

V. CONCLUSION

This chapter has reviewed the application of antitrust law to trade secrets. That review found more history than one might have predicted and less careful analysis than one might have hoped. Trade secrets cases raised competition issues even before the passage of the Sherman Act. Although the initial Sherman Act cases reveal a careful understanding of the legal properties of trade secret protection and a desire to limit the ability of trade secret holders to use trade secret licenses to restrict competition, once past these early cases the courts have too often fallen into a reflexive pattern of protecting trade secret holders at the expense of competition and consumer welfare.

Much of the problem with antitrust analysis of trade secrets has come from the failure to appreciate the differences between trade secret protection and other forms of intellectual property protection. As an economic matter, trade secrets are, of course, intended to provide some protection for innovations, thereby acting as an incentive for their production, but they have never been intended to provide monopoly rents. Rather, the core purpose of trade secret protection has been to protect against misappropriation and thereby promote relationships of trust. These relationships have important economic and social benefits, enabling cooperative

---

license those APIs necessary for interoperability with Windows as well as its communication protocols used to control communication between desktop PCs and servers).

[245] See *id.* at 698–704.

enterprises to succeed, but protection against misappropriation does not require giving monopoly profits to the trade secret holder.

This chapter has suggested some general principles for analysing trade secret claims in antitrust cases, the first and most important of which is to begin the analysis without presuming that the trade secret is innovative. Instead, trade secret holders would need to show that their secret is innovative and that the benefits of enforcing secrecy outweigh the costs of restricting competition. More careful analysis of the economic costs and benefits of protecting particular trade secrets should lead the courts to pay more attention to the effect of the trade secret owner's conduct, not only on consumer welfare but also on the competitive process, which, in itself, is important for stimulating innovation.

15 The troubling consequences of trade secret protection of search engine rankings

*Frank Pasquale**

> Search is the watchword of the information age. Among the many new information technologies that are reshaping work and daily life, perhaps none are more empowering than the new technologies of search . . . Whereas the steam engine, the electrical turbine, the internal combustion engine, and the jet engine propelled the industrial economy, search engines power the information economy.[1]

INTRODUCTION

Trade secrecy law has focused on promoting 'commercial ethics' in markets. One of its central goals is to avoid wasteful or unfair competition. For example, rather than triple-locking every vault or biometrically assessing the credentials of all encountered, a trade secret owner can bind employees, customers and others not to misappropriate or disclose valuable processes and products. A legal entitlement to trade secrecy cuts down the costs that would be incurred by zealous pursuit of 'real secrecy'.

Yet trade secrecy creates other costs. Some scholars have commented on secrecy as an impediment to incremental innovation, and have promoted patent rights as a better alternative. A smaller group has addressed the negative consequences of trade secrecy for society; for example, a firm might prevent health and safety regulators from adequately investigating

---

* Schering-Plough Professor in Health Care Regulation and Enforcement, Seton Hall Law School; Visiting Fellow, Princeton University's Center for Information Technology Policy. I am very grateful to participants at workshops at Fordham Law School, Loyola Law School and the Annenberg School of Communications at the University of Pennsylvania for their insightful comments on and critiques of this work, and to Stephen Gikow, Margot Kaminski, Adrienna Wong and Sonya Berenfeld for superb research assistance. Maja Basioli at the Seton Hall Law Library also provided valuable advice on sources.

[1] DAVID STARK, THE SENSE OF DISSONANCE: ACCOUNTS OF WORTH IN ECONOMIC LIFE 1 (Princeton University Press, 2009).

its practices or products by using trade secrecy protections to deflect investigations. This chapter will focus on a subset of cases where trade secrecy can undermine the public good: namely, the competitions sparked by search engine ranking. Opaque methods of ranking and rating online entities make it difficult for those who feel (and quite possibly are) wronged to press their case.

It may seem odd to characterize search results as a competition; they are often thought of as a neutral map of the Web. However, the growing 'search engine optimization' industry reveals the pressures that individuals and corporations experience as they struggle for salience in results associated with certain queries. The primacy of dominant search engines make them *de facto* sovereigns over important swathes of social life. Legal challenges to their power have emerged in some cases, and both government agencies and public interest groups have begun investigating the possibility that they are acting inconsistently with relevant law or their stated missions. But these challenges and investigations may never end conclusively given the secrecy at the core of the companies' operations.

Such secrecy has also compromised inquiries into the validity of factual determinations made by voting machines and intoxication-detection instruments. Both judicial decisions and secondary literature have investigated the degree of secrecy needed in these fields in order to balance the proprietary rights of software owners and the right of the public to know exactly how given actions have been interpreted by machines. Though voting and intoxication detection are more exact sciences than search engine ranking, proposals for the regulation of the former can help shape litigation over the latter.[2] This chapter focuses on two possible

---

[2] For a characterization of search engines as 'cultural voting machines', see Frank Pasquale, Internet Nondiscrimination Policies for Competition Online, Testimony before the U.S. House Judiciary Committee's Task Force on Competition Policy, July 15, 2008. The fact/opinion dichotomy is important in this area of law, as the owners of the ranking systems described in this chapter are almost certain to offer a First Amendment challenge to any governmental regulation of the results they provide. They will claim that intoxication detection and vote validity are factual determinations, whereas a search engine ranking is an opinion that cannot be punished or controlled by the state under current First Amendment doctrine. Though such defenses have protected entities like credit rating agencies in the past, they are coming under increasing pressure. Nathan Koppel, Andrew Edwards and Chad Bray, *Judge Limits Credit Firms' First Amendment Defense*, WALL ST. J., September 7, 2009 ('The judge said ratings are typically protected from liability and subject to an actual malice exception because their ratings are considered matters of public concern. "However, where a rating agency has disseminated their ratings to a select group of investors rather than to the public at large, the rating agency is not afforded the same protection", the

administrative solutions to the problems raised by opacity in search engine ranking methods.

First, challenged public uses of trade secret protected software have sometimes resulted in the appointment of a special master who can analyse the conduct at issue without revealing the trade secrets embedded in it. This chapter proposes an evolution of the special master from an occasional adjunct to courts to a permanent official presence at a relevant agency where its expertise is also needed. In the case of search engines, the Federal Trade Commission (FTC)'s commitment to assuring a separation between paid and editorial content can only be effectively enforced if some official entity can on occasion audit and fully understand the ranking decisions of search engines. A trusted institution in this field would help assure the integrity of online advertising, enable quicker resolution of cases that implicate trade secret protected methods, and potentially help the owners of trade secrets themselves by centralizing analysis of their methods rather than dispersing it among hundreds of individual courts and litigants. The pioneering work of David Levine and Danielle Citron, which addresses qualified transparency in the context of public institutions using proprietary and trade secret-protected methods, can be applied to some features of search engine disputes.[3] Mary Lyndon's analysis of the EPA's regulation of entities with trade secret protected products and services should also inform the actions of the FTC in the future if its consumer protection division begins auditing search engines more carefully.[4] As long as such powers exist in the background, regulation need not be administered only or even primarily by the state – as Google's StopBadware program has

---

judge said'). The limited dissemination of personalized search rankings is similar to the situation in that case. For a fuller discussion of personalized search, see Frank Pasquale, *Reputation Regulation*, in THE OFFENSIVE INTERNET: SPEECH, PRIVACY, AND REPUTATION (Martha Nussbaum and Saul Levmore eds., Harvard University Press, 2010).

[3] David Levine, *Trade Secrets in Our Public Infrastructure*, 59 FLA. L. REV. 135 (2007); Danielle Keats Citron, *Technological Due Process*, 85 WASH. U. L.R. 1249 (2008). For a general jurisprudential account of the value of transparency in decisions that have the effect of law, see Christopher Kutz, *Law and the Value of Publicity*, 22(2) RATIO JURIS 197 (2009).

[4] Mary L. Lyndon, *Information Economics and Chemical Toxicity: Designing Laws to Produce and Use Data*, 87 MICH. L. REV. 1795 (1989); see also Dennis Hirsch on the environmental metaphor applying to privacy theory generally, given the pervasiveness of surveillance-based business models with pervasive externalities. Hirsch, *Protecting the Inner Environment*, 41 GEORGIA L. REV. 1 (2006). The need for expertise, and extensive externalities, make regulatory models particularly relevant here, though trusted non-governmental standards bodies might offer a 'third way' between market and state.

already proven, a creative intermediary can partner with NGOs to provide 'rough justice' to sites that feel they have been treated unfairly.[5] Trusted institutions can provide both policy-makers and courts with information essential to the resolution of search-centered disputes.

To the extent that search engines resist such scrutiny, governments should consider establishing public alternatives to them. Here, lessons from recent debates over health insurance may be instructive. There are structural parallels between the intermediary role of private health insurers (which stand as a gatekeeper between patients and providers of health products and services) and that of search engines (which stand between searchers and providers of information). As the United States debates health reform, there is a tension between regulation-focused approaches (which would require revelation and alteration of private insurers' unfair practices) and a public option that would compete with existing insurers. A public option in search could play a role in search parallel to the role that Medicare plays in the health system: guaranteeing some baseline of transparency in pricing and evaluation.

I. SEARCH, SECRECY AND ACCOUNTABILITY

Many worry about search engines' growing power.[6] How are worldviews being biased by them?[7] Do search engines have an interest in getting

---

[5] JONATHAN ZITTRAIN, THE FUTURE OF THE INTERNET AND HOW TO STOP IT (Yale Press, 2008) (describing how sites tagged by Google's bots as harboring malware can appeal the decision to an NGO). The FTC already works with NGOs to increase the efficiency and fairness of dispute resolution. For example, the National Advertising Division of the Council of Better Business Bureaus vets the claims of advertisers, and in most cases it is able to pressure misleading ads off the air. See Seth Stevenson, *How New is 'New'? How Improved is 'Improved'?: The People Who Keep Advertisers Honest*, Slate.com, July 13, 2009, available at www.slate.com/id/2221968/. ('The rule is that the advertiser must have substantiated any claims before the ad was put on the air, so the NAD will first ask for any substantiating materials the advertiser can provide. If the NAD lawyers determine that the claims aren't valid, they'll recommend that the ad be altered. The compliance rate on this is more than 95 percent. But if the advertiser refuses to modify the ad (this is a voluntary, self-regulating body, not a court of law), the NAD will refer the matter to the Federal Trade Commission').

[6] See Andrew Sullivan, *The Black Box of Google*, Andrew Sullivan's The Daily Dish Blog, http://andrewsullivan.theatlantic.com/the_daily_dish/2008/12/bizarro-google.html (December 1, 2008 15:26 EST) (citing Jeffrey Rosen and Frank Pasquale).

[7] Consider Philipp Lenssen, *Google's Opinion Operator, Circa 2009*, Google

certain information prioritized or occluded?[8] A recent news article on Baidu illuminates how an unscrupulous search engine can exert a great deal of power once it attains dominance. Baidu has over 60 percent of the market in China, and can make or break an online business. Some allege that Baidu uses that power to force businesses to buy prominence on its results:

> Salespeople working for Baidu drop sites from results to bully companies into buying sponsored links [a form of paid advertising], say some who have been approached. Former clients say their rankings fall precipitously after they stop buying search-related ads from Baidu. At least one Baidu salesperson acknowledges they're right. 'The key is whether a company buys Baidu's sponsored links', says Zhong Hongjun, a salesman from a company that represents Baidu in the central city of Wuhan. 'If they don't, the search engine won't find them. If they do, they'll be in there'.[9]

These may seem like speculative worries in the United States, where Google's 'Don't Be Evil' motto translates into public assurances that the company would never do such a thing to the entities it indexes. However, there have been several notable disputes about the company's ranking policies, and at least two have been litigated in cases resulting in published opinions.[10] A book on Google by John Battelle gives some concrete examples of complaints from those disgruntled with low or falling rankings.[11]

Blogoscoped Blog, http://blogoscoped.com/archive/2006-09-21-n55.html (September 21, 2006); see Frank Pasquale on Google's leading 'net neutrality' results in *Internet Nondiscrimination Principles*, U. CHI. L. FORUM (2008).

[8] ALEX HALAVAIS, SEARCH ENGINE SOCIETY 85 (2008) ('In the process of ranking results, search engines effectively create winners and losers on the web as a whole. Now that search engines are moving into other realms, this often opaque technology of ranking becomes kingmaker in new venues'); see Posting of Aaron Greenspan, *Why I Sued Google and Won*, The Huffington Post, March 6, 2009, www.huffingtonpost.com/aaron-greenspan/why-i-sued-google-and-won_b_172403.html (March 6, 2009) (discussing a small claims court case regarding AdSense and a request for Google's policies to be more transparent).

[9] See Chi-Chu Tschang, *The Squeeze at China's Baidu*, BUSINESSWEEK, 2009, available at www.businessweek.com/magazine/content/09_02/b4115021710265.htm.

[10] *Kinderstart; SearchKing*. For a discussion of these cases, see Oren Bracha and Frank Pasquale, *Federal Search Commission: Access, Fairness and Accountability in the Law of Search*, 93 CORNELL L. REV. 1149, 1151 (2008); Frank Pasquale, *Asterisk Revisited: Debating a Right of Reply on Search Results*, 3 J. BUS. & TECH. L., 61, 69 (2008).

[11] See John Battelle, *The Search: How Google and Its Rivals Rewrote the Rules of Business and Transformed Our Culture* (New York Pub., 2005) (available for

The secrecy of search ranking algorithms has made full, conclusive and informative resolution of such disputes impossible.[12]

Neither markets nor common law are likely to hold search engines accountable under present circumstances. Oftentimes these intermediaries operate at the hub of multisided markets. For example, in a given situation where a Yahoo user is searching for flowers nearby, Yahoo's search engine might block one florist for illicit 'search engine manipulation' (as defined by a trade secret protected algorithm), but still deliver several relevant results. The searcher is unlikely ever to know of the blockage, and advertisers that benefit from increased custom may be pleased by it. Though early search engine prototypes that rested entirely on paid ads were quickly routed by more objective sources of information, few are likely to detect or mind subtle manipulation now. Given the trend toward dynamically personalized search results, it is hard to imagine how one-off monitoring could effectively detect untoward conduct here.

The legitimate reasons for search engines' general emphasis on keeping ranking algorithms confidential throw some light on the divergent rationales for adopting patent or trade secrecy protection for any given instance of intellectual property. While Google's foundational technology in search (the PageRank method) is patented, its continual tweaking of search is usually not.[13] Keeping the search algorithm private is the key to defeating

---

purchase at www.amazon.com/Search-Rewrote-Business-Transformed-Culture/dp/1591840880).

[12] Many complaints come from pseudonymous accounts, due both to Web norms and possibly because of fear of retaliation. See, e.g., Jan_Jaap, *Google So Unfair and Unstable*!, www.webmasterworld.com/google_adwords/3085690.htm (posted on September 16, 2006) (last visited February 10, 2011) (complaining about AdWords pricing and asking for greater transparency due to large price fluctuations); see Kewlguy, *Google Cancelled my Adsense Account*, www.gidforums.com/t-6174.html (posted June 27, 2005); see Allanp73, *Google's Unfair Discrimination*, www.webmasterworld.com/forum3/12654.htm (posted May 7, 2003) (complaining that a Canadian business cannot compete with an American business in an American market (in violation of the Canada – United States Free Trade Agreement) because Google ranks differently depending on what region you're searching from); see Seldo.com, *Google Knol is Evil*, http://seldo.com/weblog/2008/07/28/google_knol_is_evil (posted July 28, 2008) (complaining that PageRank is favoring Google Knol despite inferior content); see Aaron Wall, *Google Caught Selling High PageRank Links, Again & Again*, www.seobook.com/archives/002403.shtml (posted August 2008).

[13] See Bill Slawski, *Pagerank Patent Updated*, www.seobythesea.com/?p=207 (posted June 6, 2006) (last visited February 10, 2011) (discussing the updated Pagerank Patent); Bill Slawski, *Google Patents*, www.seobythesea.com/?p=1138 (posted on October 24, 2008) (last visited July 4, 2008) (last updated March 4, 2009) (categorizing and listing the 187 patents owned by Google at

gamers who might propagate link farms or other disfavored methods to gain salience in search results.[14]

Given the opacity guaranteed by trade secrecy protections, it is difficult to speak with certainty about exactly how search engines order organic (i.e., non-paid) results.[15] The number of pages linking to a given page is important, as is the number of pages linking to the linking pages, recursively. But there are also several incidental indicators of a page's relevance (and relevance-granting authority), such as its policies on selling links, its age and the frequency of fresh content on it. Search engine optimizers (SEOs) are in business to assure that those qualities are enhanced (or appear to search engines' crawlers to be enhanced) so as to increase the salience of a webpage.

Search engineers tend to divide the SEO business into 'good guys' and 'bad guys', often calling the former 'white hat SEO' and the latter 'black hat SEO'.[16] Some degree of transparency regarding the search engine's algorithm is required in order to permit white hat SEO, and these rules

---

that time); Saul Hansell, *Google Keeps Tweaking its Search Engine*, NEW YORK TIMES, available at www.nytimes.com/2007/06/03/business/yourmoney/03google.html ('[Amit] Singhal is the master of what Google calls its "ranking algorithm" – the formulas that decide which Web pages best answer each user's question. It is a crucial part of Google's inner sanctum, a department called "search quality" that the company treats like a state secret. Google rarely allows outsiders to visit the unit, and it has been cautious about allowing Mr. Singhal to speak with the news media about the magical, mathematical brew inside the millions of black boxes that power its search engine').

[14] See James Grimmelmann, *The Structure of Search Engine Law*, 93 IOWA L. REV. 1 (2007).

[15] *Id.* (The 'system for ranking pages . . . involves more than 200 types of information, or what Google calls "signals". PageRank is but one signal. Some signals are on Web pages – like words, links, images and so on. Some are drawn from the history of how pages have changed over time. Some signals are data patterns uncovered in the trillions of searches that Google has handled over the years').

[16] See Elizabeth van Couvering, *Is Relevance Relevant?*, http://jcmc.indiana.edu/vol12/issue3/vancouvering.html (search engineers' 'animosity towards the . . . guerilla fighters of spamming and hacking, is more direct' than their hostility toward direct business competitors); see Posting of Aaron Wall to SEOBook, *Google Thinks YOU are a Black Hat SEO. Should You Trust Them?*, www.seobook.com/to-google-you-are-a-spammer (April 17, 2008) (claiming that Google discriminates against self-identified SEOs); Posting by Duncan Riley on TechCrunch, *Google Declares Jihad on Blog Link Farms*, www.techcrunch.com/2007/10/24/google-declares-jihad-on-blog-link-farms/ (October 24, 2007); Rand Fishkin, *Paid Links – Can't be a White Hat With 'em, Can't Rank Without 'em*, www.seomoz.org/blog/paid-links-can-you-rank-well-without-them (posted July 10, 2007) (last visited February 10, 2011) (due to the relationship between SEO and Google, it

are generally agreed upon as practices that 'make the Web better'; i.e., have fresh content, don't sell links, don't 'stuff metatags' with extraneous information just to get attention. However, if there were complete transparency, 'black hat' SEOs could elevate the importance of their clients' sites – and even if this were only done temporarily, the resulting churn and chaos could severely reduce the utility of search results. (On a more mundane level, this is a good reason for getting a new email account every few years; as an address leaks out to more and more spammers, it attracts more junk mail.) Moreover, a search engine's competitors could use the trade secrets to enhance its own services.

This secrecy has led to a growing gray zone of Internet practices with uncertain effect on sites' rankings. Consider some of the distinctions shown in Table 15.1, based on current literature on search engine optimization.

As these practices show, search engines are referees in the millions of contests for attention that take place on the Web each day. There are hundreds of entities that want to be the top result in response to a query like 'sneakers', 'top restaurant in New York City', or 'best employer to work for'. Any academic who writes on an obscure subject wants to be the 'go-to' authority when it is googled – and for consultants, a top or tenth-ranked result could be the difference between lucrative gigs and obscurity. The top and right hand sides of many search engine pages are open for paid placement; but even there the highest bidder may not get a prime spot because a good search engine strives to keep even these sections very relevant to searchers.[17] The organic results are determined by search engines' proprietary algorithms, and preliminary evidence indicates that searchers (and particularly educated searchers) concentrate attention there. Businesses can grow reliant on good Google rankings as a way of attracting and keeping customers.

---

makes sense for an SEO to use paid links, and it also makes sense for Google to try and filter them out).

[17] Steven Levy, *Secret of Googlenomics: Data-Fueled Recipe Brews Profitability*, Wired, www.wired.com/culture/culturereviews/magazine/17-06/nep_googlenomics (May 22, 2009) (in the AdWords program, advertisers' 'bids themselves are only a part of what ultimately determines the auction winners. The other major determinant is something called the quality score. This metric strives to ensure that the ads Google shows on its results page are true, high-caliber matches for what users are querying. If they aren't, the whole system suffers and Google makes less money'); see also Google, *What is the Quality Score and How is it Calculated*, http://adwords.google.com/support/aw/bin/answer.py?hl=en&answer=10215 (last visited February 10, 2011) ('The AdWords system works best for everybody – advertisers, users, publishers, and Google too – when the ads we display match our users' needs as closely as possible').

Table 15.1 *Acceptable, unacceptable and gray area practices in search engine optimization*

White hat (acceptable)[a]	*Gray area (unclear how these are treated)*[b]	*Black hat (unacceptable; can lead to down-ranking in Google results or even the 'Google Death Penalty' of De-indexing)*
Asking blogs you like to link to you, or engaging in reciprocal linking between your site and other sites in a legitimate dialogue.[c]	Paying a blogger or site to link to your blog in order to boost search results and not just to increase traffic.	Creating a 'link farm' of spam blogs (splogs) to link to you, or linking between multiple sites you created (known as link farms) to boost search results.[d]
Running human-conducted tests of search inquiries with permission from the search engine.	Doing a few queries to do elementary reverse engineering. (This may not be permitted under the terms of service).	Using computer programs to send automated search queries to gauge the page rank generated from various search terms (terms of service prohibit this).[e]
Creating non-intentional duplicate content (through printer-friendly versions, pages aimed at mobile devices, etc.)[f]	Intentionally creating permitted duplicate content to boost search results.	Intentionally creating unnecessary duplicate content on many pages and domains to boost results.
Generating a coherent site with original and informative material aimed at the user.	Creating content or additional pages that walk the line between useful information and 'doorway pages'.	Creating 'doorway pages' that are geared towards popular keywords but that redirect to a largely unrelated main site.[g]
Targeting appreciative audience.[h]	Putting random references to salacious or celebrity topics on a blog primarily devoted to discussing current affairs.[i]	Distracting involuntary audience with completely misleading indexed content (akin to 'initial interest confusion' in Internet trademark law).[j]
Influencing search engine by making pages easier to scan by automated bots.[k]	Creating 'hidden pages' when there may be a logical reason to show one page to search engine bots and another page to users who type in the page's URL.	Using 'hidden pages' to show a misleading page to search engine bots scanning a page, and another page to users who type in the page's URL.

Table 15.1 (continued)

Notes:

[a] See Phil Craven, 'Ethical' Search Engine Optimization Exposed!, www.webworkshop.net/ethical-search-engine-optimization.html (last visited February 10, 2011).

[b] Grey Hat SEO, http://greyhatseo.com/ (last visited February 10, 2011) (claiming a Grey Hat SEO is someone who uses black hat techniques in an ethical way).

[c] Webmaster Guidelines: Quality Guidelines – Specific guidelines, www.google.com/support/webmasters/bin/answer.py?answer=35769 (last visited February 10, 2011) ('The best way to get other sites to create relevant links to yours is to create unique, relevant content that can quickly gain popularity in the Internet community. The more useful content you have, the greater the chances someone else will find that content valuable to their readers and link to it').

[d] Posting by Duncan Riley on TechCrunch, *Google Declares Jihad on Blog Link Farms*, www.techcrunch.com/2007/10/24/google-declares-jihad-on-blog-link-farms/ (October 24, 2007).

[e] Webmaster Guidelines: Quality Guidelines – Specific Guidelines, www.google.com/support/webmasters/bin/answer.py?answer=35769 ('Google's Terms of Service do not allow the sending of automated queries of any sort to our system without express permission in advance from Google'); Google Terms of Service: Use of the Services by You, www.google.com/accounts/TOS (last visited February 10, 2011) ('You agree not to access (or attempt to access) any of the Services by any means other than through the interface that is provided by Google, unless you have been specifically allowed to do so in a separate agreement with Google').

[f] Webmaster Guidelines: Quality Guidelines – Specific Guidelines, www.google.com/support/webmasters/bin/answer.py?answer=35769 (last visited February 10, 2011) ('Examples of non-malicious duplicate content could include: Discussion forums that can generate both regular and stripped-down pages targeted at mobile devices, Store items shown or linked via multiple distinct URLs, Printer-only versions of web pages').

[g] Posting on Google Blogoscoped, *German BMW Banned from Google*, http://blogoscoped.com/archive/2006-02-04-n60.html (February 4, 2006); Posting by Matt Cutts on Matt Cutts: Gadgets, Google, and SEO, *Ramping Up on International Webspam*, www.mattcutts.com/blog/ramping-up-on-international-webspam/ (February 4, 2006) (Google employee confirming BMW's ban).

[h] Webmaster Guidelines: Design and Content Guidelines, www.google.com/support/webmasters/bin/answer.py?answer=35769 (last visited February 10, 2011) ('Think about the words users would type to find your pages, and make sure that your site actually includes those words within it').

[i] Daniel Solove, *Thanks, Jennifer Aniston (or the Manifold Ways to Do the Same Search)*, Posting at Concurring Opinions, www.concurringopinions.com/archives/2006/01/thanks_jennifer.html ('One of my more popular posts is one entitled *Jennifer Aniston Nude Photos and the Anti-Paparazzi Act*. It seems to be getting a lot of readers interested in learning about the workings of the Anti-Paparazzi Act and the law of information privacy. It sure is surprising that so many readers are eager to understand this rather technical statute. Anyway, for the small part that Jennifer Aniston plays in this, we thank her for the traffic'); Dan Filler, *Coffee or Nude Celebrity Photos: A Tale of Two Evergreen Posts*, www.thefacultylounge.org/2008/04/coffee-or-nude.html ('significant amounts of traffic arrived in the form of web surfers seeking out pictures of Jennifer Aniston').

[j] Posting of Jason Preston to Blog Business Summit, *Google Punishes Squidoo for Having Too Much Spam*, http://blogbusinesssummit.com/2007/07/google-punishes-squidoo-for-having-too-much-spam.htm (July 11, 2007).

[k] Webmaster Guidelines: Design and Content Guidelines, www.google.com/support/webmasters/bin/answer.py?answer=35769 (last visited February 10, 2011) ('Create a

Table 15.1 (continued)

useful, information-rich site, and write pages that clearly and accurately describe your content'); Webmaster Guidelines: Design and Content Guidelines, www.google.com/support/webmasters/bin/answer.py?answer=35769 ('Try to use text instead of images to display important names, content, or links. The Google crawler doesn't recognize text contained in images'); Webmaster Guidelines: Technical Guidelines, www.google.com/support/webmasters/bin/answer.py?answer=35769.

For example, John Battelle tells the story of the owner of 2bigfeet.com (a seller of large-sized men's shoes), whose site was knocked off the first page of Google's results for terms like 'big shoes' by a sudden algorithm shift in November 2003, right before the Christmas shopping season. Neil Moncrief attempted to contact Google several times, but said he 'never got a response'. Google claimed that Moncrief may have hired a search engine optimizer who ran afoul of its rules – but it would not say precisely what those rules were.[18] Like the IRS's unwillingness to disclose all of its 'audit flags', the company did not want to permit manipulators to gain too great an understanding of how it detected their tactics.

So far claims like Moncrief's have not been fully examined in the judicial system, largely because Google has successfully deflected them by claiming that its search results embody opinions protected by the First Amendment. Several articles have questioned whether blanket First Amendment protection covers all search engine actions, and that conclusion has not yet been embraced on the appellate level in the United States.[19] The FTC's

[18] BATTELLE, *supra* note 11. See also Joe Nocera, *Stuck in Google's Doghouse*, NEW YORK TIMES, September 13, 2008 ('In the summer of 2006 . . . Google pulled the rug out from under [web business owner Dan Savage, who had come to rely on its referrals to his page, Sourcetool] . . . When Mr. Savage asked Google executives what the problem was, he was told that Sourcetool's 'landing page quality' was low. Google had recently changed the algorithm for choosing advertisements for prominent positions on Google search pages, and Mr. Savage's site had been identified as one that didn't meet the algorithm's new standards . . . Although the company never told Mr. Savage what, precisely, was wrong with his landing page quality, it offered some suggestions for improvement, including running fewer AdSense ads and manually typing in the addresses and phone numbers of the 600,000 companies in his directory, even though their Web sites were just a click away. At a cost of several hundred thousand dollars, he made some of the changes Google suggested. No improvement'). Savage has now filed suit against Google on an antitrust theory. Tradecomet.com, LLC v. Google, Inc., 693 F.Supp.2d 370 (S.D.N.Y. 2010) (district court granted Google's motion to dismiss complaint for improper venue because of a forum selection clause in the parties' advertising contract).

[19] Frank Pasquale, *Rankings, Reductionism, and Responsibility*, 54 CLEVELAND ST. L. REV. 115, 125 (2006); Bracha and Pasquale, *supra* note 10; Jennifer A.

guidance to search engines promoting the clear separation of organic and paid results suggests that search engines' First Amendment shield is not insurmountable here.[20] While a creative or opportunistic litigant could conceivably advance a First Amendment right to promote products or positions without indicating that the promotion has been paid for, such a challenge has not yet eliminated false advertising law, and even political speakers have been required to reveal their funding sources.[21]

II. CULTIVATING AGENCY EXPERTISE ON SEARCH ENGINE PRACTICES

The FTC has long engaged in regulation of online advertising. Almost a decade ago, the agency claimed that '[t]he same consumer protection laws that apply to commercial activities in other media apply online. The FTC Act's prohibition on unfair or deceptive acts or practices encompasses Internet advertising, marketing and sales'.[22] This agency commitment requires a good deal from all purveyors of online ads, including search engines. They must assure that paid content's identity is 'clear and conspicuous'.[23] The agency has offered guidelines for mitigating consumer

---

Chandler, *A Right to Reach an Audience: An Approach to Intermediary Bias on the Internet*, 35 HOFSTRA L. REV. 1095, 1109 (2007).

20 See Bracha and Pasquale, *supra* note 10 (discussing the implications of Ellen Goodman's work on 'stealth marketing' for search engines, and how the Hippsley Letter of 2002 inadequately addressed such concerns in the industry).

21 In early cases alleging an array of unfair competition and business torts claims against search engines, the First Amendment has proven a formidable shield against liability. Search engines characterize their results as opinion, and lower courts have been reluctant to penalize them for these forms of expression. In other work, I have described why this First Amendment barrier to accountability should not be insurmountable. Search engines take advantage of a web of governmental immunities that they would be loath to surrender. FAIR v. Rumsfeld and cognate cases stand for the proposition that such immunities can be conditioned on agreement to certain conditions on an entity's speech. Whatever the federal governments will, it is within its power to regulate ranking and rating entities in some way when they are so deeply dependent on governmental action. Frank Pasquale, *Asterisk Revisited*, 3 J. BUS. & TECH. L. 61, 69 (2008).

22 Federal Trade Commission, *Dot Com Disclosures: Information About Online Advertising* (May 2000) at 1 (available at www.ftc.gov/bcp/edu/pubs/business/ecommerce/bus41.pdf) ('[d]isclosures that are required to prevent an ad from being misleading, to ensure that consumers receive material information about the terms of a transaction or to further public policy goals, must be clear and conspicuous').

23 *Id.*

confusion, including the suggestion that 'advertisers should . . . [p]lace disclosures near, and when possible, on the same screen as the triggering claim [and u]se text or visual cues to encourage consumers to scroll down a Web page when it is necessary to view a disclosure'.[24]

In order for the FTC to determine whether its guidance is actually being followed, it will need to develop sophisticated methods of understanding how organic results are determined. Without such an understanding, it will be impossible to distinguish between paid and organic content. This monitoring needs to happen in real time, rather than after a dispute arises, for many reasons. First, data retention may be spotty. Second, the history of regulation of high technology industries indicates that government lag in understanding how critical infrastructure functions can effectively neuter even a strong regulatory regime. Just as Danny Weitzner has called for an 'independent panel of technical, legal and business experts to help [the FTC] review, on an ongoing basis, the privacy practices of Google',[25] the agency needs to develop the capacity for understanding the search ranking practices of Google and its competitors. This capacity could, in turn, enable litigants to submit focused queries to a non-biased third party that could quickly give critical information to courts now mired in discovery disputes in search-related lawsuits.[26]

---

[24] *Id.* With regard to hyperlinks that 'lead to disclosures', the link should be 'obvious', appropriately labeled and well-situated. *Id.* at 1–2. In general, site operators should '[p]rominently display disclosures so they are noticeable to consumers, and evaluate the size, color and graphic treatment of the disclosure in relation to other parts of the Web page'. *Id.* at 2.

[25] At http://people.w3.org/~djweitzner/blog/?p=95 ('In the 1990s, the FTC under Christine Varney's leadership pushed operators of commercial websites to post policies stating how they handle personal information. That was an innovative idea at the time, but the power of personal information processing has swamped the ability of a static statement to capture the privacy impact of sophisticated services, and the level of generality at which these policies tend to be written often obscure the real privacy impact of the practices described. It's time for regulators to take the next step and assure that both individuals and policy makers have information they need').

[26] But see David S. Levine's skepticism about such state-sponsored trusted entities, given the experience of those challenging Diebold in North Carolina. David S. Levine, *Secrecy and Unaccountability: Trade Secrets in Our Public Infrastructure*, 59 FLORIDA L. REV. 135, 183 (2007) ('the notion that a government-controlled or designated entity could adequately protect the interests of the general public is dubious, and would turn on many variables that might undermine the third party's ability to operate in a completely public-oriented fashion. Indeed, where a state agency effectively nullifies a law designed to protect the public's interest, the entire basis upon which an escrow regime would be built – that is, trusting the entity charged with examining the escrowed material – is undermined. Thus,

Some recent cases have demonstrated the weakness of the normal protective order process in litigation involving search engines' trade secrets. In *Viacom v. YouTube*, the plaintiff's claim that YouTube could more effectively filter allegedly infringing videos depended on its discovering the nature and extent of the sorting done by the defendant. The court decided that Viacom did not deserve access to the relevant source code, even under a protective order:

> Plaintiffs seek production of the search code to support their claim that 'Defendants have purposefully designed or modified the tool to facilitate the location of infringing content'. However, the predicate for that proposition is that the 'tool' treats infringing material differently from innocent material, and plaintiffs offer no evidence that the search function can discriminate between infringing and non-infringing videos . . .
>
> Plaintiffs argue that the best way to determine whether those denials are true is to compel production and examination of the search code. Nevertheless, YouTube and Google should not be made to place this vital asset in hazard merely to allay speculation. A plausible showing that YouTube and Google's denials are false, and that the search function can and has been used to discriminate in favor of infringing content, should be required before disclosure of so valuable and vulnerable an asset is compelled.[27]

Like the court here, many writers have recognized Google's innovation.[28] The company rolls out new, free services regularly, and the design elegance of Gmail or the engineering acumen evident in its Chrome web browser is easy to grasp.[29] Yet the core of Google's business model is its

---

it is not readily apparent that a third-party (governmental or otherwise) might adequately protect the general interests of the public').

27 Viacom Intern. Inc. v. YouTube Inc., 253 F.R.D. 256 (S.D.N.Y. 2008); see also Ray v. Allied Chem. Corp., 34 F.R.D. 456, 457 (S.D.N.Y. 1964) ('The end result of disclosure, where ultimately it develops that the asserted claim is without substance, may be so destructive of the interests of the prevailing party that more is required than mere allegation to warrant pretrial disclosure').

28 Note Jeff Jarvis's comparison of Google with Jesus in the book title 'What Would Google Do?'. For a more skeptical view, see Frank Pasquale, *Sources of Google's Success*, www.concurringopinions.com/archives/2008/01/sources_of_goog.html ('the more I study the search market, the more I see fortuitous legal and regulatory decisions paving the way to Google's success. Perhaps its technology in search was and is better than any search engine competitor. But its uniquely dominant place in the internet ecology could have been snuffed out at many points over the past 10 years' by alternative developments in key legal doctrines of copyright and communications law).

29 See Tim Anderson, *Chrome: A New Force for Web Applications*, www.theregister.co.uk/2008/09/04/chrome_review/ ('This is not just a browser: it is a vehicle for delivering web applications, and it significantly changes the balance of power between those trying to build modern client platforms'); Scott McCloud,

search engine, and no one outside the company truly understands how that works. The company prides itself on keeping its algorithms confidential, and trade secrecy law has helped it defeat or limit even governmental requests for more data on how it operates.[30] Thus, Viacom was put in a 'Catch 22',[31] unable to make a plausible showing about the nature of 'search function' given its inability to access information about it.[32] Theoretically, it could guess at what could be done here, and subsequently algorithms could be disclosed in a protective order.[33] But even in that best-case scenario, it is hard to imagine a court with the institutional competence to understand whether a given set of results has been manipulated or not. Search engine algorithms are enormously complex, and sometimes embody artificial intelligence that even their inventors have a difficult time fully understanding.[34]

The Google Chrome Comic, www.scottmccloud.com/googlechrome/index.html; but see Team Register, *Google's Comic Capers: What They Really Meant to Say*, www.theregister.co.uk/2008/09/02/google_chrome_comic_funnies/.

[30] Gonzales v. Google, Inc., 234 F.R.D. 674 (2006) ('As trade secret or confidential business information, Google's production of a [limited] list of URLs to the Government shall be protected by protective order. Generally, the selective disclosure of protectable trade secrets is not per se "unreasonable and oppressive", when appropriate protective measures are imposed').

[31] Other courts have been more sympathetic to plaintiffs in such a dilemma. See Michrotech International, Inc. v. Fair, 1992 WL 239087 (Conn. Super. Ct. 1992) ('Both of these proposed protective orders disregard the fact that in order for the plaintiff to demonstrate any wrongdoing on the part of the defendant, the plaintiff must first discover the very information which the defendant seeks to preclude').

[32] Compare a similar result in voting machine litigation in Florida in 2006–7. Jessica Ring Amunson and Sam Hirsch, *The Case of the Disappearing Votes: Lessons from the Jennings v. Buchanan Congressional Election Contest*, 17 WM. & MARY BILL OF RTS. J. 397, 398 (2008) ('the litigation ultimately was utterly inconclusive as to the reason for the 18,000 electronic undervotes because discovery targeting the defective voting system was thwarted when the voting machines' manufacturer successfully invoked the trade-secret privilege to block any investigation of the machines or their software by the litigants').

[33] According to Federal Rules of Civil Procedure (FRCP) 26(c)(1), protective orders may be issued in the discovery process 'for good cause' in order 'to protect a party or person from annoyance, embarrassment, oppression, or undue burden or expense'. FRCP 26(c)(1)(G) specifies the issuance of a protective order to structure the discovery of trade secrets: orders may be issued 'requiring that a trade secret or other confidential research, development, or commercial information not be revealed or be revealed only in a specified way'. For a general discussion of trade secrets and protective orders, see MELVIN F. JAGER, TRADE SECRETS LAW § 5:33 (updated in September 2008).

[34] The difference between explanation and understanding is key here. See G.H.

Commercial disputes like the ones mentioned above are only the tip of an iceberg of political and cultural clashes that will likely arise over search engine rankings. Consider some Republicans' fears that Google, a culturally liberal company,[35] is skewing search results to favor Barack Obama and marginalize the right.[36] Fox News has reported conservative discontent at Google's rapid response to manipulated search results related to Barack Obama, after its glacial efforts to defuse a 'google bomb' aimed at George W. Bush.[37] There are many good reasons for the difference in treatment; nevertheless, political google-bombing merits some attention. Campaigns are a struggle for salience, a competition with considerable stakes.[38] As more people form an image of candidates from search results

---

von Wright, Explanation and Understanding (2004) (distinguishing natural and human sciences); Chris Anderson, *The End of Theory: The Data Deluge Makes the Scientific Method Obsolete*, Wired, June 23, 2008, www.wired.com/science/discoveries/magazine/16-07/pb_theory ('At the petabyte scale, information is not a matter of simple three- and four-dimensional taxonomy and order but of dimensionally agnostic statistics. It calls for an entirely different approach, one that requires us to lose the tether of data as something that can be visualized in its totality. It forces us to view data mathematically first and establish a context for it later . . . Google's founding philosophy is that we don't know why this page is better than that one: If the statistics of incoming links say it is, that's good enough. No semantic or causal analysis is required. That's why Google can translate languages without actually 'knowing' them (given equal corpus data, Google can translate Klingon into Farsi as easily as it can translate French into German)'); Jaron Lanier, *One Half of a Manifesto*, Edge, www.edge.org/documents/archive/edge74.html ('There is a real chance that . . . the ideology of cybernetic totalist intellectuals will be amplified from novelty into a force that could cause suffering for millions of people').

[35] See, e.g., Sergey Brin, *Our Position on California's No on 8 Campaign*, Official Google Blog, http://googleblog.blogspot.com/2008/09/our-position-on-californias-no-on-8.html (September 26, 2008 15:23 EST).

[36] See Michelle Malkin, *Google News: Not So Fair and Balanced*, Michelle Malkin Blog, http://michellemalkin.com/2005/02/05/google-news-not-so-fair-and-balanced/ (February 5, 2005 18:49 EST).

[37] Joshua Rhett Miller, *Unlike Bush's 'Google Bomb', Google Quickly Defuses Obama's*, FoxNews.com, www.foxnews.com/story/0,2933,485632,00.html (January 30, 2009). See also *Discussion about 'Google Quickly Defuses Obama's Google Bomb'*, Technorati Blog, http://technorati.com/articles/vsKqmOgmb%2BC8VmxIBNkko3mR%2BthIfUvxxs824v1MxDc%3D?sub=Zp4RPNF9ImpoHvEWipOIDONWcXFUCDVoyvhSeb04XR0%3D (January 30, 2009).

[38] I collect literature on the 'struggle for salience' model of campaigning in *Reclaiming Egalitarianism in the Political Theory of Campaign Finance Reform,* 2008 Ill. L. Rev. 599, 644 (2008) ('Utilizing statistical evidence from several campaigns, John Petrocik concludes that, to candidates, "the campaign [is] a marketing effort in which the goal is to achieve a strategic advantage by making problems that reflect owned issues the criteria by which voters make their choice"'); see

(or related Google properties like YouTube), we might worry that allegedly neutral, algorithmic representations of authority and popularity are really being influenced by a hidden agenda.[39]

Compare these dilemmas to those posed by national security law – another area where we struggle to balance the values of openness and confidentiality.[40] Just as the FISA Court has the right to review even sensitive national security data to assure the rule of law, an analogous institution should be developed to enable regulators at the FTC or FCC to comprehend how dominant search engines' algorithms are developing – and to detect untoward manipulation.

A trusted advisory committee within the FTC could help courts and agencies adjudicate coming controversies over search engine practices. Qualified transparency here is the only chance we have to develop what Christopher Kelty calls a 'recursive public' – one that is 'vitally concerned with the material and practical maintenance and modification of the technical, legal, practical, and conceptual means of its own existence as a public'.[41] Questioning the power of a dominant intermediary like Google

---

also Frank Pasquale, *Political Google Bombing*, www.concurringopinions.com/archives/2006/10/political_googl.html (complaining that search engine optimization 'often boils down to the commodification of salience: if you give enough money to the SEO, they try to get you ranked high in response to certain queries. Given the already overwhelming influence of the "dollar primary", the thing we need to do is to extend that dynamic into the world of online politics').

[39] In *Federal Search Commission?*, Oren Bracha and I briefly mention some complexities caused by Google's purchase of YouTube. For example, does Google weight its merger with a company in its ranking algorithm? How well are YouTube's rivals doing in searches on Google for videos? Will business partners of Google be treated better in search results than, say, entities suing the company for one reason or another?

[40] In a hearing addressing competition on the Internet, House Judiciary Committee Chairman John Conyers made the comparison explicitly. At a recent hearing on the proposed Google-Yahoo joint venture, House Judiciary Chairman John Conyers complained that neither he nor other committee members were allowed to inspect the terms of the deal in a practicable manner. See Opening Statement of Chairman John Conyers, House Judiciary Committee, *Competition on the Internet*, Hearing of July 15, 2008, at 5:16–5:20, video available at www.c-spanvideo.org/program/competition (last visited February 10, 2011) (Chairman Conyers complained that the members of the Committee were only permitted to inspect the deal if they viewed its terms 'at a law firm, with no notes allowed'. He stated that the Committee was given 'more ready access to documents surrounding the President's terrorist surveillance program'). Clip available at www.c-spanvideo.org/program/competition (last visited February 10, 2011).

[41] Christopher M. Kelty, Two Bits: The Cultural Significance of Free Software (2007).

is not just a prerogative of the anxious. Rather, it's a prerequisite for assuring a level playing field online. Advocates of network neutrality would never think of permitting carriers to assert a blanket trade secrecy privilege to avoid any FCC regulation of 'network management', even though growing security concerns make the confidentiality of such strategic decisions important in many contexts. As search engines increasingly become the hubs of traffic on the Web, and assert the same Communications Decency Act and Digital Millennium Copyright Act immunities that carriers do, their actions need to become similarly subject to regulatory review.[42]

III. FROM REGULATION TO A PUBLIC OPTION

Like search engines, both law enforcement officials and agencies must gather data about individuals and events in order to make decisions about penalties and benefits. As the scope and intensity of this data collection and analysis increases, more duties are outsourced to private entities. When such entities use trade secret protected methods to analyse the data, the transparency and legitimacy of administrative processes can be threatened. For example, Danielle Citron has critiqued Colorado's adoption of a benefits management system that wrongly denied benefits to hundreds of deserving individuals.[43] Citron also describes the problems caused by automated decision-making by the 'data-mining algorithms of the Terrorist Surveillance Program' and the automated Federal Parent Locator Service's erroneous stigmatization of individuals as 'dead-beat' parents.[44] She argues that in many of these cases, the problems go beyond mere 'glitches' that are inevitable in any automated system. Rather, they amount to an illicit, *sub rosa* rule-making by programmers. Because agencies' legislative rules have the force and effect of law, they must usually be

---

42 Frank Pasquale, *Internet Nondiscrimination Principles: Commercial Ethics for Carriers and Search Engines*, U. CHI. LEGAL F. 263, 265 (2008) (arguing 'that the safe harbors that shield dominant search engines from liability also suggest patterns of responsibility for the results they present [because dominant search engines] and carriers are infrastructurally homologous . . . [acting] simultaneously [as] stable conduits, dynamic cartographers, indexers, and gatekeepers of the internet'); Frank Pasquale, *Beyond Innovation and Competition*, 104 NORTHWESTERN U. L. REV. 105 (2010) (discussing cultural and political dimensions of search engines and carriers that are not adequately addressed by economic analyses of regulation).

43 Citron, *supra* note 3.

44 *Id.*

subject to a process of notice, comment and opportunity for revision in response to comments.

After thoughtfully reviewing a number of situations where critical infrastructure needed to be scrutinized by concerned citizens and authorities, David Levine concluded that 'trade secrecy must give way to traditional notions of transparency and accountability when it comes to the provision of public infrastructure'.[45] For example, Levine has described a situation where 'the public's right to access [information concerning a vital security lapse in routing systems] was completely subjugated to the marginal claim that some of this information might qualify as a trade secret'.[46] Levine's approach may work in situations where the government directly contracts for a service and can use its procurement authority to demand certain specifications for the products and services it buys.

Commentary on voting machine controversies can also provide some guidance here. James Grimmelmann makes the case that governments can separate the need for secrecy in voting from the need for secrecy in software for voting.[47] Michael Carrier has done insightful work on the topic, proposing a series of standards, including 'voter-verified paper trail[s], random audits, [and] open source software'.[48] Danielle Citron's

---

[45] *Id.*

[46] David Levine, *Trade Secrets in Our Public Infrastructure*, 59 FLORIDA L. REV. 135 (2007). Levine also describes how trade secrecy interfered with proper testing procedures for voting machines ('Diebold's response to being informed of four successful hacks of their machines, which one hacker likened to "prestuffing a ballot box", was to say that these tests were "invalid" and "potential violations of licensing agreements and intellectual property rights"'). See also Michael Carrier, *Voting Counting Technology, and Unintended Consequences*, 79 ST. JOHN'S L. REV. 645, 655 (2005), available at http://papers.ssrn.com/sol3/papers.cfm?abstract_id=792324 ('Software is critical to DREs, with the success of elections hinging on the correctness, robustness, and security of the software. But flaws in software are not easily detectable, as malicious computer code may be disguised as useful code or may be difficult to locate. These dangers are heightened in programs as complex as those used by DREs and in software that the voting machine vendors have jealously guarded as proprietary trade secrets').

[47] James Grimmelmann, comment on *Black Box Voting Bleg,* Madisonian.net, http://madisonian.net/2006/09/25/voting-black-boxes-bleg/ ('the secrecy of the ballot booth creates some requirements for less than complete transparency. Those requirements, however, don't translate into a similar requirement that the source code of the voting machines be secret. That's just ill-advised security by obscurity').

[48] Carrier, *supra* note 46 ('I propose for electronic voting machines a voter-verified paper trail, random audits, open source software, and other recommendations. Only after these proposals are adopted can voters have confidence that the promise of vote counting technology will match its perils').

important piece *Open Code Governance* argues that open software is a keystone of legitimacy for automated processes.[49] Citron observes that U.S. 'e-voting systems use proprietary software' protected from inspection by trade secrecy and restrictive licensing.[50] She worries that the opacity denies 'election officials, candidates, technical experts, and interested citizens' the opportunity to inspect the source code to ensure the software works correctly. Citron finds a model alternative in Australia's more open system, which acknowledges the flaws in 'security via obscurity':

> Open code e-voting systems . . . generate interest due to the reputational advantages of participating in such projects. Consider Australia's open code e-voting project. A private company designed Australia's e-voting system and posted its source code online for review and criticism. The vendor posted all of its drafts of the source code, including its final version. Interested programmers and independent auditors studied the source code and provided feedback. An Australian National University professor caught the most serious problem. The vendor, in turn, fixed the source code, shoring up the system's security. Australia's e-voting system has received broad praise for its reliability and security. Similarly, computer scientists working for the Open Voting Consortium have begun programming open source software for election systems in the United States.[51]

The success of Australia's system of public-private cooperation in voting technology suggests another path for resolving concerns about the opacity of search engine rankings. Rather than trying to cabin dominant search engines' arbitrariness or unfairness indirectly (by promoting competition or regulation), policy-makers could try to outflank them by supporting a wholly transparent system of organizing the Web.

Admittedly, government entities are not major customers of search engines, and therefore would find it difficult if not impossible to use procurement authority to increase their transparency, regardless of how critical they are to the nation's information infrastructure. Yet there are several routes to a 'public option' in search that would at least provide an alternative to dominant search engines if their practices prove impossible to regulate.

For example, the recent Google Book Search settlement negotiations have led Siva Vaidhyanathan to characterize Google's archive project

---

[49] Danielle Keats Citron, *Open Code Governance*, U. CHI. LEGAL FORUM 355 (2008).

[50] *Id.* ('Courts provide trade secret protection to the source code, refusing access to it even in cases where programming errors allegedly caused election irregularities').

[51] Citron, *supra* note 49, at 383.

as evidence of a 'public failure'.[52] Whereas government intervention is often necessary in cases of 'market failure', Vaidhyanathan argues that the reverse can occur: market actors can step into a vacuum where government should have been. In the case of digitized books, the problem is presented starkly: why has the Library of Congress failed to require *digital* deposit of books, instead of merely accepting paper copies? We can debate when such a requirement became plausible; however, had the government required such deposit as soon as it became feasible, the problematic possibility of a Google monopoly here would be much less troubling. If digital deposit ever is adopted, the government could license its corpus to alternative search services. There is no good reason why the company that is best capable of reproducing books should have a monopoly on search technologies used to organize and distribute them.

More ambitiously, an NGO or quasi-administrative NGO could undertake to index and archive the Web, licensing opportunities to search and organize it to various entities that promise to maintain open standards for ranking and rating websites and other Internet presences.[53] Wikipedia, Slashdot and eBay all suggest methods of evaluating relevance and authority that could be employed by open search engines. If such a search engine became at least somewhat popular (or popular within a given niche), it could provide an important alternative source of information and metadata on ranking processes.

The need for a public option in search becomes even more apparent when we consider the waste and inefficiency causes by opaque intermediaries in other fields. Like private health insurers, Google is a middleman, standing between consumers and producers of knowledge. In programs like Book Search, it will effectively collaborate with copyright owners to

---

[52] SIVA VAIDHYANATHAN, THE GOOGLIZATION OF EVERYTHING (University of California Press, 2009) ('"Public failure" [is a] phenomenon in which a private firm steps into a vacuum created by incompetent or gutted public institutions. A firm does this not for immediate rent seeking or even revenue generation. It does so to enhance presence, reputation, or to build a platform on which to generate revenue later or elsewhere. It's the opposite of "market failure". And it explains a lot of what Google does')

[53] For a cultural case for government intervention here, see Mário J. Silva, *The Case for a Portuguese Web Search Engine*, http://xldb.fc.ul.pt/data/Publications_attach/tumba-icwi2003-final.pdf (describing the value of a Portuguese-oriented search engine); JEAN NOEL JENNENY, GOOGLE AND THE MYTH OF UNIVERSAL KNOWLEDGE: A VIEW FROM EUROPE (2007). Whereas these authors believe that English-language bias is a particularly problematic aspect of Google's hegemony in the field, I argue that the possibility of many kinds of hidden bias counsel in favor of at least one robust, publicly funded alternative here.

determine what access people get, how much they have to pay, and on what terms. In the health field, providers and private insurers are both very concentrated in the United States, and consumers (i.e., the businesses and individuals who buy insurance plans) are not. Insurers and providers also jealously guard the secrecy of many pricing decisions.[54] That is one key reason why the United States spends so much more on health care than other industrialized nations, without getting consistently better results, access or quality.

In contemporary debates on health reform in the United States, reformists split into two camps: those who believe that regulation of middlemen like insurers can bring about fair results, and those who believe that only a public option can serve as a benchmark for judging the behavior of private insurers. While the public option in health care is faltering now, it will remain a policy option in the future if new regulations on private insurers fail to improve their efficiency and quality, or to expand access to care. If search engines consistently block or frustrate measures to increase their accountability, governments should seriously consider funding public alternatives.

IV. CONCLUDING REFLECTIONS ON GOOGLE'S SECRET LAWS OF INTERNET ORDERING

> Everything has value only when ranked against another; everyone has value only when ranked against another . . . The real world appears as a video arcadia divided into many and varied games. Work is a rat race. Politics is a horse race. The economy is a casino . . . Games are no longer a pastime, outside or alongside of life. They are now the very form of life, and death, and time, itself.[55]

Reputations are created or destroyed, highlighted or obscured, by search engines. Traditional restrictions on data and information flows, be they in the form of privacy or intellectual property laws, inadequately constrain these important intermediaries. In considering the balance of power

---

[54] See, e.g., Uwe Reinhart, *The Pricing of US Hospital Services: Chaos Behind a Veil of Secrecy*, http://healthaff.highwire.org/cgi/content/abstract/25/1/57; Annemarie Bridy, *Trade Secret Prices and High-Tech Devices: How Medical Device Manufacturers are Seeking to Sustain Profits by Propertizing Prices*, 17 Tex. I.P. L.J. 187 (2009) (discussing 'recent claims by the medical device manufacturer Guidant that the actual prices its hospital customers pay for implantable devices, including cardiac pacemakers and defibrillators, are protectable as trade secrets under the Uniform Trade Secrets Act').

[55] Mackenzie Wark, Gamer Theory (Harvard University Press, 2007).

between search engines and those whom their actions affect, scholars have focused on either strengthening or weakening extant doctrines of copyright, trademark, contract, antitrust and privacy law. However, a critical mass of doctrine in these fields (along with established patterns of consumer behavior and the advent of cloud computing) has freed up so much information that law needs to be concerned not only with information aggregation, but also with rankings and evaluations that flow from it. We should be troubled when trade secrecy obscures the basis of these rankings.

The archetypal idea of a trade secret is a non-disclosed business practice that results in a more efficient or effective manufacture of product. As the economy grew more service-oriented, intangible advantages over competitors (such as client lists) rose in importance. Trade secrecy also moved from the commercial to the non-profit realm, as even churches have argued that certain scriptures and genealogical information are to be protected from prying eyes of skeptics and competitors. This chapter has focused on one particularly troubling rise in the popularity of trade secrets – their use as undisclosed 'rules of the game' in competitions for prominence in search engine results.

In an era of information overload, consumers clamor for reliable guides to quality goods and services. Google, Amazon and eBay have risen to the top of the Internet ecosystem by providing them with filtering services. We tend to think of entities like Google as elevating the salience of certain sites, but like Robert Cover's jurispathic judges, they also exist to reduce attention to the entities behind the first few pages of search results.[56] Many feel wronged or unduly slighted by their ultimate place in the pecking order that search engines create. McKenzie Wark's *Gamer Theory* begins to articulate the feeling that one is trapped, unable to escape an all-pervasive 'gamespace' whose opaque rules vitiate players' autonomy.[57] These Kafkaesque features of the Internet illuminate a trou-

---

[56] Robert M. Cover, *Nomos and Narrative*, 97 HARVARD L. REV. 4 (1983).

[57] WARK, *supra* note 55, para. 1.5 ('Ever get the feeling you are playing some vast and useless game to which you don't know the goal, and can't remember the rules? Ever get the fierce desire to quit, to resign, to forfeit, only to discover there's no umpire, no referee, no regulator, to whom to announce your capitulation? Ever get the vague dread that while you have no choice but to play the game, you can't win it, can't even know the score, or who keeps it? Ever suspect that you don't even know who your real opponent might be? Ever get mad over the obvious fact that the dice are loaded, the deck stacked, the table rigged, and the fix – in? Welcome to gamespace. It's everywhere, this atopian arena, this speculation sport . . . You are a gamer whether you like it or not, now that we all live in a gamespace that is everywhere and nowhere').

bling asymmetry at the heart of present search engine rankings. Quotidian decisions have consequences determined by entities which pair ever-more-pervasive surveillance of us with aggressive deflection of inquiries about them.

In a more egalitarian society, such unknown unfairnesses might be dismissed as marginal concerns. But we live in an age of competition and stratification. A power law distribution of attention on the Web, like ever-more-extreme polarization of wealth and poverty, has to be legitimated by markets, democracy, or some combination of the two.[58] Such forms of spontaneous coordination are perceived as fair because they are governed by knowable rules: a majority or plurality of votes wins, as does the highest bidder. Yet our markets, elections and life online are increasingly mediated by institutions that suffer a serious transparency deficit. When a private entity grows important enough, its own secret laws deserve at least some scrutiny.

Search engines have some good reasons for keeping their algorithms confidential: if they were public, manipulators of results could quickly swamp searchers with irrelevant results. However, the problem of gaming has been addressed in the past and these older solutions should guide policy here. Litigation in many fields reveals that there are ways of developing a qualified transparency permitting a trusted third party to examine a search engine's conduct without exposing its business methods for all the world to see. Nevertheless, if their past conduct is any guide to the future, search engines will vigorously fight even partial and limited disclosure of their methods to administrative agencies. Even if they succeed in resisting these regulatory moves, a public option may provide a competitive benchmark for evaluating their behavior.

Calls for increasing public responsibility for search engines are presently being channeled in two reformist directions: promoting competition among intermediaries (by lowering barriers to entry and challenging incumbents' anticompetitive practices), and tinkering in particular doctrinal areas in order to promote responsible behavior by intermediaries. The troubling consequences of trade secrecy protection undermine the validity of both these approaches. While competition may maximize the 'consumer welfare' of users of intermediaries, it may do worse than nothing for third parties (since one competitive strategy of search engines may be to make it easier for users to harm third parties). Moreover, the intermediary may

---

58 For a leading attempt to provide such a justification, see Yochai Benkler, The Wealth of Networks (2006). For a critique of Benkler's optimism here, see Bracha and Pasquale, *supra* note 10.

effectively be a natural monopoly, and any competition in the space it occupies is bound to be contrived. Doctrinal adjustment risks either over- or under-correcting current trends. Particularly in a field as dynamic and complex as search, it may prove beyond the institutional competence of courts unable to deal with rapidly shifting business practices occluded by trade secret protection. All these factors point toward the development of a public option in search, or a more regulatory approach, including teams of lawyers, engineers and programmers, that would complement extant litigation and competition.

16 The impact of trade secrecy on public transparency

*David S. Levine**

I. INTRODUCTION

During his first day as President of the United States, Barack Obama issued a 'memorandum for the heads of executive departments and agencies' regarding the Freedom of Information Act (FOIA). In the first sentence of the memorandum, President Obama noted that a 'democracy requires accountability, and accountability requires transparency'. The memorandum went on to state that FOIA 'should be administered with a clear presumption: in the face of doubt, openness prevails'. As part of the directive, President Obama ordered the Attorney General to issue new FOIA guidelines and the Office of Management and Budget to 'update guidance' to the agencies to effect his directive.[1] If President Obama's memorandum is to have the impact that is apparently desired, then the Attorney General and Office of Management and Budget will have to squarely consider the current impact of trade secrecy doctrine on public transparency. If state and local governments have similar concerns, they (perhaps even more than the federal government) will also need to examine the impact of trade secrecy on their conceptions of open government.

Trade secrecy, by its very name, invokes two core interests: secrecy and commerce. It is a singularly commercial doctrine designed to protect

---

* Assistant Professor of Law, Elon University School of Law and Affiliate Scholar, Center for Internet and Society, Stanford Law School. The author thanks Steven Bimbo and Dan Nicotera for research assistance and Elizabeth Townsend Gard, David Olson, the participants at the Workshop on Trade Secrecy at New York University School of Law and the participants at the works-in-progress talk at Charlotte School of Law for their comments. I especially thank editor Katherine Strandburg for her thoughtful comments and suggestions. As always, I thank my wife Heidi for her support and editorial comments. This chapter is in part adapted from a previous article, David S. Levine, *Secrecy and Unaccountability: Trade Secrets in Our Public Infrastructure*, 59 FL. L. REV. 135 (January 2007), as well as David S. Levine, *What Can the Uniform Trade Secrets Act Learn from the Bayh-Dole Act?*, 33 HAMLINE L. REV. (forthcoming 2011) (discussing many of the scenarios analyzed herein in the context of reform to the Uniform Trade Secrets Act).

1 Freedom of Information Act, 74 Fed. Reg. 4683 (January 21, 2009).

commercial interests by allowing companies and individuals to keep secret, for a potentially unlimited time, those formulas, processes and inventions that afford them pecuniary gain, especially when not known by competitors.[2] Standing in stark contrast to those methods and goals, the ideals, if not the daily practice, of democratic government minimize commercial interests and generally abhor secrecy as a default position. Especially in the last several decades, transparency and accountability are acknowledged to be among the core values that drive the fundamental model of a publicly-elected and properly operating democratic government.

But these fundamental ideals are strained in the present day. No longer does government operate in a bubble where its operations are fundamentally distinct from those of private industry. Government is increasingly intertwined with the private sector through its regulatory and supervisory requirements, direct partnership with or funding of private entities, and the direct provision of public infrastructure by wholly private entities. Although it appears to be a current aberration necessitated by the massive worldwide financial crisis, the government now even has significant ownership interests in private entities. Thus, government and the private sector do not operate without regard for the operations or interests of the other; quite the opposite, each increasingly can and does regard the other as a direct partner in achieving their largely divergent goals. This intersection of the private entity and government is causing doctrinal conflicts in the rules that have governed these two areas.

Fixed at the intersection of these increasingly intertwined worlds is trade secret law. Private businesses are continually displacing government in providing and operating public infrastructure, but utilizing commercial law standards and norms to do so, including the key tool of trade secrecy. Indeed, countless examples of modern infrastructure, from telecommunications in the form of the Internet, to traditional government operations in the form of voting machines, are now being provided by the private sector, and the list of industries that are regulated by or in direct partnership with government continues to expand. These industries, such as those in the financial and energy worlds, are using trade secret exemptions in open government laws to prevent the public from accessing basic information about the use of taxpayer money. Governments are funding private-sector research, or even providing the facilities in which

---

[2] As the seminal definition of trade secrets found in the Restatement (First) of Torts states, 'A trade secret may consist of any formula, pattern, device or compilation of information which is used in one's business, and which gives him an opportunity to obtain an advantage over competitors who do not know or use it'. 4 Restatement (First) of Torts § 757 cmt. b (1939).

the research is conducted, and yet the public is denied access to the results of that research because of trade secrecy doctrine. Because of these shifts in the way in which infrastructure is provided, trade secrecy doctrine has intruded into activities that traditionally have been conducted in the relatively open realm of public institutions like government.

The immediate impact of trade secrecy on public transparency can be adduced by noting the prevalence of secrecy as a core business method. The use of trade secrecy by the business world is expanding. In one empirical study of 1,478 manufacturing firms, secrecy was ranked 'first or second in importance for product innovations in 24 of the 33 industries'.[3] Significantly, secrecy was generally emphasized over patents and lead time in the development of new processes, while secrecy was tied with lead time for new products.[4] Indeed, one study concluded that by the mid-1990s, secrecy was used to protect product innovations 'much more heavily' than in the early 1980s.[5] Even in Silicon Valley, the center of the technology world, the use of trade secrecy to maintain a 'competitive edge' is on the rise.[6] Thus, secrecy is increasing in use and importance as a core business tool.[7]

The detrimental effect of trade secrecy on access to information grows as private industry and, by extension, government itself increasingly rely on secrecy to achieve their goals, while the breadth of application of the trade secrecy doctrine continues to expand. The looming problem begs the question: Can we reasonably expect private companies to adhere to public values like transparency and accountability in the provision of public infrastructure when the current trade secrecy framework allows for its

---

[3] Gerald Carlino *et al.*, *Matching Learning in Cities: Evidence from Patent Data*, Federal Reserve Bank of Philadelphia Working Paper No. 04-XX, 5 (Draft September 2004) (on file with author) (citing Wesley Cohen *et al.*, *Protecting their Intellectual Assets: Appropriability Conditions and Why U.S. Manufacturing Firms Patent (Or Not)*, National Bureau of Economic Research Working Paper No. 7552, 13 (February 2000)).

[4] Cohen, *supra* note 3, at 10.

[5] *Id.*

[6] See Hanna Bui-Eve, *To Hire or Not to Hire: What Silicon Valley Companies Should Know About Hiring Competitors' Employees*, 48 Hastings L.J. 981, 993 (1997) (noting this trend).

[7] See Josh Lerner, *The Choice of Intellectual Property Protection: Evidence in Civil Litigation* 1–2 (1994) (on file with author) (in a study of the importance of certain intellectual property protections for 530 manufacturing firms based in Middlesex County, Massachusetts, noting that 'cases involving informal protection – through the mechanism of trade secrecy rather than patents, trademarks or copyrights – are commonplace, figuring in 43% of the intellectual property disputes').

application to core government functions such as the provision of voting machines?

In such contexts, the people and the government are not simply buying a product or service which incorporates trade secrets. Rather, the products and/or services being regulated, funded and/or procured, and their attendant trade secrets, are inextricably bound up with infrastructure that people have traditionally turned to a publicly accountable government to provide or at least render transparent, involving core democratic activities such as voting, communications and access to governmental services and information. Undoubtedly, trade secrecy law and practices serve many useful and important purposes in private industry, but their use in the public infrastructure context has a vast and indelible impact on basic transparency across a wide variety of traditional governmental activities and operations.

The remainder of the chapter will explore this basic conflict. In Part II, key aspects of trade secrecy law doctrine will be explored, followed by specific current examples of this conflict in Part III. In Part IV, some possible solutions to the problem will be outlined, with suggestions as to future research that could help to clarify the best road from here.

II. RELEVANT ELEMENTS OF TRADE SECRECY DOCTRINE

Before identifying examples of the direct impact of trade secrecy on public transparency, it is important to highlight the ways in which trade secrecy, as a doctrine, conflicts with transparency. The ever-expanding definition of a trade secret, through a broadening of what constitutes 'secrecy' and 'commercial use', amplifies the impact of trade secrecy on commerce. Additionally, the fact that a trade secret can be held forever magnifies trade secrecy's ability to hinder disclosure and public dissemination of information. Inasmuch as trade secrecy is playing a major role in business operations and strategy, and businesses are increasingly entering the market for public infrastructure, the growing breadth of trade secrecy is a harbinger of increasing conflict as the worlds of private and public life mesh.

A. Trade Secrecy's Definition of 'Secrecy'

As discussed above, the seminal definition of a trade secret is 'any formula, pattern, device or compilation of information which is used in one's business, and which gives him an opportunity to obtain an advantage over competitors who do not know or use it'.[8] While secrecy is at the core of the trade secrecy doctrine,[9] the Restatement (First) of Torts noted that the protection of trade secrets is 'not based on a policy of rewarding or otherwise encouraging the development of secret processes or devices. The protection is merely against breach of faith and reprehensible means of learning another's secret'.[10] Yet, the explanation in the Restatement begs the question: isn't the encouragement of creating 'secret processes or devices' precisely the result of a law that values secrecy as its 'most important consideration' in order for its protection to be operational? It would seem so, if the previously discussed empirical data derived from industry is to be believed.[11]

In the context of public transparency, the operative problem is not only the possibility that the information deemed a trade secret may never be publicized, but that even if the owner's claim of trade secrecy is unfounded, the time, expertise and resources necessary to challenge and correct the designation would be prohibitive to all but the extremely well-funded or connected. And even if trade secrecy is successfully challenged, creating public access, it could be too late – decisions could have already been made, actions could have already occurred, and the core need to have the information could be largely mooted. Transparency in government requires not just eventual access, but timely and relatively easy access.

Secrecy results in lost opportunities to easily gain information and knowledge, a critical problem when the information involves governmental operations.[12] In the commercial context, the benefits of trade secrecy accrue with no requirement of easy access to information. This point can be illustrated by briefly comparing patent and trade secrecy law. The basic patent trade-off – public disclosure of all elements of the patented work, be it a product, business method or invention, in return for a limited-time monopoly granted to the patent owner – achieves (albeit imperfectly) the dual goals of public dissemination (transparency) and the ability to

---

8 *Supra* note 2.

9 Lehman v. Dow Jones & Co., Inc., 783 F.2d 285, 298 (2d Cir. 1986) ('the most important consideration remains whether the information was secret').

10 Restatement (First) of Torts § 757 cmt. b.

11 See *supra* notes 3–7 and accompanying text. Of course, trade secret law keeps nothing secret per se; rather, it encourages and enables the protection of secrets and protects information that has lost its secrecy. In that way, trade secrecy can be a boon for innovation, when it is used in its proper context and in traditional private enterprise.

12 Easy access would be, for example, a simple request of the information or its general public availability by way of the Internet or another communication device. No significant effort would be required.

examine and confirm (if not necessarily profit from such knowledge, i.e., accountability) that are largely absent in trade secrecy. While one may not reproduce the patented work for profit, one may at least access the patent information relatively easily and attempt to build upon or critique it. But under trade secrecy law there is no opportunity for the general public to *easily* examine that information deemed secret. As the Supreme Court noted in 1933, although monopoly rights are not granted with trade secrecy, there is no need for the trade secret holder ever to disclose the secret to the public.[13]

This difference has been discussed with reference to patents. In the context of patents, one early commentator distinguished between using patentable information *in* public versus the use of information *by* the public, explaining: 'A use in public is not necessarily a use by the public. It is distinguished not from an individual, but from a secret use. It is *a use which places the invention in such a relation to the public that if they choose to be acquainted with it, they can do so*'.[14] Patent law allows the real possibility, and perhaps likelihood, of a use in public by virtue of the existence of prior art as an element to be considered before a patent issues. Thus, patent law offers relatively easy opportunities for knowledge gained by the public. Trade secrecy, however, as applied to public infrastructure, is a use *in* public with little easy opportunity for knowledge gained *by* the public. It offers no such simple opportunity and there is no 'trade secret prior art'; its impact here is to deny the public the ability to 'choose to be acquainted' with the relevant knowledge – to keep information secret.

Moreover, trade secrecy doctrine, when applied to public infrastructure, exacerbates the loss of public information because it encourages strict efforts to hide information from public view. The ease with which one may ascertain information generally determines whether the information may be deemed a secret. Thus, the right to trade secrecy protection is 'defined by the extent to which the owner of the secret protects his interest from disclosure to others'.[15] Indeed, the Restatement (First) of Torts listed six bases for determining whether information constitutes a trade secret, which reflect a clear focus on the owner's activities and a heavy burden placed on the owner of the secret to maintain secrecy:

---

[13] U.S. v. Dubilier Condenser Corp., 289 U.S. 178, 186–7 (1933).

[14] 1 William C. Robinson, The Law of Patents for Useful Inventions 434 (1890), quoted in Louis Burgess and Ralph Dinklage, *Secret Use in its Relation to the 'Public Use' Provisions of R.S. 4886*, 28 J. Pat. Off. Soc'y 815, 818 (1946) (emphasis in original).

[15] DVD Copy Control Assoc., Inc. v. Bunner, 31 Cal. 4th 864, 880 (Ca. 2003) (quoting Ruckelshaus v. Monsanto, 467 U.S. 986, 1002 (1984)).

> (1) the extent to which the information is known outside of [the] business; (2) the extent to which it is known by employees and others involved in [the] business; (3) the extent of measures taken by [the business] to guard the secrecy of the information; (4) the value of the information to [the business] and [its] competitors; (5) the amount of effort or money expended by [the business] in developing the information; (6) the ease or difficulty with which the information could be properly acquired or duplicated by others.[16]

This places the onus squarely on the holder of the secret to prove that he has made efforts to keep the secret. In fact, only the sixth factor (the ability to reverse engineer) does not depend, at least in some part, on the efforts made to keep the secret.

But trade secrecy doctrine has taken an unusual course, and in doing so has created alternate possible methods by which to establish a trade secret, such as finding a trade secret based largely on the fact that the information is difficult to duplicate. The importance of that sixth factor is greater than one might expect, and its importance relative to other considerations can increase the possibility of protecting information as a trade secret. Although this list of factors is still cited today,[17] its contours are often altered such that proving a secret can be achieved with less reference to the actual activities of the owner than one might expect, or, put another way, with less reference to the first five factors.[18] Referring to the definition of a trade secret in the landmark case *Kewanee Oil Co. v. Bicron Corp.*[19] as an 'early basic tenet of trade secrets law', one court recently explained:

> Modern courts, however, have taken a different approach: '"Secrecy" may be measured by "the ease with which information can be developed through

---

[16] Ashland Mgmt. Inc. v. Janien, 82 N.Y.2d 395, 407 (N.Y. 1993) (quoting Restatement (First) of Torts § 757 cmt. b at 6 (1939)) (brackets in original).

[17] See Australian Gold, Inc. v. Hatfield, 436 F.3d 1228, 1245 (10th Cir. 2006) (noting that Oklahoma utilizes these six factors).

[18] See Amoco Prod. Co. v. Laird, 622 N.E.2d 912, 918 (Ind. 1993) ('Although all of the Restatement's factors no longer are required to find a trade secret, those factors still provide helpful guidance to determine whether the information in a given case constitutes "trade secrets" within the definition of the statute') (quoting Optic Graphics, Inc. v. Agee, 591 A.2d 578, 585 (Md. App. 1991); *In re Bass*, 113 S.W.3d 735, 740 (Tex. 2003) ('We agree with the Restatement [(Third) of Unfair Competition cmt. d] and the majority of jurisdictions that the party claiming a trade secret should not be required to satisfy all six factors because trade secrets do not fit neatly into each factor every time').

[19] 416 U.S. 470, 474–5 (1974) (citing the Restatement's definition of a trade secret, *supra* note 2).

proper means: if the information can be readily duplicated without involving considerable time, effort or expense, then it is not secret"'.[20]

Indeed, the modern Restatement (Third) of Unfair Competition supports this alternate basis for establishing a trade secret.[21] Thus, the sixth factor can be more important relative to the first five.[22] The result is that courts are increasingly tasked with the highly subjective job of determining what constitutes 'difficult or costly' reverse engineering, leading to varying results.[23]

In sum, the definition of a 'secret' takes on unusual connotations under trade secrecy doctrine. The effect of these counterintuitive and ambiguous definitions is clear: more, and not less, information has the possibility of being protected by trade secrecy doctrine from unfettered and easy public disclosure and examination.[24]

B. What is 'Commercial Use'

The basic theory of trade secrecy has maintained a singular focus on commercial activity from its inception as a doctrine. Among the many variables defining what constitutes a trade secret, commercial concerns have been the one bedrock constant throughout the law's development, as the primary concerns of trade secret law are maintaining business ethics and the encouragement of the inventive spirit and innovation in businesses.

---

20 Crane Helicopter Servs. v. U.S., 56 Fed. Cl. 313, 323–4 (Fed. Cl. 2003) (quoting C&F Packing Co., Inc. v. IBP, Inc., 224 F.3d 1296, 1302 (Fed. Cir. 2000)).

21 Restatement (Third) of Unfair Competition § 39 cmt. f at 431 (1990) ('the requirement of secrecy is satisfied if it would be difficult or costly for others who could exploit the information to acquire it without resort to . . . wrongful conduct').

22 See Amoco Prod. Co. v. Laird, 622 N.E.2d 912, 915 (Ind. 1993) ('In determining whether information is protectable as a trade secret, "the first and foremost consideration is whether the . . . information is readily accessible to a reasonably diligent competitor"') (quoting Surgidev Corp. v. Eye Tech., Inc., 648 F.Supp. 661, 682 (D. Minn. 1986)).

23 See Flotec, Inc. v. Southern Research, 16 F.Supp.2d 992, 1001 (S.D. In. 1998) ('Whether information is "readily ascertainable by proper means" is a matter of degree').

24 See Vincent Chiappetta, *Myth, Chameleon or Intellectual Property Olympian? A Normative Framework Supporting Trade Secret Law*, 8 Geo. Mason L. Rev. 69, 89 (1999) (noting that 'trade secret protection extends to an extremely wide variety of information' in comparison to patents); Don Weisner *et al.*, *Stealing Trade Secrets Ethically*, 47 Md. L. Rev. 1076, 1125 (1988) ('The legal definition of a trade secret is very undiscriminating and allows nearly all business ideas to qualify').

Perhaps as a result, the definition of 'commercial use' as a prerequisite to trade secret protection has expanded greatly over the last 75 years, with the result that more and more information falls under the protection of trade secrecy doctrine. In the context of transparency, the impact of this expansion is to create greater impediments to easy and unfettered access to information. The extension of 'commercial use' can be seen by briefly tracing its contours in the Restatements and significant model codes and federal laws.

The decades since publication of the Restatement (First) of Torts[25] have seen an erosion of the requirement that the information actually be 'continuous[ly] use[d] in the operation of a business'. The Uniform Trade Secrets Act (UTSA), promulgated in 1979 and revised in 1985, effected a sea change in the contours of trade secrecy by qualifying 'information, including a formula, pattern, compilation, program, device, method, technique, or process' as a trade secret so long as the information has 'independent economic value, *actual or potential*'.[26] The comments to this section explained: 'The broader definition in the proposed Act extends protection to a plaintiff who has not yet had an opportunity or acquired the means to put a trade secret to use'.[27]

Thus, by 1985, the definition of a trade secret could include information that had not even been established in the business as commercially useful, as well as 'business plans'.[28] In fact, utilizing similar definitions, courts have rejected arguments that information cannot be a trade secret where its value is merely a 'hypothetical possibility'.[29] Moreover, the definition includes negative data or information, such as 'the results of lengthy and expensive research which proves that a certain process will *not* work'.[30] In

---

25 Restatement (First) of Torts § 757 cmt. b at 5 (1939) ('A trade secret is a process or device for continuous use in the operation of a business').

26 Uniform Trade Secrets Act § 1(4), 14 U.L.A. 433, 438 (1990) (emphasis added).

27 *Id.* at 439.

28 See Carbo Ceramics, Inc. v. Keefe, 166 Fed. Appx. 714 (5th Cir. 2006) (holding that 'there was abundant evidence for a reasonable jury to conclude that [plaintiff] had a trade secret in its business plans and strategies, including pricing for its products as well as detailed information regarding industry trends, customers and customer preferences').

29 See Joint Stock Soc'y v. UDV N. Am., Inc., 104 F.Supp.2d 390, 409 (D. Del. 2000) (upholding application of trade secrecy protection for sealed recipes to make 'flavored vodkas and liqueurs' under the Delaware Trade Secrets Act, in part because while 'these vodka recipes may be old, they are nevertheless a source of potential value to the defendants').

30 Uniform Trade Secrets Act § 1, 14 U.L.A. at 439.

sum, the UTSA solidified the fact that an abundance of information, far beyond the unambiguously commercially useful, would be protected by trade secrecy. In the present context, the application of this broad definition of the phrase 'commercial use' means that more otherwise publicly accessible information has the possibility of being withheld from public inspection under trade secrecy law.

Evidencing how much lower the economic threshold for trade secrecy protection has gone, 1995's Restatement (Third) of Unfair Competition explicitly stated that the economic advantage afforded the trade secret owner 'need not be great', and it would be 'sufficient if the secret provides an advantage that is more than trivial'.[31] Thus, virtually all information that may, in some 'more than trivial' way, have any value to a company could qualify as a trade secret. The federal Economic Espionage Act of 1996 (EEA), which criminalizes most forms of misappropriation, is perhaps the ultimate culmination of the elimination of the 'continuous use' requirement in trade secrecy law. It builds upon the UTSA definition, and includes virtually all business information, including business plans and customer lists.[32]

By 2006, a form of the UTSA had been adopted in 45 states and the District of Columbia.[33] The Restatement's 'continuous use' requirement is largely dead.[34] Untethering the 'commercial use' factor from actual 'economic value' has substantially expanded the potential application of the trade secrecy doctrine to virtually any form of information connected to a business.[35] The public suffers from an increasing inability to access information, which in the context of, for example, whether a voting machine is properly tabulating votes, is troublesome. Regardless of this concern, the current trend is towards more, rather than less, business information

---

31 See RESTATEMENT (THIRD) OF UNFAIR COMPETITION § 39 cmt. e.

32 18 U.S.C. § 1839(3) (2005).

33 Uniform Trade Secrets Act (amended 1985), Table of Jurisdictions Wherein Act Has Been Adopted, 14 U.L.A. 529, Supp. 25 (Supp. 2009). It should be noted that the states have made alterations to the UTSA on a state-by-state basis, but, as one commentator has noted, the similarities in substance between the states are greater than differences in the language used. JAMES POOLEY, TRADE SECERTS § 2.03[7] (2001).

34 See Robert G. Bone, *A New Look at Trade Secret Law: Doctrine in Search of Justification*, 86 CALIF. L. REV. 241, 249 (1998) (noting that the 'continuous use' requirement has been 'relaxed or ignored' in recent years).

35 See *id.* at 248 (noting that 'almost anything can qualify as a trade secret, provided it has the potential to generate commercial value'). Given the above, it is possible that even this statement is too narrow, as commercial value is now required at something just above trivial.

being subject to trade secret protection. The myriad complications that this creates are discussed in Part III.

C. The Infinite Possible Duration of a Trade Secret

Along with the broad definition of 'secret' and the limited need for information to have commercial currency, one consistent element in trade secrecy doctrine is the theoretically unlimited duration of a trade secret. So long as the elements of trade secrecy are met, the right to keep a secret for an infinite period of time underscores the real power of enjoying trade secret protection. For instance, the prototypical example of a trade secret is the 'secret combination of flavoring oils and ingredients known as "Merchandise 7X"', the formula for Coca-Cola, which is not patented and has existed as a trade secret for over 100 years.[36] Why would Coca-Cola choose trade secrecy over patents? Precisely because of the infinite duration of trade secret protection; Coca-Cola bet on its ability to maintain the secret, and by doing so afforded itself protection (and the concomitant pecuniary gain attendant to a monopoly) far beyond the 20-year limit of patent protection.[37]

State statutes also prescribe that a 'trade secret endures and is protectable and enforceable until it is disclosed or discovered by proper means'.[38] Because a trade secret lasts, at least in theory, as long as a trade secret holder maintains its secrecy, the possibility that the information will never enter the public domain is very real. Whatever benefits the public might gain from unfettered access to the information is lost, so long as secrecy is maintained, the possibility of independent discovery of the trade secret

---

[36] See Coca-Cola Bottling Co. v. Coca-Cola Co., 107 F.R.D. 288, 289 (D. Del. 1985). Noting the efforts that Coca-Cola has undertaken to protect its secret, the court explained that the formula 'has been tightly guarded since Coca-Cola was first invented and is known by only two persons within The Coca-Cola Company' and that the 'only written record of the secret formula is kept in a security vault at the Trust Company Bank in Atlanta, Georgia, which can only be opened upon a resolution from the Company's Board of Directors'.

[37] Daniel N. Christus, *Intellectual Property in the Americas*, 13 AM. U. INT'L L. REV. 1095, 1099 (1998) ('The decision of whether or not to patent the Coca-Cola formula came down to a question of whether they wanted to have a 17-year monopoly or whether they wanted to rely on their ability to keep this a trade secret forever') (comments by Robert Wagner). Again, unlike trade secrecy, patent affords the public the ability to examine the information, and after the 20-year term of the patent, to use that information in commerce. Thus, the public can design around the information to create new processes that can expand our knowledge base.

[38] S.C. Code Ann. § 39-8-30(A) (2004).

is low, and active efforts like reverse engineering are unsuccessful. Thus, the choice of trade secrecy offers the possible benefit of a monopoly on the information for a potentially infinite period of time. This possibility becomes even more pernicious in the context of public infrastructure, like voting machines, where there are few competitors and therefore less of a chance of independent invention negating the existence of a trade secret.

In sum, trade secrecy, as currently configured, is a pervasive and powerful tool for businesses, and as currently applied, for governments as well. Its contours and scope of protection are expanding along with its power as a device to maintain privacy and secrecy. Although one may quibble at the margins regarding the likelihood of independent discovery of a trade secret, whether a trade secret may really be kept forever, or whether trade secrecy is chosen over patent in every sector important to public infrastructure, there is little dispute that trade secrecy remains a dominant intellectual property strategy for many businesses. We turn now to examine how the values that animate trade secrecy align with those animating the provision of public infrastructure.

III. IMPACT ON TRANSPARENCY

In order to assess the current and future impact of trade secrecy on public transparency, it is important to note the increasing interaction between what we have traditionally considered to be 'private industry' and government. Particularly, the involvement of private industry in the provision of 'traditional' public infrastructure, which runs the gamut from roads to waste treatment facilities to website and informational services, is rapidly increasing in the United States, as well as in Europe and South America.[39] In most parts of the world, the public sector is now viewed as incapable of providing and maintaining infrastructure on its own and, when that view is combined with the need to keep taxes down, the result is ever-increasing

[39] Sidney M. Levy, Build, Operate, Transfer: Paving the Way for Tomorrow's Infrastructure 8 (1996). In a telling scenario, for several days hundreds of automobiles were trapped in a parking garage owned by the City of Hoboken, New Jersey, when the employees of the company which owned the software that operated the 'fully automated parking structure', Robotic Parking, were booted by the City during a contractual dispute. The Robotic employees took with them the 'intellectual property rights to the software that made the giant robotic parking structure work'. The City eventually settled, agreeing to pay a U.S.$5,500/month fee to Robotics for a three-year license to operate the software. Quinn Norton, *Giant Robot Imprisons Parked Cars*, Wired, August 8, 2006, www.wired.com/news/technology/1,71554-0.html.

responsibility for public infrastructure in the hands of private entities. Indeed, current privatization proposals and actions include 'privatizing services which, in some countries, have historically been considered to be largely, sometimes almost exclusively, the domain of the public sector', like waste disposal and prisons.[40]

Additionally, indicating this greater reliance on the private sector for the development and provision of public infrastructure, according to comments submitted to Congress by the United States General Accounting Office, the government's share of research and development dollars in the United States has fallen from 60 percent in 1960 to 26 percent in 2000.[41] The result: '[i]nstead of driving research and its outcomes, the government must increasingly rely on the commercial sector'.[42] The combination of increasing reliance by the private sector on trade secrecy and increasing private sector involvement in public infrastructure provision and research renders transparency a challenge.

Furthermore, the capabilities of public infrastructure are increasing because of its use of information technology such as the Internet. Information technology has enabled public infrastructure to expand both in its geographical scope and its capabilities.[43] The impact of information technology impact is visible everywhere, from the management of the flow of traffic on roads to the day-to-day operations of local government.[44] As one commentator has noted, computer networks are fundamental to the operations of such public infrastructure as transportation, water supply, power and emergency services; without functioning computer systems, they would stop working.[45] Given the vast capabilities of public infrastructure, aided by technology but provided by public entities, trade secrecy has the potential to keep much vital information from public scrutiny.

Additionally, and more broadly, society increasingly relies on public infrastructure, whether provided by the government or not. It is omnipresent in all aspects of our lives, from walking down the street to being

---

40 A.J. Smith, Privatized Infrastructure: The Role of Government 4–5 (1999).

41 Intellectual Property: Industry and Agency Concerns over Intellectual Property Rights Before the Subcomm. on Technology and Procurement Policy of the H. Comm. on Government Reform, 107th Cong. (May 10, 2002) (testimony of Jack L. Brock, Jr., United States General Accounting Office).

42 *Id.*

43 Rae Zimmerman and Thomas Horan, *What are Digital Infrastructures?*, in Digital Infrastructures 3 (Rae Zimmerman ed., 2004).

44 *Id.*

45 Mark G. Milone, *Hacktivism: Securing the National Infrastructure*, 58 Bus. Law. 383 (2002).

able to contact emergency services if the need arises. It provides the basic conditions for people to live and for businesses to exist; its potential for failure is considered one of the major security vulnerabilities today.[46]

For all these reasons, it is difficult to underestimate the reliance that we now place on technology, provided by private entities, for the operation of public infrastructure. The impact of trade secrecy on transparency manifests itself primarily in three particular scenarios: (a) the private provision of public infrastructure (its arguably most significant impact); (b) publicly-funded research conducted by the private sector and its related contracting; and (c) the use of trade secrecy as an exemption to FOIA by regulated entities.[47] Each will be discussed below, in turn.

A. Private Provision of Public Infrastructure

1. The voting machine example

Secrecy, with its attendant goals of pecuniary gain and commercial competition, conflicts directly with the methods and purpose of transparent and accountable democratic governance. This conflict is crystallized in the private provision of voting machines. Voting machines are perhaps the signature example of a device designed to advance governmental and democratic interests. Diebold Election Systems, Inc.'s voting machines ('Diebold', now doing business as Premier Election Solutions) are replacing older and archaic (but not necessarily less reliable) pull-lever and punch-card systems. These voting machines are the public infrastructure through which elections are conducted, counted and verified. They form the backbone upon which one can exercise the right to vote with the confidence that one's vote will not be disregarded, lost or erroneously tabulated.

As examined below, however, public access to the internal workings of these machines is difficult, or in some cases impossible, to obtain. In November 2005, for example, Diebold refused to comply with a North Carolina law that requires vendors of electronic voting machines to place, among other items, their software and source code in escrow 'with an

---

[46] P.M. Herder and W.A.H. Thissen, *Critical Infrastructures: A New and Challenging Research Field,* in CRITICAL INFRASTRUCTURES: STATE OF THE ART IN RESEARCH AND APPLICATION 1 (W.A.H. Thissen and Paulien M. Herder eds, 2003).

[47] It also manifests itself when government designates information that it creates as a trade secret, but this anomalous situation is far less prevalent (although equally if not more disturbing), and will not be examined in detail in this chapter.

independent escrow agent approved by the State Board of Elections'.[48] The law is designed to 'restore public confidence in the election process' by requiring that such information be provided to the state so it can support and test voting systems.[49] In the ensuing action brought by Diebold against the North Carolina State Board of Elections (BOE) to seek a temporary restraining order and preliminary injunction against the enforcement of the statute,[50] Diebold contended that it could not provide some of the required information because the information was not controlled by or in custody of Diebold and/or belonged to third parties.[51] Diebold argued that because of this it could not submit a vendor proposal meeting all state law requirements without 'being in violation of state law'.[52]

The court eventually held, in essence, that Diebold must comply with the law if it wanted to do business with the state.[53] Diebold responded, however, that it could not disclose source code because of license agreements, and because some of the code belonged to third parties who would be unwilling to disclose it.[54] Accordingly, after another round of court battles that ensued after the BOE *approved* Diebold notwithstanding its inability to comply with the law, Diebold chose to withdraw from competing for business within the state.[55]

That trade secret law and/or principles of secrecy are at play here, even if not explicitly stated, is confirmed by Diebold's explanation to the BOE upon its withdrawal that 'we believe it is impossible for any vendor of an election system to say that they have access to all of the source code in

---

48 N.C. Gen. Stat. §§ 163–165.9A(a) (2005).

49 2005 N.C. Sess. Laws 323.

50 Diebold Election Systems, Inc. v. N.C. State Bd. of Elections, No. 05-CVS-15474 (N.C. Sup. Ct. Nov. 16, 2005), Memorandum of Points and Authorities at 1–2.

51 Diebold Election Systems, Inc. v. N.C. State Bd. of Elections, No. 05-CVS-15474 (N.C. Sup. Ct. November 4, 2005), Complaint at 6–8, 10, available at www.eff.org/cases/diebold-v-north-carolina-board-elections.

52 *Id.* at 10.

53 Gary D. Robertson, *N.C. Judge Declines Protection for Diebold*, ABC News, November 28, 2005, http://abcnews.go.com/Technology/wireStory?id=1354023; see also Diebold Election Systems, Inc. v. N.C. State Bd. of Elections, No. 05-CVS-15474 (N.C. Sup. Ct. 2005), Order of Dismissal.

54 Anne Broache, *North Carolina Defends E-voting Certifications*, News.com, December 2, 2005, http://news.com.com/North+Carolina+defends+e-voting+certifications/2100-1028_3-5980671.html?tag=mainstry.

55 Letter from Charles R. Owen, Division Counsel, Diebold, to Gary Bartlett, Executive Director, North Carolina State Board of Elections (December 20, 2005), www.votetrustusa.org/pdfs/Diebold%20Folder/Barrett%20Letter%2012-21-05-1.pdf.

question or that it is all in escrow somewhere'.[56] A truly pyrrhic victory: although the state won the initial court battle, the applicability of trade secrecy principles presumably remained, because protection of secrets was not overruled or overridden by the concerns of the public as manifested by the laws of the state. Rather than establishing a precedent eliminating the option of having a trade secret in the context of a voting machine, Diebold was able to dodge that issue and logically chose to focus on states where trade secrecy law is completely impermeable to public law overrides.

More recently, computer hackers successfully broke into Diebold's voting machines owned by Leon County, Florida to test their vulnerability to manipulations such as fraudulently changing the results of an election. What made this event particularly unusual was that the hackers were given access to the Diebold machines by Leon County Supervisor of Elections Ion Sancho so that they could test the security of the machines.[57] Diebold's response to being informed of four successful hacks of their machines, which one hacker likened to 'prestuffing a ballot box', was to say that these tests were 'invalid' and 'potential violations of licensing agreements and intellectual property rights'.[58] Sancho subsequently commented that '[m]ore troubling than the test itself was the manner in which Diebold simply failed to respond to my concerns or the concerns of citizens who believe in American elections'. Identifying the heart of the problem, Sancho also lamented, 'I really think they're not engaged in this discussion of how to make elections safer'.[59]

---

[56] *Id.* Diebold has argued that such information is akin to trade secrets in other cases. See Online Policy Group v. Diebold, Inc., No. 03-4913JF (N.D. Ca. November 24, 2003), Response to Plaintiffs' Post Hearing Letter at 3, ('Diebold has informally encouraged the students to refrain from publishing passwords, source codes, information protected by employees' privacy interests and trade secret-type information, none of which is essential for purposes of criticism'). Of course, as discussed above, access to source code is essential for understanding how a voting machine operates. *Id.* at 3 ('Access to source code supports independent technical evaluation of voting systems that, in turn, facilitates oversight and accountability of software').

[57] Zachary Goldfarb, *As Elections Near, Officials Challenge Balloting Security*, Washington Post, January 22, 2006, available at www.washingtonpost.com/wp-dyn/content/article/2006/01/21/AR2006012101051.html.

[58] Marc L. Songini, *Q&A: E-voting Systems Hacker Sees 'Particularly Bad' Security Issues*, Computerworld, January 19, 2006, www.computerworld.com/securitytopics/security/hacking/story/0,10801,107881,00.html.

[59] *Id.; see also supra* note 56. Diebold, and two other voting machine vendors, apparently now refuse to deal with Leon County, which has prompted the Florida Attorney General to issue subpoenas to those companies. Marc L. Songini, *Florida Attorney General Questions E-voting Vendors' Decision to Shun County*,

It is difficult to find a more fundamental public infrastructure than a voting machine. But again, even when the very ability to conduct an accurate and verifiable election is at issue, trade secrecy wins the day. Secrecy supported by the law resulted in a private actor being able to argue against traditional governmental notions of transparency and accountability and disengage from public discussion about proven vulnerabilities of its products. True, one could conceive of lawful ways, such as reverse engineering, to access this trade secret information in the absence of contractual prohibitions. But the fact that legislatures have to pass laws mandating that source code about voting machines should be available to the state, and state boards of elections and officials charged with operating fair and accurate elections have to jump through such legal hoops – and may not be successful in doing so – reflects a balance that is skewed in favor of commercial interests and against those of the public. The risk of being able to 'prestuff' a ballot box was not enough for Diebold to concede that public disclosure of the inner workings of the machines might be appropriate, even if for no other reason than to prove that it took the issue seriously and had nothing to hide from the public. The law must step in to proactively force such change, rather than operate as a potential bulwark against continued secrecy after transparency has been unjustly denied.

One significant additional element in the Diebold-North Carolina scenario underscores the inability of government be a third party ombudsman for or protector of the public's interest in every instance. As mentioned earlier, immediately after Diebold refused to comply with the law, and in the face of its refusal to do so, the BOE in effect ignored the law by *approving* Diebold as a vendor, noting that 'none' of the 'winning applicants' were capable of placing all of its source code in escrow, as required under the law.[60] Only after a court challenge to the Board's decision was begun did Diebold choose to withdraw from the state because it could not escrow all code as per the state's law. [61]

Thus, aside from trade secrecy law defeating the disclosure law in practice, the notion that a government-controlled or designated entity could adequately protect the interests of the general public by enforcing

---

COMPUTERWORLD, April 4, 2006, www.computerworld.com/governmenttopics/government/legalissues/story/0,10801,110192,00.html?SKC=privacy-110192.

[60] Anne Broache, *North Carolina Defends E-voting Certifications*, NEWS.COM, December 2, 2005, http://news.com.com/North+Carolina+defends+e-voting+certifications/2100-1028_3-5980671.html?tag=mainstry. See also McCloy v. BOE, No. 05-CVS-16878 (N.C. Sup. Ct. December 19, 2005), Amended Complaint at para. 17.

[61] See www.eff.org/cases/diebold-v-north-carolina-board-elections.

the disclosure requirement is dubious, and would turn on many variables that might undermine such an entity's ability to operate in a completely public-oriented fashion. Where, as here, a state agency effectively nullifies a law designed to protect the public's interest, the entire basis upon which an escrow regime would be built – i.e., trusting the entity charged with examining the escrowed material – is undermined. In this instance, but for the voluntary withdrawal of Diebold in the face of court orders, the citizens of North Carolina might very well have ended up with a voting machine vendor whose machines' operations were a mystery to all. A third party auditor (governmental or otherwise) may not adequately protect the interests of the public.[62]

2. The breathalyzer example

More recently, conflicting court decisions involving the use of breathalyzer machines to measure the intoxication levels of automobile drivers suggest a different approach. In a number of states, defendants have challenged the validity of breathalyzer tests used to prosecute them for driving while intoxicated (colloquially known as 'drunk driving' cases) and, as with voting machines, have sought the 'source code' of the machines to determine their validity and accuracy. An examination of two state appellate decisions involving breathalyzer machines suggests the scope of the problem and its contours.

In *Nebraska v. Kuhl,*[63] the defendant was charged with speeding and driving under the influence (DUI) under an Omaha city ordinance. Defendant sought, among other information, the 'source code' of the DataMaster breathalyzer machine used in his prosecution. After motion practice, the parties stipulated to the fact that the manufacturer of the DataMaster would not provide the source code to the State of Nebraska. In effect, the state was using machines to support criminal prosecution

---

[62] See also Joseph Lorenzo Hall, *Transparency and Access to Source Code in Electronic Voting* at 6 (on file with author) (noting that it is unclear whether the North Carolina statute will be enforced). While one could argue that my concern is more with government than with the operation of trade secrecy doctrine, it is again the idea that laws must be passed, litigation must be commenced, and extensive effort must be made for companies to reveal such information that makes trade secrecy doctrine problematic in this context. For transparency to be most valuable, it needs to be achieved with little effort on the part of an under-resourced public (beyond perhaps a request for the information to the appropriate entity). A solution that removes the impediment of trade secrecy without resort to litigation is the solution that would best and most expeditiously achieve the type of transparency advocated here.

[63] 741 N.W.2d 701 (Neb. App. 2007), *aff'd*, 755 N.W.2d 389 (Neb. 2008).

the operations of which were unknown to it. The lower court found the defendant guilty of DUI because it was convinced 'beyond a reasonable doubt' that the defendant had a 'concentration of alcohol' beyond 'allowable limits'.

On appeal, the Nebraska Court of Appeals considered whether the lower court erred in not requiring the state to turn over the source code to the defendant. The defendant presented the issue as a conflict, in essence, between his Sixth Amendment right of confrontation and 'any trade secret right that the manufacturer of the machine in question might have', explaining the need to 'in a way, cross examine the machine and determine if it was in proper working order'. The court declined to reverse the lower court, under an abuse of discretion standard, explaining that:

> the record is clear that the source code is not in the State's possession and that the manufacturer of the machine in question considers the source code to be a trade secret and the proprietary information of the company. We find no abuse of discretion in the county court's decision with respect to the discoverability of the source code.

Thus, primarily on the manufacturer's say so, the undisputed trade secret rights of the manufacturer of the DataMaster breathalyzer machine trumped the need of defendants – and, one would think, the state – to verify the accuracy of its law enforcement devices and prevent the possibility of a wrongful conviction. To the extent that the public at large would want access to how the State of Nebraska is determining whether an individual should be charged with DUI, the unfriendly precedent in *Kuhl* would seem to be an impenetrable barrier to transparency, unless, of course, a proper challenge were brought and resources were available to successfully mount an appeal to the highest court in the state.

More recently, the Court of Appeals of Kentucky reached a slightly more favorable result from the perspective of public transparency. In *House v. Commonwealth,*[64] a defendant charged with DUI was given a breathalyzer test using CMI Inc.'s Intoxylizer 5000. Again, the defendant sought the source code for the machine from the state to determine if there were any '"bugs" or flaws in the code's logic', and again the state did not produce it. Both the state *and* the manufacturer, CMI, succeeded in quashing subpoenas for the source code issued by the defendant.

On appeal of his conviction, the court noted that an error in the source code would be 'consequential to the accuracy of the reading intended to be relied upon by the Commonwealth'. With regard to Kentucky's and CMI's

---

64 No. 07-417, 2008 Ky. App. LEXIS 19 (Ken. January 18, 2008).

argument that the source code was a trade secret, the court tacitly agreed. But, in contrast to the ruling in *Kuhl*, the court in *House* provided that the defendant, his attorney and an expert witness could 'enter into a protective order stipulating that the code or its contents are not to be shared with any party outside of the case' and that 'the order may provide that any copies or work product generated as a result of the software engineer's review be returned to CMI upon completion of the review'. Thus, the defendant was provided some ability to properly defend himself against the charges brought by the state; the public at large, however, remained in the dark.

Kuhl and *House* illustrate the tension inherent in the private provision of public infrastructure. While individual defendants would certainly have an interest in assuring that the evidence used against them is accurate, the public at large also has a strong interest in assuring that law enforcement is doing its job properly and not abusing the significant power of the state to deny individuals life, liberty and property. There is little doubt, however, that the source code of a breathalyzer would be the kind of information that we'd call a trade secret based upon its basic definition. In *Kuhl*, we thus see the rank power of trade secrecy in its ability to trump basic Constitutional rights. *House* represents something a bit more pernicious, as the state and the manufacturer allied to use trade secrecy in an effort to prevent the defendant (and the public) from knowing how the state conducts law enforcement. From the perspective of the public at large, they were successful as, under the court's order, even the work product of the defendant's expert, which could reveal significant problems with the machines, will remain hidden from public view.

The provision of voting and breathalyzer machines by private entities illustrates the application of trade secrecy doctrine to private entities providing public infrastructure. In both cases, the value of transparency is undermined by the commercial trade secrecy doctrine. Equally disturbing, the state runs the range from complete complicity in preventing transparency to begrudging acquiescence to the need for transparency, suggesting a divergence between the interests of the government itself and the interests of its citizens. In either instance, the public's interest in transparency is marred by trade secrecy doctrine, providing a very powerful tool to prevent wide dissemination of basic information about governmental operations. Access, in sum, is largely denied absent extraordinary effort, and even that does not render full public transparency.

B. Public Funded or Sponsored Research and Contracts

'American taxpayers are entitled to open access on the Internet to the peer-reviewed scientific articles on research funded by the U.S. Government.'

So claims the Alliance for Taxpayer Access, a 'diverse and growing alliance of organizations representing taxpayers, patients, physicians, researchers, and institutions that support open public access to taxpayer-funded research'.[65] On the surface, this sounds like a fairly straightforward proposition, but again, when trade secrecy is engrafted on this seemingly uncontroversial idea, the issues become more complex and troublesome. Then, the question becomes: open access to all taxpayer-funded research, or only that taxpayer-funded research that does not include the taxpayer-funded trade secrets held by the private entity conducting the research?

In *Mississippi State University (MSU) v. People for the Ethical Treatment of Animals (PETA)*,[66] the Mississippi Supreme Court reversed a lower court's order requiring MSU to turn over documents to PETA relating to the treatment of animals in research and testing conducted at MSU by the Iams Company ('Iams'), a pet food manufacturer. MSU and Iams had entered into a series of agreements ('the agreements') regarding the research, providing for the 'secrecy of information' and no disclosure of 'intellectual property rights'. Under the agreements, MSU had also warranted that its facilities complied with the federal Animal Welfare Act[67] and other applicable laws 'regarding the care and use of vertebrate animals for research and training purposes'. PETA sought, *inter alia*, records prepared by MSU for 'projects, tests, and experiments funded by Iams, the creation of which were a requisite condition under MSU's agreements with Iams'.

MSU is a public university that receives both state and federal funds. Under Mississippi's Public Records Act ('the Act'),[68] Iams sought a court order prohibiting the disclosure to PETA of trade secrets, which are exempt from disclosure under the Act. Iams argued that the information constituted Iams' 'strategic product development portfolio'. Noting that the '[t]he subjects that Iams is studying at MSU have independent economic value because they are not generally known by competitors in the marketplace', Iams argued that the 'studies would indicate, among other things, its formulations, improvements, and product development'. Thus, argued Iams, the information included trade secrets.

In reversing the lower court, the Mississippi Supreme Court found that the records were created by MSU under the agreements, thus meeting an exemption from disclosure in the Act for trade secrets resulting from a

---

65 See Alliance for Taxpayer Access website, www.taxpayeraccess.org/.

66 992 So. 2d 595 (Miss. 2008), *reh'g den.*, 2008 Miss. LEXIS 553 (Miss., October 30, 2008).

67 7 U.S.C. § 2131 *et seq.* (1976).

68 Miss. Code Ann. § 25-61-1 *et seq.* (1972).

contractual relationship between colleges and businesses.[69] It also noted that the records were required to be created under the federal Animal Welfare Act, which also exempts trade secrets from disclosure. Moreover, the Court found that PETA had failed to refute the argument that the 'data and information' found in the records were trade secrets 'developed by MSU under contract with Iams', further rendering them exempt from disclosure under the Act. However, in a dissent, Presiding Justice Diaz noted that PETA could not refute the trade secret designation because it never had a chance to inspect the records.

Justice Diaz made another point that goes to one of the basic problems with trade secrecy in the context of public transparency. He noted that the:

> majority accepts at face value Iams' and MSU's blanket assertion that the [records] constitute . . . 'proprietary information' with 'independent economic value'. As the [lower court] noted, 'MSU and Iams have chosen to simply label the protocols as trade secrets. They do not articulate, particularize or specify a justification so as to establish with specificity that the protocols are a trade secret'.

Indeed, the majority admitted that 'we do not presume to possess the scientific or commercial acumen to discern or evaluate what may be of interest or value to a known competitor or a third-world start-up company'. This admission is both admirably candid and distressing. In fact, it is often quite difficult for courts – and governments – to assess, much less challenge, a trade secrecy designation by a private entity, for reasons ranging from lack of resources, to lack of time, to lack of expertise. That, in and of itself, is very problematic as it can prevent information that may not actually be a trade secret (that is, information that is not of value to a competitor) from being disclosed.

PETA illustrates another challenge to transparency posed by trade secrecy. There is no question that taxpayers have a presumptive right to know what is happening on publicly-funded college campuses. Nonetheless, the power of trade secrecy, backed by contracts entered into by public entities requiring them to protect the intellectual property interests of their private partners, easily means that the public may not discover trade secrets funded or supported by taxpayer revenue in otherwise public

---

[69] 'Trade secrets and confidential commercial and financial information of a proprietary nature developed by a college or university under contract with a firm, business, partnership, association, corporation, individual or other like entity shall not be subject to inspection, examination, copying or reproduction under the [Act]'. Miss. Code Ann. § 25-61-9(3) (1972).

spaces. In that way, the public cannot discover what is happening on its state college campuses, with its money, and in its name.

As seen in the *PETA* scenario and in the examples involving FOIA, *infra*, governments can be bound to assert and defend the trade secret interests of their private partners because of contractual terms and/or the applicable laws. While it would be nice if governments did not enter into contracts with such terms, contract terms like those in *PETA* are common and Mississippi's interpretation of them not unusual. Of more fundamental concern, *PETA* illustrates that governments can start to look like private entities with commercial interests, requiring trade secrecy when relationships with private entities are created.

Moreover, as private industry and government form partnerships, an additional reason for government acquiescence to blanket designations of information as trade secrets can develop: conflict of interest regarding the designations. In public-private partnership contexts, a troublesome mutuality of perceived interest can develop wherein government actors may perceive that their personal (not public) interests dovetail with the interests of private entities in protecting their trade secrets. Government actors may conclude that it is far easier to function without the public watching over them and scrutinizing their activities. Arguing that information that might otherwise be subject to disclosure constitutes the trade secrets of private partners is an easy and powerful way to prevent public disclosure of information.

Regardless of the reasons, the failure or inability of courts and governments to challenge trade secrecy assertions leaves a powerful weapon for avoiding transparency in the hands of entities operating in partnership with government.

C. The Trade Secrecy Exception to FOIA

Perhaps the best modern-day codification of public transparency and accountability is found in the passage of the Freedom of Information Act (FOIA). FOIA, enacted in 1966 as a result of increased interest in allowing investigative journalism,[70] is designed to force disclosure and 'permit access to official information long shielded from public view'[71] by permitting any citizen (and indeed, businesses) to request information from the

---

[70] Christopher J. Lewis, *When is a Trade Secret Not So Secret? The Deficiencies of 40 C.F.R. Part 2, Subpart B*, 30 Envtl. L. 143, 152 (2000).

[71] EPA v. Mink, 410 U.S. 73, 80 (1973); see also Dep't of the Air Force v. Rose, 425 U.S. 352 (1976).

government by way of a FOIA request.[72] As explained in the introduction to one of the core studies of the rights of citizens to government information, 'Few aspects of government-citizen relations are more central to the responsible operation of a representative democracy than the citizen's ability to monitor governmental operations. Critical in this regard is the existence of a general individual right of access to government-held information'.[73]

Indeed, FOIA can be the avenue for journalists and private citizens alike to discover exactly what the government is doing. As one reviewer quoting a book on investigative journalism has noted, in the wake of FOIA and a few other significant events of the 1960s, 'major media . . . began accepting "a duty to report beyond the superficial handouts from those with social and political power"'.[74] Thus, any impediment to the operation of FOIA can have devastating effects on the ability of citizens to accurately analyse and critique the activities of government.

Notwithstanding the goal of transparency, FOIA recognizes that some information in the possession of government should be kept from public disclosure. Therefore, FOIA includes a number of exemptions from disclosure, including those for certain documents and information regarding national defense, foreign policy,[75] law enforcement,[76] and, as determined by the federal agency holding the information, commercial trade secrets.[77] As explained by the Supreme Court, Congress felt the need for a trade secret exemption because 'with the expanding sphere of government regulation and enterprise, much of the information within [government] files has been submitted by private entities seeking [government] contracts or responding to unconditional reporting obligations imposed by law'.[78] Despite the protection of trade secrets,[79] the fact that FOIA sets a default

---

[72] *Supra* note 69.

[73] *Government Information and the Rights of Citizens*, 73 MICH. L. REV. 971 (1975).

[74] Carl Sessions Stepp, *Is Investigative Reporting Here to Stay?*, AM. JOURNALISM REV. 67 (Dec.–Jan. 2006) (quoting JAMES L. AUCOIN, THE EVOLUTION OF AMERICAN INVESTIGATIVE JOURNALISM (2005)).

[75] See 5 U.S.C. § 552(b)(1) (2005).

[76] *Id.*. § 552(b)(7).

[77] *Id.* § 552(b)(4).

[78] Chrysler Corp. v. Brown, 441 U.S. 281, 292 (1979).

[79] See Citizens Comm'n on Human Rights v. FDA, No. 92-5313, 1993 U.S. Dist. LEXIS 21369 (C.D. Cal. May 10, 1993) ('the documents which are part of the Prozac New Drug Application that have been withheld by the FDA are exempt from disclosure because they contain trade secrets'), *aff'd in part and remanded in part on other grounds*, 45 F.3d 1325 (9th Cir. 1995).

of disclosure[80] unless one of the exemptions applies effectively orients government towards disclosure and away from secrecy – the opposite of trade secrecy, which protects secrecy except in limited circumstances.

As in the *PETA* scenario discussed above, public transparency has been stymied in some cases by questionable use of FOIA's trade secrets exemption outside of the traditional regulatory sphere. An illustrative example of the direct impact on transparency of the trade secrets exemption to FOIA can be found in *McDonnell Douglas Corporation v. Widnall*.[81] *Widnall* involved an arena in which trade secrecy often may become problematic: public contracting. In *Widnall*, the United States Air Force (USAF) received a FOIA request from General Dynamics Corporation regarding pricing and unexercised options under a contract between the USAF and McDonnell Douglas Corporation ('McDonnell'), a competitor. The USAF contacted McDonnell, which advised the USAF that certain 'line item prices' contained in the contract were, among other designations, trade secrets. The USAF decided that a separate federal regulation required it to release the information. As a result, McDonnell wound up suing the USAF in a 'reverse' FOIA action to enjoin disclosure of, among other information, the line item prices.

For a variety of unusual administrative and procedural reasons not relevant to the present discussion, the USAF never explicitly took a position as to whether the line item prices were trade secrets. As a result, and because of the administrative posture of the case, the court found that it was not required to issue a holding on the issue. While the court noted that the USAF 'implicitly' contested the designation of the line item prices as trade secrets, it stated in dicta that '[a]lthough the idea that a price charged to the government for specific goods or services could be a "trade secret" appears passing strange to us, we agree with the government that it is not open to us to attempt to decide that issue at this stage'.[82] The case was remanded to the district court and ultimately back to the USAF so that the USAF could provide a 'considered and complete statement' of its position; however, the court never resolved the question.

It is indeed 'passing strange' that such information could be designated as a trade secret.[83] Yet at the administrative level at which the FOIA

---

[80] The very existence of a trade secret definition designed specifically for FOIA, see *infra*, suggests that the commercial definition is inappropriately applied to entities that operate in the governmental or public infrastructure spheres.

[81] 57 F.3d 1162 (D.C. Cir. 1995).

[82] *Id.* at 1167.

[83] See Gregory H. McClure, *The Treatment of Contract Prices under the Trade Secrets Act and Freedom of Information Act Exemption 4: Are Contract Prices*

request was evaluated, the designation of the line item prices as trade secrets by McDonnell determined the disposition of the FOIA request. As a result, the disclosure of basic information regarding the prices paid by the USAF for goods and services was delayed and might have been forever halted. While the court, in a different procedural and administrative posture, might have ruled that the information was not a trade secret, McDonnell's position appears to have been at least colorable – the designation was *de facto* accepted by the USAF, necessitating litigation to challenge the trade secrecy assertion.

Widnall highlights a fundamental problem: the broad modern definition of a trade secret controls in light of the lack of a trade secret definition within the FOIA statute itself. If a court applies the broad modern definition of a trade secret,[84] it is quite conceivable that, based upon the descriptions afforded by the putative owner of the trade secret, it could find a wide swath of requested information with significant public importance to constitute trade secrets. Applying the letter of the law, such a court might end up denying taxpayers the ability to discover what the USAF (and hence taxpayers themselves) are paying for goods and services. Such as result does not seem to serve the purpose of FOIA; it is certainly not transparency.

More broadly, it is important to remember that FOIA pertains only to the federal government. The states have their own versions of FOIA (as in *PETA, supra*) and, of course, to the extent that they include an exemption for trade secrets, may define a trade secret as they choose. Therefore, the definition of a trade secret again becomes the fundamental question. If a state does not have a statutory definition, or as well-developed a body of cases as is found in the federal courts, then the possibility for abuse of a trade secret exemption is manifest.

An additional and related problem arises at the administrative level. As illustrated in *Widnall* and discussed earlier, the government often relies in the first instance upon the designation by the party submitting the information that the information is a trade secret. There is little, if any, incentive for the government to challenge such a designation, especially as FOIA and the Trade Secrets Act (TSA), a criminal statute, act in tandem to prohibit the government from releasing any information that meets a

---

Really Trade Secrets?, 31 PUB. CONT. L.J. 185 (2002) (taking the position that contract prices are not trade secrets).

[84] See *supra* notes 2 and 25 *et seq.*; *cf.* Public Citizen Health Research Group v. FDA, 704 F.2d 1280, 1289 (D.C. Cir. 1983) (articulating a narrower definition of a trade secret tailored to FOIA requests that is followed by many courts and has been accepted as the definition of a trade secret for purposes of FOIA).

FOIA trade secret definition.[85] The result is that much information that may or may not be validly designated as a trade secret is not disclosed based upon the unchallenged say-so of a private entity. Unless successful time-consuming and costly litigation ensues,[86] the alleged 'trade secrets' may never see the light of day.

The ambiguous and increasingly intrusive trade secret exemption in FOIA is a serious blow to our conception of a transparent and accountable government. Moreover, as the government increasingly regulates and partners with private industry, we can expect that the trade secrets exemption will be of mounting importance.[87] As it stands today, we sacrifice transparency on the altar of protecting the commercial interests of trade secrets owners. While it would be difficult to advance a position that calls for the complete absence of a trade secret exemption under FOIA, in light of the danger of disclosing a legitimate trade secret to the trade secret holder's competitors, we currently have a FOIA scheme that gives short shrift to concerns about transparent and accountable government. As public-private partnerships and regulation increase, every day that passes without otherwise-disclosable information being made public is another day where policies and practices that may not stand up to public scrutiny may be permitted to continue and expand in the absence of input from the public.

IV. POTENTIAL SOLUTIONS AND FUTURE RESEARCH

Given the ways that trade secrecy can prevent disclosure of information in which the public may have a legitimate interest, a logical question is how to address the competing interests of the legitimate trade secret holder and the public. In considering possible solutions, it is important to note that, as the above examples illustrate, there is no cookie cutter, catch-all

---

85 18 U.S.C. § 1905 (1996); see *Widnall*, 57 F.3d at 1164. The TSA renders the disclosure of a trade secret potentially punishable by criminal sanctions.

86 See Finkel v. U.S. Dept. of Labor, No. 05-5525, 2007 WL 1963163 (D. N.J. June 29, 2007). After the U.S. Occupational Health and Safety Administration (OHSA) failed to respond to plaintiff's FOIA requests and action against OHSA ensued, the court held that alleged commercial trade secrets found in OHSA records were not exempt under FOIA because, *inter alia*, the government failed to explain how such information were trade secrets.

87 A focus of future research should include a detailed study of the actual use of FOIA's trade secret exemption by the federal government. Of course, that would require filing many FOIA requests.

solution to address every conceivable scenario in which trade secrecy could interfere with public transparency. Moreover, it is beyond the scope of this chapter to discuss all possible solutions; indeed, further research, as identified below, is required to flesh them out.

Nonetheless, there are some possible solutions to consider, the most extreme being eliminating trade secrecy protection for public infrastructure. If democratic transparency is the public's primary goal, the law might simply require those whose activities are of public concern to find proper protection in another intellectual property law doctrine, such as copyright or, more likely, patent, if possible.[88] At least from a theoretical standpoint, if not from the purely practical perspective, the idea of patents as the primary substitute for trade secrecy has appeal. Patent law is arguably a more democratic doctrine than is trade secrecy in the above contexts, because of its public disclosure requirements and limited duration of monopoly. A patent application, which becomes public 18 months after filing, must 'describe, enable, and set forth the best mode for carrying out the invention',[89] thus providing substantial public disclosure to anyone who wishes to understand the operations of the invention. Patents would also allow companies to capture the full economic value of their patented efforts for a significant but not unlimited time, thereby militating against any assertion of a 'takings' claim.[90]

---

[88] To the extent that there are exceptions under freedom of information laws for intellectual property rights, it is presumably based on the notion that those works of authorship, ideas, processes, and so forth are worthy of some modicum of protection in the law, including perhaps protection from inspecting eyes. Therefore, if the alleged trade secret information is neither patentable or copyrightable and not otherwise exempt from disclosure under FOIA, it would seem that transparency should unquestionably win the day as there would be no countervailing reason for the exemption from public scrutiny to exist.

[89] Festo Corp. v. Shoketsu Kinzoku Kogyo Kabushiki Co. Ltd., 535 U.S. 722, 736 (2002) (citing 35 U.S.C. § 112 (1975)).

[90] A concern might be raised that by eliminating trade secrecy protection for private entities engaged in public infrastructure altogether, the effect constitutes a 'taking' by the government and/or public under the Fifth Amendment to the United States Constitution. The Supreme Court has recognized that extinguishing a property interest, including a trade secret, may constitute a taking. *Monsanto*, 467 U.S. at 1003. Generally, subject to certain conditions, so long as there is a 'regulatory scheme with both burdens and benefits', a 'give-and-take exchange' as such will not be considered a 'taking'. Phillip Morris Inc. v. Reilly, 113 F.Supp.2d 129, 144 (D. Mass. 2000). The argument against a takings claim is that the voluntary submission of non-patentable trade secret information in return for the pecuniary advantages of providing public infrastructure without government competition (a give-and-take) is not a taking. See Megan E. Gorman, *Going Up in Smoke: The Effect of Phillip Morris, Inc. v. Harshbarger and Phillip Morris,*

One major argument against eliminating trade secrecy protection is that its elimination would discourage private entities from entering the market for public infrastructure. While this critique may have some validity, it is not necessarily the case that companies would not engage in such activities if trade secrecy were not available; rather, a company might simply charge more for the good or service and/or the government might have to buy all rights to the goods and services from the provider.[91] Admittedly, the possibility of trade secrecy in the public contracting context likely encourages more competitive bids, which might lead to cheaper and/or better services, suggesting the possibility that transparency may require some economic sacrifices. To address such concerns, Brett Frischmann's work suggests that, in the absence of market-based incentives, those who risk public disclosure of valuable trade secret information by providing public infrastructure could be rewarded by: (a) direct government subsidization; (b) tax incentives; (c) cooperative research plans; and/or (d) encouraging joint ventures.[92] Future research in this area should include an examination of such solutions in the context of minimum specifications for government goods and services, combined with an analysis of (1) the relevant markets for a given good or service (such as the limited market for Diebold's voting machine versus the larger market for Iams' pet food), and (2) the potential that a technology will be used in both commercial and public contexts. Such research would be very helpful in addressing the potential economic impact of eliminating trade secrecy in favor of patent protection.

Another criticism of a proposal to abandon trade secrecy altogether in the public infrastructure context is that particular technologies used in public infrastructure, such as the code in Diebold's voting machines,

---

Inc. v. Reilly on the Takings of Intellectual Property, 33 RUTGERS L.J. 771, 796–8 (2002) (approving the First Circuit Court of Appeals' analysis of a takings challenge that 'the voluntary submission in exchange for advantages of a registration [to do business in Massachusetts] could "hardly be called a taking"' in the context of the Massachusetts government's requirement that tobacco companies reveal the ingredients of cigarettes and smokeless tobacco) (quoting Phillip Morris, Inc. v. Reilly, 267 F.3d 45, 59 (1st Cir. 2001)). Moreover, the continued availability of patent protection would militate against the argument that public infrastructure providers have lost all protection of their trade secrecy rights.

91 See Mark Fenster, *The Opacity of Transparency*, 91 IOWA L.R. 885, 919 (2006) (noting that 'efforts to extend the burdens of public law procedural and disclosure requirements to private entities inevitably reduce the economic and administrative advantages that originally led government agencies to privatize or contract out previously public services').

92 Brett M. Frischmann, *Infrastructure Commons*, MICH. ST. L. REV. 121, 136 (2005).

might also be used in normal private commercial markets with minor modifications. In such a case, a provider would face a choice: forgo trade secrecy, patent the invention and sell it to the public and governments, or keep the trade secrets (thereby challenging competitors) and forgo the public infrastructure market. While a supplier may choose the latter option in some cases, it is reasonable to assume that other entities will fill the void. In any case, transparency would be achieved. An examination of the substitutability of trade secrecy and accountability in this limited scenario, and more generally in the research and development stage, is warranted.

Despite these concerns, there is no question that transparency would be significantly improved were trade secrecy abandoned in the public infrastructure context. While trade secret law allows reverse engineering and independent discovery (an often time-intensive and/or impossible endeavor), trade secrecy by its very definition abhors both transparency and public accountability. Therefore, abandoning trade secrecy for private entities engaged in activities such as providing voting or breathalyzer machines to the government and limiting protection to that which is patentable is likely the best, if not perfect, answer.[93] Whether eliminating trade secrecy in this context would be accomplished by adding a 'not public infrastructure' element to the definition of a trade secret or by creating an affirmative defense to an action alleging misappropriation is less significant than the notion that there is a theoretical disconnect and that patent law may be a ready-made salve to much of the sting of the loss of trade secrecy for affected entities. Indeed, even where there is a limited market for the specialized device, like a voting or breathalyzer machine, patentability would still allow an inventor to sell the product to

---

[93] It is important to recognize that businesses face real alternatives to secrecy that are the subject of recent scholarly works. See HENRY CHESBROUGH, OPEN INNOVATION 170–4 (2006) (discussing Intel, Inc.'s practice of publishing, rather than patenting, those inventions that they would 'prefer to put in the public domain', in an effort to benefit their business); see Jim Chen, *Biodiversity and Biotechnology: A Misunderstood Relation*, MICH. ST. L. REV. 51, 79–81 (2005) (discussing the public benefits of patent law over trade secrets, noting that trade secret law, 'by design, keeps information concealed [and] by contrast, [patent law is] designed to deliver privately held information into public hands'. But see Dan L. Burk and Mark Lemley, *Is Patent Law Technology-Specific?*, 17 BERKELEY TECH. L.J. 1155, 1161–1163 (2002) (noting that section 112 of the Patent Act imposes minimal disclosure requirements for software). Patent law has been subject to much criticism in recent years, for reasons ranging from the overuse of patents in the computer software context to the amount of information that is actually revealed in a patent application, and is therefore not the perfect solution.

its customers and license the product to its competitors. Whether this is the most efficient way to provide public infrastructure is, for purposes of this chapter, secondary to the fact that transparency and accountability would be increased under such a system.[94]

By this proposal, I am not suggesting that patents are purely democratic, that all patent applications are informative, thorough and complete, or that patents constitute the perfect substitute for trade secrecy in the public infrastructure context. Indeed, patent law has been subject to much criticism in recent years, for reasons ranging from the overuse of patents in the business method and computer software contexts to the amount of information that is actually revealed in a patent application.[95] As discussed previously, there are certain ideas and processes that are better suited to trade secrecy protection.[96] However, the fact remains that trade secrecy law serves commercial interests that are not aligned with some fundamental and basic public values, like transparency, and thus greater public accountability unavoidably diminishes some commercial advantages.

Finally, it is worth noting that trade secrecy doctrine is not needed as a vehicle to protect sensitive or potentially dangerous information from falling into the hands of people or entities who may seek to do harm to the United States' public infrastructure. For example, the Critical Infrastructure Information Act (CIIA)[97], passed as part of the Homeland Security Act of 2002, regulates 'the use and disclosure of information submitted to the Department of Homeland Security (DHS) [by businesses] about vulnerabilities and threats to critical infrastructure'.[98] While the CIIA has been criticized for being superfluous[99] and having an overly

---

94 Alternative solutions may be to retain trade secrecy in the research and development stage only, where it has enormous potential value to a commercial entity and can allow for first-mover advantages, or limit the amount of time that trade secrecy protection may be applied to public infrastructure trade secrets. Such solutions would address some of the problems that industry would face were trade secrecy eliminated in its entirety for public infrastructure projects.

95 For a detailed discussion and critique of various criticisms of patent law, see DAN L. BURK & MARK A. LEMLEY, THE PATENT CRISIS AND HOW THE COURTS CAN SOLVE IT (2009).

96 See Carlino, *supra* note 3 and accompanying text.

97 6 U.S.C. § 131 *et seq.* (2002).

98 Gina Marie Stevens, Cong. Research Serv., *Homeland Security Act of 2002: Critical Infrastructure Information Act* (2003), available at www.fas.org/sgp/crs/RL31762.pdf.

99 See Brett Stohs, *Protecting the Homeland by Exemption: Why the Critical Infrastructure Information Act of 2002 Will Degrade the Freedom of Information Act*, 2002 DUKE L. & TECH. REV. 18 (2002) (arguing that 'the private sector

broad definition of 'critical infrastructure information' that will allow an enormous amount of information to be protected from disclosure to the public,[100] the existence of the CIIA shows that trade secrecy doctrine is not needed to protect sensitive information regarding our public infrastructure from being accessed by those who could use that information to do harm.[101]

Short of abandoning trade secrecy altogether, there are other potential partial solutions, though each has its own problems. One possibility would be to institute an affirmative 'public concern' carve-out from trade secrecy. Courts have had a difficult time determining what a 'public concern' is for purposes of First Amendment protection of disclosure of trade secrets by the press, however. Eugene Volokh has argued persuasively that the courts have consistently run into problems when considering situations in which a media entity is sued for publishing a trade secret leaked to it by someone in violation of his or her duty of confidentiality, but without encouragement from the news media.[102] Therefore, a possible doctrine permitting dissemination of trade secrets deemed a 'public concern' would likely

---

exemptions are redundant and unnecessary. The Freedom of Information Act contains several exemptions that protect information given to the government by private entities').

[100] See *id.* (quoting Representative Jan Schakowsky as saying that this definition is a 'loophole big enough to drive any corporation and its secrets through'); Editorial, *Overkill in the Name of Security*, St. Petersburg Times, July 14, 2002, at 2D, available at www.sptimes.com/2002/07/14/news_pf/Perspective/Overkill_in_the_name.html (criticizing the legislation as providing an incentive for companies ' to share all sorts of irrelevant information' with the government because it would then be protected from public disclosure); Beryl A. Howell, *Information Overload*, Legal Times, June 2, 2003, at 52 (suggesting that DHS will become a 'dumping ground for large amounts of irrelevant and improperly marked business information').

[101] It is beyond the scope of this article to analyse whether the CIIA is a proper method to protect trade secret information. Nonetheless, the existence of this law suggests that one could craft an exemption under FOIA that protects certain public infrastructure trade secrets from disclosure, and thereby dispense with using the commercial definition for such purposes.

[102] Eugene Volokh, *Freedom of Speech and Intellectual Property: Some Thoughts After Eldred, 44 Liquormart, and Bartnicki*, 40 Hous. L. Rev. 697, 739–49 (2003) (commenting that the courts have a myopic view of what constitutes a 'public concern', and, in any case, should not be the entity deciding what is a 'public concern' for purposes of First Amendment analysis). See also Alex Eaton-Salners, Note, *DVD Copy Control Association v. Bunner: Freedom of Speech and Trade Secrets*, 19 Berkeley Tech. L.J. 269, 282–3 (2004) (criticizing decision of the California Supreme Court because its 'formulation and application of the public concern doctrine was incorrect').

run into similar subjectivity problems regarding where the line between a 'public concern' justifying disclosure and a 'private concern' prohibiting disclosure should be drawn.[103] While it would be nice to assign the ability to make such a determination to the courts, the difficulty in line drawing (for example, determining whether the public is sufficiently concerned about the number of hours that MSU employees devote to Iams' research such that trade secrecy protection should be curtailed) may prove subject to regular appeal and spur endless litigation. Given the judiciary's track record, caution should be exercised in assigning this responsibility to the courts.

Another partial solution would be to narrow the definition of a trade secret in the public infrastructure context so that trade secrecy would apply, as in *Public Citizen*,[104] only to information that is actually used in commerce or the disclosure of which would pose an immediate threat to the security of the public infrastructure itself. In this way, the information that would be protected from disclosure would be less than that covered by the prevailing all-encompassing definition and would reflect more respect for the legitimate needs of the public.

Alternatively, the duration of trade secret protection could be limited. For example, Iams' research could be protected for up to five years, after which time Iams would be required to submit the trade secret to a government agency to hold in escrow. Of course, under such a regime the information would not be immediately available, making public input and scrutiny impossible, and by the time the information was publicly available, potentially moot. Nonetheless, either or both of these solutions in tandem would help mitigate the most pernicious aspects of trade secret protection in this context, namely, the overly broad definition and potentially unlimited duration of trade secrecy, without wholesale abandonment of the doctrine.[105]

---

[103] Of course, by way of analogy, the U.S. Supreme Court has struggled with the definition of a matter of 'public concern' in First Amendment jurisprudence. See Dun & Bradstreet, Inc. v. Greenmoss Builders, Inc., 472 U.S. 749, 758–9 (1985) (applying the 'public concern' test to a private plaintiff who alleged defamation based upon the defendant sending an errant credit report to five subscribers, and noting that 'speech on public issues' is of primary concern to the First Amendment). For example, it seems reasonable to assume that the operation of a voting machine and its impact on one's ability to cast a recorded vote would have to qualify as a 'public concern' under First Amendment analysis.

[104] See *supra* note 84 and accompanying text.

[105] Of course, any alteration of the contours of trade secret protection would have to pass Constitutional muster by not 'frustrat[ing] the achievement of the congressional objectives served by patent law'. Bonito Boats, Inc. v. Thunder

A final partial solution would be to change the remedies allowed under a trade secret claim, by denying injunctive relief for the misappropriation or innocent release of such trade secrets and limiting relief to monetary damages. This change would be nearly as drastic as denying trade secret protection altogether, as injunctive relief is the most sought after, and most important, remedy in trade secret misappropriation cases. The typical trade secret injunction, which prevents the further dissemination or use of the subject trade secret, attempts to return the trade secret holder to its state prior to the misappropriation. The effect, in the public infrastructure context, is to put a lid on further examination of the trade secret – again contravening a core value of public governance. While denying injunctive relief does not prevent the public harm of keeping such knowledge secret from a deserving public, this solution would at least prevent the quashing of public examination once it has begun. Therefore, limiting relief to monetary damages when public infrastructure trade secrets are misappropriated should be considered. Assuming appropriation by a competitor (as opposed to a whistleblower), damages would be paid by the misappropriating competitor, and could include the complete disgorgement of profits earned by the misappropriating entity, but the public benefit of disclosure would remain. The public knowledge gained and, by dint of the public disclosure of the secret, the possible improvements therein, would not be denied.

To be sure, none of the proposed solutions, save abandoning trade secrecy altogether in the context of public infrastructure, are fully satisfactory, as they do not fully harmonize the differing theoretical underpinnings of trade secrecy and transparency. The proper goal is to obtain public transparency in the first instance, without the need to put the figurative gun to the head of the entity claiming the trade secret by way of regulatory/administrative or legal process after the fact. None of these options, save complete elimination of trade secrecy in the area of public infrastructure, resets the system to a default of transparency; rather, they force some modicum of disclosure where it would not otherwise exist. The better goal, however, is transparency by default, and the absence of complete solutions short of eliminating trade secrecy entirely in this area is perhaps the best argument that trade secrecy is simply an irreconcilable theoretical mismatch with the values and goals inherent in the provision of public infrastructure. Further research as outlined above would help

---

Craft Boats, Inc., 489 U.S. 141, 154–6 (1989) (reaffirming Kewanee Oil Co. v. Bicron Corp., 416 U.S. 470, 484, 489–90 (1974) and its analysis of why the subject trade secret law did not conflict with Congress' patent objectives and goals).

policy-makers ascertain the best solution to this vexing but significant problem.

V. CONCLUSION

Although secrecy is sometimes justified (and despite the spotty and haphazard application of democratic values by governments recently), the concepts of transparency and openness are central to the system of government that the United States regards as most legitimate and stable. But, as the above discussion illustrates, when trade secrecy impedes public disclosure of relevant information, the public's right to meaningful public debate, the ability of government officials to explain their decisions based upon evidence (and for the public to demand the same), and the resultant benefits of full and informed consideration and implementation of policy options and alternatives are suppressed.

Aside from foreclosing meaningful debate and discussion and keeping people guessing, secrecy can engender distrust and suspicion at a level productive neither for businesses and their customers nor for government and its citizens. In the contexts discussed in this chapter, secrecy means that we must guess at how elections are run, whether the evidence used in a DUI prosecution is accurate, and how taxpayer resources are being allocated in public universities and the military. There are countless other examples of potential 'trade secrets' in the public infrastructure arena. Lack of information can create paranoia because guesswork replaces real and verifiable information. As to what is actually happening, the public is left in the dark. The late Senator Daniel Patrick Moynihan, in his excellent historical analysis of secrecy as a form of government regulation, explained that the conflict created by such a scenario is akin to 'ignorant armies clash[ing] by night'.[106]

The above discussion brings into stark relief the sacrifices of public transparency that are made on the altar of commercial trade secrecy. The trend toward secrecy is likely to continue absent real discussion among policy-makers about trade secrecy's undesirable and perhaps unintended impact on public transparency. For now, the result is that the public may worry about issues that, with adequate information, could be discarded (or confirmed) as real concerns. Potentially wasting energy and resources, people under our current system of pervasive trade secret rights must

---

[106] Daniel Patrick Moynihan, Secrecy16 (1998) (discussing at length the benefits to society of less governmental secrecy).

choose between trust by faith and suspicion by ignorance. Even more worrisome, it is clear that the guise of the trade secret is sometimes being used to hide information about which we, as citizens, should be aware and concerned. Until the above issues are addressed and rectified, we simply won't know what we're missing and what is really happening in and around our government – the antithesis of public transparency.

17 Trade secrets and information access in environmental law

*Mary L. Lyndon**

I. INTRODUCTION

Businesses often assert a privilege to withhold information that would identify their own effects on human health and the environment. Access to data (including chemical identity, volume and locations of discharges, and data on health and ecological effects) is crucial to environmental, health and safety (EHS) management. Secrecy undermines risk management, yet proprietary interests often prevail in direct conflicts over data. In this chapter I outline a case for a rule that would favor access over secrecy, namely when the data describes an environmental impact or exposure.[1]

The petrochemical industry provides a good context for examining the issues. On one hand, the ingredients of a chemical formula are a classic trade secret, though patents may also be a good fit. On the other, many trillions of pounds of chemical substances are distributed each year throughout the globe, so that exposure to them is widespread.[2] Of the approximately 75,000 chemicals in use, only a relatively small number have been well characterized for potential toxicity, though many are thought to pose health risks.[3] Given these facts, should the identity of chemicals or data on their effects be covered by trade secrecy or its progeny, 'confidential business information' (CBI)?

* Professor of Law, St. John's University.

[1] I use 'EHS' and 'environmental' as synonyms, but my focus will be on the environment. Occupational health and safety and consumer product and food and drug management face similar problems in managing and distributing information. David Levine has analysed related issues in public infrastructure and other non-EHS settings. See David S. Levine, Chapter 16.

[2] U.S. companies produced or imported 15 trillion pounds of chemical substances in 2002 (42 billion pounds per day) and 27 trillion pounds in 2005 (74 billion pounds per day), not including fuels, pesticide products, pharmaceuticals or food products. Michael P. Wilson and Megan R. Schwarzman, *Toward a New U.S. Chemicals Policy: Rebuilding the Foundation to Advance New Science, Green Chemistry, and Environmental Health*, 117 ENVTL. HEALTH PERSP. 1202 (2009).

[3] Richard Judson *et al.*,*The Toxicity Data Landscape for Environmental Chemicals*, 117 ENVTL. HEALTH PERSP. 685 (2009).

This chapter poses questions about the way we have been treating information about EHS risks. The discussion is necessarily broad, but I hope it will provoke discussion among trade secret scholars and others about how to move to a new arrangement.[4] Part II describes some basic informational challenges in environmental law, including the inherent asymmetries and complexity that make continual EHS learning both difficult and essential. It then outlines the ways that secrecy creates holes in society's efforts to manage environmental risks. Part III examines the roots of the law supporting access to EHS data and its fairness and efficiency rationales. It then considers the limitations of trade secrets in this setting. Secrecy is out of place in EHS risk regulation; trade secret law itself compels this conclusion. Part IV points to alternative arrangements, some of which are already in place in limited situations. The rest of this introduction outlines the context of the issue.

Three background dimensions are particularly relevant. One is the relationship between environmental quality and technical change. Environmental law emerged in the 1960s, a period of intense technological optimism.[5] The prevailing view was that growth would bring innovation, which, in turn, would solve environmental problems.[6] Given this expectation, perhaps it was logical to enable private control over proprietary information in order to facilitate innovation. Since trade secrecy was not widespread and early environmental challenges seemed to present few mysteries, the arrangement was apparently seen as no more than an inconvenience to environmental management.

A second dimension is the federal Freedom of Information Act (FOIA), enacted in 1966, which has provided the template for agency disclosure

---

[4] There is a large literature on this topic. For general overviews, see David C. Vladeck, *Information Access: Surveying the Current Legal Landscape of Federal Right-to-Know Laws*, 86 TEX. L. REV. 1787 (2008); Mary L. Lyndon, *Secrecy and Access in an Innovation Intensive Economy: Reordering Information Privileges in Environmental, Health and Safety Law*, 78 U. COLO. L. REV. 465 (2007) (hereinafter Lyndon, *Secrecy and Access*). For more detailed analyses, see Wendy E. Wagner, *Commons Ignorance: The Failure of Environmental Law to Produce Needed Information on Health and the Environment*, 53 DUKE L.J. 1619 (2004); Mary L. Lyndon, *Secrecy and Innovation in Tort Law and Regulation*, 23 N.M.L. REV. 1 (1993) (hereinafter Lyndon, *Secrecy and Innovation*)

[5] The 'moonshot' space program and the establishment of the Environmental Protection Agency (EPA) emerged from a common paradigm. See Richard J. Lazarus, *The Greening of America and the Graying of the United States*, 20 VA. ENVTL. L.J. 75, 81 (2001); Mark Sagoff, *The Principles of Federal Pollution Control Law*, 71 MINN. L. REV. 19, 44 (1986).

[6] James E. Krier and Clayton P. Gillette, *The Uneasy Case for Technological Optimism*, 84 MICH. L. REV. 405 (1985).

policies.[7] FOIA directs agencies to disclose information upon request, but it also allows them to withhold some information, such as trade secrets and CBI, covered by FOIA's Exemption 4.[8] Courts reviewing FOIA cases have tended to leave disclosure to agencies' discretion, while regulated firms have pressed agencies for broad confidentiality: selective invisibility serves their competitive and their regulatory interests. As discussed more fully in Part III, agencies are poorly positioned to resist this pressure and often capitulate, even when they have a statutory mandate to disclose the information.

The Toxic Substances Control Act (TSCA) is the third influence on disclosure relating to chemicals in the environment. Enacted in 1976, it directed the Environmental Protection Agency (EPA) to establish a comprehensive inventory of chemicals and to develop toxicity data. However, TSCA exempted from any research requirements the 62,000 chemicals that were in use in 1976 and imposed only minimal reporting requirements for new chemicals.[9] The statute also made it costly for the EPA to demand testing by manufacturers.[10] Thus TSCA, a statute ostensibly designed to generate information and support environmental innovation, is disabled by its own provisions. With respect to trade secrets, TSCA seems to require disclosure of health and safety studies relating to any chemical in commercial distribution, whether they are claimed as proprietary or not.[11] However, the EPA has not consistently implemented this part of its mandate; indeed, secrecy is pervasive in chemicals regulation.[12]

The overall effect of these limitations is that chemical pollution can con-

---

[7] 5 U.S.C. § 552 (2006).

[8] *Id.* § 552(b)(4).

[9] Toxic Substances Control Act § 4 (codified as amended at 15 U.S.C. § 2603) (TSCA); see also Wilson and Schwarzman, *supra* note 2, at 1205.

[10] Toxic Substances Control Act §§ 4–6 (codified as amended at 15 U.S.C. § 2603-26-5). Sections 2 and 6 create a 'Catch 22' situation in which the EPA must prove that a chemical 'may present an unreasonable risk of injury to health or the environment' before the agency may require testing by the manufacturer.

[11] 15 U.S. C. § 2613(b). EPA's disclosure regulations are consolidated at 40 C.F.R. §§ 2.105–2.311 (2008). Pursuant to their separate authorizing statutes, the regulations provide for public availability of air emissions data, 40 C.F.R. § 2.301; water effluent information, 40 C.F.R. § 2.302; contaminants in drinking water, 40 C.F.R. § 2.304; and chemical health and safety information, 40 C.F.R. § 2.306, whether or not the data is claimed as proprietary.

[12] For useful overviews, see generally John Applegate and Katherine Baer, *Strategies for Closing the Chemical Data Gap* (April 2006), www.progressive-reform.org/articles/Closing_Data_Gaps_602.pdf; Rena Steinzor and Matthew Shudtz, *Sequestered Science: Secrets Threatening Public Health*, (April 2007), www.progressivereform.org/articles/Secrecy_703.pdf.

tinue until someone proves it harmful. The public must essentially 'reverse engineer' pollution problems to ascertain their origins. With no incentives to replace the old chemicals, the original 62,000 are still in use.[13]

In the decades since this framework was established, much has changed. Business use of secrecy has become widespread, while the environmental scene has become more complex. We have more varied environmental problems today and more awareness of the physical complexity and limitations of the world we live in.[14] Innovation is still a core environmental strategy, but we no longer expect environmental remedies or preventive environmental strategies to emerge automatically from economic growth.[15] Also, we have found that regulation has not been ruinous, but instead can contribute to innovative technical change.[16]

An important development is the increased role of research and information distribution in environmental management.[17] Today administrative agencies coordinate research and deploy information through reporting requirements, public listing of pollution discharges, ingredient labeling and product rating and certification. These 'information strategies' open up the conventional relationship between the agency and the regulated firm and use information to engage the market and public opinion in responses to pollution.[18] The fit between information distribution and environmental law is a good one, since the burdens of pollution are widely distributed.

A sign of the times is the European Union (EU)'s recent enactment of its ambitious program, Registration, Evaluation, Authorization and Restriction of Chemical Substances (REACH), which reverses the burden of proof for chemicals in EU markets.[19] The basic principle of REACH is

---

[13] Wilson and Schwarzman, *supra* note 2.

[14] Recent research on the effects of low-level chemical exposures is particularly relevant. See, e.g., CARL F. CRANOR, LEGALLY POISONED: HOW THE LAW PUTS US AT RISK FROM TOXICANTS (forthcoming 2011), which is discussed *infra*.

[15] See Kenneth Arrow *et al.*, *Economic Growth, Carrying Capacity, and the Environment*, 268 SCI. 520, 520–1 (1995).

[16] FRANK ACKERMAN, POISONED FOR PENNIES: THE ECONOMICS OF TOXICS AND PRECAUTION (2008).

[17] Allen L. White, *Why We Need Global Standards for Corporate Disclosure*, 69 LAW & CONTEMP. PROBS. 167 (2006) (describing development of information function in EHS risk management).

[18] Paul R. Kleindorfer and Eric W. Orts, *Informational Regulation of Environmental Risks*, 18 RISK ANALYSIS 155 (1998); Peter S. Menell, *Structuring a Market-Oriented Federal Eco-Information Policy*, 54 MD. L. REV. 1435 (1995).

[19] Council Regulation (EC) 1907/2006, on the Registration, Evaluation, Authorization and Restriction of Chemical Substances (REACH) [2006] O.J. L396 establishes a comprehensive set of requirements for chemicals and their safe use.

'no data, no market', as all chemicals must be registered and studied, or they may not be traded in the EU. REACH is forcing long-overdue change in the petrochemical industry and it makes the EU the pace-setter in the global chemicals market.[20] A number of legislative proposals in the United States would revise TSCA and follow the EU's lead, as well as introduce other reforms, including expanded access to information.[21] This is a good time to re-examine the role of secrecy in regulation.

II. THE KNOWLEDGE PROBLEM IN ENVIRONMENTAL LAW

A. Pollution and Information

Environmental management is concerned with the physical condition of earth systems and the health of their inhabitants. Pollution can be understood as extended physical activity in these systems. Terry Collins has described chemicals' environmental activity this way:

> Imagine all of Earth's chemistry as a mail sorter's wall of letter slots in a post office, with the network of compartments extending toward infinity. Each compartment represents a separate chemistry so that, for example, thousands of compartments are associated with stratospheric chemistry or with a human cell. An environmentally mobile persistent pollutant can move from compartment to compartment, sampling a large number and finding those compartments that it can perturb. Many perturbations may be inconsequential, but others can cause unforeseen catastrophes, such as the ozone hole or some of the manifestations of endocrine disruption. Most compartments remain unidentified and even for known compartments, the interactions of the pollutant with the compartment's contents can usually not be foreseen, giving ample reason for scientific humility when considering the safety of persistent mobile compounds.[22]

Circumstances change when a chemical substance is physically added to a person or an environmental situation. Will the change be temporary and

---

It requires and supports collaborative research by all companies using the same chemical and will then publicly rank chemicals based on their toxicity.

[20] See Mark Schapiro, Exposed: The Toxic Chemistry of Everyday Products and What's at Stake for Americana Power (2007). Countries that do not follow the EU's lead will fall behind and become dumping grounds for low quality and hazardous chemicals.

[21] See, e.g., Richard A. Denison, *Ten Essential Elements in TSCA Reform*, 39 Envtl. L. Rep. 10,020 (2009).

[22] Terry Collins, *Toward Sustainable Chemistry*, 291 Sci. 48 (2001).

benign or lasting and harmful? If a chemical is persistent, bioaccumulative or toxic (BPT), it is more likely to cause EHS impacts.[23]

The three illustrations below show how secrecy affects identification, assessment and responses to chemicals.

Hydraulic fracturing To retrieve natural gas from shale, where gas is trapped in tiny pockets in the rock, hydraulic fracturing, or 'fracking', pumps million gallons of fluid or gel deep into each well under great pressure.[24] The impact breaks open the rock and releases gas, which is pulled back to the surface. Fracking is associated with a number of environmental problems. Two stem from the fluids, which contain chemical mixtures that are considered proprietary but contain at least some toxins. Fluid that remains in the ground will migrate and affect groundwater.[25] Fluid that is retrieved must be disposed of, but there are limited options for handling such large amounts of contaminated water.[26] The costs of hydraulic fracturing cannot be assessed without knowing the identity and amounts of the chemicals in the fracking fluid. Disclosure would also give drilling companies an incentive to innovate to minimize the risks to water supplies.[27]

---

[23] 'Persistence' refers to the length of time the chemical can exist in the environment before being destroyed (i.e., transformed) by natural processes and 'bioaccumulation' refers to the process by which organisms may accumulate chemical substances in their bodies. See 64 Fed. Reg. 58,666 (October 29, 1999) (lowering reporting thresholds for certain persistent bioaccumulative toxic chemicals).

[24] See *Current Water Issues in Oil and Gas Development and Production: Will Water Control What Energy We Have?*, 49 Washburn L.J. 423 (2010) (explaining that energy production consumes great amounts of water, an increasingly scarce resource).

[25] Despite the risks that fracking poses to water, it was exempted from the Safe Drinking Water Act (SDWA) in 2005. See Energy Policy Act of 2005, Pub. L. No. 109-58, § 1(a), 119 Stat. 594 (2005) (codified as amended at 42 U.S.C. § 300h(d) (2006)).

[26] See New York City Comments on: Draft Supplemental Generic Environmental Impact Statement (DSGEIS) on the Oil, Gas and Solution Mining Regulatory Program: Well Permit Issuance for Horizontal Drilling and High-Volume Hydraulic Fracturing to Develop the Marcellus Shale and Other Low-Permeability Gas Reservoirs, available at www.nyc.gov/html/dep/pdf/natural_gas_drilling/nycdep_comments_final_12-22-09.pdf.

[27] The EPA has begun to study fracking and its effects. See Abrahm Lustgarten, *EPA Launches National Study of Hydraulic Fracturing*, Propublica, March 18, 2010, available at www.propublica.org/article/epa-launches-national-study-of-hydraulic-fracturing. Episodes of water contamination have sparked interest in Congress and at the EPA in re-examining the special confidentiality provisions. See Editorial, *The Halliburton Loophole*, New York Times, November 3, 2009, at

'Inert' pesticide ingredients Pesticides are designed to kill, repel or otherwise harm living organisms. Monitoring studies in the United States have found pesticides in one or more samples from every stream sampled and in more than 70 percent of common foods.[28] The Federal Insecticide, Fungicide and Rodenticide Act (FIFRA), which authorizes the regulation of pesticides, distinguishes between 'active' ingredients (those intentionally designed to kill or control the target pest) and 'inert' ingredients, which may be fragrances, dyes, aerosol propellants, solvent, desiccants, carriers and other substances.[29] The word 'inert' does not carry its common meaning here, as 'inert' pesticide ingredients may have their own biological activity, may be toxic to humans and may be chemically active. In 2004 the EPA identified almost 3,000 substances used as inert ingredients. Some of these are known to be highly toxic; about 50 percent are considered moderately risky. Some studies have found that common pesticides consist of between 50 and 86 percent inert ingredients.[30]

FIFRA requires that labels identify active but not inert ingredients, and requires less testing of inert ingredients.[31] Pesticide manufacturers maintain that inert ingredient information is proprietary, but independent assessment of pesticide toxicity is hindered by lack of public access to product-specific information about inert ingredients.[32]

Cosmetics and consumer products Regulation of consumer products has developed incrementally, with different statutes regulating different kinds of products.[33] The safety and availability of information about ingredi-

---

A28, available at www.nytimes.com/2009/11/03/opinion/03tue3.html (explaining that proposed Fracturing Responsibility and Awareness of Chemicals Act would remove exemption from Safe Drinking Water Act and require oil and gas firms to disclose chemicals used).

[28] See Caroline Cox and Michael Surgan, *Unidentified Inert Ingredients in Pesticides: Implications for Human and Environmental Health*, 114 ENVTL. HEALTH PERSP. 1803 (2006).

[29] 7 U.S.C. § 136(a), (m); see also Cox & Surgan, *supra* note 28.

[30] Cox & Surgan, *supra* note 28; *see also* Caroline Cox and Michael Surgan, '*Inert' Ingredients Threaten Human and Environmental Health*, 75 PESTICIDE PEWS 12, 12–14, n.4 (March 2007).

[31] Inert ingredients and whole formulations are not required to be tested for chronic effects. Yet synergistic effects of combinations of chemicals are likely to occur and inert ingredients can also increase exposure to pesticide formulations. Cox and Surgan, *supra* note 28, at 1804.

[32] In December 2009, the EPA opened a rule-making proceeding to consider requiring disclosure of inert ingredients. See 74 Fed. Reg. 68,215 (December 23, 2009).

[33] See, e.g., Rachael Rawlins, *Teething on Toxins: In Search of Regulatory*

ents is uneven. For instance, personal care products, such as shampoos and cosmetics, generally need not disclose the chemical composition of fragrances and labels also omit other ingredients.[34] Consumers who try to make healthy choices in personal care products have little to go on.[35]

The EU has recently taken a more assertive regulatory stance on cosmetics. Its revised Cosmetics Directive proscribes the use of listed suspect chemicals in cosmetics and directs the industry to collaborate to develop better and less expensive testing methods.[36] Some U.S. companies now sell products in Europe that comply with the EU Directive, but continue to sell products in the United States that have the EU's suspect chemicals in them.[37]

B. Expanding Information Deficits

The examples illustrate a recurring pattern. Polluting firms and EHS interests interact with exposures at different times, in different spaces and with different motivations and costs. Secrecy enables one activity and obstructs the other.

Firms tend to create the environmental or health exposures that their business model entails and the law allows. Market incentives encourage firms to enter the market sooner rather than later and then to leave behind efforts that are no longer paying off. A firm values control over information in order to serve its competitive position, though a particular secret's role may range from crucial to merely convenient or may be impossible

---

Solutions for Toys and Cosmetics, 20 Fordham Envtl. L. Rev. 1 (2009); Sarah E. Schaffer, *Reading Our Lips: The History of Lipstick Regulation in Western Seats of Power*, 62 Food & Drug L.J. 165, 202–25 (2007).

[34] See, e.g., Anne C. Steinemann, *Fragranced Consumer Products and Undisclosed Ingredients*, 29 Envtl. Impact Assessment Rev. 32, 32–8 (2009) (discussing chemical analysis of six best-selling products which identified nearly 100 volatile organic compounds (VOCs), none of which were listed on any product label, one of which was listed on one notice form, ten of which are regulated as toxic or hazardous under federal laws, and three of which are classified as hazardous air pollutants); Delia Gervin, *You Can Stand Under My Umbrella: Weighing Trade Secret Protection Against the Need for Greater Transparency in Perfume and Fragranced Product Labeling*, 15 J. Intell. Prop. L. 315 (2008).

[35] Skin Deep, a safe cosmetics campaign associated with the Environmental Working Group, rates cosmetics for toxicity based on information that is publicly available; its website demonstrates the dearth of information available for most products. See www.cosmeticsdatabase.com/.

[36] Council Directive 2003/15/EC [2003] O.J. L66; see also Schapiro, *supra* note 20, at 21–41.

[37] Schapiro, *supra* note 20, at 31–4.

to ascertain. The secret's commercial value usually will expire, perhaps within months or a few years. The possibility of liability will discourage firms from revealing past exposures when proprietary information is no longer commercially valuable. The costs of research, the uncertainties of research outcomes and the specter of liability combine to discourage firms from researching or disclosing EHS effects.[38]

On the EHS side, secrecy obscures the nature and the location of a physical change in the environment, removing key information from those concerned with responding to it. Although it may be abandoned by its commercial source, often the impact does not disappear. It may persist and be active; repeated releases of pollutants will generate wider distribution and more complex interactions. The social costs of the original secret become greater with the passage of time, as the effect becomes more costly to identify and remedy.

C. Small Doses with Large Effects

The effects of low doses of chemicals in the environment used to be just part of the 'uncertainty' that pervades regulation, but research and technical development are yielding new understanding. Today we know that ordinary people carry a 'body burden' of chemicals, including a number that are considered health risks at some levels of exposure.[39] The levels of some that have been detected appear to be medically significant, especially for fetuses and children.[40] The types of chemicals that are causing concern range from the familiar, including lead and mercury, to new categories,

---

[38] See John S. Applegate, *Bridging the Data Gap: Balancing the Supply and Demand for Chemical Information*, 86 Tex. L. Rev. 1365, 1380–5 (2008); Mary L. Lyndon, *Information Economics and Chemical Toxicity: Designing Laws to Produce and Use Data*, 87 Mich. L. Rev. 1795, 1810–16 (1989) (hereinafter Lyndon, *Information*).

[39] The Centers for Disease Control (CDC) has identified more than 300 chemicals in the blood and urine of the population. See Ctrs. for Disease Control and Prevention, National Report on Human Exposure to Environmental Chemicals (2009); Cranor, *supra* note 14, ch. 2.

[40] The developing bodies of fetuses and children have numerous critical periods of susceptibility, during which exposures to low levels of toxicants (levels that would have no effect on adults) may cause damage. Among the factors that affect their susceptibility to toxic exposures are their faster metabolism and breathing rate, body mass ratio, immature systems like kidney function and skin permeability, more years of future life and maternal changes during pregnancy, such as the 'calcium stream' from mother's bones to child which will include concentrated lead from her bones. Cranor, *supra* note 14, ch. 4.

like endocrine disruptors, which are substances that mimic or alter hormonal effects in the body.[41]

An example of harm from endocrine disruptors is the epidemic of reproductive abnormalities and cancers suffered by women who were exposed *in utero* to the pharmaceutical DES, a synthetic hormone. DES generated distinct types of injuries in daughters, some of whom were compensated by the courts, because of negligent testing by manufacturers.[42] As the DES disaster was unfolding, a group of physicians conducted autopsies of 281 female fetuses and neonates; they found vaginal tissue abnormalities (*adenosis* or incomplete development) in about 70 percent of those whose mothers had taken DES, compared with 4 percent of those whose mothers had not taken it. The *adenosis* was later understood to be the precursor of the abnormalities that emerged when surviving girls matured. The study demonstrated that exposure *in utero* could cause changes that would become apparent later in life.[43]

It now appears that fetal and early childhood exposures may contribute to a number of diseases. The early damage may consist of changes in cells that will lead to later malfunctions or even to gene expressions that will surface in the next generation.[44] It may alter the development of tissue that should later supply resistance to infections or compensate for aging processes, as in Parkinson's or Alzheimer's disease, so that the actual illness occurs decades later.[45]

Low level exposures may also cause disease in mature individuals through additive and synergistic exposures. These effects have been largely ignored in environmental regulation, but current research shows that some biological receptors are affected over time by repeated exposure to the same or different toxicants. Breast cancer is an example of a disease that is caused by cumulative exposures, as estrogen exposure is apparently additive.[46] Exposures to pesticides, DES, hormone replacement therapy and synthetic 'environmental estrogens', such as Bisphenol A (BPA),

---

[41] See *id.*; David A. Schwartz and Kenneth Korach, *Emerging Research on Endocrine Disruptors*, 115 ENVTL. HEALTH PERSP. A13 (2007), available at www.ncbi.nlm.nih.gov/pmc/articles/PMC1797850/pdf/ehp0115-a00013.pdf.

[42] See Hymowitz v. Eli Lilly & Co., 539 N.E.2d 1069 (1989) (articulating 'public risk' version of market share liability).

[43] CRANOR, *supra* note 14, ch. 4.

[44] *Id.*; Mark A. Rothstein *et al.*, *The Ghosts in Our Genes: Legal and Ethical Implications of Epigenetics,* 19 HEALTH MATRIX 1 (2009).

[45] CRANOR, *supra* note 14, ch. 4.

[46] *Id.* Studies indicate that about 67 percent of breast cancers are the result of avoidable environmental factors rather than genetic causes.

therefore may also contribute to breast cancer rates.[47] Other diseases have also been associated with low doses of environmental estrogens.[48]

These findings challenge the existing regulatory paradigm, which has assumed that low level chemical exposures are generally tolerable. Certainly, one implication is that we can no longer accept ignorance about chemical effects. Instead, we need a system that provides the greatest support for research and the earliest possible warnings.

D. Weakened Risk Management

Environmental management requires a broad commitment to continual, society-wide learning.[49] Broad access to basic information is essential to this process. People who are exposed to pollution, people who study it, like researchers and doctors, and people who are interested in it for policy debates, such as journalists, are important participants in environmental risk management.[50] EHS information also evolves over time; risk management is an iterative process. Access to the stream of information, not a peek or a snapshot, is needed.[51]

---

47 *Id.* Current body burdens of BPA in adults are 'within the range that is predicted to be biologically active in over 95% of people sampled'. *Id.* BPA is produced and used at the rate of about 2.3 billion pounds annually in the United States and most people are contaminated with it. See Rawlins, *supra* note 33.

48 These include prostate and breast cancer, uro-genital abnormalities in male babies, a decline in semen quality in men, early onset of puberty in girls, metabolic disorders including insulin resistant (type 2) diabetes and obesity, and neurobehavioral problems such as attention deficit hyperactivity disorder (ADHD). CRANOR, *supra* note 14, ch. 4; Philippe Grandjean and Philippe Landrigan, *Developmental Neurotoxicity of Industrial Chemicals*, 368 LANCELET 2167 (2006).

49 Daniel A. Farber, *Environmental Protection as a Learning Experience*, 27 LOY. L.A. L. REV. 791 (1994); Lyndon, *Secrecy and Access*, *supra* note 4, at 510–16.

50 See e.g., Current Science on Public Exposures to Toxic Chemicals: Hearing Before the Subcomm. on Superfund, Toxics, and Environmental Health of the S. Comm. on Environmental and Public Works, 111th Cong. (2010) (statement of Charles McKay, Medical Review Officer, Hartford Hospital), available at http://epw.senate.gov/public/index.cfm?FuseAction=Files.View&FileStore_id=0da04862-d2b1-41c7-a660-8824b8f2c326 (explaining that the state poison control center receives more than 30,000 calls per year from the public and medical personnel concerning possible or known toxic exposures); Lyndon, *Secrecy and Innovation*, *supra* note 4, at 26–34 (explaining that manufacturers, unions and public health experts argued for chemical identity disclosure in early federal hazard communication proceedings).

51 See John S. Applegate, *The Temporal Dimension of Land Pollution: Another Perspective on Applying the Breaking the Logjam Principles to Waste Management*, 17 N.Y.U. ENVTL. L.J. 757 (2008); Daniel A. Farber, *Probabilities Behaving Badly:*

The EPA plays a central role in setting the research agenda and synthesizing information, as well as coordinating data collection and distribution, but risk management cannot be conducted from the top down or from one central location.[52] Information distribution is widely seen as an important regulatory innovation.[53]

However, regulatory efforts to limit and disclose chemical uses have provoked extended 'science wars'. [54] As a result, the EPA's effectiveness has been compromised. A major factor has been the increase in proprietary claims that restrict the use of the available data. For instance, 95 percent of the TSCA premanufacture submitted to EPA contain some information that is claimed as confidential.[55] Each confidentiality claim

---

Complexity Theory and Environmental Uncertainty, 37 U.C. DAVIS L. REV. 145 (2003) (explaining that complex systems require careful monitoring and repeated interventions as they evolve).

[52] The National Research Council has used the metaphor of a tree for the environmental information system: information flows from the tree's roots (its dispersed sources in the physical world), through its trunk and branches (the agencies and professional experts that synthesize it), producing the foliage of useful knowledge. See, e.g, BOARD ON EARTH SCI. & RES., COMM. ON GEOPHYSICAL AND ENVTL. DATA, NAT'L RESEARCH COUNCIL, RESOLVING CONFLICTS ARISING FROM THE PRIVATIZATION OF ENVIRONMENTAL DATA § 11 *et seq.* (2003). Both expert and lay knowledge contribute and expert interpretation and further research are not always necessary. Steven Shavell has noted that much regulation can be justified by common knowledge or non-expert information. See Lyndon, *Secrecy and Access*, *supra* note 4, at 512–13.

[53] JAMES T. HAMILTON, REGULATION THROUGH REVELATION: THE ORIGIN, POLITICS, AND IMPACTS OF THE TOXICS RELEASE INVENTORY (2005); David W. Case, *Corporate Environmental Reporting as Informational Regulation: A Law and Economics Perspective*, 76 U. COLO. L. REV. 379 (2005); Bradley C. Karkkainen, *Information as Environmental Regulation: TRI and Performance Benchmarking, Precursor to a New Paradigm?*, 9 GEO. L.J. 257 (2001); Kleindorfer and Orts, *supra* note 18.

[54] See THOMAS O. MCGARITY, SIDNEY SHAPIRO AND DAVID BOLLIER, SOPHISTICATED SABOTAGE: THE INTELLECTUAL GAMES USED TO SUBVERT RESPONSIBLE REGULATION 34–65 (2004); David Michaels, *Doubt is Their Product*, 292 SCIENTIFIC AMERICAN 96, 96–101 (2005). Firms also withhold information. In 2005, the EPA fined DuPont U.S.$16.5 million for violating TSCA § 8(e) by not reporting data on the health risks posed by a chemical ingredient in Teflon. See Thomas O. McGarity, *The Complementary Roles of Common Law Courts and Federal Agencies in Producing and Using Policy-Relevant Scientific Information*, 37 ENVTL. L. REV. 1027, 1035–49 (2007) (describing the interplay between courts and agencies in this case); see also Marianne Lavelle, *E.P.A.'s Amnesty Has Become a Mixed Blessing: Be Careful What You Wish For*, NAT'L L.J., March 3, 1997, at A1 (explaining that, under an amnesty program in place from 1991 to 1996, manufacturers handed in 11,000 old, unpublished studies and adverse reaction reports).

[55] See U.S. GOV'T ACCOUNTABILITY OFFICE, CHEMICAL REGULATION: OPTIONS

means that the agency must take special care to handle the data separately, segregating bits of trade secrets and CBI from the general work of the agency.[56] The Government Accounting Office (GAO) has found that the EPA's chemical review program under TSCA has only limited ability to share the information it receives with other agencies, let alone the public.[57] In addition, sharing information is chilled by the possibility that a mistake would be punished.[58]

Secrecy makes scientific research more difficult and more costly.[59] Some key tools, such as mass balance accounting, have been blocked. Resistance to reporting the amounts of chemicals firms discharge has hindered assessment of environmental loading and ecosystem effects.[60]

Exist to Improve EPA's Ability to Assess Health Risks and Manage its Chemical Review Program 32 (2005).

[56] Proposed Rules on Public Information and Confidentiality Regulations, 59 Fed. Reg. at 60,446, 60,447 (November 23, 1994) (explaining that the EPA receives more than 40,000 FOIA requests a year, a large number of which are requests for confidential business information); see also Wagner, *supra* note 4.

[57] The GAO has repeatedly criticized the chemical management system established under TSCA and its confidentiality restrictions. See, e.g., U.S. Gov't Accountability Office, Chemical Regulation: Options for Enhancing the Effectiveness of the Toxic Substances Control Act (February 26, 2009) (arguing that the EPA needs greater authority to require production of toxicity data and share information with states and the public); GAO, Chemical Regulation, *supra* note 55, at 31–4 (explaining that agency efforts to challenge CBI claims are costly).

[58] TSCA § 14(d) (codified as amended at 15 U.S.C. § 2613(d) (2006)) imposes a penalty of U.S.$5,000, one year in prison, or both for knowing willful disclosure of protected information. The 1996 Economic Espionage Act, 18 U.S.C. § 1832(a)(5), extended the 1918 Trade Secrets Act, 18 U.S.C.A. § 1905 (2006), to expand criminal liability for disclosures. However, in Chrysler Corp. v. Brown, 441 U.S. 281 (1979), the Supreme Court found that agencies with general rule-making authority may disclose information claimed to be protected by the Trade Secrets Act.

[59] See, e.g., Andrew Vickers, *Cancer Data? Sorry, Can't Have It*, New York Times, January 22, 2008, at F8; Barry Meier, *Contracts Keep Drug Research Out of Reach*, New York Times, November 29, 2004 (describing effects on data availability of contracts between drug companies and academic researchers); Eric. G. Campbell and Eran Bendavid, *Data Sharing and Data Withholding in Genetics and the Life Sciences: Results of a National Survey of Technology Transfer Officers*, 6 J. Health Care L. & Pol'y 241 (2003); Sheila Jasanoff, *Transparency in Public Science: Purposes, Reasons, Limits*, 69 Law &. Contemp. Probs. 21 (2006).

[60] Robert K. Klee, *Enabling Environmental Sustainability in the United States: The Case for a Comprehensive Material Flow Inventory*, 23 Stan. Envtl. L.J. 131, 156 (2004) (arguing that material flow/mass balance information would enable transition to more efficient system); Uwe M. Erling, *Approaches to Integrated Pollution Control in the United States and the European Union,* 15 Tul. Envtl. L.J. 1, 19 (2001) (explaining that lack of mass balance data for model facility blocked

Secrecy also imposes costs on individuals and puts their health at risk. For instance, in 2009, Cathy Behr, a nurse in Colorado, fell seriously ill after treating a worker who had been injured in a chemical spill. Her doctors diagnosed chemical poisoning, but the manufacturer of the product she was exposed to would not disclose its full ingredients, because it considered them proprietary. Ms. Behr has partially recovered, but she continues to have respiratory problems. She has been left with uncertainty about her future health and an awareness of the limitations on her political options. 'I'd really like to know what went wrong', Ms. Behr has said, 'As citizens in a democracy, we ought to know what's happening around us'.[61]

Secrecy also has systemic economic effects. Trade secrecy has increased chemical products' inherent low visibility. As George Akerlof pointed out in *A Market for Lemons*, products with latent defects may penalize their whole product category. Products that have no defects will bear a burden or stigma, because buyers cannot tell which ones may be defective.[62] The petrochemical industry continues to manufacture products that may or may not be toxic, while non-toxic products and new 'green' chemicals are affected by the uncertainty created by the prevalence of untested chemicals.[63] Secrecy distorts the market, the R&D agenda and society's management of health and the environment.

Viewed from either an individual or a systemic perspective, disclosure is the best solution, as it aligns social needs with market and innovation imperatives.

III. THE LEGAL REGIME

In conflicts over secrecy and access the two sides invoke separate legal traditions and neither addresses the concerns of the other. Access is rooted in the common law concerned with harms and with fair and efficient risk communication; these have been extended by regulation and contemporary tort law. Confidentiality and trade secrecy have been part of unfair competition law and are now fortified by their association with patent

---

EPA experiment with a multimedia permit that would integrate and simplify permit requirements).

[61] Lyndsey Layton, *Use of Potentially Harmful Chemicals Kept Secret Under Law*, WASHINGTON POST, January 4, 2010, at A1.

[62] See George Akerlof, *The Market for 'Lemons': Quality Uncertainty and the Market Mechanism*, 84 Q.J. ECON. 488 (1970).

[63] See Collins, *supra* note 22; Michael P. Wilson and Megan R. Schwarzman, *New Science for Chemicals Policy*, 326 SCI. 1065 (2009).

law. The third legal factor, agency disclosure, is shaped by FOIA. FOIA provides for broad information access with general exceptions, but it does not provide substantive guidance on EHS disclosure. In fact, it tends to confuse the issues. This section looks at each in turn.

A. Access and Communication

Information access and communication obligations are pervasive in the common law and environmental statutes have built upon this foundation. Both the common law and regulation affirm the importance of access to information about risks. Environmental impacts follow predictably from a firm's decision to distribute pollution or product ingredients in circumstances that will lead to exposure. Exposure is expected, not a surprise. The choice to release pollutants therefore triggers familiar obligations.

Risk communication is a strong requirement in tort law. Negligence law imposes a duty to act with reasonable care with respect to third parties.[64] There is a duty to warn those who may be affected by one's actions.[65] Related information entitlements include warranty,[66] fraud[67] and the law

---

[64] See RESTATEMENT (THIRD) OF TORTS, Liability to Physical Harm § 7 (2005) (providing that an actor ordinarily has a duty to exercise reasonable care when the actor's conduct creates a risk of physical harm); *id.* § 12 (providing that an actor's skills or knowledge are to be taken into account in determining whether the actor has behaved as a reasonably careful person).

[65] *Id.* § 18 (providing that, under the 'negligent failure to warn' doctrine, a defendant whose conduct creates a risk of harm can fail to exercise reasonable care by failing to warn of the danger if the defendant knows or has reason to know of the risk, those encountering the risk will be unaware of it and a warning might be effective in reducing the risk of harm). In addition, even if the defendant adequately warns of the risk, the defendant can fail to exercise reasonable care by failing to adopt further precautions to protect against the risk if it is foreseeable that despite the warning some risk of harm remains. Warning obligations have been strengthened by case law and also retained as a strong requirement in the RESTATEMENT (THIRD) OF TORTS, Products Liability §§ 2(c), 10, 13, 18 (1998).

[66] Warranty law requires that information about latent risks be transmitted to buyers. 9 WILLIAM R. GINSBERG AND PHILIP WEINBERG, ENVIRONMENTAL LAW AND REGULATION IN NEW YORK § 2:9 (2d ed. 2009) (explaining that breach of implied warranty is closely related to the 'duty to warn' cause of action in negligence and strict product liability).

[67] See, e.g., RESTATEMENT (FIRST) OF TORTS § 529 cmt. a (1939) (pointing out that a statement containing a half-truth may be as misleading as a statement wholly false; the recipient of the statement is entitled to know the undisclosed facts insofar as they are material).

of informed consent.[68] These conventional requirements laid the foundation for contemporary rules on distribution of EHS risk information.

Tort law's effectiveness in deterring risky exposures has been limited, though tort litigation has addressed some cases. Adjudication requires evidence and this has been scarce.[69] We cannot know how many cases might have been identified or proven if the law required identification and study as a condition of exposure. Instead, regulated industries have been able stay out of court and maintain the posture, 'Who, me?'. Procedural fairness dictates that secrecy, at least, should not be legitimate in these circumstances.

Access to EHS information is efficient. It provides a non-intrusive way to correct costly market failures and it enhances a wide array of essential social and market activities. In contrast, secrecy in risk management is inefficient. It subsidizes current technologies by obscuring their costs. It allows the secret keeper to impose risks and then hoard information about them. In effect, it transfers the health and safety options of those who are exposed to those who create and profit from the exposure.

Access rules express a robust normative imperative. In Cathy Behr's case, familiar legal and ethical principles would seem to require a different outcome. When her illness went undiagnosed, what was missed? Ms. Behr's concerns about the social and civic implications of her experience are well taken.[70]

Disclosure and warning enable victims to protect themselves. Keeping chemical risks secret shifts the burden of uncertainty to those with little capacity to bear it and then withholds the data necessary to study and respond to the exposure. This imposes 'total risk bearing', to use Guido Calabresi's term. Discussing the placement of responsibility for the initial risk of harm from the behavior of others, he has observed:

> Of course, if victims were chosen to bear *all* risk initially, total atomism would be possible. Such a starting point – essentially a might makes right entitlement – is not *logically* impossible. But no atomistic *laissez-faire* society can, in fact, tolerate it. Total risk bearing by victims would neither avoid injuries cheaply

---

[68] Margaret A. Berger and Aaron D. Twersky, *Uncertainty and Informed Choice: Unmasking Daubert*, 104 Mich. L. Rev. 257 (2005).

[69] See Wendy Wagner, *When All Else Fails: Regulating Risky Products Through Tort Litigation*, 95 Geo. L.J. 693 (2007). However, tort law and regulation can be mutually supportive. See McGarity, *supra* note 54; Mary L. Lyndon, *Tort Law and Technology*, 12 Yale J. on Reg. 137 (1995).

[70] Access to knowledge may be seen as a human right. See Lea Bishop Shaver, *Defining and Measuring A2K: A Blueprint for an Index of Access to Knowledge*, 4 I/S: J.L. & Pol'y for Info. Soc. 235 (2008).

> (be efficient) nor result in an acceptable wealth distribution (be fair). At its extreme it would entail no property or bodily integrity.[71]

Ostensibly, the current system provides chemical manufacturers with a power to expose with the correlative of liability, to use Hohfeld's terms.[72] However, in practice it is a power without liability, as the power claimed is the entitlement to secrecy, which prevents the development of evidence. Liability is suppressed and the entitlement becomes a simple power to expose.

The law effectively allows polluters to anonymously deposit chemicals everywhere, including in our bodies. Whether or not firms might be held liable in court for particular exposures, this is not a tolerable situation. To change it, the law must, at a minimum, require meaningful disclosure of exposures and their effects.

B. Commercial Secrecy

Does trade secret law authorize blocking disclosure when the secret describes risks the firm is creating? There is little to indicate that it does.

As other chapters in this volume demonstrate, trade secrecy's essential functions are basically established: it supports incentives to innovate by facilitating data sharing in business relationships and providing control over information that is associated with patents. It works through a cause of action for misappropriation of trade information that is secret. It has nothing to say, however, about matters outside its own boundaries.

When trade secret interests conflict with other values, confidentiality interests often have been compromised or overridden.[73] That is to say, the doctrine operates within normal jurisprudential boundaries. The Third Restatement of Unfair Competition states:

> The disclosure of another's trade secret for purposes other than commercial exploitation may implicate the interest in freedom of expression or advance another significant public interest . . . a privilege is likely to be recognized . . . in connection with the disclosure that is relevant to public health or safety, or

---

[71] Guido Calabresi, *Torts: The Law of the Mixed Society*, 56 TEX. L. REV. 519, 525 (1978) (emphasis in original).

[72] Wesley Newcomb Hohfeld, *Fundamental Legal Conceptions as Applied in Judicial Reasoning*, 26 YALE L.J. 710 (1917).

[73] For instance, trade secret law balances the rights of employers to control the use of information and employees' right to work and use their skills and knowledge. Steven Wilf, *Trade Secrets, Property, and Social Relations*, 34 CONN. L. REV. 787 (2002).

to the commission of a crime or tort, or to other matters of substantial public concern.[74]

Furthermore, under the Restatement, the decision to award injunctive relief takes into account the interests of third persons and of the public.[75] The 'public welfare' certainly includes the individual and systemic EHS risks that are exacerbated by lack of information, including confidential or trade secret data. In the current economy, companies routinely create large-scale risks, so this exception and the need for transparency are greater than ever.

Nor is it clear that EHS information qualifies as a trade secret in the first place. Trade secret law is about commerce and the flow of information within commercial relationships.[76] Information that describes environmental risks or damage is not 'trade' or 'commercial or financial' information within the meaning of trade secret law or FOIA's Exemption 4. On their face, these terms could apply to any information that a firm or its rival may find useful, but 'trade' in this context refers to the market relationship, not the creation of physical risks to third parties. The fact that a firm's competitors might be interested in information does not insulate a firm from the implications of the activity that the information describes. It does not exempt a firm from participation in the larger legal system, including warning and harm prevention.

The term 'secrecy' is also limited.[77] To read 'secret' to include damaging externalities that are invisible, simply because they are poorly understood, would extend the doctrine beyond its function. Moreover, discharging pollutants without sufficient research and communication effectively abandons any secrecy claim that does attach.[78]

Trade secrecy's association with intellectual property seems to lift

---

[74] RESTATEMENT (THIRD) OF UNFAIR COMPETITION § 40 cmt. c (1995) (discussing improper use of disclosure).

[75] *Id.* § 44(e)(2).

[76] *Id.* §40 cmt. c ('The unauthorized disclosure of a trade secret ordinarily occurs as part of an attempt to exploit the commercial value of the secret through use in competition with the trade secret owner or through a sale of the information to other potential users . . . The disclosure of another's trade secret for purposes other than commercial exploitation may implicate the interest in freedom of expression or advance another significant public interest').

[77] Pamela Samuelson and Suzanne Scotchmer, *The Law and Economics of Reverse Engineering,* 111 YALE L.J. 1575 (2002).

[78] Where high-tech reverse engineering is available, 'secret' data is more available to commercial rivals than to exposure victims. See Lyndon, *Secrecy and Innovation*, *supra* note 4, at 30.

individual claims above the fray, but in the EHS setting this effect is more rhetorical than practical. Secrecy generally works against the basic thrust of the patent system, as it limits diffusion of information that enables further innovation. EHS assessment is an important impetus for sustainable technical change.[79] If accommodation for confidentiality about pollution rests in part on the expectation that technology will solve environmental problems, this would seem to require a showing that the particular secret actually enables improved environmental performance. As discussed in Part IV, where environmental programs are crafted to expressly stimulate environmental innovations, secrecy may have a role.

Does a conventional property frame yield a different result?[80] It is no defense to excessive risk creation that it was done using one's own property. Even full-blown conventional property rights do not legitimate harming third parties or avoiding duties to them; they have rights as well.[81]

Also, trade secrecy reverses the recommended relationship between property and the commons. Secrecy blocks efficient or sustainable allocation of resources, by hiding the actual costs of the secret keeper's uses. It is, in effect, a claim to unregulated access to resources, some of which are already in the possession of others who are more suited and inclined to provide stewardship for the resource. Instead of participating in a system that works to preserve the scarce resources of the commons, secrecy claimants assert an entitlement to use without accountability, perhaps to waste.[82] They assert a right to appropriate others' entitlements as sinks

---

79 See Lyndon, *Secrecy and Access*, *supra* note 4, at 476, 490.

80 The debate over trade secrecy as a property entitlement continues to develop. See, e.g., Charles Tait Graves, *Trade Secrets as Property: Theory and Consequences*, 15 J. INTELL. PROP. L. 39 (2007). Scholars writing on this topic generally are concerned with standard commercial relationships, such as employment. Analysis of this literature as it might apply to EHS data is beyond the scope of this chapter, but an earlier analysis can be found at Lyndon, *Secrecy and Innovation*, *supra* note 4, at 39–50.

81 'I own the bat' is irrelevant to the battery charge; 'it's my land', likewise, is not a defense to negligently caused harm. One owes a duty of reasonable care even to intruders on one's property. Katko v. Briney, 183 N.W.2d 657 (Iowa 1971). For an overview of the environment-property rights debate, see David M. Driesen, *What's Property Got to Do with It?*, 30 ECOL. L.Q. 1003 (2003).

82 Generally we now have a common space with weak or non-existent limits for technological uses, combined with protection for invisibility – seriously inappropriate access rules. If we treat the existing stock of knowledge as a 'commons of the known', new technologies and uses can be developed. Lyndon, *Secrecy and Innovation*, *supra* note 4, at 50. The work of Michael J. Madison, Chapter 10, and others forge a path forward, and in EHS research, secrecy may have a limited role in this effort. See Part IV *infra*.

for their externalities. Rather than supporting secrecy, property principles compel disclosure.[83]

The U.S. Supreme Court's decision in *Ruckelshaus v. Monsanto* has been cited in support of the assertion that trade secrets are property, but this misreads the case.[84] The Court considered a compensation claim based on the EPA's use of Monsanto's data to evaluate a rival's later pesticide registration and on the possibility that the EPA might disclose the data to the public. The Court found that trade secrets may be property for purposes of the Takings Clause, if the relevant state law would treat it as property. The Court also held, however, that trade secret protection would only be valid in the EHS regulatory setting under limited conditions set by Congress. Otherwise companies should expect regulation and disclosure.[85]

Legal secrecy in EHS regulation provides firms with an unfair but virtually perpetual procedural advantage. The underlying information asymmetry in environmental problems and the idiosyncrasies of the administrative setting make it easy for firms to assert and maintain apparent entitlements. The lag time between exposure and full understanding of effects enables firms to argue that no action should be taken, since no harm has been proven. When 'owners' affirm that disclosure will harm the firm, agency officials are understandably deferential, since property rights carry the gravitas of potential 'takings'.[86] The property frame itself, which tends to bypass complexity, reduces cases to the question of the firm's right to the information.

In addition, agencies are not positioned to evaluate confidentiality claims. Trade secrecy is inherently context-dependent, relying on the participation of knowledgeable commercial rivals to produce evidence of

---

[83] Since exposures often affect resources that are already owned and ostensibly protected by conventional property rules, it seems that a battery, trespass or nuisance model is apposite, with the secrecy claimant as the defendant. Consideration of this topic is beyond the scope of this chapter.

[84] Ruckelshaus v. Monsanto, 467 U.S. 986 (1984).

[85] *Id.* at 1009–10; see also United Steelworkers of Am. v. Auchter, 763 F.2d 728, 739 (3d Cir. 1985) (holding that trade secrets are not constitutionally protected from the regulatory process). But see Phillip Morris v. Reilly, 312 F.3d 24, 44–6 (1st Cir. 2002) (holding that state law that required tobacco companies to submit ingredient information failed a cost-benefit test and was therefore a taking).

[86] The prospect of a constitutional dispute and the possibility of prosecution, fines and imprisonment, discussed *supra* note 58, chills agencies' exercise of their discretion to disclose. See, e.g., Roger Dobson and Jeanne Lenzer, *US Regulator Suppresses Vital Data on Prescription Drugs on Sale in Britain*, Independent (UK), June 12, 2005 (explaining that ibuprofen related documents were considered proprietary and release would be a criminal offense, explained FDA official).

competitive value and secrecy. Rivals are the only insiders; agencies and others concerned with EHS risks are outsiders and do not have access to key evidence of competitive value and secrecy. Rivals are unlikely to step forward to help out, however, as they share an interest in limiting regulatory oversight. Effectively, confidentiality claims in regulation are one-sided, unchecked options to remove information from the system.[87]

Other procedural factors skew the outcome of disclosure conflicts. Secrets have their own 'aura' effect: they are dramatic and inherently intimidating.[88] Secrets must be 'protected'. If the secret is uttered, a relationship or a business may unravel. Who can gauge the effects of revealing it? This 'Pandora's Box' effect puts additional pressure on agency officials. Indeed, the idea that businesses are 'too fragile to disclose' is a persistent theme, one of the spells secrecy casts.

Finally, some pressure to assert proprietary claims stems from the structure of trade secret law. Companies have incentives to claim broadly in any event: they do not actually know whether the information is available to others; it is less costly to claim broadly; they wish to forestall later suggestions that they have not protected their information sufficiently to claim that it is secret.

C. FOIA

FOIA was enacted to promote government transparency and to put to use the information lying idle in government files.[89] At the time, trade secrecy was a relatively minor field and environmental law did not exist. Most courts reviewing agency actions under Exemption 4 have followed the plain terms of the statute and looked to see if government transparency will be served or commercial competitive interests harmed by disclosure. However, these two concerns alone cannot support a coherent approach to information access. Later environmental law has explicitly provided for disclosure of some EHS data that is claimed as trade secrets and this

---

[87] Thus, trade secrecy is particularly available in the agency context. The ability to fill in the blanks on an agency form produces the privilege.

[88] Secrecy gains influence from its rhetoric. It is a form of power in relation to those who do not know the secret's content or even, perhaps, that it exists. See Lyndon, *Secrecy and Innovation*, *supra* note 4, at 2, 35, 49, 55; SISELLA BOK, SECRETS: ON THE ETHICS OF CONCEALMENT AND REVELATION (1983).

[89] Martin E. Halstuk, *When Secrecy Trumps Transparency: Why the Open Government Act of 2007 Falls Short*, 16 COMM. L. CONSPECTUS 427 (2008); Patricia M. Wald, *The Freedom of Information Act: A Short Case Study in the Perils and Paybacks of Legislating Democratic Values*, 33 EMORY L.J. 649 (1984).

development should inform courts' and agencies' view of what is public and what is commercial or trade information.[90]

While courts often defer to agencies in disclosure cases, FOIA's intent is to get the information to the public, to counter the influence of agency capture. Leaving the choice to the agencies is especially unworkable in the environmental arena because the agency is only one of many players, with an important but limited perspective. Also, courts and agencies speak of 'balancing the interests' in these conflicts, but the 'balancing' metaphor obscures the underlying information asymmetry in EHS cases and the fact that the need for the information is caused, at least in part, by the secret itself. Secrecy prevents the development of the very information needed to make a balanced assessment.

The Court of Appeals for the D.C. Circuit has articulated its own view of Exemption 4. [91] Among other things, the court has found that the term 'confidentiality' includes (1) an agency's belief that it will be easier to get information later if confidentiality is promised now,[92] and (2) the firm's own past practice, that is, whether the firm would normally disclose the information.[93] The court apparently intended to put administrative agencies in a position to negotiate for more information by offering confidentiality. While it seems logical, this is not a workable strategy in the environmental arena. The whole subject matter of environmental regulation consists of information that firms would rather not reveal and much of this must be distributed widely for risk management. The D.C. rule leads to burdened agencies and deprives the market and researchers of EHS data. Instead, disclosure rules should clearly signal to firms that they need to know and reveal the health and environmental effects of their activities.

---

[90] See *supra* note 11.

[91] Other circuits have rejected the D.C. Circuit's approach, but it has been influential. Agency regulations today largely follow it and agency practices reflect considerable solicitude for industry preferences. See Lyndon, *Secrecy and Access*, *supra* note 4, 504–8.

[92] Nat'l Parks Conservation Ass'n v. Morton, 498 F.2d 765 (D.C. Cir. 1974). Under this ruling, agencies can negotiate for information and reach agreements to take custody of proprietary information.

[93] Critical Mass Energy Project v. Nuclear Regulatory Comm'n, 975 F.2d 871, 880 (D.C. Cir. 1992) (en banc) (confining the reach of National Parks to information that is furnished to the government under legal obligation and categorically protecting voluntarily submitted information, provided that it is not customarily disclosed to the public by the submitter). *Critical Mass* intensifies disincentives to disclose EHS data: it pays to stop revealing things now, as your practice will determine later FOIA outcomes.

Because proprietary interests and EHS disclosure are both important in their own realms, it may seem appropriate to compromise by splitting the entitlement or 'balancing' the two interests on a case-by-case basis. However, these approaches do not solve the problem. The secrecy-access predicament involves mutually exclusive uses of the same data by two separate bodies of knowledge. They are independent, except for the fact that one causes the need for the other. The commercial strategy relying on secret technology or know-how has a focused interest in the data and is funded by the underlying commercial enterprise. The EHS interest is spread out over space and time, is underfunded and often is caught unaware by the problem. As a legal matter, the problem seems to be a dispute over data. At another level, however, it is about managing technologies' social costs, including uncertainty.

IV. ALTERNATIVES

However valid their commercial rationales, proprietary privileges do not survive the transition to environmental regulation. They run afoul of basic principles of fairness and efficiency and they function as a pass to opt out of the larger learning system. Instead, the rule should be 'no secret exposures'.[94] A clear disclosure imperative would present firms with a choice among (1) avoiding exposures, (2) patenting or other appropriability strategies and (3) investing in research to prove safety or compliance with a regulatory standard. Record keeping incentives would change and administrative costs would be reduced. Firms would be less likely to postpone considering the effects of exposures. Indeed, confidentiality reform should be done in tandem with expanded research requirements.

Alternative supports for appropriability could also be developed. One approach would be to adapt the exclusive use and compensation system in pesticide regulation.[95] Under FIFRA today, data submitted when a particular active ingredient is first registered are covered by an 'exclusive use' provision; the EPA cannot consider the data to support additional registrations during the statutory period of exclusive use. However, to

---

[94] Removing commercial secrecy from EHS risk management has been recognized as desirable by many legal scholars, including those cited in this chapter. See, e.g., Thomas O. McGarity and Sidney A. Shapiro, *The Trade Secret Status of Health and Safety Testing Information: Reforming Agency Disclosure Policies*, 93 HARV. L. REV. 837 (1980).

[95] Professors McGarity and Shapiro proposed this approach in 1980. See *id.* at 883–6.

avoid duplicative research, FIFRA provides that applicants may reach agreement through binding arbitration on joint data development; new registrants may also agree with original submitters on compensation for the use of previously submitted data.[96] In 1996, this program was expanded to include a newly mandated review of pesticide levels in food.[97] By regulation, the EPA then broadened the coverage of the scheme to data submitters who are not registrants, including manufacturers of inert ingredients.[98]

Revised confidentiality rules might acknowledge firms' research and innovation efforts. Periods of exclusive use could be tailored to reward production of toxicity research.[99] If a chemical is part of a supervised innovation initiative, for example part of a 'green chemistry' research and development strategy, this could also be considered. Any privileges should have clear expiration dates and when the commercial reasons for confidentiality expire, the firm should formally withdraw the claim.[100]

An alternative would be to adjust the current private law liability system.[101] Mini-patent or registration systems also have been proposed for information about exposure that would otherwise be considered a trade secret.[102] In any event, reform in this area should be structural,

---

[96] 7 U.S.C. § 136a(c)(1)(F)(iii) (2006).

[97] See 21 U.S.C. § 346a(i)(1) (2000).

[98] Notice of Availability, Pesticides, 68 Fed. Reg. 18,977 (April 17, 2003). Arbitration is initiated by filing a request with the Federal Mediation and Conciliation Service (FMCS), but because FMCS has delegated its authority to the American Arbitration Association (AAA), requests are filed with AAA and conducted pursuant to its rules. See 3 LAW OF ENVIRONMENTAL PROTECTION § 18:38 (Sheldon M. Novick *et al.* eds., 2004).

[99] Proof of safety need not be as arduous as the struggles that have occurred over proof of harm; perhaps the arbitration model could be adapted to broader purposes. See Wendy Wagner, *Using Competition-Based Regulation to Bridge the Toxics Data Gap*, 83 IND. L.J. 629 (2008).

[100] Time limits and sunset provisions were proposed by the EPA in 1994, see *supra* note 56, and supported by the GAO and others, see, e.g., GAO, CHEMICAL REGULATION, *supra* note 55, at 34 (noting that company representatives told the GAO that after a certain date, confidentiality may no longer be necessary).

[101] See David S. Levine, Chapter 16; Jerome H. Reichman, *Rethinking the Role of Clinical Trial Data in International Intellectual Property Law: The Case for a Public Goods Approach*, 13 MARQ. INTELL. PROP. L. REV. 1, 32–3 (2009).

[102] See Lyndon, *Secrecy and Innovation*, *supra* note 4, at 50–5; Rochelle C. Dreyfuss, *Information Products: A Challenge to Intellectual Property Theory,* 20 N.Y.U.J. INT'L L. & POL. 897 (1988) (proposing an international safety net registration system for information products). David Levine discusses in Chapter 16 the issues raised by relying on patents instead of secrecy in public infrastructure and recommends further research; see also Lyndon, *Secrecy and Innovation*, *supra*

building from acknowledgement that the commercial and EHS interests are incompatible, and that EHS disclosure is the more fundamental of the two. Additional changes, such as stronger data production and disclosure requirements and greater supervision, would also be useful.[103] However, because of the diverse and dynamic quality of the data and the broad distribution that is necessary for environmental learning, removing secrecy from regulation is the best way forward.

CONCLUSION

Secrecy subsidizes existing technologies, disguising their costs and suppressing incentives to develop better technologies. It delays accountability and response, obscuring risks that become more costly with time, like the 'toxic assets' of recent financial crises. These distortions are particularly significant in environmental risk management, where latent externalities are endemic. Trade secrecy law has no place in this realm. Instead, access and disclosure rules should conform to principles of risk communication.

---

note 4, at 16–21; Lyndon, *Secrecy and Access*, *supra* note 4, at 488–9 (discussing literature on patenting and secrecy practices in relation to environmental needs).

[103] See, e.g., Frank A. Pasquale, Chapter 15, who proposes 'qualified transparency', with a trusted advisory committee located within the agency to address conflicts between proprietary interests and legitimacy and ethical principles in search engines. Such an institution could be very useful in EHS regulation, though not to decide on disclosure, which should occur with any physical exposures. For other useful suggestions, see Vladeck, *supra* note 4, at 1828–36; Wagner, *supra* note 4, at 1717–45; Lyndon, *Secrecy and Innovation*, *supra* note 4, at 50–5; McGarity and Shapiro, *supra* note 94, at 883–8.

18 Data secrecy in the age of regulatory exclusivity

*Rebecca S. Eisenberg**

INTRODUCTION

Drug regulation works in tandem with the patent system to defer generic entry in the market for pharmaceutical products, thereby preserving lucrative market exclusivity more effectively than the patent system could do without the regulatory assist.[1] Firms need regulatory approval to sell their products,[2] and to get that approval they need data showing that their products meet regulatory standards.[3] Prior to passage of the Drug Price Competition and Patent Term Restoration Act of 1984 (commonly known as the Hatch-Waxman Act)[4] drug developers relied upon confidential treatment of the data they submitted to the Food and Drug Administration (FDA) in support of a New Drug Application (NDA) to keep their data out of the hands of generic competitors who might otherwise use it to get competing versions of the same products approved. Although competitors could conduct their own trials and submit their own data, the costs of such trials were generally prohibitive for generic products that would be sold at competitive prices rather than at the premium prices charged for drugs available from only one source. As a result, the regulatory entry barrier often continued to exclude competition even after relevant patents expired.[5]

The Hatch-Waxman Act changed the rules, striking a new balance between the interests of innovators and generic competitors. To facilitate generic entry, the Hatch-Waxman Act lowered the regulatory entry barrier for generic versions of previously approved products, allowing approval of an 'Abbreviated New Drug Application' (ANDA) upon a showing

* Robert and Barbara Luciano Professor of Law, University of Michigan Law School.

1 Rebecca S. Eisenberg, *The Role of the FDA in Innovation Policy*, 13 MICH. TELECOMM. & TECH. L. REV. 345 (2007).

2 21 U.S.C. § 355(a).

3 21 U.S.C. § 355 (b), (j).

4 Pub. L. No. 98-417, 98 Stat. 1585 (1984).

5 Gerald J. Mossinghoff, *Overview of the Hatch-Waxman Act and its Impact on the Drug Development Process*, 54 FOOD & DRUG L.J. 187 (1999).

of 'bioequivalence' to a previously approved product without repeating clinical trials to prove safety and effectiveness.[6] To protect innovators, it provided patent term extensions and charged the FDA with administering periods of regulatory exclusivity before allowing use of an ANDA.[7] These provisions calibrated the duration of regulatory exclusivity to balance the competing goals of innovation and competition, formalizing and fortifying regulatory entry barriers during the period of exclusivity and explicitly permitting free riding by imitators thereafter.

Since that time, regulatory exclusivity has become an increasingly important source of protection against generic competition for the biopharmaceutical industry, as is apparent from its growing role in trade negotiations[8] and in recent legislation for the regulation of follow-on biological products.[9] In 1984, Congress provided in the Hatch-Waxman Act for periods of regulatory exclusivity, ranging from four years before an ANDA could be submitted to seven and a half years before it could be approved.[10] In 2010, Congress provided 12 years of regulatory exclusivity before the FDA could approve generic versions of biological products.[11]

Efforts to expand regulatory exclusivity have provoked skeptical opposition from critics who believe it poses a superfluous obstacle to affordable generic drugs.[12] These critics see regulatory exclusivity as redundant to patents and an undeserved extension of patent-like rights that defers competition in drug markets, to the detriment of public health.

Regulatory exclusivity creates another redundancy in protection that

---

[6] 21 U.S.C. § 355(j).

[7] 21 U.S.C. § 355(j)(5)(F). Although sometimes referred to as 'five-year exclusivity', these provisions typically provide more than five years of effective exclusivity. See *infra* note 94 and accompanying text.

[8] Jerome H. Reichman, *Rethinking the Role of Clinical Trial Data in International Intellectual Property Law: The Case for a Public Goods Approach*, 13 MARQUETTE I.P. L. REV. 1 (2009); Aaron Xavier Fellmeth, *Secrecy, Monopoly, and Access to Pharmaceuticals in International Trade Law: Protection of Marketing Approval Data under the TRIPs Agreement*, 45 HARV. INT'L L.J. 443 (2004).

[9] The Biologics Price Competition and Innovation Act of 2009, Patient Protection and Affordable Care Act, Title VII, Subtitle A, §§ 7001–3, Pub. L. No. 111–48 (H.R. 3590) (2010).

[10] For a fuller explanation of these provisions, which are codified at 21 U.S.C. 355(j)(5)(F), see *infra* notes 93–7 and accompanying text.

[11] Patient Protection and Affordable Care Act, § 7002(a)(2), to be codified in pertinent part at 42 U.S.C. § 262(k)(7)(A) and (B).

[12] Data Exclusivity: A Major Obstacle to Innovation and Competition in the EU Pharmaceutical Sector, EGA Position Paper (2000), posted at www.egagenerics.com/doc/ega_dataex-2000-12.pdf (visited February 8, 2011); Reichmann, *supra* note 8; Fellmeth, *supra* note 8.

has been less remarked upon: with regulatory exclusivity to protect against free riders, it is difficult to justify the continuing treatment of data submitted in pursuit of regulatory approval as trade secret or confidential information belonging to the submitter.[13]

Before passage of the Hatch-Waxman Act, confidential treatment made a certain amount of sense. The clinical trials necessary for NDA approval require costly and risky investments. If competitors were free to appropriate the value of successful trials to get their own copies of these products on the market without incurring the same costs and risks, free riding could undermine incentives to invest in trials in the first place. Data secrecy solved this problem.[14]

This justification for data secrecy lost its force with the introduction of regulatory exclusivity and ANDAs. Regulatory exclusivity offers an alternative means of preserving the competitive value of investments in clinical trials without the need for secrecy. Moreover, the Hatch-Waxman Act arguably destroyed the primary competitive value of secrecy once regulatory exclusivity expires. At that point, the statute permits free riding on an innovator's prior showing of safety and effectiveness by allowing generic competitors to gain market approval through the use of a less costly ANDA.[15] In this altered regulatory environment, it is much harder to argue that data secrecy is either promoting investments in clinical trials or protecting innovators against free riders.

---

13 Mustafa Ünlü, *It is Time: Why the FDA Should Start Disclosing Drug Trial Data*, 16 MICH. TELECOMM. TECH. L. REV. 511 (2010); Department of HEW, FDA, Public Information, Notice of Proposed Rulemaking, 37 Fed. Reg. No. 88, 9128, 9130 (May 5, 1972) ('1972 Proposed Rulemaking') ('Since 1938, FDA has taken the position that such data ordinarily represent valuable commercial property and trade secrets that must be retained as confidential and may not be disclosed to the public'); Thomas O. McGarity and Sidney A. Shapiro, *The Trade Secret Status of Health and Safety Testing Information: Reforming Agency Disclosure Policies*, 93 HARV. L. REV. 837 (1980); James T. O'Reilly, *Knowledge is Power: Legislative Control of Drug Industry Trade Secrets*, 54 U. CINCINNATI L. REV. 1 (1984). Judicial decisions interpreting the Freedom of Information Act (FOIA) have rejected the characterization of data from clinical trials as 'trade secret' within the meaning of FOIA, but have nonetheless held the information exempt from disclosure under a separate exemption for 'commercial or financial information . . . [that is] privileged or confidential'. Pub. Citizen Health Research Group v. FDA, 704 F.2d 1280, 1288 (D.C. Cir. 1983) (interpreting 5 U.S.C. 552(b)(4)). See also Anderson v. Dep't of HHS, 907 F.2d 936 (10th Cir. 1990).

14 Department of Health, Education and Welfare, Food and Drug Administration, Public Information, 39 Fed. Reg. 44602, 44634 (1974) ('1974 Public Information').

15 21 U.S.C. § 355(j).

Data secrecy has attracted a torrent of criticism in recent years.[16] Critics worry that secrecy can hide a multitude of sins; that firms have powerful incentives to suppress adverse results and to spin their data in their own favor to make their products look safer and more effective than they are;[17] that secrecy leads to injuries and loss of life that could be avoided if doctors and patients had full access to data;[18] that public scrutiny will supplement the efforts of regulators and enhance the soundness and credibility of their decisions;[19]and that secrecy undermines democratic values of accountability and transparency.[20] Secrecy also truncates the social value of information, limiting its contributions to future innovation. Disclosure of data from clinical trials would permit more users to learn more from it, allowing them to make better informed choices about current treatments[21]

---

[16] James M. Wood and Roxanne M. Gariby, *Hoarding Away Science: Towards a More Transparent View of Health and Online Registries for Independent Postmarket Drug Research*, 60 Food & Drug L.J. 547 (2005); American Medical Association Council on Scientific Affairs, *Enhanced Physician Access to Food and Drug Administration Data* (2005), available at www.ama-assn.org/ama/pub/category/15152.html; Editorial, *Next Stop, Don't Block the Doors: Opening Up Access to Clinical Trials Results*, 5 PLoS Medicine 1007 (2008); Howard Mann, *Hidden Data at the FDA*, 39 Hastings Center Report Bioethics Forum (June 15, 2006), retrieved on March 16, 2009 from www.thehastingscenter.org/Bioethicsforum/Post.aspx?id=184; Jeanne Lenzer, *Drug Secrets: What the FDA Isn't Telling*, www.slate.com (posted September 27, 2005); Erik H. Turner, *A Taxpayer-Funded Clinical Trials Registry and Results Database: It Already Exists Within the US Food and Drug Administration*, 1 PLoS Medicine 180 (2004).

[17] Erick H. Turner *et al.*, *Selective Publication of Antidepressant Trials and Its Influence on Apparent Efficacy*, 358 New Eng. J. Med. 252, 256–7 (2008); Wendy Wagner and David Michaels, *Equal Treatment for Regulatory Science: Extending the Controls Governing the Quality of Public Research to Private Research*, 30 Am. J.L. & Med. 119, 123–8 (2004).

[18] Janene Boyce, *Disclosure of Clinical Trial Data: Why Exemption 4 of the Freedom of Information Act Should be Restored*, Duke L. & Tech. Rev. 3 (2005), available at www.law.duke.edu/journals/dltr/articles/pdf/2005DLTR0003.pdf; Margaret Witherup Tindall, *Breast Implant Information as Trade Secrets: Another Look at FOIA's Fourth Exemption*, 7 Admin. L.J. Am. U. 213, 221–31 (1993).

[19] Wagner and Michaels, *supra* note 17, at 134–5.

[20] David S. Levine, *Secrecy and Unaccountability: Trade Secrets in Our Public Infrastructure*, 59 Fla. L. Rev. 135 (2007); see also David S. Levine, Chapter 16.

[21] Stanley S. Wang and John J. Smith, *Potential Legal Barriers to Increasing CMS/FDA Collaboration: The Law of Trade Secrets and Related Considerations*, 58 Food & Drug L.J. 613 (2003); Mitchell Oates, *Facilitating Informed Medical Treatment Through Production and Disclosure of Research into Off-Label Uses of Pharmaceuticals*, 80 N.Y.U. L. Rev. 1272 (2005).

and future research,[22] as well as permitting better public oversight over regulatory decision-making.[23]

The standard countervailing justification for secrecy as serving to protect innovators against free riders considers only one side of the ambiguous effects of secrecy on innovation. Welfare losses associated with secrecy are familiar in the intellectual property (IP) literature, and are frequently invoked as a justification for the patent system.[24] Patents provide enforceable rights that survive public disclosure, allowing innovators to profit from new technologies without having to suppress the dissemination of new knowledge. Indeed, the patent system positively requires patent applicants to disclose their inventions fully[25] and makes these disclosures freely available to the public through publication of patents and patent applications.[26] Patent law promotes innovation not only through the exclusive rights that make new inventions profitable, but through the disclosure that facilitates further innovation by others.[27] Regulatory exclusivity could likewise do more to promote innovation if it were linked to a robust disclosure requirement.

Congress, the FDA, state governments and the pharmaceutical industry have each taken steps to promote greater public disclosure of the results of clinical trials,[28] but so far they have stopped short of calling for disclosure of raw data that are submitted to the FDA, as distinguished from summary reports.[29] The FDA is currently reviewing its policies on public

---

22 Mary L. Lyndon, *Secrecy and Access in an Innovation Intensive Economy: Reordering Information Privileges in Environmental, Health, and Safety Law*, 78 U. Colo. L. Rev. 465 (2007). See also Mary L. Lyndon, Chapter 17.

23 Peter Lurie and Allison Zieve, *Sometimes the Silence Can be Like the Thunder: Access to Pharmaceutical Data at the FDA*, 69 L. & Contemp. Prob. 85 (2006).

24 Steven Cheung, *Property Rights in Trade Secrets*, 20 Econ. Inquiry 40 (1982); William M. Landes and Richard A. Posner, The Economic Structure of Intellectual Property Law 326–31 (2003).

25 35 U.S.C. § 112.

26 35 U.S.C. §§ 10, 12, 122.

27 Kewanee Oil v. Bicron, 416 U.S. 257 (1974); Aronson v. Quick Point Pencil, 440 U.S. 257 (1979).

28 For a summary of some of these initiatives see Marc J. Scheineson and M. Lynn Sykes, *Major New Initiatives Require Increased Disclosure of Clinical Trial Information*, 60 Food & Drug L.J. 525 (2005). See also Food and Drug Administration Amendments Act of 2007 § 801, Pub. L. No. 110-85, 121 Stat. 823, 904 (2007), codified at 42 U.S.C. § 282(j) (requiring submission of information about clinical trials to a public database maintained by the National Institutes of Health at www.ClinicalTrials.gov).

29 See Alastair J.J. Wood, *Progress and Deficiencies in the Registration of Clinical Trials*, 360 N. Eng. J. Med. 824 (2009).

disclosure of information as part of a Transparency Initiative[30] in response to the Obama administration's Open Government Directive.[31] As part of that process the FDA has invited public comment on a proposal to:

> convene a group of internal and external stakeholders to discuss the possible uses of non-summary safety and effectiveness data from product applications, the circumstances under which it would be appropriate for sponsors to disclose non-summary safety and effectiveness data from applications submitted to FDA, and if appropriate, the format and the method by which disclosure should occur.[32]

In the FDA's framing of the issue, the challenge is to strike the right balance between 'significant public health benefits associated with the disclosure of this information, including reducing the costs and increasing the efficiency of research', and 'other factors [that] may weigh more strongly' including 'the impact disclosure may have on innovation'.[33] Although this skeptical framing hardly sounds like a call for change, they are at least inviting a conversation that is long overdue.

This chapter reviews the history and legal basis for the FDA's confidential treatment of data from clinical trials and evaluates competing arguments for and against broader disclosure with a focus on promoting innovation. The effects of secrecy on innovation are ambiguous. Secrecy promotes innovation by protecting innovators from competition from free riders, but it also suppresses innovation by restricting access to information for use in subsequent research. Prior to the Hatch-Waxman Act, the innovation-promoting effects of data secrecy were almost certainly greater than the innovation-suppressing effects. But the situation today is quite different. Regulatory exclusivity offers an alternative and superior source of protection from free riders without the need for secrecy, while ANDAs permit free riding once regulatory exclusivity comes to an end irrespective of secrecy. Meanwhile, advances in information technology

---

30 Department of Health and Human Services, Food and Drug Administration, Food and Drug Administration Transparency Task Force; Public Meeting, 74 Fed. Reg. 26712 (June 3, 2009); FDA Transparency Initiative: Draft Proposals for Public Comment Regarding Disclosure Policies of the U.S. Food and Drug Administration (May 2010), retrieved on August 12, 2010 from www.fda.gov/downloads/AboutFDA/Transparency/PublicDisclosure/GlossaryofAcronymsandAbbreviations/UCM212110.pdf ('Transparency Task Force Draft Proposals').

31 Presidential Documents, Memorandum for the Heads of Executive Departments and Agencies on Transparency and Open Government (January 21, 2009) (74 F.R. 4685, January 26, 2009), available at www.whitehouse.gov/open/.

32 Transparency Task Force Draft Proposals, *supra* note 30, at 49.

33 *Id.*

make it possible to learn much more from aggregated databases than can be learned from sequestering safety and effectiveness data for individual products in proprietary silos.[34] The FDA currently has the authority (and arguably a statutory mandate) to make more non-summary safety and effectiveness data available right now. But further legislation could allow it to do more, simultaneously expanding public availability of information and providing greater protection against free riders for firms submitting valuable data to the FDA.

I. ORIGINS OF CURRENT ADMINISTRATIVE PRACTICE

The FDA has been treating submitted safety and effectiveness data as confidential since Congress first provided the agency with premarket approval authority in 1938.[35] Two statutory provisions arguably support this treatment: first, the federal Trade Secrets Act (TSA) prohibits any federal employee from divulging 'to any extent not authorized by law any information coming to him in the course of his employment or official duties . . . which information relates to the trade secrets . . . or to the . . . confidential statistical data . . . of any person' on penalty of fines, imprisonment and removal from office;[36] second, section 301(j) of the Federal Food, Drug and Cosmetic Act (FDCA) prohibits 'revealing, other than to the Secretary or officers or employees of the Department or to the courts when relevant . . . any information acquired under authority of section . . . 505 [requiring submission of data for approval of new drugs] . . . concerning any method or process which as a trade secret is entitled to protection'.[37] Although neither of these provisions by its terms clearly applies to safety and effectiveness data, they put FDA staff in potential legal jeopardy. So long as the FDA was under no obligation to disclose information to the public, the safest course of action was non-disclosure.

---

[34] See, e.g., Gina Kolata, *Rare Sharing of DataLeads to Progress on Alzheimer's*, NEW YORK TIMES, August 13, 2010, at A1.

[35] Federal Food, Drug and Cosmetic Act of 1938, Ch. 675, 52 Stat. 1040. For a historical review of food and drug legislation, see Richard A. Merrill, *The Architecture of Government Regulation of Medical Products*, 82 VA. L. REV. 1753 (1996). For an account of the history of the FDA's confidential treatment of data, see 1972 Proposed Rulemaking, *supra* note 13.

[36] Codified as amended at 18 U.S.C. § 1905.

[37] Codified as amended at 21 U.S.C. § 331(j).

Following passage of the Freedom of Information Act (FOIA),[38] with its mandate to make information available to the public, the FDA re-evaluated its disclosure policies in the 1970s, culminating in a regulatory framework that remains substantially the same to this day.[39] The new regulations greatly liberalized the disclosure policies of the FDA,[40] but continued to withhold from disclosure trade secrets and confidential information pursuant to Exemption 4 of FOIA.[41] The FDA concluded that the FOIA exemption was at least as broad as the statutory prohibitions on disclosure under the TSA and the FDCA.[42]

The FDA's initial proposal and responses to comments provide an interesting window on the views of the agency, regulated firms and persons seeking access to data on the functions of data secrecy prior to the Hatch-Waxman Act. The FDA received a barrage of submitted comments on both sides of the difficult question of what to do about disclosure of safety and effectiveness data submitted in support of Investigational New Drug applications (INDs)[43] and New Drug Applications (NDAs).[44] Following the approach of the Restatement of Torts,[45] the FDA decided

---

38 Pub. L. 89-487, 80 Stat. 250 (1966), codified as amended at 5 U.S.C. § 552.

39 1974 Public Information, *supra* note 14; Department of Health, Education and Welfare, Food and Drug Administration, Public Information Final Regulations, 42 Fed. Reg. 3094 (1977) ('1977 Final Regulations'); 1972 Proposed Rulemaking, *supra* note 13. Current versions are in 21 C.F.R. §§ 20.61, 312.130, 314.430, 601.50–1.

40 According to the FDA, prior to the new regulations the FDA retained approximately 90 percent of its records as confidential, and afterwards approximately 90 percent of its records were available for public disclosure. 1977 Final Regulations, *supra* note 39, at 3094.

41 Current version at 21 C.F.R. 21.61; 1974 version set forth at 39 Fed. Reg. 44647, § 4.61. Exemption 4 of FOIA, 5 U.S.C. § 552(b)(4), provides that FOIA 'does not apply to matters that are . . . trade secrets and commercial or financial information obtained from a person and privileged or confidential'.

42 1974 Public Information, *supra* note 14, at 44612 ('The Commissioner concludes that the Freedom of Information Act trade secrets exemption is as least as broad as, and is perhaps somewhat broader than, the confidentiality provisions of the other two statutes. The major difference between them is that, whereas the Freedom of Information Act exemption is discretionary, the other two statutes embody mandatory requirements').

43 An IND is an application for permission to ship in interstate commerce a drug that has not yet been approved for sale as safe and effective so that it may be used in clinical trials. 21 C.F.R. Part 312.

44 An NDA is an application for approval to market a new drug based on a showing of safety and effectiveness in clinical trials. 21 C.F.R. Part 314.

45 4 Restatement of Torts § 757 cmt. b (1939) ('A trade secret may consist of any formula, pattern, device or compilation of information which is used in one's

that submitted data could potentially qualify as a 'trade secret' under FOIA Exemption 4, but only if non-disclosure conferred a competitive advantage. Data qualified as 'confidential information' under Exemption 4 if it was commercial information of a sort generally held in the strictest confidence, which the FDA also took to mean that it conferred a competitive advantage.[46] If the data conferred a competitive advantage, the FDA could not disclose it under the TSA and the FDCA; otherwise, it was obliged to disclose it under FOIA.[47] The FDA reasoned that non-public safety and effectiveness data confers a competitive advantage if a competitor could use it to gain regulatory approval for a competing product. Data about a drug for which an NDA could be filed satisfies this standard because a competitor could not market or use the drug without first submitting such data to the FDA for approval. On the other hand, data about 'old drugs', drugs that could be marketed on the basis of an abbreviated application, or drugs for which approval has been withdrawn do not confer a competitive advantage because the data may not be used to obtain pre-market approval for these products. Data for such drugs would therefore be publicly available 'unless extraordinary circumstances can be shown'.[48]

Because an NDA requires submission of 'full reports of investigations which have been made to show whether or not such drug is safe for use and whether such drug is effective in use',[49] the FDA concluded that so long as it withheld the 'full reports' from disclosure, it could disclose summary information without inflicting competitive harm. The FDA introduced a new requirement that firms submitting data include in their NDAs a comprehensive summary of all safety and effectiveness data, which would become publicly available upon approval of the NDA. Since this summary would not constitute the 'full reports' necessary to obtain NDA approval, its disclosure would not inflict competitive harm and it would not constitute a trade secret.[50]

The FDA retained the same basic approach in final regulations in the face of comments urging both greater secrecy and greater disclosure.[51] It rejected numerous arguments for greater secrecy that did not relate

---

business, and which gives him an opportunity to obtain an advantage over competitors who do not know or use it').

[46] 1974 Public Information, *supra* note 14, at 44614.

[47] 1972 Proposed Rulemaking, *supra* note 13, at 9130.

[48] *Id.* at 9130–31.

[49] 21 U.S.C. § 355(b)(1)(A).

[50] 1972 Proposed Rulemaking, *supra* note 13, at 9130–31.

[51] 1974 Public Information, *supra* note 14.

to competitive use to gain regulatory approval, including that disclosure 'would increase product liability and other litigation problems for companies',[52] that disclosed records 'could be distorted, misconstrued, and quoted out of context',[53] that public availability would prevent investigators from thereafter publishing the data in scientific journals;[54] that disclosure of summaries would ease the burden subsequent applicants face in getting regulatory approval for competing products in the United States and abroad;[55] and that disclosure of adverse information might adversely affect sales.[56] At the same time, it rejected arguments for broader disclosure of 'full reports' because of the competitive harm that would result to data submitters if competitors could use the same data to get their identical products approved at a fraction of the cost.[57] Observing that '[p]resent law contains no provision that would permit the Food and Drug Administration to refuse to approve a "me-too" product on the basis of information obtained from the first manufacturer, once that information from the first manufacturer is disclosed', the FDA concluded that any change in the handling of 'full reports' should be made by Congress through new legislation rather than by the FDA through regulations.[58]

The same analysis led the FDA to take a different approach to data from clinical trials of biologic products, which were licensed under the Public Health Service Act[59] rather than the FDCA. Because all biological

---

52 *Id.* at 44602 ('The Commissioner advises that the question of whether this type of litigation would increase or decrease is not a factor to be considered in determining the disclosure of information to the public under the Freedom of Information Act').

53 *Id.* ('The Commissioner realizes that all public information can be abused. This is, however, not a reason for declining to comply with the requirements of the Freedom of Information Act').

54 *Id.* at 44602–3 ('The Freedom of Information Act contains no exemption permitting the Food and Drug Administration to withhold data from public disclosure solely on the ground that it is not yet published. Accordingly, unless data fall within one of the specific statutory exemptions from disclosure, the only positive means for a scientist to protect his first publication rights is to publish the information before submitting it to the Food and Drug Administration').

55 *Id.* at 44636 ('The Commissioner concludes that the possibility of competitive advantage abroad is speculative and remote').

56 *Id.* at 44637.

57 *Id.* at 44634.

58 *Id.*

59 Codified in pertinent part as amended at 42 U.S.C. § 262. Biologic products are defined by statute to include 'a virus, therapeutic serum, toxin, antitoxin, vaccine, blood, blood component or derivative, allergenic product, or analogous product, or arsphenamine or derivative of arsphenamine (or any other trivalent

products were required to undergo clinical testing in order to demonstrate safety, purity, potency and effectiveness prior to licensing, and could not be approved based on data for another manufacturer's product, the FDA concluded that safety and effectiveness data for such products conferred no competitive advantage and thus could not be trade secrets.[60] Moreover, since such data were 'routinely published in the scientific literature', they did not qualify as confidential information.[61] All safety and effectiveness data for such products would therefore be available for public disclosure once a license was issued, 'unless extraordinary circumstances are shown'.[62]

A 1977 report of a Review Panel on New Drug Regulation criticized the FDA's policy of secrecy for safety and effectiveness data for drugs and questioned whether it rested on sound legal analysis.[63] Subsequent judicial opinions indicated that the FDA had greater authority to disclose information than it was willing to claim. The U.S. Supreme Court held in *Chrysler v. Brown*[64] that the FOIA exemptions do not bar agencies from disclosing exempt information,[65] and that a Trade Secrets Act exception for disclosures authorized by law may apply to disclosures authorized by substantive agency rules that have the force and effect of law.[66]

Other courts rejected the FDA's expansive interpretation of 'trade secrets' in FOIA Exemption 4 to cover safety and effectiveness data. In *Public Citizen Health Research Group v. FDA*,[67] the Court of Appeals for the D.C. Circuit held that the Restatement definition of 'trade secret' that the FDA relied upon was inconsistent with the language and intent of Congress in passing FOIA, and that as used in FOIA, 'trade secret' has its narrower common law definition of 'a secret, commercially valuable plan, formula, process, or device that is used for the making, preparing,

---

organic arsenic compound), applicable to the prevention, treatment, or cure of a disease or condition of human beings'. 42 U.S.C. § 262(i).

60 1974 Public Information, *supra* note 14, at 44641.

61 *Id.*

62 For the 1974 proposed version, see *id.* at 44656. For the current version, see 21 C.F.R. § 601.51(e).

63 Review Panel on New Drug Regulation, Department of Health, Education and Welfare, Final Report, 33–8 (May 1977).

64 441 U.S. 281 (1979).

65 *Id.* at 293–4.

66 *Id.* at 295–303. To have this effect, the regulation must be 'reasonably within the contemplation of [the] grant of [rulemaking] authority from Congress', *id.* at 306, and must be properly promulgated under the requirements of the Administrative Procedure Act. *Id.* at 313.

67 704 F.2d 1280 (D.C. Cir. 1983).

compounding, or processing of trade commodities and that can be the end product of either innovation or substantial effort'.[68] Safety and effectiveness data were not 'trade secrets' under this definition, but might nonetheless fall within the 'confidential information' prong of Exemption 4 if disclosure would either 'impair the Government's ability to obtain necessary information in the future' or 'cause substantial harm to the competitive position of the person from whom the information was obtained'.[69] After rejecting the FDA's broad interpretation of the 'trade secrets' prong of Exemption 4, the court thus seemed to restore the same coverage under the 'confidential information' prong of the exemption.[70]

More important than whether Exemption 4 allows the FDA to withhold safety and effectiveness data from disclosure is the question, left open by the *Public Citizen* decision, of whether either the TSA or the FDCA prohibits such disclosures. Although neither of these statutory prohibitions is as broadly worded as FOIA Exemption 4,[71] the FDA decided to treat the three provisions as co-extensive.[72] A number of contemporary commentators disagreed, arguing that the disclosure prohibitions of the TSA and the FDCA did not properly apply to safety and effectiveness data.[73] If the FDA was wrong, and if the TSA and FDCA prohibitions did not cover safety and effectiveness data, then the FDA could disclose the data. On the other hand, if the data fell within the TSA and/or FDCA prohibitions, the FDA might still be able to authorize disclosure of the data through formal rule-making that has the force of law.[74] Because the FDA did not seek to

---

[68] *Id.* at 1288–9.

[69] *Id.* at 1290–2.

[70] See Ünlü, *supra* note 13, at 527–8.

[71] The TSA prohibits disclosure of 'trade secrets' and 'confidential statistical data', while the FDCA prohibits disclosure of a 'method or process which as a trade secret is entitled to protection'. See *supra* notes 36–7 and accompanying text.

[72] 1974 Public Information, *supra* note 14, at 44612 ('The Commissioner concludes that it is not feasible or practical to determine the differences, if any, between the confidentiality provisions in 18 U.S.C. § 1905 and 21 U.S.C. § 331(j), and in the Freedom of Information Act. If there are any differences, they are extremely subtle and small. Accordingly, the Commissioner intends, for practical reasons of daily administration of the law, to regard the coverage of these provisions as identical').

[73] See, e.g., McGarity and Shapiro, *supra* note 13; Richard S. Fortunato, *FDA Disclosure of Safety and Efficacy Data: The Scope of Section 301(j)*, 52 FORDHAM L. REV. 1280 (1984); cf. Robert M. Halperin, *Note: FDA Disclosure of Safety and Effectiveness Data: A Legal and Policy Analysis*, 1979 DUKE L.J. 286 (1979) (arguing that application of TSA and FFDCA prohibitions to safety and effectiveness data was uncertain).

[74] The Secretary of Health and Human Services has rule-making authority under 21 U.S.C. § 701(a) and (e).

disclose safety and effectiveness data,[75] its authority to do so has not been challenged or adjudicated. Instead, proponents of disclosure sought, with little success, to compel the FDA to disclose more data, while the FDA has joined industry in arguing that more disclosure is prohibited.[76]

While holding firm over the years to its policy of non-disclosure of 'full reports' of safety and effectiveness data, however, the FDA has become more willing to consider disclosure of summary information about clinical trials, even prior to product approval. In 2001 the FDA proposed a rule that would make available for public disclosure redacted versions of certain data and information from INDs related to human gene therapy and xenotransplantation.[77] The FDA noted that the proposed rule did not extend to trade secrets because it would not affect the confidentiality of manufacturing methods and processes,[78] and that safety and effectiveness data from human gene therapy trials were not confidential because such data had routinely been made available to the public through the oversight of the NIH Recombinant DNA Advisory Committee (RAC).[79] Moreover, the FDA asserted that its proposed rule would make disclosure 'authorized by law' under the TSA because it was within its statutory authorities to protect the public health and its general rule-making authorities.[80] In

---

75 For a brief period of time during the Carter administration, the FDA sought explicit legislative authority to permit disclosure of non-summary data from clinical trials of drugs. See Letter from FDA Commissioner Donald Kennedy to Senator Edward M. Kennedy (May 5, 1978), *reprinted in* Drug Regulation Reform Act of 1978: Hearings on S. 2755 before the Subcomm. on Health and Scientific Research of the Senate Comm. on Human Resources, 95th Cong., 2d Sess. 841–2 (1978); O'Reilly, *supra* note 13, at 12 n.63.

76 See, e.g., Pub. Citizen Health Research Group v. Food & Drug Admin., 185 F.3d 898 (D.C. Cir. 1999) (substantially approving, with limited exceptions, the FDA's refusal to release documents concerning preclinical and clinical studies for all prescription drugs for which clinical trials were discontinued because of death or serious injury of patients or because of safety concerns). But cf. Teich v. Food & Drug Admin., 751 F. Supp. 243 (D.D.C. 1990) (compelling disclosure of 20-year-old animal studies of silicone gel breast implants that court concluded would not cause substantial harm to competitive position of manufacturer).

77 Availability for Public Disclosure and Submission to FDA for Public Disclosure of Certain Data and Information Related to Human Gene Therapy or Xenotransplantation, 66 Fed. Reg. 4688 (January 18, 2001). For a full account of this episode, see Evan Diamond, *Reverse-FOIA Limitations on Agency Actions to Disclose Human Gene Therapy Clinical Trial Data*, 63 FOOD & DRUG L.J. 321 (2008).

78 66 Fed. Reg. at 4692.

79 *Id.* at 4693.

80 *Id.* at 4694, citing 21 U.S.C. §§ 355(i), 371(a), 903(b)(1).

the face of vehement opposition from the biotechnology industry,[81] the FDA never implemented its proposed rule, but the analysis accompanying the proposal sketched out a legal argument that might well have prevailed if it had pursued the matter.[82]

The FDA's Transparency Task Force recently took note of developments that have brought about greater public disclosure of information that the FDA has long treated as confidential, including 2007 legislation[83] requiring firms to disclose information about clinical trials in a public database, medical journal requirements for registration of clinical trials as a precondition for publication, and recommendations from the industry trade group PhRMA for the timely submission of summary information about clinical trials of investigational products in public databases.[84] Disclosures as a result of these initiatives call into question the continuing confidential treatment of information about unapproved products. The Task Force has issued draft proposals for broader disclosure of summary information about pending and withdrawn applications.[85] So far, however, the Task Force has stopped short of proposing broader disclosure of non-summary safety and effectiveness data.[86]

II. THE HATCH-WAXMAN ACT

Congress fundamentally altered the rules for competitive entry into the market for new drugs with passage of the Hatch-Waxman Act in 1984.[87] Prior to Hatch-Waxman, the FDA generally required the same 'full reports' of investigations showing safety and effectiveness for a generic

---

81 See Biotechnology Industry Organization, Comments of the Biotechnology Industry Organization Re: Availability for Public Disclosure and Submission to FDA for Public Disclosure of Certain Data and Information Related to Human Gene Therapy or Xenotransplantation (2001), available at www.bio.org/bioethics/background/tstm041801.asp.

82 Diamond, *supra* note 77, at 358–70.

83 Food and Drug Administration Amendments Act of 2007, *supra* note 28.

84 Transparency Task Force Draft Proposals, *supra* note 30, at 33–4.

85 See *id.* at 40–9 (draft proposals 8–16).

86 *Id.* at 49, draft proposal 17 (calling for 'a group of internal and external stakeholders to discuss the possible uses of non-summary safety and effectiveness data from product applications, the circumstances under which it would be appropriate for sponsors to disclose non-summary safety and effectiveness data from applications submitted to FDA, and if appropriate, the format and the method by which disclosure should occur').

87 See *supra* note 4.

version of a previously approved drug as it required for the pioneering drug.[88] This entry barrier discouraged generic competition long after relevant patents had expired, because the costs of clinical trials were prohibitive for generic products that would be sold at competitive prices.[89] This was the regime that informed the FDA's conclusion that full reports of investigations showing safety and effectiveness conferred a competitive advantage (and should therefore be treated as trade secrets); if the full reports were publicly disclosed, competitors could use the data to obtain approval of their copies of previously approved products at a fraction of the cost born by the originator.

The Hatch-Waxman Act profoundly altered that regime. In a historic compromise, the Hatch-Waxman Act gave innovators patent term extensions of up to five years to compensate for time lost to the regulatory approval process for NDAs,[90] while giving imitators a less costly path to regulatory approval by permitting the use of ANDAs after a statutory head-start period.[91] By using ANDAs, competitors could avoid the burden of submitting their own full reports of clinical investigations to show safety and effectiveness so long as they could show that the ANDA product is bioequivalent to the previously approved NDA product.[92]

The duration of exclusivity depends upon whether the NDA product is patented and whether the ANDA filer is challenging the validity or scope

---

[88] Generic versions of drugs approved prior to 1962 could be approved under an Abbreviated New Drug Application. 35 Fed. Reg. 11273–4 (1970). For a fuller account of this practice see Carlen S. Magad, *Generic Drugs: Breaking the Definitional Barriers to FDA Regulations*, 76 Nw. U.L. Rev. 613, 618–19 (1981). Sometimes generic versions of products approved after 1962 were approved without new trials on the basis of published literature under what was known as a 'paper NDA'. 45 Fed. Reg. 82060 (December 12, 1980). Questions about the legality and reach of this mechanism were part of the impetus for the Hatch-Waxman Act. Alfred B. Engelberg, *Special Patent Provisions for Pharmaceuticals: Have They Outlived their Usefulness? A Political, Legislative and Legal History of U.S. Law and Observations for the Future*, 39 IDEA J.L. & Tech. 389 (1999).

Although the FDCA now provides for approval of paper NDAs at 21 U.S.C. § 355(b)(2), the significance of this approval pathway has until recently been largely eclipsed by ANDAs. The language of the provision is quite broad, however, and the FDA interprets it to allow approval of a drug that is similar but not identical to a previously approved product based in part on previous unpublished studies that the applicant neither conducted nor obtained the right to use. Tam Q. Dinh, *Potential Pathways for Abbreviated Approval of Generic Biologics under Existing Law and Proposed Reforms in the Law*' 62 Food & Drug L.J. 77 (2007).

[89] Mossinghoff, *supra* note 5.

[90] 35 U.S.C. §§ 155, 156.

[91] 21 U.S.C. § 355(j).

[92] 21 U.S.C. § 355(j)(2)(A)(iv).

of any relevant patents.[93] In the United States, regulatory exclusivity often runs concurrently with patent protection, although in some cases it may last longer.[94] In the absence of patents, the period of exclusivity is a minimum of five years plus approval time, or approximately six and a half years.[95] If the NDA product is patented and the ANDA filer does not challenge the patent, the ANDA may not be approved prior to patent expiration.[96] If the ANDA filer certifies that the patent is invalid or not infringed, it may file the ANDA as soon as four years after first approval of the NDA, but if the patent holder promptly sues for patent infringement, approval of the ANDA will be stayed until seven and a half years after first approval of the NDA, subject to adjustment by the court.[97]

By design, this scheme excludes generic competition during the period of exclusivity, and permits free riding on the innovator's prior showing of safety and effectiveness for the NDA product thereafter. Once free riding is permitted, the argument for continuing data secrecy as a means of preventing competitive harm loses much of its force.[98] Secrecy beyond this point would not prevent generic competitors from getting regulatory approval for their products, which was the principal harm that the FDA had sought to avoid by withholding full reports of clinical trials from public disclosure.[99] Consistent with this focus, the FDA had concluded that once a competing product could be approved on an abbreviated application without submitting full reports of clinical trials, the full reports submitted previously with the NDA would be made available

---

93 21 U.S.C. § 355(j)(5)(B),(F)(ii).

94 Valerie Junod, *Drug Marketing Exclusivity under United States and European Union Law*, 59 Food & Drug L.J. 479 (2004).

95 Although sometimes referred to as 'five-year exclusivity', the effective period of protection is generally longer than five years. The statute prohibits the *submission* of an ANDA to the FDA for the first five years following first approval of an NDA for a new chemical entity; it takes an average of 19.2 months after that point for the FDA to approve the drug for marketing, extending the time before generic entry. Food and Drug Administration, 2007 Center for Drug Evaluation and Research Update, retrieved on November 1, 2009 from www.fda.gov/downloads/AboutFDA/CentersOffices/CDER/WhatWeDo/UCM121704.pdf.

96 If the drug is patented, approval of an ANDA must await patent expiration unless the filer certifies that the patent is invalid or not infringed. 21 U.S.C. § 355(j)(5)(B).

97 21 U.S.C. § 355(j)(5)(F)(ii); 21 U.S.C. § 355(j)(5)(B)(iii).

98 Some possibilities for free riding may remain, analysed further below. Apart from protection against free riders, secrecy benefits firms by allowing them to conceal unfavorable information from the public, but it is unclear why Congress should cooperate.

99 See *supra* notes 45–50 and accompanying text.

to the public upon request – 'unless extraordinary circumstances can be shown'.[100] Congress reached the same conclusion, and directed the FDA to make the data available to the public upon expiration of the exclusivity period, 'unless extraordinary circumstances are shown'.[101]

The statutory exception for 'extraordinary circumstances', copied from the FDA's rules,[102] has turned out to provide much broader protective cover against disclosure as a matter of administrative practice than the plain meaning of the word 'extraordinary' can support. When the FDA explained the regulatory exception in 1974, it declined to define 'extraordinary circumstances', but made clear that disclosure would be the rule and that circumstances justifying non-disclosure would be unusual.[103] Experience has not born out this prediction. In 2010, the FDA

---

[100] 1972 Proposed Rulemaking, *supra* note 13, at 9130, 9135, setting forth proposed § 130.32(d) ('All such data and information are available for public disclosure when the Food and Drug Administration . . . determines that the drug is not a new drug or may be marketed pursuant to an abbreviated NDA unless extraordinary circumstances are shown'. The 'extraordinary circumstances' exception was inadvertently omitted in the 1974 version of the regulations, see 1974 Public Information, *supra* note 14, at 44654–5, setting forth § 314.14(f)(5), but later restored, 41 Fed. Reg. 9317 (1976). See Department of Health, Education and Welfare, Food and Drug Administration, Public Information, Final Regulations, 42 Fed. Reg. 3094, 3107 (1977).

[101] Current version at 21 U.S.C. § 355(l)(1)(e) ('Safety and effectiveness data and information which has been submitted in an [NDA] for a drug and which has not previously been disclosed to the public shall be made available to the public, upon request, unless extraordinary circumstances are shown . . . (E) upon the effective date of the approval of the first [ANDA] which refers to such drug or upon the date upon which the approval of an [ANDA] which refers to such drug could be made effective if such an application had been submitted').

[102] See *supra* note 100 and sources cited therein.

[103] See, e.g., 1974 Public Information, *supra* note 14, at 44603 ('It was suggested [in comments on the proposed rule] that guidelines be adopted to establish the meaning of "extraordinary circumstances". The Commissioner advises that this type of provision creates a strong presumption of disclosure and requires any person who believes that a specific record falling within the rule should not be disclosed bears the burden of overcoming that presumption by showing unusual circumstances that justify nondisclosure . . . The Commissioner concludes that general guidelines are not feasible and that this type of provision will be administered on the basis of the facts shown in each case'); cf. *id.* at 44632 (explaining 'extraordinary circumstances' exception to disclosure of food and color additive petitions and antibiotic drug forms) ('The Commissioner advises that the provision permitting a manufacturer to show "extraordinary circumstances" to justify nondisclosure was included in the event that, on rare occasions, circumstances may arise that cannot be foreseen at this time which would require, in fairness, that material not be disclosed. The Commissioner anticipates that this will happen

Transparency Task Force lamented that '[i]n practice, these provisions have been difficult to implement'.[104]

The legislative history of the Hatch-Waxman Act suggests that the House and Senate sponsors of the bill disagreed about how to interpret its disclosure provisions.[105] In a law review article published shortly after passage of the Hatch-Waxman Act,[106] attorney James T. O'Reilly explains that the provision for data disclosure at the end of the regulatory exclusivity period, added to the bill by disclosure advocates who 'acted quietly' and 'buried' the provision 'amidst many unrelated provisions',[107] took the disclosure opponents by surprise. The opponents failed to get the wording changed,[108] but tried to forestall disclosure through statements in the legislative history about the meaning of 'extraordinary circumstances'. FDA Commissioner Frank Young wrote to the Senate sponsor of the bill stating FDA's position that safety and effectiveness data would remain confidential under the statutory language if the submitter of the data showed that it would have continuing value as confidential business information, 'even though their submission is not required as a condition to the approval of a marketing application by the Food and Drug Administration'.[109] According to O'Reilly, such continuing value might arise from usefulness in seeking regulatory approval to sell a drug overseas, or in products liability actions or (less likely) in research to discover new variations on the pioneer product.[110] Looking back in a later article in 1998, O'Reilly con-

---

on very few occasions, and that in almost all instances this type of information will promptly be released to the public. In order to show "extraordinary circumstances", the manufacturer must demonstrate that release of the information will destroy a competitive advantage that he would otherwise enjoy, that he will be hurt financially as a result, and thus that it would be unlawful or unfair to release the information involved. The mere fact that the information may be embarrassing, or may require removal of a product from the market, or may disclose adverse reactions, or may be of interest to others, or that there is some remote future possibility of competitive advantage, or that others might conduct duplicative research which would be obviated by release of the information, or similar arguments, will be insufficient to justify nondisclosure').

104 Transparency Task Force Draft Proposals, *supra* note 30, at 37.

105 See Jane A. Fisher, *Disclosure of Safety and Effectiveness Data under the Drug Price Competition and Patent Term Restoration Act*, 41 Food Drug & Cosmetic L.J. 268, 281–4 (1986).

106 O'Reilly, *supra* note 13.

107 *Id.* at 16.

108 *Id.* at 19.

109 *Id.* at 19–21 and n.14, citing 130 Cong. Rec. S10988-89 (daily 3d. September 12, 1984) (letter of FDA Commissioner Frank Young).

110 *Id.* at 23–4.

cluded that 'in most cases, the U.S. innovative firm does not lose its right of ownership for its research data, and can continue to license that data or utilize it in other nations' approval systems'.[111] Most cases, in other words, present extraordinary circumstances.

This interpretation renders the statutory language meaningless[112] and contradicts the FDA's prior explanations of the regulatory language from which the statutory language was copied. The FDA explicitly rejected the argument that all data contained in an NDA should be held in confidence forever, even after its value in obtaining regulatory approval has lapsed.[113] The basis for the FDA's pre-Hatch-Waxman distinction between summary information (which would be disclosed to the public) and full reports of clinical trials (which would be withheld from disclosure) was that submission of full reports was necessary to obtain FDA approval to market a competing product.[114] The FDA rejected arguments for confidentiality based on other potential harms to data submitters, including harms arising from use to obtain regulatory approval in other countries,[115] from use in products liability litigation,[116] and from use in research to discover new products.[117] None of these arguments justified a continuing presumption of confidentiality, although with more evidentiary support they might support case-by-case determinations of extraordinary circumstances.[118]

The Hatch-Waxman statutory directive that secrecy will end once permissible free riding begins avoids all but the most speculative of competitive harms to innovators. There are so many bad reasons why firms would seek to preserve secrecy (e.g., to conceal unfavorable information[119] in order to enhance sales and profits or to avoid products liability) that policy-makers should be cautious about accepting conclusory allegations that disclosure would deprive firms of competitive value.

---

[111] James T. O'Reilly, *Implications of International Drug Approval Systems on Confidentiality of Business Secrets in the U.S. Pharmaceutical Industry*, 53 FOOD & DRUG L.J. 123, 129 (1998).

[112] See Fisher, *supra* note 105, at 284.

[113] 1974 Public Information, *supra* note 14, at 44637, 44638.

[114] See *supra* notes 47–50.

[115] See *supra* note 55.

[116] See *supra* note 52.

[117] 1974 Public Information, *supra* note 14, at 44637–8.

[118] *Id.* at 44638 ('A situation in which one IND or NDA directly affects another might be viewed as an extraordinary circumstance. Again, the possibility of foreign competitive advantage is too speculative to justify a broad exemption from the Freedom of Information Act').

[119] An-Wen Chan, *Bias, Spin, and Misreporting: Time for Full Access to Trial Protocols and Results*, 5 PLoS MEDICINE 1533 (November 2008).

Confidential treatment of data from clinical trials should be recognized as a relic of an earlier era, when it served to protect innovators against free riding by generic competitors.[120] Today, that work is better done through regulatory exclusivity. If the FDA is finding the 'extraordinary circumstances' limitation on disclosure difficult to administer in practice, perhaps it needs to define that limitation more narrowly so that routine claims of speculative harms do not have the effect of reading the word 'extraordinary' out of the statute, turning an exception to a general rule of disclosure into a general rule of non-disclosure.

III. ACCELERATING THE TIME OF DATA DISCLOSURE

A closer question is whether it makes sense to defer disclosure until the end of the regulatory exclusivity period.[121] In patent law, public disclosure ordinarily precedes the beginning of exclusivity, with most patent applications opened to public scrutiny 18 months after their filing dates,[122] while the Hatch-Waxman Act requires public disclosure only after exclusivity comes to an end. Early disclosure is often touted as a benefit of the patent system because it enriches the public knowledge base, thereby facilitating

---

[120] Indeed, the WTO Agreement on Trade-Related Aspects of Intellectual Property Rights ('TRIPS Agreement'), negotiated with the interests of the pharmaceutical industry squarely on the table, treats data exclusivity and secrecy as alternative means of protecting the value of data from clinical trials. Under that Agreement, governments may protect the data through secrecy, or disclose submitted data so long as they take other steps to ensure protection against unfair commercial use: 'Members, when requiring, as a condition of approving the marketing of pharmaceutical or of agricultural chemical products which utilize new chemical entities, the submission of undisclosed test or other data, the origination of which involves a considerable effort, shall protect such data against unfair commercial use. In addition, Members shall protect such data against disclosure, except where necessary to protect the public, or unless steps are taken to ensure that the data are protected against unfair commercial use'. Final Act Embodying the Results of the Uruguay Round of Multilateral Trade Negotiations, Art. 39(3), Annex 1C: Agreement on Trade Related Aspects of Intellectual Property Rights, 33 I.L.M. 1197 (1994), available at www.wto.org/english/docs_e/legal_e/27-trips.pdf. In other words, data exclusivity is an alternative to protection against disclosure.

[121] For an argument that the FDA has authority to disclose all data upon NDA approval because they are no longer trade secrets following passage of the Hatch-Waxman Act, see Fisher, *supra* note 105, at 277–81.

[122] 35 U.S.C. § 122(b).

further innovation.[123] By providing an exclusionary right that survives public disclosure, the patent system protects innovators from free riders without the need for secrecy. Moreover, public disclosure makes the patent system more transparent and allows interested parties to scrutinize and challenge administrative decisions to issue patents.

Disclosure of safety and effectiveness data upon NDA approval has great potential to accelerate further innovation and to create social value that is otherwise unlikely to be captured by firms submitting the data.[124] There are two reasons why safety and effectiveness data are likely to be more valuable if publicly disclosed than they are if sequestered in proprietary silos by NDA holders. First, NDA holders have an incentive to maximize product sales that is likely to compete with the goal of maximizing further innovation. Second, public disclosure permits researchers to aggregate data from multiple products and perform meta-analyses that require the use of raw data rather than summaries.

Unlicensed researchers of the data are more likely than NDA holders (or their licensees) to find negative information that would harm product sales. Learning when the risks posed by a drug outweigh its benefits is a valuable form of innovation that NDA holders have little incentive to pursue or to license others to pursue, because they cannot capture this value. Public disclosure would permit institutions with different incentives to give the raw data a skeptical reanalysis rather than having to rely on summaries provided by the NDA holder and the FDA.[125]

Safety and effectiveness data are likely to be more amenable to aggregation and meta-analysis than the more heterogenous disclosures in patent applications. NDA filers are all collecting data to meet the same regulatory standards, and data for different products are therefore likely to be highly comparable. Applying modern bioinformatics techniques to aggregations of these data could greatly increase what is learned from the data. Treating data as proprietary makes it difficult to analyse data from more than one product at a time. Combining data from multiple studies can minimize problems of statistical insufficiency and provide information about side-effects and toxicities that are too rare to give rise to statistically significant observations in any given study that is limited to a few

---

[123] Jeanne C. Fromer, *Patent Disclosure*, 94 IOWA L. REV. 539 (2009).

[124] Ünlü, *supra* note 13, at 539–44.

[125] For examples of independent researchers identifying risks through access to raw data, see Comments of Pew Prescription Project *et al.* presented to the U.S. Food and Drug Administration Transparency Task Force (June 24, 2009), Docket No. FDA-2009-N-0247-0063.1, available at www.regulations.gov.

thousand patients.[126] Drug developers could use meta-analysis of pooled data to eliminate more quickly those products that are likely to fail in clinical trials and to target their efforts on more promising candidates.[127] It would also allow them to compare their products and to make better information available for physicians and patients to use in choosing drugs.

Regulatory exclusivity could follow the example of the patent system, providing innovators with the exclusive right to use submitted data for regulatory purposes for a period of time in exchange for disclosure. In such a system it would be difficult to justify limiting the information disclosed during the period of exclusivity to a summary of the data prepared by the submitter.[128] It is arguable, however, that current law stops short of providing exclusive rights that would obviate the need for secrecy. Even after the Hatch-Waxman Act, non-disclosure may still be necessary to prevent competitors from using data submitted by an innovator to get regulatory approval to sell generic copies of the product during the period of exclusivity.[129] This is because regulatory exclusivity defers the filing and approval of ANDAs, but not of NDAs. An applicant who is able to submit 'full reports of investigations which have been made to show whether or not such drug is safe for use and whether such drug is effective in use'[130] need not wait until the end of the exclusivity period, when the statute permits the use of an ANDA, but could instead file an NDA. So long as the innovator's data are unavailable, a generic competitor is unlikely to conduct its own clinical trials to file an NDA because it could not hope to recover that cost through future sales of the generic product at competitive prices. But if the data were publicly available, the competitor could file its own NDA at reasonable cost.[131]

This gap in protection could be fixed by amending the statute to specify that during the period of regulatory exclusivity, nobody could submit an NDA for the same chemical entity using data previously submitted in support of the NDA for the reference product without the permission of the holder of the NDA for the reference product.[132] With that fortification

---

126 *Id.* at 540.

127 *Id.* at 542.

128 21 C.F.R. § 314.430(e)(2).

129 It is possible, for example, that competitors could use disclosed safety and effectiveness data to submit an NDA under 21 U.S.C. § 355(b)(2). See *supra* note 88.

130 21 USC § 355(b)(1)(A).

131 Of course, the innovator may have patent rights that it could enforce against the generic competitor and that would defer the time when the FDA could approve the Hatch-Waxman Act.

132 This change in the law would finally respond to the FDA's complaint in

in the terms of regulatory exclusivity, Congress could explicitly require public disclosure of data from clinical trials immediately upon approval of an NDA. This combination of changes would retain approximately the same level of protection from competition for innovators that they enjoy now in the U.S. market, while improving the information base for future innovation.

It is possible that some competitive harms could result from such disclosure. Industry trade groups have responded to the FDA's cautious proposal to convene a group of stakeholders for further discussion of the issue with alarm, warning that it could cause 'grave competitive harm to the research-based biopharmaceutical industry'[133] and that 'after patents themselves, raw data is a biopharmaceutical companies' [*sic*] life blood'.[134] In addition to the concern that competitors could submit the data to the FDA in support of their own NDAs, they assert that 'these data could be used to support approval in virtually every other country in the world, even after redaction of trade secret information', that 'they would provide competitors with relevant insight into how to develop other, competitive products' and that 'patent protection would be meaningless if a competitor could access the full reports of an innovator product, which it could then use to design around the patents'.[135]

Although the FDA rejected as 'speculative and remote' similar conclusory assertions of potential competitive harm from disclosure of summaries in the 1970s,[136] perhaps greater harm could flow from disclosure of raw data. Perhaps the data could be used by a competitor to secure regulatory approval to sell generic products in foreign countries where innovators are not otherwise protected either by patents or by regulatory exclusivity. Innovators might face generic competition in these other countries sooner if generic competitors could take data released by the FDA and submit it to foreign regulators immediately upon approval of a U.S. NDA. This potential harm should be measured and considered, but it

---

1974 that 'Present law contains no provision that would permit the Food and Drug Administration to refuse to approve a "me-too" product on the basis of information obtained from the first manufacturer, once that information from the first manufacturer is disclosed'. 1974 Public Information, *supra* note 14, at 44634.

[133] See Letter from Pharmaceutical Research and Manufacturers of America to Food and Drug Administration (July 20, 2010), Docket No. FDA-2009-N-0247-0252.1 ('PhRMA 2010 comments') at 30, available at www.regulations.gov.

[134] See Letter from Biotechnology Industry Organization to Food and Drug Administration (July 20, 2010), Docket No. FDA-2009-N-0247-0251.1 ('BIO 2010 comments') at 15, available at www.regulations.gov.

[135] PhRMA 2010 comments, *supra* note 133, at 30.

[136] See *supra* note 55.

should not be presumed to outweigh the benefits of data disclosure. After all, most countries are now required by international treaties to provide patent protection for drugs, and some form of regulatory exclusivity is increasingly common as well;[137] thus, the amount of money at stake in those markets without effective protection for pharmaceutical innovators today is likely to be quite small. If competitive harm can be documented with real evidence rather than sweeping assertions, perhaps the best way to correct the level of incentives for innovation is to fortify the level of regulatory exclusivity rather than to continue to maintain data secrecy.

On the other hand, there is much social value to be gained from improved data disclosure. Data disclosure offers the prospect of improving the productivity of future pharmaceutical R&D. Prompt disclosure of data from clinical trials might, for example, alert firms to hazards associated with a class of products, highlight the relative virtues of competing products, or point to potential new uses that merit further investigation. Trade secrecy permits firms to withhold this value from competitors, thereby conferring a competitive benefit on innovators. But trade secrecy achieves this benefit at considerable social cost. Public availability of data from clinical trials would allow firms to learn from each other's experience so that they could design better products and conduct better trials in the future. It would spare firms from having to continuously reinvent the wheel and steer them away from carrying out costly trials of products that are likely to fail, perhaps bringing down the staggering average costs of new drug development. It would permit reanalysis of data by skeptical competitors in ways that might challenge the spin selected by the product's sponsor. It would permit independent analysis by scientists and institutions that do not share the agenda of the sponsor, providing a valuable check on distortions that arise from the wish to profit from hoped-for product sales. It might provide answers to questions that neither the sponsor nor the FDA had thought to ask.

The foregone social value as a result of secrecy is likely to be a growing loss, as information technology improves and as growing understanding of the genetic basis of disease and drug response makes it possible to direct queries to data from multiple studies of different drugs in different patient populations.

Government initiatives to promote innovation often call for disclosure of new data.[138] Calls for public disclosure of data sometimes face

---

[137] See Reichman, *supra* note 8.

[138] See Rebecca S. Eisenberg and Arti K. Rai, *Harnessing and Sharing the Benefits of State-Sponsored Research: Intellectual Property Rights and Data*

resistance from investigators with an interest in restricting access to data to their collaborators.[139] The National Institutes of Health requires all grant applicants seeking U.S. $500,000 or more 'to include a plan for data sharing or state why data sharing is not possible' as a part of their grant applications.[140] They cite a compelling list of arguments in support of data sharing, including reinforcing open scientific inquiry, facilitating new research, encouraging diversity of analysis and opinions, enabling the exploration of topics not envisioned by the original investigators, and permitting the creation of new data sets that combine data from different sources.

Public disclosure of data from clinical trials offers all of these benefits for innovation, in addition to improving the information base for clinical decision-making. Proper regulatory design, including effective provision for regulatory exclusivity, provides an opportunity to eliminate trade secrecy and to create a valuable public information base for drug discovery, but so far that is largely a missed opportunity.

CONCLUSION

The FDA's long tradition of treating safety and effectiveness data submitted with NDAs as confidential information made sense when it was adopted, but it has outlived its original justification. Today, regulatory exclusivity offers a better way to protect innovators from unfair competitive use of their data without the need for secrecy. With effective regulatory exclusivity in place, the goal of innovation would be better served through prompt public disclosure of data than through continuing secrecy, allowing skeptical scrutiny and meta-analysis of data by innovators whose queries are not limited by the interests of NDA holders.

Sharing in California's Stem Cell Initiative, 21 BERKELEY TECH. L.J. 1187 (2006).

139 National Research Council, Sharing Publication-related Data and Materials: Responsibilities of Authorship in the Life Sciences (2003), available at http://newton.nap.edu/catalog/10613.html#toc.

140 National Institute of Health, NIH Data Sharing Policy and Implementation Guidance (2003), available at http://grants.nih.gov/grants/guide/notice-files/NOT-OD-03-032.html.

PART IV

INTERNATIONAL ISSUES

19 Trade secrets and traditional knowledge: strengthening international protection of indigenous innovation

*Doris Estelle Long**

INTRODUCTION

At the turn of the last century, a missionary, anthropologist and long-time scholar of the practices of the Hopi Indians, Reverend Heinrich (Henry) R. Voth, was allowed to witness and photograph sacred ceremonial dances as part of his study of the Hopi religion and culture. Such photography remains generally forbidden even today. Disputes over the scope of the oral understanding regarding the use of the photographs taken, including in particular Reverend Voth's right to publish them, and the extent to which the Hopis actually agreed to have such practices recorded by an outsider (or, more specifically, the extent to which the Hopis had the practical power to refuse Voth's request), remain ongoing. What remains undisputed is that the ceremonies photographed, described and published by Voth are considered sacred, and that the knowledge regarding the conduct of such ceremonies remains closely held among certain members of the tribe. Commercialization of such ceremonies is prohibited.[1]

The history of indigenous groups and the protection of their secret practices is filled with such stories of misunderstandings, mistaken trust and incomplete legal protection. Such misunderstandings have the potential to expand exponentially as the commercial value of indigenous-held knowledge is increasingly recognized in such diverse areas as biogenetics, agriculture, sustainable development and environmental protection (among

* Professor of Law and Chair, Intellectual Property, Information Technology and Privacy Group, the John Marshall Law School, Chicago. The author would like to thank Allison Schneider and Youngjoo Ahn for their research assistance on portions of this chapter. The discussion in this chapter regarding 'generational innovation' is based in part on an earlier work: *Crossing the Innovation Divide*, 81 Temple L. Rev. 101 (2008).

[1] See, e.g., Michael F. Brown, Who Owns Native Culture 11–15 (Harvard University Press, 2003) (discussing the issue and setting forth a good summary of the sensitivities on both sides).

others). Yet despite this history of conflict, and a few problematic developments resulting from well-meaning but misguided advice concerning the creation of traditional knowledge databases, a properly crafted international trade secret regime has the potential, not only to finally affirm the respect due indigenous peoples' knowledge in this era of globalization and digitization, but also to enhance the international protection of indigenous innovation generally.

I use the term 'indigenous innovation' to refer to the creative and innovative practices, knowledge, techniques, skills and works of indigenous peoples. Such innovation is generational in nature, generally held in common by the tribe and, like all innovation, changes over time. I use this term as opposed to the more common terms 'traditional knowledge' and 'traditional cultural expressions' because it is broader than those terms, and yet more specific for purposes of analysing the potential utility of trade secret protection in protecting certain forms of indigenous knowledge.

In its broadest and original sense, the term 'traditional knowledge' covers a potentially large body of knowledge and practices handed down through generations by a particular tribe or indigenous group. It includes a wide variety of spiritual and cultural beliefs and practices, tangible works, folklore, folk art, folk remedies and information and techniques regarding the use and conservation of surrounding biogenetic resources. As a result of the work of the Intergovernmental Committee on Intellectual Property and Genetic Resources, Traditional Knowledge and Folklore of WIPO (IGC), this broad categorical term has been narrowed in recent years to exclude creative expressions. Instead, works of generational creativity have been given a separate descriptive category: 'traditional cultural expressions'. Thus, according to the IGC, 'traditional knowledge' 'in the strict sense':

> refer[s] . . . to the content or substance of knowledge resulting from intellectual activity in a traditional context, and includes the know-how, skills, innovations, practices and learning that form part of traditional knowledge systems, and knowledge embodying traditional lifestyles of indigenous and local communities, or contained in codified knowledge systems passed between generations. It is not limited to any specific technical field, and may include agricultural, environmental and medicinal knowledge, and knowledge associated with genetic resources.[2]

By contrast, the term 'traditional cultural expressions' is defined as 'any forms whether tangible or intangible in which traditional culture

---

[2] IGC, *The Protection of Traditional Knowledge: Draft Gap Analysis: Revision*, Annex I, 4, para. 4 (WIPO/GRTKF/IC/13/5(b) Rev) (October 11, 2008) ('TK Gap Analysis').

and knowledge are expressed, appear or are manifested'.[3] More simply, the current definition of traditional knowledge appears to be increasingly used synonymously with the concept of biodiversity to cover practices, traditions and knowledge involving flora, fauna and other biogenetic resources.[4] Similarly, the term 'traditional cultural expressions' is increasingly used synonymously with the term folklore.[5]

While these divisions may be useful for certain purposes, such as developing appropriate analogues for protection for works of commodifiable artistry, generational based folk art or folk music and the like, for purposes of strengthening the protection of indigenous innovation, the division is inapposite. While certain indigenous innovations (such as a ceremony for the cure of a particular disease or an oral 'text' on uses of certain plants in connection with agricultural or medical activities) may include potentially copyrightable expressions, the protection I advocate in this chapter is based on concerns with innovation rather than creativity.[6] Consequently, as used in this article, the term 'traditional knowledge' is

---

[3] IGC, *Reproduction of Document WIPO/GRTKF/IC/9/4 'The Protection of Traditional Cultural Expressions/ Expressions of Folklore: Revised Objectives and Principles'*, Annex 1, art. 1 (WIPO/GRTKF/IC/12/4(c)) (December 6, 2007).

[4] See, e.g., Convention on Biological Diversity, Art. 8(j) (requiring member countries to 'respect, preserve and maintain knowledge, innovations and practices of indigenous and local communities embodying traditional lifestyles relevant for the conservation and sustainable use of biological diversity'). The work of the IGC has increasingly demonstrated this more refined focus in its various adjunct documents regarding the relationship between 'traditional knowledge' and genetic resources despite claims to reject such a narrower focus. See IGC, *Genetic Resources: Overview* (WIPO/GRTKF/IC/14/7) (June 5, 2009) (containing a list of diverse IGC documents which have dealt with genetic resource protection, all within the context of its analysis of 'traditional knowledge'); TK Gap Analysis, *supra* note 2, Annex I, 4, para. 4 ('This draft gap analysis is required to be prepared for "traditional knowledge" as such, and not any more specific concept such as biodiversity related TK').

[5] See IGC, *The Protection of Traditional Cultural Expressions/Expressions of Folklore: Overview of Policy Objectives and Core Principles* 11 (WIPO/GRTKF/IC/7/3) (August 20, 2004) (noting use of term 'traditional cultural expressions' synonymously with expressions of folklore). In a relatively recent development, some have begun to differentiate between 'traditional cultural expressions' and 'expressions of folklore' (EOF). Agnès Lucas-Schloetter suggests that narrower terms such as folklore may allow for more focused, and ultimately more successful, protection for various aspects of what she refers to as 'traditional culture'. Agnès Lucas-Schloetter, *Folklore*, in Indigenous Heritage and Intellectual Property: Genetic Resources, Traditional Knowledge and Folklore 259, 264 (Silke von Lewinski ed., 2004).

[6] For a brief discussion of the distinctions between innovation and creativity in connection with the protection of works of intellectual labor, see generally Doris

intended to include aspects of indigenous practice that might potentially be protectable as expressions, so long as protection under trade secret doctrines is appropriate. Both agricultural techniques and folk recipes may be examples of local innovation that has been under-protected in the past. Both types of innovation frequently are held by peoples who not only are minorities within present day national boundaries, but lack the political power to ensure protection for their innovations.

I. INDIGENOUS INNOVATION: AN IGNORED CONCEPT

It is undisputed that 'innovation' is prized in today's technology-driven world. The term itself is ubiquitous, appearing in advertisements, book titles, and even in copyright decisions.[7] A recent search using the Google search engine of the term 'innovation' disclosed over 107,000,000 entries in English using the term. A search for the related term 'innovative' disclosed 113,000,000 entries in English. A Google Book search of English-language books disclosed 7,439 books containing the term 'innovation' in their titles. This romance with the concept of innovation is not new. To the contrary, as countless historians have demonstrated, the pursuit of innovation for the sake of innovation, and a belief in its positive impact can be dated at least from the Middle Ages.[8]

Intellectual property has been at the heart of this innovation quest, most clearly in the form of patent protection for those innovations (inventions) which reach a certain standard of both uniqueness and individuality. Obligations of uniqueness are generally reflected in requirements that an invention demonstrate such a high degree of novelty that an individual who is skilled in the art in question would not have invented the solution at issue. Its most frequent recitation is in the tripartite obligation for protection contained in Article 27 of the Agreement on Trade Related Aspects of

---

Estelle Long, *Dissonant Harmonization: Limitations on Cash 'n Carry Creativity,* 70 ALBANY L. REV. 1163 (2007).

[7] See, e.g., Digital Communications Associates, Inc. v. Softklone Distributing Corp., 659 F.Supp. 449 (N.D. Ga. 1987) (first reported U.S. copyright case in which the term 'innovative' is used as a synonym for expressive originality).

[8] See, e.g., ROBERT FRIEDEL, A CULTURE OF IMPROVEMENT: TECHNOLOGY AND THE WESTERN MILLENNIUM (Massachusetts Institute of Technology, 2007); DAVID LANDES, THE UNBOUND PROMETHEUS: TECHNOLOGICAL CHANGE AND INDUSTRIAL DEVELOPMENT IN WESTERN EUROPE FROM 1710 TO THE PRESENT 41 (Cambridge University Press, 1969).

Intellectual Property Rights (TRIPS) which requires Member Countries to make patent protection available 'for any inventions, whether products or processes, in all fields of technology, provided that they are new, involve an inventive step, and are capable of industrial application'.[9] In today's present technological age, this uniqueness is most often, although not exclusively, demonstrated through the invention of some 'high-tech' advance. I do not mean to suggest that only high-tech advances can meet the standards of novelty modern patent regimes impose. To the contrary, there are countless patents that have been granted for 'low-tech' innovations, including backpacks, golf swings, and combs with mirrors. But the result of the emphasis on novelty has been to undervalue the generational process underlying much indigenous innovation, denying it protection on the grounds that it has been in use too long to meet present standards of valuable uniqueness.

'Generational innovation', as used here, is innovation using tradition-based knowledge, works and practices. On its face, the term 'generational innovation' appears counterintuitive, tying innovation (a concept embodying newness) with 'generational' (a concept embodying passing across generations). Yet, the generational collaboration that tradition-based innovation represents is similar to the evolutionary and collaborative creativity of the Internet era. Such collective collaboration modes as those apparent in open source software and in the creation of web-based information sites such as Wikipedia already call into question the vitality of Western concepts of individuated creativity and time-constrained uniqueness as requisites of protectable creativity. Protection of indigenous innovation is merely another example of a broadened category of collaborative activity also evident in such Internet-based collaborations. Even though generational innovation does not always create absolutely new products, it nevertheless plays an increasing role in the diffusion of new products and processes to the developed world. This diffusion takes many forms, including third party patents based on generational innovations, the products of biopiracy, and even the commodified trade items of eco- and cultural tourism in the developing world.

Rational protection for certain types of traditional knowledge, on both a local and, more significantly, an international basis, can protect and encourage indigenous innovation. It can serve as a critical linchpin to the economic development of indigenous peoples by providing legal protection for those elements of traditional knowledge that indigenous holders chose

---

[9] Agreement on Trade-Related Aspects of Intellectual Property Rights (TRIPS), Art. 27(1).

to commodify. It can also serve as crucial support for both human dignity and cultural diversity goals. But even adequate protection for indigenous innovation would not cover all traditional knowledge. To the contrary, in order to qualify for protection, the knowledge in question should be uniquely affiliated with a particular group of indigenous peoples and their culture. Requiring such identification would reduce the potential claimants for ownership of the traditional knowledge in question. It would also ensure that only innovative knowledge was protected. Thus, for example, general knowledge about the planting seasons, while undoubtedly useful, should not qualify as protectable 'traditional knowledge' since it is not the type of culturally affiliated knowledge which is limited to, or necessarily identifiable with, a particular indigenous group. By contrast, specific knowledge about the types of plants to be harvested, or methods of fertilization or irrigation techniques, might well qualify as protectable knowledge.

While indigenous innovation could be well served by a rational *sui generis* traditional knowledge regime, no such international protection scheme currently exists. In this chapter I will argue that international trade secret protection has the potential to provide *immediate* protection for certain indigenous innovations by incorporating their protection into existing national laws, and those which are in the process of being created by developing countries to meet their TRIPS obligations. To provide such protection, the flexibilities inherent in the present international trade secret regime[10] must be applied in a rational manner that recognizes and *values* some of the unique challenges such protection presents. In advocating for the creation of domestic and international trade secrecy regimes focused on indigenous innovations, I do not mean to suggest that such protection is the sole, or should even be the primary, means to provide protection for traditional knowledge. There are many reasons, other than nurturing innovation, why a strong international regime for the protection of traditional knowledge is necessary, including, among others, to correct past injustices, to promote human rights and respect for cultural diversity, and to recognize and value the role of indigenous innovation as part of a general system of equitable wealth transfer based on the economic value of the innovation in question. But trade secrecy protection, rationally created and administered, can also help provide economic support to groups who most often are found at the poverty level in many developing countries. Unless generational innovation is valued and protected, economic development will remain largely in the hands of, and be directed by, the devel-

---

[10] For a discussion of some of the flexibilities contained in the trade secret regime required under TRIPS, see Sharon K. Sandeen, Chapter 20.

oped, non-indigenous world.[11] Trade secrecy should be only one small part, although a critical one, of a much needed traditional knowledge protection regime.

II. INTERNATIONAL TRADE SECRET PROTECTION: AN EVOLVING CONCEPT

In the international arena, trade secret[12] protection is a relatively new concept, despite its age-old foundations in domestic law. Article 39 of TRIPS, which provides the basic structure for such protection internationally, was not adopted until 1994.[13] It states in pertinent part:

> Natural and legal persons shall have the possibility of preventing information lawfully within their control from being disclosed to, acquired by, or used by

---

[11] See generally Doris Estelle Long, *Crossing the Innovation Divide*, 81 TEMPLE L. REV. 101 (2008).

[12] I am using the term 'trade secret' as synonymous with the terms 'undisclosed or confidential information' and, therefore, clearly within the normative standards contained in Art. 39 of TRIPS. The term 'trade secret' is the traditional term used in the United States for the protection of such information. Since the United States tabled the first written proposal for the protection of undisclosed information, the terms of which were largely reflected in the final version of Art. 39 (see GATT Negotiating Group on Trade-Related Aspects of Intellectual Property Rights, Including Trade in Counterfeit Goods, *Compilation of Written Submissions and Oral Statements: Revision* (MTN.GNG/NG11/W/12/Rev.1) (February 1988), the term is particularly apt. Issues regarding the reasons for the ultimate change in terminology to 'undisclosed information' do not affect the normative role of Art. 39 in connection with the protection of indigenous innovation.

[13] The first international normative standard for trade secret protection per se was contained in Art. 1711 of the North American Free Trade Agreement (NAFTA). Article 1711 actually uses the term 'trade secret' in describing the 'secret information' to be protected against unauthorized uses that are 'contrary to honest commercial practices'. While its terms undoubtedly influenced Art. 39, which was finalized nearly two years after NAFTA, Art. 1711 appears in a strictly regional agreement and does not have the same international normative impact as Art. 39 of TRIPS. Moreover, its provisions are largely similar to those of TRIPS, with certain critical distinctions regarding, for example, tangibility and potential commercial value. Compare TRIPS, Art. 39 (requiring protection for information that 'has commercial value because it is secret') with NAFTA, Art. 1711 (requiring protection for information that 'has actual or potential commercial value because it is secret' and that is 'evidenced in documents, electronic or magnetic means, optical disc, microfilms, films or other similar instruments'). Consequently this chapter will focus on Art. 39 as the normative standard for the international trade secret regime to be used to protect indigenous innovation.

> others without their consent in a manner contrary to honest commercial practices so long as such information:
> (a) is secret in the sense that it is not, as a body or in the precise configuration and assembly of its components, generally known among or readily accessible to persons within the circles that normally deal with the kind of information in question;
> (b) has commercial value because it is secret; and
> (c) has been subject to reasonable steps under the circumstances, by the person lawfully in control of the information, to keep it secret.[14]

Thus, under Article 39 countries must prevent the unauthorized use or disclosure of 'undisclosed information' where such confidential information meets three basic criteria. The information must be secret. It must have 'commercial value' because it is secret; and it must have been subject to 'reasonable steps under the circumstances' by the owner to keep the information secret. The absence of any obligation of absolute secrecy, combined with flexibility in determining what type of secrecy arrangements is required to maintain the protectable nature of covered confidential information, supports the view that some indigenous innovation might qualify for initial subject matter protection under international trade secret standards.

III. THE CRITICAL FIRST STEP: THE STUMBLING BLOCK OF 'OWNERSHIP'

Before considering the critical issues raised by the tripartite test for trade secret protection under Article 39 in connection with indigenous innovation, the unique problem of 'ownership' (or in the case of indigenous peoples, the more accurate term 'custodianship') must be addressed. Unless the indigenous concept of a type of collective 'custodianship' or trusteeship for indigenous innovation is legally cognizable, the application of the tripartite test of Article 39 to indigenous knowledge remains largely a theoretical exercise. If trade secret rights cannot be held or exercised by collective entities such as indigenous tribes, then trade secrecy's utility for protecting and encouraging indigenous innovation will be largely eviscerated.

The unique issues of 'ownership' arising from the nature of generational innovation generally and indigenous innovation in particular, fall into two categories. The first deals with the nature of 'ownership' and its

---

14 TRIPS, Art. 39(2).

relationship to indigenous concepts of trusteeship and custodianship. The second deals with the methods for dealing with the potential conflicting claims of 'ownership' and use rights. These conflicts necessarily arise as a result of the history of indigenous peoples and their history of removal and territorial dispossession, and include the rights of the diaspora to utilize the knowledge of the tribe. A complete examination of these issues is beyond the scope of this chapter. However, a brief explanation of the nature of the conflict and its potential resolution is required to understand fully the need for the flexibility that TRIPS mandates for international trade secret protection if we are to grant indigenous innovation its proper protected status.

The concept of 'ownership' as embodied by present efforts to protect innovation through intellectual property laws is undeniably a Western European construct that does not fit readily within the understanding and culture of most indigenous peoples. As exemplified by the Preamble to TRIPS, the premiere international intellectual property treaty to date, 'intellectual property rights are private rights'.[15] Not only are they private rights, they are property rights, whose exclusive exercise belongs, at least, initially, to identifiable individuals.[16] In turn, the holders of these rights are given rights similar to those granted to the owners of real property, including the right of control and exclusion over their 'property'.

Neither the personal nature of innovative 'inventorship' nor the property-based rights granted such individuated ownership have much resonance among indigenous groups. As the COICA Statement on Intellectual Property Rights and Biodiversity plainly declared in its paragraph 7: 'For members of indigenous peoples, knowledge and determination of the use of resources are collective and intergenerational'.[17] Mrs. Erica Irene Daes, Special Rapporteur, UN Economic and Social Council Sub-Commission on Prevention of Discrimination and Protection of Minorities, in her Study of the Protection of the Cultural and Intellectual Property of Indigenous Peoples, similarly recognized the communal

---

[15] TRIPS, Preamble.

[16] See, e.g., Berne Convention for the Protection of Literary and Artistic Works ('Berne Convention'), Art. 5 (granting 'authors' the 'enjoyment and exercise' of diverse rights over their protected works). Cf, Paris Convention for the Protection of Industrial Property ('Paric Convention'), Art. 4*ter* (requiring that the 'inventor' of the invention must be mentioned in any patent application). Both articles were subsequently incorporated into TRIPS.

[17] COICA Statement on Intellectual Property Rights and Biodiversity, para. 7, *reprinted in* Doris Estelle Long and Anthony D'Amato, 2002 Documents Supplement to a Coursebook in International Intellectual Property 891, 892 (West Group, 2002).

nature of indigenous ownership, stating: 'Indigenous peoples are the true collective owners of their works, arts and ideas, and no alienation of these elements of their heritage should be recognized by national or international law, unless made in conformity with indigenous people's own traditional laws and customs and with the approval of their own local institutions'.[18] While each tribe has its own culture, history, practices and beliefs, current evidence suggests that many tribes eschew individual ownership of the works created using generational knowledge, and instead treat such works, as well as the foundational knowledge contained or represented by such works, as belonging to the tribe as a collective entity. Thus, for example, a morning star pole created by an aboriginal artist using generational techniques, while undoubtedly demonstrating sufficient individual creativity to qualify as a copyright protectable work under internationally accepted standards, was considered by the artist's tribe to belong to the tribe as a whole. The individual artist, who had been trained in the techniques for creating such poles, received no special ownership rights as a result of his personal creative acts. To the contrary, the tribe viewed his artistry as a type of custodianship in which he was allowed to create images using traditional techniques so long as he continued to use his talent for the common good of the tribe.[19]

International recognition of a right to collective 'ownership' of indigenous innovation is a necessary first step toward developing a workable protection system for confidential indigenous innovation. Indeed, collective ownership is not per se contrary to present protection regimes, including trade secret protection. Many intellectual property-based regimes recognize joint ownership resulting from collaborative activities. Thus, for

---

[18] U.N. Economic and Social Council (ECOSOC), Sub-Commission on Prevention of Discrimination and Protection of Minorities, Commission on Human Rights, *Study on the Protection of the Cultural and Intellectual Property of Indigenous Peoples*, para. 171 (U.N. Doc. E/CN.4/Sub.2/1993/28) (July 28, 1993) (prepared by Erica-Irene Daes).

[19] Yumbulul v. Reserve Bank of Australia (1991) 21 I.P.R. 481 (Australia). See also WIPO, Intellectual Property Needs and Expectations of Traditional Knowledge Holders, WIPO Report on Fact-Finding Missions on Intellectual Property and Traditional Knowledge 1998–1999 (WIPO, 2001) (detailing the beliefs of diverse peoples in the collective nature of their rights); Silke von Lewinski *et al*, Indigenous Heritage and Intellectual Property: Genetic Resources, Traditional Knowledge and Folklore (Kluwer Law International, 2003) (same). Such communitarian views are not limited to indigenous peoples. See Ronald V. Betty, Copyrighting Culture: The Political Economy of Intellectual Property 12–13 (1996) (discussing the communitarian view of property and culture in Indian and Balinese traditions).

example, copyright may be held jointly where two authors work together to create a work, and in cases of a work for hire may even be held by a corporate employer.[20] Perhaps more importantly for purposes of protecting jointly held confidential information, in developed countries with sophisticated trade secret regimes protected information is often held by juridical persons, including corporations and partnerships.[21] While such entities may be considered single legal entities, in practical terms trade secrecy rights are exercised collectively by their officers or boards of directors. Such analogues strongly support the extension of trade secret holder status to the members of a particular tribe, on a collective basis. Beyond simple collectivity, however, is the more difficult question of the custodial nature of the 'ownership' such collectivity gives rise to, and the impact of this custodial 'ownership' on the definitional right of who is included among the community that holds the rights. As Terri Janke explains in *Our Culture: Our Future: Report on Australian Indigenous Cultural and Intellectual Property Rights*:

> Although Indigenous Cultural and Intellectual Property is collectively owned, an individual or group is often the custodian or caretaker of a particular item of heritage. The traditional custodians are empowered as caretakers in relation to the particular item of heritage only in so far as their actions conform to the best interests of the community as a whole. This type of relationship was noted in the case of *Deceased Applicant v Indofurn* (the Carpets Case).[22] For instance, artists may have the authority to depict a traditional, pre-existing design in their artwork by virtue of their birth or by initiation. While they have this right, they hold the knowledge embodied in the work on trust for the rest of the clan.[23]

---

[20] See, e.g., Berne Convention, Art. 7 (establishing the term of protection for works of 'joint authorship'); 17 U.S.C. § 201(b) (providing for employer authorship of employee created works).

[21] See, e.g., TRIPS, Art. 39(2) (providing that '*natural and legal persons* shall have the possibility of preventing' the misappropriation of certain undisclosed information) (emphasis added); Uniform Trade Secrets Act § 1(3) (defining the person who owns a protected trade secret as 'a natural person, *corporation,* business trust, estate, trust, *partnership, association, joint venture, government*, governmental subdivision or agency, or any other legal or commercial entity') (emphasis added). The definition of an owner in the U.S. Uniform Trade Secrets Act is particularly significant since the first reported proposal for inclusion of trade secret protection during the Uruguay Round Negotiations was made by the United States and appears to follow this Uniform Act in all major particulars.

[22] Milpurrurru & Ors v. Indofurn Pty Ltd & Ors (1995) 30 I.P.R. 209 (Australia).

[23] Terri Janke, *Our Culture: Our Future: Report on Australian Indigenous Cultural and Intellectual Property Rights* 8 (ATSIC, 1997). The *Milpurrurru* case cited by Janke had facts strongly similar to the morning star pole case discussed

The custodial communitarian relationship described by Terri Janke and others does not precisely resemble the transfer-based authorization typical to intellectual property protection regimes.[24] To the contrary, communitarian ownership of indigenous innovation does not merely involve questions of authorization and control but may also include additional concerns over heritage protection and deculturization. 'Deculturization' is basically the use of traditional knowledge in a manner which removes such knowledge from its cultural meanings and creates new and unauthorized associations that are often perceived by the holders of the knowledge to be misleading and harmful, such as for example, Professor Voth's publication of photos of sacred Hopi ceremonies described in the opening paragraphs of this chapter. Other common examples of deculturizing uses include unauthorized pop music borrowings from indigenous artists, tourist souvenirs, comic book heroes and carpet designs. While these special concerns are distinctly different from those that generally govern traditional trade secret authorization considerations, in their practical effect, they bear a strong resemblance to similar community based concerns that may influence licensing decisions regarding trade secret information, such as, for example, establishing a policy of only licensing companies with a strong record on environmental protection issues. The heritage-based custodianship for indigenous innovation, however, gives rise to a second and more problematic issue regarding 'ownership' of indigenous innovation: the rights of the diaspora to own/use such innovation, even when they are no longer present on tribal homelands.

Diasporic ownership is a particularly critical issue for indigenous peoples due to the historical lack of a right of self-determination. Countless indigenous peoples, from the Cherokee of the United States to the Panará of Brazil, have faced unwanted removal from territorial homelands. Others, such as the Iroquois in the United States and Canada, and the Sami in Finland, Norway and Sweden, found territorial lands divided by national

---

earlier. In *Milpurrurru*, carpets produced in Vietnam copied aboriginal designs without authorization. The court recognized the tribe's rights to control such reproduction in accordance with their customary practices. For a more detailed description of this case and the morning star pole case (among others), see generally TERRI JANKE, MINDING CULTURE: CASE STUDIES ON INTELLECTUAL PROPERTY AND TRADITIONAL CULTURAL EXPRESSIONS (WIPO, 2003).

[24] The work for hire doctrine can be considered an exception to this general trend since the transfer to the often-corporate employer occurs automatically, without the need for any formal agreement between the natural author (the employee) and the employer. See 17 U.S.C. § 201(b). While the work for hire doctrine is strongly entrenched in U.S. law, it is not generally followed by most civil law countries.

boundaries imposed by third parties without regard to historical tribal boundaries. Still others have been forced to flee traditional homelands in the face of political events that threatened to undermine or even eliminate the group's ability to maintain its culture and traditions.

This history suggests that claims for control of indigenous innovation have the potential to give rise to a great number of legitimate conflicts over ownership, including the right of the diaspora to ownership of indigenous innovation. Given that protectable indigenous innovation is closely tied to the identity of a particular people,[25] determinations of ownership necessarily address sensitive issues of identity and culture, including whether contemplated uses are deculturizing in nature and consequently unauthorized under tribal customs and laws. Ownership conflicts regarding indigenous innovation, however, are further complicated by the issue of the extent to which members who are no longer physically present on traditional lands (or whatever physical location the tribe may presently inhabit) – the diaspora – have legitimate claims to ownership.

Diasporic ownership claims regarding indigenous innovations are premised not merely on history and the need to correct the past harms caused by colonial abuses, but also on the human rights issues raised by the denial of such ownership. The right of cultural participation, including a right to enjoy the benefits of such culture, has been recognized in numerous human rights instruments. Thus, for example, Article 27 of the Universal Declaration of Human Rights (UDHR) expressly recognizes that 'Everyone has the right *freely to participate in the cultural life* of the community, to enjoy the arts and to *share in* scientific advancement and its *benefits*'.[26] The critical relationship between cultural participation and human dignity rights is underscored in numerous other human rights documents, including Article 27 of the Covenant on Civil and Political Rights (the ICCPR) which provides: 'In those states in which ethnic, religious or linguistic *minorities* exist, persons belonging to such minorities shall not

---

[25] See IGC, *The Protection of Traditional Knowledge: Revised Objectives and Principles*, Article 4(ii), (iii), Annex, 22 (WIPO GRTK/IC/9/5) (2006) (establishing that only traditional knowledge which is 'distinctively associated with a traditional or indigenous community or people which transmits it between generations' should be protected and that such traditional knowledge should further be 'integral to the cultural identity of an indigenous or traditional community'); IGC, *Revised Draft Provisions for the Protection of Traditional Cultural Expressions/Expressions of Folklore: Policy Objectives and Core Principles* 11 (WIPO/GRTKF/IC/9/4) (2006) (establishing that only traditional cultural expressions which are 'characteristic of a community's cultural and social identity and cultural heritage' are protectable).

[26] Universal Declaration of Human Rights (UDHR), G.A. Res. 217A(III), Art. 27 (U.N. Doc. A/810) (December 10, 1948) (emphasis added).

be denied the right, in community with other members of their group, to *enjoy their own culture*, to profess and practice their own religion, or to use their own language'.[27] While the history of the UDHR and similar human rights instruments demonstrates the general absence of a clear intention to extend this cultural participation right to indigenous communities in particular,[28] I agree with Peter Yu that the failure to expressly include these groups does not mean that such a collective right is not in accordance with the continuing trend to extend human rights to groups.[29] Moreover, these instruments taken as a whole provide an international normative standard which includes a right to cultural participation that is met, in part, through the protection of indigenous innovation.[30] This international normative standard makes the issue of diasporic ownership of critical importance in determining ownership claims to trade secret information based on indigenous knowledge and practices.

Although the right of cultural participation recognized in these instruments is facially limited to members of the 'community', defined at least under the ICCPR as 'members' of the 'group',[31] there is nothing in the

---

27 International Covenant on Civil and Political Rights (ICCPR), Art. 27 (emphasis added). See also United Nations Declaration on the Rights of Indigenous Peoples, Art. 11 (U.N. Doc. A/61/L.67) ('Indigenous Peoples have the right to practice and revitalize their cultural traditions and customs'); International Covenant on Economic, Social and Cultural Rights (ICESR), Art. 15(1) (recognizing 'the right of everyone: (a) to take part in cultural life; (b) to enjoy the benefits of scientific progress and its applications; (c) to benefit from the protection of the moral and material interests resulting from any scientific, literary or artistic production of which he is the author'); American Declaration of the Rights and Duties of Man, Art. XII (OEA/ser.L/V?II.23.doc.21 rev 6) (1948) ('Every person has the right to take part in the cultural life of the community, to enjoy the arts, and to participate in the benefits that result from intellectual progress, especially scientific discoveries').

28 Peter Yu, *Reconceptualizing Intellectual Property Interests in a Human Rights Framework,* 40 U.C. Davis L. Rev. 1039, 1145 (2007) (describing the drafting history of both Art. 27 of the UDHR and Art. 15 of the ICESR and the failure to consider minority rights as part of the cultural participation right).

29 *Id.* at 1146.

30 In addition to documents which recognize the human right of cultural participation, there are numerous other international legal instruments which recognize the importance to protect culture at a general level, including the Convention for the Safeguarding of Intangible Cultural Heritage, and the Convention on the Protection and Promotion of the Diversity of Cultural Expressions. Arguably such cultural protection cannot occur without the included right of participation in the relevant culture in a meaningful manner.

31 ICCPR, Art. 27.

right that is necessarily tied to a particular geographic area or homeland.[32] To the contrary, such right of cultural participation arguably extends beyond the narrow confines of land-based physical communities and includes those members of the tribe who no longer live on tribal homelands or within the geographic confines of the community. So long as such members remain 'in community' with the home group, however that 'community' may ultimately be defined,[33] the right of cultural participation, including the benefit of ownership in communitarian-owned indigenous innovations, should extend to the diaspora.

The complexity of the ownership issues raised by conflicts over diasporic rights to control the use and disclosure of indigenous innovation, and their relationship to sensitive issues of human dignity, cultural identity and human rights, require that such issues be resolved in proceedings that do not continue historic intrusions on indigenous peoples' rights of self-determination. This suggests that current civil litigation and arbitration models presently used to resolve intellectual property ownership disputes may lack sufficiently sensitive mechanisms to accord an appropriate level of deference to the human dignity issues raised in these conflicts. Instead, as I have suggested in other fora, a mediation system should be used based on human rights conflict resolution models to determine identity-based ownership claims.[34]

The complex issue of innovation ownership, however, should not prevent the protection of indigenous innovation under international trade secret regimes. Even though the issue of ownership is a difficult one, it is

---

[32] While territorial homelands often play a critical role in the development of indigenous culture and identity, I have argued in other fora that reliance on territorial boundaries for protection for traditional knowledge may cause unintended, and undesirable, limits on the ability to protect fully indigenous innovation. See generally Doris Estelle Long, Presentation, *The Tyranny of Land and Culture,* Intellectual Property Scholars Round Table, Drake University Law School, Des Moines, Iowa (February 23, 2008).

[33] Because the definition of a member of the community is strongly tied to the right of self-determination, such definition must ultimately be made by the tribe or group itself. Yet defining members of the 'community' may be complicated where the members of the home group and those of the diaspora disagree as to the determination of who qualifies as a member of the group, or what constitutes an appropriate use of traditional knowledge.

[34] Doris Estelle Long, Presentation, *Traditional Rights and Data Access Demands: Untying the Gordian Knot,* Access to Knowledge Conference, Yale Law School, New Haven, Conn., April 21–23, 2006. Given the strong connection which indigenous innovation has to one's identity, and the critical role which such identity will play in any ownership conflicts, providing a forum which gives all participants the sense of not only fairness, but also inclusiveness, is critical.

no more difficult than many of the other complex issues regarding intellectual property rights in the digital era. Moreover, failure to protect and encourage indigenous innovation under trade secret laws would simply continue earlier practices of exclusionary conduct in the protection of such innovation. There is no reason to continue such abusive practices in the twenty-first century.

IV. SECRECY: A FLEXIBLE STANDARD?

On a fundamental level, a rational trade secret regime sympathetic to the needs of indigenous peoples could play a critical role in the future protection and encouragement of indigenous innovation. Such a trade secret regime, based on the international norms established under Article 39 of TRIPS, could be used to protect a wide variety of innovative practices. Yet the utility of this regime in protecting indigenous innovation is necessarily limited by the obligation of reasonable secrecy. On a practical level, given that indigenous innovation is held by the tribe as a whole, maintaining an acceptable level of secrecy may be problematic. While certain types of indigenous innovation may be known or practiced by a small group of persons, other types of innovation, such as those involving agricultural techniques, may not be so limited.

For example, where traditional arts are disclosed to a small number of individuals, such as the disclosure of medical information (including critical information about the uses of certain flora and fauna in treating illnesses) to shamans, and such members are generally perceived to act under a fiduciary obligation to the tribe to maintain the secrecy of these practices, the information in question would appear to qualify as potentially protectable 'undisclosed information'. Thus, the knowledge of a traditional healer practicing in the Tumkur district of Karnataka (India) regarding his treatments for various skin diseases would most likely qualify for protection where the rituals and formulas he uses are known only to his daughter and son-in-law.[35] Similarly the disclosure of certain agricultural techniques regarding fertilization, harvesting or irrigation that are maintained within a particular segment of a particular tribe should qualify as 'confidential' information even without the existence of a formal agreement.

The definition of trade secrecy does not require that the knowledge of the secret necessarily be confined to a particular number of disclosees, but instead is judged according to the level of effort imposed to keep information

35 WIPO *supra* note 19, at Report, 62.

within the designated group. Thus, knowledge which is held in common by the tribe, and which is available to all of its members, need not necessarily be excluded from potential trade secret coverage. For example, in the case of the Hopi ceremonies, Reverend Voth was only allowed to participate because he agreed to keep the information confidential. Such efforts to restrict access confer the hallmarks of protectable undisclosed information.

Although the Hopis described in the first paragraph of this chapter were unable to protect their secret ceremonies, the Pitjantjatjara People of Australia, in a similar case, were able to challenge successfully the publication of an anthropology text, *Nomads of the Desert*, which disclosed confidential information. Just as Reverend Voth had been with the Hopis, Dr. Mountford in the 1940s was allowed access to secret ceremonies of the Pitjantjatjara tribe with the understanding that such access was granted in confidence. The confidential nature of the access was confirmed by Dr. Mountford in his text where he wrote, after the acknowledgement section:

> Where Australian aborigines are concerned, and in areas where traditional aboriginal religion is still significant, this book should be used only after consultation with local male religious leaders. This restriction is important; it is imposed because the concept of what is secret or may not be revealed to the uninitiated in aboriginal religious belief and action, varies considerably throughout the Australian Continent and because the varying views of aborigines in this respect must, on all occasions be observed.[36]

In granting an injunction, Justice Muirhead, in *Foster v. Mountford*,[37] acknowledged the confidential nature of the disclosure, stating:

> I find that the defendant, [Dr.] Mountford, many years ago, was shown things and places, and given information in confidence, by people, and on occasions which perhaps cannot now be identified, save in terms of general community, and in terms of the period. I find the plaintiffs have made out a *prima facie* case that these secrets may, by continuing publication of the book in the Northern Territory, be revealed to those to whom it was always understood it would not be revealed, and that continuance of such publication in the Northern Territory and of course perhaps elsewhere, may cause damage of a serious nature, damage of a type to which monetary damages are irrelevant, and which are not, in fact, claimed in this action.[38]

What is particularly notable for purposes of this discussion is that the court found support for the confidential nature of the information based on testimony of other anthropologists regarding the general practices

---

36 Foster v. Mountford, 14 A.L.R. 71, 1976 WL 46225, 46235.

37 *Id.*

38 *Id.* at 46236–7.

of the Pitjantjatjara tribe. Further, the court granted the sought-after injunction even though it was clear that at the time of Dr. Mountford's dealings with the Pitjantjatjara:

> [t]he people were then far less sophisticated than they are, as a group, today as they had not been subjected for so long, or to such an extent, to white man influences. In other words, it is inevitable that they took Dr. Mountford into their confidence, they showed him and explained to him sacred sites and objects, paintings and rock engravings, and he recorded their myths and totemic geography by aboriginal drawings, the camera, and notebook.[39]

Lack of sophisticated methods for securing and recording confidentiality agreements, however, did not prevent the requested relief.

Foster's recognition of the practical realities of evidencing confidentiality agreements in the face of oral traditions demonstrates the appropriate approach that should be taken in the face of claims of trade secret protection for knowledge involving indigenous innovation. More importantly, the case demonstrates a critical sensitivity to the problems of indigenous peoples (and other minorities) in protecting their confidential or sacred information in the face of a power imbalance that often makes an absolute denial of access to members of the majority impossible. As Article 39 of TRIPS recognizes, the reasonableness of efforts to maintain secrecy must be judged 'under the circumstances' of each case.[40] For cases involving indigenous innovation, such circumstances must include a consideration of the actual or perceived ability of the holder to deny access to outsiders.

In *Foster*, while an injunction prohibiting the further sale of the book within the jurisdictional reach of the court issued, such injunctive relief was not based on the *economic* harm resulting from the unauthorized disclosure of confidential information. The harm at issue was described in social and cultural terms:

> The contention that the plaintiffs as individuals, and their people, will suffer damage and dislocation if some sections of the book come into the hands of the uninitiated, is a consequence I cannot now ignore, not only because of one's lay recognition gained by service in the Territory of the significance and purpose of initiation, but also because of the possible consequences of even accidental acquisition of knowledge of such matters by women and the uninitiated.[41]

---

[39] *Id.* at 46235.

[40] TRIPS, Art. 39(2)(c) (requiring that, to be protectable, undisclosed information must have 'been subject to *reasonable* steps *under the circumstances* by the person lawfully in control of the information to keep it secret') (emphasis added).

[41] Foster v. Mountford, 1976 WL at 46236.

Given the custodial nature of ownership of indigenous innovation, this recognition of harms beyond economic ones is particularly apt. It should be noted that the legal premise of the relief granted in *Foster* was breach of confidence and not precisely 'trade secrecy' per se. Such analysis, however, remains particularly pertinent given the recognized role that breach of confidence claims play in the international protection of confidential information.[42]

According to Article 39, the protection of trade secrets is limited to 'the possibility of preventing [qualified] information . . . from being disclosed to, or acquired by, or used by others without their consent in a manner *contrary to honest commercial practices*'.[43] Footnote 10 of Article 39 further defines the honest commercial practices prong for protection in a manner that directly incorporates breach of confidentiality as a test for trade secret misappropriation. It states:

> For the purpose of this provision, 'a manner contrary to honest commercial practices' shall mean at least practices such as breach of contract, *breach of confidence* and inducement to breach, and includes the acquisition of undisclosed information by third parties who knew, or were grossly negligent in failing to know, that such practices were involved in the acquisition.[44]

This definition not only underscores the commercial basis for trade secret protection, it also demonstrates a critical factor in the appropriate analysis of trade secret protection at the international level. Such protection is based on unfair competition principles, which requires flexibility in analysis of the tripartite test for protection that is critical to the utility of trade secret protection in protecting indigenous innovation.

V. INTERNATIONAL TRADE SECRET PROTECTION: UNFAIR COMPETITION OR PROPERTY RIGHT?

Because generational innovation generally falls outside the scope of present patent and copyright protection regimes, either for lack of sufficient uniqueness or for lack of individuated origin, trade secret protection may serve as a valuable source of international protection for indigenous

---

42 But see Charles Tait Graves, Chapter 4 (arguing that trade secrecy should be disentangled from other confidentiality torts).

43 TRIPS, Art. 39(2) (emphasis added).

44 *Id.* Art. 39(2) n.10 (emphasis added).

innovation. Given some of the special issues that arise from the nature of indigenous innovation, including its cultural underpinnings and the historic lack of control which many indigenous peoples have exercised over their lands, culture and identity, for such trade secret regimes to be useful, they must be applied in a flexible manner. Such flexibility is fully available under international standards, because Article 39 of TRIPS anticipates that the application of its tripartite test will be considered against the scope of 'fairness' as opposed to rigid property rights.

The first paragraph of Article 39 firmly bases trade secret protection on unfair competition principles with its direct reference to Article 10*bis* of the Paris Convention:

> In the course of ensuring effective protection against *unfair competition* as provided in Article 10*bis* of the Paris Convention (1967), Members shall protect undisclosed information in accordance with paragraph 2.[45]

The unfair competition basis of trade secret protection under Article 39 is further underscored by the reference to 'honest commercial practices' as the measure against which the legality of the acquisition and use of undisclosed information is to be judged.[46] This language is directly derived from Article 10*bis* of the Paris Convention. Article 10*bis*, incorporated by reference into TRIPS,[47] expressly requires member countries 'to assure to nationals of such countries effective protection against unfair competition'.[48] It further defines prohibited unfair competitive acts as including 'any act of competition contrary to honest practices in industrial or commercial matters'.[49] 'Honest commercial practices' is not further defined in the treaty, although Article 10*bis* does list three unfair acts which are to be prohibited 'in particular'.[50] They are:

(1) all acts of such a nature as to create confusion by any means whatever with the establishment, the goods, or the industrial or commercial activities, of a competitor;

---

45 *Id.* Art. 39(1).

46 *Id.* Art. 39(2) (requiring 'the possibility of preventing' the unauthorized disclosure or use of undisclosed information 'in a manner contrary to honest commercial practices').

47 *Id.* Art. 2(1) (requiring members to comply with Arts. 1–12, 19 of the Paris Convention).

48 Paris Convention, Art. 10*bis*(1).

49 *Id.* Art. 10*bis*(2)('Any act of competition contrary to honest practices in industrial or commercial matters constitutes an act of unfair competition').

50 *Id.* Art. 10*bis*(3).

(2) false allegations in the course of trade of such a nature as to discredit the establishment, the goods, or the industrial or commercial activities, of a competitor;
(3) indications or allegations the use of which in the course of trade is liable to mislead the public as to the nature, the manufacturing process, the characteristics, the suitability for their purpose, or the quantity, of the goods.[51]

None of these acts is directly related to the protection of trade secrets per se. Yet this non-exclusive categorization plainly underscores the competitive basis for protection under Article 10*bis*. Each resides firmly in the arena of competition regulation, particularly with regard to consumer protection against deceptive or misleading acts. And each 'particularlization' underscores the flexible nature of the protection offered under Article 10*bis*. Quite simply, when it comes to market regulation, each country is allowed to determine which acts it considers misleading (or contrary to honest commercial practices) and which fall within the range of permissible market actions.

The unfair competition basis of Article 10*bis mandates* a flexible approach in determining prohibited conduct. This flexibility is underscored by the comments of Professor G.H. Bodenhausen in his *Guide to the Application of the Paris Convention for the Protection of Industrial Property*,[52] in which he describes the examples given as 'not limitative'[53] and stresses the role of domestic discretion in determining to what extent certain acts fall within the strictures of Article 10*bis*:

> What is to be understood by 'competition' will be determined in each country according to his own concepts: countries may extend the notion of acts of unfair competition to acts which are not competitive in a narrow sense, that is, within the same branch of industry or trade but which unduly profit from a reputation established in another branch of industry or trade and thereby weaken such reputation.[54]

This flexibility includes the definition of what practices qualify as 'unfair' because they are contrary to 'honest practices in industrial or commercial matters'. Bodenhausen indicates that this criterion of honest practices is not merely a synonym for domestic market morality. To the

---

51 *Id.*

52 G.H.C. Bodenhausen, Guide to the Application of the Paris Convention for the Protection of Industrial Property (BIRPI, 1969).

53 *Id.* at 145.

54 *Id.* at 144.

contrary, Article 10*bis* was intended to establish an international standard for prohibiting unfair competition. Bodenhausen, in describing the definition of honest commercial practices, states:

> Any act of competition will have to be considered unfair if it is contrary to *honest practices in industrial or commercial matters*. This criterion is not limited to honest practices existing in the country where protection against unfair competition is sought. The judicial or administrative authorities of such country will therefore also have to take into account honest practices established in international trade.[55]

Interestingly, Bodenhausen gives no guidance as to the sources for the purported 'honest practices established in international trade'. Clearly, as demonstrated by the non-exclusive 'particular' practices defined by the Article, there are at least certain types of acts, such as misleading consumers with false information about one's product,[56] which are plainly contrary to honest practices. But there remain a great many types of potentially unfair practices that are subject to domestic discretion. Thus, for example, as Bodenhausen recognizes, while false information about a product is plainly contrary to honest commercial practices, '[i]t has been left to the domestic legislation or case law of each country to decide whether, and under what circumstances, discrediting allegations which are not strictly *untrue* may also constitute acts of unfair competition'.[57] This flexibility was reflected in the final version of Article 39 with its direct reference to honest commercial practices in the introductory foundational paragraph,[58] in the test for trade secret misappropriation in paragraph 2,[59] and in the protection of certain types of disclosed commercial data relating to marketing approvals.[60]

---

55 *Id.* at 144 (emphasis in original).

56 Paris Convention, Art. 10*bis*(3)(3).

57 Bodenhausen, *supra* note 52, at 145 (emphasis in original).

58 TRIPS, Art. 39(1) ('In the course of ensuring effective protection against unfair competition as provided in Article 10*bis* of the Paris Convention (1967), Members shall protect undisclosed information').

59 TRIPS, Art. 39(2) ('Natural and legal persons shall have the possibility of preventing information lawfully within their control from being disclosed to, acquired by, or used by others without their consent in a manner contrary to honest commercial practices').

60 TRIPS, Art. 39(3) ('Members, when requiring, as a condition of approving the marketing of pharmaceutical or of agricultural chemical products which utilize new chemical entities, the submission of undisclosed test or other data, the origination of which involves a considerable effort, shall protect such data against unfair commercial use').

While it appears that the inclusion of trade secret protection in TRIPS began as a result of a U.S. proposal, the initial U.S. proposal did not make reference to 'unfair competition'.[61] In fact, the first reported reference in negotiating documents for TRIPS to the concept of unfair competition in connection with the protection of undisclosed information appears to be in 1990 when Switzerland submitted a draft proposal that expressly proposed that proprietary information be protected 'as provided for in Article 10*bis* of the Paris Convention'.[62] This language was later reflected in the European Union's draft text,[63] and ultimately carried through to TRIPS.[64]

The timing of the Swiss proposal, coming on the heels of a challenge by developing countries that trade secrets was not 'a category of intellectual property rights'[65] arguably demonstrates an effort to create a middle ground between the U.S. proposal, which was perceived (arguably wrongly)[66] to treat trade secrecy as a property right, and the view of

---

[61] *Suggestion by the United States for Achieving the Negotiating Objective* 9 (MTN.GNG/NG11/W/14) (October 20, 1987) (proposal for trade secret protection does not contain reference to unfair competition, honest commercial practices or Art. 10*bis*); *Compilation of Written Submissions and Oral Statements: Revision*, US Submission on Trade Secrets (MTN.GNG/NG11/W/12/Rev.1) (February 5, 1988) (chart reflecting same).

[62] Terence P. Stewart, 2 The GATT Uruguay Round: A Negotiating History (1986–1992) 2307 (Kluwer Law International, 1999); Draft Amendment to the General Agreement on Tariffs and Trade on the Protection of Trade-Related Intellectual Property Rights: Communication from Switzerland, Art. 241, 17 (MTN.GNG/NG11/W/73) (May 14, 1990).

[63] Stewart, *supra* note 62, at 2307; Draft Agreement on Trade Related Aspects of Intellectual Property Rights: Submission by European Communities, Art. 28 (MTN.GNG/NG11/W/68).

[64] It is also reflected in diverse intervening drafts, including the Brussels and Dunkel drafts in various forms. See Daniel Gervais, The Trips Agreements: Drafting History and Analysis 271–3 (Sweet & Maxwell, 2d ed. 2003).

[65] Meeting of the Negotiating Group of 11, 12 and 14 December 1989, Note by the Secretariat 23 (MTN.GNG./NG11/17) (January 23, 1990).

[66] The doctrinal schizophrenia regarding whether or not trade secret protection is a property or competition right is not limited to the international arena. Even in the United States, which first tabled a proposal for trade secret protection, the property versus competition theory debate raged over the basis for protection of undisclosed information. See Sharon Sandeen, *Relative Privacy: What Privacy Advocates Can Learn from Trade Secret Law*, 2006 Mich. St. L. Rev. 667, 673–6 (2006); Pamela Samuelson, *Privacy as Intellectual Property?*, 52 Stanford L. Rev. 1125, 1153–4 (2000) (describing instances in the United States where courts held trade secrets to qualify as 'property'). Many U.S. commentators, however, have properly recognized that despite this schizophrenia, trade secret protection in the United States is firmly based on unfair competition principles. See, e.g., Sharon Sandeen, *Identifying and Keeping the Genie in the Bottle: The Practical and Legal*

certain developing countries which perceived trade secret protection to be a purely regulatory framework.[67] This compromise position is reflected in the slightly schizophrenic framework in which trade secrets are protected under TRIPS. On the one hand, 'undisclosed information' is listed as an 'intellectual property right' subject to protection under TRIPS.[68] On the other hand, Article 39 directly incorporates unfair competition principles as part of the criterion for determining the scope of protection to be afforded such proprietary information.[69]

This schizophrenia is significant when it comes to the scope of protection to be afforded trade secrets internationally because it supports a relatively high level of flexibility. This high flexibility is critical to providing the appropriate level of protection to indigenous innovation in the face of the historic and cultural challenges which such protection faces.[70] As Pierre Régibeau and Katharine Rockett recognize:

> Intellectual property law differs from competition law in both its function and its goals. Broadly speaking, the main function of IP law is to properly assign and defend property rights on assets that might have economic value. The main function of competition law is to *regulate* the use of (intellectual) property rights when these rights are sources of market power.[71]

Realities of Trade Secrets in Bankruptcy Proceedings, 44 GONZAGA L. REV. 81, 84 (2008) ('As originally conceived, the purpose of trademark and trade secret law was not to protect property per se, but to prevent competitors from engaging in activities that exceed the bounds of legitimate competition'); Samuelson, *supra*, at 1153–4 ('Despite its frequent presence in texts of intellectual property law, trade secrecy law remains firmly rooted in unfair competition law').

67 See, e.g. Katarzyna A. Czapracka, *Antitrust and Trade Secrets: The US and EU Approach*, 24 SANTA CLARA COMPUTER & HIGH TECH L.J. 207, 213–14 (2008) (describing diverse countries, including China, Germany and Japan, who protect trade secrets as part of their general competition law).

68 See TRIPS, Art. 1(2) ('For the purposes of this Agreement, the term 'intellectual property' refers to all categories of intellectual property that are the subject of Sections 1 to 7 of Part II'; Art. 39 protecting undisclosed information appears in Part II).

69 TRIPS, Art. 39 (referring to 'unfair competition', 'honest commercial practices' and/or 'Article 10*bis*' in all three paragraphs).

70 But cf. François Dessemontet, *Protection of Trade Secrets and Confidential Information*, in INTELLECTUAL PROPERTY AND INTERNATIONAL TRADE: THE TRIPS AGREEMENT 271, 277 (Carlos M. Correa and Abdulqawi A. Yusuf. eds., Kluwer Law, rev ed. 2008) (contending that Art. 39 adopts a property rights theory).

71 Pierre Régibeau and Katharine Rockett, *The Relationship Between Intellectual Property Law and Competition Law: An Economic Approach*, in THE INTERFACE BETWEEN INTELLECTUAL PROPERTY RIGHTS AND COMPETITION POLICY 505, 522 (Steven D. Anderman ed., Cambridge University Press, 2007).

This regulatory aspect of competition law allows for consideration of a wide variety of factors that might not be taken into consideration in a purely property-based evaluation of rights, including competitive morality.[72] Such competitive morality is reflected most clearly in the emphasis in Article 10*bis* on 'honest commercial practices'.[73] By incorporating this morality element into trade secret protection on an international level, Article 39 of TRIPS avoids the more 'predictable' and yet potentially more narrow strictures of a pure property-based regime.[74] While such alleged 'predictability' might make property a more desirable basis for the protection of proprietary information from the point of view of business holders of such information, it also threatens to restrict the utility of trade secrecy in protecting indigenous innovation. At a basic level, a property-based approach would most likely reflect present rigid public domain boundaries that are used to preclude protection of most traditional knowledge on the grounds that such knowledge is already beyond the scope of legal protection.[75] The necessary flexibilities required to allow protection of indigenous innovation would largely be missing from any such property-based regime. By contrast, an unfair competition basis for trade secrecy would appear to be more directly related to the purposes behind the protection of 'non-novel,

---

[72] Sandeen, *Genie*, *supra* note 66, at 84 ('As originally conceived, the purpose of trademark and trade secret law was not to protect property per se, but to prevent competitors from engaging in activities that exceed the bounds of legitimate competition'); Mary L. Lyndon, *Secrecy and Access in an Innovation Intensive Economy: Reordering Information Privileges in Environmental, Health and Safety Law*, 78 COLO. R. REV. 465, 496 (2007) ('Trade secrecy is now widely seen as having two functions: support for business ethics and limited support for innovation'); JAMES POOLEY, TRADE SECRETS para. 102[2] (2000) ('Ethics in business is one of the two primary policy concerns (along with the encouragement of invention) that underlie trade secret law'); RESTATEMENT THIRD ON UNFAIR COMPETITION § 39 cmt. a, para. (1995) ('The development of rules protecting trade secrets formed part of a more general attempt to articulate standards of fair competition').

[73] Paris Convention, Art. 10*bis*. The minimal enumeration of non-competitive practices prohibited under Art. 39 in n. 10 (breach of contract, breach of confidence and inducement to breach) further underscores the competitive morality aspect of trade secret protection internationally since these violations are based largely on what are perceived to be unfair (or at least compensable) acts. TRIPS, Art. 39 n.10 ('For the purpose of this provision, "a manner contrary to honest commercial practices" shall mean at least practices such as breach of contract, breach of confidence and inducement to breach').

[74] See Mark A. Lemley, Chapter 5.

[75] See Doris Estelle Long, *Traditional Knowledge and the Fight for the Public Domain*, 5 J. MARSHALL REV. INTELL. PROP. L. 617, 622 (2006) (describing the inhospitable treatment of traditional knowledge protection in present debates over access to knowledge and the scope of the public domain).

non-creative'[76] indigenous innovation, that is to protect such innovation against unauthorized competitive or deculturizing uses. Since unfair competition protection by its very nature is determined against a backdrop of ethical considerations, an unfair competition basis for trade secrecy offers the potential for a greater sensitivity to the ethical and human rights issues which are implicated in the protection of indigenous innovation. By supporting a competition theory of protection, the international trade secret regime, represented by Article 39 of TRIPS, enhances the potential for protecting indigenous innovation with its unique challenges, not only to concepts of ownership and secrecy, but also to the very nature of traditional trade secret protection.

VI. THE LIMITING NATURE OF 'COMMERCE'

Article 39's limitation of trade secret protection to confidential information that has *commercial* value raises two significant problems in connection with the protection of indigenous innovation. The first relates to the scope of information that falls within the potential subject matter of protection. Since much of indigenous innovation is closely tied to spiritual issues, or at least has a spiritual context, it may, by its very nature, fall outside the narrow stricture of commercial information. The second, and closely related, problem arises from the reasons why the holders of confidential indigenous innovation wish to keep it secret. In the end, though, I do not believe these problems preclude the use of a rational international trade secret regime to protect indigenous innovation. The restriction to commercially valuable information does, however, restrict the utility of trade secret doctrines as a method for protecting all confidential information that should be protected under a traditional knowledge regime. Thus, while trade secret protection is useful in protecting *some* indigenous innovation, it does not and cannot meet all needs to protect and maintain the confidentiality of traditional knowledge. This does not

---

[76] This novelty and creativity comparison is not premised on the lack of innovative value of indigenous knowledge and practices, but is instead derived from the uniqueness requirements imposed on innovative and creative works by patent and copyright regimes, respectively. Such protection is generally premised on, inter alia, the desire to encourage the creation of new works. See, e.g., U.S. Const. Art. I, § 8, cl. 8 (granting Congress the power to enact federal copyright and patent laws to 'promote the Progress of Science and useful Arts'). By contrast, encouraging innovation is *not* the primary goal of unfair competition laws – market regulation is.

mean that a rational international trade secret regime should not be used to protect and encourage indigenous innovation. It merely underscores its limitations.

At the heart of trade secrecy doctrine is a focus on the commercial value of the undisclosed information at issue. This focus on 'commercial value' is demonstrated by the limitation in Article 39 of TRIPS to protection for undisclosed information which 'has *commercial* value because it is secret'.[77] Even the theoretical antecedent to Article 39, Article 10*bis* of the Paris Convention, with its emphasis on prohibiting acts 'contrary to honest commercial and industrial practices'[78] underscores the commercial reasons for the proffered protection. Without such commercial value, the information at question cannot be protected, regardless of its secret content.

This limitation is similarly reflected in diverse domestic trade secret regimes. Thus, for example, in the United States, protected trade secrets under the Uniform Trade Secrets Act are defined as information that 'derives independent economic value, actual or potential, from that being generally known to, and not readily ascertainable by proper means by, other persons who can obtain *economic* value from its disclosure or use'.[79] Under German domestic law, 'secret information' is protected only if the owner has ' justifiable commercial interest in maintaining secrecy'.[80] In Japan, technical information which is 'useful in commercial activity' is protected.[81] Similarly,

---

[77] TRIPS, Art. 39(2) (emphasis added).

[78] Paris Convention, Art. 10*bis*.

[79] Uniform Trade Secrets Act § 1(4) (emphasis added). This provision is particularly important since it formed the basis for the initial U.S. proposal for Art. 39 of TRIPS. The U.S. Federal Trade Secret Act, called 'the Economic Espionage Act' and enacted post-TRIPS, contains a similar requirement of commercial value. 18 U.S.C. § 1839(3)(b) (limiting protectable information to that which 'derives independent economic value, actual or potential from not being generally known to, and not being readily ascertainable through proper means by, the public').

[80] Michael Knospe, *Germany,* in TRADE SECRETS THROUGHOUT THE WORLD para. 15:7 (Terrence F. MacLaren ed., 2009). The recently enacted amendments to German trade secret law maintain the obligation of commercial value. See Gesetz gegen den unlauteren Wettbewerb (Act Against Unfair Competition) §17 (German Federal Law Gazette, I, 254) (providing protection for 'trade or industrial secrets').

[81] Kazuko Matsuo, *Japan,* in TRADE SECRETS THROUGHOUT THE WORLD, *supra* note 80, at para. 23:2 ('The trade secret law provides that an entrepreneur . . . who possesses a manufacturing method, marketing method or other technical or business information useful in commercial activity that has been protected and treated as a secret . . . may request cessation or prevention of unfair acts'). See generally Unfair Competition Prevention Act of 1993, art. 2(6) (defining a trade secret as

under U.K. law only information used in trade or business is protected if it would result in significant harm to the owner.[82]

This focus on commercial utility, while a fundamental linchpin to Article 39 protection, presents unique problems in connection with the protection of indigenous innovation. If some type of commercial value is required, are some types of secret information, such as religious or educational materials, excluded categorically because they are not 'commercial' objects? Does it matter if the group that holds the information does not recognize its commercial value? What if the tribe holds the information secret for reasons unrelated to its potential commercial value? Should such factors abrogate protection?

In the traditional context of trade secret protection, information which has either potential or actual commercial value is relatively easy to identify. Commercial information, such as know-how, business plans, customer lists, formulas, patterns, designs, programs, production, manufacturing and distribution processes and techniques, blueprints and diagrams are often protected from undesired disclosure specifically because of the sensitive commercial advantages contained in the unwitting disclosure of such information to competitors. The purposes behind the establishment of such diverse protection mechanisms as confidentiality agreements, encryption, need-to-know and workshop labor divisions are precisely to assure that information that the company perceives to have value to outsiders remains within the knowledge of authorized personnel.

In many instances, information that relates to generational innovation is kept secret for a completely different reason. It is not the commercial value of the information which necessitates its controlled dissemination and use. Rather, it is its sacred or culturally sensitive nature. Thus, for example, the traditional healer in Tumkur was careful to limit access to his methodology to family members. The purpose for such limited access was not to maintain the commercial value of the knowledge, but to honor and hold sacred the teachings of the goddess whose rituals he incorporated into his cures, and whose support he invoked.

If the goal of protecting traditional knowledge is to encourage generational innovation, then sacred knowledge would appear to play little role.

'technical or business information useful for commercial activities'. This definition has not been changed by the 2010 amendments.

[82] Simon Mehigan and Mary Yeadon, *United Kingdom,* in TRADE SECRETS THROUGHOUT THE WORLD, *supra* note 80, at para. 37:2) ('The better view . . . is that . . . trade secrets amounted to (a) information used in a trade or business (b) of which the owner limits the dissemination . . . (c) and which if disclosed to a competitor would be liable to cause real or significant harm to the owner of the secret').

In the cold, hard world of commerce, protection for educational, religious or even culturally valuable information often falls outside the strictures of trade secret protection by virtue of their perceived lack of economic or commercial value. Thus, for example, in *Religious Technology Center v. Wollersheim*,[83] the U.S. Court of Appeals for the Ninth Circuit declined to grant relief against the unauthorized dissemination of certain scriptural materials access to which was restricted by the Church of Scientology for reasons of spiritual development. The court rejected the plaintiff's claim for trade secret status because there was no claim made that such restricted materials 'convey an actual or potential *commercial* advantage, presumably measurable in dollar terms'.[84] In contrast to the sensitivity shown to spiritual concerns in *Foster*,[85] discussed previously, the court expressly rejected any claim that spiritual value was sufficient to warrant protection or cause cognizable legal harm. It stated:

> We do not accept that a trade secret can be based on the *spiritual advantage* the Church believes its adherents acquire over non-adherents by using the materials in the prescribed manner . . . The injury inflicted on the Church by the new church's misappropriation of its 'secret' is the 'religious harm' that would be suffered by Church adherents from premature unsupervised exposure to the materials. The value of the confidential materials is thus spiritual not commercial, and the materials cannot be said to have the 'independent economic value' necessary to qualify as a protectible [*sic*] trade secret.[86]

Fortunately, in a subsequent appeal, the Ninth Circuit limited its holding, stressing that its denial of trade secret protection for the plaintiff's confidential religious information was not based on its sacred nature per se, but on the absence of any claim of commercial harm to the plaintiff or economic advantage to the defendant:

> The only question before the court [in *Wollersheim*] was whether a religious scripture could qualify as a trade secret under California law if it conferred a

---

83 796 F.2d 1076 (9th Cir. 1986), *cert. denied*, 479 U.S. 1103 (1987).

84 *Id.* at 1090 (emphasis in original).

85 Although, as noted previously, *Foster* was decided on the basis of breach of confidence, it is strongly analogous to the issues of trade secrecy raised in *Wollersheim*. Both cases involved confidential information of a spiritual nature, whose unauthorized publication was alleged to cause spiritual harm. Furthermore, Australian law relies on breach of confidence to protect trade secrets, and not a 'trade secret' statute per se; see generally William van Caenegem, Intellectual Property Law and Innovation (Cambridge University Press, 2007); Joellen Riley, *Who Owns Human Capital? A Critical Appraisal of Legal Techniques for Capturing the Value of Work*, 128 Australian J. Labor L. 1 (2005), making the facial analogy even stronger.

86 *Wollersheim*, 796 F.2d at 1090–1 (footnote omitted).

> spiritual, as opposed to an economic, advantage on its owner. We determined that California law did not recognize information as a trade secret unless it conferred on its owner an actual economic advantage over competitors. Because the Church made no claim that the scriptures gave it a commercial advantage over its competitors, we held that the scriptures did not qualify as trade secrets under California law. *Wollersheim* turned, therefore, on the absence of any claim of economic advantage at the preliminary injunction stage. While we expressed doubts about whether the Church could allege the competitive market advantage required without 'rais[ing] grave doubts about its claim as a religion and a not-for-profit corporation', we did not decide one way or another whether the scriptures could qualify as trade secrets should the Church allege and prove economic advantage.[87]

Subsequent decisions in the United States have similarly rejected any absolute exclusion of religious materials from trade secrecy protection.[88] Such narrowing language, however, does not fully address the difficulty of protecting sacred knowledge from unauthorized use or disclosure. A close reading of these cases demonstrates that the sacred nature of the secrets involved makes it difficult to protect such information absent evidence of some type of competitive harm. Such harm may be easy to establish where, as in many of the U.S. cases, the alleged unauthorized use is being made by a breakaway group who is offering the same religious materials, but charging reduced prices.[89] It may, however, be more difficult in the case of indigenous innovation which is being used in a deculturizing manner.

As described previously, deculturization generally occurs when indigenous knowledge is used in a manner which is contrary to local traditions. Deculturizing uses are not limited to sacred knowledge. Nor are they simply the use of traditional knowledge without attribution or acknowledgement. Instead, they are the use of indigenous knowledge and practices in a manner which is at variance with cultural meanings. Thus,

---

[87] Religious Technology Center v. Scott, 869 F.2d 1306, 1309–10 (9th Cir. 1989).

[88] See Religious Technology Center v. Netcom On-Line Communication Services, Inc., 923 F.Supp.1231, 1252 (N.D. Cal. 1995) ('there is no authority for excluding religious materials from trade secret protection because of their nature. Indeed, there is no authority for excluding any type of information because of its nature'); Bridge Publications, Inc. v. Vien, 827 F.Supp.629, 633 (S.D. Cal. 1993) ('there is at least some precedent for granting trade secret status to works that are techniques for improving oneself (though not specifically spiritually). Conversely, there is no authority for excluding religious materials from trade secret protection because of their nature. Indeed there is no authority for excluding any type of information because of its nature').

[89] See Religious Technology Center v. Netcom On-Line Communication Services, Inc., 923 F.Supp.at 1252.

for example, the use of Kachina masks and costumes as disguises for the members of a local gambling cartel in a comic book entitled *The Kachinas Sing of Doom* is deculturizing. In the Hopi religion, Kachina masks are not disguises. Instead, the wearer is transformed into the spirit represented by the mask. The mask is viewed, not as an object, but as a living spirit, incapable of commercial appropriation. The use of the masks in the Marvel comic book not only incorporated misconceptions about the role of such masks into the storyline, it used them in ways that were directly contrary to the beliefs of the culture they represented and would not have been approved by the tribe had the Hopis been consulted.[90]

While the Hopis' objection to the use of the Kachina masks was based on their sacred nature, the use at issue was undoubtedly commercial.[91] Presumably the choice to use the Hopi masks in the comic book was made as a result of some perceived commercial value in such use. There is nothing in Article 39, or in its U.S. analogues, that requires that the commercial value of the information at issue be recognized by the *holders* of the information. So long as the confidential information at issue has commercial value, even if the commercial value is perceived only by the unauthorized user, the information falls within the strictures of Article 39. Article 39 also does not rely on the secret owner's recognition of the commercial value of the information in evaluating the reasonableness of efforts to keep it confidential. The actions taken to maintain the confidential nature of protected information need only be directed to keeping it 'secret'. As the court in *Religious Technology Center v. Netcom On-Line Communication Services, Inc.*[92] held in determining whether certain confidential techniques and processes used for religious training qualified as protectable trade secrets: 'there is no requirement that a trade secret have any value to the *defendant*; the value can be to *others* who do not possess

---

90 David Howes, *Cultural Appropriation and Resistance in the American Southwest: Decommodifying 'Indianness'*, in CROSS-CULTURAL CONSUMPTION: GLOBAL MARKETS/LOCAL REALITIES 142–4 (Routledge, 1992).

91 It is not absolutely clear if the masks themselves are confidential. The ceremonies clearly are. Unlike the Iroquois who forbid any commercialization of their False Face Masks (see Haudenosaunee Confederacy Policy on False Face Masks, available at www.peace4turtleisland.org/pages/maskpolicy.htm), the Hopis have allowed some commercialization of masks which are not used in sacred ceremonies. Given the present attempts by the Iroquois to prohibit any access to their False Face Masks, it is more likely that future deculturization claims could arise from the unauthorized sale and display of masks similar to those of the Iroquois False Face Masks where any access to such items is proscribed by the tribe.

92 *Id.* 923 F.Supp. 1231.

it'.[93] Efforts to maintain the sacred nature of certain types of indigenous innovation, including its limitation to members of the tribe or of a particular segment of the tribe, such as a medical society, should easily meet the definition of reasonable efforts.

VII. PRACTICAL PROBLEMS IN TRADE SECRET PROTECTION

Because trade secret protection does not require innovation per se,[94] but only commercial value, a rational trade secret regime can serve as a strong basis for protecting a wide variety of indigenous innovation without the stumbling block of uniqueness that curtails the application of other information protection regimes. For example, generational knowledge regarding the cultivation and uses of diverse plants from a tribe's surrounding environment may be innovative vis-à-vis the developed world, but lack the novelty necessary to achieve patent protection due to its long public use. Yet such knowledge plainly has commercial value and, when subjected to appropriate access constraints, is precisely the type of information that is most easily protected under present trade secret regimes.

Consequently, some of the most prevalent examples of trade secret analogues being applied to traditional knowledge currently arise in the context of equitable benefit sharing agreements involving access to indigenous knowledge regarding the uses of diverse flora and fauna (biota) in the surrounding tribal environment. These Material Transfer Agreements (MTAs) most often deal with the transfer of biological materials, such as plants, or other genetic materials either from the tribal environs or from the tribe itself. These MTAs usually provide for prior informed consent from the affected group, as well as for some type of equitable sharing between the recipients and the tribe of the profits from any commercial products that may result from the venture. While not yet standard in such agreements, MTAs could also contain trade secret provisions that maintain the confidential nature of any disclosures by the tribe regarding the delivered materials. Thus, for example, traditional healers of Samoa were acknowledged in a benefit-sharing agreement concerning the development of prostratin, an anti-AIDS compound derived from the Samoan native

---

93 *Id.* at 1253 (emphasis in original).

94 Such information does, of course, need some minimal level of novelty or else it would be 'generally known' to the relevant group, which would abrogate trade secret protection.

mamala tree (homalanthus nutans). As part of the transfer the healers not only had provided requested samples of the tree, but also had conveyed their knowledge regarding potential uses for such materials.[95] Such knowledge sets up the required *informational* transfer that could be the subject of appropriate contract-based trade secret protection.

There is no question that MTAs can serve as valuable adjuncts to trade secret regimes in securing protection for indigenous innovation. Such agreements, where they contain express obligations of continued confidentiality of traditional knowledge regarding the sources, cultivation, harvesting or uses of transferred biological materials, fit plainly within the traditional bounds of trade secret protection under domestic law. Moreover, violations of such agreements afford the affected tribe the ability to seek relief under both trade secret and contract claims. These contract claims may prove particularly helpful to indigenous groups by removing claims regarding the unprotected nature of the knowledge or its lack of status as a trade secret. Absent fraud, once a party has agreed to the confidential nature of an indigenous group's knowledge, it should be virtually impossible to deny successfully such status post-disclosure. But despite the *theoretical* utility of MTAs in protecting indigenous innovation, the infrastructure obligations for negotiating such agreements may severely reduce their *practical* utility at least in the future.

Presently, it is doubtful that most holders of sought-after indigenous innovation have sufficient information to negotiate MTAs that protect the tribe's interest fully. As the earlier cases regarding contact between researchers and the Hopi and Pitjantjatjara peoples demonstrate, many indigenous groups have little knowledge of such agreements and are not trained to negotiate one successfully. While there are numerous NGOs that are beginning to fill this gap, not only by offering negotiation services, but also by developing useful model agreements, clearly not all MTAs are created equal. Furthermore, absent domestic laws which require some form of equitable benefit sharing in the provision of traditional knowledge, such as the obligations imposed under Biodiversity Law No. 7788 of Costa Rica,[96] or Panamanian Law No. 20 of June 26, 2000 on the Special Intellectual Property Regime Governing the Collective Rights of Indigenous Peoples for the Protection and Defense of their Cultural

---

95 Robert Sanders, *Landmark Agreement between Samoa and UC Berkeley Could Help Search for AIDS Cure* (September 29, 2004), available at http://berkeley.edu/news/media/releases/2004/09/29_samoa.shtml.

96 Available at www.grain.org/brl_files/costarica-biodiversitylaw-1998-en.pdf.

Identity and their Traditional Knowledge,[97] it is not clear to what extent third parties would be willing to acknowledge an economic or information protection debt to indigenous tribes. It is even less clear to what extent third parties would willingly concede trade secret status to this type of information unless the law also recognizes the protectable nature of traditional knowledge per se, since other people's knowledge is precisely the type of information that is most often dedicated to the public domain by dominant powers.[98]

Even if the infrastructure exists to allow indigenous groups to protect their interests in connection with the disclosure and use of indigenous innovation, given the focus on *material* transfer, MTAs, unless carefully crafted, may fail to deal with the transfer of *information* about the uses of the transferred material. Dealing with information transfer is a critical component of the application of trade secret protection. Most MTAs, by the very nature of their subject matter, deal with rights and obligations regarding the transfer of biogenetic *materials*. Any rights and obligations arising from such access focus on the biological items themselves. Thus, for example, in the 'Standard Material Transfer Agreement' adopted by the UN Food and Agriculture Organization (FAO) for plant genetic resources, the phrase 'genetic material' is defined as meaning 'any material of plant origin, including reproductive and vegetative propagating material, containing functional units of heredity'.[99] There is no language regarding the protection of any knowledge about the uses of such materials. The lack of coverage of information transfer does not appear to be the result of intentional decisions not to include such knowledge in MTAs, but of failure to consider such inclusion Rights holders should exercise caution in entering into such agreements to be certain that information transfer is included within the scope of the agreement.

Whether memorialized in a formal agreement or through indigenous practices, confidential traditional knowledge requires a more developed trade secret enforcement mechanism than currently exists in most

---

97 Available at www.grain.org/brl/?docid=461&lawid=2002.

98 See generally Anupam Chander and Madhavi Sunder, *The Romance of the Public Domain*, 92 Cal. L. Rev. 1331, 1347 (2004) (noting that the current state of intellectual property law 'favors the Western world'); Doris Estelle Long, *Curtailing the Imperialism of the Public Domain or Changing the Rules of the Great Game for the Intellectual Property Empire* 20 (May 2008) (detailing the failure to give any voice to the interests of indigenous peoples whose works and culture are 'dropped into the public domain') (working draft of manuscript, on file with the author).

99 Standard Materials Transfer Agreement, art. 2.

developing countries, where the bulk of such knowledge is presently held. Even if adequate domestic trade secret laws exist to protect indigenous innovation (which is doubtful in many developing countries at the present time), the enforcement of such laws remains virtually non-existent. Although Article 41 of TRIPS included trade secrets among the intellectual property rights for which 'effective enforcement' is required,[100] there is little evidence of such enforcement presently. Moreover, given the special nature of indigenous innovation, and the special cultural concerns regarding its unauthorized use and disclosure, effective enforcement of such rights arguably requires different or more sensitively applied measures.

In an era when Internet disclosure of trade secret information presents a serious challenge to developed countries' intellectual property enforcement mechanisms, such disclosure would have even greater consequences for much indigenous innovation. Indigenous groups would not only potentially lose the benefits of confidentiality, but given the strong cultural relationship between the use of much traditional knowledge and the tribe's spiritual or sacred practices, these groups may also suffer the types of social and spiritual dislocations from such unauthorized disclosures that concerned the court in *Foster*. Deculturization would be assured in such an uncontrolled dissemination. Consequently, rapid and effective relief to prevent such disclosures is needed. The lengthy court delays that currently accompany much civil intellectual property litigation would not only destroy any economic benefits inhering in the information at issue, it could have a severe impact on the tribe's human right to practice their culture or exercise their own self-determination over the uses of their traditional knowledge.

For trade secret protection to serve as a valuable method for protecting indigenous innovation, issues regarding the evidentiary value to be given traditional practices and customs must also be handled in a manner that recognizes that the absence of documentation does not necessarily evidence a lack of reasonable efforts to maintain the confidentiality of given information. Moreover, reasonableness must be judged with a sensitivity to perceived past power inequities in the ability to control access to one's land and culture.

---

[100] TRIPS, Art. 41(1) (requiring 'enforcement procedures . . . so as to permit effective action against any act of infringement of [covered] intellectual property rights . . . including expeditious remedies').

VIII. TRADE SECRETS AND THE PATENT CONUNDRUM

Unfortunately, even if the infrastructure for effective and rational protection of indigenous innovation were established tomorrow, much of the traditional knowledge which could have been protected under such a system may already be lost. Such loss is not due to any failure by indigenous peoples to appreciate the need to maintain the confidential nature of their traditions or practices. Instead, some of this loss is due to the perceived lack of power by often marginalized indigenous groups to prevent unauthorized access or use by dominant cultures. Other, more recent losses, however, may be due to a failure to appreciate that efforts to secure their traditional knowledge from 'theft by patent' may well have consigned such knowledge to the public domain, at least for purposes of trade secret protection.

Just as the Internet serves as a potential threat to the ability of indigenous peoples to maintain the confidentiality and cultural meanings of their traditions and practices, it has also served as a tremendous resource for preserving cultural traditions. Countless indigenous groups have created databases in which information regarding their traditional knowledge is maintained. Many of these databases are readily accessible to the general public. Other groups maintain active websites that serve as repositories for their traditional knowledge. There is no question that many of these websites have been created and maintained for the dual purpose of preservation and education. Thus, for example, the Proyecto Orinoco website[101] provides pictures, materials and dimensions of a wide variety of crafts from 12 indigenous groups from the Venezuelan Amazonia. The purpose of the website is 'to preserve – and share – the stories of their culture'. Other websites have been created for the purpose of preventing companies from the developed world from obtaining patent protection for inventions utilizing traditional knowledge. Probably one of the most well known of these is the Traditional Knowledge (TK) Digital Library[102] which focuses on Indian traditional medicines and practices. The express purpose of the website is to create a source of information about traditional knowledge that can be used by patent examiners in determining the patentability of inventions that may contain traditional knowledge.

Aside from preservation, probably the most significant reason for the explosion of traditional knowledge websites is the desire to avoid 'theft

---

[101] Available at www.orinoco.org.

[102] Available at www.tkdl.res.in.

by patent'. In the 1990s, several notable patents were granted for inventions that were based on traditional knowledge for which the holders of such knowledge received no compensation. Among the more notable of these were patents granted for fertilizers using ingredients derived from Neem seed (European Patent 043623; U.S. Patent 5124349) and for the use of turmeric for wounds (U.S. Patent 540504). While many of these patents were subsequently revoked for lack of novelty, they raised an international thunderstorm regarding the ability of developed countries to utilize traditional knowledge without disclosing the source of such knowledge. As a result, numerous databases of traditional knowledge, including the TK Digital Library, have been prepared specifically to combat such improvidently granted patents by making traditional knowledge publicly available. Such public availability presumably removes any claim of novelty and consequently prevents the issuance of patents based on this knowledge. These freely available public databases, however, unless carefully crafted to avoid the problem, also remove any potential claim for trade secret protection for the knowledge so disclosed. In its Draft Toolkit for Documentation of Traditional Knowledge, the World Intellectual Property Organization (WIPO) warned that 'ill-considered documentation projects may damage TK holders' interests, including cultural, economic and IP interests. One important need is therefore to clarify the point that documentation can have different purposes'.[103] It is impossible to know how many groups considered the potential loss of trade secret protection when they created and posted their websites. While it may be too late to rescue information improvidently posted on freely accessible websites, it is not too late to begin to consider these critical issues in subsequent Internet postings.

Websites facilitate varying degrees of public access to traditional knowledge. Thus, for example, the Project Orinoco database appears to reflect a judgment by the holders of the traditional knowledge contained therein as to which aspects of their cultural information and practices will be freely available and which will be retained by the tribe. Such databases do not necessarily resolve the 'theft by patent' issue that served as a motivation to collect traditional knowledge in publicly accessible forms. But they do allow the holders of such knowledge to make careful, reasoned decisions about the knowledge that they will disclose to outsiders and the terms under which such knowledge may be used.

---

[103] IGC, *Draft Outline of an Intellectual Property Management Toolkit for Documentation of Traditional Knowledge* para. 5 (WIPO/GRTKF/IC/4/5) (October 20, 2002).

Similarly, the BioZulua database project was created as a repository for traditional knowledge gathered by the database creator, Fundación para el Desarrollo de las Ciencias, Fisicas y Naturales (FUDECI) from diverse indigenous groups in Venezuela.[104] BioZulua recognized the right of indigenous groups to keep their information confidential. The purpose of the BioZulua database was 'to make TK more accessible' and 'to encourage innovation using TK'.[105] Yet, while promoting access, FUDECI initially maintained the right to keep non-public domain TK confidential. The TK Digital Library similarly appears to limit its disclosure of traditional knowledge to publicly available materials. When the determination to disclose the information contained in a database is made with the knowing participation of the indigenous peoples, and with their full understanding of the consequences of the various levels of disclosure,[106] then recognition of the right of indigenous peoples to maintain certain knowledge in such databases under conditions of confidentiality is not only a positive step, but a necessary one to assure adequate protection for indigenous innovation.

The potential threat to confidentiality posed by public aggregations of traditional knowledge is not limited to Internet websites. To the contrary, many domestic *sui generis* regimes for protecting traditional knowledge contain registration obligations. Thus, for example, the Peruvian Law of Protection of the Collective Knowledge of Indigenous Peoples, designed to assist indigenous peoples in protecting their knowledge about biological resources, requires that such peoples register their knowledge to document both the knowledge and the tribe's ownership claims.[107] Fortunately, the Peruvian law also provides for three different types of registrations, including one on a 'national confidential register', the contents of which

---

[104] See, e.g., UNITED NATIONS UNIVERSITY INSTITUTE OF ADVANCED STUDIES (UNU-IAS), THE ROLE OF REGISTERS AND DATABASES IN THE PROTECTION OF TRADITIONAL KNOWLEDGE: A COMPARATIVE ANALYSIS 16–17 (2003); IGC, *Inventory of Existing Online Databases Containing Traditional Knowledge Documentation Data* paras. 43–8 (WIPO/GRTKF/IC/3/6) (May 10, 2002).

[105] UNU-IAS, *supra* note 104.

[106] This knowing participation seems particularly unlikely in the case of the BioZuala Project since there was no contractual or legal obligation to require prior consent or even the active participation of knowledge holders in the initial information gathering. See Standord Zent and Egleé L. Zeni, *On Biocultural Diversity from a Venezuelan Perspective: Tracing the Interrelationships among Biodiversity, Culture Change and Legal Reforms*, in BIODIVERSITY AND THE LAW: INTELLECTUAL PROPERTY, BIOTECHNOLOGY AND TRADITIONAL KNOWLEDGE 91, 105–7 (Charles McManis ed., Earthscan Publications Ltd, 2007).

[107] Available at www.grain.org/brl/?docid=81&lawid=2041.

are not publicly available.[108] Since the rights to control one's heritage and to self-determination of its use lie at the heart of most traditional knowledge issues, it is critical not only that the holders of indigenous innovation control the disclosure of information about it, but also that any choice to document the information is fully informed, made with a full appreciation of the potential loss of control over such documented knowledge.

Despite their utility, TK databases, however created or maintained by third parties, may prove a threat to the ability of indigenous holders to control the information contained in them. In the BioZuala Project, there is a troubling claim that ownership rights in the database reside with FUDECI. Given the uncertain status of database rights, and more particularly, the scope of rights a compiler may claim in the use of the compiled information, such claims could complicate future ownership and use claims. There is currently no international treaty or model regarding the legal protection to be afforded compilers of databases. Perhaps the most well-known, and controversial, data protection regime is the *sui generis* EU Database Directive.[109] The Directive, which formed the basis for a proposed Draft Database Treaty in 1996,[110] provides database makers with rights over the unauthorized extraction or reutilization of the data itself.[111] Such protection has the potential to transfer effective control over included innovations from the indigenous holders to the data compilers. Ultimately, the BioZuala Project, which began as a workable model for TK databases, reportedly became abusive due, in part, to the absence of indigenous peoples on the management board for the project and to ownership claims to the database itself.[112] The BioZuala Project serves as both a positive and negative example of how to manage traditional knowledge databases and other similar repositories. On the positive side, in its initial stages, FUDECI properly acknowledged the vital need to recognize that access to some traditional knowledge must remain restricted absent sufficient guarantees of either confidentiality or non-deculturizing uses. On the negative side, claims to own the data and failure to include indigenous

---

108 Peruvian Law, arts. 15, 18.

109 Council Directive 96/9/EC on the Legal Protection of Databases [1996] O.J. L77/20 ('EU Database Directive'), available at http://eur-lex.europa.eu/LexUriServ/LexUriServ.do?uri=CELEX:31996L0009: EN:HTML.

110 WIPO Draft Database Treaty, available at www.bitlaw.com/source/treaties/database.html.

111 EU Database Directive, Art. 8.

112 See, e.g., Otimio Castillo, *An Assessment of the Implementation of International Commitments on Traditional Forest-Related Knowledge in Venezuela* (2004), available at www.international-alliance.org/documents/Venezuela-finaledit.pdf; Zent and Zeni, *supra* note 106, at 105–7.

peoples in the actual governing of the database, not only ignored indigenous rights to cultural determination, but may complicate indigenous rights in the future.

The present unsettled state of database protection internationally further supports a measured approach to the adoption of 'database trusts' for traditional knowledge. As envisioned by United Nations Institute of Advanced Studies (UNU-IAS), such 'database trusts' would provide management, control and ownership rights in a database to its creator, while maintaining rights to the traditional knowledge in its indigenous holders.[113] While such trusts would appear to establish useful working relationships between those who maintain TK registers and databases and the indigenous creators of the knowledge, vesting ownership rights in the collection in anyone other than the traditional knowledge holders is destined to further complicate an already complex issue, most likely to the detriment of the groups intended to be protected by trade secret regimes – the original holders of indigenous innovation rights.

For those groups which have improvidently granted public access to otherwise protectable information as a result of the clamor over 'theft by patent', it may be too late to rescue such knowledge from the public domain. Even the flexibility provided by Article 39 of TRIPS does not necessarily provide the means for recovering control of such disclosed information. When the tribe had no practical ability to deny use of its knowledge in such databases, disclosure should not eliminate continued claims for protection so long as the tribe utilized other reasonable efforts to maintain the confidential nature of the information in question. By contrast, disclosure with the consent of the tribe in the misguided desire to prevent future thefts by patent, absent fraud, most likely cannot be undone in the light of new information about the loss of trade secret protection for indigenous innovation. Such loss of right does not eliminate the valuable role that TK databases play in the preservation and control of traditional knowledge. But it does underscore the need for cautious deliberation – and truly knowing consent – before any knowledge is made publicly available.

CONCLUSION

While trade secret protection may be criticized for its ability to 'lock up' information so long as sufficient confidentiality measures are in place, it may serve as a critical link between 'traditional' intellectual property

---

113 See UNU-IAS, *supra* note 104, at 36–7.

doctrines and 'traditional knowledge'. With its focus on secrecy without the strong uniqueness obligations of other intellectual property-based regimes, trade secret laws may serve to protect confidential practices that have commercial value to others. Nevertheless, the challenges in crafting an effective trade secret mechanism for traditional knowledge and indigenous innovation are daunting. Aside from the considerable infrastructure such a system demands, sufficient protection is only possible if protection determinations regarding secrecy and commercial value are made with a sensitivity to indigenous traditions, and the necessary limits of minority groups to exercise power over the land and culture.

Not all generational knowledge is, or should be, protected against use by third parties, but it is imperative that tribes be given the opportunity to determine the terms and conditions of access, if at all, to their culturally significant knowledge. MTAs need to be more fully developed so that they acknowledge informational transfers from indigenous providers and secure the information's continued confidential nature. The purpose of trade secret protection for generational innovation is *not* to lock away such knowledge from the public, but to assure that such innovation is used *and valued* on terms that respect the rights of indigenous holders. In addition, efforts to preserve and share traditional knowledge with the public through the creation of publicly accessible websites and databases should be supported. However, the creation of such information sources must be undertaken with the knowing consent and active participation of the relevant indigenous group. Confidential practices should not be readily disclosed without careful consideration of the potential effect such disclosure will have on the tribe's ability to commercialize such practices, or even its ability to prevent deculturizing future uses.

Indigenous innovation, or more precisely, recognition of its *value*, offers a strong potential for indigenous peoples to control and support their own economic development. The foundational nature of indigenous innovation in the protection of minority rights, however, requires that a rational international trade secret regime be interpreted and applied with a recognition of the cultural sensitivities underlying ownership, use and access issues in connection with the protection of traditional knowledge. A trade secret regime with the necessarily flexibility to adequately protect indigenous innovation may be less predictable than a property-based regime. In some instances, such a regime may cover information that some might previously have considered public. A trade secrecy approach may even be perceived to fly in the face of current movements to secure greater access to information in the digital era. But these concerns result from a failure to understand the nature of trade secret protection for traditional knowledge. Both the access to knowledge and traditional knowledge movements have, at their core, a fundamental goal of creating greater flexibility in intellectual property rights regimes.[114] A rational protection regime might actually encourage the disclosure of indigenous innovations where holders can be assured of protection of their interests. Moreover, allowing the two movements to inform, as opposed to contradict, each other may ultimately develop a stronger and fairer system – one that allows access, recognizes welfare benefits, and allows the development of new technology and all of the new works one wants.[115]

Trade secret protection, applied with the full flexibility required under its unfair competition basis under TRIPS, does not answer all the needs for adequate protection of indigenous innovation. It does, however, provide the initial underpinning for a more fulsome protection of generational knowledge. Such protection provides the critical legal foundation for the control by indigenous peoples of their innovation. More importantly, as a source for sustainable development, such protection is long overdue.

114 Long, *supra* note 75, at 320.

115 *Id.*

20 The limits of trade secret law: Article 39 of the TRIPS Agreement and the Uniform Trade Secrets Act on which it is based

*Sharon K. Sandeen**

I. INTRODUCTION

All intellectual property rights (IPRs) have limits that are designed to achieve a balance between the benefits of IPR protection and other public policy objectives.[1] During the negotiations leading to the adoption of the World Trade Organization (WTO) Agreement on Trade-Related Aspects of Intellectual Property Law ('TRIPS Agreement'),[2] the need for balanced intellectual property policies was raised on numerous occasions by a variety of participants, notably in detailed submissions by Brazil in late 1988 and Peru in late 1989.[3] Nonetheless, while U.S. negotiators acted to ensure that trade secrecy was covered by the TRIPS Agreement, there was little discussion of the need for limitations to ensure that trade secret protection would not unduly conflict with principles of free competition or the objectives of patent and copyright law.

While it is tempting to suggest that the lack of attention to limitations on trade secret protection was the result of the developed world's desire to expand the scope of IPRs, it can also be explained by the need for compromise in international negotiations and a concomitant willingness to

* Professor of Law, Hamline University School of Law, St. Paul, Minnesota.

1 For a critique of the balance arguments in the context of international norm-making, see Graeme B. Dinwoodie, *The International Intellectual Property System: Treaties, Norms, National Courts, and Private Ordering*, in INTELLECTUAL PROPERTY, TRADE AND DEVELOPMENT: STRATEGIES TO OPTIMIZE ECONOMIC DEVELOPMENT IN A TRIPS PLUS ERA 87–9 (Daniel Gervais ed., Oxford University Press, 2007).

2 Agreement on Trade-Related Aspects of Intellectual Property Rights, Part VII art. 70 § 9, April 15, 1994, Marrakesh Agreement Establishing the World Trade Organization, Annex 1C, 1869 U.N.T.S. 299, 33 I.L.M. 1197 (1994) ('TRIPS Agreement').

3 See Submission from Brazil (MTN.GNG/NG11/W/30) (October 31, 1988), paras. 13–22 and Communication from Peru (MTN.GNG/NG11/w/45) (October 27, 1989), para. IX.

allow some flexibility in the design of trade secret laws.[4] In other words, the less detailed a proposed provision on trade secrets was, the less it was necessary to discuss limitations because the lack of detail automatically provided WTO members with flexibility to define the scope and limits of their trade secret laws. An interesting, but misunderstood, aspect of the trade secret provision of the TRIPS Agreement, Article 39, is that even when details based upon U.S. law were added, significant flexibility in the design of trade secret laws was preserved. Of course, in order to exercise this flexibility, WTO members need to know all of the limitations on the scope of trade secret protection that are available.

Article 39 consists of three sections and one footnote. Pursuant to Article 39(1), the requirement that WTO members protect 'undisclosed information' and 'data submitted to governments' is explicitly tied to the pre-existing obligation of Article 10*bis* of the Paris Convention, which requires member countries to assure effective protection against unfair competition. Thus, it is similar to Article 10*bis* (3) in that it seeks to define a particular instance of conduct that is deemed 'contrary to honest practices in industrial or commercial matters'.[5]

The purpose of Article 39(2) is to create a right of individuals and companies to prevent 'information lawfully within their control from being disclosed to, acquired by, or used by others without their consent in a manner contrary to honest business practices'. Subsections (a) through (c) of Article 39(2) are modeled after the definition of 'trade secret' that is contained in the Uniform Trade Secrets Act (UTSA) and are used to define the type and scope of information that must be protected. Footnote 10 of the TRIPS Agreement sets forth a non-exclusive list of the practices that are deemed conduct contrary to honest business practices and is similar to the UTSA's definition of misappropriation.

Article 39(3) is not focused on the right of individuals and companies to prevent undisclosed information from being improperly disclosed, acquired or used, but is designed instead to impose an obligation on governmental officials to protect a subset of such information, namely, 'undisclosed test or other data, the origination of which involves a considerable effort' when such information is submitted 'as a condition of approving the marketing of pharmaceutical or of agricultural chemical products

---

[4] See Peter K. Yu, *TRIPs and Its Discontents,* 10 Marq. Intell. Prop L. Rev. 369 (2005), discussing four narratives typically associated with the TRIPS negotiations, including a 'bargain' narrative.

[5] See Art. 10*bis*(2) of the Paris Convention (1967) which states that '[a]ny act of competition contrary to honest practices in industrial or commercial matters constitutes an act of unfair competition'.

which utilize new chemical entities'. As such, it does not alter or change the definition of 'undisclosed information' that is contained in Article 39(2).

This chapter details the limitations on the scope of trade secret protection that are expressly spelled out in Article 39 of the TRIPS Agreement and those that might be used without violating its purpose and intent. Part II of this chapter presents a detailed discussion of the negotiating history of Article 39.[6] In Part III, the language and negotiating history of Article 39 is matched with the predominant law governing trade secrets in the United States, the UTSA, to identify the limitations on the scope of U.S. trade secret law that are expressly or implicitly part of Article 39. An additional constraint on the scope of U.S. trade secret law, the pre-emption doctrine, is discussed in Part IV. The chapter continues in Part V with suggestions for ways in which the negotiating history of Article 39 and the limits of U.S. trade secret law may be used to understand the test data obligations of Article 39(3) of the TRIPS Agreement.

II. NEGOTIATING HISTORY OF ARTICLE 39 OF THE TRIPS AGREEMENT

Before the TRIPS Agreement, there was no mention of trade secrets in any multilateral or bilateral agreements.[7] Typically, international agreements dealing with IPRs focused on industrial property (principally patent and trademark rights) and copyrights. The effort to add trade secrets to the mix of IPRs that would be a part of the Uruguay Round negotiations, and ultimately the TRIPS Agreement, began well before the first meeting of the TRIPS Negotiating Group (NG11). As detailed in several accounts, it was a group of U.S. industry leaders who conceived of the idea of tying IPRs to international trade and who advocated for an international system for the protection of IPRs that was based upon the laws of the United States.[8]

---

[6] 'Trade secrets' are denominated 'undisclosed information' in the TRIPS Agreement but, for consistency, are referred to throughout this chapter as trade secrets unless otherwise noted.

[7] The General Agreement on Tariffs and Trade, October 30, 1947, Art. XX(d), 61 Stat. A-11, A 61, 55 U.N.T.S. 194, 262; Art. XX(d) mentions only 'the protection of patents, trademarks, and copyrights, and the prevention of deceptive practices'. See also Work Undertaken at GATT Concerning Trade-related Aspects of Intellectual Property Rights (MTN.GNG/NG11/W/) (May 6, 1987) at 7. Trade secret protection was first included as a topic in a bilateral (or trilateral) agreement in the North American Free Trade Agreement (NAFTA) of 1994, Art. 1711.

[8] PAT CHOATE, HOT PROPERTY: THE STEALING OF IDEAS IN AN AGE OF GLOBALIZATION 223–4 (Alfred A. Knopf, 2005) (noting 'Throughout the

This advocacy led to efforts by the United States to ensure that the Punte del Este Declaration included the protection of IPRs within its scope.[9]

When NG11 met for the first time in March 1987, the United States quickly staked out its position, calling for a comprehensive, enforceable agreement for the protection of IPRs 'including patents, trademarks, trade dress, copyrights, mask works and trade secrets'.[10] In a submission later that year, the Office of the United States Trade Representative detailed its proposed negotiating objectives with respect to trade secrets:

> Trade secrets should be broadly defined to include undisclosed valuable business, commercial, technical or other proprietary data as well as technical information. Misappropriation, including the unauthorized acquisition, use or disclosure of a trade secret, must be prevented.
>
> Trade secrets submitted to governments as a requirement to do business shall not be disclosed except in extreme circumstances involving national emergencies or, in the case of public health and safety, provided that such disclosure does not impair actual or potential markets of the submitter or the value of the submitted trade secrets.[11]

From late 1987 until late 1989, most conversations concerning the TRIPS Agreement revolved around the proper scope of NG11's work. The United States argued that strong and enforceable protection of IPRs was essential to free trade and economic development and, therefore, it was appropriate for the TRIPS Agreement to contain standards for the

---

negotiations, the IPC [the U.S. industry group known as the Intellectual Property Committee] was adamant that the system must have strong protections similar to those found in the United States'). See also PETER DRAHOS (with John Braithwaite), INFORMATION FEUDALISM chs. 7, 8 (Earthscan, 2002); DUNCAN MATTHEWS, GLOBALISING INTELLECTUAL PROPERTY RIGHTS: THE TRIPS AGREEMENT ch. 1 (Routledge, 2002); JAYASHREE WATAL, INTELLECTUAL PROPERTY RIGHTS IN THE WTO AND DEVELOPING COUNTRIES 14 (Kluwer, 2001); Gail E. Evans, *Intellectual Property as a Trade Issue: The Making of the Agreement on Trade-Related Aspects of Intellectual Property Rights*, 18 WORLD COMPETITION (1994).

[9] Ministerial Declaration (Doc. MIN.DEC) (September 20, 1986) Part 1(D), paras. 72–3, at 7–8 ('In order to reduce the distortions and impediments to international trade, and taking into account the need to promote effective and adequate protection of intellectual property rights, and to ensure that measures and procedures to enforce intellectual property rights do not themselves become barriers to legitimate trade, the negotiations shall clarify GATT provisions and elaborate as appropriate new rules and disciplines').

[10] See Statement by the United States at the Meeting of March 25, 1987 (MTN. GNG/NG11/W2) (April 3, 1987).

[11] Suggestion by the United States for Achieving Negotiating Objective (MTN.GNG/NG11/W/14) (October 20, 1987) at 20.

protection of IPRs.[12] Other countries, principally India and Brazil, argued that the focus of the TRIPS Agreement should be on how IPRs impact free trade and that it should not be used as a means to establish or strengthen IPR standards.[13] In their view, it was up to the World Intellectual Property Organization (WIPO) to establish substantive IPR standards.

As a consequence of the debate concerning the scope of NG11's work, substantive discussions regarding standards for the protection of IPRs were delayed for more than 18 months. Once they occurred,[14] they were dominated by developed countries and most of the attention was focused on issues of counterfeiting, enforcement and IPRs other than trade secrets, leaving little time for the parties to gain a complete understanding of the purpose, scope and limitations of trade secret protection.[15] As further detailed in the subsections that follow, the discussions about trade secrets can be divided into three phases: (1) the *early phase* consisting of initial proposals by the United States, the European Community (EC) and industry groups; (2) a *mid-term phase* that focused on whether trade secrets are a form of intellectual property, but also included some discussion concerning standards for trade secret protection; and (3) a *drafting phase* where proposed treaty language was suggested and multiple draft agreements tabled, ultimately leading to the existing language of Article 39.

A. The Early Phase (Early-1987 Through Late-1988): Sketching the Potential Scope of Trade Secret Protection

The United States' initial written statement on the purpose and scope of trade secret protection consisted of a general statement in three parts, the first two of which appear to have been taken directly from the UTSA: (1) it broadly defined the nature of the information to be protected; (2) it identified the wrong to be prevented as 'misappropriation' (defined as

---

[12] See, e.g., MTN.GNG/NG11/4, paras. 5–6.

[13] MATTHEWS, *supra* note 8.

[14] It was not until pressure was brought to bear by the United States on some recalcitrant countries and the issue of the scope of NG11's work was referred to the Trade Negotiations Committee that NG11 began to consider 'standards and principles concerning the availability, scope and use of trade-related intellectual property rights'. Drahos, *supra* note 8, ch. 8; and Matthews, *supra* note 8, at 31–4. See also MTN.TNC/9 (April 11, 1989) and MTN.GNG/NG11/10 (November 30, 1988) para.27.

[15] Of the ten meetings of NG11 held between March 1987 and November 1988, only three included discussions concerning trade secrets issues. See MTN.GNG/NG11/4, MTN.GNG/NG11/8 and MTN.GNG/NG11/9.

the unauthorized *acquisition*, *use* or *disclosure* of a trade secret); and (3) it included a provision that was designed to address concerns regarding trade secrets that are submitted to governments.[16] From the formal record of the meetings of NG11, it appears that very little discussion of the U.S. proposal occurred between December 1987 and July 1989.[17] According to one account, however, three issues concerning the U.S. proposal were raised but left unresolved at the meetings in spring 1988.[18] The first involved the definition of misappropriation and the conditions under which it might be presumed. Related to this issue was whether liability should be extended to innocent (i.e., unknowing or non-intentional) possessors of trade secret information. Controversy also arose concerning the proposed restrictions on the use of trade secrets submitted to governments.

In early March 1988, representatives of the EC and 23 industrialized countries, together with representatives of various industry groups, participated in meetings to discuss standards for the protection of IPRs.[19] These meetings and other informal discussions among industry representatives led to the issuance in June 1988 of a document titled *Basic Framework of GATT Provisions on Intellectual Property, Statement of Views of the European, Japanese and United States Business Communities* ('*Basic Framework*').[20] In contrast to the initial proposal by the United States, the *Basic Framework* provisions on proprietary information included a list of fundamental principles together with rationales for each principle. What is most telling about the principles is that they are broader in scope than U.S. trade secret law and reflect industry concerns that transcend a desire to protect trade secrets. For instance, based upon stated Principle 2, a major concern of industry groups was that companies might be compelled by governments to disclose proprietary information as a condition of doing

---

16 MTN.GNG/NG11/W/14.

17 MTN.GNG/NG11/4–11. Informal discussions between various countries may have occurred for which there is no written record.

18 Rudolf Krasser, *The Protection of Trade Secrets in the TRIPS Agreement*, in 18 IIC Studies in Intellectual Property and Copyright Law, From GATT to TRIPS: The Agreement on Trade-Related Aspects of Intellectual Property Rights 216 (F. Beier and G. Schricker eds., 1996).

19 See *Notes on Informal Meeting on Intellectual Property Standards, March 7–11, 1988*, in 11 IIC Studies in Intellectual Property and Copyright Law, GATT or WIPO? New Ways in the International Protection of Intellectual Property 181, 186 (Weinheim, 1989). See also Drahos, *supra* note 8, Chronology of Key Events.

20 A copy of the *Basic Framework* provisions dealing with proprietary information, at 80–90 (produced by the U.S. Trade Representative in response a Freedom of Information Act request) is on file with the author.

business in a country.[21] There was also concern that where legitimate reasons existed for the disclosure of information to governmental authorities, the governmental authorities would fail to protect the secrecy of such information.[22] Principle 6 went beyond a general fear of government treatment of information to suggest the creation of a *sui generis* right of data exclusivity for all data submitted as a condition for registering a product.[23]

Of the eight principles of proprietary information listed in the *Basic Framework*, only two reflected established principles of U.S. trade secret law. Principle 5 states: 'A person who has acquired proprietary information without the consent of the owner shall be effectively deterred from using or disclosing it further when such acquisition was contrary to honest practices in industrial and commercial matters'. Principle 7 details well-established limits on the scope of trade secret protection, including the observation that it does not extend to publicly available information or to information that can be reverse engineered.[24] The *Basic Framework* also directly addressed two of the points of controversy that were raised at the spring 1988 meetings of NG11; namely, whether liability should be presumed and the potential liability of innocent infringers. Apparently sensing that the imposition of a strict liability standard for trade secret misappropriation might prevent trade secrets from being included in the

---

21 Principle 2 of the *Basic Framework* reads: 'Disclosure or licensing of information shall not be required of a patent owner by a government in connection with the compulsory or voluntary licensing of a patent'.

22 Principle 1 of the *Basic Framework* reads: 'Information required by a government to be disclosed to any party shall not be used commercially or further disclosed without the consent of the owner'. As detailed in SECRET FORMULA, there was the highly-publicized request by India for the Coca-Cola Company to disclose its formulas for its soft-drink products as a condition of being allowed to sell its products in India. See FREDERICK ALLEN, SECRET FORMULA: HOW BRILLIANT MARKETING AND RELENTLESS SALESMANSHIP MADE COCA-COLA THE BEST-KNOWN PRODUCT IN THE WORLD (HarperCollins, 1995).

23 Principle 6 of the *Basic Framework* reads: 'Information disclosed to government as a condition for registration of a product shall be reserved for the exclusive use of the registrant for a reasonable period from the day when government approval based on the information was given. The reasonable period shall be adequate to protect the commercial interests of the registrant'. See also TRIPS, Art. 70(9) which requires market exclusivity for pharmaceutical and agricultural chemical products.

24 Principle 7 of the *Basic Framework* reads: 'It is not a violation of adequate and effective protection of confidential information to derive or use commercially information from any publicly available material, whether for example in the form of documents or samples, or embodied in a product, provided use or derivation of such information is not protected by any laws or rules for protecting intellectual property or by contract, the enforcement of which is not prohibited by law'.

TRIPS Agreement, the *Basic Framework* included the following proposed limitations:

> A person is not necessarily assumed to know that particular information he receives is proprietary and being kept secret.
>
> Thus, purely accidental acquisition of information is not under consideration here but wrongfully taking commercial advantage of confidential information is regarded as a fault which gives rise to a cause of legal action on the part of the owner.[25]

Following the issuance of the *Basic Framework*, the EC submitted a proposal ('EC Guidelines') which took a less detailed approach toward trade secret protection than either the United States' or *Basic Framework* approaches. It provided, simply:

> Trade and business secrets shall be protected by law at least by providing their proprietor the right to prevent these secrets from becoming available to, or being used by, others in a manner contrary to honest commercial practices.[26]

The appeal of the EC's language was that it simultaneously added trade secrets to the list of IPRs that would be protected by international agreement while circumventing the disagreements about trade secret protection that had arisen earlier. At the meeting of NG11 in July 1988, the EC representative explained that the EC Guidelines were stated as a set of 'principles' rather than a set of 'substantive standards' and that there was an important difference between the two approaches:

> First, principles should be expressed in more general terms than would be a typical substantive standard in an international convention dedicated to substantive standards, such as for example the Paris Convention. Secondly, the translation of the proposed principles into national law would not be verbatim or even close to verbatim; rather parties would be required to follow the thrust of these principles in drafting national legislation in the required detail, taking into account the greater precision often contained in international conventions and in the national legal system in question.[27]

In effect, the EC's proposal raised the question of how detailed the treatment of trade secrets (and for that matter other IPRs) should be in

---

[25] *Basic Framework*, at 89.

[26] Guidelines and Objectives Proposed by the European Community for the Negotiations on Trade Related Aspects of Substantive Standards of Intellectual Property Rights (MTN.GNG/NG11/W/26) (July 7, 1988) at 10.

[27] MTN.GNG/NG11/8 (August 29, 1988) para. 27.

the TRIPS Agreement and whether a general principles or code approach should be followed.[28]

When NG11 next met, in September 1988, there was little movement toward agreement about the protection of trade secrets and continuing controversy concerning the proper scope of the TRIPS Agreement.[29] Although both the *Basic Framework* and the EC Guidelines included language that required countries to prevent 'acts contrary to honest business practices', a revised submission by Japan excluded such a provision or any other language dealing with trade secrets.[30] At least one country raised the issue whether trade secrets are a form of intellectual property, and a number of countries urged that the TRIPS Agreement should focus on IPRs for which there was 'universal recognition' and 'established substantive standards', suggesting that trade secrets did not fall into those categories.[31]

Undaunted by a lack of enthusiasm for a trade secret provision in the TRIPS Agreement, the United States tabled a new proposal in October 1988 which took a detailed, code approach.[32] Whereas its initial submission consisted of three general statements, the new submission addressed six topics: (1) the scope of protection; (2) the term of protection; (3) maintenance of rights; (4) the definition of misappropriation; (5) the rights conferred; and (6) conditions of government use. It also contained a provision requiring the protection of confidential information during enforcement proceedings.[33] Unlike the EC Guidelines, which circumvented earlier disagreements about the potential liability of third parties and government use of trade secrets, the United States' new proposal included provisions that addressed both issues.[34]

---

[28] See also Proposal by Switzerland (MTN.GNG/NG11/W/25) (June 29, 1988) (calling for the creation of 'indicative lists').

[29] Draft Agreement to Discourage the Importation of Counterfeit Goods (MTN.GNG/NG11/W/9) (June 25, 1987).

[30] Suggestion by Japan, MTN.GNG/NG11/W/17/Add.1.

[31] MTN.GNG/NG11/W/9, paras. 11 and 40. See also Communication of the Nordic Countries (MTN.GNG/MG11/W/29) (October 20, 1998) para. 5 ('The level of specification of the reference points to substantive standards/norms in GATT should be derived from generally internationally accepted and applied standards/norms . . . The concept of generally internationally accepted and applied standards/norms includes both existing standards and norms provided in international treaties and/or international guidelines, *as well as commonly applied national provisions and practices*') (emphasis added).

[32] MTN.GNG/NG11/W/14/Rev. 1. Although the *Basic Framework* is not cited in the U.S. submission, the language of section III tracks the structure and order of the *Basic Framework*.

[33] MTN.GNG/NG11/W/14/Rev. 1, section IV, 5(c).

[34] The proposal included the following language: 'In assessing liability for

B. The Mid-Term Phase (Mid-1989 to Mid-1990): What are Trade Secrets?

Due to the impasse regarding the scope of NG11's work, there were no meetings of the group between November 1988 and May 1989. Once the impasse was broken, the next challenge was to reach agreement on the identity of the IPRs to be included in the TRIPS Agreement and the scope of the protection to be provided. On the subject of trade secrecy, two areas of conflict emerged during the mid-term phase: whether trade secrecy is a form of intellectual property that should be included in the TRIPS Agreement; and how detailed a trade secret provision should be.

Until mid-1989, the only proposals that had been made regarding substantive IPR standards were by developed countries. Thus, the submission by India in July 1989 was an important milestone in the TRIPS negotiations as it was the first time a developing country submitted written comments concerning substantive IPR standards.[35] With respect to trade secrecy, however, India argued that it is not a form of intellectual property right and should not be a subject of the TRIPS Agreement.[36] India, like many courts and commentators in the United States,[37] viewed trade secret law as a form of unfair competition law and was unwilling to apply property principles to trade secret misappropriation claims.

By some accounts, the United States insisted that trade secrets were a form of property and resisted tying trade secret protection to unfair com-

---

misappropriation involving use or disclosure of a trade secret disclosed by mistake or by one who had misappropriated it, authorities may take into consideration whether the recipient has in good faith paid value for the secret or changed position to his detriment as a result of its receipt'. MTN.GNG/NG11/W/14/Rev. 1. Compare language of section III.D.5. of the United States' proposal with section 2(ii)(A)(C) of the UTSA.

35 While India continued to assert that NG11's charge was narrow and that it should only focus on 'the restrictive and anticompetitive practices of the owners of intellectual property rights', it recognized that substantive discussions were occurring and decided to weigh in on each of the areas of intellectual property addressed by the United States. Standards and Principles Concerning the Availability, Scope, and Use of Trade-related Intellectual Property Rights (MTN.GNG/NG11/W/37) (July 10, 1989) para. 2. See also MTN.GNG/NG11/14 (September 12, 1989) paras. 89–90.

36 Communication from India (MTN.GNG/NG11/W/37) para. 46 ('secrecy and confidentiality should be governed by contractual obligations and the provisions of appropriate Civil Law and not by intellectual property law').

37 See, e.g., J.H. Reichmann and Pamela Samuelson, *Intellectual Property Rights in Data,* 50 VAND. L. REV. 51, 139–45 (1997).

petition principles.[38] In actuality it appears there was merely a difference of opinion about the import of a property designation. In response to India's argument, the U.S. representative used the term 'intellectual property' in a broad, colloquial sense to refer to a wide range of intangible matter, arguing:

> the essential fact [is] that trade secrets were designed to protect a form of intellectual endeavor, that either was not eligible for protection under one of the normal forms of protection of intellectual property or would lose its value through the public disclosure required to receive such protection.[39]

Thus, whereas India's argument focused on the word 'property' in 'intellectual property', the United States' argument focused on the word 'intellectual', essentially arguing that all forms of intellectual endeavor are entitled to some form of legal protection.[40]

Ultimately, 14 countries adopted India's position and expressed their unwillingness to negotiate concerning trade secrets,[41] thereby further truncating the discussions concerning substantive standards for the protection of trade secrets. In effect, the developing world allowed the developed world to dictate the terms of the trade secret provisions by continually insisting that trade secrecy was not a form of IPR and therefore refusing to join the debate about the terms of the trade secrecy provisions.[42] What remained to be determined, however, was whether the general approach of the EC or the code approach of the United States would be adopted.

---

[38] Resource Book on TRIPS and Development, UNCTAD-ICTSAD Project on IPRs and Sustainable Development ch. 28, 523 nn. 1019–20 (Cambridge University Press, 2005) (citations omitted).

[39] MTN.GNG/NG11/9 (October 13, 1988) para. 11.

[40] See also MTN.GNG/NG11/16 (December 4, 1989) para. 61 ('The issue underlying the protection of trade secrets was the same as that underlying the protection of intellectual property rights generally, namely that of not benefiting from the fruits and labours of others improperly').

[41] MTN.GNG/NG11/26 (October 31, 1990). See also Guidelines for Negotiations that Strike a Balance Between Intellectual Property Rights and Development Objectives (MTN.GNG/NG11/w/45) (October 27, 1989); Communication from Argentina, Brazil, Chile, China, Columbia, Cuba, Egypt, India, Nigeria, Peru, Tanzania and Uruguay (MTN.GNG/NG71) (May 14, 1990); and MTN.GNG/NG11/21 (June 22, 1990) para. 26 (noting the joinder of Zimbabwe and Pakistan in the submission of Argentina *et al.*).

[42] See Pires de Carvalho, The TRIPS Regime of Antitrust and Undisclosed Information para 39.2.27 (Wolters Kluwer, 2008) ('developing countries may have made a strategic mistake in refusing to negotiate the protection of trade secrets, but the repercussions of that mistake are necessarily much more serious in regard to test data than of trade secrets').

As noted in the formal minutes of the meetings of NG11, not much consensus was reached on trade-related aspects of intellectual property before the Brussels Ministerial meeting in late 1990. However, negotiations concerning trade secret standards were advanced somewhat by two events: an agreement to have the Secretariat prepare a document 'setting out in synoptic form the specific proposals submitted to the Group on standards and enforcement, along with the relevant provisions of existing international conventions',[43] and the submissions of additional countries. The synoptic tables were significant because, for the first time, reference was made to Article 10*bis* of the Paris Convention and the existing obligation of Paris Convention members to prevent acts contrary to honest business practices.[44] The significance of the submissions by various countries, including a number of draft agreements (discussed in more detail below), was that they provided the basis for a discussion of substantive IPR norms which included more of the perspectives of developing countries.

The most detailed reported conversation concerning trade secrets occurred at the meetings in the fall of 1989 when a proposal by Canada was considered.[45] In its proposal, Canada expanded upon the earlier EC Guidelines by including a rough definition of trade secrets and stating: '[p]rotection for trade and business secrets is . . . an important aspect of providing a secure environment for the transfer of technology'.[46] More importantly, although the United States continued to assert a Lockean view of trade secrets, it conceded that the repression of unfair competition was one method by which trade secrets could be protected. The U.S. representative also cited to the UTSA for a useful definition of a trade secret and acknowledged that trade secret protection is limited by the concepts of reverse engineering and independent development. This discussion set the stage for the EC to propose new language that was an apparent compromise between its earlier general principles approach and the code approach preferred by the United States. Thus, in the same way that Article 10*bis* of the Paris Convention evolved from a general statement

---

43 MTN.GNG/NG11/12 (June 13, 1989) para. 15. See also the three resulting synoptic tables: MTN.GNG/NG11/W/32 (June 2, 1989); MTN.GNG/NG11/W/32/Rev. 1 (September 29, 1989); and MTN.GNG/NG11/W/32/Rev. 2 (February 2, 1990).

44 Paris Convention for the Protection of Industrial Property, as revised at Stockholm in 1967.

45 MTN.GNG/NG11/16 (December 4, 1989).

46 Standards for Trade-related Intellectual Property Rights (MTN.GNG/NG11/w/47) (October 25, 1989).

to include an illustrative list of wrongdoing,[47] the proposed trade secret provisions began to take a similar form.

In January 1990, Mexico became the first developing country to support the inclusion of a trade secret provision in the TRIPS Agreement when its submission called for an agreement to protect trade secrets 'which establishes conditions of general legal security so as to encourage associations among enterprises and the transfer of technology between them'.[48]

C. The Drafting Phase (Spring 1990 Through Late 1991): How Specific Should the Trade Secrets Standards Be?

The process of drafting the TRIPS Agreement began with the submission of a draft agreement by the EC in March 1990 which included a provision on trade secret protection that, although maintaining a general requirement to prevent acts that are contrary to honest commercial practices, included a definition of a trade secret and a restriction on the government use of test data.[49] Judging from its subsequent draft, the United States was not yet willing to give up on its goal of code approach. Instead, it proposed a trade secret provision with three detailed articles.[50] The first article, labeled 'Trade Secrets', was nearly identical to section (a) of the EC draft with the exception that it included a provision that prohibited limitations on the duration of trade secrets and, in a footnote, a definition of 'a manner contrary to honest commercial practices'. The second article, labeled 'Licensing', adopted the principle of the *Basic Framework* which precluded countries from impeding the licensing of trade secrets. [51] The third article was labeled 'Exceptions' and dealt with

---

47 See DI CARVALHO, *supra* note 42, paras. 39.1.4–39.1.14.

48 Communication from Mexico (MTN.GNG/NG11/W/60) (January 22, 1990).

49 Draft Agreement on Trade-Related Aspects of Intellectual Property Rights, Part G, Art. 28 (MTN.GNG/NG11/W/68) (March 29, 1990). Section (a) of Art. 28 contained both the obligation to protect undisclosed information and a definition of undisclosed information. Section (b) concerned the protection of 'test or other data' by contracting parties (i.e. WTO members).

50 Draft Agreement on the Trade-Related Aspects of Intellectual Property Rights (MTN.GNG/NG11/W/70) (May 11, 1990). See also the submission of Switzerland, which was similar to the U.S. submission. Draft Amendment to the General Agreement on Tariffs and Trade on the Protection of Trade-Related Intellectual Property Rights (MTN.GNG/NG11/W/73) (May 14, 1990).

51 Principle 3 of the *Basic Framework* reads: 'Voluntary licensing or transfer or technology shall not be discouraged by governments by imposing on any party to an agreement for such licensing or transfer, terms or conditions which are unreasonable or discriminatory'.

the issue of the government use of trade secrets. The first section of this article was similar to section (b) of the EC draft because it proposed to protect all trade secrets 'submitted to carry out governmental functions'. The other two sections of the third article were apparently designed to provide balance to the broad prohibition on the use of trade secrets by governments by specifying limited exceptions in the case of public emergencies.[52]

How TRIPS negotiators got from the draft agreements to Article 39 is not entirely clear because, by the end of 1990, much of the negotiation moved from formal meetings to informal and more secretive 'consultations'.[53] The process began with the creation of a draft composite text which reflected all of the submissions and many of the formal and informal discussions, known as 'The Anell (or Chairman's) Draft'.[54] In preparing the composite draft, Chairman Lars Anell restated all of the draft provisions as alternatives and showed particular points of disagreement in brackets. Even the concerns of the countries that objected to including substantive IPR standards in the TRIPS Agreement were recognized when two options were presented: one that focused on issues of counterfeiting and the other that included substantive IPR standards.

The bracketed items in the Anell Draft reveal at least two points of disagreement concerning the substantive standards for trade secret protection. The first concerned the economic value prong of the definition of a trade secret, namely, whether trade secret protection should extend to secrets with only potential commercial value (e.g., those secrets that are not yet used or licensed commercially). The draft agreements by the EC, the United States and Switzerland each included the terms 'actual or potential commercial value'. Thus, the issue whether trade secret protection should extend to information with potential commercial value must have been raised during informal consultations. More broadly, the issue concerned the definition of a trade secret and whether the protected information should be denominated 'trade secrets' as proposed by the United States,

---

52 This approach has been criticized for suggesting that all test data was protected and, therefore, exceptions were needed to protect the public interest.

53 For an explanation of the course of negotiations in late 1990 through December 1991, see Adronico Oduogo-Adede, *Origins and History of the TRIPS Negotiations*, in TRADING IN KNOWLEDGE: DEVELOPMENT PERSPECTIVES ON TRIPS, TRADE AND SUSTAINABILITY 28–9 (Christophe Bellmann, Graham Dutfield and Ricardo Melendez-Ortiz eds., Earthscan, 2004).

54 Chairman's report to the Group of Negotiation on Goods (MTN.GNG/NG11/W/76) (July 23, 1990). See also Matthews, *supra* note 8, at 36–7.

'proprietary information' as proposed by Switzerland or 'undisclosed information' as suggested by the EC.[55]

The second bracketed issue concerned the illustrative list of acts 'contrary to honest commercial practices' that was first introduced as a footnote in the United States' draft.[56] As originally proposed, third parties could be held liable for trade secret misappropriation if they 'knew, or had reasonable grounds to know' that the information was acquired in a manner contrary to honest commercial practices. In the Anell Draft, the language 'or had reasonable grounds to know' was bracketed. This means the early controversy concerning the imposition of trade secret liability on persons or companies that did not have actual knowledge of the misappropriation of trade secrets continued.

When comparing the drafts prepared by the EC, the United States and Switzerland to each other and the UTSA, an additional difference appears. Whereas the UTSA and the United States' proposal use the phrase 'generally known or readily ascertainable', the drafts by the EC and Switzerland use the phrase 'generally known or easily accessible'. It is not clear, however, if this was a difference in language or substance.

Following the distribution of the Anell Draft, additional consultations led to the creation of another draft agreement known as the 'Brussels Draft'.[57] Although, for the most part, the Brussels Draft reflects only minor changes from the Anell Draft, there were four significant changes to the provisions concerning trade secrets. First, the bracketed reference to secrets with 'potential' commercial value was removed. Second, the illustrative list of dishonest commercial practices was placed in a note as originally proposed by the United States, and the standard for imposing liability on third parties that was contained in the original note was changed to require either actual knowledge or gross negligence. Third, the language 'readily accessible' was adopted over the language 'readily ascertainable' proposed by the United States and 'easily accessible' proposed by the EC and Switzerland. Finally, all but one of the proposed provisions regarding government use of trade secrets was deleted, leaving only the provision requiring governments to protect certain test data

Following the breakdown of Uruguay Round negotiations due to

---

[55] De Carvalho, *supra* note 42, para. 39.2.22 ('some participants believed that a mere reference to the term "trade secrets" might imply the acknowledgement of proprietary or exclusive rights, which are not accepted in civil code countries').

[56] See *supra* note 50.

[57] Draft Final Act Embodying the Results of the Uruguay Round of Multilateral Trade Negotiations (MTN.TNC/W/ 35/Rev. 1) (December 3, 1990). See also Matthews, *supra* note 8, at 37.

disputes over the agricultural provisions, the TRIPS negotiations continued in a modified format throughout most of 1991.[58] Ultimately, to move matters toward a final agreement, a stripped-down version of a draft agreement was prepared and presented to countries on, essentially, a take-it-or-leave-it basis.[59] As reflected in this final draft, often referred to as the 'Dunkel Draft', the provisions governing trade secrets were reduced to the three sections that are set forth in Article 39 of the TRIPS Agreement.[60] Article 39(1) speaks to the general obligation of WTO member countries, in accordance with Article 10*bis* of the Paris Convention, to prevent conduct contrary to honest business practices. Article 39(2) identifies the wrongful acquisition, disclosure and use of 'undisclosed information' as a specific instance of conduct contrary to honest business practices and defines the type of information that qualifies for protection. Article 39(3) imposes an obligation on government officials to protect a specific type of undisclosed information, namely, test and other data required as a condition of approving the marketing of pharmaceutical or agricultural chemical products.

III. LIMITED SCOPE OF TRADE SECRET LAW IN THE UNITED STATES

To some, including the industry groups behind the *Basic Framework*, Article 39 is evidence of an international consensus to protect wide swaths of business information. However, while the history of the TRIPS negotiations reveals that the United States succeeded in having trade secret protection included in the TRIPS Agreement, the seemingly detailed language of Article 39 obscures the fact that the required scope of protection is limited. Based upon the language of Article 39, including its incorporation of UTSA principles, WTO member countries are only required to adopt laws which protect a discrete subset of business information. While industry leaders may lament this fact, the limited scope of Article 39 is entirely consistent with the U.S. law that inspired it, as explained in the sections which follow.

---

[58] Matthews, *supra* note 8, at 37–8 (explaining that the original working groups were streamlined into seven groups, and NG11 was renamed the 'TRIPS Working Group').

[59] Daniel Gervais, The TRIPS Agreement: Drafting History and Analysis paras. 1.28–1.29 (3rd ed., Sweet & Maxwell, 2008).

[60] *Id.* Annex 10.

A. A Brief History of U.S. Trade Secret Law

Consistent with the placement of international trade secret principles under the rubric of unfair competition, the development of trade secret law in the United States began at common law as a branch of the law of unfair competition.[61] Thus, its development is more akin to U.S. trademark law than to the constitutionally based laws governing patents and copyrights. As with trademark law (and consistent with the position India took during the TRIPS negotiations), the principal impetus behind U.S. trade secret law was not the protection of 'property' per se, but the development and maintenance of fair business practices. Although the nature of free competition gives competitors wide latitude to attract customers away from competing businesses, the illegal or otherwise improper acquisition of confidential information and know-how was seen by many U.S. courts as crossing the line between aggressive competition and wrongful competition.

Unfortunately, drawing the line between mere aggressive competition and wrongful competition is not easy and the early record of trade secret cases in the United States includes numerous examples of the over-assertion of trade secret rights as a means to quell legitimate competition. An early effort to improve U.S. trade secret law and harmonize it among the states is reflected in the Restatement (First) of Torts, published by the American Law Institute in 1939.[62] As expressed therein, the original conception of a trade secret was fairly narrow because only information that was secret, non-ephemeral and used in a business was protected.[63]

Although the Restatement First helped improve the application of trade secret law within the United States, a number of developments in the mid-twentieth century led to calls for a uniform, and therefore more predictable, set of trade secrecy principles.[64] First among these developments was a persistent divergence of views concerning the doctrinal basis of trade secret law, which resulted in a lack of predictability.[65] Second, was the recognition

---

[61] For a brief history of the common law development of trade secret law in the United States, see Sharon K. Sandeen, *A Contract by Any Other Name is Still a Contract: Examining the Effectiveness of Trade Secret Clauses to Protect Databases*, 45 IDEA 119, 126–44 (2005).

[62] Restatement (First) of Torts §§ 757–9 (1939).

[63] *Id.* § 757 cmt. b.

[64] The uniform law-making process in the United States is a process that results in the creation of proposed state laws that must be adopted by state legislatures in order to be effective in a given state. The Restatement differs from uniform laws in that it merely 'restates' existing common law principles and need not be formally adopted by Congress or state legislatures.

[65] See Comment, *Theft of Trade Secrets: The Need for a Statutory Solution*, 120

that the U.S. Supreme Court's decision in *Erie R.R. v. Tompkins* prevented the common law development of federal principles of unfair competition.[66] Most important were the Supreme Court's decisions in *Sears, Roebuck & Co. v. Stiffel Co.* and *Compco Corp. v. Day-Brite Lighting, Inc.*, which held that federal patent law pre-empted state unfair competition claims brought to prevent the copying of unpatented products.[67]

Given the apparent breadth of the *Sears/Compco* doctrine, there was great concern in the late 1960s that state trade secret law could not co-exist with U.S. patent law. Thus, members of the Patent, Trademark, and Copyright Section of the American Bar Association ('PTC Section') initiated an effort to draft a uniform trade secrecy law to replace the patch-work quilt of common law principles that then existed. The PTC Section, and later the National Conference of Commissioners of Uniform State Laws, was particularly cognizant of the need to draft the proposed law narrowly so that it would not interfere with U.S. patent policies. Accordingly, the limits on the scope of trade secret protection that are expressed in the UTSA cannot be easily dismissed without threatening the viability of U.S. trade secret law itself.[68]

B. Limitations on the Scope of U.S. Trade Secret Law that are Reflected in the Language of Article 39

1. Requirement of secrecy

The principal limitation on the scope of U.S. trade secret law is the threshold requirement of secrecy. Although this requirement has always been a part of U.S. law, historically it was not always applied due to the emphasis

---

U. PA. L. REV. 378 (1971) ('the body of state and federal law that has traditionally coped with the problem languishes in a deepening maze of conflict and confusion').

[66] John R. Peterson, *The Legislative Mandate of Sears and Compco: A Plea for a Federal Law of Unfair Competition*, 56 T.M.R. 16, 25 (1966) ('The effect of [the *Erie*] decision was to nullify the whole body of well-reasoned common law of unfair competition . . . The result of *Erie* in the field of unfair competition, has been a bewildering hodge-podge of conflicting decisions which defies harmonization into a uniform natural body of law').

[67] Sears, Roebuck & Co. v. Stiffel Co., 376 U.S. 225, 231 (1964) ('To allow a State by use of its law of unfair competition to prevent the copying of an article which represents too slight an advance to be patented would be to permit the State to block off from the public something which federal law has said belongs to the public') and Compco Corp. v. Day-Brite Lighting, 376 U.S. 234, 237 (1964) ('when an article is unprotected by a patent or a copyright, state law may not forbid others to copy that article').

[68] See *supra*.

that many courts placed on the asserted 'unfair' aspects of trade secrecy cases. Concerned that an imprecise application of the law was leading to the protection of information that was not secret, the framers of the UTSA carefully defined the type of information that could be protected to include only secret information.[69]

Although secrecy is the lynch-pin of every trade secret, the information that is claimed as a trade secret need not be absolutely secret. Because trade secrets have little value unless they can be used and such usage often requires the trade secrets to be disclosed to others, 'relative' or 'substantial' secrecy is all that is required.[70] The UTSA incorporates the principle of relative secrecy in its definition of a trade secret by using the terms 'generally known' and 'readily ascertainable'.[71] The generally known requirement precludes protection for information that is generally known either by the public at large or within a particular industry. The readily ascertainable limitation focuses on the nature of the information that is claimed to be a trade secret and whether it can easily be found in published materials such as trade journals and reference books or in publicly distributed products.

The secrecy limitation of trade secret law is built into the TRIPS Agreement by virtue of Article 39(2) which adopted, nearly verbatim, the UTSA's definition of a trade secret. Consistent with the wording of the UTSA, the definition of undisclosed information contained in Article 39 precludes protection for information that is 'generally known among or readily accessible to persons within the circles that normally deal with the kind of information in question'. However, Article 39 includes a restriction on the application of the generally known and readily accessible limitations that is not in the text of the UTSA. Specifically, such limitations apply only to information that is publicly available 'as a body or in the precise configuration and assembly of its components'. It is not clear where this language originally came from, but apparently it was designed to preclude the argument that information is not a trade secret if its component parts are publicly available. Nonetheless, because the definition of 'undisclosed information' is much more precise and detailed than the inexact and confusing definitions of 'proprietary information' and 'confidential information' that were proposed in the *Basic Framework*,[72] Article

---

[69] Sandeen, *supra* note 61, at 126–44.

[70] See Restatement (First) of Torts § 757 cmt. a ('a substantial element of secrecy must exist, so that, except by the use of improper means, there would be difficulty in acquiring the information').

[71] UTSA § 1(4), definition of 'trade secret'.

[72] *Basic Framework*, at 83 (defining proprietary information as 'information generated by businesses or individuals that is required to be disclosed by a

39 does not protect all of the information that industry groups initially sought to protect.

2. Economic value limitation

The UTSA definition of a trade secret is often cited as an example of how the UTSA expanded the applicable scope of trade secret protection from that which existed at common law. Actually, the UTSA merely substituted one limitation on the scope of protection (a requirement that the information be used in one's business) for another limitation (the requirement that the information derive economic value from its secrecy).[73] As a result, a theoretically broader set of information can be protected as trade secrets, but only if the more stringent requirements for protection are met. Pursuant to the UTSA, in addition to the requirement of secrecy, a trade secret owner must prove that the information it claims to be a trade secret 'derives independent economic value, actual or potential, from not being generally known to, and not being readily ascertainable by proper means by, others who can obtain economic value from its disclosure or use'.[74] It is not enough to prove that the information has actual or potential economic value generally; it must be shown that the value results from the secrecy of the information.[75]

While it is not stated in exactly the same words, the economic value limitation of the UTSA is captured in Article 39(2)(b) of the TRIPS Agreement, which requires that the information 'has commercial value because it is secret'. As noted above, although originally proposed by the EC, the United States and Switzerland, the words 'actual or potential' are not included in Article 39(2)(b). Thus, unlike the UTSA, the TRIPS Agreement only requires protection for information with actual commercial value resulting from its secrecy. This is not only a subset of all business information, but also a subset of all secret information.

3. Reasonable efforts limitation

One of the obstacles that the drafters of the UTSA faced was specifying how a court could verify the existence of a trade secret when the information that is claimed to be a trade secret would, by definition, be kept secret. In early drafts of the UTSA, the idea of a tangibility requirement

---

government to any party including the government itself' and confidential information as 'secret technical information of any type and in any form').

[73] Sandeen, *supra* note 61, at, 141–2.

[74] Compare Restatement (First) of Torts § 757 with UTSA § 1, definition of 'trade secret'.

[75] See, e.g., Buffets, Inc. v. Klinke, 73 F.3d 965 (9th Cir. 1996).

was discussed but ultimately discarded.[76] Although tangibility was seen as a way to verify the existence of a trade secret, the drafters of the UTSA quickly realized that a tangibility requirement would preclude protection for trade secrets that are not recorded. Instead, the reasonable efforts requirement was fashioned as a means of requiring evidence that the information actually existed and was an object of concern before the filing of a lawsuit.[77]

Consistent with the UTSA's definition of a trade secret, the reasonable efforts limitation is set forth in Article 39(2)(c) of the TRIPS Agreement. It requires proof that the information to be protected was 'subject to reasonable steps under the circumstances, by the person lawfully in control of the information, to keep it secret'. As with the UTSA, what constitutes reasonable efforts is not specified in the text of the TRIPS Agreement. Under U.S. law, courts are required to determine what is reasonable on a case-by-case basis with some guidance from common law and the commentary that accompanies the UTSA.[78] In practice, what is reasonable depends upon an analysis that is partly based upon the facts and partly upon the court's perception of fairness. In effect, the reasonable efforts requirement encompasses the 'general principles' approach initially proposed by the EC because it allows WTO member countries latitude to determine what is reasonable in light of their own definitions of honest and dishonest commercial practices.

4. Misappropriation limitation

In order to plead and prove a claim for trade secret misappropriation in the United States, a trade secret owner has the burden of proving both that he owns a trade secret and that the trade secret was misappropriated by the defendant. Proving that the defendant merely possesses or interfered with a trade secret is not enough; the acts of the defendant in acquiring, disclosing or using the plaintiff's trade secrets must have been wrongful acts. There are two types of wrongful acts under the UTSA: the acquisition of trade secrets by improper (i.e., illegal or tortious) means, and the disclosure or use of trade secrets in violation of a duty of confidentiality.[79] These requirements serve to ground trade secret law in its original purpose as a means of preventing unfair business practices.

---

[76] A tangibility option is included in the trade secret provisions of NAFTA, Art. 1771(2).

[77] National Conference of Commissioners of Uniform State Laws, First Reading of Uniform Trade Secret Act, August 10, 1972.

[78] See Comment to UTSA § 1.

[79] UTSA § 1(1) and (2), definitions of 'improper means' and 'misappropriation'.

Although a definition of misappropriation is not contained in the main text of the TRIPS Agreement, a definition is spelled out in footnote 10.[80] As stated therein, the alleged acquisition, disclosure or use of a trade secret must be coupled with a dishonest commercial practice, defined to mean 'at least practices such as a breach of contract, a breach of confidence, and inducement to breach'. As noted by one commentator, this provision reflected a major concession by the United States to adopt the 'continental' approach rather than the U.S. approach.[81] However, the provision is entirely consistent with the UTSA which limits the imposition of trade secret liability to situations in which the defendant engaged in a wrongful act and reflects the fact that U.S. trade secret law is not, and never has been, based purely on a property model.

Whereas the UTSA includes an illustrative list of five 'improper means' of acquiring trade secrets (theft, bribery, misrepresentation, breach or inducement of a breach of a duty to maintain secrecy, and espionage through electronic means), footnote 10 to Article 39 includes only three. One of the wrongful acts mentioned in the TRIPS Agreement is a breach of contract, something that is not mentioned in the UTSA definitions and which was not listed in the United States' proposal of October 1988.[82] This does not mean that breach of contract claims cannot be brought in the United States for an alleged failure to abide by an agreement of confidentiality. Rather, it recognizes that the remedies for a breach of contract in the United States are different from the remedies for trade secret misappropriation and that there is a general need to distinguish between the two causes of action.[83]

One reason a reference to breach of contract may have been added to Article 39 is that several countries noted that their laws already protected trade secrets under principles of contract law.[84] Another explanation is that the United States came to believe that it was important for WTO members to formally agree that the breach of a secrecy agreement or the

---

80 According to Michael Kirk, a member of the U.S. TRIPS negotiating team, he could not recall any particular reason for placing the definition of misappropriation in a footnote other than, perhaps 'it was more elegant'. Notes of interview with Michael Kirk, October 1, 2007, on file with the author.

81 Krasser, *supra* note 18, at 221.

82 MTN.GNG/NG11/W/14/rev. 1, para. 4.

83 See Sandeen, *supra* note 61, at 146–7.

84 See, e.g., Trade-Related Intellectual Property Rights, Submission by Austria (MTN.GNG/NG11/W/55) (December 8, 1989) at 4–5 and Communication from Brazil (MTN.GNG/NG11/W/57) (December 11, 1989) paras. 48 and 49. This may have been the 'continental approach' that was referred to by one commentator. See *supra* note 81.

inducement of such breach constituted a wrongful act. The reference to 'breach of contract' raises the issue whether Article 39 requires secrecy agreements to be enforced if they do not involve information that meets the definition of undisclosed information. Under U.S. law, parties to a contract cannot convert information that would not otherwise qualify for trade secret protection into a trade secret simply by designating it as such in a contract.[85] The same, apparently, is true under Article 39, providing yet another example of its limited scope.

Another fact that can be surmised from the limited list of wrongdoing that is specified in footnote 10 is that, consistent with a general principles approach, some countries were reluctant to include a specific list of wrongdoing in Article 39, preferring instead to have the flexibility to define 'a manner contrary to honest commercial practices' in accordance with their own social norms. The use of the language 'at least practices such as', in contrast to the use of the word 'includes' in the UTSA, seems to emphasize this point.

5. Limitation on third party liability

As some have argued, there is no need for trade secret laws when an enforceable contract exists between the owner of information and the individuals or companies with whom it chooses to share that information.[86] Pleas for trade secret protection are motivated by concerns about how trade secret owners can protect information when it falls into the hands of individuals or companies with whom there is no privity of contract. Judging from its early proposals, the United States wanted to ensure that trade secrets were protected against disclosure not only by those who owed a duty of confidentiality, but also by those who acquired trade secrets by mistake.

Under U.S. patent, copyright and trademark law, the issue of third party usage of IPRs is solved by creating what amounts to a strict liability tort. Anyone who violates an exclusive right that attaches to a patented invention, a copyrighted work or a protected trademark is liable for infringement whether or not he or she knew of the existence of the IPRs. By imposing a form of strict liability, the burden is placed on third parties to research the status of information they acquire to determine if it is protected by a patent, copyright or trademark. Given the secrecy of trade

---

[85] See Roger Milgrim, Milgrim on Trade Secrets, para. 1.03 n.8 (Matthew Bender, 2004).

[86] See Robert Bone, *A New Look at Trade Secret Law: Doctrine in Search of Justification*, 86 Cal. L. Rev. 241, 302 (1998).

secrets, the ability of third parties to search public records or public usage to determine if information they acquire is a trade secret of another is limited. For this reason, the UTSA is not a strict liability tort. Rather, a person can only be held liable for trade secret misappropriation if he had actual knowledge or a 'reason to know' of wrongdoing.[87]

The issue of potential third party liability for trade secret misappropriation was one substantive issue that was raised early during the TRIPS negotiations. Indeed, it was at the heart of the argument that trade secret law is a form of unfair competition law and not a type of IPR.[88] By treating trade secret misappropriation as a form of unfair competition and not as a property claim, the need to prove *mens rea* was established. Unlike the UTSA, however, Article 39 only requires countries to protect trade secrets under circumstances where the defendant either 'knew' or would be 'grossly negligent in failing to know' that trade secret misappropriation was involved. Thus, the scope of third party liability that is required under Article 39 is narrower than that specified in the UTSA.

C. Additional Limitations on the Scope of U.S. Trade Secret Law

The limitations on the scope of U.S. trade secret law discussed above are specifically incorporated into Article 39 of the TRIPS Agreement. The following limitations, while not specifically mentioned in Article 39, are arguably consistent with its purpose and intent as reflected in the negotiating history of TRIPS. In any event, since Article 39 retains much of the general principles approach first proposed by the EC, and the United States is unlikely to argue that its trade secret laws do not comply with Article 39, WTO members should be free to adopt the same limitations on the scope of trade secret law that exist under U.S. law, except to the extent that their obligations may have been altered by a Free Trade Agreement.

1. Reverse engineering and independent invention

The reverse engineering and independent invention limitations of U.S. trade secret law are closely linked. Both limitations focus on the means by which a defendant came into possession of alleged trade secrets. If information is acquired through a process of reverse engineering or independent invention, it is not 'dishonestly' acquired and cannot be said to have been misappropriated. The difference between reverse engineering and

---

[87] UTSA § 1, definition of 'misappropriation'.

[88] See *Notes on Informal Meeting on Intellectual Property Standards, March 7-11, 1988*, *supra* note 19, at 223.

independent invention is based upon how a person acquires the alleged trade secret information. If a set of information is developed without any access to the trade secrets, then it was 'independently invented'. If the information is derived from studying or taking apart a publicly distributed product or body of information in which the trade secrets are embedded, then the information was 'reverse engineered'.

As noted above, there are two places in the negotiating history of Article 39 where the reverse engineering and independent invention limitations were favorably discussed. The first is in the *Basic Framework,* the document developed by industry groups from the United States, Japan and the EC.[89] The second is in the minutes of the meeting of NG11 in the fall of 1989, at which the United States and Canada engaged in an extensive discussion of trade secret principles.[90] Referring to a number of cases in the United States for the purpose of defining the parameters of trade secret protection, a U.S. representative explained: 'a person may use his competitor's secret process if he discovered the process by reverse engineering applied to the finished product or by his own independent research'.

The text of Article 39 does not expressly mention the reverse engineering or independent invention limitations of U.S. trade secret law. However, the fact that they did not make their way into Article 39 is not surprising given the fact that they are not included in the text of the UTSA either. Because reverse engineering and independent invention are the antithesis of 'improper means', they need not be stated explicitly as exceptions in the text of trade secret laws. In the UTSA, they are set forth in the commentary as examples of the proper means of acquiring trade secrets.[91] Thus, in the same way that WTO member countries are generally free to define what constitutes acts contrary to honest business practices, they can also define proper means to include reverse engineering and independent invention.

2. Duration of injunctive relief

A major concern of the drafters of the UTSA was the duration of injunctive relief that was available for trade secret misappropriation. Because trade secret law is supposed to provide weaker protection than U.S. patent law, they were worried that if the duration of injunctive relief was not

---

89 See *supra* note 20.

90 MTG.GNG/NG11/16, para. 61.

91 UTSA, Comments ('Proper means include: 1. Discovery by independent invention; 2. Discovery by "reverse engineering". . .; 3. Discovery under license from the owner of a trade secret; 4. Observation of the item in public use or on public display; 5. Obtaining the trade secret from published sources').

limited, a trade secret claimant could obtain protection for information that was better than that provided under U.S. patent law. Accordingly, the injunction provision of the UTSA limits the duration of available injunctive relief to the life of the trade secret and provides a process by which an enjoined party may request that an injunction be lifted.[92] This principle was partially recognized during the TRIPS negotiations in a synoptic table that reads, in part: 'A trade secret should be protected so long as it is not public knowledge, general knowledge in an industry, or completely disclosed by use'.[93] However, there is no formal record of the issue being discussed. To the contrary, it appears that the United States was more concerned that countries might adopt trade secret laws with a fixed term of protection, i.e., it was concerned that protection would be too short, not too long[94]

The fact that the appropriate duration of injunctive relief for trade secret misappropriation was not set out in Article 39 does not preclude WTO members from applying the rule of the UTSA. According to the enforcement provisions of the TRIPS Agreement (Part III), while countries are required to provide for provisional and injunctive relief, they are given latitude to determine the circumstances under which such relief will be granted. Specifically, Article 44 states: 'the judicial authorities shall have authority to order a party to desist from an infringement'. It does not specify either a minimum or a maximum duration for such injunctions. Thus, WTO members which are concerned that the grant of injunctive relief to protect trade secrets may be used in anticompetitive ways to extend protection beyond the secrecy of the information can follow the lead of the United States and rescind injunctive relief when the trade secrets cease to exist.

3. Limitations on non-compete agreements

In the United States, as elsewhere, IPRs are sometimes used as the basis for restrictions on free competition that go beyond the scope of the IPRs. In the case of trade secrets, such restrictions often go beyond the exaction of a promise to keep trade secrets confidential to include a promise not to compete. As a general matter within the United States, where a promise not to compete is designed to protect legitimate trade secrets or is coupled with the sale of a business, it will be enforced.[95] However, where a non-

---

92 UTSA § 2(a).

93 MTN.GNG/NG11/W/32 (June 2, 1989) at 28.

94 See *supra* note 32.

95 Milgrim on Trade Secrets, *supra* note 85, para. 4.02[1][d][vi] n. 40. See also Sandeen, *supra* note 61, at 151–4.

compete agreement unreasonably restrains employment mobility, it will not be enforced.

In the later stages of the TRIPS negotiations, the problem of restrictive business practices was raised in a submission by Peru.[96] Peru proposed that 'in order to limit the impact of restrictive business practices, a patent or trademark owner should be prohibited from imposing conditions on the licensee'. At the time of Peru's submission, however, it continued to insist that trade secrets were not a proper subject of the TRIPS Agreement. As a result, the potentially restrictive business practices of trade secret licensees were not specifically discussed. Ultimately, Peru's initial idea was made more general and incorporated into Article 40 of the TRIPS Agreement which allows countries to prohibit anticompetitive licensing practices. This should include the type of restrictions on non-compete agreements and trade secret licensing practices that are applied in the United States.

IV. ADDED IMPACT OF PRE-EMPTION PRINCIPLES

The limitations that are imposed on the scope of U.S. trade secret law do not simply reflect the policy choices of the state legislators who adopted the UTSA; they are necessary to prevent U.S. trade secret law from being pre-empted by federal patent and copyright law. As explained by the U.S. Supreme Court in *Kewanee Oil Co. v. Bicron*, states may regulate in the area otherwise covered by federal patent and copyright law as long as the regulations do not interfere with the laws passed by the U.S. Congress.[97] Because U.S. trade secret law is limited in the manner described above, the Supreme Court concluded in *Kewanee* that it does not unduly conflict with federal patent policies. This does not mean, however, that any form of trade secret law can be adopted by the states, but only those laws that are sufficiently limited in their scope so that they are not 'an obstacle to the accomplishment and execution of the full purposes and objectives of Congress'.[98]

While the scope of trade secret law involves issues of federalism within the United States, it also raises the general question how WTO members should deal with information to which multiple IPRs attach. Before the

[96] Communication from Peru (MTN.GNG/NG11/W/45) (October 27, 1989) para. IX.

[97] 416 U.S. 470, 479 (1974).

[98] *Id.*, citing Hines v. Davidowitz, 312 U.S. 52 (1941).

implementation of the TRIPS Agreement and the requirement that WTO members adopt comprehensive laws to protect a variety of IPRs, the possibility of overlapping IPRs was slight. In countries that did not provide patent protection, for instance, there was absolutely no possibility that the protection of information under principles of contract law or unfair competition would conflict with the disclosure principles of patent law. Now that this possibility exists, the question arises how conflicts arising from overlapping IPRs should be resolved.

Under U.S. law, when different forms of IPRs overlap, the pre-emption issues are resolved by requiring 'extra elements' or 'independent wrongdoing' before an overlapping claim based upon state law will be allowed to proceed. In other words, the wrong to be remedied by the state claim must be different from the wrong to be remedied by U.S. patent or copyright law. Sometimes this is clear from the nature of the information sought to be protected, such as, for instance, when a trade secret claimant seeks to protect information that is a compilation of facts that would not be protected under U.S. copyright law. Other times, the difference is demonstrated by the nature of the defendant's wrongful actions. In the case of trade secret law, both the definition of a trade secret and the requirement of misappropriation distinguish trade secret claims from patent and copyright infringement claims and prevent trade secret law from being pre-empted by federal law.

Beyond the possibility of overlapping IPRs, trade secret laws conflict with patent law by discouraging some inventors from seeking patent protection and, therefore, trade secrecy is inconsistent with the disclosure objectives of patent law. Although the issue of the potential conflicts between the disclosure purposes of patent law and the secrecy objectives of trade secret law was raised by India in July 1989 and at the meetings of NG11 in January 1990, it was only briefly discussed.[99] Like the U.S. Supreme Court in *Kewanee*, which assumed that the overlap between patent and trade secret protection was slight, the U.S. representative argued that trade secret protection was needed 'to protect a form of intellectual endeavor, that either was not eligible for protection under one of the normal forms of protection of intellectual property or would lose its value through the public disclosure required to receive such protection'.[100] Importantly for purposes of the present discussion, the United States also argued that the risk of conflict was slight because the rights conferred under trade secret law were more limited than the rights provided under

---

[99] MTN.GNG/NG11/W/37 and MTN.GNG/NG11/14.

[100] MTN.GNG/NG11/9, para. 11.

patent law.[101] Thus, the United States' negotiators adopted, whole-cloth, the arguments that the U.S. Supreme Court used in *Kewanee*. They also cited with favor the proposal of Switzerland to limit trade secret protection to information 'which is not protected under other intellectual property laws' and argued that the narrow definition of trade secrets proposed by the United States would prevent major overlaps. Accordingly, it would not be inconsistent with the purpose of Article 39 for WTO members to adopt laws which define undisclosed information in ways that reduce potential conflicts with other IPRs.

V. LIMITED TEST DATA OBLIGATIONS OF ARTICLE 39.3

As reflected in the *Basic Framework* and early proposals by the United States, the industry groups that advocated tying IPRs to trade and using the TRIPS Agreement to increase standards for the protection of IPRs proposed principles for the protection of proprietary information that exceeded the scope of U.S. trade secret law.[102] Like the issue of potential third party liability, the proposals to limit government use of proprietary information were controversial from the start and, judging from the differences between the Anell Draft and the Dunkel Draft, continued to be a major point of contention through the end of the TRIPS negotiations.[103] In the end, only one such provision was included in Article 39: a restriction on the use or disclosure of certain undisclosed test results or other data which is submitted to government officials.[104] Additionally, Article 42 provides that 'civil judicial procedures concerning the enforcement of any intellectual property right . . . shall provide a means to identify and protect confidential information, unless this would be contrary to existing constitutional requirements'.

At the time of the first meeting of NG11 in March of 1987, the presumptive rule within the United States was (and still is) that information submitted to the government becomes part of the public record and can

---

[101] MTN.GNG/NG11/17 (January 23, 1990) para. 50.

[102] See *supra* notes 20–23.

[103] At the time of the first meeting of NG11 in March 1987, a norm had not yet developed in the United States that was consistent with a broad prohibition on the use of business information submitted to governments or a general right of data exclusivity.

[104] See TRIPS, Art. 39(3).

be obtained pursuant to a Freedom of Information Act (FOIA) request.[105] Although FOIA includes a provision that allows government officials to refuse to disclose documents if they constitute trade secrets,[106] the assertion of such an exemption is generally within the discretion of governmental authorities. Absent a special agency-specific law or regulation, or a binding confidentiality agreement between the trade secret owner and a federal agency (often offered as part of a public bidding process), there is little that a trade secret owner can do to prevent FOIA disclosures if the relevant government officials do not choose to assert the trade secret exemption. The general sentiment is that companies that choose to conduct business with the government waive trade secret protection.

Although the presumptive rule of freedom of access to information submitted to the government was beginning to change in the United States (and the European Union) in the mid 1980s,[107] the nature of the information that can be exempted from possible disclosure is circumscribed. A similar approach is reflected in the language of Article 39(3) of the TRIPS Agreement. Article 39(3) applies only to: (1) undisclosed test or other data (2) the organization of which involves considerable effort (3) which is submitted as a condition of approving the marketing of pharmaceutical or agricultural chemical products and (4) which utilizes new chemical entities. Viewed in light of the scope and limits of the UTSA, Article 39(3) should not be seen as creating a general right of data exclusivity but as a limited *sui generis* obligation.[108]

CONCLUSION

As has been noted elsewhere, international trade negotiations are all about getting a deal done and have little to do with ensuring that such agreements are consistent with domestic laws. For those who believe that public policy and democracy still have a role in the international law-making

---

105 5 U.S.C. § 552.

106 5 U.S.C. § 552(b)(4).

107 See Carlos Maria Correa, *Public Health and International Law: Unfair Competition and the Trips Agreement – Protection of Data Submitted for the Registration of Pharmaceuticals*, 3 CHI. J. INT'L L. 69, 70–2 (2002).

108 When asked why the test data obligations of Art. 39(3) were placed in the same section as the obligations to protect undisclosed information, Michael Kirk, a member of the U.S. negotiating team, responded: 'Where else would you put it. All provisions concerned undisclosed information'. Notes of interview with Michael Kirk, October 1, 2007, on file with the author.

process, this observation highlights one of the benefits of international agreements that are written in broad terms. Flexibilities are useful in international agreements because they give each party the ability to exercise some discretion in drafting domestic laws that take account of issues of local public interest. If the standards required by international agreements are too specific, there is a risk that legislators will be forced into the choice of adopting laws that either are inconsistent with the will of their constituents or which do not comply with the specifics of the international agreements.[109]

Generally, the TRIPS Agreement is an example of an international agreement that exalts specificity over flexibility. Indeed, when compared to the international intellectual property agreements that preceded it, the TRIPS Agreement is remarkable for its detail. However, as the foregoing discussion of Article 39 reveals, some provisions of the TRIPS Agreement are less detailed than others. Apparently, Article 39 represents all that the U.S. negotiators and industry groups could get. As a result, countries implementing the undisclosed information provisions have flexibility to design their laws. Ironically, if developing countries model their laws after the Uniform Trade Secrets Act, they will adopt a set of laws that is limited in ways that address many of the objections toward trade secret protection that they raised during the negotiations.

---

[109] As an example of this, see the Fairness in Music Licensing Act of 1998 (Pub. L. 105-298, 112 Stat. 2827, S. 505, Title II, enacted October 27, 1998), which the U.S. Congress adopted at the urging of small bar owners, portions of which were subsequently found to violate the TRIPS Agreement.

21 Test data protection: rights conferred under the TRIPS Agreement and some effects of TRIPS-plus standards

*Carlos M. Correa**

INTRODUCTION

Article 39(3) of the TRIPS Agreement introduced the first-ever international set of binding rules on the protection of 'undisclosed information'.[1] This provision covers two different categories of information: what is generally known as 'trade secrets', that is, information (including of a technical nature) valuable for a commercial activity; and the information that is the focus of this chapter, test data, that is, the results of clinical trials made to demonstrate the efficacy and safety of pharmaceutical and agrochemical products. The introduction of specific rules on test data reflects the influence of the powerful lobbying of the pharmaceutical industry during the TRIPS negotiations.[2]

The protection of test data was one of the issues that divided the North and the South during the negotiations of the Uruguay Round. It also raised controversies among the developed countries themselves. At the time of the negotiations, many developed countries, including Australia and Canada, did not grant specific protection to test data equivalent to the *sui generis* regimes of 'data exclusivity', which the United States and the European Communities (EC) instituted in 1984 and 1986, respectively. Divergences included operational as well as basic issues, such as the adequacy of the concept of 'proprietary' confidential information, suggested by the U.S. delegation.[3]

* Director of the Centre for Interdisciplinary Studies on Industrial Property and Economics (CEIDIE), University of Buenos Aires.

[1] Agreement on Trade-Related Aspects of Intellectual Property Rights, Art. 39(3), April 15, 1994, Marrakesh Agreement Establishing the World Trade Organization ('WTO Agreement'), Annex 1C, Legal Instruments – Results of the Uruguay Round, 33 I.L.M. 1197 ('TRIPS Agreement').

[2] See C. Deveraux, R. Lawrence and M. Watkins, Case Studies in US Trade Negotiation, vol. 1, Making the Rules 37–134 (2006).

[3] This concept was suggested in the influential Statement of Views by

The provision on test data proposed by the United States during the Uruguay Round negotiations required a minimum term of data exclusivity and prohibited not only the use of third party's test data but also reliance on such data to obtain marketing approval of a pharmaceutical or agrochemical product.[4] However, the United States failed to obtain support for this proposal, and the final text suggested by GATT Director General Dunkel adopted a lower standard of protection; that approach became the TRIPS obligation. Article 39(3) stipulates the following:

> Members, when requiring, as a condition of approving the marketing of pharmaceutical or of agricultural chemical products which utilize new chemical entities, the submission of undisclosed test or other data, the origination of which involves a considerable effort, shall protect such data against unfair commercial use. In addition, Members shall protect such data against disclosure, except where necessary to protect the public, or unless steps are taken to ensure that the data are protected against unfair commercial use.

Notwithstanding that Article 39(3) fell short of U.S. ambitions, it represented a major achievement for the proponents of test data protection. As discussed below, although the only obligation imposed by that provision is protection against unfair commercial practices, Article 39(3) gave the United States and the EC a platform from which to push, through bilateral agreements and the WTO accession processes, data exclusivity protection in a growing number of countries.

This chapter discusses the different interpretations given to Article 39(3) of the TRIPS Agreement with regard to the type of protection that must be conferred by WTO members.[5] The main argument made is that the use

---

the European, Japanese and United States Business Communities. Intellectual Property Commission *et al.*, *Basic Framework of GATT Provisions on Intellectual Property, Statement of Views of the European, Japanese and United States Business Communities* (1988).

4 The U.S. proposal, as reflected in a text submitted for consideration by the Brussels Ministerial Meeting of GATT (December 1990) read as follows: 'Parties, when requiring, as a condition of approving the marketing of new pharmaceutical products or of a new agricultural chemical product, the submission of undisclosed test or other data, the origination of which involves a considerable effort, shall [protect such data against unfair commercial use. Unless the person submitting the information agrees, the data may not be relied upon for the approval of competing products for a reasonable time, generally no less than five years, commensurate with the efforts involved in the origination of the data, their nature, and the expenditure involved in their preparation. In addition, Parties shall] protect such data against disclosure, except where necessary to protect the public]'.

5 The chapter does not examine the requirements that need to be met to trigger the obligation to protect test data. For information on the subject, see

of data by a government for the purpose of approving the generic version of a drug product for marketing is not an unfair commercial use and that the provision does not mandate either exclusive rights or compensation. The chapter also briefly addresses the economic, ethical and legal impacts of data exclusivity.

I. INTERPRETATION OF ARTICLE 39.3

Soon after the adoption of the TRIPS Agreement, divergences about the proper interpretation of Article 39(3) arose among governments, academics and other organizations. The Office of the U.S. Trade Representative, which had a key role in the negotiations, interpreted Article 39(3) as requiring a period of exclusivity. It suggested that according to this provision:

> [T]he data will not be used to support, clear or otherwise review other applications for marketing approval for a set amount of time unless authorized by the original submitter of the data. Any other definition of this term would be inconsistent with logic and the negotiating history of the provision.[6]

However, the U.S. Government Accountability Office (GAO), in addressing the question whether the requirements imposed in Free Trade Agreements (FTAs) went beyond the TRIPS Agreement, admitted that the provision was not amenable to such a clear interpretation:

> [W]hether FTA provisions on data exclusivity go beyond TRIPS is less clear . . . There are different interpretations of the obligations under TRIPS 39(3), and exactly what practices can be considered a fulfillment of this obligation. One interpretation of TRIPS 39(3) requires members to grant the originator of the data a period of exclusive use similar to that provided by data exclusivity laws in the United States. Under this interpretation, FTA provisions do not go beyond TRIPS. Others do not believe that Article 39(3) of TRIPS confers exclusive rights, but instead simply requires countries to prevent third parties from using the originators' data for unfair commercial purposes. This interpretation suggests that the FTA provision goes beyond the TRIPS requirement.[7]

Carlos Correa, Protection of Data Submitted for the Registration of Pharmaceuticals: Implementing the Standards of the TRIPS Agreement (South Centre/WHO, Geneva, 2002).

[6] Office of the General Counsel, U.S. Trade Representative, *The Protection of Undisclosed Test Data in Accordance with TRIPS Article 39.3* (May 1995).

[7] U.S. Government Accountability Office, *U.S. Trade Policy Guidance on WTO Declaration on Access to Medicines May Need Clarification*, GAO Report 07-1198 (2007) ('GAO Report') (footnotes omitted).

The EC has also argued that Article 39(3) establishes an exclusivity obligation. In its view, the only element to be determined by national laws is the *duration* of exclusivity:

> The only way to guarantee that no 'unfair commercial use' within the meaning of Article 39.3 shall be made is to provide that regulatory authorities should not rely on these data for a reasonable period of time, the determination of what is a reasonable period of time being left to the discretion of the Members . . . In theory, any country maintaining an effective system to implement obligations under 39.3 even if different from non-reliance over time, would not be in breach of its TRIPS obligations, but we are not aware of many alternatives and it is clear that what the TRIPS-negotiations had in mind was data exclusivity over a certain period of time. On the other hand, as it does not set any time limit, Article 39.3 would not prevent a country from providing for data exclusivity for an unlimited period of time.[8]

The EC admitted, however, that there were substantial disagreements during the negotiations:

> It must be admitted that the following of Article 39.3 does not, from a *prima facie* reading, appear to impose data exclusivity during a certain period of time. This lack of clarity is the obvious result of a difficult negotiation process where divergences of views arose between developing and industrialized countries as to the necessity of EC/US like type of data protection as well as among industrialized countries on the length of the data exclusivity period.[9]

Developing countries have generally held the opposite view. In a submission made by a group of these countries to the TRIPS Council for the special discussion on intellectual property and access to medicines, they stated that:

> Article 39.3 of the TRIPS Agreement leaves considerable room for Member countries to implement the obligation to protect test data against unfair competition practices. The Agreement provides that 'undisclosed information' is regulated under the discipline of unfair competition, as contained in article 10*bis* of the Paris Convention. With this provision, the Agreement clearly avoids the treatment of undisclosed information as a 'property' and does not require granting 'exclusive' rights to the owner of the data.[10]

---

[8] European Commission, *Issue Group on Access to Medicines, Questions on TRIPS and Data Exclusivity* 4–5 (2001), available at http://trade.ec.europa.eu/doclib/docs/2006/may/tradoc_122031.pdf.

[9] *Id.* at 3.

[10] Council for Trade-Related Aspects of Intellectual Property Rights, *TRIPS and Public Health, Submission by the African Group, Barbados, Bolivia, Brazil, Dominican Republic, Ecuador, Honduras, India, Indonesia, Jamaica, Pakistan,*

A large number of developing countries have, in fact, refused to grant data exclusivity. For that reason, the International Federation of Pharmaceutical Manufacturers and Associations (IFPMA) has issued complaints about many of these countries, leading the United States Trade Representative (USTR) to list these countries in its Special 301 Reports – that is, to identify these countries as engaging in unfair trade practices.[11] The number of countries without data exclusivity has, however, notably decreased as a result of unilateral pressures,[12] FTAs and concessions made by countries in the process of accession to the WTO.

The issue of data protection has been particularly controversial in India, a major world supplier of active ingredients and medicines. The Indian government set up a commission to consider what kind of protection should be conferred on test data for pharmaceuticals, taking both the obligation to comply with the TRIPS Agreement and its own national interests into account. The commission's report concluded that data exclusivity was neither required nor advisable. It noted that:

> [T]here is enough flexibility in the provisions of the TRIPS Agreement for a country to determine the appropriate means of protecting test data. In terms of paragraph 4 of Doha Declaration, the provisions are to be 'interpreted and implemented in a manner supportive of WTO Members' right to protect public health and, in particular, to promote access to medicines for all'.[13]

Paraguay, Philippines, Peru, Sri Lanka, Thailand and Venezuela (IP/C/W/296) (June 29, 2001), available at www.wto.org/english/tratop_e/trips_e/paper_develop_w296_e.htm.

[11] Special 301 Reports are made pursuant to the United States Trade Act of 1974 §§ 301–4, 19 U.S.C. §§ 2411–20. The lack of data exclusivity has been a regular complaint in USTR reports on the Special Section 301. See, e.g., the 2009 Report, where most countries on the 'Priority Watch List' (including Chile, which signed an FTA with the United States) and on the 'Watch List' are deemed to provide inadequate protection to test data. Office of the U.S. Trade Representative, *2009 Special 301 Report* (2009), available at www.ustr.gov/sites/default/files/Full%20Version%20of%20the%202009%20SPECIAL%20301%20REPORT.pdf.

[12] A dramatic example may be found in the case of Guatemala, one of the poorest countries in Latin America, which was induced to enact data exclusivity for pharmaceuticals for a period longer than that applied in the United States and EU. See International Center for Trade and Sustainable Development, *La Proteccion de Productos Farmacéuticos y Agroquímicos ('Productos Regulados') en DR-CAFTA*, Taller Regional para el Desarrollo de un Modelo sobre Datos de Prueba (August 21, 2006), available at www.iprsonline.org/unctadictsd/dialogue/2006-08-21/Correa%20datos%20de%20prueba%20rev%20(3).pdf; Doctors Without Borders, *Data Exclusivity and Access to Medicines in Guatemala* (February 2005), available at http://doctorswithoutborders.org/news/2005/access_guatemala_briefingdoc.pdf.

[13] Satwant Reddy and Gurdial Singh Sandhu, *Report on Steps to be Taken by*

The report concluded that:

> Hence, the policy decision should be taken keeping in view the national interest of the country by making use of the flexibilities in the TRIPS Agreement, in particular, the need to ensure rapid and timely response to public health needs by facilitating timely entry of generics and encouraging competition. The ethical issues of conducting repeated human trials when data on quality and efficacy already exists should also be kept in mind. At the same time, the need to adequately promote innovation and R&D in pharmaceuticals and agrochemicals by utilizing the rich human capital and the infrastructure available in the country should also be considered. This will help build India's strength in these areas on a long term sustainable basis.[14]

Despite the interpretation adopted by the United States and the EC, as well as the fact that a large number of WTO members do not provide for exclusive rights over test data, there has been no WTO ruling on the meaning of Article 39(3). Neither the United States, the EC nor any other WTO member has requested the establishment of a panel under the WTO Dispute Settlement Understanding against any of the numerous countries that do not confer exclusive rights over test data. Although the United States filed a complaint against Argentina in 2000, Argentina did not accept the U.S. claim that exclusive rights should be granted for test data. It maintained its law and the dispute was settled at the consultation stage.[15]

Admittedly, some corporate lawyers and other trade specialists have held the theory that Article 39(3) requires some form of exclusive rights. For instance, Antony Taubman (currently Director of the Intellectual Property (IP) Division at the WTO) proposed a 'heterodox reading' of Article 39(3) based on an interpretation that he considers would ensure a 'fair relationship between competitors' and meet the 'trading nations' expectations about access to IP protection'.[16] Thus, Taubman has argued that:

Government of India in the Context of Data Protection Provisions of Article 39.3 of TRIPS Agreement, para. 1.11 (2007) ('India Report'), available at http://chemicals.nic.in/DPBooklet.pdf. The Report refers to the Doha Declaration, World Trade Organization, Ministerial Declaration of 14 November 2001, WT/MIN(01)/DEC/1, 41 I.L.M. 746 (2002), available at www.wto.org/english/thewto_e/minist_e/min01_e/mindecl_e.htm.

[14] *Id.* para. 1.12.

[15] World Trade Organization Dispute Settlement Body, *Notification of Mutually Agreed Solution According to the Conditions Set Forth in the Agreement*, WT/DS171/3, WT/DS196/4, IP/D/18/Add.1, IP/D/Add.2 (June 20, 2002).

[16] Antony Taubman, *Unfair Competition and the Financing of Public Knowledge Goods: The Problem of Test Data Protection*, 3 J. INTELL. PROP. L. & PRACTICE 591,

> Competitors' commercial use of or benefit from regulatory data should be considered unfair and fit to be legally suppressed if it is likely systematically to deter submission and future production of such data: when the prospect of a competitor's immediate use of or benefit from the data is sufficient to render it irrational or unprofitable to generate the data initially, on the part of the originating firm, or when any competitor's use or benefit from test data that would, if systematically applied, deter future submissions. This conceptual basis reconciles utilitarian policymaking with legitimate claims of limited exclusive rights, because they are strictly limited by public interest, and are defensible in terms of actual public welfare, while offering data originators fair commercial opportunities.[17]

The author's logic is, however, flawed. Since research and development in pharmaceuticals and agrochemicals is essentially driven by markets in *developed* countries, the argument would, in fact, support the opposite position: that data exclusivity should not be applied in *developing* countries. In the case of pharmaceuticals, in particular, developed countries account for nearly 85 percent of the global market for prescription drugs.[18] The lack of data exclusivity in one or more developing countries is thus unlikely to be determinant for a company's decisions to invest in test data production. In addition, the lead time gained by the company originating the test data,[19] and the existence of patent protection, will, in most cases, suffice to recover any costs incurred in developing such data.

As important, the suggested 'heterodox' reading of Article 39(3) is not congruent with the interpretive method mandated by the Vienna Convention on the Law of Treaties,[20] which has been systematically applied in GATT and WTO jurisprudence.[21] Thus, in the *U.S. India*

---

601 (2008).

[17] *Id.* at 606.

[18] See Bharat Book Bureau, Achieving Success in the Developing Asian Pharmaceutical Sector 2007–2011 (2007).

[19] Dinca has noted that 'there is no empirical evidence that, in the absence of data exclusivity, the mechanisms of the free market would be definitely incapable of providing the originator with adequate reward for its investments in providing such data. Even if the free market were not capable of offering such reward, there are still other means of protection besides a strong monopoly. The exclusivity could be attenuated or completely replaced by other means'. Razvan Dinca, *The 'Bermuda Triangle' of Pharmaceutical Law: Is Data Protection a Lost Ship?,* 8 J. World Intell. Prop. 517, 547 (2005).

[20] Vienna Convention on the Law of Treaties, May 23, 1969, 1155 U.N.T.S. 331, 8 I.L.M. 679.

[21] See Mohamed Gad, *TRIPS Dispute Settlement and Developing Country Interests*, in Intellectual Property and International Trade: The TRIPS Agreement 331 (Carlos Correa and Abdulqawi Yusuf eds., 2008).

Mailbox case, the panel relied on the doctrine applied in the few 'non-violation' cases decided under the GATT dispute resolution system[22] and concluded that the United States had 'legitimate expectations' that the Indian patent legislation had not adequately fulfilled.[23] The Appellate Body reversed. It stated that the 'expectations' of the members were only those contained in the TRIPS provisions; that it was not the task of the panel or the Appellate Body to find other expectations outside the text of the Agreement itself. It held that:

> The legitimate expectations of the parties to a treaty are reflected in the language of the treaty itself. The duty of a treaty interpreter is to examine the words of the treaty to determine the intentions of the parties. This should be done in accordance with the principles of treaty interpretation set out in Article 31 of the Vienna Convention. But these principles of interpretation neither require nor condone the imputation into a treaty of words that are not there or the importation into a treaty of concepts that were not intended.[24]

Indeed, the negotiating history of Article 39(3) shows that the negotiating parties *rejected* the U.S. proposal to subject test data to a period of exclusivity. They opted for an unambiguous reference to the application of unfair competition rules. Unfair competition law does not imply the recognition of any exclusive rights.

Not surprisingly, as mentioned, the 'brand name' pharmaceutical industry (often called 'Big Pharma') has championed the view that Article 39(3) of the TRIPS Agreement does require the grant of an exclusive right. According to IFPMA:

> Even prior to the conclusion of the WTO TRIPS Agreement in 1993, some countries had already recognized the proprietary nature of registration data and enacted laws that precluded their regulatory authorities, for a fixed period of time, from relying on or otherwise using the data submitted by the originator for the approval of copies of the medicine without the permission of the originator. This concept was embodied in TRIPS Article 39.3, which all WTO Member States committed to implement in their national legislation by January 1, 2000.
>
> The requirement that WTO Member State governments not rely on the originator's data for a specified period of time is reflected in the concept of 'unfair commercial use'. A brief review of the negotiating history of the TRIPS

---

22 On the application of this doctrine, see Note by the WTO Secretariat, *Non-violation Complaints and the TRIPS Agreement* (IP/C/W/124) (January 28, 1999).

23 *India – Patent Protection for Pharmaceutical and Agricultural Chemical Products*, Panel Report, WT/DS50/R (September 5, 1997), para. 8.41.

24 *India – Patent Protection for Pharmaceutical and Agricultural Chemical Products*, Appellate Body Report, WT/DS50/AB/R (December 19, 1997), para. 45.

> Agreement reveals that the drafters of Article 39.3 envisioned 'unfair commercial use' to be any direct or indirect reliance by a country's regulatory authority on the innovator's dossier and accompanying test, clinical and pharmacological data, in the review of a subsequent generic application for a health registration on the innovator's product. A further review of the negotiating history of TRIPS Article 39.3 reveals that the drafters envisioned the period of protection at a minimum of five years (the United States model) to 10 years (the European Union model) from the date of marketing approval of the innovator's product.[25]

While the brand name industry has actively supported the introduction of five or more years of 'data exclusivity' through changes in national legislation and FTAs, the generic segment of the pharmaceutical industry has strongly disagreed with this view.[26]

Most of the academics who have addressed the issue of interpretation of Article 39(3) of the TRIPS Agreement have likewise read this provision as not requiring any type of exclusive rights.[27] In their view, the conferred

---

[25] International Federation of Pharmaceutical Manufacturers and Associations (IFPMA), *Data Exclusivity: Encouraging Development of New Medicines* 3 (June 2007), available at www.fifarma.org/cms/images/stories/Prop_Intelectual/ifpma_data%20exclusivity.pdf.

[26] Amendments introduced in October 2006 to the Canadian Food and Drug Regulations expanded data exclusivity granted in Canada from five to eight years (plus six months of pediatric exclusivity). According to the Canadian Generic Pharmaceutical Association (CGPA), taxpayers, provincial governments and consumers would pay more than U.S.$100 million each year for this three-year extension. See Canadian Generic Pharmaceutical Association, *Study on Science and Technology, Submission to the Standing Committee on Industry, Science and Technology* (2009), available at www.canadiangenerics.ca/en/news/apr_16_08.asp; see also European Generic Medications Association, *Data Exclusivity: A Major Obstacle to Innovation and Competition in the EU Pharmaceutical Sector* (December 2000), available at www.egagenerics.com/doc/ega_dataex-2000-12.pdf.

[27] See generally CARLOS CORREA, PROTECTION OF DATA SUBMITTED FOR THE REGISTRATION OF PHARMACEUTICALS: IMPLEMENTING THE STANDARDS OF THE TRIPS AGREEMENT (South Centre/WHO, Geneva, 2002); UNCTAD-ICTSD, RESOURCE BOOK ON TRIPS AND DEVELOPMENT 520 (June 2005), available at www.iprsonline.org/unctadictsd/ResourceBookIndex.htm ('RESOURCE BOOK'); Charles Clift, *Data Protection and Data Exclusivity in Pharmaceuticals and Agrochemicals*, in INTELLECTUAL PROPERTY MANAGEMENT IN HEALTH AND AGRICULTURAL INNOVATION: A HANDBOOK OF BEST PRACTICES (A. Krattiger *et al.* eds., 2007); JAYASHREE WATAL, INTELLECTUAL PROPERTY RIGHTS IN THE WTO AND DEVELOPING COUNTRIES 185–206 (2001); Lucas Arrivillaga, *An International Standard of Protection for Test Data Submitted to Authorities to Obtain Marketing Authorization for Drugs*, 6 J. WORLD. INTELL. PROP. 139 (2005); Jean-Frédéric Morin, *Tripping Up TRIPS Debates: IP and Health in Bilateral Agreements*, 1 INT. J. INTELL. PROP. MGMT. 37 (2006); Jerome Reichman, *Rethinking the Role*

protection would not impede a generic company from referring to or relying on test data submitted by another company, nor would it prevent the use of such data by the national authorities to evaluate subsequent applications of marketing approval. Their arguments, which are based on a literal reading (as mandated by the Vienna Convention on the Law of Treaties) of the obligation contained in Article 39(3), start from the premise that the discipline of unfair competition does not require recognition of exclusive rights and that the granting of exclusivity constitutes a drastic derogation to the principle of free competition. Even compensation is not necessary because the contemplated activities do not constitute 'unfair commercial use' (the terminology utilized as stated in Article 39(3)): relying on test data by a commercial company is not the same as 'use' of the data and use of data by a governmental entity to assess a subsequent applicant of marketing approval is not 'commercial'. Furthermore, obtaining a commercial advantage cannot be condemned unless it involves 'dishonest' practices, and the definition of what is 'unfair' or 'dishonest' is contingent upon the social perceptions in a particular country at a given point in time. In short, the only reasonable way to read Article 39(3) is as an obligation to refrain from obtaining undisclosed test data by means of dishonest practices (such as bribing employees, espionage) and putting such data to commercial use.

Several documents elaborated by United Nations organizations have indicated that Article 39(3) does not prevent use of or reliance on test data for the marketing approval of generic products, that is, they too have rejected the theory of exclusive rights.[28] Other reports produced within the UN system have addressed this issue with the same approach, including the 2006 Report by the WHO Commission on Intellectual Property, Innovation and Public Health (CIPIH)[29] and the Third Report of the Panel of Eminent Experts on Ethics in Food and Agriculture established

---

of Clinical Trial Data in International Intellectual Property Law: The Case for a Public Goods Approach, 13 Marq. Intell. Prop. L. Rev. 1 (2009); Pedro Roffe and Christoph Spennemann, *The Impact of FTAs on Public Health Policies and TRIPS Flexibilities*, 1 Int. J. Intell. Prop. Mgmt. 75 (2006); *Issues in Data Exclusivity*, 8 J. Intell. Prop. Rights 142 (2003).

[28] See, e.g., Resource Book, *supra* note 29, at 520; UNCTAD, *The TRIPS Agreement and Developing Countries* 46–8 (U.N. Doc. UNCTAD/ITE/1, U.N. Sales No. 96.II.D.10) (1996); World Health Organization, *The TRIPS Agreement and Pharmaceuticals* (2000), available at www.who.int/medicinedocs/en/d/Jh1459e.

[29] WHO Commission on Intellectual Property, Innovation and Public Health ('WHO Commission'), *Public Health, Innovation and Intellectual Property* (April 25, 2006), available at www.who.int/intellectualproperty/documents/thereport/ENPublicHealthReport.pdf (the author was a member of this Commission).

by the Director-General of the Food and Agriculture Organization (FAO).[30]

Similarly, the UN Special Rapporteur on the right to health held in a recent report that:

> Although developed countries proposed the inclusion of data exclusivity in TRIPS, it was not adopted. TRIPS does not require countries to provide data exclusivity. Where a national DRA [Drug Regulatory Authority] requires the submission of undisclosed data for the registration of a medicine, TRIPS only requires countries to protect such data against 'unfair commercial use' in case it relates to a 'new chemical entity' and if the origination of such data involved a 'considerable effort'. Countries can therefore determine how to protect such data. Reliance by the DRA on the clinical trial data of the originator company to approve a subsequent medicine does not amount to unfair commercial use.[31]

The understanding that the TRIPS Agreement does not impose an obligation to confer exclusive rights can also be found in the 2004 Report by the UK Commission on Intellectual Property Rights (CIPR).[32]

Despite the efforts made by the United States and the EC to promote an expansive interpretation of Article 39(3), very few scholars have embraced their interpretation. For example, Ingo Meitinger has argued that, correctly interpreted, Article 39(3) requires members to either ensure the exclusive use of the data for a period or to establish a compensation for such a use.[33] Other authors acknowledge that exclusivity is not required but hold that Article 39(3) imposes the payment of a compensation for the use of the data. Aaron Fellmeth, for instance, has suggested that 'the drug

---

[30] Panel of Eminent Experts on Ethics in Food and Agriculture ('Eminent Experts'), *Report of Eminent Experts on Ethics in Food and Agriculture, Third Session* 23 (September 14, 2005), available at ftp://ftp.fao.org/docrep/fao/010/a0697e/a0697e.pdf (the author was a member of the panel when it issued this report).

[31] Human Rights Council, *Promotion and Protection of All Human Rights, Civil, Political, Economic, Social and Cultural Rights, Including the Right to Development: Report of the Special Rapporteur on the Right of Everyone to the Enjoyment of the Highest Attainable Standard of Physical and Mental Health* (A/HRC/11/12) (March 31, 2009) para. 79 (prepared by Anand Grover) (footnotes omitted), available at www2.ohchr.org/english/bodies/hrcouncil/docs/11session/A.HRC.11.12_en.pdf.

[32] Commission on Intellectual Property Rights, *Integrating Intellectual Property Rights and Development Policy* (2002), available at www.iprcommission.org/graphic/documents/final_report.htm (the author was a member of this Commission).

[33] Ingo Meitinger, *Implementation of Test Data Protection According to Article 39.3 TRIPS: The Search for a Fair Interpretation of the Term 'Unfair Commercial Use'*, 8 J. World Intell. Prop. 123 (2005).

regulatory authority must ensure that adequate compensation renders the disclosure and use of the data economically fair'.[34] Along the same lines, Shamnad Basheer has argued that:

> [T]he minimum standard mandated by Article 39.3 is neither one of data exclusivity (as argued by the U.S. and EU) nor one of 'permissive reliance' (as argued by Professor Carlos Correa and others). Rather the term 'unfair commercial use' in Article 39.3 in effect envisages a 'compensatory liability' model, whereby regulatory data that complies with the pre-requisites of Article 39.3 (i.e. it relates to pharmaceutical or agricultural new chemical entities, is undisclosed and its origination involves considerable effort) cannot be used by any person, including a regulatory authority that uses such information to approve another product, without some compensation being paid to the originator of such data.[35]

It is hard to see, however, what the legal basis, quantum and mode of calculation for such a compensation would be. It is difficult to believe that an obligation of this type was left implicit in the TRIPS Agreement, which has spelled out in other provisions the situations where a remuneration or compensation was due.

Other authors therefore argue that, although the TRIPS Agreement does not require *either* exclusivity *or* compensation, providing for the latter may offer a compromise solution that balances the interests of the originator against those of generic companies.[36] Thus, Razvan Dinca has argued that:

> [A]s States have the general freedom to decide the methods of complying with any of their obligations under the TRIPS Agreement, it results that, in respect of the implementation of the Article 39.3, they have a large margin of

---

[34] Aaron Fellmeth, *Secrecy, Monopoly, and Access to Pharmaceuticals in International Trade Law: Protection of Marketing Approval Data under the TRIPS Agreement*, 45 HARV. INT'L L.J. 443, 464 (2004). Fellmeth does, however, acknowledge that 'it most certainly never occurred to the diplomats negotiating the TRIPs Agreement that drug manufacturers in WTO members should share in the costs of developing new drugs in foreign countries. Such a notion is 'foreign' indeed to the concepts of trade secret law'. *Id.* at 496.

[35] SHAMNAD BASHEER, PROTECTION OF REGULATORY DATA UNDER ARTICLE 39.3 OF TRIPS: THE INDIAN CONTEXT 4–5 (2006).

[36] A system of compensation is applied in the United States after ten years of the approval of agrochemical products under the Federal Insecticide, Fungicide, and Rodenticide Act (FIFRA). Upon expiry of that period any third party may use the data and register products containing the same chemical entity by relying on the test data, subject to payment of an adequate remuneration to the originator within a limited period of time. See Judit Rius Sanjuan *et al.*, *A Cost Sharing Model to Protect Investments in Pharmaceutical Test Data* (2006), available at www.essentialaction.org/access/uploads/policybrief-no1-cost-sharing.pdf.

> options, including remedies for unfair competition, data exclusivity, compulsory licenses, automatic compensatory liability or different ways of calculating the royalties.[37]

By the same token, Robert Weissman has suggested a compensation model based on a 'cost sharing' approach that, in his view:

> takes maximum advantage of TRIPS flexibilities. While providing for the non-disclosure of registration data, it does not impede generic firms from getting quickly to market. Generic companies are able to rely on approval by regulatory agencies of originator products, establish bioequivalence, and thereby obtain marketing approval.[38]

The compensation modality has been incorporated, as an alternative to data exclusivity, into the FTAs signed between the European Free Trade Association (EFTA) and a number of countries.[39] Although following the same approach, the obligation to pay compensation is formulated in varying ways in different FTAs. Thus, the FTA with Lebanon provides for a minimum six years of exclusivity 'unless the first applicant is adequately compensated' without further clarification about the way in which the adequateness of compensation will be determined. The provision explicitly prevents a party from 'relying on or referring to undisclosed test or other undisclosed data' of another party.[40] The FTA signed with Tunisia also refers to adequate compensation for the first applicant, but for a minimum of five years.[41] This agreement also establishes that such a term 'shall not exceed the period applying to the identical product in the country of origin or in the exporting country'.[42] In other words, this provision creates a modality of what has been called 'concurrent' protection, which would generally provide for a period of exclusivity shorter than that enforceable if the term of protection were counted from the date of marketing approval in Tunisia. Interestingly, in the FTA between EFTA and South Korea, the

---

[37] Dinca, *supra* note 19, at 527. For a similar opinion, see Krishna Ravi Srinivas, Test Data Protection, Data Exclusivity and TRIPS: What Options for India (2006).

[38] Robert Weissman, *Public Health-Friendly Options for Protecting Pharmaceutical Registration Data*, 1 Int'l J. Intell. Prop. Mgmt. 113 (2006).

[39] The signed FTAs are available at www.efta.int/content/free-trade/fta-countries.

[40] Free Trade Agreement between the EFTA States and Lebanon, June 24, 2004, available at www.efta.int/content/free-trade/fta-countries/lebanon.

[41] Free Trade Agreement between the EFTA States and Tunisia, December 17, 2004, available at www.efta.int/content/free-trade/fta-countries/tunisia.

[42] *Id.*

determination of the term of protection is not made in the treaty itself, but is left to 'the relevant laws and regulations of the Parties'.[43]

If compared to data exclusivity, the compensation model has a clear advantage: any party that is able and willing to pay the required compensation may use or rely on the test data to obtain the marketing approval of products containing the same chemical entity. However, the approach also presents distinct disadvantages. First, as noted earlier, the TRIPS Agreement does not establish a metric for calculating the adequacy of compensation. Indeed, apart from the United States' experience with the Federal Insecticide, Fungicide and Rodenticide Act, there is no experience anywhere in the world on implementing such a system.[44] Second, any agreed system would require proof of the investment incurred in generating the data utilized, but originator companies are likely to be reluctant to supply the evidence necessary to support their claims. Third, any such regime is likely to compromise access. Compensation obligations may put such a heavy financial burden on generic companies, and especially on small and medium generic firms in developing countries, that they may delay entry into the market until the protection ends.[45] Alternatively, if compensation is paid, the final prices of medicines and agrochemicals are likely to increase. Fourth, administration of the system may put a considerable burden on the government, particularly as it would ultimately be bound to determine the level of the compensation to be paid. Finally, as discussed more fully below, data exclusivity obligations may interfere with the latitude that members enjoy to award compulsory patent licenses under certain circumstances.

Clearly, a system based on unfair competition, without exclusivity or compensation, as permitted by the TRIPS Agreement, is the most suitable to developing countries. Companies that develop new chemical entities should be compensated, where genuine innovations exist, through patent protection, rather than by the creation of an additional layer of exclusive rights.

---

[43] Free Trade Agreement between the EFTA States and Korea, December 15, 2005, available at www.efta.int/content/free-trade/fta-countries/the-republic-of-korea.

[44] See 17 U.S.C. § 136a(c)(1)(F)(iii) (2006); Weissman, *supra* note 38, at 121.

[45] See Dinca, *supra* note 19, at 556.

II. FTAs AND WTO ACCESSION

The previous discussion shows that Article 39(3) of the TRIPS Agreement was an insufficient basis for the multilateral adoption of the data exclusivity model sought by the 'Big Pharma' and the agrochemical industry. As a result, the United States and the EC have actively engaged in achieving that target through unilateral actions such as the negotiation of FTAs and, in the case of the United States, the threat of trade sanctions under Special Section 301. All the FTAs signed by the United States include data exclusivity provisions. According to the USTR, imposing data exclusivity and other TRIPS-plus requirements such as patent term extensions and 'patent linkage' is consistent with the Doha Declaration's intent and meaning.[46]

The evolution of the provisions on test data in the U.S. FTAs clearly shows the United States' intention to fill in all the gaps left in Article 39(3). The provisions in the FTA with Jordan and Chile, for instance, refer (as Article 39(3) does) to 'undisclosed data'. This qualification disappeared in the most recent FTAs. Presumably this is because the USTR acknowledged that some test data are published by the Food and Drug Administration and other regulatory agencies upon the approval of a new product; omitting the qualifier 'undisclosed' eliminated the opportunity to minimize the effective scope of the provision's application.[47]

The list of countries required to provide data exclusivity was also enlarged as a result of conditions imposed in negotiations for accession to WTO. That is, acceding countries were required to accept this TRIPS-plus standard in order to be admitted into the multilateral system. Thus, the Working Party dealing with China's long process of accession took note of the commitments of China to:

> the introduction and enactment of laws and regulations to make sure that no person, other than the person who submitted [undisclosed test or other] data, could, without the permission of the person who submitted the data, rely on such data in support of an application for product approval for a period of at

---

[46] See GAO Report, *supra* note 7, at 28.

[47] Some have argued that, in order to be protected, the test data only needed to be undisclosed at the time of their first submission to a drug regulatory authority. See Lee Skillington and Richard Wilder, Derechos de Autor, Propiedad Intelectual, Derechos de Propiedad Intelectual Relacionados con el Comercio (2003). There is no basis, however, in Article 39(3) for this interpretation, which is obviously aimed at overcoming one of the difficulties that the U.S. government and pharmaceutical industry had to face in demanding protection for data already published by the Food and Drug Administration or other drug authorities.

least six years from the date on which China granted marketing approval to the person submitting the data. During this period, any second applicant for market authorization would only be granted market authorization if he submits his own data. This protection of data would be available to all pharmaceutical and agricultural products which utilize new chemical entities, irrespective of whether they were patent-protected or not.[48]

During the accession process, Cambodia committed to introduce protection of undisclosed and other data submitted for approval purposes;[49] Saudi Arabia adopted the required legislation during its accession process; Albania, Lithuania, Nepal, Georgia, Oman and Bulgaria also made non-specific indications of their readiness to adopt the necessary legislation on data protection.[50] In a bilateral exchange of letters between the United States and Russia, the latter agreed to implement a six-year term of protection for undisclosed pharmaceutical data, with an express prohibition of 'public' use of such data. The priority given to this issue by the *demandeurs* of data protection led in some cases (e.g. Cambodia) to the obligation on the acceding country to implement such a protection even before the end of the transition period agreed upon for other obligations in the field of intellectual property rights (IPRs).

---

[48] Working Party on the Accession of China, *Report on the Working Party on the Accession of China* (WT/ACC/CHN/49) (October 1, 2001), para. 284.

[49] Working Party on the Accession of Jordan, *Report of the Working Party on the Accession of the Hashemite Kingdom of Jordan to the World Trade Organization* (WT/ACC/JOR/33) (December 3, 1999), para. 215; Working Party on the Accession of Cambodia, *Report of the Working Party on the Accession of Cambodia* (WT/ACC/KHM/21) (August 15, 2003), para. 205. It is worth noting that Cambodia is a Least Developing Country which, under WTO rules, would have enjoyed a transitional period to introduce data protection for pharmaceuticals until 2016 and until July 2013 for agrochemicals. See Council for Trade-Related Aspects of Intellectual Property Rights, *Extension of the Transition Period under Article 66.1 of the TRIPS Agreement for Least-Developed Country Members for Certain Obligations with respect to Pharmaceutical Products* (IP/C/25) (July 1, 2002), available at www.wto.org/english/tratop_e/trips_e/art66_1_e.htm; WTO Press Release, *Poorest Countries Given More Time to Apply Intellectual Property Rules* (November 29, 2005), available at www.wto.org/english/news_e/pres05_e/pr424_e.htm.

[50] See Frederick Abbott and Carlos Correa, *Trade Organisation Accession Agreements: Intellectual Property Issues*, available at www.quno.org/geneva/pdf/economic/Issues/WTO-IP-English.pdf. Nepal, a Least Developed Country, declared its right to use the flexibility provided under the Doha Declaration on the TRIPS Agreement and Public Health. See Working Party on the Accession of Nepal, *Report of the Working Party on the Accession of Nepal Statements* (WT/ACC/NPL/17) (August 28, 2003).

III. EFFECTS OF TRIPS-PLUS STANDARDS

The effects of TRIPS-plus provisions will depend on the way in which key concepts of the system of protection, such as 'undisclosed' and 'new chemical entities' are interpreted.[51] There is room for maneuver that even countries that have adopted data exclusivity may use.[52] Although these issues will not be dealt with here, it is important to bear in mind that the impact of data exclusivity requirements will be aggravated or attenuated depending on the way in which they are operationalized.

(1) Economic impact Data exclusivity is likely to have an adverse impact on access to medicines and agrochemicals, as products that may otherwise be subject to competition would be under the exclusive control of the originator of the data for a certain period. This is particularly relevant in developing countries that did not grant patent protection to such products until recently, since data exclusivity may *de facto* become a substitute for patents that were not granted in the past.

At the same time, granting data exclusivity in a developing country is unlikely to promote additional research by large pharmaceutical firms nor attract foreign direct investment or transfer of technology to the country. It is also unlikely to substantially change the number and type of applications for marketing approval submitted to the local regulatory agency. For example, a study conducted in Jordan on the impact of data exclusivity in pharmaceuticals showed that:

> [D]ata exclusivity, a TRIPS-plus rule, delayed generic competition for 79 per cent of medicines launched by multinational pharmaceutical companies between 2002 and mid-2006, which otherwise would have been available in an inexpensive, generic form. The public health system and individuals, owing to a lack of generic competition, had to pay higher prices for new medicines. There have been no benefits from introducing strict IP rules in Jordan. There has been nearly no foreign direct investment by drug companies into Jordan between 2002 and mid-2006 to develop medicines with local companies. TRIPS-plus

---

[51] An interesting study has shown, with concrete examples, how 'defining the concept of 'new chemical entity' in a manner that excludes substances already known or described in the literature, as well as close structural analogues of existing molecules, can dramatically reduce the scope and impact of a data protection or data exclusivity regime'. See WHO Regional Office for South-East Asia, *Defining the Concept of 'New Chemical Entity' in the Drug Regulatory and Patentability Contexts: A Discussion Paper* (2008).

[52] See generally Carlos Correa, *A Model Law for the Protection of Undisclosed Data*, in INTELLECTUAL PROPERTY AND SUSTAINABLE DEVELOPMENT: DEVELOPMENT AGENDAS IN A CHANGING WORLD (Pedro Roffe ed., 2009).

> rules have not encouraged Jordanian generic companies to engage in research and development for medicines. Finally, new product launches in Jordan are only a fraction of total product launches in the United States and the European Union and are unaffordable for ordinary people. TRIPS-plus rules contributed to a 20 per cent increase in medicine prices between 2002 and 2006.[53]

Other studies that examined the probable impact of data exclusivity also predicted increases in the prices of drugs and agrochemicals and a consequent decrease in access.[54] For instance, a study for Peru relating to 43 pharmaceutical products estimated that their average price would have been between 94.3 percent and 114.4 percent higher if they had been subject to data exclusivity.[55]

(2) Ethical issues The protection of test data under exclusive rights raises not only economic but also ethical issues. In the case of pharmaceuticals, the impossibility of relying on existing data may oblige generic producers to repeat trials in humans, and thus create unnecessary risks to their life or health. Duplicative trials that are not scientifically justified would contradict the ethical principles of the medical profession as codified in the Helsinki Declaration of the World Medical Association.[56] These principles are taken into account by many drug regulatory agencies for the approval of clinical trials. This means that while the data exclusivity regime in theory leaves generic producers the option of developing their

---

[53] Rohit Malpani, *All Cost, No Benefits: How the US-Jordan Free Trade Agreement Affects Access to Medicines*, 6 J. GENERICS MEDICINES 206 (2009).

[54] See generally APOYO Consultoría, *Impacto de las Negociaciones del TLC con EEUU en Materia de Propiedad Intelectual en los Mercados de Medicamentos y Plaguicidas* (2005), available at www.congreso.gob.pe/historico/cip/tlc/3_TR/3_3/01.pdf; Centro Internacional de Politica Economica *et al.*, *Evaluación del Impacto de las Disposiciones de ADPIC + en el Mercado Institucional de Medicamentos de Costa Rica* (June 2009), available at http://new.paho.org/hq/index.php?option=com_docman&task=doc_download&gid=2425; ICTSD *et al.*, *Medicamentos y Propiedad Intelectual: Evaluación del Impacto de los Nuevos Estándares Internacionales de Propiedad Intelectual en el Precio de los Medicamentos: El Caso de la República Dominicana* (2009); Misión Salud and IFARMA, *Impacto del Tratado de Libre Comercio Firmado por los Gobiernos de Colombia y Estados Unidos sobre la Esperanza de Vida de los Pacientes Viviendo con VIH-sida en Colombia* (2007), available at http://mision-salud.org/mision/new0001.pdf; CATALINA DE LA PUENTE *ET AL.*, PROPIEDAD INTELECTUAL Y MEDICAMENTOS: EL CASO DE ARGENTINA (2009).

[55] APOYO, *supra* note 54, at 5.

[56] World Medical Association, World Medical Association Declaration of Helsinki: Ethical Principles for Medical Research Involving Human Subjects (2008), available at www.wma.net/en/30publications/10policies/b3/index.html.

'own' data, this may be impossible in practice. Even if this barrier were overcome, the costs of producing new test data may be unaffordable for generic companies, particularly in developing countries, where the scale of such companies is insufficient to fund long trials, even if the outcome is already known.

The ethical implications of a TRIPS-plus standard have also been highlighted in relation to agrochemicals. The FAO Panel of Eminent Experts on Ethics in Food and Agriculture stated in its Third Report that Article 39(3) of the TRIPS Agreement does 'not require the granting of exclusive rights'.[57] It further noted that:

> in some countries and, notably, in the context of free-trade agreements recently established with some developing countries, such test data cannot be used or relied on for at least ten years (counted from the date of marketing approval), even in cases where the relevant product is off-patent. This form of 'data exclusivity' restrains competition and leads to higher prices for inputs that farmers in developing countries need, eventually making them uncompetitive and forcing them out of production. Such exclusivity may, in practice, amount to another impoverishing trade barrier, as morally objectionable as other barriers that restrict agricultural exports from poor countries. Reducing poverty is an imperative. IPRs, including on test data, should be implemented in a way that contributes to such an objective and not to the further marginalization of farmers in the developing world.[58]

(3) Compulsory licenses In addition to the direct and other costs generated by data exclusivity, this form of protection may interfere with the utilization of compulsory patent licenses, which constitute one of the main instruments that governments may use to protect public interests where patents have detrimental effects on consumers or competitors. Several developing countries have granted compulsory licenses since 2000, in order to ensure access to medicines otherwise unaffordable to patients, namely in relation to medicines for HIV/AIDS.[59] However, if data exclusivity is granted, the beneficiary of a compulsory license may not be able to obtain the marketing approval of the product to be imported or produced under the license, unless the originator of the test data authorizes the use of the latter.

---

57 Eminent Experts Report, *supra* note 30, at 23.

58 *Id.*

59 Thailand, for instance, granted several compulsory licenses on antiretrovirals and on a patent covering a polymorph of the heart disease drug clopidogrel ('Plavix') held by Sanofi-Aventis. See Ministry of Public Health *et al.*, Facts and Evidences on the 10 Burning Issues Related to the Government Use of Patents on Three Patented Essential Drugs in Thailand (2007), available at www.moph.go.th/hot/White%20Paper%20CL-EN.pdf.

This issue has been addressed in 'side letters' on public health to the majority of FTAs signed by the USA with developing countries.[60] Further, the FTAs signed by the United States with Peru and Panama state that 'a Party may take measures to protect public health in accordance with the Doha Declaration on the TRIPS Agreement and Public Health'.[61] This general statement was introduced as a result of a bipartisan agreement reached in June 2007 between the Republican administration and Democratic leaders in the U.S. Congress.[62]

There may, however, be less here than it seems. In a report prepared for U.S. Representative Henry A. Waxman, it was noted that although the trade agreements negotiated by the Bush Administration do not specifically limit compulsory licensing,

> they also do not protect this right from potential conflicts with other intellectual property obligations such as market exclusivity. A 'side letter' provided in CAFTA [the Central America Free Trade Agreement] and the Morocco and Bahrain agreements provides that the obligations of the intellectual property chapter of the agreement do not affect the parties' ability 'to take necessary measures to protect public health'. This language, however, is more limited than the Doha Declaration, which does not use the restrictive qualifier 'necessary'. Furthermore, the letters have only interpretive value. In the event that a brand name drug company challenges a decision to approve a generic drug produced under a compulsory license, the Bush Administration has acknowledged that the conflict will only be 'informed' by the letter and will have to be 'resolved on the merits of a particular case'.[63]

---

60 The United States and Morocco, for instance, exchanged letters in June 2004 indicating that '[t]he obligations of Chapter Fifteen of the Agreement do not affect the ability of either Party to take necessary measures to protect public health by promoting access to medicines for all, in particular concerning cases such as HIV/AIDS, tuberculosis, malaria, and other epidemics as well as circumstances of extreme urgency or national emergency'. Letter from Taib Fassi Fihri, Minister Delegate for Foreign Affairs and Cooperation to Robert B. Zoellick, U.S. Trade Representative (June 15, 2004), available at www.ustr.gov/sites/default/files/uploads/agreements/fta/morocco/asset_upload_file258_3852.pdf.

61 United States–Peru Trade Promotion Agreement, Art. 16.10(2)(e) (April 24, 2004), available at www.ustr.gov/webfm_send/1031; United States–Panama Trade Promotion Agreement, Art. 15.10(2)(e) (June 28, 2007), available at http://ustraderep.gov/Trade_Agreements/Bilateral/Panama_FTA/Final_Text/Section_Index.html.

62 See www.hktdc.com/info/mi/a/baus/en/1X0078EY/1/Business-Alert-%E2%80%93-US/Congress--Administration-Announce-Trade-Policy-Agreement.htm.

63 Minority Staff Special Investigations Division of House Committee on Government Reform, 109th Cong., *Trade Agreements and Access to Medications under the Bush Administration* 11 (2005) (footnotes omitted). The report makes reference to a letter from USTR General Counsel John K. Veroneau to Representative

The GAO Report mentioned earlier also confirms that:

> USTR officials noted that they use the side letters to further clarify that the provisions of the agreement leave intact a series of methods a country can use to respond to public health emergencies. However, according to a USTR official, these side letters do not create exceptions to the provisions in the FTA.[64]

The extent to which a 'side letter' may influence the interpretation and application of the intellectual property provisions in FTAs is thus uncertain. As noted in the GAO Report, they would not create exceptions that are not otherwise provided for in the treaty itself. Hence, whether a compulsory licensee in a FTA signatory could effectively obtain market approval for a product covered by data exclusivity remains an open question.

The EC is also demanding data exclusivity in its negotiations of a FTA with India[65] and the Andean countries.[66] This was not the case, however, in the CARIFORUM Economic Partnership Agreement, where only provisions on enforcement of intellectual property rights were included. Interestingly, an EC regulation provides for a waiver of data protection provisions where a compulsory license is granted in a European country to export medicines.[67]

Sander M. Levin concerning the United States – Morocco Free Trade Agreement (July 19, 2004) in its response to the eleventh question, where it was stated that the side letter was deemed a 'subsequent agreement between the parties regarding the interpretation of the treaty or the application of its provisions' that should 'be taken into account together with the context' per Art. 31.3(a) of the Vienna Convention on the Law of Treaties.

[64] GAO Report, *supra* note 7. Footnote 28 of the same report adds: 'The side letter on public health constitutes a formal understanding that forms part of the interpretive context of a signed/implemented FTA as described in the Vienna Convention on the Law of Treaties, Article 31'. *Id.* at 32 n.28.

[65] See Oxfam, *Negotiation of a Free Trade Agreement European Union–India: Will India Accept TRIPS-plus Protection?* (2009), available at www.oxfam.de/download/correa_eu_india_fta.pdf.

[66] See HAI International and Oxfam, *Trading Away Access to Medicines: How the European Commission's Trade Agenda has Taken a Wrong Turn* (2009), available at www.oxfam.org/en/policy/trading-away-access-medicines.

[67] Commission Regulation 816/2006/EC on compulsory licensing of patents relating to the manufacture of pharmaceutical products for export to countries with public health problems [2006] O.J. L157/1. This Regulation was adopted by the European Parliament to implement the WTO Decision of August 30, 2003 see Art. 18.

CONCLUSIONS

Article 39(3) is probably the most controversial provision in the TRIPS Agreement. Different views on the scope of the rights conferred have been expressed by governments, international organizations, scholars and other experts.

The TRIPS Agreement mandates the protection of test data on the safety and efficacy of pharmaceutical and agrochemical products (when a number of requirements are met) under the discipline of unfair competition. If Article 39(3) is interpreted in the light of the Vienna Convention on the Law of Treaties, as applied by the GATT/WTO jurisprudence, it is difficult to avoid the conclusion that, whatever the intention of the proponents of said article were, the only obligation under this provision is to refrain from obtaining another party's undisclosed test data by means of dishonest practices (such as bribing employees or espionage) and not to make direct commercial use of such data. Thus, the provision does not require the establishment of a period during which such data are subject to exclusive rights, nor the payment of a compensation to the originator of data for using or relying on them. There is no reasonable way in which Article 39(3) can be read as imposing such obligations.

The absence of any request to establish a panel under the WTO Dispute Settlement Understanding against the numerous countries that have not granted data exclusivity is a strong indicator that developed countries are conscious that a WTO panel or the Appellate Body is unlikely to rule that the TRIPS Agreement imposes data exclusivity or compensation. This may also explain why FTAs signed by the United States, the EC and the EFTA have been used as a platform to obtain TRIPS-plus recognition of data exclusivity or compensation in developing countries.

The economic impact of TRIPS-plus protection of test data may be significant. Pharmaceuticals are essential for public health; agrochemicals are important for food security and one of the determinants of the level of competitiveness in agricultural production. The cost of data exclusivity or a compensation system to patients and consumers in poor countries may be disproportionately high in comparison to the additional benefits obtained by the companies that may benefit from such a protection. The ethical implications of TRIPS-plus protection, often overlooked, also need adequate consideration.

Data exclusivity systems may also create other barriers, notably for the effective application of compulsory licenses and government use. A great deal of ambiguity has surrounded the treatment of this issue in FTAs negotiated with the United States. General references to the protection of public health in the text or in side letters to such agreements may be insufficient to effectively lift the restriction created by the grant of exclusive rights over test data.

Index